History of the Town of

Bristol, Grafton County,

New Hampshire

(Volume II) Genealogies

Richard Watson Musgrove

Alpha Editions

This edition published in 2020

ISBN : 9789354008344

Design and Setting By
Alpha Editions
email - alphaedis@gmail.com

HISTORY

OF THE

TOWN OF BRISTOL

GRAFTON COUNTY

NEW HAMPSHIRE

IN TWO VOLUMES

VOLUME II – GENEALOGIES

BY

RICHARD W. MUSGROVE

BRISTOL, N. H.
Printed by R. W. Musgrove
1904

INTRODUCTION

In this volume are presented the genealogies of Bristol. The author has sought to include every family that ever resided within the limits of the town; and while this has not been possible the result has been that the following pages contain the records of 368 family names; more than 1,500 families and over 12,000 individual names.

The statistics here presented have been gathered from every available source — from family records, printed genealogies, tombstones, records of deeds and wills, church records, and records of clergymen officiating at funerals and marriages; a few from the meagre vital statistics of the town, and many by extensive correspondence with widely scattered former residents, and by personal interviews. The difficulties of its compilation makes the value of the work more apparent.

In all cases the aim has been to give the line of descent from the earliest known ancestor to the first settlement of the family in the territory now known as Bristol, and from that time to give a full record to the present, if the family continues to reside in town. In case of removal the children and in many cases the grandchildren of natives and residents are given after having left town. In but few cases has more than this been attempted.

From the nature of the case these records must be imperfect and errors will appear. They are not complete for the work of the genealogist is never finished; changes are constantly occurring. In the appendix is given the records of births, marriages and deaths that occurred while this volume was in press, in order to bring the volume up to date, but even while the index was in preparation several deaths occurred of which no record could be made.

This work is intended to be strictly genealogical and in no sense biographical. All the genealogical data obtainable has been given in each case, with very brief additional information. Only in the case of a few distinguished public men has anything more than this been given.

EXPLANATIONS

The genealogical arrangement in the following pages is self-explanatory. All members of each family are numbered consecutively to the latest descendant. In the case of children who became heads of families, a star is placed at the commencement of the line, which indicates that the name with the same number (in parenthesis) occurs again where the family is given in full.

Where no state is given, New Hampshire is to be understood; exceptions may occur in the case of large cities where it would seem superfluous to name the state. A mark of interrogation (?) implies uncertainty. Figures after "ae." indicate the age in years, months and days, thus, 5?-10-20.

Abbreviations are those usually found in works of this character, as "b." for "born"; "m." for "married"; "d " for "died"; "ae." for "aged"; "dau." for "daughter"; "res." for "resides" or "resided"; "rem." for "removed."

CONTENTS

PORTRAITS

HISTORY OF BRISTOL

GENEALOGIES

THE ABBOTT FAMILIES

Rev. Charles Frederick Abbott, son of Walter Stewart and
Dorcas (Ladd) Abbott, was b. Lemington, Vt., Nov. 27, 1831.
Mr. Abbott came to Bristol in 1861, as acting pastor of the Congregational church. Sept. 6, 1863, he m. Harriet Minot, dau.
of Solomon Cavis. (See.) After a service of a little more than
five years, he was compelled by failing health to resign his pastorate, and he d. of consumption, Sept. 20, 1866, ae. 34-9-23.
During his residence here he held a warm place in the hearts
of the people. He served two years as superintending school
committee. His death was a great loss to the town. (See
Congregational church.) Mrs. Abbott resides on Pleasant street.

---

1. Rev. George J. Abbott, the son of Isaac Abbott, was b.
in Jackson, Mich., in 1830. In September, 1861, he m. Mary
Elizabeth, dau. Jefferson Bartlett, b. in 1839, in Unity, Me.
He was pastor of the Free Baptist church in Bristol from June,
1870, till September, 1873. He d. at Oakland, Me., Nov. 3,
1883, ae. 54.

CHILDREN

2. Elmir, b. Dover, Me., 1865; m. in 1892, Susie Seavey; now in
provision business in Lynn, Mass.
3. Charles, b. Rochester; d. in infancy.
4. Winifred, b. B., August, 1878; res. Lynn.
5. Maud Elizabeth, b. Apponaug, R. I., in May, 1881; a student at
Boston University, class of 1904.

THE ACKERMAN FAMILIES

1. Fred Hale Ackerman, son of Shem G. and Joanna
(Clark) Ackerman, was b. Sept. 13, 1860, in Alexandria, under
the shadow of Mount Cardigan. He came here about 1882,
and entered the printing-office of the *Bristol Enterprise*, of which
he was for many years foreman. Here he remained, with the
exception of about one year in Pennsylvania, till July 1, 1899,
when he became postmaster at Bristol, which office he now fills.

I

He has been for several years chairman of the Republican town committee and is a past master of Union Lodge, A. F. & A. M.; has been a member of the board of education. (See Town Officers.) He m. Dec. 27, 1883, Mary Ellen, dau. Lorenzo D. Day. (See.) In 1895, he purchased the Wm. L. Chase residence on Pleasant street where he now resides.

CHILDREN

2. Helen M., b. Bristol, July 14, 1884.
3. Laurence Day, b. B., Aug. 8, 1886.

———

1. Jacob Hanson Ackerman, son of Jacob and Sarah (Hall) Ackerman, was b. Farmington, Dec. 12, 1835. He removed to Alexandria with his parents when young and there m. May 15, 1862, Mary D., dau. Heman J. and Abigail (Gray) Welton, b. Alexandria, Nov. 29, 1841. In the spring of 1891, he purchased the J. Martin Sleeper farm in Bristol where he resided till he d. Oct. 22, 1902, ae. 66-9-10.

CHILDREN

2. Annette Mary, b. Alexandria, Apr. 14, 1863; unm.; keeping a boarding-house in Winchester, Mass.
3. Frank Leslie, b. A., May 14, 1865; res. Burlington, Vt., where he was manager of the Hygienic Milk company. Unm.

THE ADAMS FAMILIES

1. Joel Coolidge Adams, son of Guy and Sarah (Cross) Adams, was b. Charlestown, Vt., Oct. 15, 1819 (Oct. 16, 1820). He m. Apr. 30, 1846, Sarah Ann, dau. Levi Cross. He came here in 1854, and was in the employ of Warren White. He d. May 22, 1879, ae. 59-7-7. She d. Bristol, Nov. 1, 1885, ae. 61-7-10. Republican, Congregationalist.

CHILDREN

2. Frances Ann, b. Nashua, Apr. 26, 1849; m. Joseph McClary. Res. Gilmanton Corner. Six children.
3. Ella Jane, b. Nashua, Aug. 5, 1851; d. Oct. 11, 1851, ae. 0-2-6
4. Sara Ella, b. Bristol, Feb. 24, 1853; d. Aug. 16, 1854, ae. 1-5-22.
5. Ida Lizzie, b. B., Oct. 13, 1854; m. Arthur O'Leary. (See.)
6. Levi Guy, b. B., Nov. 7, 1856; m. Hattie Gray; res. B. till 1900, now Nashua. Child:
    a. Georgia Edwin, d. diphtheria, Aug. 20, 1895, ae. 9-0-5.
7. Lela Ivanette, b. B., June 13, 1858; m. Frank P. Haley. (See.)
8. Carrie Jane, b. B., Sept. 19, 1859; d. Oct. 24, 1859, ae. 0-1-5.

———

1. Felix Adams was b. Gaspe Basin, Province of Quebec, May 5, 1819. He m. June 16, 1840, Rosanna Crunier, b. Gaspe Basin, Aug. 3, 1821. They removed to Haverhill, in 1873, and there he d. in 1874, ae. 65. She removed to Bristol, and

FRED H. ACKERMAN

here d. Oct. 10, 1894, ae. 73-2-7. In 1903, five farmhouses on the west side of Newfound lake, on Fowler's river, were all owned and occupied by the Adams's, and the neighborhood is now known as Adamsville. All Catholics. Children all born Gaspe Basin.

CHILDREN

*2. Felix, b. Aug. 19, 1842.
*3. Benard James, b. Oct. 8, 1844.
4. Rosanna, b. Aug. 8, 1846; m. Alexander Adams. (See.)
5. Nicholas, b. Sept. 13, 1848; m. Alma Blake, and res. East Hebron. Child:
   a. Ellen.
6. Agnes, b. July 26, 1851; m. Patrick M. Kenney. (See.)
7. Thomas, b. Nov. 8, 1853; m. Phebe Johnston, and removed to Manchester. Five children.
8. Eliza, b. Dec. 6, 1855; m. three times; now res. Tamworth.
9. William, b. Apr. 18, 1857; m. Mary Ann Johnston and removed to Manchester, where he d. Five or six children.
*10. Joseph, b. Aug. 5, 1859.
11. Alfred, b. Feb. 3, 1862; res. Hebron; unm.
12. John Battise, b. Apr. 3, 1867; has been twice m.; res. Laconia. No children.
*13. Ambrose S., b. Apr. 11, 1871.
   At a public gathering in Bristol six of the above sons stood in a row. Each was over six feet in height and each weighed over 200 pounds.

(2) Felix Adams, b. Aug. 19, 1842, m. Nov. 5, 1864, Mary Crawford, b. Ireland. Is a farmer in Adamsville.

CHILDREN

14. Emily, b. Gaspe Basin, Aug. 17, 1865; m. Oscar S. Roby. (See.)
15. Melissa, b. G. B., June 9, 1866; d. Feb. 11, 1867.
16. Nicholas, b. Feb. 1, 1869; d. at about 13 years of age.
17. Alice, b. Nov. 8, 1872; m. (1) Charles P. Rice; (2) Wm. H. Welch. (See.)
18. Patrick, b. Haverhill, Feb. 7, 1874; m. Leona Ackerman, dau. of Enoch; res. Bristol. No children.
19. Maggie W., b. Bristol, 1885.

(3) Benard J. Adams, b. Oct. 8, 1844, m. Mary Jane, dau. of William and Sophia Stanley, b. May 12, 1848. He went from Haverhill, in 1873, to Hill; came to Bristol in June, 1880, and is a farmer in Adamsville.

CHILDREN

20. William Felix, b. Gaspe Basin, Oct. 25, 1865; m. June 11, 1887, Agnes Adams, dau. of Alexander. Came to Bristol with his parents; is a farmer in Adamsville. No children.
21. Benard Ernest, b. G. B., Nov. 16, 1868; m. Florence Ethel Dustin, b. E. Concord, June 21, 1875; res. East Hebron.
22. Albert, b. G. B., Sept. 20, 1871; m. Ellen, dau. Nicholas Adams.
23. Edward, b. Haverhill, Sept. 16, 1873; m. Nov. 27, 1892, Lena Bell Emery, b. Lebanon. Came to Bristol 1880; returned to No. Haverhill, now farmer in Adamsville. No children.
24. Isaac Joseph, b. Hill, Aug. 28, 1875; d. Apr. 10, 1877.

25. Frank Joseph, b. H., Oct. 31, 1877; m. Dec. 25, 1900, Katherine Ahern. Farmer in Adamsville. Child:
  a. Leon Buddington, b. Tilton, Apr. 17, 1902.
  26. Mary Ann, b. H., Nov. 22, 1879; m. Nov. 7, 1897, James J. Johnson, b. Boston, Mass., May 9, 1876; res. Whitman, Mass. Three children.
  27. Emily Julia, b. Bristol, Feb. 3, 1881.
  28. Leon Alfred, b. B., Apr. 23, 1885; d. June 5, 1899, ae. 14-1-12.
  29. Ethel Isabel, b. B., July 17, 1888.

  (10) Joseph Adams, b. Aug. 5, 1859, m. Nov., 1889, Mary, dau. Hiram Gordon, b. Alexandria. He came here from Haverhill, about 1877. He res. in Bristol about five years; in Hill, five years; Laconia, two, and since 1890 in Hebron.

CHILDREN

  30. Wilson Joseph, b. Hebron, Oct. 2, 1893.
  31. Vera May, b. H., Nov. 9, 1898.

  (13) Ambrose S. Adams, b. Apr. 11, 1871, m. June 15, 1891, Katie A., dau. Robert Stanley, b. Gaspe Basin, Mar. 3, 1867. They removed from Bristol to Hebron in April, 1892, where he is a farmer. He is also owner and captain of steamer Stella Marion, on Newfound lake.

CHILDREN

  32. Stella Marion, b. Hebron, July 19, 1894.
  33. Marion Annet, b. H., June 8, 1896.
  34. Rodney Stanley, b. H., Mar. 6, 1898.

  35. Alexander Adams, son of Abram and Lucy (Simpson) Adams, and a cousin of Felix Adams, 2nd., was b. Gaspe Basin, 1836. In 1861, he m. Rosanna, dau. Felix Adams, b. Aug. 8, 1846. (See.) He came to Bristol in 1872, and is a farmer in Adamsville. Catholics.

CHILDREN

  36. Agnes, b. Gaspe Basin, Feb. 1, 1866; m. William F. Adams. (See.)
  37. Alexander F., b. G. B., Dec. 16, 1872; m. June 8, 1901, Rose, dau. John and Philena (Naddo) Charland, b. St. Johns, Province of Quebec, May 12, 1876. Farmer in Adamsville. No children.
  38. George, b. No. Haverhill, Mar. 8, 1879; unm.
  39. Ernest, b. No. H., July 4, 1882; unm.
  40. Arthur, b. G. B., 1883 (?); m. Stella, dau. Daniel Rowen and res. Plymouth. No children.
  41. Joseph, b. Bristol, Dec. —, 1884 (?); unm.
  42. Henry, b. B., 1886 (?).
  43. Wilson, b. B., Dec. 29, 1889.
  44. Anna Jane, b. B., May 11, 1891.

THE ALDEN FAMILY

  1. George Martin Alden, son of Hosea and Martha (Howard) Alden, is a descendant of John Alden and Priscilla

Sergt. Charles Francis Alexander
Hospital Corps, U. S. Army
(Died Apr. 16, 1904)

Molines of Puritan fame. He was b. in Randolph, Mass., Sept. 30, 1823. He came to Bristol in 1854, and m., Dec. 31, 1854, Jane, dau. of Alexander Hutchinson. (See.) He served during the Civil war as a private in the 12th Regt. Conn. Vols.; shoemaker; was a salesman some years for David P. Prescott, and later in business as a repairer of shoes.

CHILDREN

*2. George Francis, b. Bristol, Apr. 23, 1856.
*3. Charles A., b. High Ridge, Conn., Jan. 5, 1861.

(2) George F. Alden, b. Apr. 23, 1856, m. Dec. 24, 1878, Abbie E. Call, dau. John Q. and Abigail Twombly, b. Loudon, Sept. —, 1851, and d. Bristol, Sept. 27, 1884, ae. 33 years. He m., Jan. 23, 1886, Mary E., dau. of George M. Breck. (See.) She d. June 24, 1900, ae. 38-6-12. He was for many years an operative in Train-Smith company's paper-mill.

CHILD

4. Eleanor Maud, b. Bristol, Sept. 12, 1888.

(3) Charles Adrian, b. Jan. 5, 1861; brick mason; m. Sept. 28, 1882, Emma M., dau. Henry A., and Ellen M. Alden, b. Randolph, Mass., Jan. 23, 1856. He d. Bristol, July 2, 1898, ae. 37-5-17. She res. Pleasant street.

CHILDREN

5. Marion Ellen, b. Randolph, May 27, 1883, m. Charles H. Decato. (See.)
6. Frank Adrian, b. R., Feb. 16, 1885.
7. Georgia Averell, b. Bristol, July 7, 1890.
8. Jennie Louise, b. Quincy, Mass., June 21, 1892; d. May 28, 1894.
9. Charles Theodore, b. Bristol, June 13, 1895.

THE ALEXANDER FAMILY

1. Lucius Cary Alexander, son of Thaddeus and Mary (Cary) Alexander, was b. at Athens, Vt., Nov. 21, 1794. He m., in 1825, Sarah Hill, dau. Abraham, who d. in Grafton, Vt., about 1837, and he m. (2) Sophia Goodnoe, who d. Nashua, about 1885, ae. about 82. He was a manufacturer at No. Bristol, 1860-'64. He d. Medford, Mass., Nov. 9, 1872, ae. 77-11-18.

CHILDREN

2. Sarah, b. Grafton, Vt., June 10, 1826; res. Nashua.
3. George Cary, b. G., Sept. 9, 1829; m. March, 1874, Adeline Corey; d. Lowell, Mass., Apr. 9, 1901, ae. 71-7-0.
4. Charles Herbert, b. G., Dec. 10, 1831; d. in Nashua in 1856, of yellow fever contracted in Virginia.
*5 Don Pedro, b. G., Sept. 5, 1834.
*6. Horace Taylor, b. G., Aug. 1, 1836.

(5) Don P. Alexander, b. Sept. 5, 1834, m. Martha Jane,

1*

dau. of David Clement, b. Hudson in 1834, and d. Bristol, June 16, 1874, ae. 40. He m. June 22, 1875, Emily George. He was a manufacturer in No. Bristol, 1860–'64; and till 1874, a machinist on Water street. He res. Nashua.

CHILDREN

7. Charles Herbert, b. Bristol, Mar. 23, 1863 ; m. Oct. 10, 1883, Delia F. Wheelock, and d. Chester, Vt., Oct. 23, 1884, ae. 21-7-0.
8. Lillian Mabel, b. B., June 23, 1866; m. Jan. 1, 1889, George F. Parkson.
9. Will George, b. B., Jan. 31, 1871 ; m. July 11, 1894, Clara Freeman Crowell.
10. Fanny Taylor, b. B., May 24, 1874; d. September, 1874.
11. Emily George, b. June 22, 1875.
12. Kathrena, b. Dec. 19, 1876 ; d. Mar. 1, 1879.
13. Harvey Lucius, b. Oct. 17, 1878.

(6) Horace T. Alexander, b. Aug. 1, 1836, m. Jan. 1, 1860, Martha, dau. of Nathan and Hannah (Parker) Dane, b. Amherst, Mass., May 24, 1840, and d. Bristol, Apr. 15, 1885, ae. 44-10-21. They came here in 1870. He was a clerk in store of George M. Cavis ten years, and later a clerk in store of C. Taylor two years. He was in trade in Cavis's block six years and in trade in Robie's block twelve years, first in company with Charles A. George and after five years, with Charles E. Davis. Odd Fellow. Congregationalist.

CHILDREN

14. Mary Lizzie, b. Nashua, July 13, 1861 ; m. Nov. 23, 1886, John Moses Cheney, son of Joseph Y. Cheney, b. Jan. 6, 1859, in Milwaukee, Wis. He is a lawyer in Orlando, Fla., where they have resided since m. Children :
   a. Glen Alexander, b. Oct. 6, 1887.
   b. Donald Alexander, b. Jan. 23, 1889.
   c. Joseph Young, b. Aug. 4, 1891.
15. Charles Francis, b. N., June 24, 1866; was a salesman in carpet department of Jordan-Marsh Co.'s store in Boston, and at Birmingham, Ala.; enlisted in U. S. army in March, 1901, and has served as hospital steward in the Philippine Islands.
16. Jessie Dane, b. Bristol, Dec. 1, 1878; graduated New Hampton Institution in 1897, and Concord Normal school. Teacher.

THE AMES FAMILY

1. James Marston Ames, son of Caleb and Sarah (Burley) Ames, was b. New Hampton, July 13, 1817, and m. Feb. 17, 1845, Abigail F. Batchelder, dau. of Benjamin, b. Bridgewater, June 8, 1824. (See.) They came to Bristol in 1866, and settled at the North End on the farm now owned and occupied by their son, where they spent the remainder of their lives. He d. Dec. 28, 1881, ae. 64-5-15 ; she d. Jan. 10, 1886, ae. 61-7-2.

CHILDREN

2. Mary Comfort, b. New Hampton, Jan. 7, 1852 ; m. Jan. 1, 1872, Laurin C. Tilton. (See.)
*3. Burley Marston, b. N. H., Mar. 8, 1848.

BURLEY M. AMES

(3) Burley M. Ames, b. Mar. 8, 1848, m. Feb. 14, 1869, Mary Ann, dau. Orren Locke. (See.) He was a manufacturer of straw-board for six or seven years from fall of 1867, and in 1875 was manufacturer of gloves; since a farmer and dealer in wood, coal, ice, etc. He is a trustee and vice-president of the Bristol Savings bank, and a director of the First National Bank of Bristol. Democrat, Mason, Odd Fellow, Free Baptist.

CHILDREN

4. Aletea Elfra, b. Bristol, Feb. 27, 1872; m. Nathan P. Smith. (See.)
5. Ethel Winnifred, b. B., Nov. 17, 1879; m. Charles E. Spencer. (See.)

THE ANNIS FAMILY

1. Royal Bradley Annis, son of John B. and Sophronia (Buell) Annis, was b. Groton, Oct. 26, 1842. He m. Aug. 15, 1861, Sarah M., dau. Cyrus and Olive (Jesseman) Gordon, b. Lyme, Mar. 21, 1845, and d. Dorchester, Mar. —, 1864. He m. Aug. 18, 1867, Nancy R., dau. William and Clarissa (Smith) Braley, b. Grafton, Oct. 17, 1845. They came to Bristol from Haverhill in 1882. He has been teamster and paper-mill workman. In 1887, purchased the Luther J. Wadleigh residence on Cedar street where he now resides; Free Baptist; Democrat.

CHILDREN

2. Carlos Royal, b. Dorchester, July 27, 1863; d. February, 1865.
3. Ernest Royal, b. Natick, Mass., Dec. 3, 1868; unm.
*4. Robert Leslie, b. Danbury, Oct. 26, 1871.

(4) Robert L. Annis, b. Oct. 26, 1871, m. Jan. 15, 1899, Jessie May, dau. William H. and Almira (Preston) Welch, b. Canaan; spinner at Penacook; Democrat.

CHILDREN

5. Clifton, b. Bristol, July 28, 1899.
6. Vern Leslie, b. B., Sept. 19, 1901.

THE ASPENWALL FAMILY

Rev. Nathaniel W. Aspenwall, the son of John H. and Hannah (White) Aspenwall, was b. Bradford, Vt., Jan. 26, 1801. Nov. 19, 1826, he m. Laura, dau. of Philip and Mary (Babb) McGaffey, b. Lyndon, Vt., Aug. 7, 1802. He was pastor of the Methodist Episcopal church in Bristol in 1843 and '44. He united with the New England conference in 1823, and for 41 years took effective work in that conference and in the New Hampshire and Vermont conference. His conference membership lacked but four months of half a century. They removed to Chicago, Ill., in 1868, where he d. Nov. 17, 1873, ae. 72-9-21. She d. Mar. 3, 1886, ae. 84-6-26.

2. Samuel Augustus, b. Feb. 4, 1828; d. Jan. 5, 1831.
3. Amy, b. July 20, 1829; m. Oct. 12, 1856, Lester L. Bond; res. Chicago, Ill.
4. Laura Diantha, b. Aug. 5, 1833; m. Henry C. Ayres.
5. Mary White, b. Nov. 14, 1835.
6. John, b. Mar. 29, 1838; d. May 5, 1841.
7. Sarah Caroline, b. Apr. 2, 1843; m. Alonzo Wygant.

THE ATWOOD FAMILY

1. John Atwood, the progenitor of the Atwoods of Bristol and Alexandria, was b. in England. In 1749, he was in Hampstead and was named as one of the incorporators of the town. A son,

2. Moses, b. Hampstead, was a Revolutionary soldier from that town. He m. Judith Wadleigh, and after two or three children were b. removed to Alexandria, where he was a farmer and miller. He d. in the family of his son, John, ae. 86–7–0.

3. Nancy, b. Hampstead, Aug. 17, 1786; m. Jonas Hastings. (See.)
4. Thomas, b. H.; d. Bristol, while on a visit to the family of David M. Chase, about 1869, ae. about 80 years.
*5. Moses, b. H., June 2, 1790.
6. Joseph, m. Sabrina Corless. Children:
    a. Joseph, d. at 17.   *b.* John, m. Eliza Cawley.
    c. Sabrina, b. Alexandria, May 3, 1820; m. Samuel Dix Farrar.
(See.)
*7. Jonathan, b. A., 1800.
*8. John, b. A., Oct. 15, 1802.
9. Sophia, m. —— Patten.
10. Judith, b. A., Aug. 26, 1805; m. David C. Ladd. (See.) She m.
(2) Abel Ford, Orange.

(5) Moses Atwood, b. June 2, 1790, m. Mar. 26, 1818, Mary Sanborn, dau. Josiah, b. Alexandria, Aug. 29, 1796; d. Hill, Apr. 12, 1853. He was a farmer and miller; first settler on the C. H. Mudgett farm, west side of lake. He built the farmhouse now standing there. He d. Bristol, Nov. 30, 1872, ae. 82–5–28.

11. Moses Eli, b. Bristol, Aug. 4, 1820; m. Feb. 27, 1845, Sabrina J., dau. Daniel Clough; b. Alexandria, 1823; d. Hooksett, Nov. 30, 1873. He m. May 12, 1876, Lydia L. Elliott, Manchester. He was a farmer in Alexandria, and later in Hooksett, where he d. Jan. 27, 1887, ae. 66–5–23. Child:
    a. Moses W., b. Alexandria, Nov. 25, 1847; res. E. Concord.
12. Mary E., b. Bristol, Apr. 21, 1823; d. Alexandria, June 9, 1832.
13. Sally Emeline, b. B., Oct. 18, 1825; m. George W. Clifford. (See.)
14. Josiah S., b. B., Jan. 14, 1828; d. Alexandria, June 25, 1840, ae. 12–5–11.
15. Hannah E., b. B., Sept. 8, 1830; d. unm. Sanbornton, Oct. 30, 1851, ae. 21–1–32.
16. Dorothy A., b. Alexandria, July 31, 1832; d. May 13, 1841, ae. 8–9–12.
17. Eliza A., b. A., Aug. 24, 1834; m. May 12, 1859, Henry D. Haynes, Epsom. Children:

a. Charles W., b. Feb. 7, 1862; d. Apr. 9, 1872, ae. 10-2-2.
b. Ada H., b. Apr. 25, 1875; d. Apr. 25, 1875.
c. George H., b. Dec. 15, 1878.
18. John R., b. A., Aug. 14, 1837; m. Jan. 20, 1860, Diantha Holt, and d. Hooksett, June 6, 1864, ae. 26-9-22. No children.
19. Mary F., b. A., Mar. 5, 1840; m. Nov. 18, 1860, William N. Barcley, Danbury. He d. Jan. 8, 1869, ae. 28-10-3. She m. Oct. 26, 1881, James Carr, Hooksett.

(7) Jonathan Atwood, b. 1800, m. Mar. 18, 1826, Huldah, dau. of Jacob Gurdy. (See.) He was a farmer in the Locke neighborhood and there d. Nov. 9, 1834, ae. 34-7-0. His widow d. at Cape Elizabeth, Me., June 14, 1873, ae. 76-9-2.

CHILDREN

※20. Luther, b. Bristol, Nov. 7, 1826.
21. Daughter, d. in infancy.
22. Son, d. in infancy.
23. William, b. B., Nov. 6, 1830. He was a chemist and was associated with his brother, Luther, in many ventures; was long the superintendent of the Portland Oil Refinery and subsequently of one in New York; member of Maine legislature. He m. Mrs. Julia A. Steeper, nee Norton, and d. Cape Elizabeth, Me., about 1873. She res. with her son in California. Child:
    a. Edward Norton, m.; three children; res. Oakland, Cal.
24. Augustus, b. B., Feb. 19, 1833; d. B., June 19, 1856, ae. 23-4-0.

(8) John Atwood, b. Oct. 15, 1802, m. Elizabeth Corless, b. Mar. 16, 1806, who d. "Mar. 18, 1883, ae. 77-0-1." He was a farmer in Alexandria; lost both eyes by a premature discharge of a blast at the lead mine in Bristol.

CHILDREN

25. Elizabeth, d. at 18.
26. John Wadleigh, b. Alexandria, Aug. 22, 1832; m. about 1857, Susan, dau. Daniel Bailey; b. A., Apr. 5, 1838; d. May 12, 1892, ae. 54-1-7. He m. (2) Mrs. Sarah Ann Williams. Four children by first wife.
27. Mary, m. Charles Keezer, Francestown.
28. George W., b. A., Aug. 17, 1843; m. Nov. 28, 1868, Emily A., dau. David F. Tilton. (See.) He is a farmer in Bridgewater. Children:
    a. Harry G., b. Chicago, Ill., Aug. 16, 1869.
    b. David T., b. C., Nov. 14, 1872.
    c. Everett E., b. Woodstock, Dec. 17, 1883.

(20) Luther Atwood, b. Bristol, Nov. 7, 1826, m. Jan. 1, 1857, Katherine Lucy, dau. of Thomas Jefferson and Nancy F. (Lewis) Marsh, b. Lynn, Mass., Feb. 13, 1837. He d. of consumption, Cape Elizabeth, Me., Nov. 5, 1868, ae. 41-11-28. She removed to Exeter.

Luther Atwood received only such education as the limited schools of Bristol afforded. When quite a lad he commenced the study of medicine with Dr. Moody C. Sawyer, but he cared more to experiment with chemicals than study the effect of drugs. In 1849, following an explosion of chemicals that aroused the family at night, Dr. Sawyer suggested that he was not cut out

for a doctor, and young Atwood went to Boston and entered
upon the manufacture of chemicals for Philbrick & Trafton.
Two years later he became a member of the firm. About this
time Mr. Atwood took out a patent for a process of purifying
alcohol, and the U. S. Dispensary is authority for the statement
that the best alcohol used in the arts is that made by his process. He took out several patents for the manufacture of various products from coal tar, and for purifying kerosene oil. He
spent the winter of 1854-'5 in France and Germany, and made a
long sojourn in Glasgow, Scotland, where he superintended the
erection of works for the manufacture of "coup" oil by one of
his patents. In 1857, he took charge of coal oil works at Brooklyn, N. Y., and took out other patents for the distillation of coal
oil by the "pipe" process. In his latter years he was superintendent and chemist of petroleum refineries at Boston, Mass.,
and Maysville, Ky. The *Scientific American* said of him : "He
was a natural chemist ; and component parts, under his manipu-
lation, seemed to assume their proper correlation, almost by
magic. . . . . The high standard of purity which has been
reached by the oils, known under the trade mark of 'kerosene,'
is owing in a very large degree to the original, scientific far-
sightedness and laborious efforts of Luther Atwood."

CHILDREN

29. Charles Edward, b. Waltham, Mass., Jan. 11, 1858; was graduated
from Harvard in 1880 ; since 1869, resident of Exeter, where he has been
an editor on *Exeter News-Letter*. Unm.
30. Luther, b. New York City, Nov. 1, 1859; was graduated from
Harvard, 1883; submaster in classical high school, Lynn, Mass. He m.
Nov. 27, 1889, Nellie Josephine, only child of Joseph M. Taylor, Lynn.
31. Isabel Louise, b. Waltham, Mass., Nov. 22, 1861 ; a teacher in
public schools of Melrose, Mass.

THE BADGER FAMILIES

1. Leander Badger, son of Thomas, was b. in Gilmanton
May 26, 1789. He came to Bristol in 1836. He was a blacksmith and farmer, but for many years had charge of the Central
bridge toll-gate, and resided in the toll-gate house, still standing. He m. Abigail, dau. of Noah Connor, b. New Hampton,
June 19, 1788, and d. in Bristol, June 14, 1836, ae. 47-11-25. He
m. (2) Ruth Knights, of Portsmouth, who was b. June, 1800,
Newburyport, Mass., and d. in Lowell, Mass., Sept. 13, 1887,
ae. 87-3-0. He d. in Bristol, Nov. 24, 1861, ae. 82-5-28.

CHILDREN

2. Irene Carter, b. Epping, Mar. 30, 1816; m. John S Shores in 1842.
He was the son of Peter and was b. New Hampton, in 1820 and d. N H.,
Dec. 5, 1852, ae. 32-3-13   She m. Nov. 1855, Parker Perry, a descendant

of Commodore Perry. He d. Worcester, Mass., in 1876; she d. May 30, 1872, ae. 56-2-0. Children:

    a. Martha Ann, b. No. Chelmsford, Mass., Sept. 2, 1845; m. Sidney A. Brown. (See.)

    b. John Wayland, b. New Hampton, July 10, 1848; d. Sept. 14, 1851, ae. 2-2-4.

    c. Parker Wayland, b. Sept. 29, 1856; m. Dec. 9, 1880, Amy Catherine Vawter. Two children: Wayland, b. Sept. 18, 1883, and Junia Geniveo, b. Apr. 10, 1895.

  3. Benjamin, b. in Epping, Apr. 18, 1818; m. Abigail, dau. James Gordon; located in Laconia where he d.; had six children.

  *4. Leander, b. E., Feb. 4, 1820.

  5. James, b. E., July 25, 1824; m. Aseneth Stempson in Lowell, Mass.; went to Fond du Lac, Wis., where he res. many years, thence to Milwaukee, Wis., where he d. May, 1889; had three dau. and one son.

  6. Abbie Preston, b. Meredith, Nov. 14, 1827; m. Israel T. Rice. (See.)

  7. Mary A., b. M., Aug. 15, 1829; d. Nov. 11, 1858, ae. 29-2-26.

  8. Jane, b. Bridgewater, July 25, 1834. She m., Mar. 21, 1852, John Everleth, who was b. in Amherst, Mass., Jan. 1, 1821. In the Civil war he was a soldier in the 15th Mass. Battery and served 22 months. He d. at Holyoke, Mass., Mar. 16, 1880. She res. in Bristol. Child:

    a. George Parker Everleth, b. Lowell, Mass., July 23, 1853. (See in alphabetical position.)

  *9. Frank Sherburne, b. Bristol, Oct. 13, 1839.

  10. Hester Ann, b. B., Nov. 8, 1843; has been a saleswoman for many years in Lowell, Mass; unm.

    (4) Leander Badger, b. Feb. 4, 1820, came to Bristol with his parents; carpenter; he m. Aug. 8, 1845, Sephronia H., dau. Benjamin Emmons. (See.) He d. Bristol, Nov. 17, 1864, ae. 44-9-13. She m. (2) William Tibbetts. She res. during her last years in Lowell, Mass., where she d.

CHILDREN, all born in Bristol

  11. Ellen Maria, b. June 7, 1847; d. Sept. 11, 1848.

  12. Myron Curtis, b. Apr. 16, 1850; d. May 17, 1850.

  13. Warren Silas, b. Apr. 16, 1850; d. Apr. 28, 1850.

  14. Edward Frank, b. Sept. 16, 1860; m. Nov. 7, 1883, Lillie M. Small, at Lowell, Mass. He was head clerk in advertising department of the firm of J. C. Ayer & Co. He d. in Lowell, Oct. 13, 1887, ae. 27-0-27. She was b. in China, Me., Feb. 1, 1860. Child:

    a. Carl Vaughan, b. July 24, 1886.

    (9) Frank Sherburne Badger, b. Oct. 13, 1839, m. Oct. 16, 1860, S. Jennie, dau. Rowland T. Pomroy, who was b. Jan. 23, 1839, in Levant, Me. He settled in Lowell, Mass., in 1858, and in 1861 enlisted in the 12th Mass. Infantry. (See Roll of Honor.) He was in business in Lowell for many years after the war as a wood worker; later res. in Hiawatha, Kan., now in Lynn, Mass.

CHILDREN

  15. Genieve Frances, b. Lowell, Mass., Oct. 9, 1861; m. Geo. F. Barron, Lowell.

  16. Leander Boardman, b. L., Dec. 3, 1865; d. at Lowell, August, 1866.

17. Ralph Parker, b. Groton, Mass., Jan. 9, 1869; m. Mymie Wallace; res. Lynn, Mass.
18. Harry Orlando, b. G., Mar. 23, 1872; m. May 8, 1898, Kittie Bowers, of Kansas, now res. Lynn.
19. Allyn Studley, b. Lowell, Mass., June 22, 1876; m. June—, 1900, Annie M. Pardy, Horton, Kan.; res. Lynn.

THE BAILEY FAMILIES

1. Abel Bailey, son of Abel and Elizabeth (Swain) Bailey, was b. Groton, July 9, 1845. He m. (1) Martha J. Willoughby; (2) Feb. 17, 1889, Josie M. Fellows, b. Dorchester, Mar. 3, 1870. He was a farmer in Groton and Dorchester till October, 1902, when he took possession of the Levi Locke farm on Summer street. He d. in hospital in Concord, Feb. 27, 1903, ae. 57-7-18.

CHILDREN

2. Nellie M., m. Frank Ford.
3. Charles Gordon, b. Groton, July 20, 1873; m. Apr. 13, 1895, Sarah Lizzie, dau. of Lafayette and Emma F. (Colburn) Bailey, b. Groton, Apr. 14, 1878. They removed to Bristol in September, 1894. Finisher in woolen-mill and farmer. No children.
4. Effie Ardella, b. G., May 5, 1876; m. Ervin H. Reed. (See.)
5. Alice Corinne, b. Dorchester, Aug. 1, 1889.
6. Elizabeth Sarah, b. D., Jan. 25, 1897.

---

1. George Harold Bailey is a son of George Ozro and Mary Ann (Woods) Bailey. George O. served four years in the 84th Regt., Ohio Vols., in the Civil war, including the seige of Vicksburg. George H. was b. in Groton, Nov. 24, 1852, and m. Nov. 27, 1877, Ada Frances, dau. of E. Bradley and Aurilla E. Butterfield, b. Apr. 20, 1855, in Natick, Mass. They came to Bristol in March, 1891. For four years he was an employee of Dodge-Davis Manufacturing Co., later at the Mason-Perkins Paper Co.'s mill. In 1896, he built a residence on Hillside avenue, where they have since resided.

CHILD

2. Annie Eliza, b. Groton, Aug. 19, 1879; is a member of the Congregational choir and a soprano singer and organist.

THE BALLOU FAMILIES

1. The Ballous of Bristol and vicinity are the descendants of Maturin Ballou, the progenitor of the Ballous of New England. Maturin was a descendant of the Norman French, and was a co-worker with Roger Williams in Rhode Island, as early as 1645. He was one of the proprietors of the Providence Plantation of the Colony of Rhode Island. Of his children the second was

2. John, b. probably in Providence, R. I., 1650, m. Hannah Garrett, and was the father of six children, of whom the third was

3. Peter, b. Aug. 1, 1689. He m. Rebecca Asten, or Esten, May 13, 1714, and had eleven children. The tenth was

4. Peter, b. 1730; m. Elee Bucklin, and had seven children. The second was

5. Oliver, b. Springfield, R. I., in 1759. He m. —— Tiffany, and settled in Hanover. After the death of his first wife, he m. Mary Simonds, and removed to Enfield, and thence to the Borough, in Hill, where he d. June 19, 1818, ae. 59. His widow d. in Hill, about 1863, ae. 89.

CHILDREN

*6. Oliver, b. Hanover, Mar. 6, 1789.
7. Nathaniel, d. at Enfield, ae. 19.
8. Sarah, m. Jan. 31, 1791, David Sawyer, and settled in Mt. Tabor, Vt.
9. Achsah, m. Dudley Davis, and settled in Grafton.
10. Jane, m. (1) —— Blodgett; (2) —— Morgan, and removed to the West.
        By second wife
*11. Hosea, b. Hanover, Oct. 1, 1800.
*12. Horace, b. H., Nov. 8, 1801.
*13. Zara, b. Enfield, Dec. 10, 1802.
*14. John W., b. Hanover, Mar. 4, 1807.
15. Mary, b. Enfield, June, 1808; m. Aaron Kidder. (See.)
*16. Elijah, b. probably in Enfield.
17. Elisha, twin brother of Elijah; m. Lucinda Watts and res. Alexandria, where seven children were b.
*18. William P., b. probably Enfield, Oct. 20, 1816.
19. Eliza, b. Hill; m. Mar. 13, 1832, George W. Corless; they res. Hill, where he d. December, 1846. Children:
        a. Philinda B., b. H., Dec. 13, 1832; m. George A. White; she res. many years in Boston, Mass., and last years in Bristol, where she d. May 25, 1896, ae. 63-23-12.
        b. Rhoda, b. H., Apr. 1, 1837.
        c. George W., b. Bristol, May 29, 1839; d. in the army, unm., Feb. 20, 1862, ae. 22-8-21. (See Roll of Honor.)
        d. Mary, b. Apr. 23, 1840; m. Horace Dufer, and d. in Hill.
        e. James, b. May 25, 1844; d. in H., unm., about 1899.
        f. Alvin, b. Aug. 5, 1846; farmer, res. in H., unm.
20. Cynthia, b. Alexandria; m. John Peaslee. (See.)
21. Philinda, b. A.; m. —— Quimby. He went to sea and there d.; she d. 1873 (?).

(6) Oliver Ballou, b. Mar. 6, 1789, m. Oct. 12, 1813, Elizabeth, dau. Samuel Heath. (See.) She d. Dec. 30, 1818, and he m., Nov. —, 1819, Dorothy, dau. Benjamin Kidder. (See.) Oliver res. on south road in Alexandria, where his children were b. He was a tanner and shoemaker. He d. Alexandria, May 30, 1872, ae. 83-2-24.

CHILDREN

22. Sarah H., b. June 21, 1814; m. Apr. 16, 1845, Samuel A. Howard.
23. Laura, b. Jan. 18, 1816; m. (1) Joseph Johnson; (2) Silas Rhoades

24. Elizabeth, b. Jan. 21, 1818; m. Oct. 25, 1839, Alexander W. Wright.

25. Nancy, b. Mar. 25, 1822; m. Apr. 11, 1842, Varus Stearns, b. Landaff, Oct. 9, 1818. They res. Passaic, N. J. Six children.

26. Jane, b. Feb. 14, 1824; m. William Long, Feb. 8, 1846. He d. and she m. (2) Ira Morgan. She res. Lowell, Mass.

27. Dorothy, b. Sept. 19, 1825; m. July 14, 1849, Sylvester B. Leonard, and res. Lowell, Mass. Two children.

＊28. Oliver, b. Sept. 3, 1828.

29. Nathaniel, b. June 14, 1830; m. Mar. 24, 1855, Eda Ann, dau. Foster Averill, b. Londonderry, Dec. 22, 1834. In 1876, they removed to Iowa, and res. Sanborn, Iowa. Children :

    a. Edgar Nathaniel, b. Alexandria, Apr. 10, 1863; m. Mary Horner, Apr. 10, 1892; farmer in Sanborn, Iowa.

    b. Dora Belle, b. A., Dec. 25, 1866; m. July 4, 1886, John Holmes, a banker at Archer, Iowa.

    c. Frank Henry, b. A., Jan. 11, 1872; a farmer at Sanborn, Iowa.

30. Benjamin Kidder, b. Mar. 14, 1832; m. Mar. 14, 1858, Lavinia Elder, and res. Anoka, Minn.

31. Achsah, b. Feb. 11, 1833; m. James Bartlett, Sept. 14, 1853; res. Detroit, Mich.

(11) Hosea Ballou, b. Oct. 1, 1800, m. Apr. 6, 1822, Cynthia P., dau. Joseph Sanborn (See.), b. Jan. 19, 1807. He came to Bristol in 1834. He built the house next beyond the cemetery on same side of highway, and res. there ; was a speculator and farmer ; was one of the contractors for the construction of the Franklin and Bristol railroad. He went West April, 1855, and d. at Beaver Dam, Wis., Oct. 18, 1855, ae. 55–0–17. She d. Alexandria, Nov. 13, 1892, ae. 85–9–24.

CHILDREN

32 Ira Persons, b. Hill, Sept. 10, 1823; kept hotel for a time where is now Hotel Bristol ; went West in 1846 ; thence to Cuba, where he was a railroad contractor and builder. He m. in 1853, Ellen Compton, and d. of yellow fever at Matansas, Cuba, Sept. 5, 1860, ae. 36–11–25.

33. Mary Jane, b. H., Mar. 8, 1827 ; d. Oct. 24, 1829.

34. Sarah Jane, b. H., Nov. 28, 1829 ; d. Nov. 11, 1831.

35. Charlotte Augusta, b. Alexandria, Sept. 7, 1833 ; m. July 22, 1853, George F. Preston. He was in the U. S. army, and d. at Fort Bridger, Utah, Dec. 17, 1860. She res. many years in Alexandria, till 1898 ; now in New Hampton.

36. Ellen Maria, b. Bristol, July 23, 1837 ; m. Andrew F. Burpee. (See.)

37. Luisde Leon, b. B., Dec. 4, 1842. (See Roll of Honor.) Was a farmer in Alexandria till 1898, now New Hampton ; unm.

38. Anna Belle, b. B., Aug. 24, 1852; d. Oct. 14, 1854.

(12) Horace Ballou, b. Nov. 8, 1801, m. May 27, 1827, Mary Bean, dau. Caleb and Lois (Phelps) Simonds. She was b. Alexandria, Apr. 12, 1809. They came to Bristol in 1869, where he d. Feb. 6, 1891, ae. 89–3–29 ; she d. Bristol, June 30, 1894 ae. 85–2–18.

CHILDREN, all born in Alexandria

39. Caleb, b. Dec. 10, 1828 ; d. Sept. 4, 1832, ae. 3–9–24.

40. Horace Selden, b. June 27, 1833 ; d. Apr. 22, 1854, ae. 20–9–25.

LUCIAN A. BALLOU

41. Levi Bartlett, b. July 17, 1839; d. Mar. 2, 1841, ae. 1-7-15.
*42. Lucian Augustus, b. May 4, 1844.

(13) Zara Ballou, b. Dec. 10, 1802, m. Jan. 19, 1834, Caroline Tenney, b. Nov. 10, 1810. They were farmers in Hill, where he d. Sept. 7, 1866, ae. 63-8-27; she d. Alexandria, Dec. 17, 1886, ae. 76-1-7.

CHILDREN, all born in Hill

43. Warren, b. Oct. 29, 1834; d. unm. at Manchester, Feb. 15, 1859, ae. 24-3-16.
44. Mary Jane, b. Mar. 21, 1837; m. William Saltmarsh. He d. Lawrence, Mass.; she res. Waltham, Mass.
45. Persis Garland, b. Apr. 10, 1839; d. Jan 31, 1852, ae. 12-9-21.
46. Silas, b. July 28, 1841; m. Abbie Simonds; res. So. Alexandria.
47. James T., b. Dec 12, 1843; was a laborer in Bristol; unm. He d. Apr. 2, 1893, of accidental gunshot wound received while hunting, ae. 49-3-14.
*48. Zara Marshall, b. Aug. 28, 1845.
49. Ada K., b. July 24, 1847; res. Lawrence, Mass.; unm.
50. Hiland, b. Apr. 25, 1850.
51. Eveline, b. Nov. 8, 1852; m. Alexander Healey, and d. Waltham, Mass., leaving two children.

(14) John W. Ballou, b. Mar. 4, 1807, m. Mar. 24, 1833, Thirza, dau. of Gardner and Lavina (Wells) Evans, b. Hill, Apr. 25, 1813. He was a farmer; d. Bristol, Aug. 25, 1887, ae. 80-5-21. She d. Bristol, Apr. 3, 1895, ae. 82-0-8.

CHILDREN

*52. Hiram P., b. Alexandria, Oct. 25, 1833.
53. Frederick W., b. Jan. 21, 1835; m. Mary A. Holmes, widow of Silas, and dau. David and Lucy A. Huntoon, b. Lempster, Mass., May, 1835. He was a jeweler in Bristol, 1868-'74; later in Salisbury, where he d. in February, 1892, ae. 57. She d. while on a visit in Contoocook, in December, 1892, ae. 57. No children.
54. John Wesley, b. Hill, Oct. 21, 1837; m. May 12, 1860, Helen E., dau. Henry and Mary L. (Locke) Nye, b. Gaysville, Vt., May 29, 1837. He is a knitter, and inventor of knitting machinery at Bristol, Pa. Child :
    a. Minnie F., b. Gonic, May 29, 1861; d. Aug. 1, 1863.
55. Horace Augustus, b. H., Feb. 4, 1840; m. Jan. 4, 1876, Sula A., dau. Rice and Sarah (Page) Courser, b. Webster, 1849; she d. Apr. 13, 1880, and he m. (2) Carrie J. Atwood, dau. Stephen T. and Catherine (Hutchinson) Atwood. He is a policeman in Nashua. No children.
56. Isaac Clark, b. H., Apr. 25, 1842; m. Mar. 2, 1873, Ida I. Hastings, dau. of Robert S. (See.) He is a farmer in H. Children :
    a. Herman U., b. H., Aug. 29, 1874.
    b. Fred C., b. H., July 15, 1876.
    c. Edgar R., b. H., June 15, 1882.
57. Rufus M., b. Sept. 21, 1847, drowned in Franklin, Aug. 11, 1859.
*58. George Winslow, b. H., Mar. 31, 1851.

(16) Elijah Ballou m., Aug. 24, 1834, Elizabeth Peaslee, who d. childless, and he m., Mar. 1, 1840, Nancy, dau. of Samuel Tirrell. (See.) She d. Franklin, Sept. 14, 1880. He d. Hill.

59. Maria A., b. Bristol, Apr. 5, 1841; m. Martin M. Nelson, and res. Franklin Falls.

60. Weston, b. B., June 5, 1843; m. Mary Boswell of Hill, who d. Aug. 3, 1872, ae. 32. (See Roll of Honor.) He removed to the West.

61. Wayland, b. B., Oct. 16, 1844; m. Emma, dau. James W. Griffith. He was a workman in paper-mill, and d. July 4, 1883, ae. 38-8-18. A Mason. (See Roll of Honor.) She m. (2) Amos Tirrell and res. Nashua.

62. Nellie, b. B., Sept. 1, 1848; m. Napoleon Burleigh, res. Concord.

63. Alfred N., b. B., June 12, 1850; m. Zilpha White and res. Franklin.

64. Emma J., b. B., Jan. 12, 1852; d. Franklin, June 2, 1875, ae. 23-4-20.

65. Clara, b. Hill, May 28, 1855; m. Carlos S. Morey; res. Boscawen.

(18) William P. Ballou, b. Oct. 20, 1816, m. May 15, 1847, Mrs. Sophronia M. Sanborn, dau. of Moses M. Smith (See), and widow of Gustavus B. Sanborn. (See.) William P. was a farmer and shoemaker in Alexandria, and Bristol from 1867. He d. Bristol, Dec. 7, 1879, ae. 63-1-17. She was a milliner here many years; now res. Church street.

*66. LaForest Scott, b. Alexandria, Feb. 9, 1849.
*67. Quincy Arthur, b. A., Jan. 23, 1852.

(28) Oliver, b. Alexandria, Sept. 3, 1828, m. Sept. 20, 1855, Emily W. Heath, dau. of Robert. (See.) She d. Sept. 2, 1890, ae. 54-9-18, and he m. Mar. 1, 1892, Ida Gertrude, dau. of Levi N. Heath. (See.) He was a manufacturer of organs in Concord for ten years, and later was engaged in the art business. He d. Concord, Oct. 5, 1902, ae. 74-1-2. She res. Concord.

68. Hattie Annette, b. July 27, 1858; m. Jan. 18, 1881, Robert Allen Ray. Child:

a. Agnes Ellen, b. Mar. 18, 1883.

69. Helen Emogene, b. May 21, 1860; m. Dec. 24, 1891, Albert Edward Bodwell.

(42) Lucian A. Ballou, b. May 4, 1844, came here in 1868, and was a trader on Lake street. He m. Aug. 20, 1864, Mary Ellen, dau. Ansel and Mary (Mills) Fish, b. Lowell, Mass., Feb. 16, 1846. She d. Bristol, Aug. 23, 1880, ae. 34-6-7. He removed to the West in 1881, and m. (2) Annie Maria Pierce, who d. at Colorado Springs, Col., in 1889. He d. at Grinnell, Iowa, July 13, 1890, ae. 46-2-9. Republican; Mason.

70. Mary Eva, b. Alexandria, July 25, 1867; m. Feb. 5, 1891, Orpheus Edward Bell, of South Norwood, O. They res. Appleton, Wis.

71. George Alfred, b. Jan. 4, 1871; d. of diphtheria, Apr. 6, 1882.

72. Martha Grace, b. Nov. 25, 1874.

Zara Marshall Ballou

73. Harry Burchard, b. Nov. 5, 1876. Graduated Dartmouth college, 1902; m. Dec. 31, 1902, Ada R. Eaton, of Minneapolis, Minn. Is now, 1904, attending Medical school, University of Minnesota, Minneapolis, Minn.

74. Susie Gertrude, b. Apr. 6, 1878; m. Fred H. Bean. (See.)

(48) Zara Marshall Ballou, b. Aug. 28, 1845, m. May 8, 1877, Hannah Frances, dau. Thomas W. and Mary (Cheney) Shattuck, b. Waterville, Vt.. Nov. 14, 1845. He is a manufacturer of picker-sticks. Represented Bristol in the legislature of 1889. She d. Bristol, Aug. 1, 1902, ae. 56-8-17.

CHILDREN

75. Frank Marshall, b. Bristol, Nov. 9, 1881.
76. Walter Thomas, b. B., Dec. 13, 1885.

(52) Hiram P. Ballou, b. Oct. 25, 1833, m. Oct. 4, 1857, Sarah Augusta, dau. of Jacob and Nancy (Sanborn) Heath, b. New Hampton, Mar. 25, 1836. He was a workman on knit goods and an inventor, and d. Bristol, Dec. 28, 1899, ae. 66-2-3. She res. New Hampton.

CHILDREN

77. Arthur William, b. New Hampton, Apr. 21, 1861; was a druggist clerk; went to Pueblo, Col., for his health, and there m. Mar. 15, 1887, Emma Davis, of Laconia. He d. of consumption, Bristol, Apr. 17, 1887, a few days after his return. She d. Dec. —, 1895, at Laconia.

78. Minnie Ella, b. Needham. Mass., Dec. 18, 1876; m. Arthur W. Seavey. (See.)

(58) George W. Ballou, b. Mar. 31, 1851, m. May 6, 1874, Emma H., dau. Wilson Foster. (See.) She d. Apr. 27, 1887, ae. 34-1-26, and he m. Aug. 28, 1893, Florence L., dau. Horace L. and Mary (Corless) Dufer, b. Hill, Jan. 22, 1872. He is a farmer at Profile Falls.

CHILDREN

79. Oscar F., b. Hill, June 30, 1876. He is janitor of city library, Nashua; unm.
80. Grace M., b. H., Oct. 27, 1878; m. Burton E. Foss. (See.)
81. Herbert Hadley, b. Bristol, Feb. 13, 1884; is an employee in shoe factory, Nashua.
82. Harriet E., b. B., Mar. 6, 1885.
83. Lula May, b. B., Dec. 10, 1893.
84. Daughter, b. B., Jan. 8, 1895; d. Apr. 9, 1895.
85. Daughter, b. B., Feb. 4, 1896; d. May 8, 1896.
86. Pearl Lou, b. B., May 23, 1897.
87. John Wesley, d. B. Dec. 13, 1898.
88. Son, b. B., Sept. 18, 1900; d. in infancy.

(66) LaForest S. Ballou, b. Feb. 9, 1849, m. Feb. 6, 1870, Elvira B., dau. Hiram and Elvira (Simonds) Gale, b. Danbury, Jan. 14, 1848, and d. Oct. 14, 1882, ae. 34-9-0. He m. Sept. 8, 1886, Mary E. Kennedy, Concord. He came to Bristol about 1870; blacksmith; liveryman; deputy sheriff, 1891-'3; now farmer on farm at outlet of Newfound lake; Democrat.

2

89. Lola M., b. Alexandria, Apr. 1, 1873; d. Nov. 28, 1883, ae. 10-7-28.

(67) Quincy A. Ballou, b. Jan. 23, 1852, m. Oct. 19, 1881. Lisette Sophronia, dau. Stephen N. Colby. (See.) He has practiced dentistry in Bristol since spring of 1880; is member of New Hampshire Dental Society; Odd Fellow; K. of P.; Democrat. She is a milliner; a member of Methodist choir.

CHILDREN

90. Hazel Rae, b. Bristol, Dec. 22, 1891.
91. Elizabeth Belle, b. B., Dec. 25, 1894.

---

1. Jamin Ballou, son of William Jirah and Sarah Jane (Hazelton) Ballou, was b. Dorset, Vt., Feb. 22, 1842. He m. Florence Lenora, dau. William F. Town, b. Dorset, July 28, 1851. Laborer in Bristol, now farmer in Alexandria.

CHILDREN

2. Celia, b. Dorset, Vt., Apr. 4, 1867; m. Feb. 16, 1884, Benjamin F. Hemenway.
3. George W., b. Goshen, Nov. 3, 1869. Is a farmer in Alexandria.
4. Jerome, b. Chester, Vt., Nov. 22, 1871; m. Nov. 21, 1891, Amy Ann, dau. of Charles R. Hammond. Laborer in Bristol.
5. Clarence Jamin, b. Lempster, July 31, 1879; d. Bristol, Dec. 6, 1884, ae. 5-4-5.
6. Edgar, b. Bristol, June 10, 1890.
7. Florence, b. B., Feb. 8, 1892.

---

1. Frederick Jirah Ballou, son of William Jirah and Sarah Jane (Hazelton) Ballou, was b. Pawlet, Vt., Apr. 1, 1852. He m. Aug. 20, 1873, Janey A., dau. of Joseph Reid, b. Chesterfield, N. Y., Sept. 5, 1857. They came to Bristol, Nov., 1887. Laborer; res. Lake street.

CHILDREN

2. Edgar, b. Clintonville, N. Y., Dec. 5, 1874; d. in Keene, N. Y., Sept. 11, 1878, ae. 3-9-6.
3. Marion May, b. Keene, N. Y., May 12, 1876; m. Jan. 21, 1893, Weston J. Braley. (See.)
4. George Henry, b. Mineville, N. Y., June 5, 1880; m. Feb. 24, 1900, Elizabeth, dau. William C. Kelley. (See.) Killed Jan. 19, 1901, by being struck by engine at railroad crossing in Franklin. She m. (2) May 17, 1902, George Bucklin, Alexandria.
5. Agnes Eveline, b. Montague, Mass., Mar. 5, 1885; m. Apr. 25, 1903, Edward O. Lord; res. Bristol, laborer.

THE BARNEY FAMILY

1. Ahira Barney, son of James W. and Eliza B. (French) Barney, was b. in Grafton, May 18, 1845. He m., June 14,

1866, Mary Jane, dau. of Charles and Betsey Newell, b. Dec. 5, 1845. Divorced 1877. In the Civil war he served in the 15th Regt., N. H. Vols., on the quota of Grafton from Sept. 20, 1862, to Aug. 13, 1863. He was promoted to corporal on the field in March, 1863 ; was wounded at Port Hudson with a buck shot in the arm and lost the end of one finger by a minie ball. He was a resident of Bristol 1880–'86, and has been here since 1899. Carpenter, Republican, Odd Fellow, G. A. R.

CHILD

2. Leona Miriam, b. Newport, June 14, 1876; m. George E. Twombly, June 14, 1902.

THE BARRETT FAMILY

1. Amos Emery Barrett, the son of Emory A. and Martha K. (Ferrin) Barrett, was b. Bridgewater, Aug 7, 1860. He m. Mar. 29, 1882, Nellie G., dau. James and Martha Weston, b. Reading, Mass., Apr. 2, 1864. He was a res. of Bristol some years ; now a farmer in Alexandria.

CHILDREN

2. Howard E., b. Bristol, Mar. 18, 1883; d. Dec. 28, 1899, ae. 16–9–15.
3. Eva M., b. B., June 14, 1884.
4. Elsie M., b. Alexandria, Mar. 6, 1891.

---

1. David Luther Barrett, son of Emory A. and Martha K. (Ferrin) Barrett, b. Bridgewater, Oct. 9, 1854, m. July 2, 1886, Lavinia Winnifred, dau. of Frank J. and Hattie L. (Gilman) Smith, b. Plymouth, Jan. 11, 1868. Was a farmer in Bridgewater till 1896 ; a laborer in Bristol.

CHILDREN

2. Fred Morton, b. Bridgewater, Sept. 23, 1888.
3. Harry Edward, b. B., June 21, 1890.
4. Emory Francis, b. B., Sept. 19, 1892.
5. Hattie Emma, b. B., Aug. 21, 1894.
6. Rena Martha, b. B., Mar. 30, 1896 ; d. Aug. 11, 1896.
7. Lester Amos, b. Bristol, Mar. 25, 1897 ; d. Apr. 5, 1897.
8. Mildred Aneeta, b. B., Apr. 3, 1899.
9. Lena Alice, b. B., Dec. 2, 1901.

THE BARTLETT FAMILIES

From records in existence the Bartletts of Bristol can clearly trace their genealogy from Adam Bartlett, who d. in England in the year 1100. He was an Esquire to Brian, a Knight, and landed in England with him, with William the Conqueror, and seated himself in Ferring, Co. Sussex. Brian's name appears on the "Battle Abbey Roll." Both received grants of land, Stopham, in Sussex, being the principal grant. Brian, the Norman Knight, assumed the name of Brian de Stopham.

In the 14th century, John Bartlett married a daughter and heiress of the Stophams and came into possession of the whole property, the male line of the Stophams having failed. The Bartletts have lived on the estate since the Conquest, and fought at the battles of Crecy in 1346, and at Poitiers in 1356, and subscribed liberally towards the fund to defend England against the attack of the Spanish armada in 1588. The records in the stone church, built by the family in the 13th century, is complete from John Bartlett, born early in 1300, to the present. Sir Walter B. Bartlett, the present representative of the family, is a member of the House of Commons. In 1514, Richard Bartlett, heir of the estate, died. He left several children, one of whom was Edmund, who d. leaving, with other children two sons, John and Richard, who came to America in ship Mary and John, and settled in Newbury, Mass., about 1634. The Bartletts of Bristol are the descendants of

1. Richard, b. 1590, who came to America as above. He d. May 25, 1647, leaving five children. One son

2. Richard, b. England, 1621, came to America with his father. He was representative in the Colonial legislature of 1679, 1680, 1681, and 1684. He d. Newbury, Mass., 1698. His wife, Abigail, d. Mar. 1, 1687. His second son was

3. Richard, b. Feb. 21, 1649. He m. Nov. 18, 1673, Hannah Emery of Newbury, Mass. He d. leaving ten children, of whom the eighth was

4. Stephen, b. Apr. 21, 1691, in Newbury, m. Hannah Webster of Salisbury, Mass. He left several children, of whom the second was

5. Joseph, b. Apr. 18, 1720; m. Jane Colby, dau. of Ichabod Colby, a physician in Salisbury, Mass. He left several children of whom the oldest was

6. Levi, b. Apr. 25, 1745. Of his children one was

7. Ichabod Colby Bartlett, b. Amesbury, Mass., Mar. 29, 1779. His father died when he was a mere boy and he removed with his mother to Boscawen. He commenced life as a clerk in the store of Andrew Bowers, in Salisbury, Mass., where he remained till 1800, when he came to Bristol. He soon after commenced trade in a very humble way, in a building that stood on east side South Main street, where is now Frank W. Bingham's harness shop. In 1802, he erected a wooden building in Central square, just in front of the present store in this square. Here his business rapidly increased and about 1823 he erected the brick part of the present store. Here he continued in trade till 1838; engaged in farming and quite extensively in the cattle trade, and accumulated a large property. "Cato," Dr. J. S. Eaton, in

ICHABOD C. BARTLETT

a letter to *The Enterprise*, Dec. 7, 1878, thus speaks of Mr. Bartlett: "The name of Ichabod C. Bartlett was a tower of honor and strength in the commercial world. His strict methods of business taught the people providence and the importance of paying their debts. Each fall Mr. Bartlett and his aids would gather up a great herd of cattle for market, taken largely for debt, and woe to the luckless debtor who did not call at the captain's office and settle. He was a gentleman of the old school in dress and manners, just but tenacious. When the question of the color of paint for the pews of the new church was discussed, Mr. Bartlett said 'white,' the majority said 'green,' so all the pews were painted green except Mr. Bartlett's which was painted white, which color was later approved by all. Excommunicated from the church for selling rum, he later became a strong temperance man and reunited with the church." He was succeeded in business by his sons. He represented Bridgewater three years in the legislature and served as town clerk, and served Bridgewater and Bristol as treasurer. Nov. 11, 1801, he m. Anna S., dau. of Col. Peter Sleeper. (See.) She d. in Bristol, Oct. 8, 1869, ae. 86-1-26; he d. Bristol, Mar. 20, 1860, ae. 80-11-21. His residence was on the north side of Pleasant street, the same as now occupied by his son. (See Mercantile Industries.)

CHILDREN, all born in Bristol

8. Mary, b. June 7, 1802; m. William M. Lewis, of Bristol. They removed to Gainesville, Ala., where she d. May 31, 1831, ae. 28-11-34. He m. (2) a lady in Michigan and d. there. Child:

    a. William Frederic.

9. Jane, b. July 19, 1804. She res. at the old homestead, unm., where she d. Feb. 23, 1881, ae. 76-7-4.

*10. Levi, b. Jan. 8, 1807.

11. Frederick K., b. Sept. 5, 1808; d. June 11, 1811.

*12. Gustavus, b. Oct. 22, 1810.

13. Anna, b. Dec. 14, 1812; m. Jonas Minot. (Sec.)

*14. Frederick, b. Nov. 29, 1815.

(10) Levi Bartlett, b. Jan. 8, 1807, m. Martha P. Haines, dau. Stephen and Mary (Pickering) Haines, b. Canterbury, Feb. 16, 1815. She d. Bristol, May 8, 1865, ae. 50 years; he d. Bristol, Nov. 14, 1868, ae. 61-10-6. He was educated at Norwich (Vt.) Military Academy. He was a man of large business enterprises and acquired his estate in the same mercantile business as his father. He sold his business to his brother, Gustavus, and Cyrus Taylor. He was a selectman of the town six years; town clerk one year, and represented his town in the legislature two years. He was an active member of the Congregational church and for many years its most liberal supporter. He was interested in enterprises to improve the

2a

town, and was ready to assist by moral or financial support. He res. east side Central square.

CHILDREN, all born in Bristol

15. Frederick Haines, b. May 25, 1840. He was in lumber business at Profile Falls. Studied for ministry at Andover Theological Seminary 1872-'74. Licensed to preach by the Hopkinton association July 9, 1872; ordained as an evangelist at Bristol, Feb. 20, 1879. Was a missionary Central City, Dakota, in 1879; acting pastor, Breckenridge, Minn., 1883-'84. While at Breckenridge he was elected surveyor of Wilkins Co., Minn. He engaged in civil engineering and land surveying from 1884 till Oct. 1887; in business at Avalanche, N. H., Oct. 1887-'91; for some years has been in business at Silverton, B. C. Unm.

16. Levi Scott, b. Jan. 4, 1842; d. Sept. 9, 1846, ae. 4-8-5.

17. Annie Pickering, b. Nov. 30, 1843; d. Sept. 15, 1882, ae. 38-9-14. Unm. She was for some years organist at Congregational church.

18. Mary Elizabeth, b. Feb, 5, 1849; res. at her father's homestead. Unm.

(12) Gustavus Bartlett, b. Oct. 22, 1810, m. Nov. 25, 1834, Clarinda Jane, dau. of Nicholas M. and Sally (Eastman) Taylor, b. New Hampton, Mar. 9, 1815, and d. Bristol, Nov. 1, 1837, ae. 22-7-22. He m. Nov. 24, 1839, Martha, a sister of his first wife, b. New Hampton, June 17, 1820, and d. Bristol, Oct. 23, 1856, ae. 36-4-6. He m., Dec. 3, 1861, Susan A. Nicholas. He was in trade for several years in the Central square store, and his residence was on South side of Pleasant street. He removed to Lowell, Mass., Oct. 26, 1863. In May, 1867, he settled in Milford, where he d. Dec. 11, 1893, ae. 83-1-19. She res. Milford. Congregationalist, Republican.

CHILDREN, all born in Bristol

19. Mary Lewis, b. Aug. 10, 1837; d. Aug. 12, 1837.

*20. Ichabod Colby, b. Sept. 10, 1841.

21. Mary Clarinda, b. May 1, 1843; d. July 24, 1844, ae. 1-2-23.

22. Sarah Eastman, b. Feb. 4, 1845; m. Charles Moses Proctor, Nov. 24, 1869. He was b. Aug. 12, 1844, in West Cambridge, Mass., the son of Moses and Elizabeth (Conant) Proctor. They res. in Milford twenty years after marriage, then removed to Wilton where they now live. Farmer. Children:

    a. Elizabeth Martha, b. Milford, July 21, 1870.

    b. Charles Owen, b. M., Sept. 30, 1873.

    c. Walter Bartlett, b. M., Mar. 17, 1879; d. Apr. 20, 1900, ae. 21-1-3.

23. Clara Anstris, b. Apr. 5, 1847; d. June 20, 1848, ae 1-2-15.

24. Ann Minot, b. Aug. 7, 1849; m. John S. Conner. (See.)

25. Charles Henry, b. Nov. 3, 1862, was educated at the common schools of Milford; Chauncey Hall school, and Mass. Institute of Technology and Association Law school, Boston. He has been connected with the engineering of a number of railroads, including the New York and New England; Providence and Worcester; Boston and Lowell; Providence, Webster and Springfield; Concord; Lake Shore; New Boston; Concord and Montreal, and Boston and Maine. He was associated with N. W. Ellis and ex-Gov. Weston, of Manchester, in engineering

GUSTAVUS BARTLETT

and contracting. In 1889, he formed a partnership with Frank A. Gay at Manchester, succeeding N. W. Ellis & Co., and did a general engineering business, building many of the water works and sewer systems throughout New Hampshire. Removed to Boston in 1895, where he was connected with the Boston Transit Commission in the construction of the Subway. Later was appointed by the United States government to take charge of the engineering of the new plant for the construction and repair department at the Charlestown Navy Yard. In 1901, he was admitted to the Mass. bar; has now a law and consulting engineering office at 607 Pemberton Building, in Boston, and an engineering office in Manchester. He is a member of the Society of Naval Architects and Marine Engineers; New England Water Works Association; United Order of the Golden Cross; Knights of Pythias; I. O. O. F.; Sons of the American Revolution, a Mason of the 32nd degree; and a member of other organizations. He m. Dec. 17, 1890, Gertrude B., dau. of Joseph C., and Frances M. Jones, b. Claremont, Sept. 9, 1871. No children.

(14) Frederick Bartlett, b. Nov. 29, 1815, m. Dec. 10, 1845, Jane Eliza Sutherland, dau. of Daniel S. Smith. (See.) She was b. Mar. 12, 1824, and d. Bristol, Mar. 25, 1867, ae. 33-0-13. He was graduated from Dartmouth college in 1835 and has always res. in Bristol. (See Lawyers.) Represented the town in legislatures of 1851 and 1860, and in state constitutional convention of 1850. Was selectman two years. Farmer, Congregationalist.

CHILDREN, all born in Bristol

26. Ella Jane, b. Nov. 29, 1846; m. Augustus W. Evans, Concord, who d. Apr. 17, 1880, ae. 31-1-0. She d. Bristol, Nov. 28, 1896, ae. 49-11-29. One child, d. 1880.

27. William, b. Jan. 28, 1848; m. Mar. 25, 1874, Eva Eliza, dau. John P. Taylor. (See.) He left Bristol for Minn. about 1876; has a general store and is a dealer in real estate at Beardsley, Minn. No children.

28. George Smith, b. Nov. 12, 1849; studied medicine; druggist at Meredith. Unm.

29. Levi Scott, b. Feb. 8, 1852; farmer; d. unm., July 18, 1885, ae. 33-5-10.

*30. Gustavus, b. May 27, 1854.

31. Martha, b. Mar. 11, 1857; d. Mar. 25, 1870, ae. 13-0-4.

(20) Ichabod C. Bartlettt, b. Sept. 10, 1841, m. Oct. 20, 1862, Ellen Augusta, dau. Moody C. Sawyer. (See.) She d. in Malden, Mass., Oct. 20, 1873, ae. 30-0-0. He left Bristol March, 1864, and has res. in Malden, Mass., since 1871.

CHILDREN

32. Martha Relief, b. Bristol, Dec. 30, 1863; m. John S. Conner. (See.)

33. Anna, b. Cambridge, Mass., Apr. —, 1865; d. Sept. 15, 1865.

34. Ichabod Roy, b. Charlestown, Mass., Sept.—, 1869; d. Sept. 15, 1870.

35. Philip Guy, b. Charlestown, Mass., Mar. 1, 1871; res. Malden; Mass., connected with a wholesale flour store in Boston.

(30) Gustavus Bartlett, b. May 27, 1854, m. May 29, 1873,

Susan Frances, dau. David P. and Harriet N. (Griffin) Sargent. b. Haverhill, Mass., Sept. 6, 1853. He was in trade in Concord ; now res. Bristol at his father's homestead. Republican, Congregationalist, farmer.

CHILD

36. Hattie, b. Concord, Feb. 18, 1875; m. Feb. 23, 1896, George Arthur Ballard, b. Concord, Aug. 27, 1873. He is a printing-office pressman. Child :

    a. Frances Ella, b. Portsmouth, Aug. 18, 1901.

---

1. Nathaniel Bartlett, the son of Thomas and Ann (Donnel) Bartlett, was b. Dec. 29, 1830, in Eliot, Me. Nov. 17, 1856, he m. Caroline Eliza, dau. of Lemuel and Philinda (Hastings) Kendall, b. Hebron, May 12, 1836. He was a shoe manufacturer in Natick, Mass., with his son, George N., till they came to Bristol in 1894, and prosecuted same business here. He d. Bristol, Feb. 2, 1900, ae. 69-1-3. After his death, the son continued the business.

CHILDREN

    *2. George Nathaniel, b. Natick, Mass., Sept. 15, 1857.
    3. Anna Florence, b. N., July 27, 1860 ; d. Groton, Oct. 2, 1860.
    4. Oscar Spaulding, b. Eliot, Me., May 11, 1862 ; m. Clara Isabel Dennett, dau. of Jeremy, of Taunton, Mass. He d. Feb. 26, 1888, ae. 25-9-15. Child :

    a. Georgia, b. Sept. 18, 1887.

(2) George N. Bartlett, b. Sept. 15, 1857, m. Sept. 12, 1887, Ella Josephine, dau. George Champney, b. Ayer, Mass., Oct. 8, 1861. He was a shoe manufacturer in Natick till 1894, subsequently in Bristol till spring of 1902, when he removed to East Holliston, Mass., where he is a farmer.

CHILDREN

    5. Nathaniel Champney, b. Natick, Mass., Apr. 6, 1890.
    6. Stephen Wyman, b. Bristol, Oct. 3, 1894.
    7. Charles Oscar, b. B., June 4, 1896.

---

1. Frank Giles Bartlett, the son of Corbin and Sarah Jane (Nicholas) Bartlett, was b. Newbury, Apr. 13, 1876. He is a locomotive fireman on the Bristol branch of the Boston & Maine railroad. Came to Bristol, July, 1900, and m. Feb. 12, 1903, Sadie Maria, dau. of Albert and Sarah J. (Maxfield) Hussey, b. Goshen, Mar. 20, 1877.

THE BATCHELDER FAMILY

1. Benjamin Batchelder, b. Hampton, Nov. 9, 1729, settled in Deerfield, removed to Meredith and there d. He was the father of ten children. One was

2. Simeon, who m. (1) Mary Marston, (2) Miss Powell. He settled in New Hampton, and removed to Bridgewater about 1795.

CHILDREN, all except first born in Bridgewater

*3. Benjamin, b. Meredith (New Hampton), June 2, 1787.
  4. Minor, or Jemima, b. Bridgewater, Apr. 14, 1789, m. Seth Glover.
  5. Patty, b. Apr. 6, 1790, m. —— Cummings. Child :
     a. Martha Cummings, 5 Durham street, Boston.
  6. Caleb, b. Aug. 24, 1791, m. (1) Hannah Moses, (2) Mary Rollins, widow of Noah ; d. July 31, 1868, ae. 76-11-7.
  7. Polly, b. June 29, 1793 ; m. Folsom Swain.
*8. Simeon, b. Aug. 29, 1795.
*9. David, b. Sept. 24, 1797 (Sept. 12, 1798).
 10. Betsey, b. Mar. 18, 1803 ; m. Benjamin E. Tilton. (See.)
 11. Phebe, b. Nov. 26, 1807 ; m. John Boynton. Children :
     a. George O., res. Boston.
     b. Augusta Ann, b. Bridgewater, Apr. 25, 1836 ; m. David S. Kidder. (See.)
 12. Nancy, m. Sherburn W. Tilton. (See.)

(3) Benjamin Batchelder, b. June 2, 1787, m. 1815, Mary Spaulding, b. Merrimack, Jan. 24, 1790 ; d. Sept. 26, 1849, ae. 59-7-12, in Bridgewater. He was a farmer in Bridgewater, and there d. Aug., 1859, ae. 72-2-.

CHILDREN

13. Benjamin Spaulding, b. July 6, 1816 ; m. Nancy C. Batchelder of Whitefield. Three children.
14. Daniel, b. July 24, 1818 ; m. Mary J. Plumer of Thornton. Farmer and Free Baptist minister in Ashland ; three children.
15. Simeon, b. Sept., 1820 ; m. Eliza H. Colby. A farmer in Hooksett. No children.
16. Abigail Frost, b. June, 1824 ; m. James M. Ames. (See.)
17. Putnam, b. Mar. 16, 1826. Farmer in Sanbornton ; three children.
18. John Boynton, b. Jan. 20, 1832 ; m. Sarah Colby, Oct. 5, 1864. Res. Bridgewater, Somerville, Mass., and Tilton.
19. Mary b., Oct. 12, 1835 ; m. Beniah P. Burley, Sanbornton.

(8) Simeon Batchelder, b. Aug. 29, 1795, m. Mar. 6, 1822, Sarah Spaulding. She was b. Nashua, Feb. 18, 1798, and d. Bridgewater, July 14, 1852, ae. 54-4-26 ; he d. Bridgewater, Jan. 13, 1864, ae. 68-4-14.

CHILDREN

20. Benjamin, b. Jan. 29, 1825 ; d. July 10, 1828.
21. Solomon, b. Sept. 25, 1826 ; d. July 7, 1828.
22. Benjamin Spaulding, b. Jan. 30, 1829. Res. Hardin, Clayton Co., Iowa.
23. Solomon, b. July 14, 1830 ; d. May, 1832.
24. Mary Marston, b. July 13, 1832 ; d. Dec. 17, 1868, ae. 36-5-4.
25. Simeon Dana, b. Feb. 23, 1834 ; d. Nov. 1, 1856, ae. 22-8-8.
26. David Spaulding, b. Bridgewater, July 22, 1836 ; m. May 20, 1858, Abbie A., dau. Rodney and Abigail (Frost) Hammond, b. Bridgewater, July 31, 1836. Res. Plymouth. Children :

    a. Annabel, b. Nov. 23, 1862; d. Jan. 5, 1864.
    b. Addie Ann, b. Oct. 26, 1864; m. Apr. 15, 1893, Curtis A. Gordon; res. Ashland.
    c. Abbie Frost, b. May 3, 1871; d. July 4, 1893, ae. 22-3-1.
    d. Mary Esther, b. Oct. 17, 1873.
    e. Sadie Hammond, b. Aug. 28, 1877.
  27. Sarah Ann, b. Aug. 15, 1838; d. May 18, 1840, ae. 1-9-3.
  28. Sarah Ann, b. May 24, 1840; d. June 18, 1850, ae. 10-0-24.

    (9) Dea. David Batchelder, b. Sept. 24, 1797, m., in 1821, Sally Thompson, dau. of Moses Thompson Willard, who was killed at the battle of Plattsburg, Sept. 11, 1814. She was b. in Bow, Feb. 21, 1802. He d. Bridgewater, July 12, 1833, as the result of a mistake of a druggist in filling a prescription with a poison, instead of a harmless remedy ordered, ae. 35-9-18. She m. (2) Rev. Paul Perkins, a Free Baptist clergyman, who d. Hebron, Apr. 3, 1843. She d. Concord, in Feb., 1883, ae. 81. One child Ruth, was b. of this marriage.

CHILDREN, all born in Bridgewater

  29. Louisa Lavina, b. Sept. 16, 1822; m. (1) Orrin Gordon, (2) Joseph Kidder. (See.)
  30. David W., d. aged two years.
 *31. Charles Willard, b. Aug. 30, 1825.
  32. Lucinda Thompson, b. Apr. 5, 1826; m. Levi Nelson. (See.)
  33. David, b. Nov. 3, 1829; m. May 1, 1855, Eliza A., dau. John Hastings. (See.) He came to Bristol in 1846, worked at his trade, that of a wheelwright. In 1853, went to Concord, where he was an employee in the Abbott-Downing carriage manufactory. In 1884, went to Florida, where he d., June 30, 1890, ae. 70-7-27.
 *34. Nathan Hammond, b. Apr. 20, 1833.

    (31) Charles W. Batchelder, b. Aug. 30, 1825, m. in 1850, Huldah T. Emmons, dau. Benjamin. (See.) She was b. Bristol, Nov. 23, 1826, and d. Concord, Sept. 27, 1856, ae. 29-10-4. He m. (2) Olive Adeliza, dau. Alexander White, of Clarendon, Vt. She d. Sept. 5, 1882, and he m. in July, 1883, Mrs. Rebecca G. Swain, of Hebron, who now res. in Concord. He came to Bristol from Concord fall of 1861. He was a carpenter and builder, and surveyor of lumber. In 1880, removed to Concord, where he was city surveyor. He d. Concord, Apr. 12, 1890, ae. 64-7-12. Republican; a life long member of the Free Baptist church.

CHILDREN

  35. Mary Anna, b. Concord, Dec. 23, 1850; m. Sept. 26, 1870, in Bristol, Edwin Edgar Clark, b. Newbury, Vt., Dec. 16, 1847. He was a harness-maker, in shop in Central square next to the bridge; removed to Concord, where he was auctioneer and commission merchant. Res. Concord.
  36. Frank Edwin, b. C., July 3, 1853; d. July 27, 1855.
 *37. Charles Frank, b. C., Sept. 19, 1855.

    (34) Nathan H. Batchelder, b. Apr. 20, 1833, m. Dec. 20

1856, Isabelle Barron, dau. Dudley and Ruby Hovey, b. Bradford, Vt., Aug. 1, 1836. He was a resident of Bristol as a boy, 1844-'48, and was in business as a manufacturer of sleighs at the No. End, 1872-'78. He removed to Haverhill, where he d. Feb. 20, 1899, ae. 65-10-0. She res. Haverhill.

CHILDREN

38. Fred Perkins. b. Haverhill, Dec. 17, 1864; master of Ingalls School, Lynn, Mass.
39. Mary Hovey, b. H., Aug. 3, 1869; d. Oct. 27, 1869.

(37) Charles F. Batchelder, b. Sept. 19, 1855, came to Bristol 1861; m. Dec. 24, 1879, Florence Adelaide Coombs, b. Richmond, Dec. 30, 1862. He returned to Concord, 1880, where he now res.

CHILDREN

40. Grace Emmons, b. Oct. 7, 1880; d. August, 1881.
41. Louise Lawrence, b. Aug. 22, 1882.
42. Charles Walter, b. Dec. 27, 1885; d. Sept. 23, 1891, ae. 5-8-26.

THE BEAN FAMILIES

1. Dea. Elisha Bean, son of Jeremiah, of Deerfield, b. 1740, was one of the early settlers in Plymouth. He m. (1) Ruth, b. 1740; d. May, 15, 1808; (2) Aug. 29, 1808, Jemima Daft, of Rumney, who d. Jan. 8, 1817. He d. Sept. 15, 1817, ae. 77. Elisha and Ruth had eleven children. Of these, two were

CHILDREN

*2. Elisha, b. Plymouth, 1773.
*3. Jeremiah, b. P., 1774

(2) Elisha Bean, b. 1773, m. Nov. 17, 1796, Polly, dau. Simeon Cross. (See.) He was the first settler on the William H. Abel farm in Bridgewater, first taxed in 1811, and there d. June 20, 1853, ae. 80 years. She d. Bridgewater, 1861, ae. 87.

CHILDREN

*4. Simeon C.
5. Abigail C., m. July 13, 1826, David C. Ferrin.

(3) Jeremiah Bean, b. 1774, came to Bristol from Hebron about 1802. He m. Elizabeth West, b. 1769. He was a farmer and d. Bristol, Mar. 8, 1861, ae. 86-5-0. She d. Bristol, Apr. 3, 1861, ae. 91-8-0.

CHILDREN

6. Huldah W., b. Hebron, Dec. 6, 1796; m. Amos Boardman of Bridgewater, and removed to New York state.
7. Hannah F., b. H., Mar. 31, 1799; m. Pliney Roberts, and removed to Meredith. He d. Jan. 9, 1828, ae. 28-9-8.
*8. Peter M., b. H., Mar. 14, 1801.

9. Jeremiah, b. Bristol, Mar. 9, 1803; m. Sally Tirrell, and removed to Boston, Mass. He d. Jan. 28, 1834, ae. 30-10-19.
10. Sally, b. B., May 6, 1805; m. John Sleeper. (See.)
*11. Philip Cilley, b. B., Feb. 19, 1807.
12. Orrisa W., b. B., June 10, 1809; d. Feb. 15, 1831, ae. 21-8-5.
13. Ruth, b. B., Jan. 26, 1813; d. July 9, 1830, ae. 17-5-13.
14. Eliza W., b. B., July 11, 1815; m. Jan. 17, 1837, Peter Tirrell, b. Feb. 23, 1811, Nashua. He d. May 18, 1849, Nashua, ae. 38-2-25, and she m. Jan. 1, 1850, John D. Brown. (See.)
15. George M., b. B., Nov. 21, 1818; d. Mar. 2, 1843, ae. 24-3-11.

(4) Simeon C. Bean, m. Polly Harron, b. Warner. He was a farmer on the W. H. Abel farm in Bridgewater. After his death she removed to New Hampton, and there d. Oct. 31, 1882, ae. 79 years.

CHILDREN

16. Clarissa, b. Bridgewater, Apr. 17, 1843; m. Slyvester Cross. (See.)
17. Mandana, m. (1) Enoch Gordon, and had two children by him. He went to California and there d. and she m. (2) John Fuller, Bridgewater. One child. They res. Earlville, Iowa.
18. Dearborn, m.; d. 1886, of consumption, in Earlville.
19. Nancy, m. W. H. Abel, and d. Bridgewater.
20. Milton, m.; res. for a time in Bristol, and d. of consumption in Earlville, in Dec., 1886.

(8) Peter M. Bean, b. Mar. 14, 1801, m. July 13, 1826, Judith F., dau. Simeon Cross. She was b. Aug. 13, 1792. (Cross record, Aug. 17, 1791.) They removed to Berea, Ohio, 1852, where he d. July 31, 1872, ae. 71-4-17; she d. same place, Apr. 8, 1880, ae. 87-7-25. Farmers, Methodists.

CHILDREN

21. Sally M., b. May 13, 1827; d. Feb. 13, 1829.
22. Simeon C., b. May 10, 1830; killed by lightning, Aug. 2, 1850, at house of Jeremiah Bean in Bristol, ae. 20-2-23.
23. Elizabeth W., b. Sept. 5, 1831; m. Squires S. Brown. (See.)

(11) Rev. Philip C. Bean, b. Feb. 19, 1807, m. May 22, 1827, Nancy, dau. John and Nancy (Pressey) Harron, b. Bridgewater, May 4, 1809. He was a farmer in District No. 7, and Methodist local preacher; was licensed to preach in 1838 by the Methodist Episcopal church in Hanover; was ordained local deacon by Bishop Waugh in Claremont in 1843, and ordained local elder by Bishop Hedding at Northfield in 1847. He left Bristol in 1852, and d. East Manchester, 1879, ae. 72; she d. same place, 1896, ae. 87.

CHILDREN

24. Lydia Ann Cross, b. Bristol, Feb. 20, 1829; m. about 1863, George Washington Dearborn; res. East Manchester. Child:
    a. George Philip, m. Aug., 1894, Eva Martin, Alexandria, and d. 1901. (?)

*25. John Harron Sleeper, b. Bristol, Sept. —, 1831.
*26. George Moses, b. B., May 30, 1842.
27. Jeremiah, b. Bridgewater, d. young of scarlet fever.
28. Moody Marshall, b. B., d. young of scarlet fever.
29. Harrison Pressey, b. Oct. 22, 1857; m. Emily J. Rogers, Hebron. While residing in Manchester, in 1878, he went away and was never heard from. She d. Hebron, 1882. Son, Walter.

(25) Lieut. John H. S. Bean, b. Sept. —, 1831, m. Nov. 25, 1856, Eliza W. Parker, of Rumford, Me. They resided at Rumford till 1862, when he enlisted in the 12th Regt. Maine Vols. (See Roll of Honor.) After the war he was postmaster at Bridgewater, then removed to Bristol to the Nelson neighborhood, where his buildings were destroyed by fire. Was three years on police force in So. Boston, where he d. May 26, 1872, ae. 40-6-0. She res. Nashua.

CHILDREN

30. Orrisa Ann, b. Rumford, Me.; m. James Healy. Three children. Res. Nashua.
31. Oretta Nina, b. R. Unm. Res. Nashua.
32. Clarence Irving, b. Bristol, m. Kate Smith. He d. Adams, Oregon, 1886, ae. 22. Child:

    a. Clarence Alvin, res. Adams.

33. Frank Marshall, b. Bridgewater; d. South Boston, 1872, ae. 8 years.
34. Fred Parker, b. B.; m.; res. 5 Pleasant street, Nashua.

(26) George M. Bean, b. May 30, 1842, m., Dec. 6, 1865, Mary Frances, dau. of Caleb Sawyer. (See.) He came to Bristol from Bridgewater, 1853, and removed to East Manchester, 1870, where they res.

CHILDREN

35. Arthur Philip, b. Bristol, Jan. 21, 1867; d. Manchester, Apr. 23, 1873, ae. 6-3-2.
36. Alvin George, b. B., Sept. 21, 1868; m. Apr. 12, 1893, Jennie Maud Reid, and res. Manchester. Child:

    a. Norman Reid, b. Mar. 1, 1895.

37. Harry Oscar, b. East Manchester, Sept. 15, 1870; m., June 6, 1892, Rose Leilia Still, and res. Manchester. Child:

    a. Charles Douglas, b. Mar. 12, 1893.

38. Ina Florence, b. E. M., July 15, 1872.
39. Frank Perry, b. E. M., Aug. 5, 1875.
40. Albert Stuart, b. E. M., May 28, 1878.
41. Warren Marshall, b. E. M., Apr. 21, 1884.
42. Howard Sawyer, b. E. M., May 17, 1886.

———

1. Reuben C. Bean, son of Sinclair, was b. 1807, in Newport. He m. Sarah Follansbee, dau. of Benjamin. (See.) He resided in Bristol from 1834 till 1864. She d. Bristol, July 22, 1862, ae. 49, and he m. (2) ——— ———, who res. Franklin Falls. He was a dealer in shoes, and a cutter in Warren

White's shoe shop; was an abolitionist, and class leader in Methodist church. Died in Penacook, July 20, 1871, ae. 64.

2.   Mary S., m. James P. Dustin, and d. Nov. 24, 1865, ae. 20.
3.   Sarah Etta, d. Sept. 17, 1855, ae. 2-2-9.
4.   George F. was a conductor on Northern railroad and landlord Elm House, Concord. He d. Raymond, Sept. 15, 1882, leaving widow and two children.
5.   Ann Maria, m. and res. in Hillsboro.
6.   Charles H., son by second wife. Res. Franklin Falls.

---

1.   Fred Herman Bean, son of Herman Orvil and Mary (Storrer) Bean, was b. Reed's Ferry, June 2, 1878. He came to Bristol in September, 1899, and was, till spring of 1903, a salesman in store of Cavis Bros., now of firm of Bean & Noyes, successors of Alexander & Davis, merchants. He m. Nov. 25, 1899, Susie G., dau. Lucian A. Ballou. (See.)

THE BECKFORD FAMILY

1.   Henry Shedd Beckford, son of Capt. David and Sally (Edmonds) Beckford, was b. in Salem, Mass., Sept. 8, 1806. He m., Feb. 15, 1830, Mary Ann, dau. of Benjamin and Ann Perry, of Salem, Mass., b. Apr. 26, 1807, and d. No. Salem, N. H., Aug. 23, 1855, ae. 48-3-27. Capt. David Beckford was lost at sea. When a boy, Henry S. Beckford commenced work in a flannel-mill at Salem, Mass., said to be the first flannel-mill in New England. When twenty-one years of age he started a flannel-mill for himself in Loudon, N. H., but later operated a mill in Salem, N. H., for thirty years. He represented Salem, N. H., in the legislature of 1860 and '61. He came to Bristol in 1863 and engaged in the manufacture of frocking at No. Bristol in company with his son, Benjamin P., under the firm name of H. S. Beckford & Son. Soon after the death of his son and partner, in 1867, he removed to Grafton, where he d. Mar. 23, 1883, ae. 76-6-4.

2.   Jacob O., b. Nov. 26, 1830; d. Salem, Mar. 7, 1862, ae. 31-3-11.
3.   Henry P., b. Dec. 27, 1832; was a Baptist clergyman; d. Nov. 1, 1860, ae. 27-11-4.
4.   Phebe E., b. Dec. 25, 1834; d. Oct. 14, 1852, ae. 17-9-19.
5.   Mary Ann, b. Nov. 1, 1837; d. July 29, 1855, ae. 17-8-28.
6.   Benjamin P., b. May 27, 1839; d. Bristol, Jan. 21, 1867, ae. 27-7-24.
7.   Sarah E., b. June 19, 1841; d. Haverhill, Mass., Nov. 17, 1883, ae. 42-4-28.
*8.   William Augustus, b. May 15, 1843.
9.   Martha M., b. Dec. 27, 1847; d. Aug. 27, 1848, ae. 8 mos.
*10.   Frank Mahlon, b. Oct. 13, 1851.

CAPT. WILLIAM A. BECKFORD

(8) Capt. William A. Beckford, b. May 15, 1843, ran away from home before he was eighteen years of age and enlisted, Mar. 29, 1861, as a private in Co. B, 3rd U. S. Infantry. When serving in this organization, he was present at the first Bull Run fight. He was discharged for disability Sept. 5, 1861, and Nov. 8, 1861, enlisted as a private in Co. F, 8th Regt., N. H. Vols., and was mustered in as a sergeant; was appointed first sergeant June 1, 1863, and commissioned first lieutenant Dec. 16, 1863, and was mustered out Jan., 1865. Capt. Beckford served with the 8th Regt. in the Department of the Gulf in Louisiana and Mississippi. He was with his regiment in six general engagements, including the seige of Port Hudson, May 23, to July 9, 1863, besides many skirmishes. June 14, 1863, while serving as a first sergeant, he took command of his company, and was in command when commissioned. In March, 1864, in a skirmish at Plackerman, La., was wounded in the leg with a minie ball. At Bayou de Glaize, La., May 17, 1864, he was severely wounded, a minie ball passing through his right lung and shattering the shoulder blade, causing a running sore that still troubles him. He came to Bristol in 1865, and engaged in manufacturing stocking yarn a few years at No. Bristol. He organized the Head Rifles in Bristol in 1866, and was made its captain; was deputy sheriff four years; postmaster one term; represented Bristol in constitutional convention of 1876, and legislature of 1880. He has been an active Republican politician and a member of the Republican State Central committee; G. A. R.; K. of P. He m. (1) Mary J. Nowell, of Derry, who d. Bristol, Jan. 5, 1879, ae. 41. He m. (2) Feb. 18, 1880, Bessie, dau. of Dea. Gardner J. Bowers, b. Alexandria, July 28, 1840. She d. Bristol, Dec. 20, 1899, ae. 59-4-22. He m. (3) July 9, 1902, Grace Anna, dau. B. Smith and Mary E. (Eastman) Stevens, b. Hill, June 6, 1868. They res. Lake street.

CHILD

11. Nellie A., b. Derry, Aug. 14, 1862; m. Moses Southard. (See.)

(10) Judge Frank M. Beckford, b. Oct. 13, 1851. He m. (1) Kittie Mooers Buswell, of Haverhill, Mass.; divorced May term of court at Plymouth, 1884, and m. (2) Mrs. Elvira A. Sanborn, of Bristol. He came to Bristol with his father, read law in office of Hon. Lewis W. Fling, removed to Laconia in 1884, and continued his studies in the office of Hon. Thomas J. Whipple, and was admitted to the bar in 1889; was a member of the state constitutional convention in 1888, from Laconia; was appointed judge of the Laconia police court, 1892; resigned May 21, 1895. Is now practicing law in Laconia.

CHILD

12. Henry Shedd, b. Haverhill, Mass., Oct. 5, 1874; m. May 15, 1900, Eleanor R., dau. John H. and Hannah Robinson, b. Laconia, Apr. 12,

1878. Was educated at Tilton Seminary and at Dartmouth Medical school; is a practicing physician at Belmont, and medical referee of Belknap county. Child:

  a. Hortense Robinson, b. Mar. 15, 1901.

THE BEEDE FAMILIES

  1. Rev. Caleb S. Beede, son of John and Olive (Tuttle) Beede, was b. in Vermont, July 26, 1805. He first came to Bristol, in 1829, as a Methodist circuit preacher, being sent here by the New England conference, with which he united that year. He remained on this circuit one year, and July 1, 1830, m. Mary, dau. of Moses Worthen. (See.) He continued a member of the New England conference five years and then located, and in 1838 settled in Bristol. Here he was a contractor and builder. He built the Methodist church on Spring street and other buildings. In 1850, he removed with his family to Lenox, Ohio, where he engaged in lumbering. Twice his mills were consumed by fire, but he built the third. He served in the Civil war as a private in the 29th Ohio Infantry. He d. at Lenox, Apr. 17, 1877, ae. 71-8-21; she d. same place, June 2, 1889, ae. 80-0-27.

CHILDREN

  *2. John Wesley, b. New Hampton, June 2, 1831.
  3. Wilbur Fisk, b. Loudon, Oct. 30, 1832; m. June 13, 1855, Weltha A., dau. Ephraim Ward. She was b. Green River, N. Y., Sept. 16, 1836, and d. Jefferson, O., Mar. 7, 1876, ae. 39-5-21. He m. (2) Aug. 2, 1878, Jennie S., dau. Orren Smith. She was b. Trumbull, O., Mar. 15, 1848. They res. Gregg's Corner, O. No children, but adopted two. He d. Austinburg, O., Jan. 29, 1897, ae. 64-3-9.
  4. Charles Worthing, b. Chichester, Aug. 31, 1834. He went to Ohio three years before his parents and Oct. 6, 1858, m. Phebe Jane, dau. Erastus Norton. She was b. Lenox, O., Sept. 19, 1835. They res. Dorset, O. No children.
  5. Ann Orrilla, b. Pembroke, Sept. 16, 1836; d. May 13, 1837, ae. 0-7-27.
  *6. Moses Worthing, b. Bristol, Aug. 28, 1839.
  7. Frances Ann, b. B., July 20, 1841; d., unm., Lenox, O., Aug. 10, 1877, ae. 36-0-20.
  8. Laura Hulda, b. B., Dec. 5, 1844. She m. July 18, 1866, David Darrow, b. Coitsville, O., Oct. 4, 1841. They res. Lowellville, O. Children:
    a. Charles Reuben, b. Poland, O., June 13, 1867.
    b. Vernice May, b. P., Feb. 16, 1870; m. Sept. 29, 1879, Charles F. Wilkins. Res. Youngstown, O., 134 Carroll street.
    c. George Caleb, b. P., Dec. 29, 1874; d. Oct. 22, 1876, ae. 1-9-23.
    d. Grace Cora, b. P., Mar. 27, 1878.
    e. Ralph Hayes, b. P., Sept. 13, 1879; m. Jan. 12, 1900, Helen Bryson, Lowellville.
  9. Mary Maria, b. Bristol, Aug. 25, 1846; m. Mar 4, 1875, George Henderson, son of Cook Henderson, who d. Apr. 18, 1888. Res. 319 W. Chestnut street, Leadville, Col. Children:

MOSES W. BEEDE.

REV. CALEB S. BEEDE.

a. Wilbur Wesley, b. Oro, Col., Jan. 4, 1877.
b. George Beede, b. O., Mar. 1, 1878.
c. Mary Eliza, b. Leadville, Col., Sept. 20, 1880.
d. Beulah Bernice, b. L., Nov. 4, 1884; d. Nov. 9, 1886, ae. 2-0-5.

10. Sarah Jane Manson, b. Bristol, Dec. 11, 1848. Unm. Res. 1309 Hillman street, Youngstown, O.

(2) John W. Beede, b. June 2, 1831, m. Feb. 12, 1857, Parmelia Maria Darrow, b. Aug. 10, 1836, Ellington, N. Y. They res. Youngstown, O., where she d. May 24, 1899, ae. 62-9-14. He served four months in 29th Ohio Infty. and 100 days in 155th Ohio Infty. during Civil war.

CHILDREN

11. Henry Darrow, b. Youngstown, May 10, 1858; m. Polly Richter. Three children.
12. George Moses, b. Y., Oct. 10, 1860; m. Emma Phillips. Four children.
13. Mary Elizabeth, b. Y., Jan. 5, 1863; m. Charles Osborn, killed on railroad in 1893. Four children.
14. Hattie Caroline, b. Lenox, O., June 8, 1867; m. George Blunt. Four children.
15. Theodatus Giles, b. Youngstown, Mar. 21, 1871; m. Mary Pfundt. Three children.
16. John Wesley, b. Y., Oct. 5, 1873; m. in 1893, Mary Jenkins.
17. Bates Worthing, b. Lenox, Feb. 23, 1876.

(6) Moses W. Beede, b. Aug. 28, 1839, m. Jan. 1, 1863, Eliza, dau. Grove and Mary (Webster) Henderson, b. Austinburg, O., July 21, 1835, and d. Sept. 14, 1874, at Lenox, O., ae. 39-1-23. He m., July 5, 1876, Mrs. Frances L. Watson, widow of Harlow Watson, and dau. Amos Curtis, b. Feb. 27, 1843. Res. Lenox, O. All Congregationalists. (See Roll of Honor.)

CHILDREN

18. George Owen, b. Lenox, O., Feb. 28, 1865. He was one of the discoverers of the great iron deposits of Colorado, and is now interested in mining at Leadville, Col.
19. Bernice Gertrude, b. L., June 14, 1868; m. May 23, 1889, Leonard Worcester, Jr., a teacher in public schools of Leadville, Col. She is a music teacher.
20. Martha Frances, b. L., May 20, 1878.
21. Lulu Edith, b. L., Nov. 10, 1879.

---

1. William Penn Beede, son of William Taylor and Irene Quimby (Smith) Beede, was b. Fremont, Apr. 17, 1839. He m. in May, 1892, May Etta, dau. Augustus Remick, b. Oct. 17, 1867. He was a merchant, lumber dealer, farmer and hotel keeper before coming to Bristol about 1894, since which time has been liveryman and stage driver.

CHILD

2. Eva Maud, b. Mar. 28, 1891, and d. Bristol, Dec. 31, 1899, ae. 8-9-3.

3

THE BENNETT FAMILIES.

1.   Daniel Bennett, son of William and Olive (Merrick) Bennett, b. in New Hampton, Jan. 28, 1802, m. Mar. 27, 1823, Rhoda, dau. of Samuel and Mary Connor (Fuller) Clifford. He was a farmer and laborer and came to Bristol in 1841, and resided one year near Moore's Mills, then in Bridgewater, and after five years returned to Bristol, and res. in the village, where he d. Mar. 26, 1865, ae. 63-1-28.   She was b. in Alexandria, Feb. 23, 1803, and d. in Bristol in the family of Charles P. George, Apr. 5, 1886, ae. 83-1-12.

CHILDREN, all born in New Hampton

2.   Mary Clifford, b. Oct. 5, 1824; m. John W. Sanborn.   (See.)
*3.   William Leavitt, b. Dec. 16, 1827.
4.   Samuel Clifford, b. Oct. 18, 1828; m. Nov. 15, 1858, Mary, dau. Alexander Hutchinson.   (See.)   Res. on Lake street.   Has been a stage driver, and for 32 years a teamster in employ of the Mason-Perkins Paper company.   No children.
5.   Olive Jane, b. May 28, 1831; m. Charles P. George.   (See.)
*6.   Cyrus Magoon, b. Aug. 12, 1834.

(3)   William L. Bennett, b. Dec. 16, 1827, m. Nov. —, 1847, Lauretta Jane Dolloff, of Meredith.   She d. and he m. in Dec., 1863, at Manchester, Martha Thorn, who d. about 1881, in Boston.   William L. enlisted at Manchester, Aug. 9, 1861, in Co. A, 3rd Regt., N. H. Vols., Civil war, and served as wagoner till mustered out at Morris Island, S. C., Nov. 23, 1863.   Was wagoner in ammunition train at battles of Morris Island and Fort Wagner and under fire.   After the war res. Manchester and Boston till about 1883, when he came to Bristol and made his home with his sister, Mrs. John W. Sanborn.   Farmer.

CHILDREN

7.   George, b. Bristol, Sept. 7, 1848.   In 1865, went from home with a menagerie and never heard from.
8.   Jonathan Robinson, b. Meredith, June 6, 1850; m. Jennie, dau. Thomas E. Osgood.   (See.)   He is a hairdresser in Milford, Mass.
*9.   William Joseph, b. Laconia, Nov. 28, 1852.

(6)   Cyrus M. Bennett, b. Aug. 12, 1834, m. Nov. 15, 1858, Lydia Ann, dau. Smith Emmons.   (See.)   He was a farmer and laborer, and d. Bristol, Oct. 17, 1883, ae. 49-2-5.

CHILDREN

10.   Evora, b. Bristol, Aug. 17, 1863; m. July 8, 1891, Walter M. Wotton, son of Warren and Cordelia (Morton) Wotton.   Shoemaker.   They res. Dover, Mass.   Child:
a.   Arland Merl, b. Sept. 26, 1894.

(9   William J. Bennett, b. Nov. 28, 1852, m. (1) Mary Noyes, who d. Mar. 14, 1874.   He m. (2) Caroline Augusta, dau. Henry Plumer, b. Manchester, Jan. 31, 1851.   He m. (3)

Sept. 20, 1880, Jemima LaCourt, dau. Joshua M., and Eliza-
beth (Jedlen) LaCourt, b. Dec. 20, 1860, in Windsor Mills, P.
Q., and d. Bristol, Jan. 31, 1897, of consumption, ae. 36-1-11.
He committed suicide June 1, 1894, ae. 41-6-4.

CHILDREN

11. Alice Maud, b. Franklin, Nov. 30, 1874; m. Alphonzo G. Wallace.
12. Hattie Belle, b. Hill, Nov. 26, 1876.
13. William Joshua, b. Whitefield, Feb. 9, 1881 ; d. July 1, 1890.
14. John Thomas, b. W., June 13, 1884.
15. Frank Leavitt, b. Wells River, Vt., Jan. 13, 1886.
16. Irving, b. Woodsville, Feb. 17, 1888.
17. Mary Elizabeth, b. W., Sept. 8, 1890.
18. Grace, b. Bristol, Oct. 26, 1892. After death of the mother was
adopted by E. L. March, Lowell, Mass.

---

1.   Robert Winthrop Bennett is the son of Rev. Robert and
Ruth (Beless) Bennett. He was b. in Thompson, Conn., Oct.
21, 1875, and m. June 19, 1899, Louise Haines, dau. of Charles
E. and Martha Annette (Haines) Doying, b. St. Johnsbury,
Vt., Apr. 12, 1883. He came to Bristol in October, 1898. Had
a fish market in 1899 ; now in employ of George A. Dow, as a
meat cutter.

CHILD

2. Robert Gordon, b. New Hampton, July 18, 1900.

---

1.   Fred Joseph Bennett, son of Joseph and Excelia (Viey)
Bennett, was b. Waldon, Vt., June 28, 1877. He m. Sept. 10,
1900, Nellie Rose, dau. Frank and Ellen (Goodard) Hill, b.
Canaan, June —, 1877. He came to Bristol in October, 1895,
and was an employee of C. N. Merrill ; now at pulp-mill of the
Train-Smith company.

CHILD

2. Florence Ellen, b. Bristol, June 11, 1901.

THE BENTON FAMILY

1.   William Wesley Benton was the son of Hiram and Jan-
nette (Wallace) Benton. He was b. Compton, P. Q., in 1851,
and in 1871, m. Etta, dau. of John and Julia (Barton) Knights,
b. Concord, 1853. He was a wood turner. Since 1894, has res.
Danbury.

CHILDREN

2. Annie, b. Eliot, Me., 1871 ; m. 1894, in Cincinnati, O., Dr. Frank
X. Kern, who died May, 1903. Res. C.
3. Lucy, b. Hebron, 1873; m. Jan. 28, 1896, Edward R. Stebbins, b.
Newbury, Vt., son of E. H. and Martha (Townsend) Stebbins. Res.
Danbury.

4. Elizabeth White, b. Bristol, 1875; m. Jan. 2, 1895, William J. Webster, b. 1876, Boston, Mass., son of John W. and Sarah E. (Fox) Webster.

5. William Perrin, b. B., 1877; d. B., 1882.

6. Angie, b. B., 1879; m. Apr. 15, 1900, Myron M. Moshier, b. Groton, 1882, son of Ira and Mary (Phelps) Moshier. (See.)

THE BERRY FAMILIES

1. Hon. Nathaniel Springer Berry was b. in Bath, Me., Sept. 1, 1796. His father was Abner, son of Capt. John, who served in the Revolutionary war; one of three brothers who came from Scotland and settled in Bath, Me. His mother was Betsey, dau. of Capt. Nathaniel Springer, who commanded a company of artillery in the Revolutionary war and was killed in action. His father was a ship builder at Bath, Me., and was killed by the careening of a vessel on which he was at work, when Nathaniel was about six years of age. Nathaniel was one of four children. Mrs. Berry m. (2) in 1808, Benjamin Morse, a ship joiner, who went to Bath, Me., from Lisbon, N. H., and they removed to Lisbon, in March, 1810, where Nathaniel remained a few months and then went to Bath, N. H., and became an apprentice of a Mr. Morrison to learn the saddle and harness maker's trade. This situation soon failed him and he became the apprentice of Eben Carlton, to learn the tanner's trade. He was now 16 years of age, and he bound himself to work during his minority for $40 a year and his board. He was to find his own clothes, but to have six months of schooling each year during this time. This contract was carried out by both parties. He worked as a journeyman two years after learning his trade, and in March, 1818, when 22 years of age, he came to Bristol and worked one year for Robert Brown for $200 and then worked at his trade one year at Littleton. In 1820, he bought the tannery on Central St., Bristol, for $800, paying $300 down and giving his note for the remainder. His purchase included not only the tan yard but a large tract of land embracing nearly the whole of Spring street, and including the residence recently occupied by Clarence N. Merrill and removed by him to make way for a new one. In this residence he commenced to keep house, his sister, later Mrs. Teresha Ladd, being his housekeeper. Jan. 26, 1821, he m. Ruth, dau. James and Ruth Smith, b. Bath, Jan. 1, 1800. In March, 1823, both Mr. Berry and his wife professed religion and in September following united with the Methodist church in full membership. During all his long life he was a liberal supporter and active worker in the church of his choice, and noted for his devoted piety and humble spirit. He was a delegate to the Methodist General Conference in 1872.

Mr. Berry continued business at his tannery in Bristol till,

1836, when he sold to Warren White and removed to Hebron in 1840. (See Manufacturing Industries.) At Hebron he continued in the tanning business with his son and was twice burned out. The last fire occurred in 1857, and he did not rebuild, or engage in active business thereafter.

Politically Mr. Berry was highly honored. He represented Bristol in the legislature of 1828, 1833, 1834, and 1837, and Hebron in 1854. He was elected senator from the 11th district in 1835 and 1836. He was a delegate to the Democratic National convention at Baltimore in 1840, which nominated Martin Van Buren for president. He was appointed associate justice for the court of common pleas in 1841, and served nine years. He served five years as judge of probate for Grafton county, ending June 5, 1861, when he was inaugurated governor. He served as lieutenant, captain, and lieutenant-colonel of the old 34th regiment of militia. He was for 23 years justice of the peace and quorum in New Hampshire, and five years in Massachusetts.

He acted with the Democratic party till the convention at Baltimore, when the action of the convention on the subject of slavery caused him to break his party ties, and he became one of the organizers of the Freesoil party. At the first state convention of this party, in October, 1845, Mr. Berry was nominated for governor. The Liberty party also nominated him, and at the election in March following, he received enough votes to prevent a choice by the people, and he was nominated at the four succeeding conventions of his party. At the Republican convention in January, 1861, he was nominated for governor, and in March was elected by a majority of 3,000. He was re-elected in March, 1862. During his term of office as governor, he enlisted, armed, clothed and equipped 15 regiments of troops, and issued over 700 commissions. In the spring of 1862, Gov. Berry was one of 22 Northern governors who held a consultation at Altoona, on the state of the Union. At this conference an address was prepared to the president and taken to Washington, and Gov. Berry was selected to present it, which he did in a characteristic way, asking if they, as governors, were doing all that they could do to further the Union cause.

He was noted for the same scrupulous honesty in public affairs as in his private business. When the state voted $1,000,-000 for war expenses, he was urged by influential men to place the bonds with them at a discount of five per cent. This he refused to do, and, finally, with the aid of John E. Lyon, he sold the whole at par, thereby saving a large sum and preserving the credit of the state. In an address before the state Prohibition convention, June 19, 1888, he stated he had never asked a man to vote for him, nor written a letter to secure the influence of any man in his behalf.

3a

His wife d. July 26, 1857, ae. 57-7-0, and he m. January, 1860, Mrs. Louise Farley, of Andover, Mass. In April, 1864, he removed to Andover, and in 1872, to Worcester, Mass., where his second wife d., Apr. 6, 1878. He then spent six years with his daughter, in Milwaukee, Wis., but the last twelve years of his life he passed in the family of his son in Bristol, where he d. Apr. 27, 1894, ae. 97-7-26.

His last years were sunny and happy and exceptionally free from the infirmities of old age; his mind clear and active to the last. On Tuesday, Apr. 17, while taking a walk, he contracted a cold which settled on his lungs, and he gradually failed till the end came.

The funeral services were held at the Methodist church Monday afternoon, Apr. 30, and were attended by a large concourse of people. The services opened with prayer by Rev. J. M. Durrell, Scriptures were read by Presiding Elder J. E. Robins. Rev. J. D. LeGro, pastor of the church, gave a review of his life as a Christian man; Presiding Elder S. C. Keeler spoke of him as a public man; Rev. J. W. Merrill, D.D., read an original poem, and Rev. J. M. Durrell gave a summary of his life. Among those present were Gov. John B. Smith, ex-Govs. Frederick Smythe, P. C. Cheney, and Hiram A. Tuttle, and many other public men. Nelson Post, G. A. R., and Train Rifles did escort duty. The remains were laid to rest in the Pleasant Street cemetery.

CHILDREN

⁂2.   William Augustus, b. Bristol, Oct. 23, 1824.

3.   Emeline Smith, b. B., June 17, 1823; m. in June, 1852, Charles E. Morse, of Indiana, formerly of Lisbon. They removed to Fort Wayne, Ind., where Mr. Morse was road master of the Pittsburg, Fort Wayne and Chicago railroad five years, then moved to Milwaukee, where he held same position on Northern Division of Chicago, Milwaukee & St. Paul railroad till his death, which occurred in June, 1876, at Horricon, Wis. She d. Milwaukee, Wis., Apr. 23, 1888, ae. 64-10-0.

(2)   William A. Berry, b. Oct. 23, 1824, m. in Hebron, Oct. 7, 1851, Laura Ann, dau. of Varnum and Elizabeth (Lovejoy) Pratt, b. Hebron, Oct. 22, 1831. She is the great-grand-daughter of Thomas Pratt, a captain in the Revolutionary war. Mr. Berry was a manufacturer of leather in Hebron with his father till 1858, when he returned to Bristol and engaged in the manufacture of buckskin gloves and mittens with J. C. Draper. This continued for 10 years. He was later in the same business nine years with Milton A. Kent of Boston. He was a manufacturer of pulp from 1881 to 1891 with David Mason, and succeeded Wm. T. Taylor in the manufacture of picker-sticks. He represented Hebron in the legislatures of 1855, '57, and '58. In Bristol has served 17 years as moderator of the annual town meeting, and seven years as selectman; has been a director of

the Bristol Savings bank from its organization, and a member of its committee on investments. He was assistant assessor of internal revenue from 1862–'72, and has been justice of the peace and quorum since 1858, sitting as justice at many hearings, and has been administrator of many estates. He has been an official member of the Methodist Episcopal church since 1853. Republican, Mason, and Odd Fellow. Now retired from business, residing on South Main street.

CHILD

4. Emma Pratt, b. Bristol, June 17, 1866; pursued studies at Tilton Seminary; has been librarian of Minot-Sleeper library eleven years.

---

1. Samuel Berry was b. in Strafford, June 10, 1810, and d. in Watertown, Mass., Oct. 10, 1874, ae. 64–4–0. He m. Oct. 11, 1836, Mahala Huckins, b. New Hampton, Feb. 23, 1809, and d. Bristol, Apr. 29, 1871, ae. 62–2–6. He was a shoemaker and came to Bristol, about 1835, and res. here till 1871, when he went to Watertown, Mass. Methodist.

CHILDREN, all born in Bristol

2. Sarah Ann, b. Aug. 18, 1837; d. Dec. 20, 1856, ae. 19–4–2.
3. Ellen Frances, b. Jan. 1, 1840; m., 1865, Charles Henry, son of Francis Kimball, b. Exeter, 1840. Children :
    a. Frank Wesley, b. Brighton, Mass., 1868; m., 1889, Mary Etta Wyman, Boothbay, Me. Res. Natick, Mass.
    b. George Arthur, b. Watertown, Mass., 1871; d. Watertown, 1890.
4. Charles Wesley, b. Sept. 30, 1842; m. Mar. 18, 1868, Mary Abby, dau. Luther and Mary (Eaton) Gleason, b. Wayland, Mass., July 1, 1838. He removed to Watertown, Mass., 1861, and was in trade there some years. In 1891, went to Holliston, Mass., where he now res. (See Roll of Honor.) Children :
    a. Guy Staples, b. Watertown, Mass., Sept. 4, 1869; d. Aug. 9, 1870.
    b. Florence Emeline, b. W., May 23, 1872.
    c. Adelaide Brevard, b. W., Apr. 28, 1876.
5. Mary Emily, b. Sept. 23, 1844; d. Nov. 15, 1856, ae. 12–1–22.
6. George Henry, b. May 5, 1847; d. Jan. 5, 1898, Naval Hospital, Philadelphia, Pa., ae. 50–7–0. (See Roll of Honor.)

---

1. Freeman Enoch Berry, son of Levi and Abigail (Page) Berry, was b. Oct. 7, 1831, in Alexandria. Oct. 26, 1854, he m. Betsey Aiken, dau. of Reuben and Irena G. (Healey) Locke, b. Alexandria, Mar. 28, 1836. Freeman E. Berry res. on a farm in Alexandria till 1890, when he came to Bristol, making his home in the old Fisk block, where he d. Jan. 3, 1902, ae. 70–3–26. His widow res. Bristol. Free Baptist.

CHILD

2. Martha Etta, b. Alexandria, May 24, 1856, m. Rev. Frank E. Briggs. (See.)

1. John Page Berry, son of Levi and Abigail (Page) Berry, was b. in Alexandria, Aug. 20, 1833. He m. in 1861, Rosetta, dau. of Isaac P. and Nancy (Page) Greenleaf, b. in Groton, in 1834, and d. in Alexandria, Aug. 18, 1880, ae. 46 years. He m., Nov. 2, 1882, Emma R., dau. of John W. Atwood (See.), b. Apr. 15, 1858, in Alexandria. He was a farmer and lumber dealer in Alexandria for 25 years ; came to Bristol in Feb., 1899, and here d. Oct. 12, 1901, ae. 68-1-22. She res. Bristol.

CHILDREN, by first wife

2. Ardella Angeline, b. Alexandria, Apr. 20, 1862 ; res. Boston ; unm.

3. Oscar Everett, b. A., July 3, 1865 ; m. Florence J. Allen ; dry goods merchant in Boston ; res. Brighton, Mass. No children.

4. Alma Lunette, b. A., May 7, 1872 ; m. Lester M. Slocum. He d.; she res. Boston. No children.

THE BICKFORD FAMILY

1. Elbridge Sherman Bickford, son of Joseph A. and Mary E. (Dow) Bickford, was b. Dorchester, Aug. 6, 1867. He m. Sept. 2, 1895, Mabel N., dau. of William A. Rice. (See.) She studied painting at the New England Conservatory, Boston, and is an oil painter of local note. He is an employee of Dodge-Davis Manufacturing Co. Methodist, Odd Fellow, Republican. No children.

THE BINGHAM FAMILY

1. Allen Wardner Bingham, son of Theron and Almeda (Guillow) Bingham, was b. Lempster, Feb. 28, 1825. He m. Apr. 18, 1849, Elvira F., dau. of Moses and Hannah (True) Thompson, b. Newport, Dec. 19, 1826. He was a currier in Newport, Portville, N. Y., Lebanon, Sunapee, and came to Bristol in 1866, where he worked at his trade for a while and then became a dealer in stoves and tinware till 1880, when he went to Manchester, Mass., thence to Newport, where he remained 19 years and then returned to Bristol, where he now resides. Republican, Free Mason, Congregationalist. Was five years town clerk of Bristol.

CHILDREN

2. Edward Allen, b. Newport, Jan. 26, 1850, served three years in U. S. Navy ; m. Belle Underhill, and res. in Cambridge, Mass. Is salesman for steam heating apparatus. Has six children.

*3. Fred Walter, b. Newport, July 7, 1852.

*4. Frank Wallace, b. N., July 7, 1852.

5. Hattie Jane, b. Portville, N. Y., Jan. 17, 1860 ; d. Nov. 29, 1882, of consumption, ae. 22-10-12.

FRANK W. BINGHAM

6. Violetta Maud, b. Lebanon, Oct. 2, 1864; d. of consumption, Nov. 17, 1887, ae. 23-1-15.
7. Mary Elvira, b. Bristol, May 25, 1868; d. Nov. 8, 1888, of consumption, ae. 20-5-13.

(3) Fred W., b. July 7, 1852, m. Sept. 1, 1874, Lizzie E., dau. Oscar F. Morse. (See.) Was a dealer for some years in stoves and tinware; in the livery business, grain business, now agent American Express company. Republican, Mason.

CHILDREN

8. Myrtie Morse, b. Nov. 29, 1875.
9. Fred Walter, b. Sept. 27, 1877; is a clerk in counting-room of the Dodge-Davis Manufacturing Company. Republican, Mason.
10. Oscar Allen, b. Dec. 23, 1880; is a clerk in employ of Boston & Maine railroad, Boston.
11. Harriet May, b. Feb. 7, 1882; was graduated June, 1903, from Concord High school.

(4) Frank W., b. July 7, 1852, m. May 6, 1879, Aldonna, dau. William C. Lovejoy. (See.) She is a teacher of the piano. He has been in trade as a harness maker since January, 1878. Republican.

CHILD

12. Lucile, b. Bristol, Sept. 15, 1884; d. Jan. 20, 1890, ae. 5-4-5.

THE BISHOP FAMILY

1. Dr. James Monroe Bishop was the son of John and Abigail (Parker) Bishop. He was b. in Hanover, May 14, 1821. Nov. 11, 1852, he m. Margaret Ayer, dau. of Samuel B. and Betsey (Philbrick) Locke, b. Concord, Aug. 13, 1832. He was a practicing physician in Bristol 43 years. (See Physicians.) He d. in Stamford, Conn., June 16, 1891, while on the train *en route* to attend the International Medical Association at Atlantic City, N. J., ae. 70-1-2.

CHILDREN

2. Mary Abbie, b. Bristol, Aug. 11, 1854; graduated classical department of Tilton Seminary, 1877; was a teacher in the graded schools of Bristol one year. (See.) Graduated New England Conservatory of Music, Boston, 1892, and has taught instrumental music at Bristol and at Lynn, Mass., where she now res.
3. Daniel Locke, b. B., May 15, 1856; d. Aug. 26, 1856.
4. Lizzie Belle, b. B., Aug. 27, 1857; graduated from Chelsea, Mass., High school in 1877; and from classical department Tilton Seminary, 1878. She was a teacher four years in the Bristol graded school and one year in the Dickinson Seminary, Williamsport, Pa. She m. Aug. 23, 1893, Edwin H. Johnson, Lynn, Mass., who d. Mar. 22, 1894. She res. Lynn.
5. Channing, b. B., July 26, 1864; m. May 15, 1893, Lena B., dau. Richard W. and Nancy Jane (Emery) Cragin, b. Dec. 24, 1866. She pursued the classical course of Tilton Seminary, class of 1884. He has been a practicing physician in Bristol since 1889. (See Physicians.)

THE BLACKSTONE FAMILY

1. Benjamin Edward Blackstone, son of Daniel, was b. St. Albans, Vt., May 23, 1829. Oct. 30, 1852, he m. Nancy Jane, dau. Joseph Kidder. (See.) She d. Bristol, Nov. 27, 1893, ae. 58-6-20. He m. (2) Susan, dau. of Stephen Brock. For some years he carried on the old saw-mill on south side of New-found river in Bristol village. Served in the 12th Regt. in Civil war on quota of Sanbornton ; discharged after three months' service. He is now a farmer.

CHILDREN

*2. Orren Edward, b. Manchester, Aug. 27, 1853.

3. Henry Joshua, b. Bristol, Mar. 30, 1855 ; d. Dec. 19, 1856, ae. 1-8-19.

4. Charles Henry, b. B., Dec. 24, 1856; d. of consumption, July 1, 1894, Everett, Mass. Unm.

5. Emily Jane, b. B., Apr. 15, 1860; m. June 2, 1897, Herbert Dexter Rice, son of James B. and Sarah (Weeden) Rice, b. Jan. 6, 1850. No children. Res. Melrose, Mass.

6. Irvin Kidder, b. B., Mar. 18, 1863. Unm. Res. Manchester.

7. Anna Mabel, b. B., June 29, 1867 ; m. June 1, 1890, Bruce Valiquet, son of Thomas, b. Chicago, Apr. 16, 1864. Res. 19 Everett St., Melrose, Mass. No children.

8. Della Vera, b. B., Jan. 8, 1871 ; m. Henry E. Holbrook, Jan. 1, 1891. Res. Stoughton, Mass.

(2) Orren E. Blackstone, b. Aug. 27, 1853, m. Nov. 1, 1887, Wilhelmine, dau. John and Louisa (Bradlau) Shroedter, b. Bagniten, Germany, Mar. 31, 1864. They res. 48 Eighth street, Norwich, Conn.

CHILDREN

9. Henry Edward, b. Aug. 8, 1888.

10. Hedwig Louisa, b. Apr. 3, 1890.

11. Helen Emily, b. June 20, 1901.

THE BLAISDELL FAMILY

1. John C. Blaisdell was the son of Elijah and Mary (Fogg) Blaisdell and the grandson of Hon. Daniel Blaisdell. Daniel Blaisdell was a native and a resident of Canaan. He was a member of the governor's council five years from 1803, and represented New Hampshire in Congress two years from 1809. Elijah was a prominent lawyer. He resided and d. in Lebanon. John C. Blaisdell was b. in Pittsfield, May 13, 1805. He m. Jan. 15, 1829, Ruth S., dau. Dr. Sethus B. and Ruth (Wells) Forbes, b. Hill, Oct. 6, 1808. They came to Bristol in 1848, and resided where the bank block now stands. There Mrs. Blaisdell opened the first millinery store in town. Mr. Blaisdell was a farmer and served two terms as commissioner of Grafton county. They removed to Laconia in 1862, where he was internal revenue collector from July, 1863, till September,

HON. JOHN C. BLAISDELL.

1865. In 1866, they removed to Vineland, N. J., where he d. Mar. 1, 1893, after 64 years of wedded life, ae. 87-9-18. He was a Republican in politics, and was a Mason for 65 years. Mrs. Blaisdell was a great sufferer for more than 30 years as the result of a railroad accident. She d. at the home of her son, in Camden, N. J., May 14, 1896, ae. 87-7-8.

CHILDREN

2. Arlond, b. Mar. 20, 1831; d. Jan. 21, 1833.
*3. Arlond Henry, b. Feb. 13, 1836.
*4. Elijah Galond, b. Hill, May 4, 1847.

(3) Arlond H. Blaisdell, b. Feb. 13, 1836, m. (1) Mary Pattee, of Bristol; (2) Belle Cooper. He opened the first machine shop in town on Water street in 1859. He removed to Vineland, N. J., 1872, where he now has the largest machine shop in New Jersey.

CHILD

5. Ida May, b. Bristol, Oct. 23, 1858; m. May 5, 1879, Charles S. Brown. They res. Vineland. Child:
a. Alice Virginia, b. 1880.

(4) E. Galond Blaisdell, b. May 4, 1847, m. May 24, 1875, Julie E., daughter of Elisha C. and Ellen P. Fellows, b. Jan. 21, 1847. He was graduated from Dartmouth college 1868; editor *Vineland Weekly* for several years; went to Camden, N. J., in 1879, and entered the employment of the West Jersey railroad. Is now special claim agent West Jersey & Seashore railroad, and Pennsylvania railroad, at Camden.

CHILDREN

6. Viola Margaret, b. Vineland, Apr. 4, 1876; student Bryn Mawr college, Bryn Mawr, Pa.
7. Clara Elizabeth, b. V., Feb. 10, 1879; d. Oct. 20, 1883, ae. 4-8-10.

THE BLAKE FAMILY

1. Paine Blake m. Polly Leach in Hampton and settled in Sanbornton, where she d. Feb. 11, 1795. He removed to Maine and there d. They had eight children of whom the 6th was

2. Greenleaf. He m. July 17, 1808, Charlotte, dau. of Dr. Timothy Kelly. (See.) He was a farmer in Hill, where he d. Sept. 17, 1869, ae. 61-2-0; she d. Hill, Aug. 20, 1879, ae. 94-9-21.

CHILDREN

3. Horatio Kelly, b. Sept. 3, 1808; m. (1) Jane T., who d. Hill, May 16, 1837, ae. 26-8-26. He m. (2)
*4. Albert was b. Aug. 19, 1810, in Canada, while his parents were there temporarily.
5. Tirzah, b. Apr. 8, 1812; res. with her brother, Curtis N., in Hill.
6. Sarah L., b. Jan. 29, 1814; m. Stephen A. Oakley. (See.)

7. Rosilla S., b. May 5, 1818; m. (1) —— Godding; (2) —— Snow, Pomfret, Vt.
8. Curtis C., b. Oct. 10, 1820; d. young.
9. Curtis N., b. Feb. 11, 1826; m. Jane S. Piper, dau. Nathaniel, Apr. 20, 1865. He d. July 20, 1893, ae. 67-5-9. Children:
    a. Bertie Lancelet, b. Feb. 3, 1870.
    b. Clyde A., b. Dec. 17, 1876.
10. Gilman K., Jan. 18, 1828; d. Jan. 19, 1853. Unm.

(4) Albert Blake, b. Aug. 19, 1810, m. Adaline Sylvia, dau. Jonathan and Sylvia Smith, b. Oct. 11, 1811, and d. Bristol, Dec. 19, 1879, ae. 68-2-8. He was a trader in Hill and at one time (1855) made friction matches there. He came to Bristol, 1868, and was a large owner of real estate. He d. Bristol, June 17, 1892, ae. 81-9-28. Republican.

CHILDREN

*11. Roswell, b. Hill, Mar. 14, 1838.
12. Clinton, b. H., Aug. 2, 1839; m. Josephine L. Wadleigh, dau. of Jonathan T. and Betsey (Thomas) Wadleigh, of Sanbornton. She d. in Franklin, and he m. (2) Hattie Call. He was in trade for some years in Bristol, and was postmaster at Franklin four years, where he now res.; speculator. Republican.
*13. Albert, b. H., June 13, 1845.

(11) Roswell Blake, b. Mar. 14, 1838, m., Apr. 28, 1863, Sarah Emery Dickinson, dau. of Amos. (See.) He was a farmer and speculator. Came to Bristol in 1863 and here d. Dec. 14, 1894, ae. 56-9-. She res. Bristol, South Main street.

CHILDREN

14. Alma L., b. Bristol, May 28, 1864; m. (1) Oscar F. Sleeper. (See.) she m. (2) Albion A. Veasey. (See.)
15. Edward Arthur, b. B., Oct. 21, 1866. Was a clerk in grocery store of Alexander & Davis 11 years; now letter carrier on Free Rural Delivery Route No. 1.
16. Amos Albert, b. B., Oct. 23, 1868; has been a salesman in clothing and shoe store of C. H. Dickinson since 1890. He m. Feb. 4, 1903, Sarah A., dau. of James Fitzpatrick. (See.)
17. Lawrence, b. B., Feb. 22, 1883.

(13) Albert Blake, b. June 13, 1845, m. Apr. 23, 1873, Louise Angelina, dau. Daniel S. Mason. (See.) He was postmaster in Bristol seven years; for 18 years has been railway postal clerk. Res. Pleasant street, Bristol.

CHILD

18. Edith Mason, b. Bristol, Apr. 10, 1878; m. May 2, 1901, George Ernest Tyler, b. Weston, Mass., Dec. 12, 1876, son of Sidney and Sarah (Hanscomb) Tyler. He is a railway postal clerk.

THE BLODGETT FAMILIES

1. Rev. Ebenezer Blodgett was b. in Plymouth, Feb. 9, 1777, and d. in Bristol, Sept. 28, 1854. He was the son of Dea.

James Blodgett, an officer in the French and Indian wars, who settled in Plymouth in 1764, being one of the first settlers in that town. He m. (1) Nancy A. Penniman, of Moultonboro', who d. in Bristol, Feb. 16, 1826, ae. 45 years. He m. (2) Apr. 3, 1830, Lydia E. Barnard, of Warner, b. Feb. 5, 1787; d. in Bristol, Sept. 29, 1856, ae. 69-7-24. He came to Bristol in 1835; was a local preacher of the Methodist church, and res. at Profile Falls. He was the presiding officer at an anti-slavery meeting in the old Methodist chapel, in 1837, when Rev. George Storrs spoke and was mobbed. He is said to have preached several years in West Hill meeting-house.

CHILDREN

2. Alice, m. —— Bartlett, and settled in Woodstock.
3. Atossa, m. John H. Gill; lived and d. in Plymouth.
4. Katherine, m. Leonard Felch, of Weare.
*5. Ebenezer Kellum, b. Plymouth, Mar. 4, 1831.

(5) Ebenezer K. Blodgett, b. Mar. 4, 1831, m. Oct. 11, 1850, Rose W., dau. of Clark Merrill (See.), b. Apr. 13, 1834. He was a farmer in Hill, Plymouth and in Bristol at Profile Falls 1835-'55, 1882-'85. They now res. Suncook.

CHILDREN

6. Fred Clark, b. Hill, Nov. 19, 1854; m. Mar. 24, 1880, Serena L., dau. of Lemuel L. and Submit C. Draper, b. Roxbury, Mass., Dec. 6, 1857. He is chief clerk, motive power department, South Division, Boston & Maine railroad. Res. 26 School St., Melrose, Mass. Children:

    a. Lilla Lucina, b. Plymouth, Feb. 21, 1881.
    b. Serena Rose, b. P., Aug. 9, 1883
    c. Ernest Frank, b. Somerville, Mass., May 4, 1885.

7. Frank Edwards, b. Lowell, Mass., Nov. 20, 1858; m. Feb. 11, 1886, Jennie E., dau. of Hon. William Hazeltine, of Suncook, b. June 27, 1859. He is a dealer in coal and wholesale dealer in wood in Suncook. Children:

    a. Harriet Rose, b. Fitchburg, Mass., Dec. 24, 1888.
    b. Philip Hazeltine, b. Suncook, Sept. 5, 1893.

----

1. William Riley Blodgett was the son of Thomas and Deborah (Rowell) Blodgett. He was b. Orford, June 21, 1805, and m., Oct. 11, 1828, Deborah, dau. of Lemuel and Harriet (Crowell) Hedge, b. Chatham, Conn., Dec. 6, 1806. They came to Bristol from Kalamazoo, Mich., in 1850. He was a blacksmith. She d. Bristol, Dec. 11, 1857, ae. 51-0-5, and he m., Dec. 31, 1859, Mary Clay. He d. Bristol, Nov. 2, 1880, ae. 75-4-11.

CHILDREN

2. Thomas Lemuel, b. Naples, N. Y., Jan. 6, 1832; was in Bristol a few years when a young man; m. Charlotte Crawford, of New York City, and has res. Los Angeles, Cal.
3. William Blidore, b. Naples, May 26, 1835; res. in Michigan.

4. Susan A., b. Kalamazoo, Mich., Nov. 9, 1837; m. Sylvanus W. Swett. (See.)

5. Mary, b. K., July 5, 1842; m. Edward P. Sawyer. (See.)

*6. Frederick Eugene, b. Jackson, Mich., Jan. 5, 1846.

(6)   Frederick E. Blodgett, b. Jan. 5, 1846, left Bristol for New York before the Civil war, and was learning bank check engraving when he enlisted, Sept. 1, 1864, in Co. K, 2nd New York Cavalry. He served under Gen. Custer in Gen. Sheridan's Cavalry division, in the Shenandoah valley and participated in several cavalry engagements, including the capture of Gen. Lee's last supply trains. He was discharged June 5, 1865, and returned to New York, where he was for twelve years an expert engraver with Tiffany & Co., and ten years with Stein Bros., 23d street. He engraved his name and the letters of the alphabet on the head of a pin. He m., June 28, 1873, Lena, dau. Morris Bessunger, b. New York City, June 27, 1854. He is now with Tiffany Bros., and res. 445 4th Ave.; is captain First Mounted Veterans of New York City.

CHILDREN

7.   Eugene, b. Bristol, May 23, 1874.
8.   Estelle, b. Boston, Sept. 4, 1879. An actress.
9.   Chester, b. May 17, 1882 "Is an unrivaled trick cyclist."
10. Dorothy, b. New York city, July 12, 1884. Is an actress.

THE BOARDMAN FAMILIES

1.   Benjamin and Elias Boardman, twin brothers, settled in Bridgewater, in May, 1790, going from Reading, Mass. Their log cabin was where was later the cemetery near the meeting-house. Where was the doorway of their cabin was later the spot where Benjamin and his wife were buried. They paid for their land by raising grain in the summer and working at shoemaking winters at Reading. They moved their families to Bridgewater in the spring of the eighth season. Elias built on the Alonzo Wheeler place, which house was destroyed by fire in 1883. Benjamin was a soldier in the Revolutionary war, and had at least six children.

2.   Elias Boardman and his wife, Hannah, were the parents of

CHILDREN

3.   Elias, b. Nov. 24, 1786.
4.   Hannah, b. Mar. 21, 1788.
5.   Amos, b. Feb. 25, 1791.
*6. Benjamin Lewis, b. Bridgewater, Apr. 5, 1793.
7.   Moses, b. Sept. 29, 1794.
8.   Elizabeth Smith, b. Oct. 18, 1796.
9.   Mary Lewis, b. July 10, 1799.
10. William, b. May 6, 1804.
11. Nancy, b. Nov. 23, 1805.

(6) Benjamin L. Boardman, b. Apr. 5, 1793, m. Susan R. Moses, b. Alexandria (Pembroke). They came to Bristol from Massachusetts and occupied the Edwards farm on High street. Here he d. July 1, 1862, ae. 69-2-26. She d. same place, Dec. 9, 1876, ae. 78. They had at least seven children.

CHILDREN

*12. William L. P., b. Mar. 24, 1827.
13. Lydia, E. C., b. Pembroke; d. Bristol, Jan. 6, 1892, ae. 63-0-16. Unm.
14. Mary L., b. Reading, Mass.; d. Bristol, June 24, 1894, ae. 57-3-10. Unm.
15. Martha E., b. So. Reading, Mass., Mar. 3, 1840; d. Bristol, Feb. 20 (22), 1887, ae. 46-11-17
16. Susan M., d. Bristol, Apr. 12, 1863, ae. 28-5-.

(12) William L. P. Boardman, b. Mar. 14, 1827, m. Oct. 18, 1865, Mary G. (May) White, dau. Samuel and Mary May. He was for 35 years master of Lewis school, Boston. He d. Boston, Mar. 18, 1901, ae. 74-0-4.

CHILD

17. Samuel May, b. Dec. 27, 1869.

---

1. Edmund Boardman, the son of Stephen, was b. Portsmouth, June 30, 1806. He m., Nov. 30, 1831, Sally Phippen, b. Salem, Mass., Mar. 23, 1806. He was a soap maker in Cambridgeport, Mass., and a farmer in Alexandria. He came to Bristol about 1874. She d. Bristol, Dec. 1, 1875, ae. 69-8-8. He d. Bristol, Oct. 16, 1888, ae. 82-3-16.

CHILDREN

2. Sarah Lufkin, b. Cambridgeport, Mass., July 19, 1832; m. Sept. 8, 1866, Lucian C. Abbott, and d. Apr. 16, 1885, ae. 52-8-27.
3. Charles, b. C., Nov. 26, 1833; m. Mar. 27, 1872, Eliza Ann, dau. of Benjamin Q. Fellows (See.), b. Nov. 17, 1843. He spent five years in California, 1860-'65; was in trade in Rollins' block with Samuel D. Farrar five years previous to the fire of Dec. 7, 1871; in trade in basement of Abel's block six months; built the Robie block on Pleasant street in 1872, and in trade there till Oct. 1, 1888; dealer in furniture in basement of this block till the block was gutted by fire, Apr. 2, 1889; continued same in Blake block till 1890. Has served as town treasurer and tax-collector. Congregationalist, Republican, Mason. No children.
4. George Phippen, b. C., Mar. 15, 1835; d. Apr. 6, 1859, ae. 24-0-21.
5. Gideon, b. C., Dec. 15, 1836; m. Aug. 31, 1862, Sarah Jane, dau. of Nathan and Ruth C. Blake. She d. in Alexandria, Sept. 4, 1864, ae. 26-6-22. He m. Oct. 5, 1872, Ella A., dau. Ansel and Mahala Chandler, b. Bristol, Aug. 7, 1849. He was a carriage maker and repairer. She d. Bristol, Mar. 29, 1900, ae. 50-7-22; he d. two days later, ae. 63-3-16; both buried in one grave. Child:
   a. Emma Jane, b. Alexandria, Aug. 15, 1863; m. Mar. 23, 1885, Scott Spencer of Plymouth and res. Sloane, Iowa. Three children.
6. Helen Smith, b. Alexandria, Dec. 30, 1842; m. George M. Tewksbury and res. Westboro, Mass. Four children.

THE BOHONON FAMILY

1. Stephen Bohonon was the son of Jacob and Sarah (Judkins) Bohonon. Jacob was a cousin to Daniel Webster. Stephen was b. Boscawen, Feb. 1, 1790. He came here in 1812, and became a soldier, from Bridgewater, in the war then in progress with England. He had previously served one term of five years in the Navy. He m., May 1, 1827, Rebecca, dau. of John Willard (See.), b. June 5, 1802. He was a carpenter and farmer and res. south of Danforth brook on the Nelson road, where she d. July 27, 1851, ae. 49-1-22 ; he d. Oct. 13, 1878, ae. 88-8-12.

CHILDREN, all born in Bristol

2. Malinda Ruth, b. Mar. 31, 1828; d. Bristol, June 23, 1846, ae. 18-2-22.
3. John Willard, b. Oct. 15, 1830; d. Feb. —, 1832, ae. 1-4-. } Twins.
4. Lucy Maria, b. Oct. 15, 1830; m. Moses Emmons. (See.) }
5. Leonard Willard, b. July 16, 1835; m. Mary A. Dicey, Alexandria ; m. (2) Oct. 3, 1879, Mrs. Mary A. Danforth, Danbury.
6. Daniel Webster, b. Mar. 25, 1842; served in Co. C, 12th Regt. N. H. Vols., and d. Richmond, Va., July 26, 1880, ae. 38-4-1 ; unm. (See Roll of Honor.)

THE BOND FAMILY

1. Charles G. M. Bond was the son of Alfred Bond, and was b. Greenwich, Mass., Mar. 10, 1850. He m. Hattie Alice, dau. of Jonathan and Harriet A. (Gregg) Taylor, b. Boston, Mass., Dec. 1, 1846. He was in trade with Hon. Cyrus Taylor, one year from May, 1890; removed to Stoughton, Mass., in May, 1891 ; now in business in Hudson, Mass.

CHILDREN

2. Herbert T., b. Detroit, Mich., Mar. 13, 1873.
3. Gertrude M., b. D., June 23, 1876 ; m. Harry Moore of Hudson, Mass. One son.
4. Howard C., b. D., Sept. 2, 1880.
5. Alfred M., b. D., May 21, 1883.
6. Harold A., b. D., Mar. 29, 1887.

THE BOWERS FAMILIES

1. Jerahmeel Bowers, the son of Jerahmeel, was b. in Townsend, Mass., Nov. 1, 1773. When he was a boy, his father moved to that part of Salisbury now Franklin. At the age of 15 he commenced to teach school, and among his pupils was Daniel Webster. Teaching was his chief occupation for many years, though a cripple. "His form would have produced a fortune for his parents had they seen fit to have exhibited him for money." His ancestors came from Bath, England. He m.

Dorothy Gale, dau. Stephen, b. July 27, 1783, on Isle of Man. They settled in Hebron, where their first child was b., and then removed to Bristol, where their other children were b. During a residence in Bristol of 25 years, he was a justice of the peace, and resided in a house that stood in the lot directly in front of the present schoolhouse in Union district. She d. Boston, Mass., May 5, 1847, ae. 63–9–8; he d. Natick, Mass., Sept. 7, 1847, ae. 73–10–6.

CHILDREN

2. James, b. Hebron, Aug. 10, 1804; killed at Charlestown, Mass., May 13, 1831, ae. 26–9–3. Unm.

*3. Rufus Lewis, b. Bristol, Jan. 27, 1807.

4. Alsa Gale, b. B., Dec. 24, 1808; m. June 5, 1836, James M. Barnard, Hebron. Died a widow at Natick, Mass., Jan. 23, 1881, ae. 72–0–29. Children :

    a. James B., b. Hebron, Mar. 3, 1837; d. Mar. 4, 1837.

    b. Isaac Henry, b. H., May 22, 1839; d. Aug. 9, 1840.

    c. Julia Grace, b. H., June 24, 1842; d. Aug. 13, 1843.

5. Caroline Carter, b. Bristol, July 8, 1813; a deaf mute, educated at Deaf and Dumb Asylum, Hartford, Conn. She m. Benjamin Clough. (See.)

*6. Cyrus Russell, b. B., June 18, 1811.

7. Harriet Newell, b. B., Apr. 8, 1815; d. Dec. 26, 1815.

8. Laura Farnham, b. B., Feb. 3, 1817; m. Dec. 31, 1846, Sparrock Barney, of Boston, Mass., and d. Southboro, Mass., Aug., 1850, ae. 34–3–. Child :

    a. Laura Frances, b. Aug. 1850; m. Herbert Carpenter, Marlboro, Mass.

9. Jerahmeel Lombard, b. B., Feb. 26, 1819; m. Jane Odell, Lowell, Mass., 1844, and d. Natick, Mass., Jan. 26, 1866, ae. 46–11–.

10. Benjamin Franklin, b. B., May 30, 1821; m. Sept. 7, 1847, Abba C., dau. Timothy and Sarah Martin, b. Bremen, Me. She d. Natick, Mass., Nov. 26, 1855, and he m., Apr., 1856, Maria Coleman of Wrentham, Mass., who d. Medfield, Mass., Apr., 1872. He was a photographer at 491 Fulton street, Brooklyn, N. Y., where he was in business in 1900. By first wife had one son and one daughter.

*11. William Tenney, b. B., June 2, 1823.

12. Dorothy Ann, b. B., Nov. 23, 1825; d. B., Oct. 3, 1827, ae. 1–10–10.

(3) Rufus L. Bowers, b. Jan. 27, 1807, m. October, 1837, Eliza, dau. Levi Hutchins, b. Gilmanton, Feb. 12, 1811. He was a farmer in Bridgewater, Gilmanton, Alexandria, and Sanbornton. He d. Laconia, May 23, 1867, ae. 60–1–26.

CHILDREN

13. Charles Lewis, b. Bridgewater, Oct. 25, 1839; m. Jan. 1, 1863, Carrie Augusta Eaton. Six children.

14. Caroline Elizabeth, b. Gilmanton, Sept. 8, 1841; m. Samuel H. Lawrence. She d. Meredith, July 5, 1875, ae. 33–9–27. Two children.

15. George Franklin, b. Alexandria, June 5, 1845. Served in Co. H, 15th Regt. N. H. Vols., and d. of typhoid fever at Carrolton, La., May 9, 1863, ae. 17–11–4.

16. Laura Ann, b. A., June 8, 1848; m. William H. H. Rollins, a farmer at East Tilton, where she d. of consumption, Mar. 1, 1878, ae. 29–8–23. Both were teachers before m. Child :

    a. Clara Alice, b. May 9, 1873.

4

17. Mary Jane, b. A., Oct. 8, 1850; m. Samuel H. Lawrence, April, 1876.

(6) Cyrus R. Bowers, b. June 18, 1811; m. Catherine Brown, of Concord, and d. Houlton, Me., Dec. 23, 1890, ae. 78-11-. In 1837, he built the brick house on Lake street, where Kiah Wells lived and died, and he set out a row of maple trees from his home to Central square.

CHILDREN

18. Daughter, d. in Bristol, aged about one year.
19. Charles, res. Natick, Mass.

(11) William T. Bowers, b. June 2, 1823, m. Apr. 21, 1847, Mary Corney, Foxboro, Mass., and d. Hyde Park, Mass., in October, 1871, ae. 48-4-.

CHILDREN

20. William, res. Boston, Mass.
21. Julia Grace.

---

1. Dea. Gardner J. Bowers was born July 8, 1793. He m. (1) Betsey ———, who d. Nov. 8, 1836, ae. 39 years; he m. (2), Mar. 28, 1837, Mrs. Sarah Colby, widow of Ebenezer Colby, of Salisbury, and dau. of Dea. John Abrams, who res. in Sanbornton, near Hill village. Gardner J. Bowers was a deacon in the Congregational church in Franklin. While filling this office he settled in South Alexandria on the Kendrick Dickerson farm. While residing here, in 1842, he was elected deacon of the Congregational church in Bristol, and filled this office till his death. He res. in Bristol in the house next north of the Methodist church from 1855 till his death, Mar. 28, 1868. His age was 74-8-20. Mrs. Bowers d. Oct. 13, 1868, in her 72d year. She had six children by her first husband, and two by Dea. Bowers.

CHILDREN

2. Gardner J., d. Feb. 22, 1839, ae. 17-7-11.
3. George Brown, b. Alexandria, Mar. 11, 1838; m. in Jan. 1868, Mary Bowers, a relative. He was a dentist in Bristol for a time after his m.; res. most of his life in Iowa, and returned East a few years since, and settled on the farm in South Alexandria where he was born. Child:
      a. Ned Orville, b. Jan. 30, 1877; res. with his parents.
4. Betsey, b. Alexandria, July 28, 1840; m. Capt. William A. Beckford. (See.)

THE BOWLER FAMILY

1. Rev. John Atwood Bowler, son of Rev. George and Ann Creamer (Alley) Bowler, was b. Watertown, Mass., Oct. 25, 1852. May 19, 1879, he m. Sarah Josephine, dau. of Cyrus and Sarah W. (Tileston) Coburn, b. Allenstown, July 7, 1853. He was pastor of the Methodist church in Bristol three years from

spring of 1884, coming from Hillsboro Bridge. He was a member of the New Hampshire Conference from 1881 till 1900, when he was transferred to the New England Conference. He is at present stationed at Bondville, Mass.

CHILD

2. Bertram Evan, b. Hillsboro, Jan. 26, 1882. Is a watchmaker and optician at Manchester.

THE BRADLEY FAMILY

1. Moses Hazen Bradley, son of John and Hannah (Ayer) Bradley, was b. Concord, May 15, 1782. He m., Dec. 26, 1817, Mary Green, dau. of Dr. Peter Green, and sister of William, b. Concord, Dec. 26, 1784. They resided in the Green house, Central square, 1812 to 1834, when they removed to Concord, where he d., June 22, 1834, ae. 52-1-7; she d. Concord, about 1865. (See Lawyers.)

THE BRAGG FAMILY

1. Rev. Lyman Daniel Bragg, the son of Rev. Daniel Pitkin and Laura C. (Church) Bragg, was b. Hinesburgh, Vt., Feb. 24, 1850. His father traces his descent on his mother's side from William de la Grande, who went from Normandy to England in 1066 with William the Conqueror. John Porter, a descendant in the 16th generation from William de la Grande, was in this country as early as 1637. Mr. Bragg is also a descendant from William Pitkin, who settled in Hartford, Conn., in 1659. Rev. L. D. Bragg, was graduated from Middlebury (Vt.) college, 1875, and from Boston University, School of Theology, in 1878. He united with the New England Methodist Conference in 1880, and was transferred to the New Hampshire Conference in 1892. He was professor in Rust University, Holly Springs, Miss., two years, and with this exception, has filled various pastorates including two years in Bristol from April 1901. He m., June 16, 1880, Sarah Julia, dau. of Abram and Mary Ann (Apgar) Klotz, b. German Valley, N. J., Jan. 13, 1855. She is a graduate of Centenary College Institute at Hackettstown, N. J., with degree of M. L. A.

CHILDREN

2. Laura Mary, b. Northbridge, Mass., Oct. 9, 1881.
3. Ernest Lyman, b. Spencer, Mass., Apr. 1, 1885.
4. Barbara Klotz, b. Medford, Mass., July 7, 1886.

THE BRALEY FAMILY

1. Herbert Braley, son of Elbridge J. and Lovina (Waldron) Braley, was b. Alexandria, July 2, 1868. He m., Nov. 6,

1889, Flora M., dau. Nicholas R. and Frances (Ray) Gardner, b. Hebronsville, Mass., Nov. 6, 1866. He came to Bristol in 1884; was three years an operative in the woolen-mill; since 1890, a teamster. No children. Mason, Odd Fellow, Republican.

———

1.   Weston James Braley, son of Elbridge J. and Lovina (Waldron) Braley, was b. Alexandria, Jan. 20, 1874. He m., Jan. 21, 1893, Marion M., dau. of Frederick J. Ballou. (See.) She was b. May 12, 1876, and d. in Bristol, Sept. 25, 1902, ae. 26-4-13. He came to Bristol in 1889, and is a teamster in the employ of the Mason-Perkins Paper company. Republican.

CHILDREN

2.   Bertha Julia, b. Bristol, Aug. 6, 1895.
3.   Clyde Edward, b. B., Mar. 16, 1898.

THE BRECK FAMILY

1.   George Coolidge Breck, son of Marshall H. H. Breck, was b. Sherburn, Mass., Nov. 15, 1831, and d. in Bristol, Jan. 6, 1885, ae. 53-1-21. Feb. 20, 1856, he m. Sarah Elizabeth, dau. of William and Elizabeth (Vaughn) Wesson, b. Boston, Mass., Mar. 1, 1834. He enlisted Aug. 28, 1862, on the quota of Wentworth, in Co. G, 12th Regt. N. H. Vols. At the battle of Chancellorsville, May 3, 1863, he was twice wounded, being struck by minie balls in the calf of the leg and hip. Nov. 17, 1863, by reason of his wounds, he was transferred to the 18th Co., 2d Bat. Invalid Corps, and discharged at Albany, N. Y., Apr. 11, 1865. After the war he was a coal burner at Rumney till 1870, when he came to Bristol, and was an employee in the Mason-Perkins paper-mill. Mrs. Breck res. Bristol.

CHILDREN

*2.   Joseph Henry, b. Wentworth, Feb. 20, 1860.
3.   George Marshall, b. Rumney, Oct. 11, 1869; m. July 2, 1892, Alice May, dau. Hiram S. Tilton. (See.) Divorced. He went to Gardner, Me., in 1895, and there m., Mar. 26, 1898, Mrs. Katherine Kenniston.
4.   Mary E., b. Wentworth, Dec. 12, 1861; m. George F. Alden. (See.)
5.   Addie Gertrude, b. Bristol, Feb. 3, 1877; drowned Sept. 23, 1880, ae. 3-8-20.
6.   Jennie May, b. B., Apr. 5, 1875; d. Aug. 22, 1875, ae. 0-4-4.

(2)   Joseph H. Breck, b. Feb. 20, 1860, m. May 18, 1881, Nellie M., dau. Philip Jones, b. Loudon, July 22, 1862. He has been an employee of the Mason-Perkins paper-mill since 1874.

CHILDREN

7. Willie Henry, b. Bristol, Aug. 9, 1883; d. Oct. 20, 1884, ae. 1-2-11.
8. Lois May, b. B., Jan. 19, 1892.
9. Leslie Joseph, b. B., Aug. 20, 1896.

THE BRIGGS FAMILY

1. Sherman Shattuck Briggs, son of Amasa and Mary (Shattuck) Briggs, was b. Oct. 1, 1828. Sept. 19, 1848, he m. Abby Jane, dau. of Moses and Jane (Morse) Trussell, b. Aug. 10, 1829. He was a shoemaker, came to Bristol in 1860, and res. High street. He d. suddenly of heart disease while visiting in Methuen, Mass., Nov. 21, 1868, ae. 40-1-20. Shortly before her death she removed to Franklin, where she d. Dec. 4, 1894, ae. 65-3-24.

CHILDREN

*2. Frank Edwin, b. Boscawen, Dec. 2, 1849.
3. George Nason, b. Oct. 31, 1851; d. at Bristol, June 7, 1870, of consumption, ae. 18-7-6.
4. Alice Adelaide, b. Nov. 24, 1854; d. at Bristol, May 27, 1872, of consumption, ae. 17-6-3.
5. Ida Anna, b. Dec. 28, 1855; m. Edward Martin of Richmond, Va. She d. Aug. 5, 1876, of consumption, ae. 20-7-7.
*6. Fred Herman, b. Dunbarton, Oct. 1, 1858.
7. Jennie Eva., b. D., Mar. 12, 1860; m. Nov. 29, 1881, Leroy L. Thompson. She d. Franklin Falls, Mar. 18, 1902, of consumption, ae. 42-0-6. He is a machinist at Lakeport. Child:
a. Sherman E.

(2) Frank E. Briggs, b. Dec. 2, 1849, m. Dec. 24, 1873, Martha Etta, dau. of Freeman E. Berry. (See.) Is a clergyman of the Free Baptist denomination; was graduated at New Hampton Literary Institution, 1879; Cobb's Divinity School, Lewiston, Me., 1882; licensed to preach, May 27, 1879; ordained, July 7, 1882, by a council of the Sebec (Me.) Quarterly Meeting. He served as pastor the Abbott, Parkman, and No. Guilford, Me., church, two years from June 1, 1882; at West Lebanon, Me., two years from June 1, 1884; at No. Berwick, Me., from May, 1886, till 1889; Center Strafford, 1889-'91; Barrington, 1891-'96; Washington, Vt., 1896-1902; is now serving the church at So. Lemington, Me.

CHILDREN

8. Edward Mortimer, b. Alexandria, Oct. 23, 1878. He was graduated from New Hampton Institution, 1902; now a teacher.
9. Ena, b. A., Nov. 18, 1883.
10. Berneice, b. No. Berwick, Me., Apr. 21, 1888.

(6) Fred H. Briggs, b. Oct. 1, 1858, m. Dec. 29, 1885, Della Alice, dau. Elbridge Tilton. (See.) He is a photographer, and has been in business in Bristol; in Demorest and Harriman, Ga.; in Connecticut; now in Amesbury, Mass.

4a

11. Harold Herman, b. No. Berwick, Me., Apr. 23, 1888.
12. Bertha Lenona, b. Bristol, June 25, 1898.

THE BROWN FAMILIES

1. Samuel Browne, the progenitor of Stephen Thurston Brown and his descendants, was b. in Rowley, Mass., July 20, 1686. He m., May 17, 1716, Elizabeth Wheeler, b. July 12, 1695, dau. of Josiah Wheeler, of Salisbury, Mass. He was prominent in church and town affairs in Rowley till about 1728, when he removed to Littleton, Mass., and there resided till 1742, when he removed to West Dunstable, now Hollis, N. H., where he was one of the founders of the church. Among his children was

2. John. He was b. in Rowley, and was there baptized in Byfield church, Mar. 29, 1724. He went to Hollis with his father and m., Oct. 9, 1744, Kezia Wheeler, who d. Oct. 31, 1760. He m. Feb. 18, 1761, Martha, dau. of Ezekiel and Martha (Thurston) Jewett. He res. some years in Monson, near the Hollis line, and was selectman of the town. In 1762, in company with his brother, Josiah, who had been a lieutenant in the French and Indian war, and five others, he traveled north along the Merrimack and Pemigewasset rivers, till they reached what is now Plymouth. Here they selected land, erected log cabins, and commenced to clear the land for farms. In the spring of 1764, they took their families to their homes in the wilderness. The names of John Brown and Josiah Brown appear among the grantees or proprietors of the town. John Brown was a physician. He dropped the final letter from his name, and his orthography has been followed by all his descendants. He d. May 6, 1776; she d. in the family of her son, Stephen Thurston Brown, in Bristol, Mar. 5, 1797. Of his nine children, one was

3. Stephen Thurston, b. Plymouth, Apr. 18, 1766. He purchased 65 acres of land in what was afterward known as the Locke neighborhood in Bristol. His land now constitutes a part of the Damon Y. Emmons farm, and his log cabin stood where now stands the ell of Mr. Emmons' farmhouse. He was first taxed for this land in 1788. Dec. 18, 1788, he m. Anna Davis, of Goffstown, and here were born to them twelve children, all but one living to maturity. Mr. Brown was a man of sterling integrity — a Quaker, and he brought up his children according to the tenets of his religion. He d. in family of his dau., Martha, in South Alexandria, May 4, 1839, ae. 73-0-16. Mrs. Brown d. in the family of her son, Samuel, in Bridgewater, May 23, 1851.

CHILDREN, all born in Bristol

*4. John, b. Sept. 15, 1789.

5. Anne, b. May 27, 1791; m. Isaac Swett. (See.)

*6. Samuel, b. Oct. 28, 1793.

*7. Joseph, b. Mar. 3, 1796.

*8. Enos, b. Mar. 3, 1798.

9. Martha, b. May 15, 1800; m. Daniel Simonds. (See.)

10. Sally, b. 1802; m. Jacob Colby of Weare, in Oct., 1823; she d. Weare, 1878, ae. 76 years. He d. in W., 1884. Children:

    a. Stephen B., b. Weare, 1824; m. June 1, 1847, Mary Ann Beard; res. Quincy, Mass. Five children.

    b. John B., m. Mary J. Cochrane. Served in 14th Regt. N. H. Vols. One son.

    c. Amanda, m. Lewis Tuttle.

    d. Calvin, b. 1840. Res. So. Weare.

    e. Henry, m. ——— Brown, of Maine. ⎫ Twins.
    f. Ella, res. Henniker; unm.   ⎭

    g. Helen, m. (1) Fred Merrill, Goffstown, two children; (2) Aaron Y. Hacket, two children; (3) Hosea B. Corless, one child.

11. Hannah Locke, b. Sept. 24, 1803; m. Dec. 5, 1826, William Colby, of Bow, b. July 31, 1803. He was a shoemaker in Bow till 1850, when they removed to Michigan. She d. Van Buren, Ind., Aug. 10, 1863, ae. 59-10-16. He d. Three Rivers, Mich., Feb. 26, 1875, ae. 71-6-25. Children:

    a. Hazen, b. Bow, July 17, 1827. About 1850 he changed his name to Ion Vernon. He m., June 19, 1848, Hannah M. Butterfield; (2) Dec. 10, 1859, Agnes Wood. He was a practicing physician at Three Rivers, Mich., where he d. Apr. 16, 1893, ae. 65-8-29. She res. Three Rivers. Four children.

    b. Mary Ann Brown, b. Bow, Oct. 27, 1829; m. June 24, 1853, Thomas Bonnett, b. England, 1810. They removed to Michigan, in 1852. He d. Salem, Mich., Feb. 27, 1892, and she m., July 14, 1894, William Alx. Address, Burnips Corner, Allegan Co., Mich. One child, Martha F. E., b. Mar. 31, 1861, m. Ralph Pomeroy. Res. Dutton, Mich.

    c. Samuel Murray, b. Oct. 10, 1832; d. June 26, 1834, ae. 1-8-16.

    d. Samuel Augustus, b. Feb. 26, 1835; went to Michigan in 1852, and m., Jan. 17, 1864, Martha A. Henry. Address, Neenah, Wis.

    e. Hannah Jane, b. Bow, May 3, 1839; m. Sept. 10, 1854, John Glidden, went to Michigan, 1854, and res. 541 No. Front street, Grand Rapids, Mich. Five children.

    f. Martha Ellen, b. Concord, Jan. 14, 1843; m. Apr. 21, 1861, William H. Sprague, b. Michigan, Mar. 31, 1837. They res. 213 Fourth street, Oakland, Cal. Three children.

    g. William Warren, b. Bristol, Aug. 17, 1845; m. Aug. 10, 1868, Rosetta Jane Lovejoy, b. Oct. 31, 1853, in Indiana. They res. David City, Neb. (See Roll of Honor.) Children: (1) Warner Willis, b. Feb. 17, 1874; (2) Emma May, b. May 7, 1876; d. Feb. 29, 1877; (3) Clara Belle, b. Apr. 13, 1878; (4) Hannah Mabel, b. July 17, 1885; d. Sept. 4, 1885.

12. Stephen, d. about 1824, aged 18.

13. Mary Ann, m. Jerry B. Warner, Oct. 2, 1836. He d. 1874. Child:

    a. J. E. Warner, b. July 21, 1845; m. Daisy Ramsden, 1883.

14. Michael, d. in infancy.

15. Aseneth, b. May 20, 1814; m. Calvin Fuller, Mar. 15, 1838. He was b. Mar 1, 1812, and d. New Boston, Jan. 11, 1869, ae. 56-10-10. She d. Alexandria. Children:

a. Henry Calvin, b. Wilton, Dec. 18, 1839; m. (1) Susan C. Flagg, Nashua; (2) Martha M. Sias, Boston.

b. Edwin Stiles, b. W., Feb. 24, 1841; m. Emily Wilcox, of Flint, Mich.

c. Mary Elizabeth, b. Mason, Mar. 16, 1847; m. Walter S. Robinson, Haverhill, Mass.

d. George Burnham, b. New Boston, Aug. 16, 1849; m. Helen A. Kelso of N. B.

e. Elbridge Brown, b. N. B., Dec. 9, 1851; d. July 4, 1859, ae. 7-6-25.

(4) John Brown, b. Sept. 15, 1789, m. Sally, dau. of Jonathan Ingalls, b. July 17, 1793. (See.) He was a soldier in the War of 1812 from Bristol, went to Vermont soon after the war, and to Michigan in 1839, where he was an extensive farmer. He united with the Bristol Methodist church about 1809 and "was a Methodist of positive tpye 75 years and a day." He d. in Portland, Mich., Feb. 11, 1885, ae. 95-4-26. She d. in Derby, Mich., June 14, 1867, ae. 73-10-27.

CHILDREN

16. Sophia, b. Bristol, Mar. 4, 1813; m. Oct. 18, 1828, Nathan Wyman, St. Albans, Vt. She res. Danby, Mich., post-office address, Sebawa, Iona Co., Mich. Children:

a. William W., b. Dec. 29, 1831.

b. Julia S., b. Apr. 22, 1833; d. Oct. 15, 1852, ae. 19-5-23.

c. George W., b. Mar. 29, 1837.

d. Charles W., b. Aug. 29, 1840; d. Oct. 1889, ae. 49-2-.

e. Elliot O., b. July 20, 1843.

17. Benjamin Hazelton, b. Bristol; went West and m. Rebecca Van Horn in Indiana, removed to Nebraska and there d. The family then removed to California. Children:

a. William.   *b.* George.   *c.* Mary Jane.

18. Jonathan S., b. Grand Isle, Vt.; m. Jane Reed, Danby, Iona Co., Mich. Said to be a wealthy farmer.

19. Henry H., b. Colchester, Vt., m. Almira Cahoon, Bangor, Me., and d. in army. No children.

20. Charlotte, b. Grand Isle, Vt., Mar. 20, 1823; m. Samuel S. Haight, Apr. 12, 1840. He was a well-to-do farmer and justice of the peace at Woodland, Parry Co., Mich. He d. Nov. 12, 1865, and she m. Rev. Amos Wakefield, Methodist, Aug. 29, 1874. He was b. Wheelock, Vt., Mar. 31, 1813. She res. Middleville, Perry Co., Mich. Children:

a. George, b. July 3, 1841; d. Nov. 30, 1849, ae. 8-4-27.

b. Sophia, b. Mar. 25, 1843; m. Henry Hinkly, Mar. 24, 1861, of Howard City, Mich. Children: (1) Henry, m. Ola Norton. (2) Frank, an engineer, m. Edie Goodrich, of Kalamazoo, and res. at Parmelee, Mich. (3) Burt, b. Mar. 8, 1869. (4) Merritt.

c. Sarah, b. Aug. 26, 1844; d. July 15, 1867, ae. 22-10-19. A dau. survives, who m. L. S. Gibbs, Grand Rapids.

d. Watson, b. Oct. 3, 1849; m. Elnora Lapham. Is a large stock dealer in Ludden, Dickey Co., Dak. Three sons: Samuel, Ernest, Alonzo.

(6) Samuel Brown, b. Oct. 28, 1793, m. Nov. 9, 1819 (Bridgewater records 1820), Susanna S., dau. Abraham Dolloff

(See), b. Dec. 9, 1800. They settled on the Horace Brown farm in Bridgewater, where he d. in Oct., 1868, ae. 75 ; she d. Bristol, in family of John Roby, Mar. 14, 1879, ae. 78-3-5.

CHILDREN, all born in Bridgewater

21.   Solomon, b. June 28, 1823; graduated Jefferson Medical College, Philadelphia, 1847 ; m., in 1847, Matilda Sidney Hughes, Philadelphia ; practiced medicine in P. till Sept., 1862, when he d., ae. 39-3-. She d. Mar., 1868. Had three children.

✻22.   Horace, b. Aug. 15, 1825.
✻23.   Levi Dolloff, b. Apr. 28, 1833.
✻24.   Warren Smith, b. Sept. 11, 1839.

(7) Joseph Brown, b. Mar. 3, 1796, m., in 1825, Relief, dau. of Stephen and Mary (Brown) Ordway. She was b. 1803, and d. in Campton, May, 1867, ae. 64. He was a lumber manufacturer and dealer. He erected the first saw-mill at Moore's Mills, so called, and continued business there 14 years. He removed to Campton in 1843, and later to Whitefield, where he d. Mar. 26, 1884, ae. 88-0-23.

CHILDREN

✻25.   Alson Landon, b. Bristol, Apr. 9, 1827.
26.   Stephen, b. B., 1829; served in 40th Mass. Vols., and d. in service at Folly Island, S. C., Nov., 1863, ae. 34.   Unm. (See Roll of Honor.)
27.   Mary Ann, b. B., Nov. 10, 1830; m. May 23, 1850, Hanson S. Chase, son of Jonathan and Abiah, b. Portsmouth, Apr. 8, 1823. They settled in Plymouth about 1873, where she d. Oct. 21, 1898, ae. 67-11-11. She was a member of the Universalist church. Children :

  a. James Whitcher, b. Campton, July 6, 1851 ; d. in Plymouth, Aug. 30, 1874, ae. 23-1-24.
  b. Warren Green, b. C., Mar. 30, 1854; m. (1) June 20, 1881, Kate B. Farr, who d. Feb. 10, 1894. He m. (2) Mar. 12, 1896, Lillian M. Heath.
  c. Irving Hanson, b. C., Nov. 18, 1858 ; m. Dec. 7, 1881, Minnie Elliott.
  d. Edward Averill, b. C., May 15, 1869; m. Ruth McClure, July 12, 1894.

✻28.   Amos, b. Bristol, June 29, 1832.
✻29.   Warren G., b. B., July 27, 1834.
30.   Relief, b. B., Aug., 1839; m. Elijah Averill, Jr., in 1858. He was b. in Merrimack, Oct., 1833. Child :

  a. Maretta Frances, b. Campton, June 21, 1859; m. Oct. 16, 1877, Rutherford Byrne, of So. Durham, P. Q. Address, Seattle, Wash.

31.   John O., b. Bristol, 1841 ; d. 1841.
32.   Joseph, b. B., 1842. He served in 15th Regt. N. H. Vols., and d. Aug. 11, 1863, ae. 21. (See Roll of Honor.)
33.   Laura Augusta, b. Campton, 1845 ; m. George W. Merrill in 1865, and d. in Campton, in May, 1882, ae. 37.

(8) Enos Brown, b. Mar. 3, 1798, m. Lavinia, dau. James Heath. She was b. Stewartstown, and d. New Hampton, Sept. 6, 1885. He was a farmer in Bridgewater, an eccentric man, commonly called Doctor. He d. previous to 1890.

CHILDREN

34. Stephen Salveteus, b. 1833 ; d. about 1890.
35. Julia, b. Aug. 10, 1838; d. Oct. 10, 1849, ae. 11-2-0.
36. Edwin E., b. Bridgewater; served in Co. E, 12th Regt. N. H.
Vols. Killed at Gettysburg, July 2, 1863. He enlisted Aug. 15, 1862, at
which time his age is given as 22.
37. Simeon C., b. B., June 7, 1835. Lived on a farm that lies partly
in Bridgewater and partly in Bristol. Was formerly a voter in Bridgewater. Recently erected a dwelling on that part of his farm in Bristol
and is consequently now a voter in Bristol. Never m.
38. Ellen Augenette, b. Bristol, July 27, 1846. She m. Oct. 30, 1864,
Warren Wesley Dalton, son of John, b. New Hampton, 1843, where he d.
Oct. 29, 1870. She d. same place, Oct., 1894, ae. 48. Children :

    a. John E. Dalton, b. Alexandria, Mar. 19, 1865 ; m. Apr. 29,
1891, Ida Weilbranner. Res. Ishpeming, Mich.
    b. Frank B. Dalton, b. New Hampton, Oct. 15, 1867 ; m. Dec. 7,
1892, Hattie Merrill. Res. Ashland.
    c. Julia May Dalton, b. N. H., 1869 ; d. Feb., 1873, ae. 4 years.
    d. Nellie W. Dalton, b. N. H., Oct. 3, 1870 ; m. Dec. 16, 1896, C.
O. Hopkins. Res. Lakeport.

(22) Horace Brown, b. Aug. 15, 1825, m. June 23, 1847,
Mary Augusta, dau. of Jesse and Patience (Hobart) Fletcher,
and was b. Groton, Oct. 25, 1828. They res. on the farm where
he was born, and here he d. July 23, 1874, ae. 48-11-8. She
res. in Ashland.

CHILDREN

39. Horace Burdett, b. Bridgewater, May 13, 1851 ; m. Annie Rebecca
Cass, Mar. 17, 1873. Salesman. Res. Ashland.
40. Sarah Augusta, b. B., Jan. 24, 1853 ; d. May 17, 1854.
41. Wilfred Fletcher, b. B., May 3, 1862 ; m. Sept. 25, 1885, Minnie E.
Reed. Graduated from Mass. College of Pharmacy in 1888, and received
degree of Ph. G. Is prescription clerk in drug store in Ashland.
42. Ora Aldru, b. B., Mar. 4, 1864 ; m. June 1, 1893, Sarah Adder,
dau. Col. Thomas P. Cheney, and is in trade in Ashland. Elected treasurer of Grafton county in 1902.

(23) Levi D. Brown, b. Apr. 28, 1833, m. Oct. 11, 1855,
Eliza Ann Phinney. She was the dau. of Jabez and Jane Fisher
Phinney, and was b. Oct. 30, 1829, in Sandwich, Mass., and d.
in Philadelphia, Penn., Jan. 6, 1882, ae. 52-2-6. He settled in
New York soon after he m., and a few years later removed to
Philadelphia ; was 15 years in the tea and spice business, from
which he retired in 1878, with a competency. He is now presi-
dent of a national bank and of an electric light company in
Philadelphia.

CHILDREN

43. Susannah Jane, b. Philadelphia, Feb. 5, 1870 ; graduated at Lasell
Seminary, Auburndale, Mass., class of 1888.

(24) Warren S. Brown, b. Sept. 11, 1839, m. Oct. 29
1871, Mrs. Wilhelmina Fredricka (Popplar) Gilmore. She was
b. West Brighton, N. Y., Mar. 3, 1844. He served in Co. 1,
19th Mass. Infty., and in Co. B, Heavy Artillery, serving 16

months in all. Res. in Bridgewater till Oct., 1874, since then in Center Harbor ; farmer.

CHILDREN

44. Warren Smith, b. Bridgewater, Oct. 10, 1872.
45. Lucinda Jane, b. Center Harbor, June 18, 1875 ; d. Jan. 17, 1890, ae. 14-7-29.
46. Phebe Amelia, b. C. H., May 22, 1881.

(25)   Alson L. Brown, b. Apr. 9, 1827, m. Mary A. Currier, Sept. 11, 1849. She was the dau. of William and Sophia Currier, and was b. in Ashland, June 27, 1832. He removed from Bristol to Campton with his father in 1843 ; was engaged in the lumber business with his father till 1864, when his brother, Warren G., purchased the father's interest and the new firm removed to Whitefield, in 1872, and organized the Brown Lumber company which was largely engaged in manufacturing lumber, railroading, and other business. Mr. Brown was president of the company, and to him was largely due the growth of the company and the prosperity of the town. He was a Republican in politics and was a member of the State Constitutional Convention of 1876, and a delegate to the Republican National Convention in 1880, which nominated James A. Garfield for president. He represented Whitefield in the legislature of 1881–'82. He d. at Whitefield, Jan. 24, 1891, ae. 63-9-15.

CHILDREN, all born in Campton

47. A daughter, b. Nov. 11, 1850 ; d. same day.
48. William Wallace, b. Feb. 22, 1852 ; m. (1) Louisa Veasey, (2) Belle Follansbee. Res. in Wentworth.
49. Oscar Alson, b. Jan. 21, 1854 ; m. Ada Page, and res. in Whitefield.
50. Charles Fremont, b. Sept. 7, 1856 ; d Aug. 23, 1863, ae. 6-11-16.
51. George Landon, b. May 5, 1860 ; d. Sept. 5, 1860.
52. Alice Sophia, b. Nov. 14, 1861 ; m. Edward Ray, July 20, 1881, and res. Whitefield. Children :

    a. Edith Alice, b. Dec. 8, 1883.
    b. Richard Alson, b. Sept. 3, 1887.
    c. Mary Etta, b. Apr. 27, 1890.

53. Joseph Walter, b. May 3, 1864 ; m. (1) Katie Howland, (2) Annie Martin. Res. Whitefield.
54. Etta Condelle, b. May 17, 1869 ; m. Oct. 20, 1887, Emery Appleton Sanborn. Res. 14 Arlington street, Boston.

(28)   Amos Brown, b. June 29, 1832, m., 1868, Annie M. Peebles, b. Lake Nevers, N. Y. He went to the Pacific coast in 1858, and engaged in the lumber business till 1885. Later speculated in real estate successfully. He settled in Seattle, Wash., when it had but a dozen houses, now a population of 75,000 or more. He d. in San Francisco in spring of 1899, ae. 67.

CHILDREN

55. Alson Lemer, b. Seattle, Mar. 14, 1869. Is a practicing lawyer in Seattle.

56. Emma, b. S., Feb. 27, 1871 ; m. Sept. 18, 1893, Hon. Ritchey M.
Kennear, a leading attorney of Seattle. Res. 4th and Bell streets.
57. Ora, b. Olympia, July 20, 1878; a graduate of Stanford University,
Cal.
58. Anna, b. Aug. 19, 1880. Graduate of University, at Seattle, Wash.
59. Helen Hazel, b. Seattle, Mar. 24, 1887.

(29) Warren G. Brown, b. July 27, 1834, m. Ruth B.
Avery, Mar. 1861. She was the dau. of Stephen and Hannah
(Mitchell) Avery, and was b. in Campton, and d. in Thornton,
Sept., 1863. He m. (2) in 1865, Charlotte, dau. of Ephriam
and Eliza (Broad) Elliot, b. Brownfield, Me., Jan. 11, 1848.
He left Bristol in 1843, and res. in Campton and Thornton till
1857. Spent three years in California and Washington territory. From 1860 to 1869 farming in Thornton and lumbering
in Bellows Falls, Vt. Settled in Whitefield 1869, where he has
been engaged in lumbering, as superintendent of the Brown
Lumber company. He shipped the first cargo of lumber from
Washington territory, around Cape Horn, to eastern ports in
1876, and has since shipped many.

CHILDREN, by second wife

60. Josephine Ruth, b. Campton, June 22, 1867.
61. Dasie A., b. Whitefield, Sept. 22, 1870.
62. Carl Elliott, b. W., Sept. 10, 1878.
63. Kenneth Warren, b. W., Sept. 8, 1883.

- - -

1. Edmond Brown was b. in Kingston, Jan. 1, 1771. He
came to Bristol as early as 1797, and built on the site of the
Cavis Brothers' store the first blacksmith shop in Bristol village. He boarded at the tavern of Moses Sleeper, but soon
after built the first house on the site of Hotel Bristol, and here
a sister kept house for him till his marriage. In 1808, he
removed to North Bristol to what was later known as the Rollins farm, and here he continued the blacksmith business. He
was a large owner of real estate and, in 1832, purchased what is
still known as the Brown farm on the west side of the lake ; in
1833 he moved there and there passed the balance of his life.
He was a liberal Calvinist Baptist. He m. Nov. 12, 1799, Hannah (Merrill) Swett, widow of Benjamin Swett, b. May 24,
1765, in Hanover (?). She d. Bristol, Nov. 16, 1853, ae.
88-5-22. He d. Bristol, Mar. 12, 1857, ae. 86-2-11.

CHILDREN, all born in Bristol

*2. Amos, b. Sept. 4, 1800.
3. Hannah, b. July 16, 1802; d. Bristol, May 23, 1887, unm., ae.
84-10-7.
4. Dana, b. Feb. 9, 1804 ; m. July 28, 1832, Sarah Cheney, of Bradford, b. Apr. 2, 1810. Soon after his m. he was ordained as a Calvinist
Baptist minister, and served the church in Bradford, and later labored in
Vermont. About 1840, on account of ill health, he located in Nashua,
and united with the First Calvinist Baptist church in that city. He d. in

REV. AMOS BROWN

Nashua, Jan. 25, 1868, ae. 63-11-16. She d. Wilton, Dec. 15, 1879, ae. 69-8-13. No children.

5. Joanna, b. Jan. 12, 1806; m. Robert Patten, of Alexandria, Nov. 1848, and d. Alexandria, Dec. 28, 1867, ae. 61-11-16. No children.

(2) Rev. Amos Brown, b. Sept. 4, 1800, m. Jan. 13, 1819, Abigail, dau. David Cheney (See), b. Jan. 24, 1799. They commenced life on what has been known as the Thomas H. Wicom place, east of Newfound lake; lived for a time on the Gurdy farm in the Locke neighborhood, and, in 1825, purchased the Thomas Dimond farm, later known as the Moses Cheney farm, on the west shore of the lake next to Newfound river, and there he resided till 1830, when he moved farther north to near where Amasa Hilands now resides. In 1833, he went with his father to the Brown farm, now occupied by Silas S. Brown, and here he passed the greater part of his life. Mrs. Brown d. Dec. 14, 1845, ae. 46-10-20, and he m. Feb. 9, 1847, Lovilla, dau. of Stephen and Abiah (Putney) Collins, b. Weare, Dec. 15, 1823. Amos Brown was licensed to preach by the Sandwich Quarterly Meeting, of the Free Baptist denomination Dec. 16, 1829, and was ordained at Alexandria, Sept. 30, 1832, by a council of elders of the Sandwich Quarterly Meeting, composed of Rev. John Hill, of Alexandria, Rev. Simeon Dana, M.D., Rev. Thomas Perkins, of New Hampton, and Rev. Levi Smith. He labored one-half the time at Alexandria from 1837 till 1853, and had pastoral oversight of the church for thirty-seven years. During his labors there, 160 were added to the church. He also labored successfully in Nashua, Orange, Center Harbor, New Hampton, Hill, and Bridgewater. He represented Bristol in the legislature of 1847 and 1848. In May, 1867, he accepted a call to the pastorate of the Free Baptist church at Eaton, where a revival of religion was very general. In the midst of his success he d. of apoplexy, Dec. 7, 1867, ae. 67-3-3. Burial from the Free Baptist church at Bristol and the remains were laid to rest in the village cemetery. Rev. Ebenezer Fisk officiated at the funeral, assisted by four other clergymen. Mr. Brown was a man of great native ability. He had a heart quick to respond to the joys and sorrows of others. He was always calm, forbearing and loving, a pleasant and cheerful companion, and a great lover of God and man. Mrs. Brown d. at Bristol, Jan. 28, 1888, ae. 64-1-13.

CHILDREN all born Bristol

*6. James Harvey, b. July 3, 1819.

7. Cynthia Fellows, b. Apr. 22, 1822; m. Henry Dermis Towle, Oct. 5, 1854; d. Iowa, Nov. 6, 1890, ae. 68-6-14. No children.

8. Webster Cheney, b. Sept. 27, 1829; m. July 12, 1859, Sarah Ann, dau. William and Sarah (Bond) English, b. Boston, Mass., Oct. 4, 1818. Mr. Brown was educated in the district schools of his native town and at the academies at Andover Center, Wentworth, and East Andover. He remained on the home farm till 1854, when he went to Nashua, where he

was traveling salesman for J. C. Kempton, confectioner, six or seven years, and eleven years proprietor and manager of an eating house. Mr. Brown served Ward 6 three years as selectman, represented it in the legislature in 1867 and 1868, and as inspector of the check-list four years. He served the city three years on the board of assessors. In 1875, he was appointed assistant city marshal, which position he held three years. In 1884, he was elected county commissioner and served by re-election till Apr. 1, 1901. The county farm buildings at Goffstown were erected during his term of service, and he was accorded much credit for the prudent and economical manner in which this work was done. Mr. Brown ranks among the most popular men of that county. Republican, Free Baptist. Mrs. Brown d. at Nashua, Jan. 10, 1902, ae. 83-3-6. No children.

*9. Silas S., b. Feb. 4, 1832.

10. Sarah Ann, b. Nov. 12, 1833. She was a teacher 25 years in California ; now res. with her brother, Silas S. Brown, in Bristol.

(6) James H. Brown, b. July 3, 1819, m. Nov. 3, 1843, Mary Mooney Smith Mudgett, who d. Concord, Dec. 10, 1893, ae. 77-9-20. He was a farmer in Hill, a number of years, and represented that town in the legislature. He was a deacon in the Free Baptist church in Alexandria. He d. Bristol, Sept. 28, 1875, ae. 56-2-25.

CHILDREN

11. Arthur Noyes, adopted. Killed by lightning July 9, 1851, ae. 8 years.

12. Edward A., adopted ; was clerk in the store of C. Taylor ; went West ; was yard master of a railroad in Davenport, Iowa.

(9) Silas S. Brown, b. Feb. 4, 1832, m. Feb. 2, 1854, Kate, dau. of George and Margaret Sivright Howie, b. Keith, Scotland, Apr. 3, 1827. He was a farmer in Bristol, till 1858, when he removed to Lisbon, where he remained till about 1876 ; then returned to the old homestead where he still lives. He has served six years as selectman of Bristol, and four years as supervisor of the check-list. In 1884, he was elected county commissioner and served four years. During this time he was resident superintendent of the County farm at Haverhill.

CHILDREN

13. Fred Howie, b. Bristol, Jan. 10, 1855; d. in Lisbon, Dec. 2, 1874, ae. 19-10-22.

14. Anna Belle, b. B., Sept. 25, 1856; m. Feb. 17, 1877, William Henry Weston, and res. Lisbon. Children, all b. Lisbon :

    a. Susan Catharine, b. Oct. 12, 1878.
    b. Charles Cheney, b. May 19, 1881.
    c. Corena Isabella, b. Mar. 8, 1883.
    d. Carlie Mae, b. May 15, 1885
    e. Jane Walker, b. Aug. 29, 1887.
    f. Margaret Howie, b. Dec. 18, 1889.
    g. Helen Brown, b. May 18, 1893.
    h. Fred Webster, b. Dec. 4, 1895.

15. Cheney Clarence, b. Lisbon, Apr. 6, 1860; m. Mar. 18, 1890, Annie Granville Sides, of Portsmouth. He res. Auburn, Me. General manager Carman-Thompson Co., Steam Engineers, Lewiston, Me. Child :

    a. Stanley Sides, b. Nov. 8, 1892.

1. Robert Brown was b. Jan. 25, 1778, and came to Bristol from Bow. First taxed here in 1818. He built and operated a tannery and shoe shop on south side of Pleasant street next to the river where is now the Riverside house. He m. Apr. 24, 1799, Sarah Clement. She was b. Oct. 16, 1771, and d. Bristol, July 24, 1844, ae. 72-9-8. He d. Bristol, July 6, 1854, ae. 76-4-11. Both members of Methodist church.

CHILDREN

2. John, b. Jan. 23, 1800; d. Mar. 17, 1811.
*3. Samuel Clement, b. Mar. 13, 1802.
4. Relief, b. Aug. 11, 1804; m. Richard H. Sawyer. (See.)
5. Carleton, b. Apr. 24, 1807; drowned July 27, 1811.
6. Sarah, b. Landaff, Nov. 1, 1809; m. Dr. Moody C. Sawyer. (See.)
7. Mary, b. June 29, 1811; d. June 4, 1812.
8. Squires C., b. Nov. 13, 1813. He was in trade in this village; was married and had one child which was killed by falling down stairs. He d. in Illinois, Aug. 4, 1884, ae. 70-8-21.

(3) Samuel C. Brown, b. Mar. 13, 1802, m. Apr. 10, 1823, Martha A. Johnson. He succeeded his father as tanner and currier, and erected, in 1840, the dwelling that now stands between Lake and Pleasant streets. In 1849, he purchased the saw-mill on Lake street and converted it into a tannery. He twice represented Bristol in the legislature; served as selectman six years; ten times as moderator at the annual town meeting, and four years as town clerk. He emigrated to the West in 1854. She d. in Waukesha, Wis., Oct. 28, 1859. He d. at the home of his son, Charles, in Jackson, Mich., Mar. 19, 1887, ae. 85-0-6.

CHILDREN, all born in Bristol

9. Martha Ann, b. June 23, 1823; m. Mar. 2, 1848, Moses Colcord Hoyt, M.D., for some years a practicing physician in Bristol. She d. in Bristol, Dec. 8, 1851, ae. 28-5-15. Children:

   a. Leston L.   b. Laura.
10. Charles, b. Mar. 28, 1825, d. May 14, 1826.
*11. Charles, b. June 24, 1828.
*12. Edwin Carleton, b. Feb. 15, 1831.
13. John Henry, b. Mar. 15, 1839. No family.

(11) Charles Brown, b. June 24, 1828, m. Jane Wilson, Apr. 28, 1859. See was the dau. of Robert and Phebe (Bettey) Wilson, and was b. Orange, Mar. 1, 1828. He went West soon after his father; gave his attention to railroading and became paymaster of the Michigan Central Railroad. He d. Jan. 28, 1889, ae. 60-7-4, in Jackson, Mich.

CHILDREN

14. Kate Matilda, b. Waukasha, Sept. 9, 1860; m. Julian J. Bennett, Sept. 21, 1881.
15. Anna Martha, b. W., Mar. 7, 1862; m. Harry R. Hall, Apr. 5, 1882.

16. Willis Harvey, b. Jan. 7, 1866, at W.; m. Rose Beach, May 6, 1891.

17. Harry C., b. Dec. 3, 1867, at Brookfield, Wis.

(12) Edwin C. Brown, b. Feb. 15, 1831, m. Jan. 4, 1859, Sarah P. Blake, at Milwaukee, Wis., and now res. 859 Cass Ave., Detroit, Wis. He has been for many years superintendent of the Michigan Central railway.

CHILDREN

18. Marion Denison.   19. Frank Sherburne
20. Saidee Carleton.

----

1. Joseph Henry Brown, son of Labon, was b. in Salisbury, Dec. 13, 1795. He was in Bristol as early as 1820, and m. Feb. 29, 1822, Sally, dau. of Rowell Straw. He succeeded her father on the Horne farm just above the schoolhouse near Solon Dolloff's, and near where the schoolhouse now is, he had a cabinet shop. Mrs. Brown d., and he m., Sept. 16, 1824, Jane, dau. of Benjamin Kidder (See), b. July 30, 1797. He removed to Danbury in 1835. He was a contractor in constructing a section of the Franklin and Bristol railroad. A partner drew $1,700 from the company to pay the workmen and decamped, and Mr. Brown was obliged to mortgage his farm to make good the loss. She d. Danbury, Aug. 26, 1880, ae. 82-0-26 ; he d. Dec. 15, 1886, ae. 91-0-2.

CHILDREN

*2. Amos P. H., b. Bristol, Apr. 21, 1823.

3. Mary A., b. B., Feb. 8, 1827 ; unm.; res. Danbury.

4. David Wiggin, b. B., June 18, 1829. Res. Danbury. He m. Malinda Flanders, Wilmot. She d. Nov. 1890. Children :

  a. Charles Henry, d. in Wilmot, aged 3 years.
  b. Nellie M., m. Edward Braley, Hebron. Two children.

5. Chastina, b. B., Oct., 7, 1831 ; m. Jan. 11, 1855, Charles P. Wells, son of Josiah and Eunice (Whittemore) Wells, b. July 4, 1829. Res. New London. Children :

  a. Ella M., b. Wilmot, Oct. 7, 1855 ; m. Apr. 15, 1891, John Colby, New London.
  b. Augusta A., b. Danbury, Nov. 28, 1857. Res. N. L.
  c. Frank E., b. D., Apr. 23, 1860 ; m. Aug. 10, 1895, Sarah A. Fifield, Webster.
  d. John E., b. D., July 15, 1862 ; res. N. L.
  e. Mary C., b. D., Oct. 4, 1864, m. Frank Roberts, Aug. 15, 1882.
  f. Addie J., b. D., Dec. 29, 1867 ; m. Dec. 22, 1885, Horatio E. Luce, Woodstock, Vt.
  g. Anna L., b. Springfield, Mar. 7, 1869 ; m. June 20, 1895, Elmer A. Luce. Res. Prosper, Vt.
  h. Sarah A., b. S., July 8, 1871. Res. N. L.
  i. Lillie G., b. S., July 2, 1873 ; res. N. L.
  j. Martha E., b. S., Jan. 24, 1877. Res. N. L.

6. George G., b. Wilmot, Sept. 26, 1837 ; m. Mary Ann Goodhue. Res. West Andover. Two children, both deceased

7. Melissa J., b. W., Apr. 23, 1842. Unm. Res. Danbury.

(2) Amos P. H. Brown, b. Apr. 21, 1823, m. (1) Jane, dau. John Clay, (2) Lydia A., dau. Ralph Coburn. He has res. in Pelham since 1875. (See Roll of Honor.)

CHILDREN

8. Frank M., b. Wilmot, 1861; m. June 4, 1879, Mirah H , dau. Louis Little. Manufacturer boots, Haverhill, Mass. She d. Haverhill, Aug. 29, 1892. Child :

    a. Henry Gibbon, b. June 20, 1880. Shoe cutter, Haverhill.

9. George A., b. Thetford, Vt.; res. Pelham.
10. Phebe Jane, m. —— Messer ; res. New London.
11. Cynthia A., d. at 30, unm.

---

1. In 1771, Enoch Brown went from Seabrook to Weare and there settled. The name of his wife was Betty. They had nine children, the second of whom was

2. Enoch, b. Seabrook, June 10, 1756. He m. Sarah Davis, of Gosport. He was in Weare as late as 1803, and removed to Bridgewater with his family, where he was a farmer.

CHILDREN

3. Benjamin.   4. John.   5. Mary.
*6. Dexter, b. Weare, Oct. 23, 1803.
7. Squires. He bought land for a farm one-fourth mile north of the Bristol town farm, and went to Boston to earn money to pay for it and was never heard from later. His brother, Dexter, succeeded to the farm.

(6) Dexter Brown, b. Oct. 23, 1803, m. May -, 1819, Deborah, dau. of Benjamin and Abigail (Morgan) Smith, b. Bridgewater, June 20, 1800. He was a farmer in Bridgewater, but about 1850 removed to what is now known as the George D. Cross place near foot of the lake, and in 1852 to Willow street, Bristol village, where he d. June 7, 1858, ae. 54-7-14. She d. Bristol, July 6, 1883, ae. 83-0-16.

CHILDREN

8. David Davis, b. Bridgewater, May 29, 1821 ; d. August, 1825, ae. 4-3-.
9. Rufus, b. B., Apr. 16, 1823 ; d. Apr. 27, 1824, ae. 1-0-11.
*10. Charles Smith, b. B , Jan. 22, 1825.
11. John D Brown, b B., Feb. 25, 1827; m. Jan 1, 1850, Eliza W., widow of Peter Tirrell, and dau. of Jeremiah Bean. (See.) He was a farmer in Hudson, where he d. Sept. 29, 1900, ae. 73-7-4. She res. Hudson Center with her adopted son :

    a. Henry C., b. Delton, Wis., Feb. 25, 1859, son of Darwin R., and Rhoda M. (Bryant) Woodward. His father d. when he was three years old and he was adopted by John D. Brown. He m. Oct. 9, 1883, Clara Jane, dau. of George R. and Betsey M. (Kidder) Bryant, b. Irasburg, Vt., May 2, 1860. He is station agent at Hudson Center. Children : (1) Freddie LeRoy, b. Nashua, Mar. 20, 1886 ; d. in Irasburg, Vt., Sept. 27, 1888. (2) Ina Louise, b. Hudson Center, Oct. 6, 1889.

12. Squires Smith, b. B., Jan. 6, 1829; m. Jan. 29, 1852, Elizabeth

W., dau. of Peter M. Bean. (See.) They removed to Berea, Ohio.
He was a jeweler by trade; served as a lieutenant in the 177th Regt.
Ohio Vols., in the Civil war; was mayor of Berea in 1868, and again in
1874; was publisher of the *Berea Grit*, and a trustee of the Methodist
Episcopal church. He d. Berea, June 5, 1901, ae. 72-4-29. She res.
Berea. Children:

    a. Frank, b. Berea, Dec. 13, 1856; d. Aug. 27, 1865, ae. 8-8-14.
    b. Fred Clarence, b. Berea, Oct. 23, 1869; m. Nov. 5, 1892, Della
Cottier. Res. Berea.

    13. Deborah Locke, b. B., Feb. 26, 1831; m. Samuel H. Tilton.
(See.)
    14. David Lyman, b. B., Jan. 27, 1835; d. Bristol, Apr. 30, 1860, ae.
25-3-3, unm.
    15. Sarah Marinda, b. B., Jan. 4, 1837; m. James W. Griffith. (See.)
    16. Francena, b. B., Nov. 22, 1839; d. Dec. —, 1840.
  *17. Rufus Dearborn, b. B., May 25, 1842.

(10) Charles S. Brown, b. Jan. 22, 1825, m. Sept. 26,
1850, Orinda Carpenter, dau. of Henry and Elizabeth (Buck)
Tilton, b. Sept. 16, 1823, in Hebron. They came to Bristol
from Bridgewater about 1852, and he became an employee in
paper-mill. He served in 12th Regt. N. H. Vols. (See Roll
of Honor.) She d. Bristol, Mar. 8, 1869, ae. 45-5-22, and he
m. Sept. 11, 1869, Ruth P., widow of Merrill P. Simonds.
(See.) He d. Mar. 8, 1886, ae 61-1-16. She resides Bristol.

CHILDREN

    18. Ellen Frances, b. Bridgewater, Oct. 17, 1851; m. Hiram T.
Heath. (See.)
    19. Frank Eugene, b. Bristol, Aug. 5, 1853; m. July 4, 1888, Mrs.
Nellie M. (Gove) Jameson. He was a teamster in Bristol and was
killed by being thrown from his team, Dec. 13, 1888. A wheel passed
over his neck breaking it. His age was 35-4-8. His widow removed
to Concord. No children.
    20. John Henry, b. B., Feb. 19, 1855; m. in Boston, Mass., Sept. 22,
1892, Ellen Elizabeth Noble. Is a dealer in groceries in Boston.

(17) Rufus D. Brown, b. May 25, 1842, m. (1) Dec. 2,
1862, Lydia Ann, dau. Ozias and Lydia (Patten) Walker, b.
Alexandria, 1841; (2) in 1880, Mary Jane Calley, b. New
Hampton. He was an employee at Dow & Mason's paper-mill;
went to California in January, 1869, and returned in October,
1870. Was a spinner at woolen-mill of Holden & Co., and of the
Dodge–Davis Manf. company, and since Dec., 1897, at Franklin
Falls. Bass singer, Democrat, Odd Fellow, Fireward 10 years.

CHILD

    21. George Francis, b. Bristol, Oct. 24, 1865; m. June 10, 1899, Mrs.
Cora M. Kimball, dau. of Reuben K. and Mary Blanchard, b. Franklin,
June 12, 1869. He is a spinner at Franklin Falls.

---

    1. John Browne, said by tradition to have been a Scotch-
man, was b. in England between 1589 and 1595. He was a
baker in London. Apr. 17, 1635, he embarked on the Elizabeth,

landed at Boston, and went to Salem, Mass. In 1638, he became one of the first settlers in Hampton, where he was a farmer and stock raiser, but engaged in ship building. He was one of the largest land owners in the town and the third man in wealth on the oldest tax list of the town. He m., in 1640, Sarah Walker, who also came from London in ship Elizabeth. She was b. 1618, and d. in Hampton, July 6, 1672, ae. 54. On the town records of Hampton is recorded : "John Browne, Aged about ninetie years, Died upon the 28h Day february 1686." Of his many children, one was

2. Jacob, b. 1658, m. Sarah, dau. of William and Mary Brook, of Portsmouth ; d. Hampton, Feb. 13, 1740, ae. 82. Of their children,

3. Samuel was b. September, 1686. He m. Elizabeth Maloon, about 1708, and d. Hampton. Jan. 14, 1772, ae. 85–4–. She d. Feb. 9, 1764. A son, or grandson, of Samuel was

4. Joseph, b. Hampton, moved to what is now Danville, and in Oct., 1781, to Andover, and there d. a little later than 1800. He had seven children, of whom the fourth was

5. Henry, b. in Danville, 1775. He m. Lovey Ladd of Gilmanton, moved to Bridgewater in 1817, and settled on what is now known as the Woodman farm, on the River road. There he d. 1834, ae. 59.

CHILDREN

6. Hannah, b. Andover, 1797 (?) ; d. Bridgewater, 1862, ae. about 65.
*7. James, b. A., July 3, 1805.
8. Mary Potter, b. A., Sept. 12, 1816 ; m. Seth Spencer. (See.)

(7) James Brown, b. July 3, 1805, m. Nov. 18, 1830, Judith Blaisdell, dau. of John and Nancy (Pressey) Harron, b. Bridgewater, Jan. 12, 1807. He was a farmer in New Hampton and Bridgewater. Was deacon of the Second Free Baptist church in Bridgewater. They removed to Bristol in 1867, where she d. June 12, 1883, ae. 76–5–0. He made his home for 20 years previous to 1895, in the family of his son, John Henry, at Bristol, but spent his last days with his son, Manson S., at Plymouth, where he d. Jan. 17, 1898, ae. 92–6–14.

CHILDREN

9. Mary Elizabeth, b. Bridgewater, Dec. 5, 1831 ; m. Nov. 30, 1852, Dudley Marshall.
10. Joseph Harron, b. New Hampton, Dec. 19, 1833 ; m. May 1, 1862, Harriet Newell, dau. Joseph and Harriet Newell (Frye) Huse, b. Danville, Vt., Aug. 18, 1837. He d. Concord, Mar. 16, 1900, ae. 66–2–27. From 1862, till 1869, he was a preacher of the Free Baptist denomination. In 1870, he united with the New Hampshire Conference of the Methodist Episcopal church and filled various pastorates till 1892. The remaining years of his life were mainly devoted to Bible distribution for the New Hampshire Bible society. Mrs. Brown res. Lancaster. Child :
    a. Orlana Jane, b. Stafford Bow Lake, Sept. 10, 1863 ; m. June 16, 1895, John Merritt Morse, Lancaster.

11.   Manson S., b. Bridgewater, Nov. 29, 1835; m. Apr. 19, 1859, Ann P. E., dau. Kimball Whitney, b. May 24, 1835. (See.) During the Civil war he served as principal musician in the 13th Regt. N. H. Vols. from Aug. 15, 1862, till June 21, 1865. Is a farmer in Plymouth. Has served several terms as sheriff of Grafton County. Was a member of New Hampshire senate in 1885-'6. She d. Plymouth, May 28, 1903, ae. 68-0-4.
12.   John Henry, d. in infancy.
13.   Hester Ann, b. B., Jan. 25, 1839; m. Mar. 1, 1865, Melvin A. Dame. She d. at Stafford, Mar. 14, 1866, ae. 27-1-19.
14.   Hannah Angeline, b. B., July 31, 1841; m. Oct. 5, 1875, John D. Harris. She d. at Ipswich, Mass., Apr. 5, 1893, ae. 51-8-4.
15.   Josephine G., b. B., Feb. 5, 1844; m. Dec. 16, 1865, William H. Abel, and d. June 20, 1869, ae. 25-4-15.
16.   Lovinia G., b. B., Apr. 13, 1847; m. July 20, 1870, William H. Abel, and d. Aug. 7, 1870, ae. 23-3-24.
17.   John Henry, b. B., May 20, 1850. He came to Bristol with his parents in 1867, and m. June 10, 1872, Marietta S., dau. of Joseph and Sally C. (Cram) Lougee, b. Sanbornton, Sept. 22, 1849. He was in trade in Abel's block some years; was in the lumber business and a land surveyor; railway mail clerk on the Boston, Concord and Montreal railroad 1881-'82; postmaster at Bristol 1882-'85; selectman at Bristol eight years; was deputy sheriff 1887-'91; represented his town in the legislature of 1891. He was traveling freight and claim agent for the Boston, Concord and Montreal railroad from May, 1891, till its lease to the Boston & Maine, and since July 1, 1895, has been claim agent for New Hampshire for the Boston & Maine railroad, with office in Concord. He is a prominent Republican politician, and has served as a member of the Republican state central committee nearly 25 years. He was commissary general on the staff of Gov. Charles E. Busiel; was a delegate to the Republican National Convention in 1896, that nominated William McKinley for president, and served as presidential elector in Jan., 1901. He is a Mason and has been a justice of the peace since 1871. He removed from Bristol to Concord in 1895. No children.

----

1.   Abraham Brown was b. Franklin, Mar. 17, 1818. He m. Mar. 11, 1841, Lucinda, dau. of Jacob Batchelder of Franklin, b. Oct. 13, 1818. He learned the wheelwright trade in Franklin and soon after came to Bristol and worked at his trade; removed to Bridgewater in 1845; thence to Plymouth, where he d. Apr. 14, 1853, ae. 35-0-27. Mrs. Brown m. Feb. 26, 1857, Samuel Currier of Plymouth, where she d. Aug. 21, 1895, ae. 76-10-8.

CHILDREN

*2.   Sidney Allison, b. Bristol, Apr. 22, 1843.
*3.   George Augustus, b. B., Apr. 23, 1844.
4.   Dora Ann, b. Bridgewater, Jan. 31, 1847; m. Nov. 29, 1882, Edgar Merrill, b. Campton, Mar. 9, 1841. No children. Res. Plymouth.
*5.   Clark Jacob, b. B., May 3, 1848.

(2)   Sidney A. Brown, b. Apr. 22, 1843, m. Jan. 27, 1864, Martha Ann, dau. of John S. and Irena C. (Badger) Shores, b. No. Chelmsford, Mass., Sept. 2, 1845. He is a carriage maker; worked several years for Lovejoy & Kelley in Bristol, and has since worked in Amesbury, Mass., and other places; now res. 7 Abbott street, Medford, Mass.

GEN. JOHN H. BROWN

CHILDREN

6. Eva May, b. New Hampton, June 6, 1866; d. Plymouth, Sept. 2, 1867, ae. 1-2-26.
7. Everett Currier, b. N. H., Jan. 5, 1869. In Boston Art School.
8. Fred Clark, b. N. H., Apr. 5, 1871; d. Plymouth, Feb. 12, 1873, ae. 1-10-7.

(3) George A. Brown, b. Apr. 23, 1844, m. Nov. 18, 1869, Augusta S., dau. Thomas and Mary (Emerson) Shute, b. Bridgewater, Mar. 2, 1847. Have res. Nebraska, now in Hudson, Mass.

CHILDREN

9. Dora Estella } b. Palmyra, Neb., Aug. 24, 1875.
10. Flora Estella }
Flora E., m. Herbert F. Carter, Oct. 12, 1898. Child:
   a. Laura Mabel, b. June 21, 1900, in Quincy, Mass.
11. Melzana Frances, b. Dec. 12, 1880, in Red Cloud, Neb.

(5) Clark J. Brown, b. May 3, 1848, m. July 1, 1877, Emma Azuba, dau. of John G. and Diana (Heath) Jack, b. Meadville, Pa., Jan. 18, 1852. Res. 5 Court St., White Plains, N. Y.

CHILDREN

12. Blanche Effie, b. Randolph, N. Y., June 25, 1878.
13. Ethel Dorothy, b. R., June 12, 1880.
14. Fred Clark, b. R., July 6, 1881.
15. Reba Alice, b. Atlanta, Ga., Feb. 25, 1886.
16. Florence May, b. A., Oct. 10, 1887.
17. Carl Batchelder, b. Jamestown, N. Y., Aug. 4, 1890.

---

1. Lieut. Daniel Brown, son of Jonathan, was b. in Candia, May 10, 1771. He m. Elizabeth French, b. Kingston, Dec. 11, 1774. They settled in Bridgewater after two of their children were b. and here they passed the remainder of their lives. She d. Feb. 11, 1831, from taking a dose of tartar emetic, put up by a druggist for cream of tartar, ae. 56-2-0. He d. Mar. 14, 1860, ae. 88-10-4.

CHILDREN

2. Betsey, b. Candia, Feb. 14, 1791, m. Paul Perkins, Mar. 16, 1813. Children:
   a. Daniel.   b. Mehitable.   c. David.   d. Betsey.
3. Jonathan, b. C., Oct. 23, 1793; m. —— Pope, and lived in Bridgewater, Mass. Children:
   a. Henry.   b. Mary.
4. Nancy, b. Bridgewater, May 6, 1798; m. Daniel Cummings; d. in Ashland, in Feb., 1895, ae. 96-9-.
5. Joshua French, b. B., July 16, 1800.
6. Daniel, b. B., July 11, 1802; d. Jan. 10, 1803.
7. Daniel, b. B., Feb. 14, 1805; d. in the South of yellow fever.
*8. Richard, b. B., Sept. 4, 1807.
9. Simeon Batchelder, b. B., Mar. 1, 1812.
10. Parker Merrill, b. B., July 6, 1816.

5a

(8)   Richard Brown, b. Sept. 4, 1807, m. Nov. 2, 1833, Mary Cynthia, dau. of Charles and Margaret Mitchell, b. Bridgewater, July 28, 1809. She d. in Bridgewater, Aug. 15, 1881, ae. 72-0-17. He was a farmer in Bridgewater, but late in life removed to Bristol, res. on Lake street. He d. in family of his son, George, at New Hampton, Sept. 27, 1896, ae. 89-0-23.

CHILDREN

11.   George, b. Bridgewater, Jan. 1, 1835 ; m. Apr. 2, 1857, Susan Jane Mitchell. They res. New Hampton. Child :
    a.   Ora John, b. Oct. 15, 1865.
*12.   Daniel Mitchell, b. B., Apr. 12, 1842.
*13.   Curtis, b. B., Jan. 12, 1847.
14.   John Smith, b. B., Aug. 11, 1848 ; d. Feb. 1, 1866, ae. 17-5-20.
*15.   Herman Richard, b. B., Jan. 25, 1850.

(12)   Daniel M. Brown, b. Apr. 12, 1842, m. Nov. 10, 1869, Frances Emma, dau. John G. and Eliza A. (Dow) Marston, b. Bristol, Jan. 30, 1847. They res. Bristol, 1872 to 1876, since in Plymouth. Laborer.

CHILDREN

16.   Alberta, b. Bristol, Dec. 23, 1872.
17.   Margaret, b. Plymouth, July 1, 1876.

(13)   Curtis Brown, b. Jan. 12, 1847, m. Nov. 29, 1866, Lucy A., dau. of Isaac C. Tilton. (See.) He came to Bristol in May, 1866, was clerk in store of Geo. M. Cavis, and later in store of Lucius W. Hammond. He d. of typhoid fever, Nov. 9, 1871, ae. 24-9-27. His widow res. Webster.

CHILDREN

18.   Lora Edith, b. Bristol, May 29, 1868. Was graduated from New Hampton Literary Institution, 1888. Taught school. Bookkeeper in Concord ; m. Apr. 30, 1901, Fred Corser and res. Webster.
19.   Arthur Curtis, b. B., Apr. 13, 1870 ; m. Apr. 12, 1893, Eva Jane, dau. Stillman Clark. (See.) Salesman dry goods store, Franklin Falls.
    a.   Stuart Arthur, b. Pittsfield, Aug. 8, 1895.
    b.   Floyd Merlin, b. Laconia, July 4, 1901.

(15)   Herman R. Brown, b. Jan. 25, 1850, m. Jan. 23, 1872, Mary Addie, dau. of John McCutcheon and Mary Ann (Gilman) Fogg, b. Bridgewater, Feb. 9, 1853. He d. Bridgewater, Jan. 3, 1889, ae. 38-11-8, and his family came to Bristol with his father in April, 1889. Mrs. Brown res. Franklin.

CHILDREN

20.   Annie Cynthia, b. Bridgewater, Dec. 29, 1875. Res. Franklin ; unm.
21.   Claude Herman, b. B., Sept. 10, 1878. Res. Newton Center, Mass.

----

1.   George Gale Brown, son of Benjamin Butler and Phebe (Gale) Brown, was b. Northfield, Oct. 20, 1837. He located in Bristol in 1862. Was a merchant tailor, blacksmith, hotel

keeper, had a meat market two or three years; and was in the grain business six or eight years. He was a lover and owner of good horses. He removed to Tilton in the fall of 1888, where he now resides. In grain business at Tilton, Ashland, and Contoocook. He m. Nov., 1863, Ada Byron, dau. of Philip and Lydia Reed, b. Claremont, June 17, 1836; d. Bristol, Nov. 3, 1865, ae. 29-4-16. He m. July 16, 1867, Ellen Elizabeth, dau. Josiah D. Prescott. (See.) She d. Bristol, Nov. 7, 1874, ae. 30-9-8. He m., May 30, 1901, Mrs. Etta Frances Shaw, dau. of John W. and Ann (Dearborn) Johnson, of East Tilton.

CHILDREN

2. George Henry, b. Bristol, Sept. 15, 1865; d. May 21, 1866.
3. Ada May, b. B., Sept. 27, 1869; m. George B. Cavis. (See.)
4. Nellie Prescott, b. B., Oct. 31, 1874; m. Mar. 21, 1901, George Henry Davis, Tilton. Child:
  a. Mary Elizabeth, b. Tilton, Dec. 20, 1902.

---

1. Charles Gale Brown, a brother of above, was b. Northfield, Dec. 11, 1835. He went to sea at the age of 14 years, and spent most of his life on the water, visiting many of the principal ports of the world. Served in the United States navy 20 years. Came to Bristol in 1880, and made his home with his brother, George G., where he d. Apr. 2, 1885, ae. 49-3-21; unm.

---

1. Stewart I. Brown is the son of John S. and Sophia C. Brown, and was b. Penacook, Nov. 6, 1848. He is a lineal descendant of Peter Brown, who landed from the Mayflower at Plymouth, in 1620. Nov. 21, 1893, he m. Mary Ella, dau. of John F. and Eliza J. Danforth, b. Penacook, Apr. 11, 1869. He was in trade in Penacook, from 1886 till 1897, when he came to Bristol and became a member of the firm of Weymouth, Brown & Co., who still keep a country store in the stand formerly occupied by Cyrus Taylor.

CHILD

2. Donald, b. May 26, 1897.

---

1. William I. Brown is the son of Iddo S. and Roxana (Pingree) Brown. He was b. Wilmot, Feb. 24, 1846, and m. Dec. 20, 1874, Sarah F., dau. of Daniel and Armida J. (Prescott) Sanborn, b. Danbury, July 9, 1854. He came to Bristol from West Lebanon, in June, 1898, and is express messenger between Bristol and Concord. Iddo S. Brown was a soldier of the War of 1812.

CHILD

2. Grace F., b. Concord, June 15, 1878; m. Dec. 19, 1900, Joseph H. Folsom.

1. Clarissa Brown, dau. of Amos and Nancy Brown, b. Concord, July 18, 1800, was an operative in mill at Lowell for 22 years. She made her home with her sister, Mrs. Jacob N. Darling from 1855. Insane. She d. Bristol, June 20, 1881, ae. 80-11-2.

2. Salome E. Brown, a sister of the above, was b. Wheelock, Vt., Mar. 4, 1806 ; made her home for some years with her sister, Mrs. Darling ; d. Centennial Home, Concord, Dec. 2, 1890, ae. 84-8-28.

THE BRYANT FAMILY

1. Col. John Stephens Bryant, son of John and Eleanor (Bickford) Bryant, was b. Laconia, Apr. 11, 1800. He m., Sept. 22, 1822, Hannah P. Edwards, dau. of John (See), b. May 20, 1801. His father served in the War of 1812 ; was wounded, and afterward a prisoner. John S. commenced life as a business man in Hill, in 1820, and in summer of 1826, removed to Bristol and built "a large colonial house" on the site of the Bristol Savings bank. Here he kept hotel for a time and had a cabinet shop in the second story of the ell. The buildings were destroyed by fire Oct. 15, 1829. Though crippled financially, in less than three years he was living in another fine residence on the same site. In 1837, he built the brick house on Pleasant street recently owned by Ezekiel Follansbee, and occupied it two years, when he sold to Gustavus Bartlett, and removed to Haverhill, in 1839. Col. Bryant was a public spirited man. He was colonel of the 34th Regt. militia, and deputy sheriff several years. After removing to Haverhill, he was admitted to the bar and practiced law from 1845 till 1873. He lived to celebrate his golden wedding. He d. at Haverhill, Sept. 6, 1873, ae. 73-4-25 ; she d. same place, June 7, 1893, ae. 92-0-17.

CHILDREN

2. Ann, b. Hill, July 3, 1823; m. Gardner Elliott, Sept. 23, 1845. He was b. Jan. 20, 1814, at Thornton, and d. Brooklyn, N. Y., Jan. 14, 1876. At marriage removed from Bristol to Eutah, Ala., and here their children were born. Later resided in Brooklyn, N. Y. After death of her husband she resided with her children at Perth Amboy, N. J. Children :

a. George Frank, a captain in the United States Marine Corps. His duties have taken him from Spitzbergen on the north to the extreme south, and around the world more than once. He was captain of marines at Japan during the Chinese-Japanese war. He m. Anna Mansfield, dau. of Commodore Oscar C. Badger, U. S. Navy. One dau., Daisy Sinclair.

b. Helen Gardner, m. Augustus E. Marston, Brooklyn, N. Y., a professor of chemistry. One child, Maria Louise. He d. in early life and she m. (2) Dr. Augustus H. Buckmaster, of New York, in 1888. Children : (1) Elliott. (2) Helen.

c. Anna Bessie, m. Eugene J. Higgins, Walpole, Va. Two children : (1) Eugene Elliott. (2) John de B. He d. and she m. (2) Charles C. Hommann, a lawyer of Perth Amboy, N. J. Child : Charles Chauncey.

d. Louise Burleigh, d. Haverhill, 1870, aged nearly 6 years.

3. George Franklin, b. Bristol ; d. at 17, while a student at Dartmouth college. He was a young man of great promise.

4. Hannah Louise, b. B., Mar. 7, 1833 ; m. in September, 1854, Hon. George W. Burleigh of Somersworth, a prominent lawyer, and agent of Great Falls Manufacturing Co. for 15 years. He d. Apr. 26, 1878 ; she d. Mar. 26, 1894, at New Rochelle, N. Y., ae. 61-0-19. Children :

a. Helen Louise, m. Lieut. G. A. Merriam, U. S. Navy.

b. Sarah Noble, m. William B. Greeley, a lawyer. Res. New Rochelle, N. Y.

c. George William, a lawyer, m. 1894, Iris Yturbide Stockton. Res. New York city.

THE BRYAR FAMILY

1. Charles Albert Bryar, the son of Jonathan K., and Maria Ann (Annis) Bryar, was b. No. Groton, Feb. 12, 1862. He m., Dec. 18, 1882, Denelda May, dau. Daniel S. and Mary Ann (Pierce) Putney, b. Hebron, Dec. 5, 1861. He has been a farmer, carpenter, wood turner, blacksmith, machinist, and is now a millwright in the employ of the Dodge-Davis Manf. Co. He came to Bristol in May, 1900, and res. Crescent street.

CHILDREN

2. Ernest Kilburn, b. Hebron, July 9, 1883.
3. Merton Kitteridge, b. No. Groton, July 26, 1884.
4. Arlena May, b. Hebron, Sept. 22, 1886.
5. John Silver, b. H., June 21, 1891.
6. Harold Keith, b. H., Aug. 27, 1893.
7. Hazel Maria, b. H., July 7, 1896.

THE BRYSON FAMILY

1. John Bryson, son of James, was b. Londonderry, Ireland, in 1834. He m. Mary Ann Kelley, b. 1835, in Dublin, Ireland. Machinist. He served as a private in a Maine regiment in the Civil war. He came to Bristol about 1872, and worked at his trade, and here d. Oct. 22, 1890, ae. 56 years. She d. Bristol, May 9, 1898, ae. 63.

CHILDREN

2. Thomas Dorathy, b. Portland, Me., June 13, 1857. Came to Bristol with his parents and has been an operative in the Train-Smith Co.'s paper-mill. Unm.

3. John James, b. Portland, Me., Apr. 11, 1866 ; came to Bristol in 1872, and m., Sept. 21, 1884, Myrtie, dau. George C. and Hattie (Heath) Flanders, b. Danbury, Sept. 21, 1870. She is a dressmaker. He has operated hair dressing rooms in Bristol for 20 years.

*4. William Matthews, b. Portland, Me., May 16, 1869.

(4)   William M. Bryson, b. May 16, 1869, m. May 12, 1892, Mary Ella, dau. of Joseph A. Decato (See.), b. Apr. 13, 1875. Has been for several years operative in paper-mill.   Catholic.

CHILDREN

5.   Villa Ella, b. Bristol, June 23, 1893.
6.   Earl Edward, b. B., Oct. 27, 1897; d. Dec. 24, 1897.
7.   Esther Agnes, b. B., Apr. 6, 1901.

THE BUCKLIN FAMILY

1.   Moses Bucklin was b. in Enfield, Jan. 13, 1795.   He m. Delight, dau. of Otis Kilton, b. Grafton Center, in 1803. He was a man of more than ordinary intelligence and ability. Before the days of railroads, he was a dealer in grain, which he purchased in Enfield, and drew to Boston or Providence with his own two-horse team, and there disposed of it.   He was wide-ly known as an inventor.   He invented an improved pump, which supplanted the old wooden pump.   The Ford harrow, which was extensively used throughout the United States, was his invention, and from it he derived at one time a large income. He made several trips to Washington concerning his inventions, and on one trip he rode on the first passenger train between Baltimore and Washington.   His wife d. in 1865, ae. 62 years, and he subsequently made his home with his son, Otis K., in Bristol, till the death of the latter, when he went to reside with his son, Frank K., at East Tilton, where he d. Sept. 28, 1889, ae. 94–8–15.   He was the father of ten children.
2.   Otis Kilton Bucklin, son of Moses, was b. Woburn, Mass., July 9, 1829.   When a boy his father removed to Graf-ton, and there he resided till 1852, when he went to California. After four years he returned to Grafton, and m., Oct. 16, 1856, Elizabeth, dau. of Henry and Dorothy Gray, b. Sheffield, Vt., Apr. 7, 1838.   He was engaged in the hotel business at Graf-ton till December, 1867, when he purchased the Bristol House and removed to Bristol.   The next season he built the present hotel and was its proprietor and landlord, with the exception of a brief interval, till Oct., 1886.   (See Taverns.)   He was for some years the owner of the carriage factory on Central street, and there engaged in the manufacture of carriages.   (See Manu-facturing Industries.)   He d. May 11, 1887, ae. 57–10–2.   Mrs. Bucklin makes her home with her daughter, Mrs. Frank H. Lovejoy, on Beech street.

CHILDREN

3.   Addie Jane, b. Grafton, Dec. 11, 1857; m. Edgar O. Fowler, M. D. (See.)
4.   Etta Belle, b. G., Apr. 1, 1859; m. Dr. Charles H. White.   (See.)
5.   Hattie Louise, b. G., Oct. 2, 1860; m. Frank H. Lovejoy.   (See.)
6.   Son, b. Bristol, July 24, 1868; d. B., Aug. 4, 1868.

OTIS K. BUCKLIN

THE BUNKER FAMILY

1.   Karl F. Bunker, son of Charles, was b. Rumney, July 8, 1874. He m., Mar. 2, 1895, Edna Isabel, dau. of George Scott Tilton. (See.) He was a teamster in Bristol for a few years, and removed to Rumney.

CHILD

2.   Charles F., b. Bristol, Oct. 9, 1895.

THE BURLEIGH FAMILY

1.   James Warren Burleigh is the son of James and Nancy (Leavitt) Burleigh. He was b. Stratham, Dec. 10, 1838. Aug. 19, 1861, he enlisted in Co. D, 3rd Regt. N. H. Vols., from Brentwood, and served till Aug. 23, 1864. In the assault on Fort Wagner, S. C., July, 1863, he was wounded. A piece of spent shell struck his knee. He m. Nov. 13, 1865, Jane B., dau. of David Ham, b. Strafford, Dec. 14, 1836. He came to Bristol 1868, and carried on the John F. Merrow stock farm for fourteen years, when he bought the Gilman farm adjoining where he still lives.

CHILD

2.   Sadie Viola, b. Bristol, June 29, 1869. Graduated from New Hampton Literary Institution. She m. Charles F. Huckins. (See.)

THE BURPEE FAMILY

Andrew Fales Burpee, son of Samuel and Sally (Fales) Burpee, was b. New London, Oct. 23, 1836. He. m. Aug. 19, 1857, Ellen Maria, dau. Hosea Ballou. (See.) He served in Co. C, 12th Regt. N. H. Vols. in Civil war on quota of Alexandria. Enlisted Aug. 20, 1862, and was discharged for disability at Concord, Apr. 25, 1863. In July, 1863, he settled in Bristol, Summer street. Blacksmith. He d. Bristol, Oct. 4, 1877, ae. 40-11-11, from a gunshot wound in the back received by the accidental discharge of a gun in the hands of his son while hunting. His widow d. Bristol, Apr. 10, 1899, ae. 61-8-17.

CHILDREN

※2.   Ira Ballou, b. Lakeland, Minn., May 11, 1858.
※3.   Don Alphonso, b. Bristol, Dec. 29, 1864.
4.   Minnie Ula, b. B., June 21, 1859; d. Sept. 7, 1869.
5.   Nellie Maria, b. Alexandria, Aug. 3, 1872; m. Warren F. Keyser. (See.)

(2)   Ira B. Burpee, b. May 11, 1858, m. Jan. 10, 1880, Hattie Belle, dau. Israel Tukey. (See.) He has been, since 1886, foreman of the Train-Smith company's pulp-mill, and

has served four years as fireward of the Fire Precinct.   Republican.

6.   Annie Lora, b. Bristol, Apr. 4, 1881 ; d. Sept. 2, 1881.
7.   Frank Ira, b. B., Apr. 5, 1882. Is an employee at pulp-mill.

(3)   Don A. Burpee, b. Dec. 29, 1864, m. July 9, 1887.
Ida Frances, dau. Elbridge Braley, who d. Bristol, Sept. 10,
1896, ae. 26–4–8.   He m. Mar. 15, 1899, Aldonna Louise, dau.
Fremont A. Grey, b. New Hampton, 1879.   He is an employee
at Calley & Currier's crutch factory. Odd Fellow. Mason.
K. of P.   Republican.

8.   Lena Maud, b. Bristol, Nov. 30, 1887.
9.   Lottie Lola, b. B., June 12, 1889.
10.   Darius George, b. B., Jan. 5, 1891.
11.   Harry Don, b. B., Mar. 12, 1893.
12.   Lewis Lampson, b. B., Sept. 22, 1899.
13.   Claude Basil, b. B., Nov. 28, 1901.

THE BUTTRICK FAMILY

The founder of the Buttrick family in America was William
Buttrick, b. in England about 1617.   He settled in Concord,
Mass., in 1635, on a farm embracing the spot where the Minute-
men stood when they received the first shot fired in the Revolu-
tionary war. Maj. John Buttrick, who led the company of
Minutemen on that memorable occasion was a great-grandson of
William.   The farm still remains in the possession of the Buttrick family.   The line of descent is as follows :
    1.   William Buttrick, named above, b. in England about
1617.   He had eight children of whom the fourth was
    2.   Samuel.   Of his six children, one was
    3.   Jonathan.   He was the father of fourteen children.
One of them was Maj. John Buttrick mentioned above, and
another, the fifth, was
    4.   Nathan.   He was the father of six children, of whom
the fourth was
    5.   Eli, b. Concord.   He m. Sarah Parker. They settled
in Concord, Mass., but in the early years of the 19th century,
removed to South Alexandria and settled on what is still known
as the Buttrick farm.   He removed to Bristol as early as 1824,
and was toll gatherer for the Central Bridge corporation occupying the toll house from 1824 till 1828, or later.

6.   William Parker, b. Jan. 25, 1792; d. Feb. 4, 1815, ae. 23–0–9.
7.   Sarah, b. Oct. 17, 1793 ; d. May 20, 1866, ae. 72–7–3.
*8.   Nathan, b. Oct. 14, 1795.

9. Elijah, b. Apr. 5, 1797. He was a tax-payer in Bristol, 1825-'27; d. July 1, 1827, ae. 30-2-26.
  10. Lydia, b. Dec. 8, 1798; d. Apr. 25, 1869, ae. 70-4-17.
  11. John Bateman, b. Oct. 29, 1800; d. Jan. 25, 1861, ae. 60-2-26.
  12. Ann R. B. Aug. 25, 1802; d. Sept. 19, 1876, ae. 74-0-24.
  13. Eli, b. Oct. 9, 1804; d. Oct. 24, 1823, ae. 19-0-15.
  14. Susan W., b. Feb. 10, 1807; d. Mar. 28, 1874, ae. 67-1-18.
  15. Emily, b. May 14, 1809; d. June 12, 1863, ae. 54-0-28.
  16. Hiram, b. Dec. 17, 1811; d. Dec. 1, 1886, ae. 74-11-14.
  17. Horace, b. June 3, 1814; d. May 6, 1869, ae. 54-11-3.
  18. William P., b. Dec. 1, 1817; d. Feb. 3, 1851, ae. 33-2-2.

(8) Nathan Buttrick, b. Oct. 14, 1795, m. Mary Clifford, dau. of Ebenezer, of Alexandria, b. Mar. 29, 1793. He succeeded his father on the home farm, and here his children were b. He d. Oct. 8, 1881, ae. 85-11-24; she d. Dec. 10, 1875, ae. 82-8-11.

CHILDREN

*19. Nathan Bateman, b. Alexandria, Jan. 1, 1822.
  20. John Adams, b. A., Feb. 13, 1828.
  21. Charles Wesley, b. A., Oct. 16, 1830.
*22. George Francis, b. A., Nov. 7, 1835.

(19) Dea. Nathan B. Buttrick, b. Jan. 1, 1822, m. Nov. 25, 1847, Elizabeth Pingree, dau. Samuel and Lydia (Pillsbury) Taylor, b. Sept. 27, 1825, in Danbury. He is a carpenter and farmer. They removed to Bristol in March, 1855, and res. on Lake street. He is deacon of the Congregational church. Democrat.

CHILDREN

23. Adelaide Augustine, b. Danbury, Aug. 23, 1849; m. Sept. 30, 1884, Angus Dunkason, son of Henry, b. Pictore, Nova Scotia, Dec. 15, 1848 They res. Fitchburg, Mass. Children:
  a. Raymond Bateman, b. Fitchburg, Mass , Jan. 30, 1888.
  b. Alice Elisabeth, b. F., Oct. 27, 1890.
  24. Frank Willis, b. Grafton, July 29, 1854; d. B., Oct. 13, 1857, ae. 3-2-14.

(22) George F. Buttrick, b. Nov. 7, 1835, m. Oct. 18, 1860, Laura Ann, dau. of Benjamin and Mehitable (Huckins) Cass, b. Bristol, Oct. 25, 1836. He was a teamster in Boston five years; in trade in Rollins's block in Bristol three years from spring of 1864; was a glove-cutter for 18 years for Kent & Berry and Milton A. Kent; was a salesman in Tilton three years and then returned to Bristol. Since the organization of the Electric Light company, in 1889, has been its electrician. He was an official member of the Methodist church, and superintendent of the Sunday-school, and has been for many years a leader of the choir. Democrat. Odd Fellow.

CHILDREN

*25. Frank Clifton, b. Boston, Mass., July 2, 1861.
  26. Infant, b. Nov. 7, 1867; d. Nov. 8, 1867.
  27. Edgar Roscoe, b. Feb. 12, 1869; d. July 20, 1870. ae. 1-5-8.

(25) Frank C. Buttrick, b. July 2, 1861, m. Apr. 10, 1883, Laurette H., dau. of Arial H. George. (See.) He graduated from Boston Dental college ; practiced dentistry a few months in Iowa and several years in Bristol, where he d. Feb. 9, 1892, ae. 30-7-7. She res. Bristol. He was an Odd Fellow. Democrat.

CHILD

28. Charles Francis, b. Bristol, Dec. 28, 1884.

THE BUXTON FAMILY

1. Anson Buxton, son of Simeon Bentley and Caroline E. (Bullard) Buxton, was b. Worcester, Mass., Mar. 18, 1848. He m. Apr. 25, 1870, Adellah, dau. Josiah and Rosalinda (Chamberlin) Clough, b. Strafford, Vt., Mar. 13, 1851. He served in Co. F, 2nd Regt. Vt. Infty, enlisting Aug. 1, 1862, when but little over 14 years of age; was discharged Feb. 21, 1863, Apr. 1, 1863, he enlisted in Co. E, 17th Regt. Vt. Infty. and was discharged July 25, 1865. He came to Bristol in Dec. 1879, res. on Merrimack street, where he has been a blacksmith.

CHILDREN

2. Edith, b. Thetford, Vt., Mar. 25, 1871; d. Feb. 21, 1876, ae. 4-10-26.
3. Ulysses Grant, b. Tunbridge, Vt., Feb. 1, 1873. He m. Marguerite McKellop, b. Springfield, Mass., 1876. Children :
    a. Mae.   *b.* Lester.
4. Fred Harris, b. Franklin, May 1, 1875; m. Nov. —, 1897, Bell Call, b. Richmond, Vt. They res. Newport.
5. Willie Bradbury, b. Franklin, May 9, 1879.
6. Clarence Edward, b. Bristol, Sept. 25, 1889.
7. Bernice Isadore, b. B., Feb. 14, 1894.

THE CALL FAMILY

1. Jonas Call was b. in Boscawen, Jan. 8, 1808. He was the son of Silas Call, a captain in the war of 1812 from Boscawen, and grandson of Mrs. Philip Call, who was killed and scalped by the Indians at what is now known as the Webster place, Franklin, in August, 1754. In 1844, Jonas m. Harriet Newels, dau. of William and Hannah (Jackson) Bond, b. Jefferson, Me., Sept. 4, 1814. He was a farmer and mechanic. He came to Bristol from Andover, in October, 1865, and res. on Merrimack street, where he d. Jan. 7, 1881, ae. 72-11-29; she d. same place Jan. 8, 1882, ae. 67-4-4.

CHILDREN

2. Eva, b. Jefferson, Me., Mar. 26, 1846 ; m. May 1, 1869, Charles H. Clay, Farmington, and d. in Omaha, Neb., Oct. 1, 1901, ae. 55-6-5. He d. Cambridge, Neb., Mar. 4, 1892. Four daughters.

3. Justin Bond, b. J., May 16, 1847. He m. Emma Brown, Columbus, Ohio, and res. Denver, Col.
*4. Silas William, b. J., Apr. 3, 1849.
5. Amanda Richardson, b. J., June 9, 1850; m. George H. Knights. (See.)
*6. Harry Manly, b. J., Oct. 19, 1851.

(4) Silas W. Call, b. Apr. 3, 1849, was a dealer in stoves and tinware in Bristol for some years. He m. May 3, 1874, Ella Isabelle, dau. Stephen F. and Sophronia A. Shirley, b. Milford, Nov. 9, 1851. He left Bristol in October, 1883, res. Dover till spring of 1884, when he went to Malvern, Kansas. In fall of 1885, returned to New Hampshire, and has since res. in Manchester.

CHILDREN

7. Grace Ella, b. Bristol, Nov. 15, 1875.
8. William Bond, b. B., June 30, 1877. In 1894, entered office of *Youth's Companion*, Boston. Since 1901, foreman folding department of the "Brown Book of Boston."
9. Anabelle, b. B., May 11, 1880.
10. Justin Manley, b. B., Dec. 4, 1881; is an employee in *Youth's Companion* office, Boston.
11. Shirley Silas, b. B., Sept. 12, 1883. Is with his brother, William B. Call.
12. Ada Augusta, b. Manchester, Mar. 27, 1890; d. Oct. 3, 1890.
13. Ralph Harvey, b. M., May 22, 1891.
14. Ernest Jonas, b. M., May 1, 1894.

(6) Harry M. Call, b. Oct. 19, 1851, m. June 25, 1884, Laura Ellen, dau. Charles H. and Ellen M. Legg, b. Lowell, Mass., Dec. 12, 1861. He is a job printer, doing business at 8 Pratt street, Allston, Mass.

CHILDREN

15. Laura Ellen, b. Cambridge, Mass., July 29, 1887.
16. Leella Smith } b. Portland, Me., Feb. 5, 1889.
17. Lalia Blanche }

THE CALLEY FAMILIES

1. William Calley and William Calley, Jr., were both residents of Stratham at the commencement of the Revolutionary war, and both signed the "Association Test" in that town.
2. William Calley, Jr., served in the Revolutionary army. He was at Winter Hill, as a private in Capt. Coffin's company in December, 1775, and he served in the Saratoga campaign from Sept. 8, to Dec. 15, 1777, as a private in Capt. Rollins's company, Col. Drake's regiment. He m. —— Stevens and removed to Sanbornton, and there d. Feb. 16, 1809; she d. at a later date, at the home of her son, David, in Ashland, ae. over 90. They had at least five children : Benjamin, Comfort, Patty, Andrew, and

3. Capt. David, b. Nov. 15, 1774. He m. June 25, 1797, Sally Folsome, and they settled in New Hampton near the Dana meeting-house, and in 1814, moved to that part of Holderness now Ashland. She d. and he m. (2) Martha Marston, dau. of Jeremiah Marston, b. Feb. 29, 1785. He d. in April, 1847, ae. 72-4-. He had two children by his first wife and twelve by his second. One of the latter was

4. Rev. David Calley, b. in Ashland, Nov. 8, 1815. He m. Sept. 4, 1845, Dorcas Doubleday, dau. John and Lydia (Shepard) Shepard, b. Holderness, Mar. 8, 1814, and d. Tunbridge, Vt., Aug. 29, 1846, ae. 32-5-21. He m. Mar. 23, 1848, Mary Mooney, dau. Obediah and Eliza (Moody) Smith, b. New Hampton, July 12, 1821. She was a woman of superior gifts and endowments, and a veritable helpmeet to her husband in all his positions in life. She d. Bristol, Oct. 26, 1896, ae. 75-3-14. The father of Mrs. Calley, Obediah Smith, was a prominent man and an extensive trader in Ashland. He was the son of Stephen Smith who served in the Revolutionary war as a private in Capt. Benjamin Whittier's company in Col. Nichols's regiment. His enlistment was from July 6 to Oct. 24, 1780, and his field of service was at West Point, N. Y. Obediah was b. May 21, 1787. He m. (1) Nov. 14, 1814, Mary Mooney, who was b. Apr. 19, 1792, and d. Dec. 28, 1815. He m. (2) Aug. 30, 1820, Eliza Moody, the mother of Mrs. Calley. She was b. Apr. 21, 1797, and d. in Manchester, Sept. 21, 1888, ae. 91-5-0. Obediah d. June 2, 1853, ae. 66-0-11. Mr. Calley became a Free Baptist clergyman in 1837, and, with the exception of three years, when he was laid aside with a throat difficulty, he was continuously in the active work of the pastorate till 1892. His labors included two terms at No. Tunbridge, Vt., three terms at Bristol; Alexandria, No. Sandwich, Center Sandwich, South Tamworth, and Meredith Center. In 1892, he retired to his home in Bristol, and is enjoying a sunny old age. Even now, at 88 years of age, he occasionally preaches and officiates at funerals. (See Freewill Baptist church.) He is a Mason; in politics a Republican. He had a seat in the legislature from Holderness in 1853; from Bristol in 1872 and 1873; and from Sandwich in 1885.

CHILDREN

5. Son, b. Tunbridge, Vt., Aug. 27, 1846; d. Sept. 7, 1846.
6. Dorcas Doubleday, b. Bristol, Jan. 28, 1849; m. June 26, 1870, Charles Henry Gordon. He was a farmer in Alexandria, where he d. May 17, 1897, as the result of a fall from the scaffold in his barn, ae. 58-11-17. Children :

    a. Arthur Moody, b. Alexandria, May 29, 1871; d. Jan. 10, 1873, ae. 1-7-11.
    b. Karl Albert, b. A., June 16, 1878.
    c. Helen Mary, b. A., July 27, 1883.

*7. David Moody, b. Ashland, Mar. 12, 1850.

8. Eliza Marston, b. A., July 12, 1851; d. Bristol, June 8, 1876, ae. 24-10-26.

9. Ella Belle, b. A., Apr. 4, 1853. She was a teacher in the Bristol graded schools nine years from 1878; in Merrimack Grammar school, Concord, ten years, and has been principal of the High school in Bristol since 1899.

10. George Hoyt, b. Bristol, Dec. 11, 1854; m. Aug. 4, 1892, Mrs. Addie J. Fowler, widow of Edgar O. Fowler, M.D., and dau. Otis K. Bucklin. (See.) He has been a practicing physician in Bristol since 1880. (See Physicians.)

11. Mary Frances, b. B., June 12, 1857; d. Aug. 7, 1873, ae. 16-1-25.

12. Charles Henry, b. B., May 15, 1859; m. Nov. 29, 1887, Ella E., dau. Lucius W. Hammond. (See.) He was four years town clerk, and was in trade in the Abel block from 1882 till 1887, when he went to Denver, Colo., where he has since been a grocer. No children.

13. Martha Bartlett, b. Tunbridge, Vt., Dec. 21, 1861; m. Anson B. Pray. (See.)

(7) David M. Calley, b. Mar. 12, 1850, m. in January, 1874, Ida Abby, dau. Russell and Abby (Jenness) Moore, b. Alexandria, Mar. 2, 1856. He has been in trade in the Abel block since 1887. Is a Mason and Odd Fellow; in politics a Republican; has served as town clerk since 1891, and represented Bristol in the legislature of 1903.

CHILDREN

14. Elfleda Maud, b. St. Johnsbury, Vt., Jan. 22, 1875; m. Nov. 28, 1894, Ernest E. Pike. He is a concreter in Burlington, Vt. Children:
   a. Mildred Eunice, b. Bristol, Dec. 26, 1895.
   b. Helen Elizabeth, b. Burlington, Vt., May 23, 1900.
15. Grace Lillian, b. St. J., Aug. 18, 1877; d. Sept. 11, 1886, ae. 9-0-23.
16. George Frank, b. St. J., May 8, 1880.
17. Mary Abby, b. Wells River, Vt., Feb. 14, 1883.
18. Ralph M., b. Bristol, Jan. 4, 1885; d. Sept. 15, 1886, ae. 0-8-11.
19. Russell David, b. B., July 1, 1890.
20. Edgar M., b. B., June 29, 1892.
21. Margaret Pearl, b. B., Dec. 29, 1893.

1. Thomas Calley was the earliest known ancestor of Francis W. Calley. Thomas and his wife, Mary, were residents of Epping and emigrated to Sanbornton in the early years of the town. Of three known sons, one was

2. Jonathan, b. May 19, 1756. He m. Elizabeth Cole, Aug. 15, 1781, probably in Epping, and moved about that time to Sanbornton. He was the first settler near Cawley pond, named for him. Of his six children, one was

3. Rev. Benjamin, b. Jan. 5, 1785. He m. Polly, dau. of John Shaw. He organized the Christian Baptist churches in Sanbornton, Franklin, Hill Center, Danbury, Andover, and Warner. He is said to have baptized 1,000 persons during various powerful revivals. The *History of Sanbornton* says "he was one of the marked men of his day, both in and out of his native

town." He d., May 29, 1854, ae. 69–4–24. Of his three children, one was

4. Rev. Benjamin, b. Sept. 3, 1813. He m. Nancy E. Thomas, dau. of Joseph, Mar. 11, 1830. He was a farmer, and a Christian Baptist clergyman for 18 years, preaching at the "Chapel" in Sanbornton, at Danbury, Hill, Wilmot, and other places. He had 11 children, of whom the 9th was

5. Francis Willard, b. Sanbornton, May 11, 1851. He m. May 7, 1870, Jerutia, dau. of Dea. Levi Carter, b. New Hampton, Apr. 26, 1847. She graduated from New Hampton Literary Institution in 1868. Francis W. came to Bristol in November, 1871, and was a blacksmith in the employ of Otis K. Bucklin till Sept. 1, 1876, when he purchased the business, which he continued till Nov. 1, 1879, when he sold and went to Colorado. One year later he returned, and Dec. 1, 1880, commenced the manufacture of crutches in company with Jefferson A. Simonds. A short time later George C. Currier purchased Mr. Simonds's interest and the firm became Calley & Currier, and Mr. Calley has been the senior member of this firm till now. They do a large and prosperous business, shipping their goods to various parts of the world. (See Manufacturing Industries.) Mr. Calley is a member of Union Lodge, A. F. and A. M., and a Knight Templar. In politics he is an Independent. He res. on South Main street. No children.

THE CARLETON FAMILY

1. Ebenezer Carleton, son of Eleazer, was b. Lyndeborough, Apr. 2, 1754. His descendants claim that he was Gen. Washington's purveyor, and this claim appears to be well taken. By the *Revolutionary War Rolls* it appears that he first enlisted Aug. 1, 1775, in Capt. Benjamin Mann's company, Col. James Reed's regiment. He was in Col. Scammel's regiment from 1777 to 1781, and his company was selected by Gen. Washington as his body guard, Jan. 1, 1779, and was known as "Washington's Life Guard." That Washington should select one of this company for his purveyor was but natural. He was discharged for disability occasioned by being thrown from his horse. At his discharge Gen. Washington presented him with a pair of pistols and Mrs. Washington with a gold watch, as tokens of regard. Ebenezer Carleton m., June 3, 1784, Rebecca Farrar, b. May 29, 1754, and d. in Hill, Sept. 7, 1832, ae. 78–3–8. They res. at Danbury Four Corners, Fisk place in New Hampton; on north bank Smith's river, and in 1799 were the first settlers on a farm in the Borough, and here he d. Dec. 8, 1836, ae. 82–8–6.

Francis W. Calley

CHILDREN

2. Timothy, b. Apr. 9, 1785 ; d. unm. in Hill, ae. about 70.
3. Ebenezer, b. Mar. 9, 1787; d. Burlington, Vt., about 1848 ; m. ; no children.
4. Rebecca, b. Aug. 25, 1789; m. Samuel Wells (Published Jan. 13, 1810). She d. Waterford, Penn., Sept., 1855. Children :

    a. Charles, d. Seattle, Washington, Apr. 13, 1896, leaving four or five children.
    b. Son, d. infancy.

*5. Jeremiah, b. Danbury, Feb. 7, 1792.
6. John Montgomery, b. Oct. 12, 1795; m. Lovina, dau. Ebenezer Wells, and d. in Hill, in 1828. Children :

    a. Osgood, d. young.
    b. Rebecca, m. a Livingston, and d. in Minnesota.

(5) Jeremiah Carleton, b. Feb. 7, 1792, m. Jan., 1820, Betsey Tenney. She was b. Hill, Apr. 10, 1799, and d. Feb. 8, 1888, ae. 88-9-28. He was a farmer, and d. in Hill, Oct. 19, 1878, ae. 86-8-12.

CHILDREN

*7. Pettingill Garland, b. Hill, Dec. 23, 1821.
8. Julia Ann, b. H., Apr. 13, 1825; m. Robert S. Hastings. (See.)
*9. Samuel Wells, b. H., Nov. 19, 1828.
10. Philinda, b. H., May 25, 1830; d. Aug. 17, 1832, ae. 2-2-22. Fell into a tub of scalding water.
11. Sarah Philinda, b. Oct. 3, 1833; m. Samuel Yates. He was a soldier in Co. G, 10th Me. Vols., in Civil war and d. in Gorham, Mar. 3, 1876, ae. 46-9-. She d. Apr. 12, 1878, ae. 44-6-9.
12. Elizabeth M., b. H., Oct. 23, 1835; m. Sept. 28, 1861, John Albert Day, Bradford, Mass. Children :

    a. Mary Lizzie, b. Dec. 20, 1868.
    b. Bessie Mabel, b. Nov. 7, 1872.
    c. John Carleton, b. Dec. 30, 1873.

(7) Pettingill G. Carleton, b. Dec. 23, 1821, m. Dec. 26, 1844, Mary Elizabeth, dau. John Hastings. (See.) She d. in Waterford, Pa., Oct. 3, 1855, ae. 34-10-, and he m. Dec. 14, 1856, Sarah Philinda, sister of first wife, b. Nov. 30, 1831. He removed to Bristol in August, 1864. Painter, Republican, Odd Fellow, class leader of the M. E. church, and superintendent of the Sunday-school. He removed to Melrose, Mass., about 1880, where he d. of smallpox, July 1, 1902, ae. 80-6-8.

CHILDREN

13. Ida W., b. Merrimac, Mass., Apr. 4, 1847; d. in Haverhill, Mass., Dec. 4, 1850, ae. 3-8-0.
14. Theodore LaForest, b. Nov. 19, 1852; m. Nov. 13, 1872, Mary E., dau. of George W. Clifford, b. Mar. 6, 1852. She d. Malden, Mass., Feb. 25, 1896, as result of carriage accident a month previous, ae. 43-11-19. He m., Nov. 15, 1899, Margaret Matthews Pineo, b. New Brunswick, Aug. 15, 1875. Children :

    a. Mary Adna (adopted), b. Haverhill, Mass., Oct. 24, 1885 ; m. July 25, 1802, C. W. Cleveland ; res. Everett, Mass.
    b. Harold Everard (adopted), b. Bradford, Mass., May 8, 1891.
    c. Gladys, b. Aug. 8, 1900.

15. Eugene C., b. June 13, 1855; d. Mar. 4, 1878, ae. 22-8-21. He was a Junior at Dartmouth college, a civil engineer, and a brilliant young man.

16. Ardella, b. May 17, 1858; d. Sept. 10, 1859, ae. 1-3-23.

17. Eva Almertia, b. Dec. 5, 1860; m. Dec. 5, 1881, William N. Dawes. Res. Melrose, Mass. No children.

(9) Samuel W. Carleton, b. Nov. 19, 1828, m. Jan. 1, 1857, Mary E., dau. Alfred Kelley, b. Aug. 16, 1832. They res. on the Clark Merrill farm in the Borough, Hill. Methodists, Republican.

CHILDREN

18. Addie May, b. Hill, Jan. 18, 1858; m. Willis Fisk Calley. Child:
    a. John C., b. May 1, 1893.

19. Ella Jane, b. H., May 26, 1862; m. Frank Pray. Child:
    a. Roy, b. Aug. 16, 1889.

20. Elmer Hanson, b. H., Jan. 1, 1869; m. Mabel Patten. No children.

THE CASS FAMILIES

1. Daniel Cass, b. Candia, Aug. 8, 1789, m. Feb. 25, 1813, Lydia Clay. They settled on the James Cross place in Bridgewater soon after they were m. and later near the meeting-house. They passed their last years in the home of their son, Dea. John F., in Bridgewater. He d. Feb. 3, 1865, ae. 75-5-25; she d. Mar. 23, 1865, ae. 72-5-10.

CHILDREN, all born in Bridgewater

2. Caroline W., b. Dec. 9, 1813; d. Sept. 9, 1835, ae. 21-9-0.
*3. Calvin, b. May 21, 1815.
4. Julia Ann, b. July 26, 1817; d. Sept. 21, 1838, ae. 21-1-25.
*5. John Franklin, b. Nov. 29, 1818.
6. Melinda, b. Sept. 23, 1822; m., Mar. 27, 1843, Horace Perkins, and d. Rumney, Apr. —, 1868, ae. 44.
*7. Daniel, b. Aug. 9, 1824.
8. Lydia R., b. Jan. 8, 1829; d. Apr. 22, 1857, ae. 28-3-14.
9. Samuel N., b. May 2, 1830; d. Feb., 1898, ae. 67-9-.
10. Cyrus Alvin, b. Dec. 8, 1833; m. Jan. 3, 1857, Jane A. Hibbard.

(3) Dea. Calvin Cass, b. May 21, 1815, m. Mar. 4, 1841, Almira Richardson, b. Woburn, Mass., Feb. 28, 1812. He came to Bristol in 1851. A farmer and mechanic, Republican, deacon Congregational church. Res. Merrimack street. He d. Bristol, May 24, 1871, ae. 56-0-3; she d. Bristol, Aug. 11, 1874, ae. 62-5-13.

CHILD

11. Almira Frances, b. Bridgewater, July 11, 1842. Res. Stoneham, Mass. Unm.

(5) Dea. John F. Cass, b. Nov. 29, 1818, m. Dec. 26, 1843, Jane Locke, dau. Favor (See), b. Aug. 22, 1823. He was a farmer in District No. 7, 1847-'59, when he settled on farm

now occupied by Simeon H. Cross at North End. He was deacon of Congregational church. Republican. He d. June 6, 1876, ae. 57–6–7; she d. Sept. 10, 1890, ae. 67–0–18.

CHILDREN

12. Ellen, b. Nov. 26, 1845; m. Henry Griffith. (See.)
13. Julia Ann, b. Bristol, Mar. 9, 1849; m. Simeon H. Cross. (See.)
14. George F., b. Bristol, July 4, 1851; m. Apr. 13, 1871, Nellie A. Keezer, dau. of Geo. W. (See), b. Apr. 9, 1852. He has been for many years an overseer in woolen-mill. No children. Republican, Odd Fellow.
15. Sarah Augusta, b. B., Dec. 30, 1855; m. Otis F. Cross. (See.)
16. William F., b. July 5, 1857; m. May 1, 1880, Roxy Dolloff, dau. Solon. (See.) He d. of consumption, Apr. 3, 1881, ae. 23–8–28. She m. (2) Charles H. Dickinson. (See.)
17. Mary Martha, b. B., June 16, 1861; m. Dec. 22, 1885, Edmund Fairfield Peckham, son of Rev. Cyrus B., b. July 21, 1862. Res. 20 Dodge street, Providence, R. I. Child:
    a. Earle Winfield, b. Providence, Oct. 11, 1886.

(7) Daniel Cass, b. Aug. 9, 1824, m. Feb. 26, 1860, Francena D., dau. Joshua Kidder, b. Apr. 22, 1841. (See.) He was a farmer in District No. 7, till about 1865, when he located on Summer street, where she d. July 26, 1876, ae. 35–3–4; he d. same Oct. 17, 1881, ae. 57–2–8.

CHILD

18. Flora Dell, b. Bristol, Aug. 4, 1869; m. June 20, 1892, Luther H. Bailey, b. Jan. 27, 1870, and res. Alexandria. Child:
    a. Harry Hobart, b. Alexandria, Apr. 4, 1893.

---

1. Nason Cass, b. 1751, m. —— Hoyt, and settled on the Kendrick Dickerson farm in South Alexandria, where he d. in 1819, ae. 68. He had at least the following named

CHILDREN

2. John.   3. Cyrus.   4. Jesse.
5. Beniah.   6. Nason.
*7. Joseph, b. Alexandria, Apr. 3, 1785.

(7) Joseph Cass, b. Apr. 3, 1785, m. Feb. 23, 1809, Betsey Glidden, b. May 28, 1787. In 1807, he settled at what is still known as Cass's mills in South Alexandria, and there he was a farmer and had a saw-mill, grist-mill, carding machine, and clothing-mill, and a cabinet shop. He was a shrewd business man and accumulated a good property. In 1870, being then 85 years of age and his wife 83, he sold all his property here and emigrated to Grinnell, Iowa. There she d. Sept. —, 1871, ae. 84–4–, and he d. Sept. 7, 1879, ae. 94–5–4.

CHILDREN, all born in Alexandria

8. Emeline, b. Feb. 21, 1810; m. Darwin Forbes, who d. Grinnell, Iowa, Apr. 26, 1892, ae. 85–10–27; she d. Aug. 29, 1900, ae. 90–6–8.

*9.   Seth, b. Mar. 7, 1812.
  10.   Jane, b. Apr. 9, 1814; m. Jeremiah Flanders, b. May 27, 1814.
  11.   Sophia, b. May 11, 1816; d. Sept. 20, 1882, ae. 66-4-9. Unm.
*12.   Calvin D., b. 1820.
  13.   Harriet, b. July 1. 1822; m. Abram Goodrich. She d. June 26.
1882, at Grinnell, Iowa, ae. 59-11-25. He d. same place, Mar. 20, 1881, ae.
58-5-19.
*14.   Nason W., b. June 1, 1829.
  15.   Lewis, b. May 5, 1833; m. Mary Jane Simonds, b. Apr. 1, 1832.
They res. Grinnell.

(9)   Seth Cass, b. Mar. 7, 1812, m. Belinda B., dau. of
Jonathan Ladd. They settled in Bristol about 1863, succeeding to the Rev. Walter Sleeper homestead on No. Main street.
He served as selectman and tax collector of Bristol. Farmer,
Republican. He d. in Illinois while on his way home from a
visit to Grinnell, Iowa, Oct. 31, 1880, ae. 68-7-24. Mrs. Cass
d. Bristol, Mar. 10, 1883, ae. 70-1-.

CHILDREN

*16.   Orrison Gustine, b. Alexandria, Aug. 26, 1843.
*17.   Cyrus Newell, b. A., June, 1845.
  18.   Christie, d. young.

(12)   Calvin D. Cass, b. 1820, m. Oct. —, 1844, Theresa
Jane, dau. Sethus B. and Ruth (Wells) Forbes, b. Hill, 1818, d.
Alexandria, July 24, 1851, ae. 33. He m. (2) July, 1852, Frances
Adaline, sister of first wife, b. Hill, Mar. 6, 1823, and d. Vineland, N. J., Mar. 7, 1880, ae. 57-0-1. He settled in Bristol in
1852, was wool carder and clothier and miller, where C. N. Merrill & Son now have a grist-mill on Central street, and later
operated saw-mill on south side of river. He res. on Spring
street next west of old M. E. church. In 1867, he removed to
Laconia, where he remained four years; then started for the
West for his health, reached Manchester, and there d. Aug. 18,
1871, ae. 51. Methodist, Republican.

CHILDREN

  19.   Lizzie F., b. Alexandria, Dec., 1845; d. Dec. 18, 1853, ae. 8 years.
  20.   Frank H., b. A., Mar., 1847. Res. 131 Adams street, Chicago,
Ill.
  21.   Arthur B., b. Bristol, 1856; d. Mar. 6, 1864, ae. 7-9-11.

(14)   Nason W. Cass, b. June 1, 1829, m. in April, 1853,
Augusta H., dau. of Abram and Hannah (Fifield) Shaw, b.
Salisbury, 1835, and d. Hill, May 15, 1856, ae. 21 years. He
m., Nov. 17, 1856, Abbie E., dau. Henry and Susan (Rowe)
Emery, b. Andover, Apr. 13, 1825, and d. Bristol, May 13,
1897, ae. 72-1-0. He settled in Bristol about 1864; has res. on
Summer street; a traveling optician. Republican, Mason.

CHILDREN

  22.   Josephine Augusta, b. Hill, Jan. 15, 1855; d. Boston, Nov. 12,
1889, ae. 34-9-27. She was a brilliant scholar and poetess. See sketch
under "Literature."

(16)   Orrison G. Cass, b. Aug. 26, 1843, was a farmer, and succeeded to his father's homestead. He m. (1) —— Simonds; (2) Dorinda Bullock, b. Alexandria, Apr. 1, 1839, and d. Oct. 26, 1884, ae. 45-6-25. He m. (3) Mary Keniston; (4) May 22, 1893, Emily Lucy, dau. Salmon H. Tilton, b. New Hampton, Nov. 27, 1844. He d. Bristol, Apr. 29, 1903, ae. 59-8-3. Republican.

CHILD

23.   Ella B., b. Alexandria, Apr. 23, 1866; d. Mar. 30, 1881, ae. 14-11-7.

(17)   C. Newell Cass, b. June, 1845, m. Sept. 15, 1867, Emma H., dau. Abram Dolloff. (See.) He res. in Illinois some years; now in Spangle, Wash. Mrs. Cass returned East in 1873, and entered the office of the *Cottage Hearth* in Boston, remaining till 1875. While continuing to write for the magazine, she resumed her vocation of music teaching, having classes in Franklin, Bristol, New Hampton Institution, and Proctor Academy, Andover. In 1887, she accepted a position with the Redpath Lyceum bureau, Boston, and for a term of years had charge of the bureau's interest in New England, and has since been identified with lyceum work, making her home in Bristol.

CHILD

*24.   Harland Howard, b. Manchester, Ill., Oct. 1, 1868.

(24)   H. Howard Cass, b. Oct. 1, 1868, m. Jan. 29, 1896, Libbie Abbie, dau. of Dr. David P. and Abbie Jane Goodhue, b. West Springfield, Feb. 10, 1875. After leaving the schools of Bristol he spent three years in Boston, taking special courses of study. He fitted for an optician and began practice at Rutland, Vt., in 1896. Two years later he removed to Claremont where he is still in practice.

CHILDREN

25.   Marion Elizabeth, b. Rutland, Vt., Sept. 25, 1896.
26.   Ralph Goodhue, b. Claremont, Vt., Dec. 16, 1899; d. Oct. 12, 1900.

---

1.   Nason Cass, probably a cousin of the Nason Cass who settled in Alexandria, and Hannah, his wife, settled in New Chester, about 1773. The cellar, south of Wilson Foster's farm near the railroad, marks the place where their log house stood. He served one term in the Revolutionary war from New Chester. The following, as far as known, were his

CHILDREN

2.   John, drowned while rolling logs into the Pemigewasset river, near his home. He was a voter at the time, but unm.
*3.   Jacob, b. 1768.
4.   Sarah, b. New Chester, Sept. 14, 1778; m. Dec. 20, 1798, Moses Stevens, Enfield.

(3) Jacob Cass, b. 1768, m. Apr. 9, 1795, Betsey Bean. They were farmers on old homestead in Hill; in Canada, and on New Chester mountain, in Bristol. He d. in Hill, Mar. 23, 1853, ae. 85, and she made her home in the family of her son, Jacob, in Bristol, but d. while on a visit in Hill, Dec. 23, 1870, ae. 85.

CHILDREN

5. Betsey, m. —— Blaisdell; res. in Hill. He was a peddler; disappeared while on the road, and never heard from; supposed to have been murdered.
6. Jane, m. (1) John Tilton, Bridgewater. (See.)
7. Nason, m. Mary Tilton, and lived in Borough. Children:
   a. Edward. b. Rosan, m. Frank York. c. Dolly, never m.
8. Mary, b. Stanstead, Canada, m. (1) Benj. Gould, m. (2) George Brown, Hill.
*9. Jacob, b. S., June 16, 1811.
10. Ann, m. Jonas Abbott, lived in Hill.
11. Lovina, m. Alvin Gerry, (2) B. Q. Fellows; d. Dec. 1, 1894, ae. 79. (See.)
12. Hannah, d. unm.

(9) Jacob Cass, b. June 16, 1811, m., Mar. 13, 1836, Emily, dau. of James and Hannah (Parker) Yalding, b. Concord, Dec. 18, 1812. He was a farmer in the Borough, till about 1865, when he moved to Bristol village, Lake street, where he d. Oct. 14, 1890, ae. 79-3-28. She still lives, a hard working woman at 91 years of age. Both members M. E. church.

CHILDREN

13. Mary Ann, b. Hill, Aug. 15, 1837; m. Benjamin G. Durgin. (See.)
14. Sarah Emily, b. H., July 12, 1840; d. Jan. 6, 1846, ae. 5-5-24.
15. Lewis George, b. H., Nov. 13, 1842; d. Apr. 19, 1864, ae. 21-5-6; unm.
16. Charles Herman, b. Hillsboro, Sept. 9, 1844; d. Lawrence, Mass., Oct. 2, 1895, ae. 51-0-23; m. Dec. 24, 1871, Margaret, dau. Robert Lightbody, b. Westville, N. Y., Dec. 5, 1851.
17. Clementina A., b. H., Apr. 11, 1848; d. Apr. 29, 1863, ae. 15-0-18.

THE CATE FAMILY

1. Albert Frank Cate, son of Ammon T. and Edna P. (Clark) Cate, was b. in Franklin, Sept. 9, 1858. He m., May 5, 1883, Flora E., dau. of Merrill P. Simonds. (See.) He came to Bristol 1880. Is a machinist and painter.

CHILDREN

2. Daisy Belle, b. Bristol, Feb. 12, 1884.
3. Harry Garfield, b. B., July 20, 1886.
4. Karl Elroy, b. B., Aug. 30, 1889.

THE CAVIS FAMILY

1. Solomon Cavis, the son of Nathaniel, was b. in Bow, Nov. 22, 1800. His maternal grandmother was Dorcas Abbott,

KARL G. CAVIS

the first white female b. in Concord. She m. Ed. Hall, and his
dau., Lydia, m. Nathaniel Cavis. Solomon Cavis came to Bristol in 1820, and served as clerk in the store of Ichabod C. Bartlett three years. His compensation the first year was $30 and
board ; the second year, $140. This was thought at that time to
be great pay. In May, 1823, Mr. Cavis associated himself with
Philip Webster, and they opened a general store, under the firm
name of Webster & Cavis, where is now White's block, with a
capital of $500. For board they paid $1.25 each per week. Mr.
Cavis used to drive his own team to Boston for goods. Once,
on his return, his horse ran away and scattered his goods along
Boscawen street. He regained his horse and then gathered up
his goods. Mr. Cavis spent his long life in the mercantile business and secured a competence. (See Mercantile Industries.)
He was closely identified with the material prosperity of the
town ; he was the first in town to discontinue the sale of spiritu-
ous liquors, and he became an active worker in the temperance
cause. He was above reproach in all the relations of life and
honored in the community. He was through life a liberal supporter of the Congregational church, but did not become a member till 71 years of age. In politics he was a Democrat. He
served three years as town clerk and seven years as town treasurer ; and was postmaster 1830 to 1841. He erected the residence on Pleasant street now occupied by his daughter, Mrs.
Abbott. He m., Oct. 16, 1828, Almira, dau. of Hon. James
Minot, b. Nov. 23, 1804. (See.) He d. Feb. 2, 1884, ae.
83-2-10. Mrs. Cavis was a lifelong member of the Congregational church, and active in church and benevolent work. She
d. Sept. 13, 1884, ae. 79-9-20.

CHILDREN

*2. George Minot, b. Bristol, Mar. 5, 1830.
3. Harriet Minot, b. B., Dec. 13, 1831 ; m. Rev. Charles F. Abbott.
(See.)

(2) George M. Cavis, b. Mar. 5, 1830, m. July 28, 1856,
Abby Mansur, b. May 2, 1830. She d. in Bristol, Aug. 16,
1858, ae. 28-3-14, and he m. Oct. 18, 1866, Harriet Amelia, dau.
of Daniel M., and Mary Jane (Gordon) Dearborn, b. Sanbornton, Jan. 1, 1841. At 16 years of age, Mr. Cavis commenced a
mercantile career in his father's store, and continued till his
death. In 1875, he was elected treasurer of the Bristol Savings
bank and, in 1884, he disposed of most of his mercantile interests
to Horace T. Alexander, that he might devote his time to the
duties of the bank. He served the bank as vice-president three
years, and as treasurer from the date of his first election till his
death — 16 years. He was considered a superior financier, and
enjoyed the confidence of the community. He was a Mason
and a Democrat, and served three years as town clerk. He

erected and occupied a residence on Pleasant street, where he d.
Dec. 21, 1891, ae. 61-9-16. Mrs. Cavis was an estimable
woman, a member of the Congregational church, a teacher in
the Sunday-school, and active in all church work. She d. Jan.
15, 1892, ae. 51-0-14.

CHILDREN, all born in Bristol

*4. Harry Minot, b. May 29, 1857.
*5. Karl Gordon, b. Sept. 12, 1867.
*6. George Bertrand, b. Feb. 28, 1869.
  7. Raymond, b. Jan. 13, 1871; m. Sept. 22, 1897, Nettie Ellen, dau.
of John C. Wheet, M.D. (See.) He was for some years clerk in the
Bristol Savings bank. Res. Summer street. No children.
  8. Lawrence, b. Aug. 26, 1872; d. Feb. 11, 1883, ae. 10-5-15.
  9. Henry Taylor, b. Mar. 28, 1878; d. May. 16, 1878, ae. 0-1-18.
 10. Almira Belle, b. Mar. 22, 1881; d. Jan. 30, 1882, ae. 0-10-8.

(4) Harry M. Cavis, b. May 29, 1857, m. May 12, 1897,
at Washington, D. C., Kate, dau. of Maj. George H. Chandler,
and niece of Senator William E. Chandler, b. Baltimore, Oct.
21, 1871. He read law with Hon. H. W. Parker, at Claremont,
and with Hon. John Y. Mugridge, at Concord, and was admitted to the bar in 1881. Is a practicing lawyer in Concord.

CHILD

 11. George Chandler, b. Feb. 14, 1898.

(5) Karl G. Cavis, b. Sept. 12, 1867, m. June 27, 1894,
Bella D., dau. of Levi C. Gurdy. (See.) He is a member of
the firm of Cavis Brothers, merchants. (See Mercantile Industries.) Is president of the Bristol Aqueduct company, a Congregationalist, Democrat, Mason. He res. in the parental homestead on Pleasant street.

CHILDREN

 12. George Minot, b. Bristol, Dec. 7, 1895.
 13. Sarah Hortense, b. B., June 28, 1897.
 14. Harriet, b. B., Sept. 19, 1901.

(6) George B. Cavis, b. Feb. 28, 1869, m. Oct. 15, 1896,
Ada May, dau. of George G. Brown. (See.) He is a member
of the firm of Cavis Brothers, a director of the First National
Bank of Bristol, Democrat, Congregationalist, and a past master
of Union Lodge, No. 79, A. F. and A. M.

CHILD

 15. Myla Brown, b. Bristol, Sept. 2, 1900.

THE CHANDLER FAMILIES

1. Capt. Abiel Chandler was the son of Timothy and Elizabeth (Copp) Chandler, b. Sanbornton, Oct. 20, 1765. At 16
years of age he enlisted in the Continental army and served two

GEORGE B. CAVIS

years. He was at White Plain, West Point, and Saratoga, and was a pensioner. Dec. 25, 1788, he m. Abigail, dau. of Jonathan Thomas, of Sanbornton, a drummer in the Continental army. He settled in Bristol in 1793 or '94, on what is now the James W. Burleigh farm, in the northeast part of the town. The buildings were some distance from the highway and long since disappeared. In Bristol he was a captain in the militia. About 1819, he removed to Stewartstown, where his wife d., and he returned and made his home in the family of his son, Timothy, where he d., May 5, 1855, ae. 89-6-15.

CHILDREN

2. Elizabeth, b. Sanbornton, July 28, 1789; m. Daniel Kidder. (See.)

3. Abigail, b. S., Apr. 4, 1791; d. Aug. 17, 1791.

*4. Timothy, b. S., June 4, 1792

5. Tabitha, b. Bristol, Apr. 18, 1794; m. Stephen Caswell, b. July 17, 1799; went to Stewartstown, thence to Brompton, Canada, where they both d. Children:

    a. Abigail Sarah, b. Stewartstown, Nov. 22, 1822; m. Mar. 15, 1838, Joseph Sleeper, Stanstead, C. E., son of Hezekiah. He was a mechanic; in United States service as a sharp shooter three years. Removed to Hartland, Wis.

    b. Susan Mary, b. Brompton, Aug. 15, 1824; m. Mar. 19, 1846, David Sloan, farmer, Brompton, who was killed by a horse, Apr. 3, 1849; m. (2) Andrew Lamb, farmer, Brompton. Seven children.

    c. Ruth Ann, b. May 19, 1826; m., at Lowell, Mass., 1848, Wm. Straw, (2) at Manchester, Wm. Reynolds, b. England. Four children

    d. Berengera Dalton, b. at Brompton, Feb. 17, 1828; d. Dec., 1849, at Saco, Me., ae. 21-10-.

    e. Thais Elizabeth, b. Feb. 10, 1830; m. Dec. -, 1852, at Manchester, Ortes Tyler, dyer. He d. May 15, 1853, ae. 22-9-. She m. (2) Joshua B. Page, and removed to Salisbury. He d. in Maine. Three children.

    f. Stephen Abiel, b. Dec. 7, 1833; d. Mar. 20, 1846, ae. 12-3-13.

    g. Tabitha Almira, b. Mar. 26, 1836; d. Apr. 23, 1845, ae. 9-0-27.

    h. Isaac Washington, b. Apr. 7, 1838; m. Dec. 3, 18—, Matilda Reynolds, Windsor, C. E. Farmer, settled Brompton. Two children.

    i. Abiel Walker (adopted), b. Sept. 23, 1846.

*6. Jonathan, b. Bristol, May 14, 1795.

*7. George Washington, b. B., June 30, 1797.

8. Azuba, b. B., Sept. 29, 1800; m. Seth Tirrell, b. Nov. 12, 1798. He d. Stewartstown, Sept. 4, 1872, ae. 73-9-22; she d. same place, Jan. 19, 1891, ae. 90-3-20. He was a farmer and lumber manufacturer. Children:

    a. Mary Adrith, b. Stewartstown; m. Thos. Farrar, d. Walworth, Wis. Four children.

    b. Hezekiah Fellows, b. Feb. 16, 1826; carpenter, Jamestown, Cal.

    c. Christiana Sophia, b. Jan. 2, 1828; m. Charles L. Morse; farmer, Stewartstown. Three children.

    d. Lafayette, b. May 15, 1830.

    e. Infant, b. Mar. 13, 1832; d. Mar. 31, 1832.

    f. George Washington, b. Feb. 5, 1833; served in Co. E, 12th

Mass. Vol. Wounded at 2nd battle of Bull Run. Hatter, Natick, Mass.

    g. Allen A., b. Feb. 27, 1835. Res. Brighton, Mass.

    h. Helen Marr, b. Sept. 6, 1837; m. Apr. 6, 1865, Charles C. Tirrell, Stewartstown, farmer.

    i. Seth Walker, b. May 15, 1840. In Civil war served in 6th Me. Battery; wounded Cedar Creek.

    9. Salome, b. Bristol, Aug. 6, 1802; d. Nov. 7, 1802.

    10. Luzetta, b. B., Sept. 30, 1803; m. Aug. 27, 1823, Caleb L. Dalton, b. June 12, 1796. They res. Stewartstown, where he was town clerk ten years. He d. Mar. 28, 1847, ae. 50-9-16; she d. Aug. 13, 1864, ae. 60-10-13. Children:

    a. Cassandra, m. Harvey Gould.
    b. Berengea, b. July 10, 1825; d Aug. 1, 1827, ae. 2-0-21.
    c. Lucian Rawson, b. Sept. 10, 1827; d. at about 20.
    d. Althea, b. Nov. 10, 1829.
    e. Almeda Augusta, b. Jan. 15, 1832; d. at about 20.
    f. Ruhamah, m. Cyrus Young, Littleton.
    g. Flavius Josephus, printer; U. S. service 1862.
    h. Florentius, farmer, Colebrook.
    i. Florentia.
    j. Caleb S., in Civil war, 13th Regt. N. H. Vols., as corporal and sergeant; wounded at Cold Harbor, Va.

    11. Matilda D., b. Bristol, Jan. 7, 1805; m. Sept. 28, 1828; Joshua, Tirrell, of Stewartstown, b. Canterbury, July 29, 1800. He d. of smallpox, Mar. 18, 1860, ae. 59-7-19; she d. May 28, 1871, ae. 66-4-21. Children:

    a. Enoch T., b. Stewartown, Aug. 9, 1830, m. Apr. 10, ——, Chloe T. Harriman. Two children.
    b. Abiel W., b. May 5, 1834. Farmer in Stewartstown.
    c. Hannah, b. May 15, 1837; d. Nov. 20, 1862, ae. 25-6-5. Unm.
    d. Hiram Madison, b. Oct. 14, 1840. Farmer in Stewartstown.
    e. John A., b. Sept. 16, 1847.

    12. Abiel Walker, b. Bristol, Nov. 26, 1807, m. Feb. 8, 1855, Marinda Jane Pierce, of Haverhill. He went to Bow Creek, Knox Co., Ohio, with his brother, Jonathan, about 1853, where he d. Child:

    a. Anson, b. Bow Creek, O.

    (4). Timothy Chandler, b. June 4, 1792, m. Apr. 6, 1821, Lois, dau. of Jacob Gurdy (See), b. June 20, 1794. He settled on farm now occupied by Damon Y. Emmons, and here he d. Mar. 18, 1881, ae. 88-9-14. She d. same place May 9, 1872, ae. 77-9-19. Democrat.

CHILDREN, all born Bristol.

    13. Samantha, b. July 4, 1820; m. Frederick Kidder. (See.)

    14. Huldah Atwood, b. Nov. 14, 1823; m. Damon Y. Emmons. (See.)

    15. Hiram Peabody, b. Dec. 29, 1828; m. (1) Angeline Morse, of Friendship, Me. No children. (2) Jan. 25, 1862, Susan T. Roberts, of Goffstown. He was an edge-tool maker at Collinsville, Conn. Child:

    a. Belle Dewey, b. July —, 1866.

  *16. Meshech Gurdy, b. Mar. 9, 1830.

    17. Ann Maria, b. Mar. 29, 1834. Has made her home with her sister, Mrs. Damon Y. Emmons. Unm.

    18. Mary Augusta, d. Aug. 21, 1846, ae. 5-8-0.

(6) Jonathan Chandler, b. May 14, 1795, m. 1824, Sarah Small, of Northfield. He went to Stewartstown, where he owned a saw-mill; from there to Missouri; thence to Ohio, and Kansas, where he d.

CHILDREN

19. John L. Jefferson, b. Stewartstown.
20. Charles Wesley. 21. Timothy.
22. Frank. 23. Sarah Ann.

(7) George W. Chandler, b. June 30, 1797, m. Apr. 7, 1825, Harriet Ladd, of Stewartstown. He was a farmer in Stewartstown and in Ohio. He d. in Ohio, Jan. 25, 1832, ae. 34-6-25. She m. (2) Joseph Taylor.

CHILDREN

24. Asa G., m. in Stewartstown, Emily Roswell, of Pittsburg.
25. Hannah. An operative in Lowell, Mass.

(16) Mesheeh G. Chandler, b. Mar. 9, 1830, m. May 19, 1861, Mary Lovinia, dau. Jewell and Mary (Blodgett) Jesseman, b. in Hudson, Mar. 19, 1842. He is a stone-cutter, and res. on Chandler street, named for him. Democrat. Odd Fellow.

CHILDREN

26. Willis Dana, b. Bristol, Jan. 4, 1864; m. Sept. 8, 1882, Nancy A., dau. George W. and Elizabeth F. (Fletcher) Small, b. Unity, Me., Apr. 1, 1859. Child:
   a. George Willis, b. B., Mar. 4, 1885.
27. Addie Etta, b. B., Aug. 8, 1866, m. Dennis Haley. (See.)

THE CHASE FAMILIES

1. William Little Chase, son of Moses and Abigail (Little) Chase, was b. in South Newbury, Mass., Apr. 1, 1804. He located in Bristol in 1826 and opened a shoe store in a little building that stood where the west-side drug store now stands; later was in the same business at corner of Central square and Pleasant street, where he was also postmaster. Oct. 29, 1829, he m. Sally, dau. Capt. James Minot, b. June 19, 1809. (See.) They resided where Rev. David Calley now lives on Summer street, where their children were b. In March, 1844, he removed to Lyme, but returned to Bristol about 1867, residing on Pleasant street, where he d. June 26, 1875, ae. 71-2-25. She spent her last years in the family of her son, Hannibal, in Lyme, and there d. June 17, 1893, ae. 83-11-28. Mr. Chase was one of the early members of the Congregational church, uniting in 1827; Mrs. Chase united in 1831. In politics he was a Republican; was five years town treasurer.

CHILDREN

*2.   William Minot, b. Aug. 13, 1830.
*3.   Hannibal, b. May 14, 1832.
*4.   Josiah Brown, b. Jan. 24, 1834.
*5.   Charles Wilson, b. Aug. 29, 1836.
*6.   Henry Melville, b. June 13, 1838.
   7.   Julia Maria Minot, b. Jan. 6, 1841; m. Sept. 9, 1863, Col. now Gen. Thomas Francis Barr, U. S. Army, He was the son of Thomas and Jean (McAuslane) Barr, and was b. West Cambridge, Mass., Nov. 18, 1837. Children:
       a.   Harry Perkins, b. Carbon, Pa., July 25, 1864; m. Clara C. Jencks, Manchester, July 6, 1887.
       b.   Alice Gertrude, b. New York City, Oct. 12, 1870; m. Lieut. Frank Tompkins, U. S. Army, Jan. 4, 1893.
   8.   George Francis, b. Feb. 18, 1843, d. Lyme, Jan. 4, 1864, ae. 20-10-16. (See Roll of Honor.)

(2) William M. Chase, b. Aug. 13, 1830, m. Jan. 1, 1853, Ellen Florence, dau. Nicholas and Annette (LeCain) Choate, b. Canada, Aug. 29, 1830. He removed to Lyme with his parents in 1844. He was seven years employed by the Passumpsic railroad, residing at St. Johnsbury, Vt. He was manager of a coal mine for some years at Broad Top City, Pa.; 1868 to 1876 res. Virginia; then returned to Philadelphia, in coal business. He d. Burmont, Pa., June 22, 1895, ae. 64-10-9; interment at Bristol. His widow res. Burmont.

CHILDREN

*9.   Frank Wilson, b. Lyme, Oct. 7, 1853.
  10.   Gorge Minot, b. St. Johnsbury, Vt., Aug. 3, 1855; m. April, 1881, Minnie Allen, West Newton, Mass. He was connected with United States Arsenal, Philadelphia, Pa.
  11.   Carrie Deane, b. St. J., May 10, 1860.
  12.   Fred Melville, b. Broad Top City, Pa., Jan. 24, 1865; m. Feb. 22, 1872, Ellen Stark, Spring Brook, Pa.; res. Wilkesbarre, Pa.
  13.   Edward Berwind, b. B. T. C., Feb. 15, 1868; m. June 2, 1890, Jane Melone, Germantown, Pa. Address, Burmont, Pa.

(3) Hannibal Chase, b. May 14, 1832, m. Oct. 27, 1856, Marinda H., dau. Alvah and Mary (Hall) Jeffers, b. Lyme, July 10, 1835. He is an extensive farmer in Lyme.

CHILDREN

  14.   William Little, b. New Haven, Conn., Sept. 21, 1860; m. Dec. 18, 1901, Mary A. Place, Highgate, Vt. Res. Lyme; commercial traveler.
  15.   Sally Minot, b. Lyme, Mar. 8, 1870; m. Mar. 11, 1896, Charles E. Palmer, farmer, Lyme. Child:
       a.   Sally Marinda.
  16.   Mary Marinda Jeffers, b. L., Mar. 17, 1872; m. Sept. 4, 1898, Fred R. Graham; res. Stoneham, Mass. Agent American Express company.

(4) Josiah B. Chase, b. Jan. 24, 1834, m. Nov. 15, 1865, Elizabeth Ann, dau. of Daniel H., and Elizabeth Belknap, b. Boston, Mass., July 2, 1840. He was for many years the senior member of the firm of Porter Brothers & Co., Boston, wholesale

dealers in small wares. He d. at his home in West Newton, Mass., Sept. 16, 1899, ae. 65-7-22.

CHILDREN

17. Agnes Greenwood, b. Catonsville, Md., Feb. 16, 1867.
18. Porter Belknap, b. Boston, Mass., Feb. 20, 1872.
19. Josiah Brown, b. West Newton, Mass., Oct. 5, 1875.
20. Ralph Minot, b. W. N., Feb. 14, 1878.

(5) Charles W. Chase, b. Aug. 29, 1836, m. Feb. —, 1855, Rosan Emily, dau. of Micah and Emily (Wells) Hoyt (See), b, Bristol, Apr. 24, 1835. He d. at Lynchburg, Va., June 10, 1876, ae. 39-9-11. Mrs. Chase res. Bristol.

CHILD

21. William Henry, b. Bristol, Nov. 6, 1858; d. Bristol, June 15. 1865, ae. 6-7-9.

(6) Henry M. Chase, b. June 13, 1838, served in the First Regt. Vermont Vols., in the Civil war in 1861. He graduated at the Dartmouth Medical school in 1863, and in December, 1863, was appointed assistant surgeon U. S. Navy. (See Roll of Honor.) He graduated in medicine again at Medical College, University of Pennsylvania, in 1866, and same year settled in Lawrence, Mass., where he has since been in practice. He m., June 22, 1869, Mary Esther, dau. Irenus and Mary Esther Hamilton, b. Lyme, June 13, 1845. He was a member of the Military Order Loyal Legion of United States, Commandery of Massachusetts. He d. Lawrence, June 15, 1903, ae. 65-0-2.

CHILDREN

22. Mabel Hamilton, b. Lawrence, June 24, 1870; d. Aug. 24, 1870.
23. Mary Hamilton, b. L., Aug. 31, 1872.
24. Henry Melville, b. L., July 28, 1874; graduated Dartmouth, 1897, and from Harvard Medical school, 1901. Is house surgeon, Massachusetts General Hospital, Boston; member Boston Medical Library and Massachusetts Medical Society, and member of the Military Order Loyal Legion. Is a physician and surgeon, 308 Marlborough street, Boston. May 20, 1903, he m. Miss Blanche Knox of Andover, Mass.
25. Philip Minot, b. L., May 11, 1885.

(9) Frank W. Chase, b. Oct. 7. 1853, m. Jan. 3, 1877, Susie Blanch, dau. of Dr. Ludwel Lee, b. Lynchburg, Va., Jan. 12, 1855. He is a farmer at Sunny Side, Garrett Co., Md.

CHILDREN

26. Martha Ellen, b. Lynchburg, Va., June 20, 1879.
27. William Minot, b. L., June 15, 1881; res. Windber, Somerset Co., Pa.
28. Julia Lee, b. Philadelphia, Pa., Apr. 8, 1885; d. July 7, 1885.
29. Charles, b. P., Nov. 23, 1886; d. Nov. 23, 1886.
30. Frank Lee, b. P., Nov. 30, 1888.
31. Lucie Dean, b. P., July 8, 1892.
32. Margarett Barr, b. P., July 16, ——.

1. David Chase, son of William and Phebe (Piper) Chase, b. probably in Sanbornton, June 19, 1766, m. Anna Taylor, dau. of Jonathan, Sept. 19, 1786. She was b. Sanbornton, May 7, 1770, and d. in Bristol, Apr. 12, 1853, ae. 82-11-5. They settled in Bristol about 1826, purchasing the Chase farm in Dist. No. 9. He suffered amputation of leg as the result of a fever sore, from which he d. Dec. 19, 1835, ae. 69-6-0. He had eight children, b. in Sanbornton and New Hampton, of which the third was

2. Deacon David Chase, b. Sanbornton, Mar. 31, 1792. He m., Feb. 24, 1816, Annie Russell, of Meredith, and came to Bristol with his parents. He was a farmer and d. Bristol, Aug. 3, 1871, ae. 79-4-2. She d. Bristol, Mar. 31, 1875, ae. 82-9-.

CHILDREN

3. Mary Ann, b. New Hampton, Dec. 21, 1816; m. Hanson Beede, Dec. 17, 1839, and res. Meredith. She d. Mar. 27, 1857, ae. 40-3-6. Five daughters. He m. (2) 1858, Miss Sarah E. Hackett. He d. Jan. 26, 1903.

*4. Daniel S., b. New Hampton, Nov. 14, 1818.

5. Nathaniel Russell, b. N. H., Feb. 14, 1821; d. Nov. 29, 1845, ae. 24-9-5; unm.

*6. Nicholas Taylor, b. N. H., May 14, 1823.

7. Lovina Maria, b. N. H., Dec. 23, 1826; m. Jonas Nickelson, Feb. 24, 1859. They res. till 1893, in Tennessee, when they removed to South Lake Weir, where he d. May 2, 1896, and where she now res.

*8. David M., b. Bristol, Mar. 31, 1828.

9. Jonathan, b. B., July 17, 1830; d. Dec. 27, 1832, ae. 2-5-10.

10. Emeline Hill, b. B., Mar. 26, 1833 She was a graduate of Thetford (Vt.) Seminary, class of 1858, and taught school in Illinois. She m. Oct. 19, 1861, Capt. Joseph T. Brown. He was captain in the 52nd Illinois Vols. in Civil war, and later judge of Rone Co., Ill. He d. Sept., 1866, in Donder, Ill. She d. Gallatin, Tenn., May, 1874, ae. 41-2-. Child:

   a. Charles, b. Sept., 1865; d. Apr. 1866.

11. John Franklin, b. B., Mar. 5, 1837; d. May 7, 1842, ae. 5-2-2.

12. Matilda Jennie, b. B., Mar. 7, 1841; m. Charles Lovel Porter, Oct. 29. 1868. She graduated at New Hampton in 1860, and taught in the North and South several years before marriage. They res. Tennessee and Mississippi, and in 1874 removed to South Lake Weir, Fla. Children:

   a. Annie Mabel, b. Columbus, Miss., Oct. 7, 1870; m. Frank W. Chase, of Providence, R. I., June 29, 1890. He d. July 7, 1890, ae. 19-9-0.
   b. Florence Chase, b. Dec. 29, 1876.
   c. Maria Nicholson, b. Nov. 20, 1880.

(4) Daniel S. Chase, b. Nov. 14, 1818, was educated in schools of Bristol and the high schools of Hebron and Plymouth. He taught one year in Virginia; studied medicine with Dr. Jacob S. Eaton in Bristol, and attended medical lectures at Dartmouth College in 1843 and 1844, and at the University of New York in '45 and '46, and graduated from Dartmouth Medical school in 1846. He also studied dentistry and practiced in Augusta, Ga. Given honorary degree of D.D.S. by Baltimore

College of Dental Surgery. He manufactured gold foil and plate for the market and when the war commenced was the only one in this business in the South. He left Georgia after the battle of Bull Run and returned to Bristol in 1862, where he practiced dentistry five or six years, went to Nebraska in 1868, returning in 1869. He m. Oct. 2, 1869, Ellen Fisher, a teacher in the High school in Bristol, dau. of John E. Fisher, of Franklin, and removed to Fremont, Neb., where he practiced dentistry and superintended the city schools, and laid out the Chase addition to the city. Went to South Lake Weir, Fla., in 1876, took up a homestead in the woods, made brick for his chimneys and lime for plastering on his own land, and planted 20 acres of orange trees. After 24 years in Florida, removed to Medford, Mass.

CHILDREN

13. Annie Maria, b. Nebraska, July, 1870; d. Apr. 30, 1892, ae. 21-9-.
14. Edward William, b. N., Feb., 1872.
15. Daniel Walter, b. N., Sept., 1874.

(6) Nicholas T. Chase, b. May 14, 1823, m. Olive A. Huckins, Aug. 30, 1854. She was the dau. of Ira and Olive A. (Abbott) Huckins, b. Oct. 16, 1833, in Tamworth. He was a farmer on the family homestead, but a few years before his death removed to Laconia, where he d. Nov. 25, 1893, ae. 70-6-11. His widow returned to Bristol, where she d. May 12, 1902, ae. 68-6-26.

CHILDREN, all born in Bristol

*16. Frank Huckins, b. June 22, 1856.
17. Addie M., b. July 2, 1858; m. Leston L. Rollins. (See.)
18. Emma M., b. July 6, 1861; m. John Olin Tilton, Apr. 25, 1882; (2) June 1, —, Fred B. Huckins of Hebron.
19. Ira D., b. Sept. 16, 1863; m. Carrie Jennie Bailey, dau. Henry H., of Alexandria. She was b. Aug. 28, 1864, and d. May 6, 1887, ae. 22-8-8; m. Dec. 12, 1888, Mary, dau. Hiram L. Gordon, b. Alexandria. He d. Apr. 2, 1889, ae. 25-6-16.
20. Arthur T., b. Apr. 5, 1873. Is a printer. He m. Oct. 1, 1892, Clara J., dau. William T. Oakley (See); m. (2) July 23, 1899, Monica Mahar, of Franklin.

(8) David M. Chase, b. Mar. 31, 1828, m. Jan. 1, 1849, Mary Jane, dau. of Jonas Hastings. (See.) She was b. Apr. 19, 1829, and d. Mar. 7, 1897, ae. 67-10-18. He is a farmer and with the exception of a year or two in Florida, has always res. in Bristol.

CHILDREN

21. Jennie M. (adopted), m. Frost N. Perkins. (See.)
22. George Francis Leavitt (adopted), b. 1850; m. June 9, 1870, Nellie A., dau. James R. and Emily (Young) Adams, b. Hill, 1850. They res. St. Louis, Mo.

(16) Frank H. Chase, b. June 22, 1856, m. Nov. 24, 1887,

7

Mabel A., dau. Jonathan T. Batchelder, b. Wentworth, Aug. 16, 1869. He is a cabinet maker at Campton Village.

CHILDREN

23. Lewis Taylor, b. Bristol, Aug. 27, 1890.
24. Bertha Mae, b. Laconia, May 17, 1892.
25. Gladys Pearl, b. L., Sept. 3, 1894.
26. Arthur Taylor, b. L., Apr. 21, 1897.

---

1. Stephen Chase settled in the wilderness of Gilmanton at some time previous to 1788, and here he cleared for himself a farm. He was residing here as late as 1822. He sold his farm for $1,700, put his money in a basket, and loaded the basket with his family and a few household goods into a hayrack, and traveled to northern New York where he settled. He had three sons and three daughters. The sons were Stephen, John, and David.

2. David, was b. Gilmanton, Feb. 7, 1788, and there, like his father, he cleared for himself a farm. Mar. 29, 1814, he m. Deborah, dau. of David and Elizabeth (James) Sanborn, b. July 23, 1789. In 1831, he removed to Loudon, thence to Bristol in 1838. He bought the saw- and grist-mill at North Bristol, for $600, and added a rye bolt at a cost of $300, and then sold about 1846, at a sacrifice, and removed to Danbury, where his wife d. Mar. 20, 1847, ae. 57-7-27. After one year he returned and made his home in the family of his son, Joseph S., for a few years, but later with his daughter, where he d. Nov. 8, 1856, ae. 68-9-1.

CHILDREN

*3. Joseph Sanborn, b. Gilmanton, Dec. 31, 1814.
*4. Ira Stephen, b. G., Nov. 21, 1816.
5. Eliza Sanborn, b. G., Jan. 18, 1820; m. John M. R. Emmons. (See.)
6. David Lawrence, b. G., July 28, 1822, m. (1) Oct. 6, 1844, Mary Kendall, b. July 1, 1820; (2) Jan. 28, 1867, Salome B. Potter. He was a merchant in Boston, and d. Dec. 17, 1884, ae. 62-4-19. Five children.

(3) Joseph S. Chase, b. Dec. 31, 1814, m. Dec. 20, 1844, Charlotte Harriman, dau. of John, b. Mar. 2, 1815. He was a clothier at North Bristol till about 1847, when he built and resided in a house on North Main street, later owned and occupied by John H. Durgin. He was a workman at clothing-mill on Central street; deputy sheriff in 1855. He d. Dec. 15, 1871, ae. 56-11-14. Mrs. Chase removed to Franklin Falls, and there d. May 27 (28), 1894, ae. 79-2-25.

CHILDREN

*7. John F., b. Bristol, June 5, 1845.
8. Charles Henry, b. B., May 27, 1852. A conductor on railroad at Philadelphia, where he d. about 1887. He left a widow.
9. Ida H., b. B., Mar. 31, 1855. Res. Franklin Falls, now in Boston.

(4) Ira Stephen Chase, b. Nov. 21, 1816; m. Mar. 22, 1849, Cordelia Page, dau. Caleb and Lois (Phelps) Simonds, b. Alexandria, Mar. 7, 1824, and d. Bristol, July 17, 1893, ae. 69-4-10. He d. Bristol, Jan. 19, 1892, ae. 75-1-28. (See Physicians.)

CHILDREN

10. Ira Arthur, b. B., Mar. 25, 1854; m. July 6, 1881, Abby Maria, dau. Hon. Cyrus Taylor. (See.) He has been a practicing lawyer in Bristol since 1881. (See Lawyers.)
11. Son, b. Bristol, Nov. 16, 1855; d. Nov. 18, 1855.
12. Mary Alice, b. B., Apr. 9, 1857; m. Seymour H. Dodge. (See.)
13. Daughter, d. Mar. —, 1867.

(7) John F. Chase, b. June 5, 1845, served in Co. D, 12th Regt. N. H. Vols., in the Civil war. (See Roll of Honor.) Was for some years on the Boston Police force. He m. Dec. 20, 1865, Elizabeth Finn, dau. of John and Mary (Wilkes) Finn b. England, Apr. 2, 1836. He d. Boston, June 25, 1901, ae. 56-0-20. She res. 113 Porter street, West Somerville, Mass.

CHILDREN

14. Charlotte, b. So. Boston, Nov. 6, 1866.
15. Frank, b. Boston, June 3, 1868; m. Nov. 3, 1895, Etta Fitzgerald. He d. Charlestown, Mass., Dec. 10, 1895, ae. 27-6-7.
16. Maud, b. Boston, May 11, 1879.

THE CHENEY FAMILIES

1. The Cheneys of Bristol are descendants of John Cheney, who was in Newbury, Mass., as early as 1635, with his wife and four children, Mary, Martha, John, and Daniel, all born in England. Later six more children came to their home. The fourth child
2. Daniel, b. England, about 1633, m. Oct. 8, 1665, in Newbury, Sarah Bayley. They had eight children, of whom the third was
3. Daniel, b. Dec. 31, 1670. He married Hannah Dustin. Her father was Thomas Dustin and her mother Hannah Dustin, the heroine of Contoocook Island, and thus the Cheneys of this town are the descendants of this famous woman. To them were b. eight children, of whom the second was
4. John, b. Mar. 10, 1701, who had four children, the third of whom was
5. Daniel, b. Newbury, Mar. 10, 1737, m. Feb. 17, 1757, Elizabeth, dau. Samuel Davis, of Newbury. He was a soldier in the Revolutionary war and was one of those who responded to the "Lexington Alarm" Apr. 19, 1775, and marched that night to Cambridge, and is supposed to have been the Daniel Cheney who res. in Lancaster, in 1780, and signed a petition to

the state that year.   He purchased land in New Chester, June 20, 1796, and came here about 1799, and made his home in the family of his son, Daniel, and there d.

CHILDREN

   6.   Moses, b. Jan. 9, 1758; d. Bristol in family of his brother, Daniel, about 1814, unm.
   *7.   Daniel, b. Apr. 17, 1761.
   8.   John, b. July 7, 1764, in Newbury, where he d. July, 1833 ae. 69.
   *9.   David, b. Newbury, Mass., July 5, 1767.
   10.   Sarah, b. Nov. 15, 1770.
   11.   Elizabeth, b. May 20, 1773, m. Ebenezer Kelly.   (See.)
   *12.   Enoch.

   (7)   Daniel Cheney, b. Apr. 17, 1761, m. Nov. 16, 1788, in Chelsea, Mass., Hannah Payne, of Chelsea ; (2) Dec., 1789, Susannah Badger.   He was in Concord in 1788, and is supposed to have come to Bristol about 1798, though his name is not on the tax-list for that year.   He was a soldier in the Revolutionary war, having served two months in Capt. Silas Adams's company, in Col. Titcomb's regiment, 1777, and several other terms, and was a pensioner as late as 1833.   His home was the dwelling-house recently owned by Prof. W. L. P. Boardman, on High street.   His name last appears on the tax-list of Bristol in 1830, and he was in Lowell, Mass., in 1836.

CHILDREN

   13.   Joanna, b. Jan. 27, 1797 ; m. Apr. 15, 1812, Hazen Colby.   Went to Lowell.   Had two sons : Rufus, who m. and d. soon after, and Hazen, who d. young.
   *14.   Daniel, b. Bristol, Apr. 18, 1801.
   15.   Hannah, " m. a German, was a cook in U. S. Marine hospital about twenty years.   Died about 1856, or '57, and was buried at Lowell, Mass."   The *Cheney Genealogy* says " d. unm. at Chelsea, Mass., Jan. 10, 1857."
   16.   Susanna, m. Sept. 4, 1811, Edward Eastman, and removed to Springfield, Vt.

   (9)   David Cheney, b. July 5, 1767, m. Nov. 28, 1792, Anna, dau. of Edmond Worth, of Newbury, Mass., where she was b., Jan. 21, 1773.   Soon after their marriage they settled in Hebron, and here two children were b., when they moved to Bristol.   In 1799, he purchased of Dr. Timothy Kelly, his home place on Summer street, and the same year built the one-story house that stood till recently where Henry C. Whipple has lately erected a residence.   While doing this, Mr. Cheney occupied Dr. Kelly's old home on the site of the Wm. G. Kelley residence.   He remained here till 1812, when he moved into a house at North Bristol in January that was commenced November before, from lumber then cut in the woods.   Here he spent the remainder of his life.   She d. Nov. 4, 1847, ae. 74-9-13 ; he d. Jan. 1, 1855, ae. 87-5-26.

17. Anna, b. Hebron, Aug. 27, 1795. She lived with her sister Mary in Bristol, where she d., unm., Sept. 8, 1859, ae. 64-0-11.

18. David, b. H., May 6, 1797; m. Dec. 31, 1826, Hannah Taylor of Bridgewater. Four years later moved to Haverhill, and lived there and at Lisbon for fifty years. His wife d. at Lisbon, Jan. 10, 1878, ae. 80 years. He spent his last years in the family of his sister, Mary, in Bristol, and here he d. Apr. 28, 1884, ae. 86-11-22. No children.

19. Abigail, b. Bristol, Jan. 24, 1799; m. Amos Brown. (See.)

*20. Moses, b. May 8, 1801.

21. Joseph,   } b. Mar. 5, 1803, { d. Mar. 29, 1803.
22. Benjamin, }   { d. Mar. 26, 1803.

23. Mary, b. July 24, 1804; m. William Mudgett. (See.)

24. John Webster, b. July 9, 1806; d., unm., Apr. 9, 1828, ae. 21-9-0.

*25. Leonard, b. Oct. 25, 1808.

26. Elizabeth, b. June 12, 1811; m. Mar. 7, 1844, George Locke and removed to Alexandria, where she d., Jan. 30, 1890, ae. 78-7-18. He d. Feb. 20, 1883, ae. 71-8-8. Farmer. Children:

    a. Mary Anna, b. Apr. 23, 1845; d. Mar. 16, 1869, unm., ae. 23-10-23.

    b. Edmond Webster, b. Feb. 13, 1847; m. Mar. 31, 1870, Susan Webber, of Orange. He d. Nov. 30, 1892, ae. 45-9-17. No children.

27. Edmund W., b. Feb. 5, 1814; m. (1) Nov. 30, 1841, Sarah Johnson, b. Apr. 18, 1810; d. Nov. 3, 1848, ae. 38-6-15; (2) m. Mar. 5, 1850, Hannah U. Johnson, b. Aug. 31, 1802; d. Apr. 7, 1881, ae. 78-7-6; m. (3) Sept. 6, 1882, Laura C. Rhoades, widow of Silas and dau. of Oliver Ballou, d. June 15, 1884, ae. 68-4-26. No children. He d. in Bridgewater, Feb. 10, 1898, ae. 84-0-5.

28. Sarah, b. Dec. 25, 1815; d. in Alexandria at home of E. W. Locke, Jan. 27, 1892, ae. 76-1-2. Unm.

(12) Enoch Cheney, son of Daniel, was b. Newburyport, Mass. He came to Bristol about the same time as his brother Daniel, 1798, and settled on what is now known as the Briggs place, adjoining his brother. He m. in Bristol, Dec. 20, 1803, Betsey, dau. of John Kidder, b. May 25, 1781. (See.) She d. in Hebron, about 1817, the children were given homes by relatives. He m. (2) Widow Hoyt, and removed to Concord, where he d. about 1825.

29. Elizabeth, b. Bristol, Aug. 11, 1804; d. Nov. 26, 1804.

30. Hiram, b. B., Feb. 24, 1806; d. Jan. 28, 1807.

*31. Alonzo, b. B., Nov. 14, 1807.

32. Elvira, b. B., Apr. 18, 1809; m. in Plymouth, Jan., 1834, David George, b. Plymouth, Apr. 18, 1808; d. in Wentworth, June 6, 1883, ae. 75-1-16. She d. Concord, Sept. 2, 1890, ae. 81-4-14. Children:

    a. Elizabeth Kidder, b. May 8, 1836; m. Henry H. Lovejoy, Littleton, Dec. 11, 1858. Child, Lorena Sue, b. Dec. 29, 1869.

    b. Frank Henry, b. July 12, 1840. (See.)

    c. Sarah Augusta, b. Aug. 12, 1848. Res. Concord. Unm.

33. Hannah, b. June, 1811; m. George Dearborn, Plymouth, and d. Plymouth, Nov. 17, 1880, ae. 69-5-. Children:

    a. Edwin, drowned when young.

    b. Georgianna, b. Oct., 1847; m. Charles L. Sanborn, Holderness.

    c. Mary, b. Sept., 1849; d. unm., Apr., 1878, ae. 28-7-.

7*a*

34.   Alvin, b. Pembroke, Aug. 16, 1813 ; m. May 16, 1850, Mary Smith Murphy. Went to Illinois and was living in Parker, Turner Co., South Dakota, in 1893, aged 80.   Children :

    a.   Charles Sumner, b. Winchester, Mass., Dec. 22, 1851 ; d. Apr 2, 1857, ae. 5–3–10.

    b.   Walter Gardner, b. W., Feb. 20, 1854.

    c.   William, b. W., Sept. 28, 1855.

    d.   Howard, b. Dundee, Ill., Oct. 2, 1857.

    e.   Jennie W., b. Sept. 24, 1859, in Dundee.

35.   Mary Jane, b. Bristol, May 2, 1815. When she was four years of age she went to Boston to live with relatives. In 1839, she went from Boston to Oberlin, Ohio, to obtain an education. She obtained a scholarship and worked four hours a day for her board, and continued this for five years, until completing the Ladies' course. In the winter of 1842, she taught the first school for colored children in town of Waverly, Pike Co., Ohio, in a log house. After having taught two weeks, a mob destroyed her schoolhouse by fire. At the end of two weeks more she had obtained another log house and again her school was in operation, and the term of three months was finished, although she was in frequent receipt of threatening letters, some of which threatened her with a coat of tar and feathers if she did not desist from teaching the blacks. Aug. 29, 1844, she married Rev. Seth T. Wolcott of the Theological School at Oberlin. Having completed his labors there, he was sent as a missionary to Jamaica, West Indies, by the American Board of Foreign Missions. They left New York in a sailing vessel in Nov., 1846. On the passage the vessel was wrecked and after drifting one week, reached Charlestown, S. C., where they remained eight weeks, while the vessel was undergoing repairs. They arrived in Jamaica in Feb., 1847, and were sent to Union Station Hermitage, in the mountains. Mr. Wolcott preached half the time there and half the time at an out-station, Mrs. Wolcott conducting services at home when her husband was away. In 1855, they left Hermitage, and went to Richmond, Jamaica, W. I., to a sugar estate of 1,000 acres, and formed an Industrial school to teach children to become useful men and women. Both sexes were admitted to the day and boarding school, the girls being taught sewing and housework, and the boys working on the estate when not in school. A church was also organized at Richmond at this time. The school was continued till 1869, and during its continuance 3,000 pupils attended. After closing the school they continued to do what they could for the good of the colored people until the death of Mr. Wolcott, which occurred in Dec., 1873. Mrs. Wolcott was postmaster ten years at Richmond, where she was still living in the summer of 1903, vigorous at 88 years of age. Children :

    a.   Henry B., b. June 12, 1848. He graduated from Oberlin college in 1870, was principal of a colored school in Chattanooga, Tenn., 1872–'74 ; returned to Jamaica and was ordained as a United Presbyterian missionary at Rosehill, under the Presbyterian Board of Scotland.

    b.   George L., b. Dec. 10, 1850 ; d. Oct. 25, 1856, ea. 5–10–15.

(14)   Daniel Cheney, b. Apr. 18, 1801, m. Nov. 24, 1825, Mahala, dau. Solomon and Phebe Copp, b. Sanbornton, July, 1803, and d. Wakefield, Mass., June, 1886, ae. 83 years. He d. in 1837, ae. 36 years. She m. (2) Moses Loverin.

CHILDREN

*36.   Charles Henry Rogers, b. Bristol, Jan. 13, 1827.

37.   Sarah Hannah, d. in infancy.   38.   George Fitzgerald, d.

39.   Susan Hannah, d.   40.   George Mowe, d.

MARY J. CHENEY WOLCOTT

(20) Moses Cheney, b. May 8, 1801, m. May 15 (13), 1828, Rebecca, dau. of Abner and Lydia Colby, of Bridge-water. He lived on farm at outlet of Newfound lake, and here he d. Feb. 1, 1869, ae. 67-8-23 ; she d. June 15, 1867, ae. 74-3-.

CHILDREN, all born in Bristol

*41. John L., b. Sept. 19, 1831.
42. Charles W., b. June 28, 1834; m. Abby Spaulding. He served in Co. C, 12th Regt. N. H. Vols., and was killed at the battle of Chancel-lorsville, May 3, 1863, ae. 28-10-5. No children. (See Roll of H nor.)
43. Lydia Ann, b. May 30, 1837 ; d. June 4, 1837.
*44. Moody S., b. May 31, 1840.
45. Joseph M., b. Feb. 13, 1843 ; d. Jan. 22, 1845, ae. 1-11-9.
*46. Henry Dennis, b. Apr. 28, 1846.

(25) Leonard Cheney, b. Oct. 25, 1808, was a farmer in Alexandria. He m. Feb. 26, 1838, Rebecca B., dau. of Dea. David and Rebecca (Bailey) Haynes, b. Alexandria, Feb. 27, 1813 ; d. Alexandria, Apr. 1, 1892, ae. 79-1-4. He d. Alexandria, July 9, 1877, ae. 68-8-14.

CHILDREN

47. Christianna Melissa, b. Alexandria, Apr. 29, 1841 ; m. Aug. 28, 1862, William Porter Seavey. He d. Dover, May 22, 1880. Children :
    a. Willis Ambrose, b. Alexandria, July 17, 1863 ; d. Feb. 16, 1868, ae. 4-6-29.
    b. Weldon Worth, b. Hereford, Canada, Sept. 17, 1865.
    c. Clinton, b. Dover, Apr. 27, 1867.
    d. Leonard, b. D., Jan. 18, 1869.
    e. Minnie May, b. D., Dec. 13, 1871 ; d. Jan. 19, 1872.
    f. Christianna Blanch, b. D., June 15, 1873.
    g. Fred Heyward, b. D., May 24, 1876.
    h. Hale Norwood, b. D., Feb. 7, 1878.
    i. Nelson Stanley, b. D., June 28, 1879.
    j. William Sawyer, b. D., Sept. 24, 1880.
48. Augustus Ferrin, b. Alexandria, Aug. 7, 1849 ; m. Aug. 25, 1872, Laura Young, dau. David, b. Loudon, Jan. 25, 1851. No children.

(31) Alonzo Cheney, b. Nov. 14, 1807, on the death of his mother, was given a home by his uncle, Reuben Kidder, where he lived till his m., Dec. 25, 1833, to Theodate Powell. She was the dau. of David Powell, and was b. Nov. 25, 1814 ; d. in Bristol, Sept. 23, 1864, ae. 49-9-28. He m. May 20, 1866, Lydia H. Powell, widow of Rev. David, and dau. Jonathan Fel-lows. (See.) She d. Oct. 21, 1884, ae. 75-7-. He succeeded Reuben Kidder on a farm at the base of Bristol Peak. He early united with the Methodist church and was for some years a class leader. He d. at the home of his daughter, Olive Jane, Apr. 19, 1886, ae. 78-5-5.

CHILDREN

49. Olive Jane, b. Bristol, Jan. 1, 1835; m. Joseph M. Mason. (See.)
50. Anna Betsey, b. B., June 1, 1840; m. Mar. 17, 1870, Daniel H.

Ames, and removed to Ashland, where he d. She res. Manchester. Children:

> a. Harold D., b. Ashland, May 22, 1880; d. Jan. 26, 1882, ae. 1-8-4.
> b. Austin Cheney, b. A., June 20, 1883.

(36) Charles H. R. Cheney, b. Jan. 13, 1827, m. Jan. 18, 1846, Sarah A. E. Willey, of Lynn, Mass. He left Bristol before his marriage, and res. Wakefield, Mass.

CHILDREN

51. Sarah Adelaide, b. Lynn, Mass., Apr. 20, 1847. Res. Wakefield, Mass.
52. George Henry, b. L., Feb. 14, 1849. Res. Wakefield.
53. Charles Augustus, b. Lowell, Mass., Jan. 3, 1852. Res. Wakefield.
54. Emma Susan, b. L., Dec. 7, 1853. Res. Wakefield.
55. Clara Annetta, b. Wakefield, Mass., Jan. 19, 1856; d. Dec. 5, 1856.

(41) John L. Cheney, b. Sept. 19 1831, m. July 7, 1853, Susan Hardy Jaquith, b. May 2, 1839; d. in Bristol, May 6, 1874, ae. 35-0-4. He was a farmer and lived at No. Bristol; d. Lake street, Sept. 17, 1884, ae. 52-11-28.

CHILDREN

56. Eugene Jerome, b. Hebron, Feb. 10, 1856; m., 1878, Abbie J. Colby of Hill; (2) Mar. 6, 1891, Georgia A. Peaslee of Concord.
57. David Oscar, b. Bristol, July 11, 1858; m. Feb. 20, 1895, Cora Ida Dana of Franklin. Res. West Concord.
58. Henrietta Ermina, b. B., May 20, 1863; m. Quincy S. Dustin. (See.)
59. Georgianna Grace, b. B., Mar. 3, 1868; m. Quincy S. Dustin. (See.)

(44) Moody S. Cheney, b. May 31, 1840, m. July 22, 1866, Martha E., dau. of Uriel R. and Ann (Conner) Rollins, b. Andover, Aug. 13, 1844, and d. Franklin, Aug. 6, 1891, ae. 46-11-23. Was for many years an employee in Train-Smith company's paper-mill.

CHILDREN, all born in Bristol

60. Bertha E., b. June 16, 1874; m. Aug. 8, 1893, Bradbury M. Prescott, Jr., and lives in Franklin.
61. A. Mamie, b. June 16, 1876; m. July 26, 1896, George W. Hammond, and removed to Brockton, Mass.
62. Frank, b. Dec. 22, 1879; d. diphtheria, Dec. 30, 1883, ae. 4-0-8.

(46) Henry D. Cheney, b. Apr. 28, 1846, m. Sarah Elizabeth, dau. of John B. and Hannah Kimball, b. Meredith, 1851. He has been an employee at the Mason-Perkins paper-mill nearly 30 years.

CHILDREN

63. Emma Frances, b. Bristol, Feb. 11, 1870; m. William Hunt. Three children.
64. Anna Belle, b. B., May 19, 1873; d. Sept. 29, 1873.

STILLMAN CLARK, ESQ.

65. George Wesley, b. B., Jan. 11, 1876; m. Nov. 23, 1895, Lena B.,
dau. of Hiram M. Worthley. (See.)
66. Charles Henry, b. B., June 28, 1879.
67. Sylvania Maud, b. B., Mar. 6, 1882.
68. Austin Leon, b. B., Apr., 1886.

THE CILLEY FAMILY

1. John Mowe Cilley was the son of Charles and Betsey
(Mowe) Cilley. He was b. in Andover, Feb. 29, 1824, and m.
in 1862, Susan Cilley, dau. of Saunders Herbert, b. Nov. 18,
1833. (See.) He d. in Bristol, Aug., 1865, ae. 41-6-. He
was a druggist in east-side drug store for ten years previous to
his death. She m. (2) Aug. 7, 1880, Ebenezer W. Mason. He
was b. in Hill, in 1819, where he spent his life as a farmer and
where he d. Feb. 12, 1898, ae. 79 years; she d. Hill, May 15,
1889, ae. 55-5-27.

CHILD

2. George Herbert, b. Bristol, May 15, 1864; m. Dec. 13, 1886, Ida
A., dau. of Charles E. Currier, b. Andover, Sept. 29, 1864. He was a
farmer in Hill till 1901, since then a farmer in Concord. Children:
    a. Roy Currier, b. Hill, July 3, 1892.
    b. Leon David, b. H., Jan. 13, 1895.

THE CLARK FAMILIES

1. Stillman Clark is the son of Jonathan and Matilda
(Gale) Clark, and a grandson of Jonathan Clark, one of the
first settlers of Danbury, and a soldier in the Revolutionary war.
He was b. Nov. 20, 1833, in Dickinson, N. Y. School teacher
10 years. He m., July 4, 1866, Frances H., dau. of Richard
W. and Eleanor (Currier) Stuart, b. Danbury, July 11, 1841.
He read law with Hon. Samuel K. Mason in Bristol, 1862-'64,
and was assistant postmaster. Served on quota of Bristol in
Civil war. (See Roll of Honor.) Admitted to bar, May, '66.
Removed to Danbury, where he was postmaster 16 years from
July, '66, and merchant. Now insurance agent and farmer.
Mason, Granger, G. A. R.

CHILDREN

2. Mabel Florence, b. Danbury, Mar. 3, 1867; d. Nov. 27, 1872, ae.
5-8-24.
3. Eva Jane, b. D., July 14, 1868; m. Arthur C. Brown. (See.)
4. Helen Ervilla, b. D., Dec. 29, 1871; d. Nov. 22, 1873, ae. 1-10-23.
5. Ida May, b. D., Nov. 8, 1878.
6. Annie Garfield, b. D., July 22, 1881.

1. Samuel Marshall Clark, son of Samuel and Mrs. Mary
Ann (Arms) (Fleer) Clark, was b. Alexandria, Oct. 24, 1855.

He m., May 6, 1891, May F., dau. of John C. Heath, b. Mar.
23, 1868, in Andover. (See.) A resident of Bristol since 1897.
Woodworker, Odd Fellow, Republican. No children.

---

1. Irvin M. Clark is the son of Mrs. Mary Etta Thurston.
He was b. May 26, 1875, in Alexandria, and m., Aug. 1, 1896,
Harriet A., dau. of Charles H. and Mary A. (Phillips) Tenney,
b. Alexandria, Feb. 3, 1878. He is a laborer in Bristol. Odd
Fellow, K. of P.

CHILDREN

2. Mary Beatrice, b. Bristol, Dec. 17, 1896.
3. Cora Nettie, b. B., Nov. 21, 1898.

THE CLAY FAMILY

1. Caleb Long Clay, son of William and Betsey (Long)
Clay, was b. Salisbury, Mar. 26, 1824. Jan. 15, 1851, he m.
Mary Emery, dau. of Joseph, b. Andover, Jan. 18, 1822, and d.
Plymouth, Nov. 20, 1854, ae. 32-10-2. He m. Dec. 26, 1855,
Jane, dau. of Aaron Stearns, b. Plymouth, June 1, 1823; d.
Bristol, Mar. 11, 1900, ae. 76-9-10. He settled in the Nelson
neighborhood, Bristol, in 1855. Buildings struck by lightning
and destroyed by fire July, 1884, and in October, following, he
removed to a farm on the New Hampton side of Pemigewasset.
This farm he sold in April, 1895, and returned to Bristol, resid-
ing on No. Main street till death of his wife, when he went to
East Andover to reside with his daughter. Official member of
Methodist church, Democrat, served as selectman.

CHILD

2. Mary Helen, b. Plymouth, Nov. 5, 1854; m. Dec. 21, 1880, John
G. Bailey, res. East Andover.

Amanda Stearns, a sister of Mrs. Clay, made her home in Mr.
Clay's family and there d. Dec. 6, 1894, ae. 63-9-0.

THE CLEMENT FAMILY

1. Alphonso Clement, the son of Joseph and Mehitable
(Evans) Clement was b. Moultonboro, July 8, 1835. He m.,
Nov. 26, 1857, Clara A., dau. of John A. and Polly (Adams)
Berry, b. Moultonboro, Apr. 8, 1832. Res. in Meredith till
spring of 1868, when he came to Bristol. He built and resided
in residence now owned and occupied by Chas. W. Fling on
Union street. Removed to Plymouth in 1878; to Somerville,
Mass., in 1884; was blacksmith. He d. Nov. 19, 1900, ae. 65-
4-11. Family res. Somerville, Mass.

CHILDREN

2. Elizabeth Frances, is a teacher in Somerville.
3. Laura May, m. in 1893, Walter H. Russell, of Boston. Res. Blue Hill, Maine.

THE CLEVELAND FAMILY

1. John Cleveland was in Bristol as early as 1779. He settled next above the Hall farm, his cabin being on the west side of the highway. He was deputy sheriff for some years. He was of Scotch descent, the son of John and Betsey (Downer) Cleveland, and was b. Aug. 13 (19), 1764. Tradition says he came from Connecticut with his sister who m. Jonathan Ingalls. He m., Oct. 10, 1786, Sarah, dau. of John Kidder. (See.) He d. June 6, 1809, ae. 44-9-23, and his wife made her home in the family of Reuben Kidder, and with her dau., Betsey, at No. Bristol. Methodists.

CHILDREN, all born Bristol

2. Betsey, b. Nov. 9, 1787. Unm.
*3. Downer, b. Aug. 25, 1792.
4. John, b. Mar. 20, 1795, went to Cleveland, Ohio.
*5. Smith, b. Apr. 5, 1798.
6. Moses, b. July 9, 1802, removed to Bath, where he m. Mary Hunt. In 1836, removed to Littleton where he d. Four children.
7. Sally, b. Apr. 3, 1805; m. — Fisk, and d. in Bath.

(3) Downer Cleveland, b. Aug. 25, 1792, m. Ruth Parker, b. Jan. 30, 1802. They removed to Alden, N. Y., where he d., Oct. 24, 1851, ae. 59-1-29. She d. Lake Mills, Wis., Mar. 24, 1892, ae. 90-1-24.

CHILDREN

8. Ruth Lorette, b. Lester, N. Y., Oct. 16, 1821; m. —— Whitney.
9. John Downer, b. L., Feb. 11, 1824; m. Oct. 17, 1853, Cornelia Ferguson, b. May 11, 1834; d. Feb. 12, 1857, ae. 22-9-1. He m. (2) July 20, 1859, Nancy Jarvis, b. Dec. 14, 1835.
10. Sarah Sophia, b. Apr. 15, 1826, at Clarence, N. Y.; m. —— Towsley.
11. Washburn Parker, b. C., Apr. 8, 1828; d. Oct. 19, 1872, at Lake Mills, Wis., ae. 44-6-11.
12. Rhodes Mortimer, b. C., Feb. 8, 1831; d. Nov. 20, 1891, at Osage, Iowa, ae. 60-9-12.
13. Josephine Betsey, b. Alden, N. Y., Mar. 12, 1835; d. Monroe, Mich., Feb. 24, 1861, ae. 25-11-12.
14. Mary Frances, b. A., Dec. 22, 1838; m. —— Hoyt.

(5) Smith Cleveland, b. Apr. 5, 1798, m. Oct. 27, 1822, Hannah, dau. of William and Mary Campbell, b. New York city, Dec. 25, 1806; d. Hailesboro, N. Y., May 4, 1872, ae. 65-4-9. He d. Spragueville, N. Y., July 6, 1877, ae. 79-3-1.

CHILDREN

15. Sally Ann, b. Jan. 5, 1824; m. Jehial Carpenter; d. Mar., 1858, ae. 34-2-.

16.   Mary Jane, b. Feb. 1, 1827 ; m. Oct. 27, 1848, Benjamin Cross ; d. June, 1884, ae. 57–4–.

17.   William Downer, b. July 3, 1829 ; m. Oct., 1855, Louise Rolph.   P. O., Gouverneur, N. Y.

18.   Smith Darius, b. Mar. 22, 1832 ; d. Oct. 15, 1857, ae. 25–6–23.

19.   Margaret Maria. b. Oct. 10, 1834 ; m Mar. 3, 1858, Victory Kitts; d. Oct. 17, 1878, ae. 44–0–7.

20.   Caroline Eliza. b. Mar. 9, 1837 ; m. July 3, 1858, Louis Collins. P. O., Hailesboro, N. Y.

21.   Benjamin Dwane, b. Apr. 21, 1841 ; d. Oct. —, 1846, ae. 5–6–.

22.   Della Amelia, b. Feb. 15, 1847 ; m. Mar. 28, 1871, Jay F. Hodgkins.   P. O., Gouverneur, N. Y.   Children :

    a.   Nora May, b. Jan. 10, 1872 ; d. Mar. 29, 1897, ae. 25–2–19.

    b.   Blanche Adeen, b. Apr. 3, 1875.

THE CLIFFORD FAMILY

1.   George Washington Clifford, son of Isaac and Sally (Somes) Clifford, was b. Alexandria, Feb. 22, 1823.   He m., Mar. 8, 1845, Sally E., dau. of Moses Atwood, b. Oct. 18, 1825. (See.)   He was a carpenter and farmer in Bristol, 1864–'82, most of this time residing on farm on New Chester mountain, where she d. June 8, 1880, ae. 54–7–20.   He d. Melrose, Mass., July 27, 1890, ae. 67–5–5.   Methodists.

CHILDREN

2.   Ida F., b. Alexandria, June 1, 1846 ; d. Sept. 22, 1864, ae. 18–3–21.

3.   Ellen F., b. A., Dec. 9, 1848 ; m. Scott C. Rowell.   He d. Dec. 8, 1868, ae. 24–6–24 ; she d. Apr. 1, 1869, ae. 20–3–22.

4.   Clara Frances, b. A., Mar. 24, 1851 ; m. Albert C. Wescott.

5.   Mary Etta, b. A., July 6, 1852 ; m. Theodore L. Carleton.   (See.)

6.   Emma Eliza, b. A., Jan. 11, 1854 ; m. Oct. 12, 1872, Hosea L. Hilliard, son of George R. and Harriet G. Hilliard, b. New Hampton, Sept. 6. 1849.   They res. Deering Center.   Children :

    a.   Son, b. Bristol, May 11, 1873 ; d. May 12, 1873.

    b.   Millie Leona, b. Epsom, Sept. 22, 1879 ; m. Frank R. Hilliard, Jan. 4, 1897, and d. Oct. 13, 1901, ae. 22–0–21.   He res. Pittsfield.

    c.   Ruth Clifford, b. E., Mar. 27, 1892.

    d.   Merton Brown, b. E., Oct. 30, 1896 ; d. Feb. 22, 1902, ae. 5–3–22.

7.   Daughter, b. and d. June 1, 1857.

8.   Frank Edwin, b. A., May 5, 1859 ; m. July 4, 1882, Dora M., dau. of Gilman D. Laney.   (See.)   She res. Malden, Mass.   Children :

    a.   Frank Eldridge, d.

    b.   Karl Eugene, b. Manchester, Jan. 11, 1886.

    c.   Helen M., b. Malden, Aug. 13, 1891.

9.   Sarah Jane, b. A., Feb. 1, 1862 ; d. Mar. 12, 1862.

10.   Minnie Lee, b. Bristol, Mar. 13, 1865 ; m. June 13, 1888, Frank E. Keniston, son of Joseph F., b. July 31, 1863 ; d. Apr. 6, 1889, in Andover, ae. 25–8–5.   Dec. 15, 1891, she m. George Linton Atwood, son of Joel. Res. Malden, Mass.   Children :

    a.   Joel Clifford, b. Nov. 6, 1894.

    b.   Louis Linton, b. Sept. 21, 1900.

11.   Hattie Ida, b. Bristol, Mar. 25, 1867 ; d. Bristol, Sept., 1867.

THE CLOUGH FAMILIES

1.   John Clough came from Sandown in the early years of the 19th century and settled on the farm later known as the town farm.   He m. Mehitable Ingalls, probably a relative of Jonathan Ingalls, of whom he purchased the farm.   The family were zealous Methodists.   He was a trustee of the church in 1814. He was a drover and bought cattle for Ichabod C. Bartlett and drove them to market.   His name last appears on the inventory of Bristol in 1822.   Tradition says he went to East Concord, and from there, back to Sandown, where he d.

CHILDREN

2.   Moses, was a merchant in Concord.
3.   Phebe Muzzey, b. Sandown, Sept. 18, 1794; m. Amos Sleeper. (See.)
4.   Mehitable, m. Rev. J. C. Cromack, a Methodist clergyman.
5.   Betsey, m Samuel Ingalls, and removed to South Newmarket.
6.   Polly.   7.   Sally.
A John Clough, Jr., was taxed in 1821.

----

1.   Benjamin Clough, b. Gilmanton, Dec. 2, 1809, m. Oct. 13, 1833, Caroline Carter, dau. of Jerahmeel Bowers.   (See.) They were both deaf and dumb.   The marriage ceremony was performed by Rev. John S. Winter, of Bristol, being repeated in the sign language by her sister, Alsa.   After a short residence in Tilton, they located at No. Bristol, where he became a manufacturer of furniture.   His place of business was on the north side of the highway, east of the bridge over the west channel of the river, and his residence on the south side of the road.   They left town about 1845; he went to the gold fields of California and later to Australia.   He d. Natick, Mass., Oct. 31, 1871, ae. 61–10–29.

CHILDREN

2.   Laura Maria, b. Tilton, Nov. 25, 1834.   Res. Natick.   Unm.
*3.   James McQuestion, b. Bristol, Aug. 19, 1836.
4.   Martha Ann, b. B., Feb. 6, 1839; m. Feb. 6, 1866, Henry F. Felch, b. Natick, Mar. 18, 1839, who served as captain in Co. I, 39th Mass. Vols. in the Civil war.   Res. Natick.   Children:
     a.   Harry, b. Mar. 3, 1867.
     b.   Mattie K., b. Nov. 12, 1869; m. Feb., 1898, William B. Pratt.
*5.   William Henry Harrison, b. B., Jan. 27, 1841.
6.   George Franklin, b. Manchester, Oct. 3, 1846; d. 1847.
7.   Clarence Bradford, b. Natick, Aug. 28, 1855; d. 1856.

(3)   James M. Clough, b. Aug. 19, 1836, m. May 15, 1858, Mary, dau. of Francis C. and Bridget (Carrol) Conlin, b. Ireland, May 15, 1837.   They reside Natick.

CHILDREN

8. James Ellsworth, b. July 6, 1861.
9. Harry Wasson, b. Dec. 24, 1863.
10. George McClellan, b. Mar. 14, 1866.
11. Frederick Howard, b. July 21, 1868.
12. Mary Elizabeth, b. Aug. 26, 1870; d. Mar. 26, 1892, ae. 21-7-0.
13. Benjamin Franklin, b. Aug. 11, 1872.
14. Clarence Bradford, b. Jan. 26, 1875; d. June 20, 1879, ae. 4-4-24.
15. Walter Henry, b. May 9, 1878.
16. Lester Irvin, b. Mar. 13, 1881.

(5) William H. H. Clough, b. Jan. 27, 1841, m. in 1862, Rebecca Stearns, dau. of Thomas, b. Sudbury, Mass., Feb. 6, 1841. They live in Natick.

CHILDREN

17. Annie Laurie, b. Saxonville, Mass., Dec. 25, 1862; d. Feb. 4, 1863.
18. Alice Florence, b. Natick, Sept. 6, 1868; m. William S. Willis, June 28, 1888. Res. 6,216 Madison Ave., Chicago, Ill.
19. Sidney Stearns, b. N., Oct. 24, 1869; d. Feb. 2, 1870.
20. Jessie Marion, b. N., Dec. 1, 1872; d. Apr., 1873.
21. William Irving, b. N., Apr. 15, 1877. Is a carpet designer in Natick.

THE COLBY FAMILY

1. Stephen Nelson Colby is the son of Moody and Sarah (Arnold) Colby, and was b. Hampstead, Apr. 18, 1823. Dec. 26, 1854, he m. Adeline Marie, dau. of Thomas and Dorothy (Hoyt) Robie, b. Sept. 26, 1835, in Raymond. They have been residents of Bristol since 1865. Laborer, Democrat, Methodist.

CHILD

2. Lisette Sophronia, b. Fremont, Mar. 9, 1856; m. Quincy A. Ballou. (See.)

THE COLE FAMILIES

1. Rev. Otis Cole is the son of Joshua and Amanda (Hinds) Cole. He was b. Stark, Dec. 25, 1832, and m. Sept. 22, 1858, Lucy Jane, dau. Henry B. and Harriet (Brown) Skinner, b. East Cambridge, Mass., Sept. 26, 1838. He is a clergyman of the Methodist Episcopal church; was pastor of the Bristol M. E. church four years from spring of 1887. He united with the New Hampshire Conference in 1865, and has continued a member till now, with the exception of two years, when he was a member of the Tennessee Conference and a teacher in the Central Tennessee College. He has filled nine appointments in the New Hampshire Conference. He is a man of superior attainments, unusual devotion to his work and an eloquent divine.

CHILDREN

2.   Harry Joshua, b. Spencer, Mass., Aug. 15, 1859; m. Apr. 20, 1887, Bessie P. Garland, who d. Aug. 3, 1897. He is a practicing lawyer in Haverhill, Mass.   Children :

    a.   Margaret Frances, deceased.   *b.*   Arthur Harrison.
    c.   Luella Winnifred.   *d.*   Helen Edith, deceased.

3.   Mary Helena, b. Spencer, Mass., Nov. 12, 1860; unm. House-keeper for her brother.

---

1.   Samuel Cole, b. in Methuen, Mass., m. Sarah Phelps, and was a farmer in Alexandria.   She d. Feb. 26, 1861, ae. 67, after which he res. in Bristol, where he d. Dec. 20, 1873, ae. 83-4-.   He was a Methodist of the olden type.   He had a family of several children.

One CHILD was

2.   Sylvanus, b. Alexandria, May 18, 1836; m. Lucretia Elizabeth, dau. of Nathan and Sarah (Crosby) Moore, b. Hebron, Dec. 22, 1839.   He was a farmer in Alexandria; a teamster in Bristol, 1867-'75, and in St. Johnsbury, Vt., 1875-'88; since which time has res. Stoneham, Mass. Night watchman and clerk.   Children :

    a.   Onie Etta (adopted), d. Mar. 29, 1902, ae. 34.
    b.   Frank Raymond (adopted), b. Boston, Oct. 10, 1888; d. Aug. 14, 1902, ae. 13-10-4.
    c.   Adrian Foster Moore (given a home), b. Groton, Nov. 20, 1872.
    d.   Willie Cole Moore (given a home), b. G., July 16, 1874.

THE CONNER FAMILY

1.   John Smith Conner, son of Charles E. and Louise A. (Chessman) Conner, was b. Lancaster, Feb. 19, 1856.   He m., July 6, 1881, Ann Minot, dau. of Gustavus Bartlett.   (See.) She d. Bristol, June 6, 1893, ae. 43-9-29.   He m., Nov. 13, 1895, Martha R., dau. of Ichabod C. Bartlett.   (See.)   He was a clerk in Cyrus Taylor's store, 1878-'79; in clothing business with Mr. Taylor, in White's block, for three years, under the firm name of Conner & Co., and again clerk for Mr. Taylor one year, when he purchased the country store on Lake street and did a large business till June 1, 1900, when he sold to Fred E. Noyes.   No children.   Now lives in Bristol.

THE CONNOR FAMILY

1.   John Rollins Connor is the son of James and Hannah (Beale) Connor, b. Andover, Oct. 13, 1840.   He is a descendant of the fourth generation from Simeon Connor, the third settler in the town of Andover.   He is descended on his mother's side from Dea. Enoch Robinson, who was captain of a company of

militia in Attleboro, Mass., and marched his company to Boston, on receiving the news of the battle of Lexington. The son of Dea. Enoch was Otis Robinson, the great-grandfather of John R. Connor, who entered the Revolutionary army at the age of 14, and was later the second pastor of the First Baptist church in Salisbury. John R. was a farmer in Illinois three years; was stone mason and bridge builder for the Northern railroad seven years, and station agent at Andover two years till August, 1877, when he became station agent at Bristol; resigned Nov., 1890, and has since been assistant agent. He is a Mason and a Republican. Has served six years as supervisor of the check-list and five years as selectman. He m., Mar. 1, 1862, Lydia Frances, dau. of Eben P. and Mary (Tucker) Yeaton, b. in Dover, Feb. 15, 1844.

CHILDREN

2. Carrie Ellen, b. Kickapoo, Ill., June 27, 1862; d. Bristol, Sept. 21, 1900, ae. 38-2-24.

3. Mary Isabel, b. Andover, Sept. 21, 1864; d. July 17, 1866, ae. 1-9-26.

4. John Fred, b. A., July 27, 1866; d. Sept. 2, 1868, ae. 2-1-5.

5. Charles Eben, b. A., Nov. 26 1868; d. June 8, 1872, ae. 3-6-12.

6. John Albert, b. A., Nov. 24, 1875.

7. Lou Frances, b. Bristol, June 21, 1879; m. May 25, 1901, William H. McKenzie. They res. Natick, Mass.

THE COOLIDGE FAMILY

1.   Charles Wesley Coolidge is the son of Rev. John Wesley and Nancy (Merriam) Coolidge. He was b. Sept. 14, 1852, in Leominster, Mass. Feb. 7, 1877, he m. Kate Lucy, dau. of Cephus and Eliza (Price) Brown, b. Independence, Ohio, Dec. 13, 1857. Her father was in the U. S. Navy previous to the Mexican war, and carried for life the scar of a wound on the neck received from a poisoned arrow fired by a native in South America. He served in Maj. Ringold's battery in the Mexican war and was near him when he was killed at Palo Alto. Charles W. studied dentistry in Boston, and one year in Harvard Dental college. He practiced in Leominster, Mass., two years, 1875-'76; was admitted a member of the New Hampshire Dental Society in June, 1879, being the fourth man to pass an examination. He has practiced in Antrim, Hancock, Hillsboro Bridge, and in Bristol. He res. on the New Hampton side of the Pemigewasset. He served five years in Platoon B of Capt. Piper's Battery at Hancock; and commanded Train Rifles at Bristol.

CHILDREN

2.   Charles Wesley, b. Hancock, Sept. 22, 1877; graduated from Simonds High school at Warner, in June, 1894; enlisted May 13, 1898, in

First Regt. N. H. Vols., war with Spain, and went south with his regiment. In July, 1898, was on duty at Maj. Tetley's recruiting office, Concord; returned to his regiment and promoted corporal; discharged Nov. 1, 1898. Is a speculator and broker at No. Londonderry.

3. Eugene Leslie, b. Hillsboro, June 15, 1879; m. Jan. 14, 1903, Lenora May, dau. Leroy C. and Abbie B. (Couch) Stevens, b. Warner, Nov. 10, 1876. Assistant dentist. Address, Bristol.

4. Helen Kate, b. Bristol, Apr. 22, 1881; killed May 23, 1881, by a cupboard falling upon her.

5. Jessie May (adopted), b. Maine, Oct. 12, 1882; d. Sept. 10, 1884, ae. 1-10-28.

6. Donna Brown, b. Bristol, Nov. 22, 1884.

7. Dora Gordon, b. New Hampton, Feb. 19, 1888.

---

1. John Wesley Coolidge, a brother of Charles W., above, was b. Leominster, Mass., Dec. 16, 1864. He m., Apr. 22, 1886, Ida Elizabeth, dau. of Warner C. and Lorenzo Viola (Hayward) Goodhue, b. Hancock, May 31, 1868, and d. Hancock, May 6, 1895, ae. 26-11-5. He m., Nov. 12, 1898, Florence Cynthia, dau. of Henry Ward and Nellie (Beckwith) Ware, b. May 11, 1877. Since Apr., 1901, has been a practicing physician in Bristol. (See Physicians.)

CHILDREN

2. Francis Wilbur, b. Dec. 13, 1889; d. Dec. 16, 1889.
3. Ruth, b. Nov. 5, d. Nov. 8, 1895.
4. Eleanor, b. Bristol, Jan. 6, 1903.

THE CORLISS FAMILY

1. Rev. Cyrus LeRoy Corliss is the son of George H. and Eva Gertrude (Harvey) Corliss, and was b. in Plymouth, Mar. 22, 1876. His grandfather was Gen. Cyrus Corliss of Plymouth. June 24, 1903, he m. Gertrude Violet, dau. of Otis W. and Agnes R. Potter, b. Mar. 15, 1883, at Charlestown, Mass. She graduated from the Melrose School of Music, taking a special course on the violin. He graduated from Wesleyan University in 1900, and was one year in the School of Theology, Boston University. He was pastor of the Methodist church at Lakeport, 1901-'02, and commenced his labors in Bristol as pastor of the Methodist church in April, 1903.

THE CORSER FAMILY

1. John Corser was a tax-payer in Bristol, 1839-'45. He m., Mar. 21, 1838, Marianne A., dau. of Brackett L. Greenough (See), b. Apr. 18, 1818. He was associated with his father-in-law in the operation of mills. They had at least one

8

2. Norman D., b. Bristol, Aug. 24, 1843. He served in Co. C, 5th Regt., and was wounded at Fair Oaks and at Cold Harbor. (See Roll of Honor.) He m., Oct. 8, 1866, Emma E., dau. of Horace and Emma (Boothe) Sessions, b. Lebanon, June 7, 1842. Children:

    a. Lillian G., b. Apr. 9, 1870.
    b. Harry E., b. Aug. 13, 1871.
    c. Herbert H., b. July 17, 1872; d. Feb. 22, 1887, ae. 14-7-5.
    d. Mary F., b. June 5, 1880.

THE COX FAMILY

1. Caleb Cox, son of John and Mary Brown (Smyth) Cox, was b. Holderness, Aug. 21, 1810. He m., July 8, 1841, Caroline, dau. of Capt. Thomas and Miriam (Cox) Cox, b. Holderness, July 31, 1821. Caleb Cox was a farmer and drover. He represented Holderness in the legislatures of 1851 and '52; was selectman twelve years, and was recruiting officer for the town during the Civil war. Both he and his wife were lifelong members of the Free Baptist church. They removed to Bristol about 1883, where he d. Oct. 17, 1887, ae. 77-1-26. Mrs. Cox is living in Meredith.

2. Winfield Scott, b. Holderness, Nov. 20, 1842; m. June 5, 1869, Sarah L. Perkins, and res. Center Harbor. Farmer. Has been deputy sheriff and trader. No children.

3. Mary Abbie, b. H., Mar. 28, 1849; d. Jan. 29, 1851, ae. 1-10-1.

4. Carrie Ella, b. H., May 31, 1853; d. Oct. 28, 1876, ae. 23-4-27.

5. Wilmer Caleb, b. H., June 24, 1858; m. Mar. 5, 1882, Emma Maria, dau. John C. and Maria (Mason) Avery, b. Meredith, Dec. 9, 1863. They came to Bristol in Mar., 1883. After working one year in a paper-mill, he entered the store of Hon. Cyrus Taylor as clerk, where he remained six years. He then entered the clothing store of Charles H. Dickinson, where he has remained, with the exception of a year and a half at Meredith and Newbury, Vt., till the present time. He is a past master of Union Lodge, A. F. and A. M., and a prominent Republican. He represented Bristol in the legislature of 1901. No children.

THE CRAWFORD FAMILIES

1. The Crawfords are of Scottish descent. The name of Thomas Crawford appears in Hampstead as early as Jan. 1, 1743, when it was attached to a petition to "His Majesties Council and House of Representatives." In a muster roll of Capt. Abraham Parry's company, raised for the Crown Point expedition in 1756, is found the name of Thomas Crawford, of Hampstead. In 1764, his name appears as one of the signers of an agreement "to Settle the Long and unhappy Dispute that has Subsisted under the said freeholders of Hampstead that Settled under the Haverhill and Amesbury Titles; and the Proprietors of Kingston or Clamers under them." This is evidently

the "Thomas Crawford, of Hampstead," who settled in what is now Bridgewater, in 1768. His son,

2. Thomas Crawford, later Colonel, had preceded him and was the first settler within the present limits of that town. June 21, 1766, when only nineteen years of age, he purchased 400 acres of land in Bridgewater, and soon after settled on Lot 9, First Division, now the farm of Sherman S. Fletcher. His log cabin stood a few rods west of the buildings now standing. One hundred years ago, and a little later, the Crawfords of Bridgewater were very numerous. Ezra Crawford, Capt. Jonathan Crawford, Robert Crawford, and John Crawford had large families, but the name disappeared from the town records many years ago. Col. Thomas Crawford had a family, but the most persistent efforts, continued through several years, have failed to discover more than fragments of a genealogy. It appears from the town records that "Thomas Crawford, Jr., married, Nov. 21, 1811, Mrs. Polly Peaslee." This was probably a son of Col. Crawford. Thomas Crawford, Jr., had at least two children: Jane, b. Jan. 5, 1812, and William, b. June 20, 1813. Tradition says that the Crawfords of Bridgewater settled Crawfordville, Ind.; but all efforts to obtain information from Crawfords now living there have been fruitless.

Col. Thomas Crawford, as appears from dates given at the time of his enlistment in the continental army, was b. about 1749, probably in Hampstead. He enlisted from New Chester, July 11, 1775, and served as sergeant in Capt. Osgood's company of Rangers in the Northern army, and was discharged in December, following. In June, 1776, he was member of the committee of safety of New Chester, and signed a petition to the "Colony Committee" for arms and ammunition for local defense. In the Bennington campaign he served as sergeant major in Col. David Hobart's regiment. After the war he is said to have commanded the regiment of local militia. He served as moderator of the annual town meeting in New Chester, two years; as selectman of New Chester, 11 years, and subsequently of Bridgewater, 15 years. He served 21 years as town clerk of Bridgewater, and four years as treasurer. He represented his district or town (See Political History) in the legislature 13 times, first in 1787, and last in 1806. In 1791, he was given a seat contested by "Mr. Shattuck." He represented his district in the convention that convened at Exeter, Feb. 13, 1788, to ratify the constitution of the United States; and in the convention that convened at Concord, Sept. 7, 1791. He served as justice of the peace many years. He was one of the leaders of the house of representatives; was at the head of some of the most important committees, and frequently served on special committees. He was evidently one of the progressive men of his day, and his vote is recorded as in favor of such measures as the establishment of post-routes and liberal pay for the post-riders. He did not hesitate to protest against allowing the president of the state to fill the office of district judge of the Federal court. He voted against lotteries, and against a grant of land to Rev. Jeremy Belknap as compensation for writing the *History of New Hampshire*, and against allowing each member of the House a copy of the history when printed.

Col. Crawford was largely influential in securing the incorporation of the town of Bridgewater, and he was designated to call the first town meeting. In manner, Col. Crawford was a rough diamond even for his day. Tradition says that on one occasion he sold 40 acres of land to procure means to attend the general court. He made his trips to the sessions of the legislature on horseback, with food for himself in his saddle-bags, and for his horse in a bundle behind him.

----

1.   The earliest known ancestor of the Alexandria Crawfords was William Crawford, who came to America in company with his father-in-law, Robert Graham. Tradition says that his son, Robert, then two years old, came with them. They settled in Chester. This son was

2.   Captain Robert Crawford, who was also a resident of Sandown. July 13, 1780, he gave his son, William, a deed of 276 acres of land in what is now the east part of Hebron and west part of Plymouth. Robert m. (1) Joanna Sanborn, (2) Jane Templeton, who d. July 10, 1833, ae. 91. He d. Sept. 6, 1791, ae. 68. He had ten children, of whom the second was

3.   William, b. Mar. 1, 1759. He settled on the land above mentioned in 1782, and about 1798 exchanged this land with Dea. Zebulon Ferrin for land in Alexandria. In going to his new possessions he moved his goods across the lake in boats, because there were no roads between these two points. He m., in 1786, Joanna Melvin, who d. in 1822 ; he d. Oct. 19, 1837, ae. 78-7-18. He had ten children, among whom were :

#4.   William, b. Plymouth, Oct. 25, 1789.
5.   Susan C., b. P.; m. —— Kelly. (Mother of Joseph D. Kelly, See.)
6.   Sally, b. Alexandria, July 29, 1801 ; m. Abbott Lovejoy. (See.)

(4)   Col. William Crawford, b. Oct. 25, 1789, m. Joanna, dau. of Moses Sleeper (See), b. Bristol, Oct. 5, 1801. He was a trader and farmer and accumulated a competence at what is known as Crawford's Corner in Alexandria, where he d. Apr. 8, 1851, ae. 61-5-13. She d. Alexandria, Apr. 25, 1864, ae. 62-6-20.

CHILDREN, all born in Alexandria

7. Mary Jane, b. Oct. 10, 1826; m. in October, 1850, George G. Hoyt, and d. Meredith, March, 1887, ae. 61.

*8. George Templeton, b. Dec. 20, 1828.

9. Charles Wilson, b. Apr. 8, 1831; d. in Iowa, July 28, 1855, ae. 24-3-20.

10. Laura Ann, b. Aug. 5, 1833; d. Mar. 31, 1836, ae 2-7-26.

11. Luther E., b. July 13, 1835; d. Aug. 29, 1836, ae. 1-1-16.

12. Anna, b. May 22, 1837; m. Woodbury Sleeper. (See.)

13. Almira E., b. Dec. 22, 1843; m. Kendrick S. Bullock, and d. Feb. 3, 1889, ae. 45-1-11.

(8) George T. Crawford, b. Dec. 20, 1828, was educated at Hebron academy, Tilton seminary, and Proctor academy, Andover. He m. June 29, 1851, Hannah, the adopted dau. of William and Mary (Pattee) Simonds, b. Pawtucket, R. I., in January, 1831. He settled in Bristol in 1866, and was for ten years engaged in the flour and grain business on Central street, where are now Clarence N. Merrill & Son. He is an Odd Fellow, and was formerly one of the leading Democratic politicians of the state. He was a member of the legislature from Alexandria in 1854 and 1856. In Bristol he served two years as selectman, and three years as superintending school committee. He was two years treasurer of the county and served six years as county commissioner. He removed to Boston in 1880, where he has since resided. He was for some years connected with the New Hampshire Land company in the purchase and control of large tracts of land in New Hampshire and Maine, and for ten years held the position of timber land agent of the Fall Mountain and Winnipesaukee Paper companies. He is now associated with his son under the firm name of G. T. & C. L. Crawford, timber land experts, Boston, and in this connection has been engaged in examining and reporting upon large tracts of timber land in the Provinces of Ontario, Quebec, New Brunswick, Nova Scotia, Newfoundland and Labrador, as well as in New York and the New England states. Mr. Crawford has also been somewhat prominent in forestry matters in New Hampshire, and has at various times written articles for publication on the subject. He is a member of the Massachusetts Forestry Association.

CHILDREN

14. William George, b. Alexandria, Mar. 12, 1852; m. Nov., 1882, Harriet E. Gurdy, dau. Joel. (See.) They res. in Boston. Child:

    a. Robert Leslie, b. Aug. 12, 1887.

15. Mary Emma, b. A., Sept. 30, 1854. Res. in Boston. Unm.

16. Charles Louis, b. Sherbrooke, P. Q., Feb. 9, 1862. He m. Shuah Mansfield Towle, dau. Royal Mansfield, b. in Milford, Sept. 22, 1861. No children. He is associated with his father as above.

17. Alice Isabel, b. A., May 7, 1864. Res. in Boston. Unm.

18. Caroline Maud, b. A., July 29, 1866; m. Apr. 26, 1893, George

Henry Trask, son of John Heminway and Mary Trask, b. Rochester, Vt.,
Sept. 22, 1864. They reside in Rochester, Vt. Children:
    a. John Crawford, b. Rochester, Vt., Apr. 2, 1896.
    b. Margaret, b. R., Mar. 4, 1898.
  19. Helen Gertrude, b. Bristol, July 13, 1868. Res. in Boston. Unm.
  20. Luther, b. B., Aug. 2, 1869 ; d. Nov. 9, 1869.

THE CROCKETT FAMILY

    1. Thomas Crockett was a resident of Kittery, Me., in
1648, and of York, Me., in 1652.
    2. John Crockett, a descendant of Thomas, was b. June
28, 1739, m. Mary Lane, Oct. 26, 1762. They lived in Hampton or Stratham. He d. Mar. 15, 1817, ae. 77-8-17. She d.
Sept. 18, 1792, ae. 48-2-. They had seven children, one of
whom was
    3. Ephraim, b. Stratham, May 16, 1774 ; m. Eliza Dexter,
May, 1806. He was a physician in Sanbornton, 1802-1809.
Became a Baptist clergyman. In 1816, settled over the Baptist
church in Grafton ; removed to Danbury, where he d. June 10,
1842, ae. 68-0-24. He had three sons, one of whom was
    4. Andrew James Crockett, b. Sanbornton, May 29, 1811,
and d. Bristol, Sept. 3, 1885, ae. 74-3-4. Feb. 20, 1840, he m.
Laurinda, dau. of Nathaniel Goss and Hannah (Pillsbury)
Haynes, b. Salisbury, June 16, 1815. On the day of their m.
they came from Danbury and settled on the farm now occupied
by Mrs. John W. Sanborn, on New Chester mountain. Seven
years later, removed to Pleasant street, where he d. and where
Mrs. Crockett still resides. He was a carpenter and house joiner,
and made seraphines in a small building just north of the Congregational church. Republican. Both were members of the
Congregational church.

CHILD

    5. Ida L. (adopted), dau. of Horace L. Sleeper (See), b. Woburn,
Mass., May 25, 1852 ; m. July 15, 1875, George Woodward, a trader and
prominent man in New London for 20 years. He d. Mar. 1, 1894, ae.
51-7-2. Mrs. Woodward and dau. res. in Bristol. Children:
    a. Horace L., b. New London, Mar. 28, 1878 ; d. Jan. 8, 1880, ae.
1-9-10.
    b. Florence Edna, b. N. L., Apr. 20, 1883.

    Mrs. Mary Ann Crockett, widow of Dexter Crockett, of Danbury, d.
at the residence of Mrs. Laurinda H. Crockett, in Bristol, July 6, 1897,
ae. 84-8-16.

THE CROSBY FAMILY

    1. Capt. Jezeniah Crosby of Billerica, Mass., m. Elizabeth
Gilson of Pepperell, Mass., and settled on Tenney hill, Hebron.
They were among the early settlers of that town. The oldest

son, Rev. Jezeniah, was a Unitarian clergyman for 50 years. The fourth son was

2. Isaac Crosby, who m. Betsey, dau. of Joshua Heath (See), b. July 4, 1796, and d. Hebron, Dec. 17, 1861, ae. 65-5-13. He d. in his 80th year.

CHILDREN, all born in Hebron

3. Roswell, d. Haverhill.
4. William Sumner, d. Poughkeepsie, N. Y.
5. Elizabeth, b. Dec. 11, 1823; m. Josiah D. Prescott. (See.)
*6. Milo Heath, b. Mar. 7, 1826.
7. Willard H., d. Poughkeepsie, N. Y.
8. Caroline, m. Leonard Ferrin; d. Hebron.
9. Mary, m. B. R. Tenney; d. Poughkeepsie.
10. Martha, d. infancy.

(6) Milo H. Crosby, b. Mar. 7, 1826, m. Sept., 1846, Harriet B., dau. of Ebenezer Heath, b. Canaan, Sept. 22, 1826. She d. Bristol, Jan. 4 (7), 1878, and he m., Nov. 14, 1880, Mrs. Francena Weeks. Mr. Crosby was largely interested in the manufacture of lumber at Hebron, where his steam mills were twice destroyed by fire. In 1862, he became interested in the manufacture of bedsteads in Bristol, and in 1868, became a citizen of the town. In connection with his son, Edward D., he was a large manufacturer of bedsteads and croquet sets in a building that stood on the east side of Water street, giving employment to 40 hands, till the building was destroyed by fire, Dec. 29, 1885. The business was continued in town, and in January, 1889, he was in business in what was known as the Pray tannery on Lake street, when he was for the fourth time burned out. He now res. at No. Bristol, engaged in dairy farming. Was for some years an official member of the Methodist Episcopal church. Republican, Odd Fellow.

CHILDREN

*11. Edward Dudley, b. Hebron, Apr. 25, 1848.
12. Frank Lewis, b. H., May 1, 1850; d. at Poughkeepsie, of typhoid fever, while attending Eastman's Commercial College, in Apr., 1871, ae. 21.
13. Son, b. H.; d., ae. 14 weeks.
14. Mary Antoinette, b. H., Mar. 19, 1853; m. Orrin B. Ray. (See.)
*15. Willard Everett, b. H., Nov. 13, 1855.

(11) Edward D. Crosby, b. Aug. 25, 1848, m. Jan. 4, 1869, Ella Malvena, dau. of Dr. Alvah Cady and Lucia Malvena (Taylor) Hall, b. Rumney, May 7, 1849. She d. in Rumney, Oct. 1, 1877, ae. 28-4-24, and he m., Dec. 25, 1878, Mae Lucinda, dau. of John and Martha (Packard) Bickford, b. Orford, Dec. 25, 1853. He was largely engaged in the manufacture of bedsteads and croquet sets with his father. He went to Ontario, Cal., for his health in 1883, and there d. of consumption, Nov. 21, 1885, ae. 37-2-26. She m. (2) George G. Shute and res. Woodsville.

CHILDREN

16. Kate Frances, b. Bristol, Jan. 18, 1873. Has been a kindergartner in Boston, Mass., since 1892.

17. Fred Bickford, b. B., Jan. 16, 1881. Graduated Boston School of Technology, 1903.

(15) Willard E. Crosby, b. Nov. 13, 1855, m. May 25, 1881, Nellie May, dau. B. Frank Brown. She d. Bristol, July 21, 1886, ae. 26. He was an undertaker in Hudson, N. Y., one year, when he returned to Bristol and here d., Sept. 4, 1887, ae. 31-9-21.

CHILD

18. Nellie May, b. July 15, 1886 ; res. Concord.

THE CROSS FAMILY

The Crosses of Bristol trace their ancestry to Charlenge, now Charlinch, Somersetshire, England. The name appears in the *Domesday Book* of William the Conqueror, also in the wars of the Crusades. Sir Robert Cross, of Charlenge, was knighted by Queen Elizabeth, in 1602, for heroism, as admiral, against the Spanish Armada and at Cadiz. He died without issue. His coat of arms was brought to this country by Gen. Ralph Cross, of Revolutionary fame. From it, it may be seen that the family sprang from Norman stock and belonged to the landed gentry of England. Closely related to Sir Robert were Robert and John, who, in 1637, sailed from Ipswich, Eng., to Ipswich, Mass. Robert settled in Newburyport, Mass. John settled in Methuen, Mass., where eight generations have lived in a house still standing. The latter brother became the founder of the line, as follows :

1. John, of Methuen, b. England, m. Dorothy, dau. of Robert Swan of Rowley.

CHILDREN

2. John, b. Methuen ; m. Sarah Peacock, 1708.
*3. William, b. M.

(3) William Cross, b. Methuen, m. Apr. 9, 1706, Mary Favoli, a French Huguenot.

CHILDREN

4. Joseph, b. Methuen.
*5. William, b. M., 1710.

(5) Dea. William Cross, b. Methuen, 1710, d. Mar. 9, 1803, ae. 93. He m. Mary Corliss, Nov. 5, 1741. She d. Feb. 17, 1805.

CHILDREN, all born in Methuen

6. William, b. Aug. 4, 1742; m. Elizabeth Ladd. He d., ae. 100-7-. A soldier of the Revolution.

7.   Jonathan, b. Oct. 1, 1743 ; m. Elizabeth Bailey.
*8.   Simeon, b. Mar. 10, 1745.
9.   David, b. Mar. 8, 1746 ; m. Judith Corliss.
10.   Stephen, b. July 25, 1749 ; d. Apr. 2, 1758, ae. 8-8-7.
11.   Molly, b. July 15, 1751 ; m. —— Hastings, Alexandria.
12.   Ruth, b. June 10, 1753 ; m. Joseph Atwood, Alexandria.
13.   Lydia, b. Nov. 6, 1755 ; m. John Harvey, Dracut, Mass.
14.   Abijah, b. July 6, 1758 ; m. (1) Elizabeth Parker ; d. Feb. 21, 1848, ae. 89-7-15. A soldier in the Revolution.
15.   Deborah, b. Aug. 2, 1760 ; m. —— Hazeltine, Hebron.
16.   Benjamin, b. Aug. 24, 1763 ; d. Mar. 15, 1766, ae. 2-6-21.

(8)   Simeon Cross, b. Mar. 10, 1745, m. Abigail Corliss, who d. Mar. 9, 1834, ae. 87. He d. Feb. 22, 1837, ae. 91-11-12. He was a soldier of the Revolution, a corporal in Capt. James Jones' Co. of Minute-men that fought at Concord, Apr. 19, 1775.   In 1778, came to New Chester and made the first settlement on what is still called the Cross farm on the river road, in Bridgewater, about three miles above New Hampton bridge. At the first town meeting in Bridgewater (1788) he was elected one of the selectmen, and served in all three years.

CHILDREN

17.   Mary, called "Polly," b. Methuen, Mar. 28, 1774 ; m. Elisha Bean. (See.)
18.   Chloe, b. M., Nov. 3, 1776 ; m. Feb. 18, 1798, Samuel Harriman. (See.)
19.   Stephen, b. M., Feb. 10, 1778, was a soldier of the War of 1812. Settled in Malone, N. Y.
20.   George, b. Bridgewater, Apr. 6, 1780 ; d. Jan. 6, 1862, ae. 81-9-0. Soldier of War of 1812 ; m. Dec. 27, 1818, Nancy, dau. James Heath, b. Dec. 15, 1795 ; d. Oct. 30, 1886, ae. 90-10-15. They had 12 children, one of whom was George Darius, b. Bridgewater, July 31, 1834. In the Civil war he served as corporal in Co. E, 12th Regt. N. H. Vols., on the quota of his native town, enlisting Aug. 15, 1862. Was at the battle of Fredericksburg, and at Chancellorsville, May 3, 1863, was severely wounded. Transferred to the 114th Co., 2nd Battalion Invalid Corps Feb. 15, 1865, and discharged at Washington, July 15, 1865. He was unmarried and the last few years of his life lived alone in Bristol, in a farmhouse on the old turnpike near the foot of the lake. Apr. 3, 1898, he was found dead in his home, where he had evidently d. the evening previous of heart disease, and fallen on the hot stove. His age was 63-8-1. An unfinished letter written by him lay on the table, addressed to the Commissioner of Pensions, concerning the disease that caused his death.
21.   Abigail, b. Bridgewater, May 31, 1782 ; m. John Gordon, New Hampton, and had seven children. He d. Mar., 1852. She d. Hebron, May 30, 1855, ae. 72-11-29.
22.   Simeon, b. B., Aug. 7, 1784 ; m. Jan. 29, 1807, Elizabeth Harriman, dau. of John (See), b. Feb. 27, 1786. They settled in Stewartstown. Five children.
23.   Lydia, b. B., May 14, 1787. Res. with her sister, Judith, and d. unm.
*24.   Abijah, b. B., Mar. 14, 1790.
25.   Judith F., b. B., Aug. 17, 1791 (Bean record, Aug. 13, 1792) ; m. Peter Bean. (See.)

(24)   Abijah Cross, b. Mar. 14, 1790, m. Sarah, dau. of

Enos Ferrin, of Hebron (Published June 11, 1815). Was a farmer in Bridgewater, where he d. Apr. 6, 1837, ae. 47-0-22. She d. Stewartstown, Feb. 15, 1872.

CHILDREN, all born in Bridgewater

*26. Sylvester, b. Apr. 17, 1816.
27. Lamira, b. Dec., 1817; d. Apr., 1823, ae. 6-4-.
28. Susan, b. Sept. 7, 1818 ; m. Otis Cross.
29. Simeon, b. June, 1820; d. June, 1823, ae. 3-0-.
30. Jonathan, b. Apr., 1823 ; d. in infancy.
31. Abigail, b. May 5, 1824; m. Chas. B. Heath. Living New Hampton, 1903.
32. George, b. Apr., 1827 ; d. in infancy.
33. Abijah Ferrin, b. May 23, 1829; m. Angenette Brown. Served as Ferrin A. Cross in Co. H, 13th Regt. N. H. Vols., Civil war, and was killed at Cold Harbor, June 4, 1864, ae. 35-0-11.
34. Stephen Franklin, b. May 17, 1830; m. Lois Tyler.
35. Alma Maroni, b. Feb. 2, 1836; m. Rebecca Poor; served in Co. H, 13th Regt. N. H. Vols., Civil war. Living in Pittsburg, 1903.

(26) Sylvester Cross, b. Apr. 17, 1816, m. Apr. 17, 1843, Clarissa, dau. of Simeon and Polly (Herron) Bean. (See.) She was b. Bridgewater, July 21, 1823, and d. Bridgewater, May 10, 1878, ae. 54-9-19. He m., Apr. 17, 1886, Mrs. Cordelia (Barrett) Clough, dau. of Ezra Barrett. She d. Apr. 14, 1894. He was a farmer, and succeeded his father on the farm settled by his grandfather. He came to Bristol in 1897, and has since made his home with his son, Simeon H. Is still vigorous at 87 years of age. Republican. Was a member of the Second Free Baptist church in Bridgewater.

CHILDREN, all born in Bridgewater

36. Simeon Henry, b. May 21, 1844; m. Sept. 1, 1866, Julia Ann, dau. Dea. John F. Cass. (See.) He came to Bristol in July, 1867, and is a farmer on Lake street, succeeding his father-in-law. In the Civil war he served in Co. E, 12th Regt. N. H. Vols., on the quota of Bridgewater. Has served as selectman seven years, road agent two years, and as fireward one year. Republican. Odd Fellow. G. A. R. No children.
37. Frank Washington, b. Apr. 4, 1846; m. Ida F. Knights; res. Lynn, Mass.
38. Sylvester Warren, b. June 13, 1848; m. Anna Robinson, Newark, N. J. Res. Crawford, Neb.
*39. Otis Ferrin, b. July 15, 1850.
40. Mary Nancy, b. Feb. 8, 1853; m. Feb. 7, 1874, Jacob A. Woodman, and d. in Bridgewater, Dec. 9, 1886, ae. 33-11-1.
41. Clarissa Mandana, b. Feb. 20, 1855; d. in Bristol, unm., Dec. 5, 1897, ae. 42-9-15.

(39) Otis F. Cross, b. July 15, 1850, m. Nov. 2, 1872, Sarah Augusta, dau. of Dea. John F. Cass. (See.) He settled in Bristol in 1878, and has been an operative in woolen-mill; res. corner of Lake and Chandler streets. Republican, K. of P.

CHILDREN

42. Una Estella, b. Bridgewater, Aug. 13, 1873. She was graduated

from New Hampton Literary Institution in two courses. She m. Nov. 28, 1900, Prof. Henry W. Brown, vice-principal of New Hampton Literary Institution. She is a teacher of music at same institution. Child :

    a. Marion Doton, b. New Hampton, Apr. 14, 1903.

  43. Otis Earle, b. Bridgewater, May 28, 1877.

THE CULVER FAMILY

  1. Rev. Newell Culver was b. Pomfret, Vt., July 13, 1811. June 25, 1837, he m. Caroline, dau. of John H. and Hannah (White) Aspinwall, b. Lancaster, Feb. 8, 1812. He was a Methodist clergyman. United with the New Hampshire Conference in 1833, retaining his membership till death. He filled six appointments in Vermont and twelve in New Hampshire. Was pastor of M. E. church at Bristol 1859-'61. In 1868, he built residence corner Summer and Spruce streets, where he spent most of his remaining years. He d. while visiting his dau. at Pittsfield, Mass., Sept. 22, 1882, ae. 71-2-9. She d. Pittsfield, Jan. 14, 1890, as the result of a fall down stairs, ae. 77-11-6.

CHILDREN

  2. Caroline Sophia, b. Sharon, Vt., May 5, 1841 ; graduated Tilton seminary, 1861 ; m. John H. Musgrove. (See.)
  3. Mary Ellen, b. Hanover, Aug. 6, 1845 ; d. Lebanon, Sept. 15, 1865, ae. 20-1-9.

THE CUMMINGS FAMILIES

  1. Daniel Kidder Cummings was the son of Daniel and Lois (Kidder) Cummings, and was b. Groton, Dec. 1, 1831. He m., July 4, 1853, Mary Jane, dau. of Joseph Bradbury, b. Gilford, Dec. 15, 1829. She d. Apr. 24, 1862, ae. 32-4-9, and he m. Nov. 7, 1863, Ellen M., dau. of John Brown, b. Springfield, Aug. 24, 1830; d. Bristol, Sept. 4, 1900, ae. 70-0-10. He was a farmer, res. Wentworth, Bridgewater, Franklin, and about 1890, came to Bristol. He served in the First N. H. Heavy Artillery during the Civil war. Congregationalist, Republican, member G. A. R., and Granger.

CHILDREN

  2. Mary Lois, b. Groton, Sept. 25, 1854 ; d. July 3, 1870, ae. 15-9-8.
  3. Orville Darius, b. Wentworth, Oct. 29, 1861 ; m. Hannah French. Res. Worcester, Mass.
  4. Annie Corinna, b. Groton, Sept. 7, 1865 ; d. Oct. 25, 1865.
  5. Emma Mabelle, b. G., Mar. 8, 1867 ; m. Edward F. Kendall. (See.)
  6. Fred Wesley, b. Franklin, Dec. 12, 1868; d. Feb. 26, 1870, ae. 1-2-14.
  7. Mary Alice, b. F., Sept. 12, 1870; m. Henry C. Varney. (See.)

1.   James Alfred Cummings, brother of above, was b. No. Groton, Oct. 1, 1843. He m. Ellen Hill, of Laconia, 1865 (?). He m., Nov. 24, 1872, Mary Chambers, dau. of William and Eliza Gilbert Chambers, b. Burlington, Vt., 1846. She d. in Plymouth, Dec. 1, 1895, and he m. Aug. 30, 1899, Nettie Belle Beatrice, dau. of Stanley and Emma Louise (Chambers) Jacobs, b. Hiland, Kansas, Aug. 25, 1874. He was a farmer; came to Bristol in August, 1897. Here he was a wood worker and baker. By reason of a fever sore, his arm was amputated a few weeks before his death, which occurred in Bristol, Sept. 1, 1902. His age was 58-11-0. Mrs. Cummings went to California, where she now resides.

CHILD

2.   Mary Lois, b. Plymouth, Apr. 5, 1885. Res. Bristol.

THE CURRIER FAMILY

1.   Trueworthy Gilman Currier, son of Dr. Edmond Currier, an early physician of Hopkinton, and Betsey (Stanley) Currier, was b. in Hopkinton, May 13, 1799, and d. in Bristol, July 31, 1874, ae. 75-2-18. He m., Mar. 24, 1825, Nancy Chase, dau. of Moses, b. Leominster, Mass., Mar. 8, 1804, and d. Bristol, July 21, 1885, ae. 81-4-13. Mr. Currier was a millwright and miller. He came to Bristol in 1836 and built a grist-mill for Brackett L. Greenough — what is now the lower story and basement of the main building owned by Calley & Currier, crutch manufacturers. Jan. 18, 1838, he brought his family here and moved into a small house on site of the Abel block. He later occupied for many years the "mill house" near the grist-mill, still standing. On completion of the mill, Mr. Currier operated the same on shares till November, 1849, when he purchased and continued to operate it till 1865. (See Industries.) He was a Republican and Free Baptist.

CHILDREN

2.   Sarah Ann, b. Mar. 12, 1826; m. 1848, William Hannaford, b. Boscawen, Mar. 27, 1822. They res. for 45 years in Lowell, Mass., where she d., June 7, 1897, ae. 71-2-25. He served in 6th Mass. Infantry, and d. Soldiers' Home, Chelsea, Mass., Sept. 23, 1898, ae. 76-5-26.

*3.   Charles Ransom, b. Hopkinton, July 22, 1828.

*4.   Theodore Elliott, b. H., June 16, 1830.

*5.   Cyrus Chase, b. H., Mar. 5, 1834.

6.   Lorenzo Merrill, b. H., July 30, 1837; m. Aug. 6, 1860, Hattie Susan, dau. of Albert and Emily (Hannaford) Hunt, b. Oct. 12, 1841, in Webster, and d. Penacook, May 19, 1878, ae. 36-7-7. He m. (2) May 30, 1879, Arabella, dau. William Davis and Abigail (Hoyt) Colby, b. Concord, Oct. 7, 1857. He served in the Civil war as first class musician in 2nd Brigade Band, 10th Army Corps, called Post Band, Hilton Head, S. C., from Jan. 13, '63 to July 4, '65. No children. Was for many years leader of a cornet band. Machinist, deacon Congregational church, Republican, Mason, G. A. R. He d. Penacook, Apr. 20, 1903, ae. 65-8-20.

GEORGE C. CURRIER

*7. George Carroll, b. Bristol, Feb. 13, 1841.
8. Martha Jane, b. B., Mar. 3, 1845; m. Frank H. George. (See.)

(3) Charles R. Currier, b. July 22, 1828, m. Mar. 8, 1852, Abigail, dau. of Moses G. Edgerly (See), b. Dec. 25, 1829, and d. Bristol, May 26, 1871, ae. 41-5-1. He m. (2) July, 1874, Mrs. Eliza Ann Walker, widow of True Walker, and dau. of Josiah M. Healey, b. Alexandria, in 1840, d. June 20, 1882, ae. 42; he m. (3) Jennie E. Hoyt, Nov. 12, 1885, dau. of Albert Fifield. She d. Alexandria, July 1, 1903, ae. 64. He was for many years a miller in his father's grist-mill, now farmer in Alexandria; was drum-major of 34th Regt. Republican, musician.

CHILDREN

9. Ella Augusta, b. Bristol, Oct. 28, 1853; m. June 5, 1880, William Augustus Sumner, son of Jabez and Fannie (Babcock) Sumner, b. Dorchester, Mass., May 28, 1830; d. Tilton, Feb. 27, 1903, ae. 72-8-29. No children.
10. Clarence Moody, b. B., June 27, 1857; m.; two children. Last known address, Elkhart, Ind.

(4) Theodore E. Currier, b. June 16, 1830, m. Oct. 28, 1852, Mary Folsom, dau. of Jonathan and Lucy (Green) Sanborn, b. Concord, Dec 14, 1827. She d. Auburndale, Mass., Aug. 26, 1880, ae. 52-8-12. He m., Oct. 4, 1883, Mary Arlina, dau. of John and Mary A. Oburg, b. Boston, Mass., Dec., 1851. He left Bristol in 1844; was a clerk in Concord 12 years, then in trade there till 1863; an appraiser in custom house, New York, for two years, since then an appraiser in custom house, Boston. Res. 124 Ashmont street, Dorchester, Mass.

CHILDREN

11. Helen Melville, b. Concord, Jan. 27, 1856; d. Jan. 4, 1857.
12. Edward Theodore, b. C., July 29, 1857; d. Boston, Mass., June 25, 1879, ae. 21-10-26.
13. Frank Sanborn, b. C., Apr. 9, 1860; d. in C., June 23, 1863, ae. 3-2-14.
14. Charles Clarke, b. Brooklyn, N. Y., May 6, 1864.
15. Jonathan Sanborn, b. Cambridgeport, Mass., July 2, 1868.

(5) Cyrus C. Currier, b. Mar. 5, 1834, m. Apr. 21, 1858, Electa A., dau. of Enoch and Hannah (Prescott) Brown, b. Belmont, June 1, 1838. He was a piano-tuner and res. Manchester and Belmont. Died at Belmont, July 2, 1892, ae. 58-3-27. His widow res. Belmont.

CHILDREN

16. Elmer Brown, b. Feb. 21, 1862, d. Nov. 7, 1866, ae. 4-8-16.
17. Helen Gertrude, b. Aug. 24, 1868; d. May 30, 1875, ae. 6-9-6.

(7) George C. Currier, b. Feb. 13, 1841, m. Apr. 26, 1866, Clara Ann, dau. of Samuel and Mary A. (Moulton)

Cox, b. Holderness, July 5, 1838, and d. Bristol, Feb. 5, 1899, ae. 60-7-0. He m. (2) Nov. 18, 1899, Mrs. Anna A. (Spencer) Fowler, widow of David S. Fowler, and dau. Charles H. Spencer. (See.) Served as a musician in Co. D, 12th Regt. N. H. Vols., Civil war. (See Roll of Honor.) Was a wheelwright from 1859 till 1881 when he engaged in the crutch business, which he still continues. Is a Knight Templar. Member of G, A. R. Republican. Served five years as fireward.

CHILD

18. Clara Blanche, b. Bristol, Nov. 26, 1871; m. Ansel G. Dolloff. (See.)

THE CURTICE FAMILY

1. Alexander Curtice, the son of Stephen, was b. in Antrim, Oct. 27, 1803. He m., Sept 25, 1832, Margaret Gamble, b. Aug. 31, 1798. He was a farmer in Danbury, Hill, Vermont, and in Bristol from about 1867, and here d. Dec. 29, 1873, ae. 70-2-2. She d. Bristol, Feb. 13, 1873, ae. 74-5-12.

CHILDREN

2. William Mason, b. Nov. 15, 1833; d. July 21, 1838, ae. 4-8-6.
3. Betsey, b. July 8, 1836; d. July 12, 1840, ae. 4-0-4.
4. Margaret Jennie, b. Apr. 10, 1838; d. Bristol, July 10, 1871, ae. 33-3-0.
5. John Warren, b. Dec. 12, 1839. He m. Lydia Woodburn. Was a druggist in Hinsdale, Mass. She d. He d. Washington, D. C., Jan. 1, 1901, ae. 61-0-19. No children.
*6. James Archibald, b. Danbury, Nov. 8, 1841.

(6) James A. Curtice, b. Nov. 8, 1841, went to Illinois at his majority, and, after six years, to California, where he remained four years. Returned to Bristol to care for his parents. At their death he succeeded to the homestead, the John M. Merrill place, a half mile south of Central square. Here he carried on the meat business till his death. He m. Oct. 5, 1876, Mary Melissa, dau. of William and Mary (Gordon) Eaton, b. New Hampton, Oct. 28, 1843. She d. Bristol, Aug. 27, 1878, ae. 34-9-29, and he m. Nov. 8, 1879, Almeda M., dau. Samuel and Anna (Carter) Emerson, b. New Hampton, Jan. 25, 1848. He d. Feb. 22, 1901, ae. 59-3-14.

CHILDREN

7. Mabel Augusta, b. Bristol, Oct. 6, 1877. Res. Bristol. Unm.
8. Abbie Anna, b. B., Oct. 20, 1880. Res. Bristol. Unm.

THE CUTLER FAMILY

1. Roswell Cutler, son of Roswell W. and Marietta (Craig) Cutler, was b. Shefford, P. Q., Nov. 4, 1861. Oct. 4, 1883, he

m. Mary M., dau. of George and Mary A. (Knapp) Jackson, b. Woodford, Vt., Jan. 16, 1862. At 15 years of age he commenced work for the railroad as messenger. He was station agent eight years at No. Troy, Vt., from which place he came to Bristol in May, 1895, and has since been station agent here. He is a Mason, Methodist, and Republican.

CHILDREN

2. Raymond William, b. Sweetsburg, P. Q., Aug. 20, 1884.
3. Harrison Roswell, b. North Troy, Vt., Apr. 21, 1888.
4. Charles Wright, b. N. T., Jan. 20, 1890.
5. George Jackson, b. Bristol, Aug. 6, 1895.

THE CYR FAMILY

1. Joseph Cyr is the son of Samuel and Emily (Marcotte) Cyr. He was b. Warwick, Canada, Mar. 26, 1858, and m. May 28, 1877, Rosy, dau. of Louis L. and Mabel (Rival) LaFlamme, b. Hyacinth, P. Q., Jan. 28, 1860. He was an overseer in Washington woolen-mill, Lawrence, Mass., previous to July, 1886; since overseer of card-room in Dodge-Davis woolen-mill at Bristol.

CHILDREN

2. Oliver Arthur, b. Lawrence, Apr. 21, 1878; d. at 3 mos.
3. Bertha Florence, b. L., July 8, 1879; m. Bert H. Jewell. (See.)
4. William Ernest, b. L., Apr. 26, 1881, m. Oct. 12, 1902, Nellie M. Ballou, dau. of Hiland. Salesman in store of Weymouth, Brown & Co. No children.
5. Arthur Delmore, b. L., Feb. 21, 1884.
6. Laura Blanch, b. L., Nov. 23, 1885.
7. Edward Herbert, b. Bristol, Jan. 13, 1893.

THE DALTON FAMILY

John Martin VanBuren Dalton, the son of Samuel W. and Mahala S. (Robinson) Dalton, was b. New Hampton, June 11, 1843. He was a farmer in Bridgewater till 1894, since then in Bristol, occupying the John M. R. Emmons farm. He m. Aug. 16, 1894, Emma, dau. of John M. R. Emmons. (See.) No children.

THE DAMON FAMILY

1. Amos Damon, son of Amos and Nancy (Standish) Damon, was b. in Malden, Mass., May 31, 1814. He is the sixth generation from Miles Standish. He m. Nov. 25, 1841, Clarissa, dau. of David Batchelder, b. No. Reading, Mass., Feb. 27, 1822. In February, 1843, they settled on a farm in the Locke neighborhood, where they remained till about 1859, when they removed to the old Worthen farm three-fourths of a

mile east of Central square. In 1875, they removed to Reading, Mass., where they still reside. He was a fife major in the old 34th Regt. militia, and in the Civil war served in Co. D, 12th Regt. N. H. Vols. (See Roll of Honor.) Republican. Methodist.

CHILDREN, all but first born in Bristol

2. Hannah Marinda, b. No. Reading, Aug. 22, 1842. Res. Reading. Unm.
3. Clarington, b. Mar. 2, 1844; d. Apr. 10, 1845, ae. 1-1-8.
4. Clarington, b. Jan. 16, 1846; d. Aug. 31, 1846, ae. 0-7-15.
*5. Otis Standish, b. May 16, 1847.
6. Clara Marietta, b. Nov. 16, 1849 ; m. Samuel D. Rollins. (See.) She res. Reading.
7. Laura Ann, b. Mar. 29, 1852. Res. Reading, unm.

(5) Otis S. Damon, b. May 16, 1847, m. Mar. 16, 1869, Carrie B., dau. of Oliver S. Hall. (See.) He is a farmer in Bristol. Republican. Methodist.

CHILD

8. Everett Leon, b. Bristol, Oct. 19, 1869 ; d. of heart disease, Nov. 2, 1889, ae. 20-0-13.

THE DANFORTH FAMILIES

1. Dea. Samuel Danforth was a descendant of Nicholas Danforth who emigrated from England to Boston, in 1634, with three sons and three daughters. His wife had died five years before. He settled in New Towne, now Cambridge, and at once became prominent in public affairs. He was selectman 1635-'37, and a deputy to the General Court in 1636 and '37, and was an original member of Thomas Shephard's church. "In 1637 he was one of the twelve appointed ' to take orders for a college at New Towne.' " He died in April, 1638. A son in the line of descent was Rev. Samuel Danforth, a tutor in Harvard College. In 1650, he was ordained as a colleague to John Eliot, the "Apostle to the Indians." In this capacity he labored 24 years, and d. in November, 1674. Another distinguished ancestor of Dea. Samuel was Rev. Samuel Danforth, the 4th minister of the church at Taunton, Mass. Dea. Samuel was b. Norton, Mass., Oct. 16, 1773. He m. Apr. 12, 1808, Mehitable Marshall, b. in Framingham, Mass., Jan. 30, 1787. They came to Bristol in 1844, where most of their children had preceded them. At Norton he was deacon of the Congregational church and he was acting deacon of the church at Bristol 40 years. He brought up his family in the puritan style and was noted for his even and consistent Christian life, and unfaltering faith in God and the Bible. He resided on Spring street, his house standing where George H. White now resides, where he d. Jan. 29, 1860, ae. 86-3-13. She d. Feb. 8, 1868 ae. 81-0-8.

CHILDREN

2. Richard Sears, b. Norton, Mass., Jan. 26, 1809; d. from the kick of a horse, Aug. 4, 1818, ae. 9-6-8.

3. Henry M., b. Hopkinton, Mass., Aug. 6, 1810; m. Judith Morse, b. "New Hampshire" 1814. He attended the New Hampton Literary Institution and became a Baptist clergyman. He was pastor of the church at Evans, N. Y., from Apr. 4, 1846, till June 11, 1865; and from Feb. 1, 1868, till 1883 or '84, over 34 years in all. He d. Aug. 22, 1886, ae. 76-0-16. Mrs. Danforth d. Evans, Feb. 27, 1883, ae. 69. One child, deceased.

4. Abigail S., b. Pelham, Mass., Nov. 12, 1811; m. Warren White. (See.)

5. Benjamin, b. P., June 24, 1813; d. Mar. 9, 1814.

6. Nancy M., b. P., Jan. 24, 1815; m. at Dana, Mass., May 5, 1842, Theodore N. Patterson, later a merchant tailor in Bristol. She res. Monroeville, Ohio, then in Minonk, Ill., where she d. Nov. 1, 1864, ae. 49-9-7. One son deceased.

7. Appleton Howe, b. P., July 8, 1817; m. Aug. 11, 1847, Frances Amelia, dau. of Z. and Almira Studley, b. Worcester, Mass., Apr. 27, 1827. He was a student at New Hampton, graduated from Madison University, Hamilton, N. Y., in August, 1847. The same year he went to Gowhatti, Assam, 1,000 miles north of Calcutta, India, as a missionary of the American Baptist Missionary Union, where he remained ten years. His wife d. at Rangoon, Burmah, Feb. 3, 1874, ae. 46-9-6. In Feb., 1862, he became pastor of the Milestown Baptist church, Philadelphia, Pa. In 1864, labored in the Army of the Potomac. He d. at Milestown, Feb. 14, 1865, ae. 47-7-6. Children:

   a. Elizabeth Jane, b. Gowhatti, Apr. 22, 1849; m. Mar. 5, 1874, Joseph B. Cope; res. 168 Herman street, Germantown, Pa.

   b. Nathan Brown, b. G., Apr. 27, 1852; m. Oct., 1882, Elizabeth Jones. Res. Wilmington, Del.

   c. Appleton Howe, b. G., Apr. 14, 1854; res. Florence, Arizona.

   d. Helena Frances, b. G., Oct. 18, 1857; d. at Calcutta, India, Mar. 14, 1858.

*8. Richard Sears, b. Pelham, June 26, 1819.

9. George P., b. Dana, Mass., Oct. 18, 1821; was a workman in White's tannery. He m. Apr., 1843, Fidelia P., and d. Oct. 21, 1865, ae. 44-0-3. He m. (2) Mary Wise. Child:

   a. Fred P., b. Bristol.

10. Almon Hodges, b. Dana, Mass., June 24, 1824; m. Hannah, dau. Benjamin Rowe, Nov. 8, 1849. She was b. Gilford, June 15, 1825, and d. Minonk, Ill., Jan. 15, 1896, ae. 70-7-0. He is a banker at Minonk. No children.

11. Mehitable Jane, b. D., June 12, 1831; m. Rev. Oliver P. Pitcher, a Methodist clergyman, Mar. 10, 1852; d. Mar. 13, 1854, ae. 22-9-1.

(8) Richard S. Danforth, b. June 26, 1819, m. Jan. 16, 1843, Amanda Melvina, dau. of Josiah and Rachel (Corliss) Hill, b. Alexandria, Jan. 13, 1824. He learned the brick mason's trade at Troy, N. Y., and came to Bristol in 1841, and was for 12 years foreman of Mr. White's tannery here; then part owner in a tannery in Woodstock for 16 years. He returned to Bristol in 1868, and has since resided here. Congregationalist, Republican; has served as selectman three years.

9

CHILDREN

12. Sarah Jane, b. Bristol, Nov. 16, 1843. Res. Bristol; unm.

13. Charles Richard, b. B., Feb. 4, 1845. Went to Minonk, Ill., in 1869, where he is a banker. He m., Jan. 29, 1885, Lizzie, dau. of Jacob and Phillipena (Monk) Knapp, b. Clayton, Ill. Children:

    a. John Charles, b. Minonk, July 30, 1887.
    b. Louisa Elizabeth, b. M., July 10, 1890.

14. John Samuel, b. Bristol, Nov. 30, 1847. He was a guide on the Magalloway river, Me., for some years, then established Camp Caribou, Parmachenee lake, a famous fishing and hunting resort of which he was proprietor till 1897, when he sold and went to Florida, where he is proprietor of a hotel at Stewart. He m., Nov. 30, 1885, Sarah, dau. of Enoch B. Knapp, b. Sept. 8, 1865, in Newry, Me., and d. Stewart, Fla., Feb. 2, 1901, ae. 35-4-24. Child:

    a. Richard Sears, b. Newry, Me., May 8, 1887.

15. Georgiana, b. B., Feb. 24, 1849; d. Feb. 16, 1852, ae. 2-11-22.
16. Harry Vivanna, b. Woodstock, Apr. 21, 1857; d. July 11, 1863, ae. 6-2-20.

Rachel Pierce, mother of Mrs. Danforth, d. in her family, Jan. 4, 1880, ae. 78-0-2. She m. (1) Josiah Hill; (2) Wm. Pierce.

---

1. **Abel Danforth,** m. Mrs. Rebecca (Hubbard) Willard, widow of John Willard, and dau. of Jeremiah Hubbard. They settled on the Danforth farm, next east of Danforth brook, about 1822, and there he d. Sept. 5, 1851, ae. 74; she d. Aug. 20, 1867, ae. 89.

CHILDREN

2. Esther Rebecca, b. Bristol, Oct. 20, 1820; d. in B.; unm.
3. Mary Ann, b. B., Aug. 12, 1822; unm.; d. B., Sept. 29, 1891, ae. 69-:-17.
*4. Abel Willard, b. B., July 30, 1824.

(4) **Abel W. Danforth,** b. July 30, 1824, m. Lucinda Hadley Edgerly, of Gilmanton. (Certificate issued Sept. 11, 1852.) He succeeded his father on the farm, where she d., May 30, 1886, ae. 64; he d. Sept. 15, 1872, ae. 48-1-15.

CHILDREN

5. Ella Frances, b. Bristol, Nov. 21, 1853; m. James Calvin Nowell. (Certificate issued Apr. 16, 1870.) Res. Franklin. Children:

    a. Henry Philip, b. Bristol, Sept. 2, 1871.
    b. Charles Alfred, b. Franklin.

6. Esther Rebecca, b. Bristol, Feb. 14, 1855; m. (1) Charles Hill, (2) George Shaw. Both d. She res. Franklin Falls. Children:

    a. Mary Leila, b. Andover.   *b.* Edith Luella, b. A.
    c. Georgiana Gertrude, b. A.

*7. John Wesley, b. Bristol, June 3, 1857.

7. **John W. Danforth,** b. June 3, 1857, m. Aug. 13, 1881, Addie Leona, dau. of Timothy and Isabel (Curtis) Curtis, b. Oct. 12, 1861; d. July 11, 1886, ae. 24-8-29. He m. Apr. 5, 1887, Addie Mae Lovering, dau. of David, b. Sanbornton. She

d. of malignant diphtheria, Mar. 19, 1889, ae. 23–1–, and he m. Aug. 30, 1890, Nellie J. Golding, dau. of Calvin. (See.) He is a farmer and wood worker.

CHILDREN

8. Lena Belle, b. Bristol, May, 1882 ; d. May 12, 1889, ae. 7 years, of consumption resulting from diphtheria.
9. Blanche May, b. B., Apr. 1, 1884; d. of malignant diphtheria, Mar. 4, 1889, ae. 4-11-3.
10. Daisy Maud, b. B., July 15, 1888 ; d. of malignant diphtheria, Mar. 12, 1889, ae. 0-7-27.

---

1. Benaiah Danforth, son of Benaiah and Patience (Hoyt) Danforth, was b. Danbury, May 6, 1809. Apr. 13, 1834, he m. Abigail, dau. of Caleb and Rhoda (Currier) Sargent. She was b. in Hill, June 23, 1808. They res. Danbury and Wilmot till 1865, when they removed to Bristol. He was a farmer and tanner. He d. Bristol, Jan. 27, 1879, ae. 69-8-21. She was living in Hill in July, 1903, ae. 95.

CHILD

2. Mary E., b. Danbury, Apr. 10, 1837 ; m. Aug., 1859, Thomas Warren Sawyer. He was drowned at Laconia, Feb. 4, 1873. She d. Feb. 7, 1863, ae. 25-9-27. Child :
   a. Charles Harvey Sawyer, b. Hill, June, 1862. (See in alphabetical position.)

THE DARLING FAMILY

1. Dea. Benjamin Darling is said to have been born in England, and to have moved from Hawke to Sanbornton where he carried on the first mill, and was an original member and deacon of the Congregational church at the Square 1771-'72. He m. Mar. 8, 1758, Hannah, and d. Apr. 16, 1795. He had six children, among them
2. Ebenezer, b. Jan. 11, 1765 ; m. Abigail Morrison, dau. of Ebenezer, June 26, 1782. He was a miller at what is now Tilton, and d. of consumption, Dec. 14, 1826, ae. 61-11-3. She d. Sept. 15, 1840, ae. 76-4-. Of his twelve children, three settled in Bristol :
   *3. Ebenezer, b. Mar. 16, 1790.
   *4. Daniel, b. Dec. 2, 1802.
   *5. Jacob Newman, b. Aug. 10, 1808.

(3) Ebenezer Darling, b. Mar. 16, 1790, m. (1) Sally Clough, of Northfield ; (2) Dec. 5, 1820, Abigail Tirrell, dau. of Jonah (See), b. Bristol, Aug. 27, 1790. He came to Bristol in 1835 and was a farmer in the Kidder neighborhood. He d. of lung fever, Apr. 5, 1875, ae. 85-0-19 ; she d. Sept. 5, 1881, ae. 91-0-8.

6. Jonathan C., b. Northfield, May 13, 1813, m. Caroline Richardson, and d. Sept. 9, 1864, ae. 51-3-26. Never resided in Bristol. No children.

7. Sally C., b. Sanbornton, Aug. 13, 1822 ; m. Osman Powell. (See.)

8. Joanna Lincoln, b. S., July 20, 1825; m. Benjamin F. Sanborn. (See.)

9. Harriet S., b. S., July 7, 1830, Res. Bristol, unm.

(4) Daniel Darling, b. Dec. 2, 1802, m. June 28, 1826, Harriet, dau. of Andrew Sanborn. He was a clothier at No. Bristol, 1826-'36. He d. Lowell, Mass., May 28, 1857, ae. 54-5-26. She d. in Franklin, Oct. 8, 1867, ae. 64.

10. Eliza Ann, m. 1870, Henry C. Greene ; res. New York City. Two children, both deceased.

11. Harriet E., b. 1834; d. in Bristol, Sept. 30, 1835, being fatally burned.

12. Mary E., b. 1838 ; d. Mar. 6, 1841, ae. 3 years.

(5) Jacob N. Darling, b. Aug. 10, 1808, m. Sept. 13, 1831, Abigail Tappan Brown, dau. of Amos and Nancy Brown, of Franklin, b. Wheelock, Vt., Mar. 28, 1808. He had a clothing-mill at No. Bristol, 1830-'35: removed to Whitefield; in 1841, returned to Bristol. Was a druggist and merchant tailor where is now the west-side drug store. He was for many years a prominent member of the Methodist church. She was ever present at the bedside of the afflicted. He resided on Lake street, where he d. June 8, 1859, ae. 50-9-28 ; she d. Apr. 6, 1880, ae. 72-0-8.

13 Harriet Elizabeth, b. Whitefield, July 24, 1838 ; m. Moody O. Edgerly. (See.)

14. Charles Walker, b. W., and d., ae. 8 months.

15. Mary Minot, b. B., 1842, and d. Feb. 1, 1844, ae. 1-6-.

16. George Ambrose, b. Bristol, July 6, 1846. Merchant in Boston many years. Unm.

THE DAVIS FAMILIES

1. Rev. Hezekiah Davis, b. Stafford, Conn., June 4, 1785, was an itinerant preacher of the Methodist Episcopal church. Jan. 29, 1816, he m. Sally, dau. of Maj. Theophilous Sanborn, b. Sept. 17, 1793. (See.) He remained in Bristol till 1819, when he located in Stafford, Conn.; in 1832, went to Springfield, Mass., and, in 1835, emigrated to Hartsgrove, O., where he was one of the first settlers in the woods of that section. Both he and his wife were highly esteemed for their many virtues. He d. Hartsgrove, O., Jan. 8, 1861, ae. 75-7-4 ; she d. same place, Apr 26, 1858, ae, 64-7-9.

2. William, b. Bristol, Jan. 25, 1817; d. Trumbull, O., Nov. 14, 1875, ae. 58-9-19. He m. Martha Cook, who d. 1877, leaving a dau. who d. four years later. He m. (2) Charlotte Clark, who d. twelve years later, leaving a dau. He m. (3) Sarah Ann Andrus, who d. five years later leaving a son, who survived a few months. He m. (4) Martha Doneley, who survived him.

3. Adeline, b. B., July 7, 1818; d. from eating choke cherries, while on a visit to Bristol, Aug. 30, 1821, ae. 3-1-23.

4. Otis Sanborn, b. Stafford, Conn., Jan. 30, 1820; m. Martha Mead, and d. in Austinburg, O., Feb. 18, 1890, ae. 70-0-18, leaving two sons and two daughters.

5. Fidelia, b. S., Oct. 23, 1822, m. Jan. 1, 1844, George W. Andrus, of Trumbull, O. One dau., one son.

6. Betsey Orcott, b. Oct. 6, 1825; m. Sept. 9, 1859, Epaphras Chapman Bill, b. in Conn., Nov. 18, 1821. She d. Reelsville, Ind., Nov. 23, 1857, ae. 32-1-17. Child:

    a. Fred Adelbert, b. at Hartsgrove, O., Aug. 12, 1850; m. Sept. 1, 1877, Clara M. McMaster. He is general passenger and freight agent of the Hot Springs Railroad Company. Res. Hot Springs, Ark. Children: (1) Jesse May, b. Reed's Landing, Oct. 10, 1878. (2) Earl McMaster, b. Dubuque, Iowa, July 14, 1888.

---

1. **Orren Bean Davis**, son of Timothy and Hannah (Bean) Davis, was b. Springfield, Mar. 20. 1821. He left home with a half penny and a small bundle of clothes, and became a farmer's boy in Andover. Later he was a peddler with two tin trunks, till he came to Bristol in 1847. Was in trade in the Rollins block, 1847-'52, then went to Franklin, where he was liveryman, landlord of Franklin house and for many years of the Webster house, where he d. Sept. 12, 1882, ae. 61-5-22. He m., in August, 1847, Eliza Ann, dau. of Dea. Joseph and Huldah Weeks (Morrill) Fellows, b. East Andover, Dec. 2, 1829. She d. Hampton Falls, Aug. 22, 1854, ae. 24-8-20, and he m. (2) Lucinda F. Shaw, widow of Sylvester H., b. in Wilmot, and d. in Franklin.

2. Charles Evans Fellows, b. Bristol, May 21, 1848; m. Feb. 8, 1868, Emma Frances, dau. Jesse and Hannah (Bliss) Baker, b. New London, Feb. 9, 1849. He is a farmer and seller of granite and marble for cemetery work at Andover. Children:

    a. Harry Fellows, b. Franklin, Oct. 13, 1869; m. Mina Louretta Connor, May 29, 1893. Overseer in finishing room in Sulloway's mill at Franklin. Two children.

    b. Oscar Baker, b. May 30, 1871. Res. Andover, unm.

    c. Carrie, b. Mar. 10, 1873; d. Sept. 12, 1873.

    d. Ethel May, b. Feb. 1, 1874, m. July 6, 1896, Martin Cunningham, furniture dealer and undertaker, Franklin Falls.

3. Lucinda Ann, b. Franklin, Nov. 22, 1857; m. Fred F. Long, of Franklin. No children.

4. Orren Bean, b. F., Dec. 11, 1861; d. Mar. 12, 1862.

5. Jennie Louise, b. F., Sept. 13, 1864; m. George D. Mayo, Franklin. Three children.

1. Charles Edwin Davis, son of Martin and Lydia (Aldrich) Davis, was b. Grafton, Sept. 4, 1854; m. Aug. 28, 1875, Ella J., dau. of Charles P. George, b. Sept. 4, 1855. (See.) Mr. Davis was a farmer and served seven years on the board of selectmen in Alexandria; came to Bristol in 1888, and was four years engaged in the livery business and eight years a member of the firm of Alexander & Davis, merchants. He has served four years as selectman of Bristol; is a past master of Union Lodge; Methodist; Democrat.

CHILD

2. Edwin Martin, b. Alexandria, Oct. 13, 1877. Is a clerk in First National Bank of Bristol.

---

1. Byron Edgar Davis, son of Levi W. and Abby H. (Piper) Davis, was b. in Wentworth, June 23, 1876. He m., May 22, 1900, Florence L. Stewart, b. Wales, Mass., Aug. 9, 1882. Has res. in Bristol three years. Paper maker.

CHILD

2. Hazel Edgarine, b. Bristol, July 15, 1902.

THE DAY FAMILY

1. Lorenzo Dow Day was the son of Isaac and Polly (Davis) Day. He was b. in Mercer, Me., May 17, 1814. He m. Harriet Newell, dau. of Manley and Lovina (Davis) Stevens, b. Orford, Oct. 31, 1821. He was a marble worker in Orford, Rochester, and Concord, till 1863, when he came to Bristol, and continued same business till age compelled him to retire. He represented Rochester in the constitutional convention of 1850, and the legislatures of 1851 and '52. In politics he was a Democrat, and he was a Mason for forty years. He d. in Bristol, Feb. 26, 1887, ae. 72-9-9. Mrs. Day d. in Concord, Dec. 31, 1901, ae. 80-2-0. Lovina D. Stevens, mother of Mrs. Day, d. at the home of her dau., in Bristol, Aug. 11, 1884, ae. 83.

CHILDREN

2. Elmina H., b. Orford; m. (1) Daniel W. Steele, of Lyme, who d. El Paso, Texas, July 23, 1877. She m. (2) John S. Keaghey. They res. Jasper, Jasper Co., Texas. Children:

    a. Hattie, m. Thomas H. Nilms. Address, Pennington, Trinity Co., Texas.
    b. Daniel C., m. and res. Beaumont, Texas.
    Four children d. in infancy.

3. Eliza Jane, b. Orford; m. July 30, 1887, Col. Charles H. Roberts, son of John and Polly (Davis) Roberts, and grandson of George Roberts, who served under Paul Jones. He res. Washington, D. C., and Concord.

4. Harriet Ann, b. Orford, Feb. 4, 1842; m. Sept. 19, 1865, William Henry Niles, son of Samuel W. and Eunice C. (Newell) Niles, b. Orford, Dec. 22, 1839. Children:

    a. Florence, b. Reading, Mass., Dec. 7, 1867 ; m. George W. Moulton, of Lynn, Jan. 31, 1889. Children : (1) Gladys Niles, b. Mar. 18, 1890. (2) Pauline H., b. May 4, 1893 ; d. July 14, 1894, ae. 1-2-10.

    b. Grace, b. Lynn, June 6, 1871 ; m. June 2, 1896, Dr. Charles R. Henderson, Reading, Mass. Child : Helen, b. Feb. 18, 1898.

    c. Mary Ethel, b. Oct. 31, 1883.

    5. Emma, b. Orford, Aug. 23, 1845 ; m. Mar. 13, 1865, Thomas Abbot, son of John C. and Elizabeth (Abbot) Pilsbury, b. Derry, Dec. 4, 1845, and d. Concord, Jan. 12, 1893, ae. 47-1-8. She m. (2) George W. Colbath, Jan. 22, 1895. Child :

    a. John Abbot Pilsbury.

    6. Sarah Lavina, b. Rochester, Feb. 6, 1846. She was a teacher in the Bristol graded school for three years from 1867, and was a member of the choir at the Methodist church. She m. Josiah E. Prescott. (See.)

    *7. Charles Herbert, b. Rochester, Mar. 13, 1848.

    8. Mary Helen, b. Rochester, Jan. 31, 1854 ; m. Fred H. Ackerman. (See.)

    9. Frank, b. Bristol, Jan. 12, 1865 ; m. Jan. 17, 1894, Nancy Frye, dau. of L. A. and Addie (Johnson) Babcock, b. Littleton, June 5, 1874. They res. 271 State street, Concord. Child :

    a. Marguerite, b. Concord, Jan. 22, 1895.

    (7) Charles H. Day, b. Mar. 13, 1848, m. Hattie A., dau. of Horace M. Emmons. (See.) He came to Bristol with his father and was associated with him in the marble business. He was town clerk in 1874 ; was deputy sheriff, 1875-'76 ; register of deeds of Grafton county, 1877-'81. He removed to Haverhill on assuming the duties of register of deeds, and to Concord in January, 1887. For ten years from 1881 was a large shipper of pressed hay from Canada to all parts of New England ; was senior partner of Concord Coal company 1888-1902 ; now senior partner Concord Ice company. Owns residence in Concord, and at Haverhill, one of the finest summer homes in Grafton county. A Democrat and a Mason.

CHILDREN

    10. Arthur Newell, b. Bristol, Jan. 7, 1868. Is associated with his father in the ice business, Concord ; unm.

    11. Minnie Maria, b. B., Jan. 7, 1872 ; m. Charles L. Jackman, Esq., Concord, and d. Sept. 13, 1898, ae. 26-8-6. To her memory Mr. Jackman constituted the Minnie Maria Day-Jackman fund of the Minot-Sleeper Library. (See Libraries.)

    12. Hattie Eva, b. Haverhill, July 15, 1877.

THE DEARBORN FAMILY

    1. The Dearborns of Bristol and Hill are the descendants of Godfrey Dearborn, who emigrated from Exeter, England, to Exeter, in 1639 ; settled in Hampton in 1650, and d. 1686. Of his descendants, 34 have been physicians. A granite monument 46 feet in height now stands in the cemetery in Exeter to his memory. He had three sons, Henry, Thomas, and John.

2.   Thomas was b. England, about 1634.   He resided in
Hampton.   Among his children was
    3.   Ebenezer.   One of his sons was
    4.   Ebenezer.   He was the father of
    5.   Jonathan, b. 1746.   He m. Delia, dau. of John Robie.
They res. in Chester, where five sons were b.   One of these was
    6.   Richard, who settled in Hill.   He m. Dolly, dau. of
Samuel Underhill, of Chester.   He was the father of
    7.   Selwyn C., b. Hill, Oct., 1816.   He m., Apr. 24, 1840,
Emor J., dau. of David Trumbull, b. Warner, Jan. 7, 1822.
They were farmers in Hill, where he d. Mar. 22, 1880, ae.
63-5-.   She res. Hill.

CHILDREN

8.   Sarah A., b. Hill, July 25, 1842; m. James A. Garland, who d·
Nov. 26, 1883; (2) Robert S. Johnson.   Res. in Sanbornton.
    *9.   Kenson Eliphalet, b. H., Apr. 22, 1844.
    10.   Lyman T., b. H., Apr. 11, 1846; m. Nov., 1876, Addie G. Russell;
res. in Hill.
    11.   Emor J., b. H., Mar. 13, 1852; m. Rev. Hiram Stratton. She d.
July 8, 1887, in Pennsylvania.
    12.   Ina May, b. H., Apr. 21, 1865.   Unm.

(9)   Kenson E. Dearborn, b. Apr. 22, 1844, m. Mar. 1,
1868, Mary, dau. of William and Mary (Smith) Tibbetts, b.
Brookfield, Nov. 13, 1846, and d. Bristol, Aug. 4, 1882, ae.
35-8-21.   July 18, 1885, he m. Carrie C., dau. of Moses and
Diana VanBuren Ferrin, b. Cherry Creek, N. Y., Mar. 23,
1843.   She was a teacher at the Normal School, Fredonia, N.
Y., and at the institution at Jamestown, N. Y.   In Bristol she
was a member of the board of education.   She d. May 27,
1901, ae. 58-2-4.   He m. (3) Nov. 18, 1902, Mina, dau. of
Thomas Hill, b. Mass., July 21, 1862.   He came to Bristol in
1869, and has been a practicing lawyer here.   (See Lawyers.)

CHILDREN

13.   Daisy May, b. Bristol, Apr. 6, 1871; m. Mar. 21, 1896, Joseph Hale
Merrill, son of Charles, b. Aug. 12, 1873.   Res. Wentworth.
    14.   Leonie Laura, b. B., Nov. 22, 1872, d. June 25, 1885, ae. 12-7-3.
    15.   Grace Marion, b. B., April 17, 1876.
    16.   Selwyn Kenson, b. B., Sept. 10, 1879; graduated Dartmouth Col-
lege 1901; m. Sept. 4, 1901, Eda F., dau. of George H. Mann, of Woodsville.   He is studying medicine at Dartmouth, class of 1905.

THE DECATO FAMILY

1.   Charles Decato was the son of Charles Decato Bean,
who dropped the last name and thereafter was known simply as
Charles Decato.   He m. Tiotis Bushway.   Three children were
b. to them in Three Rivers, Canada, and nine in Canaan.   At
the time of his death in March, 1901, he had 120 descendants.
Of his children, three located in Bristol in 1885, viz:

*2. Joseph Allen, b. Canaan, Sept. 8, 1849.
*3. Henry, b. C., Jan. 4, 1852.
*4. John, b. C., Jan. 13, 1856.

(2) Joseph A. Decato, b. Sept. 8, 1849, m., Feb. 13, 1873, Agnes, dau. Frank and Derosha (Hedel) Hill, b. Mar. 4, 1857, in Stanstead, Canada. He is a blacksmith on Willow street. Catholic. Res. Lake street.

CHILDREN, all born Canaan

5. Alice, b. Feb. 14, 1874; m. Joseph Gage. (See.)
6. Ella, b. Apr. 13, 1875; m. William M. Bryson. (See.)
7. Walter J., b. Sept. 30, 1876; m. Apr. 29, 1899, Ellen, dau. C. H. Stockbridge, b. Haverhill, Mass., 1879.
8. Charles O., b. Sept. 29, 1878.
9. William J., b. May 29, 1880; m. May 29, 1902, Mrs. Catherine, widow of Charles E. Mason. (See.) Res. South Main street.
10. Otto, b. May 15, 1883.

(3) Henry Decato, b. Jan. 4, 1852, m. Oct. 12, 1874, Mrs. Virginia (Martin) Young, widow of Joseph, b. Canaan, 1848. He is a mill operative. Res. corner Crescent and Willow streets.

CHILDREN

11. Hattie, b. Canaan, Sept. 2, 1875; m. Charles E. Kimball. (See.)
12. Charles H., b. C., Aug. 13, 1879; m. Jan. 22, 1901, Marion E., dau. of Charles A. Alden. (See.) They res. Penacook. Child:
    a. Emma Marion, b. Bristol, Apr. 10, 1901.
13. Otis, b. C., Aug. 20, 1881. Operative in woolen-mill.
14. Hervey, b. C., Sept. 14, 1883. Res. Penacook.
15. Melvina, b. C., July 28, 1877; d. ae. 1-2-7.
16. Almie, b. Bristol, Oct. 6, 1887; an operative in woolen-mill.

George Adolphus Young, son of Mrs. Decato by first husband, was b. Feb., 1873, Lawrence, Mass. Now res. Franklin. Was hostler.

(4) John Decato, b. Jan. 13, 1856, m. Jan. 6, 1876, Alice, dau. of Frank Hill, b. Lebanon, May 17, 1857. A paper-mill employee. Res. Willow street.

CHILD

17. George, b. Bristol, Mar. 7, 1886.

THE DICEY FAMILY

1. Wesley Hiram Dicey, son of Hiram and Isabel (Benton) Dicey, was b. Alexandria, Nov. 22, 1869. He m. Eva A., dau. Green L. Tilton (See), b. Mar. 17, 1870. With the exception of two years on a farm in New Hampton, has been a teamster in Bristol since 1884. Republican. Free Baptist.

CHILDREN

2. Eliza Maud, b. Bristol, Aug. 19, 1888.
3. Della Bernice, b. B., Sept. 1, 1890.
4. Mildred Joanna, b. B., Nov. 11, 1893.

THE DICKERSON OR DICKINSON FAMILY

In 1638, about sixty families came to America from York-shire, England, under the leadership of Rev. Ezekiel Rogers. In April, 1639, they settled in Rowley, Mass. One of these emigrants was

1. Thomas Dickerson. He d. in 1661. The name of his wife was Janet. They had two sons and four daughters. One was

2. James, b. 164-. He m. Rebecca, and had five sons and four daughters. One son was

3. Joseph, who m. Elizabeth Platts. One of his sons was

4. Joseph, b. 1707. His wife was Sarah. They had five sons and two daughters, of whom the fifth was

5. Moses, b. 1744. He settled on the Harry M. Dickerson farm in the west part of Hill, about 1790. He m. Eunice Wood, and d. Dec. 3, 1814, ae. 70-7-0. She d. Aug. 30, 1814, ae. 66.

CHILDREN

6. Thomas, b. 1770; settled in west part of Hill about 1793, and there d. Jan. 3, 1848, ae. 78-5-. His wife, Lydia, d. Aug. 12, 1803. He evidently m. (2) Tabitha. Eight children.

7. Jonathan, b. 1771, settled in west part of Hill in 1792, and d. Mar. 16, 1857, ae. 86. He m. (1) Hepsey, who d. May 21, 1797, ae. 28; (2) Hannah, d. June 17, 1817, ae. 45; (3) Jane, d. Sept. 30, 1845, ae. 64. Seven children.

8. John, b. 1773, d. in Hill, Mar. 3, 1842, ae. 69. He m., Dec. 29, 1801, Theodora, b. Sept. 16, 1772, d. Nov. 17, 1805, ae. 33-2-1. He m. (2) Comfort, who d. Mar. 24, 1850, ae. 64-10-. Four children.

*9. Moses, b. June 12, 1775.   10. Amos, b. 1782, d. Hill.

(9) Moses Dickerson, son of Moses, b. June 12, 1775, m. Sally Kinsman, b. June 23, 1781. She d. Feb. 8, 1842, ae. 60-7-15. He d. Hill, July 12, 1852, ae. 77-1-0. He was a farmer in west part of the town.

CHILDREN, all born in Hill

11. Sewell, b. Oct. 7, 1799; m. Hannah, dau. of Jonathan Dickerson. Farmer in Hill; d. Oct. 4, 1872, ae. 72-11-27; she d. Apr. 25, 1880, ae. 76-1-. Three children.

12. Watson, b. Feb. 5, 1801.   *13. John, b. Aug. 17, 1803.

*14. Arial, b. Aug. 20, 1805.

15. Polly, b. Oct. 13, 1807; d. Oct. 2, 1848, ae. 40-11-19.

16. Amos, b. Apr. 3, 1811; d. Nov. 15, 1811.

*17. Amos, b. Mar. 8, 1815.

18. Sabra, b. Oct. 25, 1817; m. John Clement, and d. at Penacook, at about 75.

19. Sally K., b. Jan. 4, 1820; m. Julius Kinsman; res. Brookline, Mass.

(13) John Dickerson, son of Moses, b. Aug. 17, 1803, m. Adeline M. Taylor, and d. Sept. 20, 1867, ae. 64-1-3.

*20. Willis Kinsman, b. Hill, Jan. 21, 1829.
21. Elkanah, res. Philadelphia, Pa. 22. Eveline, d.

(14) Arial Dickinson, son of Moses, b. Aug. 20, 1805, m.
Feb. 8, 1832, Abigail H., dau. Nathaniel and Nancy (Chase)
Norris, b. Hardwick, Vt., June 21, 1801, and d. Bristol, Feb. 28,
1847, ae. 45-8-7. He m., June 16, 1847, Betsey W., dau.
Daniel and Betsey (Hall) Patch, b. Warner, Jan. 29, 1816.
Farmer. Came from Hill to Profile Falls in 1841, and d. Bris-
tol village, July 21, 1886, ae. 80-11-1. She d. in home of her
son, Jan. 1, 1900, ae. 83-11-2.

CHILD

*23. Joseph Norris, b. Bristol, Oct. 26, 1841.

(17) Amos Dickinson, son of Moses, b. Mar. 8, 1815, d.
Jan. 23, 1864, ae. 48-10-15. He m. Huldah Southwick, dau.
of Daniel and Ruth Bartlett, b. in Hill, Feb. 2, 1814, and d.
Bristol, Feb. 20, 1895, ae. 81-0-18. He was a farmer in Hill ;
a justice of the peace ; represented Hill in the legislature two
years. Last 20 years of her life she made her home with her
son, Charles H.

CHILDREN

24. Ellen Frances, b. Hill, Apr. 7, 1839; m. Oramel E. Eastman, and
res. E. Andover. Two children.
25. Sarah Emery, b. H., Aug. 23, 1840; m. Roswell Blake. (See.)
26. Watson Augustus, b. H., Aug. 13, 1842 ; m. Ella, dau. of Benj.
F. Sargent; is a dealer in hay and grain, and mill supplies, Lowell, Mass.
*27. Charles Henry, b. H., Apr. 7, 1844.

(20) Willis K. Dickerson, son of John, b. Jan. 21, 1829,
m. Nov. 30, 1856, Sarah J., dau. of Martin and Susan (Richmond) Perkins, b. Plympton, Mass., July 9, 1837. He resided
in Plymouth ; in Bristol, 1869-'87, manufacturer of buckskin
gloves and mittens, then in West Bridgewater, Mass., where
he d. Jan. 21, 1898, ae. 69-0-0. She res. West Bridgewater.

CHILDREN

28. Addie Jane, b. Hill, Sept. 22, 1861; m. Oct. 19, 1884, William
Abram Fowler, West Bridgewater, Mass.
29. Charles Willis, b. Rumney, Dec. 25, 1864; m. Nov. 6, 1895, Lizzie
Frances Doten ; res. Wollaston, Mass.
30. Lizzie Rebecca, b. R., Jan. 24, 1867 ; d. Nov. 10, 1868, ae. 1-9-16.
31. Alice Edena, b. R., Oct. 30, 1868.
32. Bertha Helen, b. Bristol, Apr. 30, 1878.

(23) Joseph N. Dickinson, son of Arial, b. Oct. 26, 1841,
m. Aug. 25, 1866, Clara Albertina, dau. of Eldred Roby (See),
b. Lowell, Mass., Feb. 19, 1847, and d. in Bristol, June 11,
1891, ae. 44-3-22. He was merchant tailor 15 years ; for many
years foreman of Taylor & Gordon's shop in manufacture of

picker-sticks; now solicitor for Masonic home, Manchester. Methodist. Is a past master Union Lodge. Democrat.

CHILDREN

33. Lillian Norris, b. Bristol, Oct. 13, 1867; m. Newell A. Bailey, Sept. 15, 1888. Children:
    a. Pearl Lillian, b. Bristol, Apr. 17, 1890.
    b. Elwin Newell, b. Alexandria, July 29, 1893.
    c. Eldred Joseph, b. A., Apr. 30, 1895.
    d. Arial William, b. A., June 30, 1899; d. Sept. 23, 1899.
34. Elbert Eldred, b. B., June 23, 1869; employee of American Express company, Concord. Methodist. Mason. Unm.
35. Dora Albertine, b. B., Dec. 26, 1871; m. Frank W. Towns. (See.)
36. Ionel Arial, b. B., Mar. 30, 1876; dealer in ice, job teamster, Bristol. Methodist, Mason.

(27) Charles H. Dickinson, son of Amos, b. Apr. 7, 1844, m. Oct. 28 1876, Ida May, dau. of John B. and Elizabeth Gordon; b. New Hampton, May —, 1857, and d. Bristol, Mar. 18, 1881, ae. 23–5–. He m. (2) Nellie M. Jesseman. She d. Dec. 7, 1889, ae. 22–4–19, and he m. (3) Nov. 18, 1893, Mrs. Roxy Maud Cass, widow of William Cass, and dau. of Solon Dolloff. (See.) Since 1871, he has been a prosperous merchant in Bristol, a dealer in clothing, gents' furnishing goods, boots and shoes. Telegraph agent 25 years. Has held office of town treasurer for 17 years, and represented Bristol in legislature of 1895. Republican; is a 32° Mason.

CHILDREN

37. Charles Perkins, b. Bristol, Nov. 5, 1877. Graduated from New Hampton Institution, 1898. Salesman in his father's store. Mason.
38. Amos Gordon, b. B., Oct. 11, 1880. Graduated from New Hampton Institution, 1902.

THE DODGE FAMILIES

Seymour H. Dodge, son of Elias B. Dodge, was b. Bath, Feb. 17, 1846. He m. Dec. 31, 1879, Mary Alice, dau. of Dr. Ira S. Chase. (See.) He came to Bristol in 1872, and was for many years a salesman in the store of Hon. Cyrus Taylor; is now a carpenter. Res. School street. Mason. Republican. No children.

1. John Wright Dodge was the son of Daniel and Sally (Wright) Dodge. He was b. in Hanover, Sept. 4, 1815, and m. July 1, 1855, Clementine (Chandler) Whipple, dau. of Henry H. and Anna (Wright) Chandler, b. Hanover, Nov. 12, 1818. She d. in Enfield, Mar. 6, 1893, ae. 74–3–24, and he m. (2) Mrs. Helen A. (Bridgman) Morgan, widow of Converse G. Morgan, of Enfield, and dau. of John and Augusta (Chandler) Bridgman, of Hanover. He d. at Enfield, Feb. 13, 1897.

CHARLES H. DICKINSON

ae. 81-5-9. Mr. Dodge and his first wife are interred in Pleasant Street cemetery at Bristol.

John W. Dodge was born on a farm and was the youngest
of 10 children. At the age of 17 he became manager of the
farm and main support of the large family, in which there were
several invalids and incapacitated persons, but by rigid econ-
omy and untiring industry, he carried the load for many years
with only a few dollars' aid from the town when an unfortunate
brother necessarily became an inmate of an asylum. This slight
assistance he early resolved to make good to the town which he
did many fold by endowing a free bed in Hitchcock hospital at
Hanover for the use of the poor and unfortunate of the town.
His substantial aid to several members of the family less fortunate than himself continued through his entire life and through
his wise forethought and generous provision, succeeding generations are enjoying his munificence. The worthy poor and unfortunate ever found in him a generous and unostentatious friend.

Mr. Dodge's school advantages were, necessarily, very
limited, but having a great fondness for reading and a very
retentive memory, he became well-informed and an entertaining
conversationalist on almost any subject. Being an independent
thinker and naturally skeptical, he investigated every subject of
importance to his own satisfaction and then was ready to give
reasons for his conclusions. As a strong Democrat, his faith
was based upon conclusions after deep study of the political
history of our country and formation of the government. Though
his family were of the " old school " Baptist faith, Mr. Dodge's
religious views were very broad and liberal and he affiliated
with the Universalists. In social, as well as business life, his
high moral character and strict integrity was never questioned.
His word was as good as his bond. It was his firm belief that
every man should endeavor to make the world better for having
lived in it, and, unquestionably, his efforts in that direction
were successful.

When about 32 years of age, Mr. Dodge became interested
in a country store in Hanover and continued the business with
different partners till about 1865, when he moved to Enfield and
was employed by A. Conant, as assistant manager of Shaker
Mills, manufacturing hosiery and flannels. When Mr. Conant
retired, two years later, Mr. Dodge formed a partnership with
D. L. Davis and Samuel Williams, the firm running the mills
till 1873, when Mr. Williams retired, and Dodge, Davis & Co.
succeeded, Henry C. Whipple becoming a member. This firm
continued to run the mills till 1885, when the machinery and
business were moved to Bristol.

CHILDREN

2. Infant son, b. Hanover, Jan. 21, 1857 ; d. Oct. 12, 1857, ae. 0-8-21.

3.   Fannie Louisa, b. H., Apr. 30, 1859; m. Rev. Walter Dole, in Enfield, Jan. 13, 1886.   He is a Universalist clergyman.

---

1.   George H. Dodge, son of John and Sarah J. (McVennon) Dodge, was b. Antrim, Mar. 3, 1863.   He m., June 30, 1887, Alice Roxanna, dau. of Samuel K. and Hannah (Leach) Pike, b. New London, Mar. 18, 1861.   He was in the shoe trade in Milford and in Bristol three years from November, 1899.   Emigrated to state of Washington.

CHILD

2.   Avis, b. Milford, Feb. 7, 1899.

THE DOLLOFF FAMILIES

1.   The Dolloffs are supposed to be of Russian stock, as the name indicates.   Abraham Dolloff, who settled in Bristol, was b. Aug. 27, 1768, in Rye as is supposed.   He was the son of Nicholas and Sally (Clough) Dolloff.   His father d. when he was about ten months old, and he was given a home by Abram Hook, Esq., a wealthy farmer in Kingston, who is said to have overworked and abused him.   When 16 years of age an uncle called to see him on his way from Portsmouth to his home in Andover, and Abraham took the opportunity to accompany him home.   Here he met Rachel Locke, of Sandown, who was b. in Rye, Oct. 15, 1772, and they were married Nov. 28, 1793. She was the dau. of Levi.   A brother, Benjamin, had already made his home in Bridgewater.   Abraham and his bride settled in the Locke neighborhood.   He was a carpenter as well as farmer and built the house that was afterward the home of Benjamin Locke.   The first child of Abraham and the first of Benjamin were b. in the same room, became man and wife, and both d. in the same room though in another home, at the close of a long life.   After the birth of his first child, Abraham moved to near the Prescott farm in Bridgewater, where he remained about 16 years and then returned to the Locke neighborhood, where he built, on the Dolloff farm, the large two-story farmhouse still standing, the best set of buildings in town when completed. The material for this building he cut on the farm, drew the logs to the saw-mill at Profile Falls, had them sawed into lumber, and then drew it back.   On this farm he passed the remainder of his life and here d. May 15, 1855, after nearly 62 years of wedded life, ae. 86-8-18; she d. May 11, 1860, ae. 87-6-26. He was a man of strong and unique personality.   When nearly 70 years of age, he discarded the use of cider and united with the Methodist church, and at 80 discarded tobacco.

*2. Levi Locke, b. Bristol, Nov. 9, 1795.
    3. Sally Clough, b. Bridgewater, May 30, 1798; m. Favor Locke.
(See.)
    4. Susanna Sanborn, b. B., Dec. 9, 1800; m. Samuel Brown. (See.)
*5. Nicholas Blaisdell, b. B., Feb. 6, 1803.
    6. Mary, b. B., June 9, 1805; m. Joseph Moore. (See.)
    7. Margaret Sanborn, b. B., Nov. 28, 1807; m. Jonathan Emmons.
(See.)
    8. Elmira Smith, b. B., Dec. 14, 1810; m. John Roby. (See.)
    9. Rachel Locke, b. B., Apr. 24, 1814; m. Calvin Swett. (See.)
*10. Abram, b. Bristol, Mar. 20, 1818.

(2) Levi L. Dolloff, b. Nov. 9, 1795, m. Roxy, dau. of
Benjamin Locke (See), b. Dec. 3, 1798. He lived for a time on
the home farm, then purchased the Abram Hook farm, in
Bridgewater, on the lake "Point," and here he passed his life.
He had what was called the best farm in town, delightfully
situated. He was a Methodist and Republican. He d. Apr. 6,
1880, ae. 84-4-27; she d. July 7, 1884, ae. 85-7-4.

    11. Infant son, d. Dec. 24, 1820.
    12. Infant daughter, d. Apr. 28, 1825.
*13. Solon, b. Bridgewater, Oct. 3, 1827.
    14. Hannah, b. B., Jan. 6, 1831; m. Abner Fowler. (See.)
*15. Orrin Locke, b. B., July 26, 1833.
*16. Gilbert Bruce, b. B., Dec. 7, 1835.
    Emily Jane Eaton, dau. of Cyrus W. (See), was given a home from
childhood in this family.

(5) Nicholas B. Dolloff, b. Feb. 6, 1803, m. Jan. 29, 1851,
Mrs. Harriet (Mason) Locke, widow of Benjamin and dau. of
David Mason. (See.) She d. Nov. 16, 1856, ae. 42-3-24, and
he m. (2) Rhoda Aldrich, dau. of Dr. Aldrich, of Sugar Hill,
b. Mar. 16, 1813, d. Sept. 29, 1885, ae. 72-6-13. He was a
farmer and also a school teacher and surveyor, and ranked high
as a mathematician. In 1830, he purchased an interest in the
saw-mill at Moore's Mills and continued the manufacture of lumber here for 20 years. He frequently run the river with rafts
of lumber, masts, and spars to market. He sold his interest in
the lumber business in 1850, and removed to Franconia, where
he resumed farming, and here he lived till the death of his wife,
when he made his home with his son, Mason, and with friends
in Bristol. He d. in Woodstock, July 13, 1892, ae. 89-5-7.

    17. Mason D., b. Franconia, Nov. 10, 1852; m. Dec. 14, 1876, Emma
E. Hanson. She d. Mar. 12, 1902, at St. Elizabeth's hospital, Boston, as
the result of a surgical operation. He res. Lincoln.
    18. Loren, b. F., Dec. 17, 1854; d.

(10) Abram Dolloff, b. Mar. 20, 1818, m. Feb. 22, 1838,
Lydia, dau. of Levi Nelson (See), b. Dec. 4, 1818. He has

been a farmer, drover, and dealer in meats. He commenced
at 17 years of age to buy and sell cattle, and continued this
for many years. He bought largely in Vermont, New Hampshire, and Canada, and drove his herds to market. In 1865, the
tariff being unfavorable for importing live stock, he shipped
dressed beef to the states. In 1862, he opened the first meat
market in Bristol, and later had markets also in Franklin and
Tilton. He continued in the meat business in Bristol till June,
1899, his business career covering a period of 64 years. He has
been a member of the Methodist church in Bristol for 75 years,
and was a class leader for 25 years, and is still a member of
the official board of that church, having filled this position for
nearly 62 years. Mrs. Dolloff was a woman of superior ability
and attainments, active in church and society work. After
nearly 63 years of wedded life, the wife d. Dec. 20, 1900, ae.
82–0–16.

CHILDREN, all born Bristol.

19. Almira Smith, b. Dec. 12, 1838; graduated Tilton seminary, class
of 1860; m. Rev. George J. Judkins. (See.)
20. Otis Ayer, b. Nov. 25, 1843; d. Sept. 15, 1845, ae. 1–9–20.
21. Emma Hannah, b. Feb. 14, 1846; was educated at Kingston
academy and at Music Vale Seminary, Salem, Conn. She m. C. Newell
Cass. (See.)
22. Lynthia Nelson, b. Jan. 20, 1850; d. Nov. 16, 1855, ae. 5–9–26.
23. Harlan Howard, b. June 29, 1852; d. Oct. 4, 1855, ae. 3–3–5.
24. Viola Leone, b. Jan. 3, 1854; d. Oct. 10, 1855, ae. 1–9–7.
25. Anna Maria, b. Apr. 8, 1858. She studied oil painting and crayon
drawing in Boston and New York, and was an artist of great promise.
She excelled in crayon portraits. She m. Ervin T. Drake, M.D. (See.)
26. Alma Kate, b. Apr. 8, 1858; d. of consumption, June 16, 1875, ae.
17–2–8.

(13) Solon Dolloff, b. Oct. 3, 1827, m., May 1, 1850,
Nancy, dau. of Daniel and Martha (Brown) Simonds, b. Alexandria, Mar. 1, 1829. He was a school teacher in early manhood. After his m. he lived in Bristol, then Franklin; returned
to Bristol and purchased the old Tom Locke farm, a mile or more
east of Central square, where he has since res. He also kept a
meat market in Bristol village for many years till 1902. He is
a Republican and has served on the board of selectmen. He is
active in Grange circles.

CHILDREN

27. Wilbur, b. Bristol, Apr. 1, 1854; d. Dec. 24, 1854.
28. Ida May, b. Franklin, Oct. 3, 1856; she graduated from New
Hampton Literary Institution, and was a school teacher. She m.,
May 1, 1879, Fred A. Whittemore, of Bridgewater. He graduated from
Dartmouth College, class of 1888. He has been a school teacher; now
farming at Whitinsville, Mass. Children:
   a. Wilfred, b. Bristol, Jan. 12, 1882; is a student at Dartmouth
College, class of 1904.
   b. Leila May, b. B., July 21, 1884.
   c. Aurioe Maria, b. Lonsdale, R. I., Sept. 27, 1892.

d. Fred Dolloff, b. L.., Jan., 1896; d. from the effects of a scald, Nov. 21, 1897, ae. 1-10-.

Two daughters d. in infancy.

29. Roxy, b. Franklin, Jan. 5, 1859; m. William F. Cass. (See.) He d. Apr. 5, 1881, and she m. (2) Charles H. Dickinson. (See.)

30. Levi Manson, b. F., Sept. 24, 1860; m. Nov. 14, 1894, Mary R., dau. of Daniel J. and Abbie (Persis) Worthley, b. Bradford, Nov. 15, 1867. Is the owner of a milk route in Arlington, Mass. No children.

31. Frank Daniel, b. Bristol, Sept. 7, 1862; m. Feb. 9, 1889, Nellie Florence, dau. of Levi D. Johnson. (See.) He is manager of his father's farm. Child:

　a. Frank Neil, b. B., Apr. 11, 1892.

32. Lucy Solon, b. B., Aug. 8, 1870; m. May 1, 1897, Minnie Obrien, of Newport. He had charge of his father's meat market for a time; now res. in Newport, in the meat business.

(15) Orrin L. Dolloff, b. July 26, 1833, m. May 26, 1859, Clarinda A., dau. of Daniel and Dorcas (Baker) Elliott, b. Rumney, Sept. 5, 1839. He is a farmer at the Hoyt tavern stand in Bridgewater, where for several years Mrs. Dolloff has kept a summer boarding-house—Elm Lawn.

CHILDREN

33. Alba O., b. Bridgewater, Mar. 10, 1860; m. Nellie Vose, dau. of John F. Vose, b. Alexandria, Apr. 17, 1856; and d. Dec. 10, 1886, ae. 30-7-23. He m. Jan. 12, 1889, Jennie Maud Dewar, of Manchester, b. Jan. 13, 1865. He is a letter-carrier in Manchester.

34. Myra Etta, b. B., Apr. 7, 1864; m. Dec. 25, 1882, Frank H. Elliott. They res. Concord. Child:

　a. Clarice Mae, b. Concord, May 24, 1888.

35. Mabel M., b. B., Nov. 1, 1868; m. Sept. 15, 1897, Harry P. Hathorne. Is a bookkeeper in Boston. Res. Chelsea, Mass.

36. Maud M., b. Nov. 1, 1868, a twin sister, is a milliner.

(16) Gilbert B. Dolloff, b. Dec. 7, 1835, m. Apr. 22, 1857, Margaret H., dau. of Isaac C. Tilton. (See.) She was b. Oct. 15, 1834, and d. June 1, 1867, ae. 32-7-16. He m. in July, 1868, Mary E. Vose, who d. Dec. 28, 1869, and he m. May 8, 1870, Emily Jane, widow of Charles H. Spencer, and dau. of Cyrus W. Eaton. (See.) He has represented his town in the general court, and has served as selectman. He succeeded his father on the home farm.

CHILDREN

37. Abner F., B. Bristol, July 3, 1863.

＊38. Ansel G., b. Bridgewater, Dec. 24, 1869.

39. Agnes M., b. B., Apr. 3, 1872; m. Harris W. Hammond.

(38) Ansel G. Dolloff, b. Dec. 24, 1869, m. June 6, 1891, Blanche C., dau. George C. Currier (See), b. Nov. 26, 1871. He was a dealer of stoves and tinware in the basement of Blake's block, for some years previous to 1902, when he became a member of the firm of Emmons & Dolloff, in same business, at stand next north of Newfound river, on west side of Central

square.   He is a Republican, an Odd Fellow, and a member of the K. of P.   Is now serving as fireward.

40.   Helen Mary, b. Bristol, Oct. 30, 1893.

---

1.   Samuel Dolloff, the son of Samuel and Mary Dolloff, was b. in Meredith, and d. in Waterville, October, 1895.   He m. Mary, dau. of Isaac Webster, b. in Meredith, d. Waterville.   Was a resident of District No. 5, in Bristol, 1842-'46.

2.   Charles W., b. Meredith, Mar. 20, 1833; m. Laura A., dau. of John L. Davis, b. Gilford, June 19, 1841.   Served in Co. G, 12th N. H. Vols.   Wounded Mar. 3, 1863, at battle of Chancellorsville; gunshot wound in right forearm.   Res. Concord.

3.   Levi, b. M., Mar. 2, 1835.   Was a corporal Co. H, 14th N. H. Vols., enlisting Aug. 11, 1862 ; wounded Sept. 19, 1864, at Opequan, Va.   Res. Campton Village.

4.   Benjamin, b. M., 1840 (?).   Served in Co. K, 16th Mass. Vols., from July 2, 1862, till July 27, 1864.   Res. Everett, Mass.

5.   John E., b. Bristol, July 13, 1842, m. Rowena M., dau. Nathan and Lorinda Holbrook, Aug. 2, 1866.   She was b. Milford, Mass., Aug. 31, 1848.   (See Roll of Honor.)   Res. Passumpsic, Vt.   Children :

    a.   Eugene Malcolm, b. Lebanon, Sept. 9, 1867 ; m. Mary Grow, Lynn, Mass., Sept. 25, 1889 ; is a physician at Rockport, Mass.

    b.   George Warren, b. Danville, Sept. 25, 1869 ; d. Barnet, Vt., Sept. 3, 1877, ae. 7-11-8.

    c.   Etta B., b. Barnet, Vt., Sept. 27, 1871 ; m. Nov. 19, 1887, Willie E. Demas.   He d. Sept. 19, 1890.

    d.   Inez Bertha, b. Glover, Vt., Dec. 22, 1873.

6.   Eunice, m. ——— Steele ; d. Lakeport, March, 1901.

7.   George F., b. Thornton.

DOUD

Arthur V. Doud, M.D., is the son of Sylvester S. and Mary R. (Goodell) Doud, b. New Haven, Vt., Oct. 23, 1867.   His ancestors were of English stock.   On his mother's side they settled in New England previous to the Revolutionary war ; on his father's side, they have resided in New England since 1636. Dr. Doud practiced medicine one year in Hill and came to Bristol in July, 1897, and has since been in practice here, occupying a suite of rooms corner of Central square and Spring street. Unm.   (See Physicians.)

THE DOW FAMILIES

1.   Jonathan Dow was b. in Hampton, May 21, 1734.   He m. Comfort Brown, b. Oct. 10, 1730.   He d. in New Hampton, Nov. 6, 1816, ae. 82-5-15.   A son was

2. Levi, b. New Hampton, Mar. 31, 1763, and d. same place in March, 1849, ae. 86. He m. in 1784, Abigail Godfrey, b. in Poplin, Oct. 10, 1758, and d. Dec. 17, 1822, ae. 64-2-7. Of his children, one was

3. Joseph Godfrey, b. New Hampton, Aug. 30, 1789. He m. Polly Boynton, Dec. 8, 1811. She was b. Mar. 22, 1791. He d. in New Hampton, Dec. 3, 1830 (tombstone says 1831), ae. 41-3-3. She m. (2) Robert Heath. (See.)

CHILDREN, all born in New Hampton

4. Mary Jane Boynton, b. Feb. 8, 1813; m. John C. Downing. (See.)
5. Wm. Boynton, b. Apr. 10, 1815.
*6. George Washington, b. May 6, 1817.
7. Eliza Ann, b. Dec. 2, 1819; m. Jan. 2, 1840, John B. Marston.
8. John Mooney, b. Mar. 10, 1822; d. Dec. 20, 1845, ae. 23-9-10.
9. Joseph Godfrey, b. Mar. 22, 1825; res. in California; d. June 19, 1885, in Washington Ter., ae. 60-2-27.
10. Martha Curtis, b. Dec. 20, 1827; m. Charles B. Heath. (See.)

(6) George W. Dow, b. May 6, 1817, m. Adeline C., dau. of Elisha Gurdy. (See.) She was b. Dec. 8, 1816, and d. Bristol, Sept. 10, 1865, ae. 48-9-2. He m. (2) Amanda Jane, widow of Joseph F. Rollins. (See.) He d. in Bristol, May 9, 1891, ae. 74-0-3. Mrs. Dow res. on School street. He was a farmer at Moore's Mills, 1844-'47. In 1852, in company with David Mason, he engaged in the manufacture of strawboard on Willow street, and continued this and the manufacture of paper for ten years. He was superintendent of strawboard-mills at Contoocook and in the West.

CHILDREN

11. Charles B., b. Bristol, 1842; m. Addie, dau. James and Eliza Blake. Certificate issued Sept. 26, 1863. He res. Bristol, Chicago, and for several years in California; now in Honolulu. He m. (2). Changed his name to Charles D. Stone.
12. John Mooney, b. B., 1846; m. Dec. 21, 1880, Elizabeth Flude. (See Randolph Family.)

---

1. William Lawton Dow, son of True Perkins and Eunice Canney (Brown) Dow, was b. Moultonboro, June 23, 1852. He m. Feb. 9, 1879, Sadie, dau. of Ivory and Rhoda (Philpot) Furgeson, b. Waterbury, Me. He was for 16 years a foreman in finishing department of a shoe factory at Dover. Came to Bristol in April, 1895; was interested for a time in the manufacture of shoes. In June, 1899, succeeded Abram Dolloff in meat business. Free Baptist. Odd Fellow. No children.

---

1. George Albert Dow, son of Cyrus Benjamin and Ellen M. (Couch) Dow, was b. Warner, May 4, 1870. Was farmer

in Warner; was eight years an employee of Deerfoot Farm
Creamery company in Contoocook; assumed charge of its
creamery in Bristol in April, 1900, which position he still
holds. He operates a meat market and a milk route. Unm.
Republican. Free Baptist.

Flora P. Dow, a sister and housekeeper for above, was b.
August, 1872; m. Joseph W. Johnson.

Mary Ann Dow, an aunt of above, dau. of Isaac and Polly
(Watson) Dow, b. Boscawen, Aug. 27, 1821, res. with George
A. Dow, above.

---

1.   Jacob H. Dow was b. in Sunapee, Aug. 15, 1821.   He
m. (1) Irene Angel, of Sunapee, where she d. He m. (2) Mary
Ann Stevens, of Wilmot; (3) Oct. 22, 1858, Charlotte L. Holden, dau. Ira Holden, b. Addison, Vt., Oct. 22, 1827. He
came to Bristol about 1856, and was a laborer. (See Roll of
Honor.) After the war, he settled in Hill, and there d. Apr.
20, 1884, ae. 62-8-5.

CHILDREN

2.   Irene, b. Sunapee; m. Mark Towle, of Haverhill, Mass. Res.
Hammond, Ind.
3.   Sarah, b. S.; m. Charles E. Smith, New Hampton. Res. Hammond, Ind.
4.   John.   5.   Luella, b. S.; m., and d. in New Hampton.
6.   Mary A., b. S.; m. —— Cheney; res. Newport.
7.   Arthur A., b. Bristol, Sept. 1, 1859; m. June 4, 1881, Belle Wadleigh.   Child:
      a.   Mabel E., b. July 18, 1883; m. Leston Maclinn. (See.)
8.   Horace E., b. B., Dec. 18, 1861; went to Chicago, and there m.
Feb. 15, 1885, Rosa Eagan.   In 1899, located in So. Omaha, Neb.
9.   Edward Everett, b. B., Oct. 20, 1864.   At 16 went to Hammond,
Ind., thence to Lakin, Kansas, there m. in Jan., 1890, Kate Carneys.   In
1901, went to Redlands, Cal.
10.   Alice A., b. Hill, Nov. 22, 1867; m. June, 1894, Charles P. Sargent
of Gilmanton.   Res. Lower Gilmanton.
11.   Donna E., b. H., July 8, 1870; m. Mar. 20, 1897, Walter L. Smith
of Buxton, Me.   Res. Gleasondale, Mass.

---

1.   Abram S. Dow, son of Philip, b. Nov. 10, 1816, m.
Mary Jane Moore, dau. of Joseph, b. New Hampton, Jan. 8,
1822.   He was a farmer in District No. 4, from 1874 till he d.,
Mar. 15, 1881, ae. 64-4-5.   She d. Apr. 18, 1877, ae. 55-3-10.

CHILDREN

2.   Charles G., b. Meredith, July 22, 1850.   He came to Bristol
with his father and succeeded him on the farm.   He m. (1) Sept. 2,
1877, Martha M. Clifford, dau. of Sylvester, (2) July 5, 1900, Katie A.,
dau. of Allen and Sarah (Barrett) Keyser.   Children:
      a.   Lewis Sylvester, b. Bristol, Aug. 16, 1880; m. Aug. 13, 1902,
Ethel Maud, dau. of Lyman B. and Ellen J. (Gordon) Wells.
      b.   Leon Chester, b. B., Nov. 53, 1882.
      c.   Alfred, b. B., Dec. 3, 1884.

d. Von Karl, b. B., Jan. 16, 1887.
e. Richard, b. B., Apr. 12, 1890.

3. Anna M., b. Meredith, Sept. 10, 1852; d. July 26, 1871, ae. 18-10-16.
4. John G., b. Alexandria, June 2, 1854; d. Sept. 24, 1884, ae. 30-3-22.
5. George H., b. Meredith, May 7, 1859; d. Bristol, Apr. 22, 1880, ae. 20-11-15.
6. Ellie M., b. Aug. 2, 1865; m. Edwin Smith.

THE DOWNING FAMILY

1. John Cook Downing, son of Henry and Abigail (Ellen-wood) Downing was b. Londonderry, Mar. 29, 1809. He m. Mar. 19, 1834, Mary Jane Boynton Dow, dau. of Joseph G., b. Feb. 8, 1813. (See.) He was a carpenter. Res. Alexandria, later No. Bristol, and still later built and res. in the Cass house on Merrimack street. He also built the house first occupied by Charles E. Mason on South Main street. Moved to Lowell, Mass., 1841, a pattern maker. In 1857, went to Healdsburg, Cal., undertaker; he d. Dec. 22, 1875, ae. 66-8-23; she d. same place, Mar. 10, 1894, ae. 81-1-2.

CHILDREN

2. Ellen Antoinette, b. Bristol, Dec. 22, 1838; m. Nov. 14, 1858, John Washington Bagley, son of David, b. Cayuga Co., N. Y., Oct. 2, 1827. They res. Guerneville, Sonoma Co., Cal. Children :
    a. Josephine Antoinette, b. Healdsburg, Cal., Oct. 15, 1859.
    b. Mary Louise, b. H., June 18, 1863.
    c. Herbert Lincoln, b. H., July 7, 1865.
    d. Frank John, b. H., Sept. 9, 1871.
    e. Alice Clare, b. Guerneville, Nov. 19, 1874.
    f. Carl Elmer, b. G., Sept. 21, 1877.
3. Joseph Henry, b. Bristol, Nov. 28, 1840; m. Dec. 3, 1873, at Healdsburg, Cal., Mrs. Matilda (Prince) Burlingame, dau. Thomas R. and Abigail S. (Oakes) Prince, b. Portland, Me., Nov. 29, 1842. Res. 709 10th street, Oakland, Cal.

    a. Annette Roby, b. Oakland, Cal., Dec. 16, 1882.
4. Clarence Victor Blossom, b. Lowell, Mass., May 22, 1850 ; m. May 22, 1878, Mary Ann Frances Smith, b. Sonoma Co., Cal. He d. Vallejo Sonoma Co., Cal., Nov. 30, 1882, ae. 32-6-8. Children:
    a. Fred Parsons, b. San Francisco, Cal., May 1, 1879.
    b. Lucille Antoinette, b. S. F., Sept. 27, 1880.
    c. Clare Victor, b. Vallejo, Cal., Aug. 1, 1882.

Family res. 1,031 Valencia street, San Francisco, Cal.

THE DRAKE FAMILIES

1. Jacob Burnham Drake was b. in New Hampton about 1794. He was the son of Nathaniel, b. in New Hampton, and grandson of Nathaniel, of Northwood, one of the first settlers in New Hampton. Jacob B. m. Polly Smith. In 1835, he settled

10*a*

in the Locke neighborhood ; in 1843, removed to No. Bristol, where he d., Oct. 29, 1869, ae. 75 ; she d. July 3, 1867, ae. 73.

CHILDREN

2. Nancy, b. New Hampton, 1817; m. John Spencer ; lived and d. in Berwick, Me.
*3. Philip Smith, b. N. H., Apr. 14, 1819.
4. Emily Jane, b. N. H., 1834 ; d. Bristol, Nov. 9, 1855, ae. 21-4-.

(3) Philip S. Drake, b. Apr. 14, 1819, m. Apr. 11, 1839, Harriet, dau. of Benjamin Locke (See), b. Jan. 14, 1822. They settled on the Muzzey farm in the Locke neighborhood ; in 1843, removed to the silver mine farm in No. Bristol with his father ; about 1876, sold to Abner Fowler and removed to a farm near the cemetery in No. Bristol, where he d. Sept. 15, 1882, ae. 63-5-1, and where she res.

CHILDREN

*5. Charles Norton, b. Bristol, Sept. 30, 1839.
*6. Henry Wells, b. B., May 30, 1846.
7. Abra Ann, b. B., Jan. 13, 1851 ; m. Andrew T. Nudd. (See.)
8. Frank LaForest, b. B., Jan. 10, 1855 ; m. Nov. 17, 1883, Mary Ann Webster and res. Laconia.

(5) Charles N. Drake, b. Sept. 30, 1839, m. Sept. 9, 1862, Harriet Augusta, dau. of Col. Samuel H. Rollins. (See.) At battle of Gettysburg he lost a leg and was shot through the body. (See Roll of Honor.) Farmer and carpenter. Served as selectman. He d. suddenly Sept. 1, 1896, while officiating as manager at the funeral of a neighbor — fell from his carriage while *en route* to the grave and expired from heart failure ; ae. 56-11-1. Republican, G. A. R. She d. Bristol, Mar. 18, 1900, ae. 57-11-9.

CHILDREN

9. Irene Maud, b. Bristol, May 8, 1868 ; d. Nov. 4, 1879, ae. 11-5-26.
10. William Harrison, b. B., Jan. 18, 1871 ; d. Mar. 29, 1872, ae. 1-2-11.
11. Daughter, b. B.; d. Dec. 2, 1878, ae. 4 weeks.

(6) Henry W. Drake, b. May 30, 1846, m. Sept. 25, 1869, Lavinia S. Page, dau. of Mitchel H. (See.) Divorced. (See Roll of Honor.) He is a locomotive engineer at Harrisburg, Pa. She m. (2) Oscar F. Morse. (See.)

CHILDREN

12. Minnie Eva, b. Bristol, Oct. 8, 1870 ; m. Frank E. Keezer. (See.)
13. Charles Mitchell, b. B., Apr. 6, 1873 ; m. in Boston, Sept., 1895, Ida M. Lukes. He is an electric car motorman, Somerville, Mass.

---

1. Thomas Thayer Drake, son of Ebenezer T. and Abigail (Berry) Drake, was b. Pittsfield, July 21, 1827. He m., Jan. 27, 1853, Emily Ann, dau. of Samuel and Betsey (Swett)

Jenness, b. Pittsfield, Nov. 13, 1832. In 1873, he settled in Bristol. He is a farmer, mechanic, and mover of buildings. Is a Republican, Calvinist Baptist. She d. in Bristol, Mar. 2, 1902, ae. 69-3-19.

CHILDREN, all born in Pittsfield

*2. Edward Malcom, b. June 5, 1855.
*3. Ervin Thayer, b. May, 21, 1857.
4. Herbert Elmer, b. Dec. 30, 1859; m. Aug. 25, 1886, Mary Eloise Johnson. Graduated Wesleyan University in 1886, taught six years in East Greenwich academy in East Greenwich, R. I.; studied two years in Europe, returning in 1894, and has since been teacher of Latin in the classical High school in Providence, R. I.
5. Annie Isabel, b. Dec. 5, 1861; d. July 27, 1864, ae. 2-7-22.
6. Addie May, b. June 8, 1865. Graduated Tilton Seminary 1886, studied in Europe, taught French and German in Tilton Seminary; afterwards in Drew Seminary, Carmel, N. Y.
7. John Payson, b. May 26, 1857; m. June 22, 1899, Hattie Pearl Krum, Stevens's Point, Wis. He graduated Wesleyan University, Middletown, Conn., 1894; taught the sciences three years in High school, Stevens's Point, Wis.; in Moline, Ill., High school; now in Western Illinois State Normal school. Child:

 a. Russell Payson, b. Malone, Feb. 27, 1901.

8. Amy Belle, b. June 3, 1869; graduated Tilton Seminary, 1892, and Normal school, Lowell, Mass. Is principal graded school, St. Johnsbury, Vt.
9. Arthur Knowlton, b. Mar. 11, 1872; graduated Harvard Medical school, 1898. Pathologist and assistant superintendent in State Hospital, Tewksbury, Mass.

(2) Edward M. Drake, b. June 5, 1855, m. June 5, 1883, Almira Helen Haskins, of Danbury. He was a lumber manufacturer. Removed to Tilton, 1892, where he is a carpenter. Was deputy sheriff at Tilton six years.

CHILDREN

10. Mabel Helen, b. Bristol, Feb. 16, 1886.
11. Raymond Haskins, b. B., Nov. 17, 1890.

(3) Ervin T. Drake, b. May 21, 1857, m. Nov. 5, 1884, Anna Maria, dau. Abram Dolloff. (See.) She d. of consumption, June 1, 1885, ae. 27-1-23. He m. (2) Mary Louise, dau. Jonas B. and Addie Proctor Aiken, of Franklin. He is a physician of large practice in Franklin, where he settled in 1885.

CHILDREN

12. Ruth Bradley, b. Franklin, June 4, 1890.
13. Mary Louise, b. F., Aug. 20, 1892.
14. Ervin Thayer, b. F., Nov. 3, 1894.
15. Robert Aiken, b. F., Dec. 6, 1896.

THE DRAPER FAMILIES

1. Jason Currier Draper, son of Nathaniel and Mary (Gill) Draper, was b. in Plymouth, Dec. 7, 1816. He m. Dec.

22, 1843, Hannah True, dau. of Benjamin F. and Sarah (True) Cass, b. Andover, Nov. 9, 1819. He was a glove manufacturer in Plymouth ; settled in Bristol, 1858, and continued this business, first on Lake street, and later on site of present saw-mill in Bristol village till his death. He erected the residence on School street, opposite the schoolhouse grounds, and there d. Apr. 24. 1868, ae. 51-4-17. He was a successful business man, a Republican, Mason, official member of the Methodist church, and superintendent of the Sunday-school. Mrs. Draper d. Bristol, Nov. 26, 1890, ae. 71-0-17.

CHILDREN

2. Sarah G., d. Aug. 20, 1850, ae. 1-2-18.
3. Luzetta Sarah, b. Plymouth, Dec. 29, 1852 ; m. George A. Emerson. (See.)
4. Jason True, b. Bristol, Dec. 30, 1859; graduated Boston University, 1884, receiving degree of A.B. Received from same institution, in 1889, degree of A.M. He has taught at Lyndon Institute, Lyndon, Vt.; at Berea College, Berea, Ky.; high school, Pueblo, Colo.; high school at Oakland, Cal., and is now at the head of the department of Natural Science in the high school at Holyoke, Mass. He m. June 23, 1886, Catherine Ella, dau. of Nathaniel and Philinda Morrison, b. Somerville, Mass., Jan. 15, 1860. No children.

---

1. Alvah McQuesten Draper, the son of William and Sarah (Lacy) Draper, was b. Plymouth, Nov. 20, 1828. Mar. 30, 1853, he m. Rosella Euphremie, dau. of Joseph and Mary (Hoit) Pike, b. Chateaugay, N. Y., Sept. 28, 1832. They came to Bristol in November, 1868, and he was manufacturer of buckskin gloves and mittens. Returned to Plymouth in November, 1884, and in April, 1890, emigrated to Iowa. He d. Boone, Iowa, Mar. 20, 1899, ae. 70-4-0. She res. Pilot Mound, Iowa.

CHILDREN

⁂2. Albert William, b. Plymouth, Feb. 14, 1854.
3. Eugene Cochran, b. P., May 1, 1856; m. June 11, 1887, Sarah E. Roby, dau. Lowell R. (See.) Was a workman in Taylor & Gordon's mill ; d. in Bristol, Sept. 11, 1888, ae. 32-4-10. She res. Hebron. No Children :
⁂4. Alvah Everett, b. P., Nov. 21, 1864.
5. Leslie Binford, b. P., May 24, 1867 ; m. Jan. 1, 1888, Abbie Dearborn. No children. He again m., and res. Pilot Mound, Boone Co., Iowa. Child :
   a. Alvah Leslie, b. Feb., 1900.
6. Elsie Mary, b. Bristol, Apr. 2, 1871 ; went West with her parents, and m. July 30, 1892, Rev. Harris Norton Lawrence, Congregational clergyman. They res. at Boone, Iowa. Child :
   a. Gertrude May, b. Laurens, Iowa, Dec. 12, 1893.

(2)   Albert W. Draper, b. Feb. 14, 1854, m. Lovinia A. Bayley, July 10, 1875. He m. (2) and res. Manchester.

CHILDREN, by first wife

7. Ethelyn, b. Oct. 3, 1876.
8. George Albert, b. Mar. 13, 1879; d. Aug. 29, 1888, ae. 9-5-16.
9. Edgar, b. Sept. 11, 1880; d. Oct. 1, 1881, ae. 1-0-20.
10. Inez, b. Oct. 20, 1882; d. Aug. 25, 1885, ae. 2-10-5.

(4) Alvah E. Draper, b. Nov. 12, 1864, m. June 11, 1887, Mary Alma, dau. Mark G. and Eliza A. (Sanborn) Duston, b. Salisbury, Mass., Dec. 3, 1861. He is a clergyman, a member of New Hampshire Methodist Conference since 1892. Graduated from Tilton Seminary and from Boston University, College of Liberal Arts.

CHILDREN

11. Stacy Arthur, b. June 28, 1888. 12. Helen Pike, b. Feb. 8, 1891.
13. Marion Elsie, b. Apr. 2, 1893. 14. Jason Sanborn, b. Nov. 3, 1894.
15. Ralph Lemuel, b. Aug. 23, 1896.
16. Norman Everett, b. May 2, 1898.

George Albert Draper, a brother of Alvah M., above, was b. Plymouth, Mar. 15, 1822. He came to Bristol about 1866, and was a manufacturer of buckskin gloves here a few years previous to his death which occurred Aug. 7, 1874. His age was 52-4-22, and he was unm. (See Fatal Accidents.)

THE DREW FAMILIES

1. Samuel Drew, b. Shapleigh, Me., was a Revolutionary soldier from Plymouth. His first enlistment was July 11, 1775, at which time his age was given as 19. He m. Betsey Webber, b. Methuen, Mass. In 1785, they settled a mile north of the Locke neighborhood, in Bristol, on the old road to the Bridgewater meeting-house, long since abandoned. He was the first settler on this farm, and here the first town meeting of Bridgewater was held, in 1788. He spent his last days in the family of his son, Samuel, in Northern New York. She d. in family of son John, in New Hampton.

CHILDREN

*2. Amos Webster, b. Plymouth, Dec. 20, 1783.
*3. Benjamin, b. P., Apr. 17, 1785.
4. Betty, b. Bristol, Apr. 20, 1787; m. Jacob Swain and removed to Gilmanton, where he d. She d. New Hampton. No children.
5. Samuel, b. B., Aug. 24, 1789. Had a family and removed to Northern New York.
6. Sally, b. B., Sept. 28, 1791; m. Ephraim Merrill. (See.)
7. Polly, b. B., Apr. 2, 1794; m. —— Roby, and removed to Stewartstown.
8. John, b. B., June 9, 1797. He m. a dau. of Esq. Simpson, of New Hampton, and lived and d. there. She d. in the West in family of dau. Louise. Children:

a. William.   *b.* James, who went to California when 20 years old.   *c.* Harriet.   *d.* Louise.   *e.* Sarah.   *f.* Elijah, and perhaps others.

(2)   Amos W. Drew, b. Dec. 20, 1783, m. Dorothy, dau. Jacob Gurdy. (See.) Published Sept., 1803. He m. (2) Ruth, dau. Samuel Gurdy. (See.) He was a farmer in Bristol, New Hampton, and for 20 years at Goffs Falls, where he d. Jan. 15, 1873, in family of daughter Susan, ae. 89-0-25.

CHILDREN, all supposed to have been born in Bristol

9.   Sally, b. Dec. 1, 1803; m. George B. Gordon, May 20, 1827. Res. Alexandria. Three children. Family all deceased.
10.   Betsey, b. Nov. 2, 1805 ; m. Thomas R. Emmons. (See.)
11.   Aaron, b. Apr. 27, 1808; m. Mary Colby. He d. in Manchester, she in Collinsville, Conn.
12.   Mary, m. Solomon French, a farmer in Bristol. He d. Sept. 4, 1882, ae. 69-6-3; she d. Jan. 14, 1887, ae. 76-8-27. No children.
*13.   Asa, b. Apr. 24, 1812.
14.   Ann, m. George Burns, and d. in Boston, Mass.
15.   Louise, b. 1816; m. Moses Hemmingway in 1842. She d. in Stoneham, Mass. He m. (2) 1877, Etta Paine, and res. Stoneham, Mass. No children.
*16.   Alvin, S., b. Nov. 3, 1818.
17.   Susan Hoyt, b. June 21, 1820; m. William H. Perkins. (See.)
*18.   Amasa Worthen, b. Dec. 20, 1822.
*19.   Alfred R., b. Apr. 6, 1824.
20.   Lydia, m. Enoch Nicholson. She d., and he went to Nebraska, where he was killed by lightning.
21.   Lucy, m. (1) Jesse Cross; (2) George B. McQuesten, No. Londonderry. Children :
   a. Amos Webster.   *b.* Rufus.   *c.* Webster Cross, drowned.
   d. Sarah,   *e.* Charles.   *f.* Melvina, m. John Hadley.
22.   Dorothy, d. young.   23. Melissa, d. young.

(3)   Benjamin Drew, b. Apr. 17, 1785, m. Sept. 3, 1807, Sally, dau. of John Harriman (See), b. July 6, 1788. He was a farmer in Bristol, New Hampton, and in Stewartstown, where he d. Oct. 5, 1869, ae. 84-5-18 ; she d. Dec. 10, 1870, ae. 82-5-4.

CHILDREN

*24.   Amos Webster, b. Bristol, Apr. 5, 1808.
25.   Mary Harriman, b. May 4, 1810.
26.   Lucy, b. Apr. 11, 1815; d. Dec. 9, 1842, ae. 27-7-28.
27.   Sally, b. Sept. 21, 1820; d. Apr. 16, 1839, ae. 18-6-25.
28.   Benjamin, b. Aug. 4, 1822 ; d. Sept. 10, 1822.
29.   Benjamin, b. Jan. 20, 1826.   30. Edwin W., b. Dec. 10, 1828.

(13)   Asa Drew, b. Apr. 24, 1812, m. Nov. 11, 1834. Sarah C., dau. of Peter Wells (See), b. Sept. 25, 1808. He was a farmer for many years in the Locke neighborhood, then in Hebron, and later res. some years on Lake street. She d. Sept. 7, 1890, ae. 81-11-12, in the family of her son, Harvey, in Alexandria; he d. in the family of his dau., Mrs. Samuel O. Morrill, Bridgewater, Jan. 23, 1900, ae. 87-8-29.

CHILDREN

*31.   Harvey W., b. Bristol, Sept. 2, 1835.

32.   Augustus B., b. B., Feb. 2, 1837; d. in Bridgewater, June 28, 1863, ae. 26-4-26, of disease contracted in the army. (See Roll of Honor.)

33.   Emily, } b. B., Sept. 25, 1839; { m. Samuel O. Morrill, Bridewater.
34.   Charles, } { d. Bridgewater, Oct. 18, 1850, ae. 11-0-23.

35.   Peter Wells, b. Hebron, Feb. 25, 1843. Served in Company C, 12th Regt. N. H. Vols., and d. in the service Jan. 21, 1863, ae. 19-10-26. While on the march this soldier was taken sick and fell out of the ranks, was arrested by the provost guard, and soon after died of the measles. He was reported a deserter and this record so stood till 1880, when it was amended.

36.   Hannah W., b. Hebron, Apr. 8, 1845; m. Lorenzo Flanders, Bridgewater. He. d. Jan. 22, 1902.

37.   Mary Ann, b. Bridgewater, Oct. 31, 1849; m. George F. Follansbee. (See.)

(16)   Alvin S. Drew, b. Nov. 3, 1818, m. Sept. 25, 1840, Anstrice Caroline, dau. of Russell and Polly (Flanders) Ray, b. Manchester, May 4, 1825. He was many years on the Boston police force and d. East Boston, Oct. 31, 1891, ae. 72-11-28.

CHILDREN

38.   Frances Ellen, b. Dec. 21, 1843; d. Jan. 4, 1885, ae. 41-0-13. She m. Howard Woodbury, June 1, 1862, who d. Jan. 21, 1888. Children:

a.   Mabelle Frances Augusta, b. Nov. 7, 1866; m. Benjamin H. Douglass, Apr. 29, 1891.
b.   Frank Woodbury, d. in infancy.
c   Herbert Granville, b. Nov. 10, 1868.
d.   Ethel Ward, b. Nov. 6, 1870.
e.   Franklin Howard, b. Sept. 28, 1875.

39.   Manilus Mortimer, b. Jan. 21, 1845; d. May, 1845, ae. 4 mos.

40.   George Granville, b. Aug. 16, 1847; m. Dec. 25, 1870, Elta T. Bean. He m. (2) June 17, 1883, Emily B. Baker, who d. Apr. 1, 1890. He m. (3). He is a lawyer in Boston. Children:

a.   Effie Belle, b. 1871, d. 1871.
b.   Blanche Telula, b. Sept 30, 1872.

41.   Ella, b. Jan. 23, 1849; d. July 1849.

42.   Emma Jane, b. Nov. 28, 1851; m. Osro A. Scovell. Children:

a.   Edith Ward, b. Mar. 16, 1876.
b.   Clifford, b. Feb., 1877; d. July, 1889, ae. 12-5-.

(18)   Amasa W. Drew, b. Dec. 20, 1822, m. Oct. 23, 1850, Julia Ann, dau. of Josiah Fuller (See), b. Aug. 5, 1831, and d. Boston, Mass., Sept. 24, 1888, ae. 57-1-19. He was on Boston police force; shipping clerk for large shoe firm; gate keeper and ticket agent, East Boston ferry. Res. East Boston.

CHILDREN, all born East Boston

43.   Harriet Eliza, b. June 28, 1852; d. Mar. 16, 1855, ae. 2-8-18.

44.   Charles Fuller, b. Feb. 24, 1856; m. Georgia E. Golden, March, 1880. She d. November, 1882, in East Boston. He m. Sept., 1899, Alice Lambert Rumney, of East Boston. Child:

a. Henry C., b. Nov., 1882, d. May, 1886, ae. 3-6-.

45. Hattie Ermina, b. June 6, 1858; m. Dec. 12, 1883, Henry H. Rich. Two children, d. in infancy.

46. Henry Webster, b. Aug. 17, 1864. Has been in British Columbia, mining, since about 1885.

(19) Alfred R. Drew, b. Apr. 6, 1824, m. May, 1847, Mary Gannon, dau. John. She d. in Boston in April, 1851, or '52, and he m. (2) Lucretia Jordan, of Portland, Me., who d. in Boston. He m. (3) Mary Jane Sanborn, b. Northfield. In 1849, Mr. Drew assumed the position of patrolman on the police force of Boston; was made special officer in 1870; in October, 1878, was made Chief Inspector, and therefore ranked third on the force which embraced over 800 men. He retired about 1888, and res. for a time in Canaan. In 1893, he returned to his native place and here d. Nov. 8, 1893, ae. 69-7-2; she d. Bristol, Apr. 22, 1899, ae. 68 years.

CHILDREN

47. Henrietta Frances, b. Nov. 22, 1848; m. Sept. 5, 1887, Charles W. Holmes. (See.)
48. Albert R., b. 1850, d. 1854, ae. 4 years
49. Emma R., b. 1854. Unm. Res. Boston.
50. Frank Herbert, b. 1856, killed on cars in 1878, ae. 22.

(24) Amos W. Drew, b. Apr. 5, 1808, m. Julia Esther, dau. Hubbard and Abigail (Rumford) Lovering, b. June 4, 1815, Loudon. They res. Colebrook and Lancaster. He represented his town in the legislature of 1847 and 1848; was state senator in 1862 and 1863; treasurer of Coos county in 1852 and 1853, and coroner of the county for nearly twenty years. He d. Mar. 22, 1888, in Colebrook, ae. 79-11-17; she d. Stratford, Apr. 22, 1890, ae. 74-10-18.

CHILDREN

51. Lucy Abigail, b. May 4, 1843; d. in Colebrook, Oct. 23, 1887, ae. 44-5-19.
52. Irving Webster, b. Colebrook, Jan. 8, 1845; m. Carrie H., dau. Dan S. and Sarah Merrill, b. Woodstock, Aug. 14, 1845. He is one of the prominent lawyers of the state. Was a member of the state senate in 1883; a delegate to the Democratic National convention in 1880, 1892, add 1896, and one of the commissioners for the erection of the state library building. Children:
　　a. Paul, b. Feb. 20, 1872; d. Oct. 1, 1872.
　　b. Neil B., b. Sept. 9, 1873.　　*c.* Pitt F., b. Aug. 27, 1875.
　　d. Sarah Maynard, b. Dec. 19, 1876.
53. Benjamin Franklin, b. June 28, 1848; m.; one child, Josephine.
54. Warren Edwin, b. Stewartstown, June 29, 1850; m. Abby Crawford, of Colebrook. Children:
　　a. Jennie.　　*b.* George.　　*c.* Ellen.
55. Julia Ellen, b. Aug. 21, 1855; m. F. N. Day, Stratford. Children:
　　a. Esther.　　*b.* Frederick.
56. Holman Arthur, b. Aug. 28, 1857; m. Mary Bedell, Colebrook.

57. Edward Everett, b. Sept. 24, 1859.
Six sons d. in infancy.

(31) Harvey W. Drew. b. Sept. 2, 1835, m. in 1860 (?)
Lizzie A., dau. of Mitchel H. Page (See), b. May 21, 1841.
He served in Co. C, 12th Regt. N. H. Vols. in the Civil war.
(See Roll of Honor.) He was a blacksmith in Bristol, Bridge-
water, Groton, and Alexandria. Mrs. Drew d. Alexandria,
Mar. 23, 1888, ae. 46-10-2. He m. (2) Mrs. Ruhama Alexan-
der, of Alexandria, where he d. Aug. 5, 1895, ae. 59-11-3.

CHILDREN

58. Elmer Elsworth, b. Dec. 17, 1861 ; m. Alberta Avery, of Plymouth. Has been a policeman in Somerville, Mass., since 1895.
59. Nellie Eva, b. Bridgewater, May 7, 1865 ; m. Jan. 1, 1880, Edwin
W. Farnum, and res. Lebanon. Children :
    a. James Perley, b. Mar. 13, 1885.
    b. Harry Gould, b. July 14, 1890.
    c. Helen Mary, b. Mar. 14, 1894.
60. Perley Asa, b. Jan. 14, 1867; m. Delia L. Emery, dau. Peter, b.
Canada, July 15, 1869. Res. Cornish Center. Children :
    a. Franklin Perley, b. Aug. 16, 1886.
    b. Clarence Emery, b. Oct. 26, 1888.
61. Ethel Dollie, b. Sept. 14, 1882. Res. Alexandria.

----

1. Rev. Alfred E. Drew, son of Aaron and Maria,
was b. Fairfax, Vt., Sept. 13, 1841. He m. July 17, 1867,
Anna E., dau. of Benjamin Atwood, b. Newbury, Vt., Aug.
21, 1848. He is a Methodist clergyman, and was pastor of the
Methodist church in Bristol two years from April, 1869. Has
labored in New Hampshire, Connecticut, and California ; now
pastor at Tarpon Springs, Fla.

CHILD

2. Kate, b. Littleton, Jan. 30, 1869 ; m. Dec. 6, 1895, W. C. Evans ;
res. New York city.

THE DURGIN FAMILIES

1. William Durgin is said to have come from England in
1690 and settled in Massachusetts. Of his five children
2. William, b. 1717, settled in Epping and removed to
Sanbornton in 1768, where he d., in 1789, ae. 72. He had 13
children, one of whom was
3. William, b. Sept. 5, 1750. He m. (1) Elizabeth Morrison, (2) Mrs. Hannah Clement, Nov. 4, 1798. He d. May 11,
1822, ae. 71-8-6. Of his 15 children, one by second wife was
4. John Hill, b. Sanbornton, Nov. 2, 1800. He was a
teacher, storekeeper, farmer and drover. A Whig and an abolitionist. He came to Bristol in 1870, and purchased a home on

North Main street where he d. Sept. 20, 1882, ae. 81-10-18. He m. Lucretia, dau. of Amos and Nancy Brown, b. Wheelock, Vt., and d. Bristol, June 7, 1875, ae. 72.

CHILDREN

5.　Nancy Ambrose, b. Sept. 24, 1825; d. July 4, 1826, ae. 0-9-10.

6.　Nancy Ambrose, b. Oct. 15, 1827. She was educated at Tilton Seminary; taught school many years, including three years in graded schools of Bristol; was three years superintending school committee of Bristol. Res. at the family homestead. Unm.

7.　Laura Blodgett, b. Nov. 30, 1830; m. Nov. 24, 1850, Charles D. McDuffee, b. Rochester, Mar. 4, 1829. He was agent of the Everett mills, Lawrence, and later of the Manchester mills, Manchester. He d. July 5, 1902, ae. 73-4-1. She res. Manchester. Four children.

8.　Lucretia Clement, b. July 10, 1833; m. Eusebe F. Mansean, and res. Wolton, P. Q. Six children.

9.　Clement Thayer, b. Sept. 4, 1835; m. Nov. 23, 1860, Mary E. McGonigal, (2) Maria Chickering. Two children. Res. Bridgeport, Conn.

10.　Louise Maria R., b. June 1, 1837; m. Frank L. Prince, of Amherst, Nov. 4, 1855. Four children.

11.　Horace Webster, b. Sept. 4, 1839; m. Irene Calvert, of Louisville, Ky., June 15, 1871; he m. (2) Dora H. Hibbard, who d. Feb. 10, 1888, and he m. (3) Ella F. Lee, of Manchester, Mass. He was a merchant in Taunton, Mass.; now treasurer and general manager of Granite City Soap company, Newburg, N. Y.

12.　Clara Kendrick, b. May 1, 1843; m. John M. Prince, Jan. 1, 1861; a farmer in Amherst. Five children.

13.　George Arthur, b. Sept. 24, 1844; d. Aug. 11, 1855, ae. 0-10-17.

14.　Charles Eastman, b. Feb. 24, 1847; a merchant in Taunton, Mass., now res. Cambridgeport, Mass.; agent Granite City Soap company. He m., Aug. 16, 1871, Abbie H. Pettingill of Salem, Mass., who d. at Cambridgeport, June 23, 1901, ae. 52-4-22. Child:

　　a.　Arthur Kemble, b. Sept. 11, 1873.

———

1.　Benjamin George Durgin was first taxed in Bristol in 1868. He m., Sept. 26, 1862, Mary A., dau. of Jacob Cass. He was a carpenter, and a resident of Bristol much of the time till his death, which occurred at Goffstown, Dec. 1, 1901. She res. Bristol.

CHILD

2.　Arthur Cass, b. Bristol, Sept. 19, 1868; m. Dec. 23, 1889, Maud M. Smith. He is an electrician. Children:

　　a.　Howard W., b. May 5, 1893.　　b.　Fred, b. May 3, 1895.

THE DURRELL FAMILY

1.　Rev. Jesse Murton Durrell was the son of William Henry and Sarah (Averill) Durrell. He was b. in Boston, Mass., and m. July 23, 1878, Irene Sarah, dau. of Hiram and Betsey Clark, b. Plymouth, May 17, 1852. He is a Methodist clergyman, and has been a member of the New Hampshire

Annual Conference since 1869. He has filled eleven pastorates, including three years at Bristol, 1874-'77; was president of Tilton Seminary 1891-'95; now presiding elder of Dover district, and res. Dover.

THE DUSTIN FAMILIES

1. Samuel Dustin, son of Samuel and Rachel (Sanborn) Dustin, was a descendant of Hannah Dustin. He was b. Sanbornton, Aug. 21, 1811, and m. Jan. 9, 1837, Polly D., dau. of John and Betsey (Rundlett) Morrison, b. Sept. 24, 1814, in Sanbornton. He res. in Sanbornton, Bristol, 1857-'72, and in Franklin; was engaged in buying and selling bark, etc. She d. Franklin, July 30, 1897, ae. 82-10-6. He d. Franklin.

CHILDREN

2. James Prescott, b. Dec. 1, 1843; m. Mary Bean, dau. of Reuben, June 21, 1864. She d. Nov. 24, 1865, ae. 20, and he m. Alice D. French, of Andover, Jan. 14, 1870. He was station agent for some years; removed to Plymouth about 1876, where he was a farmer. She d. Plymouth, and he d. same place, May 12, 1900, ae. 56-5-11. Child:

    a. James Morrison, b. Plymouth.

3. Florence Emily, b. Oct. 18, 1847. Res. Beardsley, Minn; unm.
4. Samuel Perry, b. Mar. 6, 1850; m. Feb., 1874, Lydia Kelley, and res. Franklin; for some years a bookkeeper. He d. at the Margaret Pillsbury hospital, Concord, Feb. 23, 1903, ae. 52-11-17. Children:

    a. Carl E., d. Franklin, June 4, 1903, ae. 26.
    b. C. Eugene.   *c.* Winonah.

---

1. Quincy Stephen Dustin is the son of Daniel Flanders and Sarah Jane (Pickering) Dustin, b. Hill, Jan. 29, 1857. He m., Oct. 31, 1878, Henrietta E., dau. of John L. Cheney (See), b. May 20, 1863, and d. in Bristol, Jan. 6, 1892, ae. 28-7-16. He m., Feb. 1, 1893, Georgianna G., sister of his first wife, b. Mar. 3, 1868. They res. in Bristol and Hill. Farmers.

CHILDREN

2. Ida May, b. Hill, Dec. 25, 1879; m. Charles R. Seavey. (See.)
3. Gerald Leonard, b. New Hampton, Oct. 10, 1881.
4. Grace Etta Maud, b. Bristol, Aug. 16, 1884; m. Frank E. Woodward, May 5, 1902.
5. Pearl Augustus, b. B., Oct. 16, 1887; d. B., Feb. 6, 1889, ae. 1-3-20.
6. Henrietta Pearl, b. B., Jan. 4, 1892.
7. Stephen Cheney, b. B., Dec. 11, 1893.
8. Harold Quincy.

THE EASTMAN FAMILIES

1. Capt. Elias Maybee Eastman, the son of Thomas Follansbee and Sarah (Maybee) Eastman, was b. Eastport, Me.,

Apr. 7, 1821. When ten years old he ran away from home and shipped as a cabin boy on ship "Samuel"; followed the sea till 1864; was then pilot four years in Portland harbor. He came to Bristol in 1871; teamster. At 82 he is still a hard working man. In November, 1842, he m. Elizabeth Harrison, dau. of Abraham, b. Belfast, Ire. She d. in 1875, ae. 40.

---

1. Horace Weston Eastman, son of Henry Hoyt and Caroline (Preston) Eastman, was b. Groton, Oct. 9, 1867. He m., Oct. 23, 1889, Martha McIntosh, b. Boston, Mass., May, 1873. He came from Plymouth 1896; blacksmith.

CHILDREN

2. Haven Sylvan, b. Plymouth, May 31, 1891.
3. Clifton Kenneth, b. Bristol, Oct. 26, 1896.
4. Roy Linwood, b. B., Apr. 20, 1903.

Susan Eastman, b. Bath, Apr. 25, 1822, made her home in the family of her sister, Mrs. Solon S. Southard, for many years. She d. June 29, 1900, ae. 78-2-4.

THE EATON FAMILIES

1. David Eaton came from Candia and settled in the Hall neighborhood about 1812. He m. Abigail Rowe, dau. of Isaac Smythe. She d. Dec. 21, 1835, ae. 48; and he m. Dec. 8, 1841, Mrs. Anne (Peaslee) Ash. He d. Mar. 22, 1857, ae. 79; she m. Joseph Sanborn, Sanbornton. He was a cooper and farmer.

CHILDREN

2. John, b. Candia, Oct., 1811; m. Judith Johnson, of Hopkinton. Seven children. He d. and she removed to Concord.
3. Ebenezer, b. Bristol, Jan., 1816; m. Mary J., dau. of Moses Sanborn. (See.) He was a farmer and trader on Summer street; d. Mar. 31, 1865, ae. 49-2-. She m. (2) David S. Fowler. (See.) Child:
   a. Henry F., d. Aug. 27, 1849, ae. 4-8-.
4. Sally, b. B., d. Apr., 1819, ae. 6 mos.
5. Sally, b. B., d. Oct., 1822; ae. 2 years.
6. Rufus, b. B., June 30, 1822; m. Sept. 19, 1848, Mary Jane Jewell, dau. of John, b. Northfield, Feb. 19, 1826. A cooper and farmer on Summer street. Republican. Children:
   a. Frank, b. Bristol, Oct. 8, 1849; d. Oct. 25, 1870, ae. 21-0-17.
   b. George H., b. B., June 30, 1852; d. Sept. 1, 1870, ae. 18-2-1.
7. Frank, b. B., 1828; d. of smallpox in Manchester, Feb. 21, 1848, ae. 20.

---

1. Jacob Sawyer Eaton, M.D., was the son of Nathaniel and Mary (Kimball) Eaton, b. in Warner, Jan. 4, 1805. Sept.

20, 1830, he m. Mrs. Harriet (Bean) Kimball, dau. of Daniel and Salley (Pattee) Bean, b. Warner, Apr. 22, 1810. He removed from Alexandria to Bristol in 1832. (See Physicians.) His wife d. Dec. 5, 1837, ae. 27-7-13. He m. Sept. 2, 1849, Alma Ellery, dau. of Edward and Alma (Holden) Tyler, b. Jan. 5, 1815 ; d. Harvard, Mass., Nov. 21, 1899, ae. 84-10-16. He d. Harvard, Sept. 5, 1888, from the shock of a carriage accident four months previous. His age was 83-8-1.

CHILDREN

2. John Marshall, b. Bristol, May 12, 1832; m. Oct. 27, 1858, Maria, dau. of Louis Wetherby, b. Concord, Mass., Mar. 9, 1837. He studied medicine with his father and at the Harvard Medical school, where he graduated in 1856. He practiced in Stow, Mass., and later in Milford, Mass. Is now retired at Harvard, Mass. (See Roll of Honor.) No children. Congregationalist.
3. Frances Amelia, b. B., June 10, 1835 ; d. Sept. 8, 1838, ae. 3-2-28.
4. Horace Augustus, b. Nov. 5, 1837; d. Mar. 4, 1839, ae. 1-3-29.
5. Lucian Kimball, b. B., Nov. 7, 1850; d. Fort Wayne, Ind., Mar. 16, 1888, ae. 37-4-9.
6. Harriet Frances, b. B., Mar., 1853; d. July 7, 1863, ae. 10-4-.
7. James Ellery, b. Stow, Mass., July 10, 1855; m. July 27, 1889, Flora Kate, dau. of Dr. Robert H. Timpany, b. Toledo, O., Oct. 27, 1858. A merchant in Toledo. Children :
    a. Ellery Timpany, b. Toledo, Dec. 23, 1894.
    b. Albert Tyler, b. T., Nov. 17, 1898.
8. Alma Tyler, b. Nov. 12, 1857, was a teacher in public schools of Harvard. She m. June 19, 1889, H. B. Royal, M.D., of Harvard. Child :
    a. Kent Tyler, b. Oct. 25, 1891.

---

1. William Eaton, son of Thomas, was b. Feb. 29, 1754, removed from Seabrook, Mass., to Sanbornton, in 1800. He was a Revolutionary soldier. He m. Betsey Eaton. He d. Oct. 11, 1837, ae. 83-7-12. She d. Dec. 14, 1839. They were the parents of 13 children, of whom one was
2. Wheeler, b. Sept. 2, 1787. He m. (1) Abigail Perkins, (2) Mrs. Nancy (Burley) Sleeper. He was a farmer two miles below Hill village. Six children, one of whom was
3. Cyrus Wheeler, b. Weare, May 23, 1813. He m. Phebe Whitcher Goodwin, of Weare. Located in Bristol in 1841 ; was a carpenter and manufacturer of seraphines. He d. Rockport, Mass., Aug. 13, 1849, ae. 36-2-20. She d. in Plymouth, Oct. 15, 1863, ae. 44-1-.

CHILDREN

4. Cyrus Perkins, b. Franklin, Jan. 19, 1839; m. Oct. 19, 1865, Henrietta Vander Woerd, dau. of Charles and Jacoba J. (Pfeiffer) Vander Woerd, Waltham, Mass. She was b. Leyden, Holland, Sept. 7, 1844, and d. Waltham, May 28, 1901, ae. 56-8-21. He has been for many years an inspector of timing in the factory of the Waltham Watch company. Child :

11

a. Louis Gill, b. Waltham, Feb. 24, 1872; m. June 6, 1899, Jessie Mabelle Downer, b. Middlebury, Vt., Nov. 17, 1872. Teacher of violin in Boston.

5. Emily Jane, b. Mar. 11, 1841; m. Charles H. Spencer. (See.)

6. George W., b. Bristol; res. in Chicago and has four children.

7. Clara Jane, b. B., May 30, 1848; m. Jan., 1866, Jonathan Hoag, a grocer in Stoneham, Mass.

---

1. William Eaton, son of Caleb and Sarah (Cass) Eaton, was b. Sanbornton, Mar. 28, 1811. He m., Apr. 19, 1839, Mary Ann Gordon, who d. May 5, 1855, ae. 42. He m. May 19, 1856, Susan Smith, of Meredith, who d. Franklin, Apr. 6, 1877, and he m., Oct. 8, 1878, Mrs. Mary Edgerly, widow of Jonathan. He res. on the Levi Locke farm, on Summer street, 1848–'52; was a deacon of the Free Baptist church.

CHILDREN

2. Mary Melissa, b. Meredith, Oct., 1842; m. James A. Curtice. (See.)

3. Sarah Ann, b. Jan. 14, 1845; d. in New Hampton, Oct. 8, 1854, ae. 9-8-24.

4. Emma Harriet, b. Apr. 29, 1854; d. June 16, 1872, ae. 18-1-17.

THE EDGERLY FAMILY

1. Moses Gilman Edgerly, son of Jonathan and Abigail (Gilman) Edgerly, was b. in Sanbornton, Nov. 23, 1798. He m., Nov. 11, 1824, Mahala Rollins, dau. of Reuben and Anna C. (Clifford) Osgood, b. Sanbornton, Sept. 21, 1805. He was a machinist in Sanbornton and Nashua, and came to Bristol about 1838 from Amoskeag. Res. Lake street, where he d. Dec. 5, 1870, ae. 72-0-12. She d. May 23, 1866, ae. 60-8-2.

CHILDREN

2. Salathiel, b. Sanbornton, Feb. 9, 1826; d. Apr. 30, 1827, ae. 1-2-21.

3. Abigail Ann, b. S., Dec. 25, 1829; m. Charles R. Currier. (See.)

4. Moody Osgood, b. S., Aug. 15, 1832; m. Sept. 29, 1856, Evelyn S., dau. of Sias and Harriet (Batchelder) Scott, b. in Vermont, and d. Denmark, Me., Nov. 22, 1864. He m. May 15, 1866, Harriet E., dau. of Jacob N. Darling (See), b. July 24, 1838, and d. Aug. 19, 1897, ae. 59-0-25. He went to Nashua, 1858, served on quota of Nashua in Co. F, 1st Regt., in Civil war; returned to Bristol in 1864; was several years in business as a machinist; now a brass worker. Republican, Methodist, G. A. R.

5. Mahala, b. S., Oct. 31, 1834; and d. Jan. 31, 1835.

6. Mary Howard, b. Amoskeag, July 26, 1839; and d. of consumption in Bristol, Mar. 4, 1858, ae. 18-7-8.

7. Ellen Frances, b. Bristol, Dec. 9, 1841; and d. of consumption, Oct. 8, 1860, ae. 18-9-29.

THE EDWARDS FAMILY

1. John Edwards was the son of John and Jemima (Wallingford) Edwards. He was b. in Bradford, Mass., Apr. 14,

1764, and m. Feb. 17, 1785, Betsey Holden, b. Aug. 29, 1767, in Pepperell, Mass. They were farmers in Gilmanton previous to 1830, when they settled in Bristol on the Boardman farm on High street, where, after 64 years of wedded life, he d. Jan. 2, 1849, ae. 84-8-18. Mrs. Edwards d. in Concord, July 11, 1855, ae. 87-10-12.

CHILDREN

2. Betsey, b. Pepperell, Mass., Aug. 23, 1786 ; m. Timothy Frisbee, came to Bristol in 1838, went to New York in 1839, and d. there Nov. 30, 1861, ae. 75-3-7. Child :

    a. John L., an eminent chemist, d. in Covington, Ky.

3. Hephzibath P., b. May 22, 1788; m. Jeremiah P. Sawyer, and res. in Bristol some years ; went to Minnesota, where she d. Dec. 27, 1865, ae. 77-7-5. Children :

a. Emeline.	*b.* John.	*c.* Jeremiah.
d. Daniel.	*e.* Hephzibath.	*f.* Olive.

4. Ruth, b. Gilmanton, May 10, 1790; m. Richard P. Bennett, and d. Haverhill, Mass., Nov. 20, 1852, ae. 62-6-10.

5. John, b. G., May 15, 1792; m. Margaret Ross, and d. in Pennsylvania, May 22, 1824, ae. 32-0-7, leaving a family.

6. James, b. G., Apr. 23, 1794; m. Alcemena Frisbee, and d. Mar. 8, 1817, ae. 22-11-15.

7. David, b. G., Aug. 2, 1796 ; m. Alcemena (Frisbee) Edwards ; res. in Bristol for a time and removed to Newbury, Vt., and there d. Oct. 9, 1883, ae. 87-2-7.

8. Jemima Wallingford, b. G., Apr. 29, 1799 ; m. (1) John C. Blake. He d. in Bristol, and she m. (2) Daniel Sanborn. (See.) Child :

    a. Ann Maria Blake, m. William C. Lovejoy. (See.)

9. Hannah Powers, b. G., May 20 (21), 1801 ; m. Col. John S. Bryant. (See.)

10. Samuel, b. July 20 (21), 1803 ; d. Sept. 30, 1805, ae. 2-2-10.

11. Mary M., b. Mar. 28, 1806; m. Elias T. Colby. Were early pioneers to Oregon and both d. there.

12. Piermont, b. Sept. 1, 1808; d. Sept. 20, 1808.

13. Melinda M., b. Nov. 21, 1809; m. James S. Blodgett ; res. in Bristol some years ; went to Concord where she d. Feb. 10, 1873, ae. 63-2-19. No children.

14. Sarah W., b. Mar. 1, 1812; m. Lewis Heath. (See.)

THE EMERSON FAMILY

Several by the name of Emerson went from Newburyport, Mass., to Weare, in the early part of the 18th century. Among the number was

1. Daniel. He had six children. Among them was

2. Jonathan, who m. Susanna Dodge. Both d. in Weare. She lost her life in their burning house. They had four children, of whom the second was

3. Isaiah, b. Dec. 24, 1800. He was a resident of Bristol, 1824-'28. Aug. 26, 1824, he m. Sarah (Sally), dau. of Moses West Sleeper (See), b. Feb. 28, 1807. He d. in Manchester,

Mar. 30, 1859, ae. 58-3-6. She m. (2) Jonathan Emmons, and d. in Bristol, Aug. 2, 1886, ae. 79-5-4.

CHILDREN

4. James A. B., b. Bristol, Feb. 7, 1826. Was a job teamster. He d. in Manchester, Aug. 1881, ae. 55-6-.
5. Nehemiah L., b. B., Sept. 4, 1827; d. in California.
6. Marcia L., b. B., May 8, 1829; m. S—— Warren, and d. Hudson, Me., Nov. 15, 1865, ae. 36-6-7.
7. Moses W., b. Jan. 19, 1831. He served in the 47th Regt. Mass. Vols., in Civil war. Res. Lowell, Mass.
8. Mary L., b. Nov. 3, 1833; res. East Saugus, Mass., unm.
9. Elizabeth A., b. Oct. 6, 1834; m. Otis E. White, and res. East Saugus.
10. Julia A., b. Sept. 1, 1836; m. Lucius B. Clogston, and d. at Bridgewater, Aug. 9, 1901, ae. 64-11-8.
11. John Dodge, b. Hermon, Me., Nov. 10, 1837; m. (1) about 1857, Almira Currier, who d. a year or two later. He m. (2) Angeline Smith, 1861 (?), and he m. (3) Apr. 5, 1877, Annie F., dau. of Alonzo and Mary Ann (Tanner) Andrews, b. Boston, Mass., Nov. 28, 1856, and d. Nashua, Oct. 25, 1880, ae. 23-10-27. He served in the 6th Regt. Mass. Vols. Was railroad conductor and hotel keeper. He d. about 1897. Three children.
12. Lucian W., b. H., Sept. 11, 1840; served in a New York regiment in Civil war; was a hotel keeper. He d. in Kansas, Feb. 3, 1875, ae. 34-4-22.
13. Joseph A., b. H., May 31, 1842; served in 10th Regt. Mass. Vols. Is yard master for Milwaukee and St. Paul Railroad at La Crosse, Wis.
14. Orrin F., b. H., July 7, 1844; m. Dec. 11, 1781, Octavia Roberts, of Hill. Was a dentist in Bristol, 1877-'81; now Franklin Falls.
*15. George Addison, b. H., Aug. 24, 1846.
16. Arthur L., b. H., Apr. 2, 1849; taxpayer in Bristol, 1877-'78; a physician in Chester. Was surgeon general on staff of Gov. Sawyer; was treasurer of Rockingham county four years; was a Knight Templar Mason, and Odd Fellow. He m. a dau. of Charles Fisk, Manchester. He d. Aug. 16, 1901, ae. 52-4-14.

(15) George A. Emerson, b. Aug. 24, 1846; m. Jan. 22, 1873, Luzetta Sarah, dau. Jason C. Draper (See), b. Dec. 29, 1852. He served four months in the 42nd Regt. Mass. Vols., in the Civil war; taught in the Bristol High school, 1872-'73; was town treasurer one year; supervisor of the check-list two years; moderator two years, and selectman three years. Removed to Everett, Mass., 1892, where he still res., though still retaining interest in Bristol real estate, and in the Bristol Electric Light company, of which he is manager. (See Lawyers.)

CHILDREN

17. Ernest Benjamin, b. Cambridge, Mass., Jan. 25, 1874. He graduated from the Everett High school, and from the School of Medicine, Harvard University in 1898. He has since served at the Mass. State hospital, at Tewksbury, one year as interne, and later on the medical staff. He has charge of the department of Women and Children, and supervision of the department for the insane.
18. Jason Draper, b. Tilton, Sept. 16, 1877; graduated at Everett High school; was two years at Tufts college, and graduated at the College of Liberal Arts, of Boston University, class of 1902, and from the Law School

of this University in 1903, *cum laude*. He m. June 19, 1901, Edith Henry, dau. Henry A. Taylor. (See.)

19. George Edward, b. New Hampton, Nov. 6, 1880; attended Everett High school and Tilton Seminary, and graduated at Medical School of Harvard University in 1903.

THE EMMONS FAMILIES

1. Lieut. Benjamin Emmons, son of Samuel and Maria (Norton) Emmons, was b. Feb. 29, 1743. He was the first permanent settler within the limits of Bristol. In the spring of 1766, he came to New Chester from Chester, and commenced a clearing on what is still the Emmons farm, on the river about three miles from the village. Apr. 6, 1769, he m. Elizabeth, dau. of Abner Fellows, of Sandown, b. Sept. 25, 1746. (See.) She d. May 19, 1783, ae. 36-7-24 (Fellows record says d. May 13, 1782), and he m. Nov. 11, 1783, Dolly Stevens, who d. Jan. 11, 1827. He d. Dec. 30, 1835, ae. 92-10-1.

Benjamin Emmons was a prominent man in his day. He was a Revolutionary soldier from New Chester, and after the war was active in the militia. When 79 years of age he united with the Methodist church, but all his children, born many years before this event, were scrupulously baptized in infancy and a record duly made in the family Bible. About 1788, Mr. Emmons erected the two-story frame house that now stands on this farm —the oldest house in town. Here he kept tavern for some years, and here his descendants have lived for three generations, his great-grandchildren, Mr. and Mrs. John M. V. Dalton, being the present occupants. (See Chapter on First Settlements in New Chester.)

CHILDREN, all born Bristol

2. Samuel, b. Feb. 20 (28), 1770. He was the first white child b. in Bristol, and was killed while logging on Hoyt hill, Nov. 3 (13), 1806, unm., ae. 36-8-13.
  *3. Abner, b. Aug. 8, 1771.
  *4. Moses, b. May 13, 1773.
  5. Ruth, b. June 8, 1775; m. Sherburn Tilton. (See.)
  *6. Reuben, b. Apr. 30, 1777.
  *7. Joseph, b. May, 13, 1779.
  8. Mary, b. May 28, 1781; m. John Dolloff, of New Hampton.
  9. Elizabeth, b. Oct. 2, 1784, d. unm., 1850. (m. Sherburn Tilton 3d)
*10. Benjamin, b. May 14, 1786.
  11. Sally, b. June 2, 1787; m. Stephen Eastman (Published Dec. 23, 1809), resided in Bridgewater; d. Dec. 10, 1824, ae. 37-6-8.
  12. John, b. Oct. 2, 1789; d. unm., Apr. 23, 1820, ae. 30-6-21.

(3) Abner Emmons, b. Aug. 8, 1771, m. Mar. 15 (14), 1799, Betsey Robinson, who d. May 6 (26), 1832. He was a farmer on east side of the lake in Bristol, and later went to Vermont.

CHILDREN

13. Elizabeth, b. Jan. 8, 1800.
14. Philena, b. July 30, 1801.
15. Ruth, b. July 10, 1803.
16. Moses, b. Nov. 9, 1805. (A Moses Emmons m. May 30, 1832, Sarah W. Glover.)
17. Judith, b. Mar. 28, 1808.

(4) Moses Emmons, b. May 13, 1773, m. Feb. 21, 1799, Sally (Sarah) Thomas. He was a farmer in the Locke neighborhood. He d. Oct. 6, 1845, ae. 72-4-23; she d. Dec. 30, 1855, ae. 73-10-.

CHILDREN, all born Bristol

*18. Benjamin, b. Dec. 16, 1799.
*19. Jonathan, b. Jan. 25, 1802.
*20. Thomas Robert, b. Oct. 28, 1803.
21. Merrill, b. 1804 (?); m. Rhoda Ann Cross, of Bridgewater, Mar. 9, 1831. She d. Nov. 7, 1854, ae. 52 years. He d in the army at Carrollton, La., Aug. 14, 1862, ae. 58. No children. (See Roll of Honor.)
*22. Smith, b. 1807.

(6) Reuben Emmons, b. Apr. 30, 1777, m. Betsey, dau. of Moses Sleeper (See), b. Mar. 6, 1780. Farmer near Pemigewasset bridge; d. Dec. 4, 1865, ae. 88-7-4.; she d. May 23, 1872, ae. 92-2-17.

CHILDREN, all born Bristol

23. Merrill, d. in infancy.
24. Merrill, b. Apr. 8, 1801; d. May 19, 1804, ae. 3-1-11.
25. Josiah, b. Nov. 28, 1803; d. unm., Oct. 17, 1842, ae. 38-10-19.
*26. Samuel, b. Sept. 25, 1805.
27. Betsey, b. Sept. 22, 1807; m. July 30, 1833, Rev. Richard Newhall, a Methodist circuit-rider; on Bridgewater circuit in 1827. He was b. July 18, 1800, and d. Dec., 1872; she d. Feb. 25, 1895, at Ocean Grove, N. J., ae. 87-5-3. Children:

　　a. Mary Elizabeth, b. May 19, 1835.
　　b. Richard Watson, b. Apr. 17, 1841, a lawyer in New York.
　　c. George Smith, b. Aug. 19, 1856.
　　d. Ellen Lewis, b. Mar. 1, 1865.

28. Pliney Swan, b. Sept. 10, 1809. Went to Illinois previous to the Civil war and has not been heard from since.
*29. Horace Merrill, b. July 30, 1811.
*30. David Atwood, b. July 10, 1814.
31. Reuben Peterson, b. Feb. 15, 1817. Kept an eating saloon in Boston, Mass. Died at home, unm., Apr. 20, 1845, ae. 28-2-5.
32. Adeline, b. July 4, 1819; m. May 7, 1842, John H. Higbee, and removed to Newport, where they res. many years. She now res. with her children, Newport, R. I. Children:

　　a. Isa Matilda, b. Nov. 29, 1844.
　　b. Charles Reuben, b. Feb. 24, 1847.
　　c. John W., b. Mar. 11, 1848.
　　d. Carrie Maria, b. May 29, 1852.
　　e. Edward Wyman, b. Dec. 26, 1853.

33. Mary Ann Atwood, b. June 6, 1821; m. May 31, 1848, David B. Mason, b. Meredith, Dec. 6, 1820. They settled in Lebanon, where he d. July 18, 1889, ae. 68-7-12, and where she was living in July, 1903. Children:

    a. Addie Minerva, b. L., Oct. 30, 1850. Unm.
    b. Arthur Smith, b. Lebanon, May 28, 1854; m. Sept. 16, 1890, Otilla Helgeson, and res. Alexandria, Minn.
    c. Julius Higbee, b. L., June 25, 1858; d. Sept. 12, 1861, ae. 3-2-17.

*34. Gustavus, b. Nov. 5, 1823.

(7) Joseph Emmons, b. May 13, 1779, m. (pub. Feb. 22, 1801), Ruth Sleeper, dau. of Moses (See), b. Dec. 6, 1782. Farmer; next east of Horace N. Emmons's. He d. in Ohio, about 1852; she d. Orange, Sept. 5, 1868, ae. 85-8-29.

35. Polly, b. Bristol, Mar. 4, 1802; m. Samuel Hartshorn, and removed to Hebron, where they d. Children:

    a. Sarah Emmons, b. Hebron, Apr. 1, 1824; m. Henry Magee, Lynn, Mass. She d. Lynn, Jan. 3, 1899, ae. 74-9-2. Four children.
    b. Wellington P., b. H., 1826. Res. Lynn, Mass.

36. Moses, b. B., Mar. 6, 1804; m. Sally Glover, and d. Apr., 1873, in Orange, ae. 69-1-. Child:

    a. Jerusha Morse, b. Aug. 23, 1832; m. Levi Lamphrey; d. Concord, Apr. 24, 1888, ae. 55-8-1. He res. Lawrence, Mass.

37. Thomas Jefferson, b. B., Jan. 19, 1806; m. Marinda Culver; d. in Lyme, 1877, ae. 71. She d. Lynn, Mass. No children.

38. Sarah (christened Kezia), b. B., Feb. 8, 1808; m. Asa H. Kendall. (See.)

(10) Benjamin Emmons, b. May 14, 1786, m. Mar. 7, 1811, Sally Sleeper, dau. of Samuel (See), b. Mar. 13, 1791. He succeeded his father on the home farm and there d. Aug. 21, 1827, ae. 41-3-7; she d. in Ashland, July 31, 1872, ae. 81-4-18. She was blind for years before her death.

CHILDREN, all born in Bristol.

*39. John Martin Ruter, b. Nov. 17, 1811.

40. Dorothy Stevens, b. July 13, 1813; m. John Hastings. (See.)

41. Elizabeth Sanborn, b. July 15, 1816; m. Feb. 14, 1843, Albert Kimball, b Holderness, Aug. 24, 1816, and d. Plymouth, Feb. 1, 1892, ae. 75-5-7. She d. Laconia, Feb. 27, 1887, ae. 70-7-12. Children:

    a. William Russell, b. Holderness, July 7, 1844; m. Apr. 17, 1867, Lydia A. Morse, Campton.
    b. Albert Myron, b. H., Feb. 8, 1846; m. Feb., 1870, Sarah A. Plummer, Campton.
    c. Marshall Emmons, b. H., Oct. 10, 1848; d. Nov. 3, 1848.
    d. Sarah Jane, b. H., Aug 25, 1849; d. in infancy.
    e. Ellen Maria, b. H., Aug. 1, 1850; d. Aug. 11, 1856, ae. 6-0-10.
    f. Mary Lizzie, b. H., Mar. 13, 1852; d. Aug. 5, 1856, ae. 4-4-22.
    g. Ida Maie, b. Concord, Aug. 22, 1857; m. May 28, 1878, Elias W. French, b. Thetford Center, Vt., Oct. 2, 1856.

42. Sally Sleeper, b. Nov. 28, 1819; d. Mar. 11, 1835, ae. 15-3-13.

43. Sophronia Huckins, b. Mar. 11, 1822; m. Leander Badger. (See.)

44. Maria Norton, b. Mar. 31, 1824; m. Apr. 13, 1849, John A. Quimby, Sharon, Vt.

45. Huldah Tilton, b. Nov. 23, 1826; m. Charles W. Batchelder. (See.)

(18) Benjamin Emmons, b. Dec. 16, 1799, m. Sept. 25, 1822, Mary, dau. of David Powell (See), b. Aug. 2, 1802. Farmer. He d. Lowell, Mass., Dec. 16, 1855, ae. 56–0–0 ; she d. Alexandria, Mar. 12, 1850, ae. 47–7–10.

CHILDREN

46. Sarah Ann, b. Stewartstown, Oct. 27, 1823 ; m. Luther Ingalls. (See.)

47. Theodate Smith, b. Bristol, Dec. 30, 1825 ; m. Louis Fernald, and res. Boston.

48. Elisha Gurdy, twin brother of Theodate ; m. Mary Jane Cook, of Ellsworth, Me., and removed to San Francisco, Cal., where he d. in July, 1877, ae. 51–7–. Four children.

49. Samuel Smith, b. Bridgewater, Jan. 18, 1829; m. (1) Susanna Goldsmith, (2) Eliza Ellerson. He d. Jan., 1874, in Lawrence, Mass., ae. 55.

50. Mahala Jane, b. Bristol, Feb. 28, 1834 ; m. June 25, 1856, Samuel P. Downs. He d. Lowell, Mass., Sept. 15, 1866. She d. about 1895, ae. about 61. Child :

a. Albert Elroy, b. Lowell, Dec. 25, 1857. An artist in So. Boston, Mass.

51. Alonzo Cheney, b. Alexandria, Aug. 20, 1840 ; m. 1866, Annie McElroy ; res. Dorchester, Mass.

(19) Jonathan Emmons, b. Jan. 25, 1802, m. Feb. 11, 1829, Margaret S., dau. of Abraham Dolloff (See), b. Nov. 28, 1807. He was a farmer on the John F. Merrow farm till 1876, when he removed to the Worthen farm, east of the village. She d. Aug. 17, 1868, ae. 60–8–19, and he m. Mar. 16, 1869, Mrs. Sarah Emerson, widow of Isaiah. (See.) He d. Oct. 19, 1880, ae. 78–8–24 ; she d. Aug. 2, 1886, ae. 79–5–5. He was for half a century prominent in religious and political circles. He thought for himself and his position on any subject was always clearly defined. His educational advantages were confined to a few weeks of the district school each year, and two years at the New Hampton Institution. He taught school 18 consecutive winters. In 1824, in company with Nathaniel S. Berry and William Lewis, he opened Sunday-schools in town and was for many years superintendent of one in the Locke neighborhood. He was also a Methodist class leader.

CHILDREN

52. Sylvester, m., and d. in Franconia at age of 32. Family all deceased.

53. Lavinia, d. young.

54. Gilbert B., d. Bristol, Jan. 31, 1835, ae. 0–4–8.

55. Leroy S., b. B., d. unm., in Franconia, about 1864, ae. 28 years.

56. Alvira ⎫ d. Nov. 10, 1848, ae. 1–2–0.
57. Charles ⎭

58. Charles G., b. B., Sept. 20, 1849. He graduated from the New Hampton Literary Institution about 1876, and read law in the office of

Judge David Cross, Manchester. He was assistant clerk of the New Hampshire house of representatives in 1878 and 1879, and clerk of same body in 1881 and 1883. While reading law he became interested in hotels and served as chief clerk of the Crawford House. Was connected with Hotel Wentworth in 1882–'83; had charge of the Summit House, Mt. Washington, in 1884–'85; of the Hamilton Hotel, Bermuda, in the winters of 1883–'84 and 1884–'85. In February, 1886, he left Manchester to take charge of a large hotel in California for the Pacific railroad. At the Fifth Avenue Hotel in New York City he was taken sick with Bright's disease and there d., Mar. 7, 1886, ae. 36-5-17. He was a man of great promise. Unm.

(20) Thomas R. Emmons, b. Oct. 28, 1803, m. May 28, 1822, Abigail, dau. of Josiah Fuller. (See.) She d. Feb. 26, 1839, and he m. (2) Betsey W., dau. of Amos Drew, b. Nov. 2, 1805. (See.) She d. Nov. 24, 1866, ae. 61-0-22. He d. Feb. 26, 1891, ae. 87-3-28. He was a farmer at No. Bristol.

CHILDREN

59. Damon Young, b. Bristol, Nov. 24, 1822; m. Jan. 15, 1845, Huldah A. Chandler, dau. of Timothy (See), b. Nov. 14, 1823. They are farmers on the Timothy Chandler farm near the Locke neighborhood. No children.

＊60. Moses, b. Hebron, May 2, 1825.

61. Lyford, b. about 1828; went to sea on a whaler at the age of 14 years and never returned. His brother, Moses, met him at the Sandwich Islands, while on another whaler, and this was the last known of him.

62. Darius, m. Kate Maxwell. They res. in Somerville, Mass., where one child was b., which d. in Lowell, Mass. She d. Charlestown; he d. in Bristol, at the home of his sister, Mrs. Rose Wooster Todd.

63. Rose Wooster, b. Bristol, July 21, 1835; m. Mar. 30, 1853, William Todd. She d. B., Jan. 23, 1877, ae. 41-6-2. Children:

a. Addie Frances, b. Amoskeag, Dec. 22, 1854; m. May 8, 1875, Charles Bartley, who d. Boston, Mass., Nov. 11, 1888. She res. San Francisco, Cal.

b. Charles Henry, b. Boscawen, June 21, 1857; d. Bristol, Mar. 20, 1870, ae. 12-8-29, as the result of injury received while coasting.

(22) Smith Emmons, b. 1807, m. Lydia Ann Ward, of New Hampton, (2) Widow Allen, who d. in the seventies. He was a farmer in New Hampton and Bristol, and d. Nov. 22, 1879, ae. 72.

CHILDREN

64. Lydia Ann, b. July 7, 1836; m. Cyrus Bennett. (See.) She d. in Bristol, July 21, 1903, ae. 67-0-14.

65. Addison S., b. Bristol, Aug. 14, 1834; d. in Union army at New Orleans, July 8, 1863, ae. 28-10-24. (See Roll of Honor.)

66. Almira, b. Mar. 13, —; d. Manchester, unm. Dressmaker.

67. Abbie, b. Oct., 1838; m. Charles Bowen, of New Hampton. He served in New Hampshire Battalion First New England Cavalry, and d. of disease, at Annapolis, Md., Nov. 22, 1863, ae. 25-1-.

68. Marcellus C., b. Bristol, about 1840; served in New Hampshire Battalion New England Cavalry; discharged for disability, Oct. 7, 1862, and reached Bristol on his way home, where he d. at the home of his sister, Mrs. Cyrus Bennett. (See Roll of Honor.)

69. Mary Amanda, b. about 1842; m. and res. Cape Ann, Mass.

(26) Samuel Emmons, b. Sept. 25, 1805, m. in Hanover, Sept. 25, 1827, Eliza, dau. of Jabez and Sarah Warren, who d. May 3, 1844. He m. (2) Oct., 1846, Eliza Hurd, of Unity. He d. Nov. 27, 1848, ae. 43-2-2, and she m. again and d. in Chicago, Ill., about 1882. Samuel Emmons bought his time of his father before he was twenty-one years of age and went to Hanover and from there, three years later, to Newport. He spent most of his life keeping hotel.

CHILDREN

70. Eliza Ann, b. Newport, July 20, 1829; m. Nov. 22, 1853, John M. Nise, b. Scotland, Aug. 16, 1822. They lived in Lawrence, where he d. July 29, 1888, ae. 65-11-13. Children :
    a. Sarah Eliza, b. Dec. 22, 1852 ; d. Feb. 27, 1854, ae. 1-2-5.
    b. Charles Emmons, b. Apr. 30, 1854 ; d. Oct. 15, 1855, ae. 1-5-15.
    c. Florence Jean, b. Oct. 1, 1856 ; d. Dec. 15, 1856.
    d. Etta, b. Apr. 19, 1858 ; m. Jan. 28, 1880, Samuel H. Bell, a druggist at Derry Depot, and d. 1900. Two children.
71. Morris Jonathan, b. Charlestown, May 13, 1833. Res. Newport.
72. Samuel Webb, b. C., June 22, 1835. A baker in Boston.
73. Augusta, b. June 6, 1836 ; d. in infancy.
74. George Warren, b. Walpole, July 12, 1837 ; m. 1863, M. Emeline Follansbee, of Enfield. Served in 3rd Regt. N. H. Vols., as 1st lieutenant and captain. Res. Dorchester, Mass.
75. Hennie, b. Newport, Feb. 25, 1839; m. Robert M. Mason. (See.)
76. Charles Lowell, b. Newport, Oct. 16, 1841. Served as sergeant in 12th Mass. Vols., and was killed at Gettysburg, July 3, 1864, ae. 22-8-17.
77. William, b. Oct. 17, 1843; d. Mar.. 1844, ae. 1-7-.
78. Arabelle, b. Mar. 1, 1848; m. Robert Flemming, Chicago, Ill. Two daughters.

(29) Horace M. Emmons, b. July 30, 1811, m. Feb. 1, 1838, Maria, dau. of David Batchelder, b. Reading, Mass., Feb. 1, 1818, d. Nov. 23, 1897, ae. 79-9-22. Farmer on the farm now occupied by his son, Horace N., two miles east of Central square, and here he d. Aug. 27, 1888, ae. 77-0-27. In politics he was a Republican. He was for many years a prominent member of the official board of the Methodist church, and stood high in the community for his personal worth and ability.

CHILDREN, all born Bristol

79. Ellen Maria, b. Sept. 14, 1842; graduated from New Hampton Institution in 1866 ; m. Prof. George M. Fellows. (See.)
80. Adeline Higby, b. May 11, 1844 ; she was a graduate at New Hampton Institution taught in the public schools, including one year in the graded schools. She m. Charles Forrest. (See.)
81. Harrison, b. Aug. 6, 1845 ; d. in infancy.
✳82. Gardner Batchelder, b. Feb. 18, 1847.
83. Harriet Ann, b. Sept. 3, 1848; m. Charles H. Day. (See.)
84. Horace N. Emmons, b. Nov. 15, 1850; m. Dec. 25, 1873, Emma E., dau. Stephen N. Heath (See), b. Apr. 24, 1853. She d. Feb. 24, 1898, ae. 44-10-0, and he m. Maude Bell Caldon, Nov. 18, 1902. He succeeded his father on the home farm and operated a large milk route for 23 years.

HORACE M. EMMONS

HORACE N. EMMONS

Is an official member of the Methodist church; a Granger and a Republican. He has served three years as road agent.   Child :

a.   Emma Maria, b. Bristol, Sept. 23, 1876.

(30)   David A. Emmons, b. July 10, 1814, m. Nov. 22, 1842, Celinda B., dau. James and Nancy (Tenney) Ramsey, of Marlow, b. Feb. 4, 1819.   He d. Oct. 17, 1845, ae. 31-3-7.   She m. (2) Mar. 4, 1876, Orville H. Peck, of Alstead, where she d. 1893, ae. 74..

CHILDREN

85.   Helen Frames, m. William Sullivan and lived in Lebanon.
86.   Ellis, d. young.   87.   Reuben, d. young.
88.   Etta, m. Warren French, and lived in Alstead.

(34)   Gustavus Emmons, b. Nov. 5, 1823, m. Nov. 30, 1851, Electa Taylor, dau. of Jonathan C. and Polly (Taylor) Smith, b. New Hampton, Jan. 30, 1834.   He served in Co. C, 12th Regt. N. H. Vols., and was killed at Chancellorsville, May 3, 1863, ae. 39-5-28.   (See Roll of Honor.)   She m. (2) William F. Harris.   (See.)

CHILDREN

89.   Cora D'Alber, b. Bristol, July 26, 1853; d. Apr. 24, 1864, ae. 10-8-28.
90.   Nellie Eyers, b. Concord, Feb. 4, 1855.   Telegraph operator at Ashland.
91.   Linda Betsey, b. Bristol, Aug. 30, 1856 ; m. Sept. 11, 1878, James B. Hughes.   They res. Concord.   Children :
a.   Howard Hill, b. Littleton, Jan. 31, 1880.
b.   James B., b. Concord, Jan. 10, 1883.
c.   Arthur Reuben, b. C., July 3, 1886.
92.   Gustavus Reuben, b. B., Feb. 15, 1859 ; res. Waterloo, Oregon.

(39)   John M. R. Emmons, b. Nov. 17, 1811, m. Mar. 7, 1843, Eliza S., dau. of David Chase (See), b. Jan. 18, 1820. He d. Dec. 10, 1888, ae. 77-0-23.   She d. Oct. 17, 1902, ae. 82-8-29.   Mr. Emmons spent his life on the same farm as his father and grandfather before him.   He was a man above the average in general intelligence and good judgment, and served six years as selectman.   He was a member of the Free Baptist church.

CHILDREN

93.   Lovertia Eliza, b. Jan. 27, 1844 ; m. May 20, 1872, Amos F. Bartlett, and d. in Bristol, June 25, 1876, ae. 32-4-28.   He m. (2) Clara A. Brackett, Great Falls.   Children :
a.   Ernest Guy, b. Bristol, Mar. 5, 1873 ; d. Sept. 16, 1894, ae. 21-6-11.
b.   Irvin Winifred, b. B., Mar. 30, 1874 ; d. Aug. 6, 1890, ae. 16-4-6.
94.   Marcus L., b. Jan. 21, 1847 ; m. Kate E. Russell, of Plymouth, where he was a manufacturer of buckskin gloves and mittens, and later a baker.   Still later, he was a baker in Tilton, where he d. July 5, 1891, ae. 44-5-14.   Republican.   Mason.   No children.
95.   Martha F., b. Aug. 7, 1849.   She was a teacher in the public schools.   She m. John F. Philbrick, Jan. 31, 1877, and res. Meredith. Children :

    a. Carl Frederick, b. Meredith, Jan. 25, 1882; d. Sept. 16, 1894, ae. 12–7–21.
    b. Arthur Emmons, b. M., Sept. 18, 1884.
    c. Ralph Clinton, b. M., July 31, 1887.

  96. Sarah Jennie, b. Apr. 29, 1853. She was a teacher in the public schools for some years. She m. Wilbur L. E. Hunt, and lives in Woodstock. No children.

  97. Ella,   } b. Apr. 21, 1855; { d. Jan. 21, 1864, ae. 8–9–0.
  98. Emma, }   { m. John M. V. B. Dalton (See), and succeeded her father on the home farm.

  99. Everett H., b. May 9, 1865; m. Feb. 24, 1885, Augusta I., dau. of Orin Nelson. (See.) Divorced. She m. (2) Scott Tirrell. (See.) He m. Aug. 7, 1895, Viola A. Pitman, of Alexandraia. He is now (1903) a carpenter in Nashua.

    (60) Moses Emmons, b. May 2, 1825, m. Dec., 1848, Lucy Maria, dau. of Stephen Bohonon (See), b. Oct. 15, 1830. In early life, he spent three years on a whaling voyage on the Pacific ocean, later a farmer and stone mason in Bristol. He d. Jan. 3, 1892, ae. 66–8–1. She res. Bristol.

CHILDREN, all born Bristol

  100. Addie, b. May 8, 1849; m. May 13, 1874, Madison Sanborn, son of Isaiah. She d. May 4, 1875, ae. 25–11–26. Child:
    a. Addie, b. Apr. 23, 1875.

  101. Abbie Malinda, b. Apr. 20, 1851; m. Charles W. Sanborn. (See.)
  102. Josephine, b. Aug. 9, 1855; m. Osgood Dale. Child:
    a. Howard Bertrand.

  103. Jennie, b. Mar. 5, 1865. Unm.
  104. Nettie, b. Apr. 25, 1868; m. Feb. 3, 1887, George Battis. Child:
    a. Clyde, b. Apr. 2, 1889.

  105. Ethel, b. July 28, 1870. Unm.

    (82) Hon. Gardner B. Emmons, b. Feb. 18, 1847, m. Nov. 26, 1868, Sarah J., dau. Charles C. Flanders, b. Concord, Oct. 21, 1847. First engaged in the meat business in Bristol, in the employ of Abram Dolloff, in 1863, where he remained three years; two years in Lowell, Mass., and two in Tilton in the same business. In Jan., 1871, he commenced business for himself in Concord, which he still continues. He is a director in the Concord Street Railway, a trustee in the Guarantee Savings bank, and was for several years interested in a cattle ranch in Montana. He is now also engaged in the coal business. He has been for many years trustee and treasurer of the First Baptist church. He has been a member of the city government four years, represented his ward in the legislature of 1887, and his district in the senate of 1897.

CHILDREN, all born in Concord

  106. Harry Gardner, b. Oct. 5, 1869; m. Maud Evelyn, dau. of Horace H. Danforth. Dry goods merchant, Concord. Children:
    a. Gardner Gage, b. Mar. 20, 1894.
    b. Helen, b. July 4, 1895.
    c. Margaret, b. May 25, 1897.

JOHN M. R. EMMONS

Hon. Gardner B. Emmons

107. Grace Lela, b. Mar. 10, 1871 ; d. Feb. 15, 1886, ae. 14-11-5.
108. Oscar Flanders, b Aug. 21, 1872 ; m. July 16, 1901, Helen Lothrop, dau. of Chas. E. Sprague. No children. He is associated with his father in the meat and coal business.
109. Hattie Sarah, b. Sept. 16, 1878. Is a teacher.

---

1. John Emmons, son of Samuel and a brother of Lieut. Benjamin, was b. Nov. 19, 1740. He m. Oct. 13, 1783, Sarah Woodman. In 1779, he was the owner of the Hiram Heath farm, but sold to Daniel Heath and removed to the west part of Hill. He had four children, among whom was

2. Aaron Emmons, b. Jan. 5, 1787, m. Betsey Somes, of Alexandria. He was a soldier in the War of 1812. Was a resident of Bristol, 1828-'39. From 1832-'37, he operated the woolen-mill on Central street. He d. Afton, N. Y., Nov. 14, 1865, ae. 78-10-9 ; she d. a few months later.

CHILDREN

3. John S., b. Bristol, Nov. 14, 1829. Is supposed to have d. in Massachusetts state prison.
4. Sarah Ann, d. unm. in Lowell, Mass.
5. Ruth C., m. James W. Preston, M.D.; d. in Plymouth, Sept., 1866. He was a druggist in Bristol, 1880-'84, and d. Woburn, Mass. Child :
    a. Carrie, m. John Burt, of West Virginia. He d. and she returned to Plymouth, and there d. Her son, Willie, d. in Bristol. May 5, 1884, of consumption, ae. 17-1-12.
6. Mary L., m. Thomas Landers ; res. Jersey City, N. J.
7. Abbie, d. in Jersey City, unm.   8. Willie, d. young.

---

1. Willie Benjamin Emmons, the son of John F. and Rachel B. (Hill) Emmons, was b. Feb. 11, 1867, in Woodstock. His grandfather was Benjamin, and his great-grandfather was John, a brother of Lieut. Benjamin. He m. Sept. 7, 1897, Frances E., dau. of Daniel W., and Eva (Currier) Hall, b. Canterbury, Nov., 1878. He was postmaster at Thornton 12 years, town treasurer four years, and selectman one year. Settled in Bristol fall of 1902, and is a member of the firm of Emmons & Dolloff, stoves and tinware.

CHILD

2. Louise Mae, b. Woodstock, June 7, 1899.

THE EVERETT FAMILY

1. Lieut. David E. Everett is the son of Dea. Dexter and Betsey (Pingree) Everett. He was b. New London, Oct. 25, 1825, and m. June 1, 1848, Harriet R., dau. of Elder Richard and Lucy (Stevens) Davis, b. Locke, N. Y., June 10, 1825.

He was a harness maker in Bristol from 1850 till 1863, when he removed to Concord, where he has since res. and followed his occupation. In Civil war he served in Co. D, 12th Regt., as first lieutenant. (See Roll of Honor.) Was town clerk five years.

CHILDREN

2. DeVolney, b. Hill, July 31, 1850; m. Oct., 1873, Abby Jane Adams, of Lancaster. He is in the piano trade in New York city and res. 1,931 Madison Ave. Child:

    a. Robert Gordon, b. Concord, Sept. 14, 1880, was corporal Co. L, 71st N. Y. Vols., War with Spain. Was in the battles before Santiago; contracted typhoid fever and furloughed for sixty days, and returned to his home in New York city, where he d. Sept. 5, 1898, ae. 17-11-21.

3. DeWitt Clinton, b. Bristol, Apr. 16, 1854; m. Martha Jane Bailey, Concord, October, 1878. Res. Concord.

THE EVERLETH FAMILY

1. George Parker Everleth, b. Lowell, Mass., July 23, 1853, is the son of John and Jane (Badger) Everleth (See p. 11.) He was a resident of Bristol some years and here m. June 23, 1880, Martha Ann, dau. of Fletcher C. Wells. (See.) He is a printer in Worcester, Mass.

CHILDREN

2. Minnie Sadie, b. Bristol, Sept. 19, 1881; m. Sept. 24, 1902, Bert Austin.

3. Chester, b. Worcester, Mass., Mar. 25, 1884.

FALL

Fred Sherwood Fall is the son of Isaac H. and Mary E. (Swasey) Fall, b. Lebanon, Me., July 27, 1856. Marble worker. Located in Bristol 1880, and worked for L. D. Day & Son till Jan. 1, 1886, when he purchased the business and has continued it till now. Republican, Mason, K. of P. Unm.

THE FARRAR FAMILY

1. Samuel Dix Farrar, son of Benjamin and Sarah (Ball) Farrar, was b. in Sutton, Mar. 21, 1817. He m. Apr. 21, 1836, Sabrina, dau. of Joseph Atwood (See), b. May 3, 1820, and d. in Bristol, Aug. 2, 1871, ae. 51-2-29. He m. Sept. 14, 1872, Mrs. Caroline P. Randlett. He was in trade in Manchester; and in Bristol in company with Charles Boardman. He d. May 9, 1884, ae. 67-1-18. He was a major and colonel of the old 34th Regt. of militia. His ancestors came from Warwick, Eng., in 1610, and settled at Charles City, Va.

ISAAC FAVOR
(First white child born in New Chester)

2. Marcus O., b. Alexandria, Feb. 26, 1838, m. Sept. 23, 1889, Mrs. Helen Abby (White) Taylor, widow of Henry A. Taylor. (See.) She d. Bristol, May 11, 1895, ae. 48-3-25. He served in the U. S. Navy during the Civil war; was three years connected with the Geological Survey of Canada and for 25 years mining and metallurgical engineer in southern and western states and Mexico. Now res. in Bristol.

THE FAVOR FAMILIES

1. Capt. Cutting Favor was b. Mar. 11, 1737, and d. in Hill, Mar. 8, 1822, ae. 84-11-27. He m. Judith Bagley, who d. in Hill, Apr. 17, 1829, "in the 90 year of her age." Capt. Cutting Favor was the first permanent settler in New Chester, having made a settlement in the early months of 1766. Mrs. Favor was, without doubt, the first white woman in the new town. The site of his log cabin is between the two dwellings now standing on the farm of Wilson Foster about a mile south of Smith's river. He owned large tracts of land in New Chester and New Hampton. He was a member of Committee of Safety in New Chester in 1776, and served as lieutenant in the Bennington campaign in 1777, and later in the same season was at Saratoga.

CHILDREN

2. Sarah, b. Newtown, Dec. 28 (24), 1759. She m. Ebenezer Wells, and d. in Hill, May 28, 1843, ae. 83-5-0.

3. John, b. N., Jan. 15 (17), 1762; m. Nov. 30, 1780, Hannah Stephens. He perished in a snow storm while going from his home on Murray hill to his father's, Jan. 15, 1782, ae. 20-0-0. Child:

    a. Judith, b. Feb. 7, 1782.

4. Mary, b. N., Jan. 21, 1764; m. Jacob Gurdy. (See.)

5. Jacob, b. N., May 21, 1766, m. Lucy Farrar. He settled in Grafton, and later lived in Danbury; was the father of 13 children, most of whom emigrated West.

. 6. Isaac, b. Hill, Aug. 24, 1768. He was the first white child b. in New Chester. He m. Sarah Webster, June 16, 1789, and went to New York state previous to 1816. He d. Manlius, N. Y., Mar. 28, 1859, ae. 90-7-4. She d. same place. They were the parents of eight children, of whom one was

    a. Ambrosia, b. Hill, 1809; m. Joseph H. Prescott, and res. Hill.

7. Judith, b. H., Sept. 17, 1770; m. Green Tilton, Apr. 25, 1787, lived in New Hampton and there d. June 15, 1850, ae. 79-8-28. He. d. New Hampton, Mar. 8, 1810. They had 14 children, of whom one was

    a. David Tilton, b. Jan. 6, 1810. (See.)

8. Elizabeth, b. H., Feb. 10, 1772; m. Nathaniel Merrill.

9. Dorothy, b. H., Oct. 6, 1774; m. Feb. 22, 1797, James Sargent.

10. Hannah, b. H., Aug. 6, 1776; m. Benjamin Locke. (See.)

11. Moses, b. H., July 11, 1778; d. Oct. 7, 1825, ae. 47-2-26. His wife, Sally, d. Sept. 24, 1809, ae. 23 years. Two children d. young.

12. Aaron, b. H., Aug. 13, 1780; m. Ruth Sanborn, dau. of Maj. Theophilus. (See.) He d. Sept. 4, 1835, in New Hampton, ae. 55-0-21, and she m. June 6, 1838, John Adams, and d. Tilton, Jan. 2, 1870, ae. 83-9-6. Children:

 a. Cutting, b. Sept. 13, 1806; d. N. H., Apr. 20, 1881, ae. 74-7-7.
Hannah, his wife, d. Aug. 21, 1882, ae. 72-9-7.
 b. Mary, b. Mar. 31, 1808; killed by roll of a log, Dec. 8, 1816,
ae. 8-8-7.
 c. Ruth, b. Nov. 14, 1809; m. Capt. Daniel Smith, Meredith.
 d. John, b. Nov. 26, 1813; d. Sept. 9, 1827, ae. 13-9-13.
 e. Sally, b. Sept. 1, 1818; m. ——— Lane, of New Hampton,
and there d.
 f. Laura, b. July 9, 1823; m. Stephen Long, Sanbornton. She
d. Dec. 28, 1863, ae. 40-5-19.
 g. Moses, d. Dec. 11, 1832, ae. 7-2-0.

1. Thomas Favor was, according to tradition, a cousin of
Capt. Cutting Favor. He came from Newtown to Hill about
1788. He m. Achsah Wadleigh. Both d. in Hill. They had
12 children, among them

 ⁂2. Daniel, b. Newtown, Sept. 9, 1787.
 ⁂3. Walter, b. Hill, Aug. 24, 1811.

(2) Daniel Favor, M.D., b. Sept. 9, 1787, m. Jan. 20,
1814, Mary (Polly) Sleeper, dau. of Peter (See), b. Mar. 25,
1793. He was a physician in Hill, where he d. Nov. 23, 1846,
ae. 59-2-14; his widow d. Bristol, Nov. 11, 1863, ae. 70-7-16.

CHILDREN

4. Frederick, b. Hill; d. in Chicago, Ill.
5. Mary A., b. H., m. Joshua T. Kendall. (See.)
6. Jersine B., b. H., Jan. 22, 1823; m. Laura J. Pattee, Sept. 7, 1849.
She was the dau. of John and Mary (Corliss) Pattee, b. Bristol, Jan. 22,
1825. He was a lumber manufacturer and laborer in paper-mill, Bristol,
till 1854, when he removed to Concord. He served in 1st Regt., N. H.
Cavalry, and d. at Frederick City, Md., Apr. 27, 1865, ae. 42-3-5. She
res. Concord. Children :
 a. Daniel B., b. Bristol, Sept. 11, 1850, m. Mary J. Casey. Was
killed in the railroad yard at Concord, July 8, 1889, ae. 38-9-27.
His widow and four children res. Concord.
 b. Frederick K., b. B., Feb. 11, 1853; m. Nellie I. Rand. He d.
Oakland, Cal., Sept. 3, 1886, ae. 33-6-22. Widow and two sons
res. 565 16th street, Oakland, Cal.
7. Nancy J., b. H., Feb. 26, 1825; m. Orrin Locke. (See.)

(3) Col. Walter Favor, b. Aug. 24, 1811, m. Elvira, dau.
Moses Webster, b. Hill. He d. Oct. 19, 1846, ae. 35-1-25.
She res. for some years in Bristol, and here d. Aug. 25, 1877,
ae. 64.

CHILDREN

 ⁂8. Moses W., b. Hill, Jan. 22, 1833.
9. Hiram Walker, b. H., Oct. 4, 1834; m. May 6, 1861, Thankful H.,
dau. of David and Clarissa S. Gage, b. Pelham, Dec. 15, 1838; was salesman in store of Bartlett & Taylor, 1850-'61 ; in clothing business with
Cyrus Taylor, where is now west-side drug store, till fall 1863, when he
went to Boscobel, Wis., where he has since been in trade ; for some years
in company with Moody A. Sawyer, formerly of Bristol. Child :
 a. Susie, b. Boscobel, June 25, 1871.

JOHN A. FAVOR

10. Rebecca W., b. H., Apr. 4, 1836; m. Nathaniel Rowe, of Andover, (2) Mark C. White, Boston, Mass., d. July 18, 1885, ae. 49-3-14.

11. Albert Martin, b. H., Jan. 2, 1838; d. Bascobel, Wis., Feb. 8, 1874, ae. 36-1-6.

12. Susan D., b. H., Dec. 9, 1840. She res. in Bristol, now Hyde Park, Mass.; unm.

13. Frederick Harvey, b. H., Jan. 2, 1842; m. Oct. 19, 1880, Mary, dau. of Anthony and Mary (Bryant) Elliott, b. Hamilton, Canada, Oct. 19, 1859. He served in the 3rd Regt., and was wounded at Secessionville, S. C., June 16, 1862. He d. Batavia, Ill., Dec. 22, 1883, ae. 41-11-20. Two children.

14. Elvira W., b. Alexandria, Aug. 2, 1845; m. Edwin S. Foster, M. D. (See.)

15. Mary W., b. A., Feb. 4, 1847; d. July 24, 1858, ae. 11-5-20.

(8) Moses W. Favor, b. Jan. 22, 1833, m. Nov. 26, 1857, Mary G., dau. of Jeremiah and Judith Davis, b. Loudon. His life work has been that of a locomotive engineer. Res. No. Main street. Was a deacon in Free Baptist church. Republican, Odd Fellow. Removed to Concord, March, 1886.

CHILDREN

16. Walter Webster, b. Concord, Oct. 31, 1859; m. June 20, 1882, Mary Edell Rowe, dau. of Joseph, b. Franklin, Nov. 16, 1861. He is a locomotive engineer. Res. No. Main street. Republican, Free Baptist, Odd Fellow. Children:

   a. Ernest Howard, b. Bristol, June 3, 1887.
   b. Alice Evelyn, b. B., Sept. 13, 1895.

17. Frank H., b. Bristol, Mar. 19, 1863; m. June, 1892, Pearl Blackwell. Is a locomotive engineer. Res. Lafayette, Ind.

18. Cora A., b. B., Sept. 2, 1867; m. Jan. 12, 1891, Ira O. Mathews, of Alexandria. Res. West Concord.

19. Nina G., b. Nov. 16, 1871; m. Nicholas I. Quint, res. Concord.

---

1. John Favor was a resident of Newtown; m. Lydia Hoyt and settled in Weare. He had 11 children, of whom one was

2. Zebediah. He m. Sarah Burnham. Of his four children, one was

3. William, b. 1800. He m. Betsey Worthley. They were the parents of six children, of whom the first was

4. Almon Moses, b. July 18, 1831, in Weare. He m. in 1861, Mary Robinson, dau. of William T. and Irene Q. (Smith) Beede, b. Hebron, July 9, 1841, who d. in Hebron, June 10, 1883, ae. 41-11-1. He d. in Hebron, Nov. 23, 1891, ae. 60-4-5.

CHILDREN

5. John Almon, b. Weare, Mar. 15, 1862; m. Mar. 23, 1890, Nora Viola, dau. of Henry Griffith (See), b. Jan. 31, 1870. Settled in Bristol in 1883. Operative in paper-mill; in livery business at North End since Apr., 1894. Is a K. of P., Republican, served three years as selectman.

   a. Corinne, b. Bristol, Oct. 31, 1895.

6. Oreste Gilbert, b. Weare, Oct. 20, 1863; m. Bertina French, Jan., 1894. Res. Brockton, Mass.

21

7. Anson Leroy, b. Hebron, June 6, 1873; m. July 3, 1893, Nettie Donahue. Res. Stoughton, Mass.

8. Willie B., b. H., Apr. 11, 1877; d. Apr. 21, 1879, ae. 2-0-10.

9. Lucy May, b. H., Oct. 1, 1879. Res. in Bristol since 1887. Compositor in *Enterprise* office; m. Nov. 26, 1902, Roy C. Horne, b. Aug. 26, 1875. He is foreman of *Enterprise* printing-office.

10. Sylvia Alice, b. H., May 26, 1883; res. Epping.

THE FELLOWS FAMILIES

The Fellowses of Bristol are the descendants of William Fellows, who was b. about 1610, and came to New England, as is supposed, in the ship Planter, about 1635. He m., probably, Mary Ayres. In 1639, or before, he was a resident of Ipswich, Mass., where he remained till his death, which occurred near Nov. 29, 1676. Willian had a brother Samuel who settled in Salisbury, Mass., who has numerous descendants. Another brother, Richard, settled in Northampton, Mass., and was killed with his only son, John, in the fight with the Indians at Bloody Brook, in 1676. William had four sons and four daughters, Ephraim, Samuel, Joseph, Mary, Elizabeth, Abigail, Sarah, and Isaac.

1. Isaac was b. about 1635. He resided in Ipswich; m. Joanna Boardman, Jan. 29, 1672, and d. Apr. 6, 1721, ae. 86. One son was

2. Deacon Jonathan, b. Ipswich, Mass., Sept. 28, 1682. In 1740, he removed to Hampton, where he d. Jan. 21, 1753, ae. 70-3-23. He had four wives: Hannah Dutch, Sarah Day, Widow Sarah (Potter) Rust, and Widow Deborah (Batchelder) Tilton, who survived him. He had three children by his first wife, the children of his second wife all d. in infancy, and he had five by his third wife. The youngest child was

3. Abner, b. Ipswich, Mass., Dec. 5, 1720; m. Elizabeth Rowe. They res. in Kingston and Sandown. In 1769, a daughter m. Benjamin Emmons and settled in New Chester, and he accompanied the young couple to their new home. He was so favorably impressed with the situation in New Chester that he resolved to settle there himself, and, in 1773, he sold his farm in Sandown, and settled on the farm now owned and occupied by Horace N. Emmons, in 1774, where he remained till his death, which occurred not earlier than 1786. Several of the early town meetings were held here, and he presided as moderator five times. He was a member of the Committee of Safety in 1776.

CHILDREN

4. Mehitable, m. Robert Dinsmore, Oct. 3, 1767. He d. in Revolutionary army of smallpox.

5. Elizabeth, b. Sept. 25, 1746; m. Benjamin Emmons. (See.)

6. Sarah, b. Dec. 12, 1747; m. Philip Huntoon, of Salisbury, about 1773. He d. of smallpox in the Revolutionary army. She came to Bristol with her father and d. here.

*7.   Josiah, b. Kingston, Nov. 3, 1757.
*8.   John, b. Sandown, Mar. 10, 1760.
9.   Moses, b. S., May 12, 1761; m. Deborah Tilton. Mar. 15, 1787. He was one of the first settlers on Bridgewater hill. No children that lived to maturity.

(7)   Josiah Fellows, b. Nov. 3, 1757, came to Bristol with his father. He m. Jemima Quimby, of Hill, dau. of Jeremiah. She was b. Oct. 9, 1757, and d. in Bristol, Apr. 3, 1814, ae. 56-5-24. He succeeded his father on the home farm, where all his children were b. He was a soldier in the Revolutionary war, and was at the battle of Stillwater. He d. Mar. 20, 1852, ae. 94-4-17. He used to drive a four-ox freight wagon to Boston loaded with freight from this section and return with goods for the store of Col. Moses Lewis.

CHILDREN

10.   Abner, b. Feb. 5, 1781; d. June 28, 1786, ae. 5-4-23.
11.   Jeremiah, b. Apr. 27, 1782; d. July 31, 1795, ae. 3-3-4.
*12.   Josiah, b. Jan. 28, 1784.
*13.   Jonathan, b. Apr. 24, 1786.
14.   Elizabeth, b. Jan. 13, 1788; d. Aug. 20, 1790, ae. 2-7-7.
15.   Molly, b. Jan. 28, 1790; d. Apr. 2, 1790.
*16.   Peter, b. Apr. 14, 1791.
17.   Ruth, b. Feb. 9, 1795; m. John Kidder. (See.)
18.   Jemima, b. Dec. 19, 1796; d. Aug. 17, 1797
*19.   Benjamin, b. Nov. 22, 1799.

(8)   John Fellows, b. Mar. 10, 1760; m. Oct. 5, 1785, Lois Tilton, of Sandown, and was an early settler on Bridgewater hill. She was b. in Hawke, Jan. 2, 1758, and d. in Bridgewater, Nov. 8, 1857, ae. 99-10-6. He was a soldier in the Revolutionary army (See) from New Chester, and d. Bridgewater, Mar. 27, 1829, ae. 69-0-17.

20.   Abner, b. Nov. 24, 1786; m. Nov. 12, 1812, Elizabeth Prescott, dau. of Joseph, and d. Nov. 30, 1830, ae. 44-0-6. Children :
      a.   Lois T., b. Dec. 14, 1818; m. William Peasley.
      b.   Daniel T.
21.   Mary, b. Dec. 25, 1788; m. Oct. 22, 1816, Joseph Brown. She d. Feb. 25, 1841, ae. 52-2-0. He and two children emigrated to Minnesota, where they were victims of the Sioux massacre in 1862. (See Stories and Incidents.) Children :
      a.   Lois, b. Dec. 1, 1819; m. David Bartlett, Plymouth, and d. Sept. 1, 1889, ae. 69-9-0. Seven children.
      b.   Jonathan, b. June 9, 1822; killed by Indians in 1862, ae. 40.
      c.   Horatio, b. Jan. 26, 1827; killed by Indians in 1862, ae. 35.
      d.   Theodore, b. Sept. 15, 1832; d. at two years of age.
22.   David, b. Oct. 5, 1792; d. Nov. 28, 1803, ae. 11-1-23.
23.   Sarah, b. Nov. 13, 1794; m. Oct. 22, 1830, Enoch Colburn, of Hebron, and d. in August, 1841, ae. 46-9-.
24.   Lois, b. July 3, 1796; m. Dec. 31, 1818, Moses Rowe. He was b. Mar. 14, 1796; d. Feb. 28, 1828, ae. 31-11-14. She d. Aug. 8, 1879, ae. 83-1-5. Four children; all d. young.
25.   John, b. Mar. 16, 1798; d. Dec. 15, 1803, ae. 5-8-29.
"Drowned, in Bridgewater, June 20, 1827, Stephen Fellows, son of John, aged 17."—*Patriot.*

(12) Josiah Fellows, b. Jan. 28, 1784, m. Mar. 23, 1809. Susanna Sanborn, dau. of Benia, b. 1789. (See.) They were the first settlers on the David H. Sleeper farm at the foot of the lake, and here all their children were born. He d. Oct. 21, 1852, ae. 68–8–23 ; she d. July 3, 1864, ae. 75.

CHILDREN

26. Cynthia, b. 1810; d. 1811.
27. Louise, b. 1811 ; m. Jesse F. Kendall. (See.)
*28. Calvin Peterson, b. June 19, 1813.
*29. Samuel Smith, b. July 14, 1818.
*30. Rufus, b. June 11, 1821.

(13) Jonathan Fellows, b. Apr. 24, 1786, m. Feb. 25, 1806, Hannah, dau. of Thomas Eastman, b. May 3, 1788: was a farmer next east of farm now occupied by Horace N. Emmons, the buildings of which were destroyed by fire. Here all their children were born, and here he d. Apr. 7, 1845, ae. 58–11–13 : she d. Nov. 27, 1856, ae. 68–6–24.

CHILDREN

31. Ruth K., b. May 18, 1807 ; d. Apr. 24, 1827, ae. 19–11–6.
32. Lydia H., b. Mar. 19, 1809 ; m. David Powell. (See.)
*33. Winthrop R., b. July 22, 1813.
*34. James Pickering, b. Feb. 29, 1816.
35. Thomas E., b. Nov. 6, 1817; d. Mar. 18, 1819, ae. 1–4–12.
36. Sally S., b. Sept. 15, 1819; m. Fred Marden, of Thornton, Apr 12, 1839; d. Feb. 9, 1859, ae. 39–4–24.
37. Nancy K., b. Apr. 26, 1821 ; m. Sawyer S. Sanborn. (See.)
38. Hannah Eastman, b. Nov. 30, 1824; m. Nov. 12, 1846, Warren Fletcher, of Westford, Mass. He d. Worcester, Mass., July 2, 1881, ae. 60. She res. Lowell, Mass. Children :
    a. Clarence Warren, b. May 27, 1854; m. Dollie I. Robinson, Nov. 15, 1886. Res. Brooklyn, N. Y.
39. Lurinda, } b. July 25, 1828 ; d. Aug. 10, 1828.
40. Lucinda, }
41. Jonathan, b. July 25, 1830; d. Nov. 15, 1830.
42. Malina, b. Jan. 6, 1832 ; d. Jan. 24, 1836, ae. 4–0–18.

(16) Peter Fellows, b. Apr. 14, 1791, m. Lydia, dau. of Peter and Rhoda (Quimby) Ladd, published Oct., 1810. She was b. Nov. 3, 1791, and d. Aug. 3, 1828, ae. 36–9–0. He m. (2) Apr. 10, 1833, Mary Townsend, who d. Aug. 31, 1863. He d. Aug. 12, 1866, ae. 75–3–28.

CHILDREN, all except last born in Bristol

43. Lorana, b. Jan. 24, 1811. She m. Nov. 5, 1829, James Berry, farmer, of Alexandria, where she d. Jan. 7, 1892, ae. 80–11–13. He d. Boscawen, Oct. 27, 1895, ae. 89–9–22. Children :
    a. Caroline M., b. July 31, 1835; m. Sullivan Ingalls. (See.)
    b. Olive Ann, b. Feb. 1, 1846; m. Elijah C. Manchester. (See.)
    c. Gilbert H., b. Dec. 2, 1850 ; m. Philena J. Hayford, Jan 12, 1871, and res. Penacook. Six children.
44. Luther Sanborn, b. Mar. 8, 1814 ; m. Sarah Ann Heath, Feb. 16,

1836. She d. in Bristol, Oct. 4, 1840, and he removed to Janesville, Wis. No children.

*45. Benjamin Quimby, b. Sept. 27, 1816.

46. Mahala, b. Apr. 17, 1819; m. Ansel Chandler, 1847, and d. Aug. 20, 1856, ae. 37-4-3. Child:

  a. Ella A., b. Bristol, Aug. 7, 1849; m. Gideon Boardman. (See.)

47. Francis Bradbury, b. Oct. 5, 1821; d. July 30, 1843, ae. 21-9-25.

48. Cynthia, b. Oct. 1, 1823; m. Ira Burnham, and removed to Janesville, Wis.

49. Lydia Ann, b. Hill, Sept. 23, 1834; m. Sept. 29, 1857, Horace H. Withington, b. Hanover, Jan. 21, 1829. She d. May 24, 1888, Toledo, Ohio, ae. 53-8-1. Child:

  a. Wallace H., b. Aug. 20, 1858, in Hanover. He m. Lillian E. Belden, Dec. 25, 1878, and res. Toledo, O.

(19) Benjamin Fellows, b. Nov. 22, 1799, m. Miriam Hoyt, the dau. of Samuel, about Apr., 1821. He was a farmer on the west side of the lake, near where Amasa S. Hilands now lives, and here his children were born. She d. in Bristol, Apr. 18, 1866, ae. 69 years. He d. in the family of his son, Milo, Dec. 19, 1880, ae. 81-0-27. Besides being a farmer he followed his father's occupation of driving a four-ox freight wagon between Bristol and Boston.

CHILDREN

*50. Milo, b. July 23, 1821.

51. Belinda, b. Bristol, Aug. 27, 1827; m. Benjamin F. Robinson and res. at North Bristol, where she d. Dec. 20, 1860, ae. 33-3-23. Children:

  a. Millard F. *b.* Roxy, m. —— Brogan and res. Ashland.
  c. Addie.   *d.* Milo, b. Dec. 17, 1860.

(28) Calvin P. Fellows, b. June 19, 1813, m. Aug. 30, 1836, Mary Jane Worthen, dau. of Samuel R. (See), b. Apr. 28, 1816. He was a farmer in Bristol and New Hampton, where both d.: he, Mar. 11, 1856, ae. 42-8-22; she, May 25, 1865, ae. 49-0-27.

CHILDREN

*52. George Marshall, b. Bristol, May 8, 1837.

53. Laura Ann, b. B., Oct. 8, 1841; m. May 4, 1864, Joseph Cleaveland. They res. Methuen, Mass. Children:

  a. Willis M., b. Lawrence, Mass., Jan. 15, 1866; m. Ida M. Robinson, June 2, 1890; clergyman, member N. H. Methodist Conference.
  b. Sylvester I., b. June 19, 1868; d. May 3, 1891, ae. 22-10-14.
  c. Joseph L., b. Mar. 13, 1871, Methuen; m. Edith Reed.
  d. Annie Laura, b. Lawrence, Feb. 10, 1874; m. Harrison Tower.
  e. Helen L., b. L., Oct. 3, 1883.

54. Frank Worthen, b. Bristol, Feb. 19, 1847. He m. Dec. 10, 1873, Betsey Jane Hall, dau. of Fletcher, of Rumney, b. Apr. 28, 1851. He d. Dec. 22, 1900, ae. 53-10-3. She res. Plymouth. Children:

  a. Charles Davenport, b. Feb. 21, 1875, in Rumney; d. Jan. 7, 1876.
  b. Mary E., b. Jan. 20, 1877. A book-keeper in Boston, Mass.

(29) Samuel S. Fellows, b. July 14, 1818, m. Oct. 28, 1841, Mary S., dau. of Joseph Rollins (See), b. Apr. 20, 1821. Farmer at No. Bristol, where he d. Mar. 15, 1893, ae. 74-8-1 ; she d. same place, June 15, 1884, ae. 63-1-25.

CHILDREN

55. Mary Frances, b. Bristol, Aug. 26, 1842 ; m. Josiah D. Prescott. (See.)
56. Samuel Scott, b. B., July 26, 1846 ; m. July 8, 1875, Henrietta Sanborn, dau. of Gilman. (See.) He has kept a livery stable in Wells River, Vt., for some years. Children :
    a. Mary Franka, b. Feb. 9, 1889.
    b. Lois Genevieve, b. Dec. 13, 1890.

(30) Rufus Fellows, b. June 11, 1821, was a physician at Hill and Lowell, Mass., and d. Boscawen, Mar. 19, 1886, ae. 64-9-8. He m. Elizabeth, dau. of Rev. William Nelson, of Hebron. She d. Lowell, Mass.

CHILDREN

57. Abbie, b. Nov. 20, 1844 ; d. Sept. 20, 1845. Poisoned by drugs taken from her father's medicine chest.
58. Willis Mott, b. Mar. 22, 1848 ; m. Aug. 19, 1867, Ella, dau. of Ira and Hannah Clough, of Lowell, b. Nov. 10, 1846, and settled in Haverhill, Mass., where he was a physician and druggist, and where he d. Apr. 20, 1890, ae. 42-0-28. Children :
    a. Bertha Emma, b. Aug. 4, 1870 ; d. Apr. 1, 1880, ae. 9-7-27.
    b. Anna Maud, b. Sept. 24, 1872.
    c. Nina Emma, b. Jan. 29, 1879.
    d. Edith, b. Aug., 1882.   *e.* Hester, b. July 2, 1884.
59. Annie, b. May 28, 1854 ; d. May 4, 1872, ae. 17-11-6.

(33) Winthrop R. Fellows, b. July 22, 1813, m. June 28, 1837, Sally D., dau. of Benjamin Locke (See), b. Sept. 4, 1814. With the exception of six years in Wentworth, he spent his life in Bristol, where he d. Jan. 11, 1891, ae. 77-5-19. He was a farmer. Res. No. Bristol and Lake street, where the last 37 years of his life were passed. He was a Republican and Methodist. She d. Apr. 18, 1898, ae. 83-7-14.

CHILDREN

60. Warren Gerry, b. Wentworth, Apr. 22, 1838 ; m. Feb. 1, 1864, Caroline L. Nutting, of Newport. She d. Jan. 2, 1891, ae. 56-2-26, and he m. June 25, 1894, Mrs. Mary J. Lewis, of Newport, dau. of Curtis Travis, b. Goshen, Jan. 13, 1835. He was for years a salesman in Boston. His health failing, he returned to his father's homestead in Bristol in 1888, where he d. July 4, 1897, ae. 59-2-12. Child :
    a. Joseph Warren, b. Nov. 17, 1866. Is m. ; manager of a theatrical troupe.
61. Jonathan Alvin, b. W., Apr. 29, 1841 ; m. Apr. 18, 1865, Louise T., dau. of William and Lois Bangs, b. Mar. 3, 1847, in Madison, Conn. He was a machinist, now a fruit farmer, Meriden, Conn. Child :
    a. Fred Winthrop, b. Bristol, Aug. 19, 1867 ; a clerk in New Haven, Conn.
62. Smith D., b. Bristol, June 6, 1843 ; d. June 20, 1844, ae. 1-0-14.

MILO FELLOWS

63. Lauretta D., b. B., Aug. 26, 1847; m. Elmer V. Pike, Oct. 7, 1883. He was b. in 1847, and d. Bristol, Mar. 27, 1894, ae. 47. She m. (2) George H. Fowler. (See.)

64. Alma L., b. B., Feb. 22, 1858; d. Apr. 4, 1865, ae. 7-1-12.

(34) James P. Fellows, b. Feb. 29, 1816, m. Dec. 25, 1838, Nancy J., dau. of Jonathan M. and Jane G. (McCutchins) Marden, of Bridgewater, b. Pembroke, Jan. 1, 1815. He res. on same farm as his father, next east of the Horace N. Emmons farm, till about 1853, when he removed to Thornton, where he d. Mar. 28, 1864, ae. 48-0-29. She d. Plymouth, Jan. 3, 1885, ae. 70-0-2.

CHILDREN, all born in Bristol

65. Frank Watson, b. Feb. 19, 1840; d. Thornton, Feb. 14, 1861, ae. 20-11-25.

66. Ann Malora, b. Aug. 14, 1841; d. Sept. 17, 1850, ae. 9-1-3.

67. Chauncey Ayer, b. May 28, 1845; m. June 26, 1870, Eliza Jane, dau. of Albert Lyford, b. Thornton, June 15, 1848. He res. Plymouth, where he has been postmaster. Children :

    a. Maud, b. Thornton, Feb. 5, 1872 ; d. Concord, July 20, 1873, ae. 1-5-15.

    b. Victor Marlburg, b. Campton, Jan. 16, 1874; m. Mar. 27, 1901, at St. Albans, Vt., Mary Beulah, dau. of Joseph C. Leslie. Res. St. Albans, Vt. Child : Marion Lyle, b. Mar. 30, 1902 ; d. Apr. 2, 1902.

    c. Lyle, b. Plymouth, June 14, 1882.

68. Roselma Jane, b. Sept. 8, 1846; d. Sept. 17, 1850, ae. 4-0-9.

69. Clementine Eastman, b. Apr. 10, 1848; d. Sept. 25, 1848.

70. Florence Ann, b. Jan. 12, 1852; m. Nov. 18, 1869, Hiram H. Gordon, son of William H. They res. Concord.

(45) Benjamin Q. Fellows, b. Sept. 27, 1816, m. July 14, 1839, Hannah, dau. of Benjamin Kidder (See), b. Nov. 29, 1801. She d. Bristol, Apr. 14, 1877, ae. 75-4-15. He m. July 4, 1878, Mrs. Lovina Gerry. He was a farmer and stone mason, and res. on Kidder hill till about 1854, when he moved to No. Main street, where he d. Feb. 10, 1888, ae. 71-4-13. She d. Dec. 1, 1894.

CHILDREN

71. Sarah Jane, b. Bristol, Feb. 8, 1841; m. Green L. Tilton. (See.)

72. Eliza Ann, b. B., Nov. 17, 1843; m. Charles Boardman. (See.)

(50) Milo Fellows, b. July 23, 1821. Left home at 19 years of age and worked as a stone cutter in Boston. Was turnkey at state prison, Charlestown, Mass., two years from Dec., 1848 ; returned to Bristol in Dec., 1850, and settled in the Locke neighborhood, where he res. till 1866 ; since then on his farm on Summer street. Has been a stone cutter as well as farmer. Methodist, Republican. Tax-collector 17 years. He m., Dec. 12, 1850, Susan D., dau. of Benjamin Locke (See), b. Feb. 11, 1828 ; d. Oct. 12, 1899, ae. 71-8-1.

CHILDREN, all born in Bristol.

73. Albert Russ, b. Sept. 8, 1851; m. Evelean T., dau. of Timothy B.

and Henrietta (Seavey) Grant, b. Prospect, Me., Dec. 29, 1853. He is a physician in Winterport, Me. Child :

    a. Timothy Grant, b. June 4, 1878.

74, Smith Drake, b. Mar. 17, 1853; m. Dec. 26, 1876, Etta B. Jewett, dau. of Jeremiah. (See.) No children. He was a tinsmith and superintendent of the Bristol Aqueduct and later, florist, having hot houses on Merrimack street. Member of the legislature in 1893. Now florist in Saugus, Mass. Republican, Mason.

75. Oscar Fowler, b. Sept. 10, 1857, m. May 24, 1883, Eva M., dau. of Hon. Lewis W. Fling. (See.) He studied in the office of Mr. Fling. Went to Bucksport, Me., in Mar., 1881 ; was admitted to the bar in 1881, and has since been in practice in that place, having met with marked success. He was county attorney four years ; collector of customs at Bucksport, district of Castine, three years; was member of the Maine house of representatives in 1901, and was made chairman of the committee on revision of the laws; was reelected member of the house in 1902, and elected speaker of that body. He made a most efficient and popular officer and his name is prominently mentioned in connection with the gubernatorial nomination. He is a Republican, Methodist, and a Mason, 32°. Children :

    a. Raymond, b. Oct. 17, 1885.   *b.* Frank, b. Nov. 7, 1889.

76. Milo A., b. Sept. 23, 1861 ; d. Mar. 24, 1864, ae. 2-6-1.

77. Leslie H., b. Dec. 11, 1863; m. Nov. 23, 1892, Elizabeth Kerr; is a florist at Hyde Park, Mass. No children.

78. Susie M., b. Apr. 21, 1866 ; m. May 30, 1897, George Jenkins, who d. Bristol, Jan. 4, 1900, ae. 76-3-17 ; she d. July 13, 1902, ae. 36-2-22.

79. Alice A., b. Mar. 16, 1873. Graduated from East Maine Conference Seminary, Bucksport, Me., 1892. Is assistant postmaster at Bristol.

(52) Prof. George M. Fellows, b. May 8, 1837, m. Aug. 12, 1862, Ellen Maria, dau. of Horace M. Emmons. (See.) He graduated from Dartmouth College in 1862, and has devoted his life to teaching, having been principal of Contoocook Academy and Franklin High school, Corinth Academy, at Corinth, Vt.; instructor in Latin, at seminary, Falley, N. Y. ; principal of Avery Grammar school, Dedham, Mass., and Grammar schools, Hyde Park, Mass., and since 1877, in Boston, as supervisor of Grammar schools, and member of school board, and sub-master of Edward Everett Grammar school. He is also secretary and treasurer of official board of the Methodist Episcopal church.

CHILDREN

80. Calvin Peterson, b. Franklin, Sept. 17, 1863; m. Apr. 27, 1898, Carrie, dau. of Francis and Sarah (Cook) York. Night agent American Express company, Worcester, Mass. Children :

    a. Dorothy, b. Apr. 24, 1900.
    b. George Marshall, b. Jan. 21, 1902.

81. Horace Emmons, b. Franklin, Jan. 2, 1865 ; m. Oct. 7, 1891, Margaret Isabella Hoogs. Is a dentist at Hyde Park. Child :

    a. Horace Weston, b. July 21, 1892.

82. Edward St. Clair, b. Lawrence, Mass., Dec. 29, 1866 ; m. Jan. 24, 1899, Alice Mabel, dau. of Francis and Sarah (Cook) York. He is an attorney in Boston ; clerk of district court, Norfolk county, Mass.; res. Hyde Park, Mass. Children :

    a. Eunice, b. Nov. 5, 1900.   *b.* Edward York, b. Apr. 12, 1903.

SMITH D. FELLOWS

83. George Frederick, b. Hyde Park, Mass., July 24, 1874; m. Oct. 8, 1902, Sadie Elizabeth Gould. Is clerk in American Surety and Trust company, Boston office, and res. Hyde Park.

84. Frank Marshall, b. H. P., July 24, 1874; clerk in the Chicago and Great Western railroad freight department, Boston, Mass.

---

1. William Henry Harrison Fellows was the son of Nathaniel and Polly (Sanborn) Fellows. He was b. Andover, Aug. 17, 1814. He m., May 20, 1837, Mary Jane Gove, dau. of Jeremiah, b. Wilmot, May 28, 1817, and d. Bristol, Oct. 29, 1863, ae. 46-5-1. He was a blacksmith in Bristol, 1860–'63. He d. Campton, Jan. 7, 1884, ae. 69-4-20.

CHILDREN

2. Joseph Prescott, b. Wilmot, Mar. 13, 1837. (See Roll of Honor.) He m. Addie J. Kimball. Res. Manchester. No children.

3. Henry Alamando, b. W., June 10, 1844; d. of wounds at Philadelphia, Aug. 20, 1863, ae. 19-2-10. (See Roll of Honor.)

4. Louise M., b. W., Oct. 16, 1847; m. Dec. 3, 1865, Fred M. Moulton, son of Nathaniel, of Concord, Me., b. May 2, 1842.

THE FELT FAMILY

1. Rev. Joseph L. Felt, son of Leander and Almira (Collester) Felt, was b. Sullivan, June 11, 1837. July 29, 1862, he m. Lucy M., dau. of Uriah B. Moore, b. Templeton, Mass., 1843, and d. Templeton, Oct. 6, 1866, ae. 23. He m., Feb. 19, 1870, Julia E. Cheney, who d. at Antrim, May 23, 1877. He m., Apr. 14, 1885, Mrs. Sara J. Robertson, who d. Suncook, Sept. 2, 1893. He m., Nov. 3, 1897, Mrs. Clara A. P. Kimball, widow of Dr. John R. Kimball, of Suncook. He joined N. H. Methodist conference spring of 1878, and has since been in the active work of the Methodist ministry. Was pastor of the church at Bristol in 1898. No children. Children of present wife are

2. Mary Lizzie Kimball, m. Oct. 7, 1896, John J. Hills, and res. Newton, N. J.

3. Edith Huldah Kimball, res. in Bristol during her stepfather's pastorate here.

THE FERNALD FAMILY

1. Rev. Samuel Pray Fernald, son of Tobias and Sally (Pray) Fernald, was b. No. Berwick, Me., May 25, 1809. He m. Mar. 28, 1838, Hannah Evans, dau. of Joseph and Lydia (Evans) Palmer, b. Tuftonboro, Sept. 12, 1810. Mr. Fernald came from Gilmanton to Bristol in 1850, and was for over three years pastor of the Free Baptist church. (See.) He d. Melvin Village, June 9, 1888, ae. 79-0-14. She d. same place, July 1, 1888, ae. 77-9-19.

2. Orlando Marcellus, b. Candia, Sept. 1, 1840; m. July 5, 1871, Mary Lathrop, dau. of Wells Lathrop, b. South Hadley, Mass., Feb. 15, 1847. He d. in Boston, Mass., Apr. 15, 1902, ae. 61-7-14. At time of his death he had been for 30 years professor of Greek in Williams college, Williamstown, Mass. No children. His widow res. Williamstown.

3. Aroline Martha, b. Alton, Sept. 27, 1844; m. Aug. 14, 1871, George Byron Files, Pittsfield, Me.

THE FERRIN FAMILY

1. Jonathan Ferrin, son of Enos, one of the early settlers in Alexandria, and Judith (Corliss) Ferrin, was b. Alexandria, Apr. 7, 1798, and d. in Temple, in May, 1882, ae. 84-1-. He m., Nov. 18, 1824, Harriet, dau. of Bailey and Elizabeth (Merrick) Webster, b. New Hampton, Nov. 10, 1802, and d. Alexandria, Mar. 29, 1849, ae. 46-4-19. He m. (2) Mrs. Josiah Sanborn. He was a farmer in Bridgewater, where his first 12 children were b., at Moore's Mills and in Bristol.

CHILDREN

2. Bailey Webster, b. Nov. 3, 1825; m. Feb. 14, 1852, and went West.

3. Augustus Jonathan, b. Nov. 20, 1826; m. May 28, 1855, Olive, dau. of John Roby (See), b. Feb. 8, 1835; d. Bristol, June 21, 1856, ae. 21-4-13. He m., June 5, 1864, Sarah M., sister of his first wife. He lived on the Dolloff farm on the hill, 1868-'87; on the Roby farm at Moore's Mills, till 1900, when he removed to New Hampton. Republican, Odd Fellow. Served five years as selectman of Bristol. Children :

    a. Fred Roby, b. Natick, Mass., Jan. 22, 1867; m. Mar. 17, 1898, Lulu, dau. of Charles F. Noyes, Franklin.

    b. Arthur Augustus, b. Bristol, Mar. 24, 1875.

    c. Walter Gustave, b. B., Aug. 29, 1878; d. July 31, 1882, ae. 3-11-2.

    d. Herman } b. B., Apr. 17, 1884.
    e. Harry }

4. Francis Legro, b. Mar. 11, 1828. Res. Natick, Mass.

5. Abralona Viana, b. Feb. 15, 1829; m. —— Pope, Aug. 31, 1856, and res. Medford, Mass.

6. Morris Tucker, b. Apr. 29, 1830; m. Apr. 29, 1860, Helen A. Gerry, b. Billerica, Mass., Feb. 5, 1834. He served three months in 6th Mass. Vols., and d. New Hampton, Jan. 20, 1876, ae. 45-8-21. She d. Natick, Mass., Apr. 11, 1871, ae. 37-2-6. Children :

    a. Nellie A., b. Lowell, Mass., Sept. 22, 1861; d. Dec. 7, 1861.

    b. Nellie A., b. Natick, June 29, 1865; m. George D. Judkins. (See.)

    c. Charles A., b. N., Mar. 30, 1868; d. June 7, 1868.

    d. Laura F., b. N., June 30, 1870; d. Sept. 9, 1870.

7. Enos, b. Oct. 25, 1831. Never m.; has lived in Bristol with his brother, Augustus J., and in family of Uriah H. Kidder. Is a farmer, Mason, Democrat. Served on quota of Bristol in Civil war. (See Roll of Honor.)

8. Judith Melissa, b. Jan. 25, 1833; d. Dec. 30, 1853, ae. 20-11-5.

9. Benjamin Franklin, b. Feb. 19, 1834.

10. Hiram Woodbury, b. Apr. 3, 1835, lives in Concord. Was corporal in Co. D, 12th Regt., serving on quota of Groton. Was severely wounded at Cold Harbor.

11. Levi Edwin, b. Apr. 25, 1836. Res. Lynn, Mass.
12. Harriet Arvilla, b. June 3, 1837; d. Maine, Mar. 28, 1849, ae. 11-9-25.
13. Mary Elizabeth, b. Dec. 5, 1838.
14. Abigail Dolloff, b. Bristol, Feb. 6, 1840.
15. Moses Albert, b. Alexandria, Aug. 1, 1841 ; res. Plymouth.
16. Laura Jane, b. A., June 15, 1844; m. —— Rockwood, and res. in Temple.
17. Ira Polk, b. A., July 29, 1845; res. in Minn.

THE FIELDS FAMILY

1. Frank Pierce Fields is the son of Smith and Mary (Moses) Fields. He was b. in Merrimack, Nov. 5, 1852, and m., Nov. 24, 1877, Clara Jane, dau. of Nathan H. and Harriet (Hackett) Weeks, b. Thornton, June 2, 1857. He was two years in the meat business in Plymouth ; came to Bristol, July, 1877, and has been connected with the Mason-Perkins Paper company, since 1897 as treasurer and general manager. He is a Democrat and a Mason.

CHILDREN

2. Mary Belle, b. Bristol, Sept. 24, 1880.
3. Charles Weeks, b. B., Dec. 14, 1883.

THE FITZPATRICK FAMILY

1. James Fitzpatrick, son of Martin and Mary (Warren) Fitzpatrick, was b. Leeds, England, Apr. 11, 1834. He m. in August, 1858, Bridget, dau. of Robert Caplis, b. Ireland, May, 1835, and d. Enfield, Oct 15, 1877, ae. 42-4-. Has res. in Bristol since 1890, and is an employee of woolen-mill. Catholic.

CHILDREN

2. Mary Hannah, b. Burlington, Vt., Sept. 10, 1860.
3. Robert William, b. B., Dec. 16, 1862; m. M. C. Nickerson, Sept. 6, 1897.
4. William, b. Enfield, Mar. 31, 1865.
5. Martin, b. E., Aug. 10, 1867 ; d. May 17, 1875, ae. 7-9-7.
6. Sarah Agnes, b. E., Jan. 26, 1871 ; m. Amos A. Blake. (See.)
7. Anna Elizabeth, b. E., May 20, 1873.

THE FLANDERS FAMILIES

1. Capt. Joseph Flanders came to Bristol from Landaff. His wife was Relief Brown, a sister to Robert Brown. They res. where Solomon Cavis lived, later, on Pleasant street. He was a captain in the War of 1812, a deputy sheriff in Bridgewater, and a prominent man in the community. He left Bristol for Cambridge, Mass., about 1824, where he was a glass worker.

CHILDREN

2. Wardwell, was a sea captain ; m. and d. in New Orleans, La.

3. Benjamin Franklin, b. Bristol, Jan. 26, 1816; m. Aug. 24, 1847, Susan Hall, dau. of Alvah Sawyer. (See.) He fitted for college at New Hampton Institution, and graduated from Dartmouth in 1842, supporting himself by teaching while obtaining an education. In 1843, he went to New Orleans, where he studied law and was admitted to the bar. He became part proprietor and one of the editors of the *New Orleans Tropic*. At the commencement of the Civil war, with his wife and children, the youngest only seven days old, he fled to the North, leaving behind property valued at $40,000. Upon the fall of New Orleans, he returned and was made treasurer of the city by the military authorities, but a few months later resigned, having been elected representative to Congress. He took his seat in that body in March, 1863. That same year Secretary Chase appointed him supervising special agent of the treasury department for Louisiana, Mississippi, and Texas, which office he filled till 1866, when he resigned. In 1867, he was appointed military governor of Louisiana. In May, 1870, he became mayor of New Orleans, and from 1873 to 1885, he was, by appointment of President Grant, United States assistant treasurer at New Orleans. The New Orleans *Times Democrat* said of him at the time of his death : "He was not one of the carpet bag politicians, for he won and retained the respect of the people. He was well liked for the very consistency with which he held his convictions, and the truthfulness and honor by which all his actions were governed." He was possessed of a fine physique, and was hale and hearty at 76 years of age. He d. at his plantation, Youngsville, La., Mar. 13, 1896, ae. 80-1-17. His wife survived him. Children :

a. Katherine Anna, b. New Orleans, La., Sept. 11, 1848; m. Edward R. Pelton, publisher and owner of the *Eclectic Magazine*, New York city.

b. Susan Elizabeth, b. N. O., Mar. 11, 1852; m. Alexander L. Ridden, of New Orleans.

c. Mary Brown, b. N. O., Apr. 22, 1856, and res. at Youngsville, La.

d. Joseph Alva, b. N. O., June 14, 1859. Res. Youngsville.

e. Benjamin Franklin, b. N. O., Dec. 29, 1861. Res. Youngsville.

f. Rufus John, b. N. O., Sept. 10, 1865; d. Brooklyn, N. Y., Jan., 1869, ae. 3-5-.

4. Rufus, went to New Orleans.

5. John, went to New Orleans.

---

1. Charles Stephen Flanders, son of James and Lucy (Whitney) Flanders, was b. Chelsea, Vt., Dec. 4, 1845. He came to Bristol in 1862, and m. Apr. 2, 1868, Amanda W., dau. Kiah Wells. (See.) Was a job teamster; deputy sheriff two years; tax collector two years. Went to Boston in 1886, where he owns a billiard hall, and where he m. (2) Oct. 23, 1891, Augusta White, dau. of William and Phebe (Covert) White, b. Nova Scotia, Apr. 14, 1865. Republican. Odd Fellow.

CHILD

2. Owen L., b. Bristol, Dec. 17, 1869. Res. Bristol.

THE FLEER FAMILY

1. George Henry Fleer, son of George and Mary Ann (Arms) Fleer, was b. Watertown, Mass., July 5, 1835. He m., Dec. 24, 1860, Antoinette Lambert, dau. of Ruel Lambert, b. Lincolnville, Me., July 11, 1839. Served nine months in the 6th Mass. Infty in Civil war. After discharge, settled in Vineland, N. J.; in 1871, came to Bristol; was 12 years a workman on engines in paper-mill. Member of G. A. R. Republican. Res. Crescent street.

CHILDREN

2. Annie Belle, b. Alexandria, Jan. 23, 1862; m. Sept. 4, 1883, Frank H. Junkins, and res. Lebanon, Me. Farmer. Children:
    a. Ola, b. Somersworth, Dec. 3, 1884.
    b. Edna, b. Newfields, Feb. 22, 1889.
    c. Elmer Hall, b. N., May 21, 1890.
    d. Annie Fleer, b. Somerville, Mass., Nov. 27, 1893.

3. Frank Henry, b. Vineland, Feb. 15, 1868; m. Sept. 3, 1887, in Dover, Zenna May, dau. of George K., and Ann (Allaway) Willand, b. Berwick, Me., Feb. 12, 1869. He was engaged in shoe manufacturing for a few years; in trade on Lake street July, 1898, till Jan., 1904. Children:
    a. Austin Elbert, b. Dover, June 13, 1889.
    b. Helen Blanche, b. D., Dec. 22, 1891.

THE FLING FAMILY

1. Abel Fling was a resident of Pomfret, Conn., and served three years in the Revolutionary army. He m., June 10, 1793, Susan Alvord, who was 87 years old at the time of her death. He d. at Winsor, Vt., at the age of 80 years. They were the parents of

2. Abel, b. Springfield, Vt., Mar. 4, 1795. He m. (1) Abigail Harlow, who bore him one child. She d. and he m. (2) Hopestill Harlow, an aunt of his first wife, and dau. of Levi Harlow, of Springfield, Vt. She d. July 19, 1865, and he passed the last 15 years of his life in the family of his son in Bristol, and here d. Aug. 8, 1880, ae. 85-5-5.

CHILDREN

3. Abbie, b. 1818; m. Stephen Hastings, of Windsor, Vt.
*4. Lewis Wells, b. Windsor, Vt., Dec. 6, 1824.

(4) Hon. Lewis W. Fling, b. Dec. 6, 1824, m. (1) Apr. 20, 1853, Maria Currier, of Wentworth, who d. in Bristol, Aug. 19, 1854, ae. 31. He m. (2) Dec. 18, 1855, Margaret, dau. of Rev. Walter Sleeper (See), b. Nov. 20, 1828. He entered the office of Chief Justice J. E. Sargent, at Canaan, in the spring of 1847. Soon after Judge Sargent removed to Wentworth and he went with him, and continued in his office there. In Nov., 1851, he was admitted to the bar, and became a partner with Judge Sargent, and so continued until Feb. 13, 1853, when he

located in Bristol. Since that date, he has been in the practice of his profession here, and during all this time—over 50 years—has occupied the same office in White's block. (See Lawyers.) He is a Mason and Democrat; has served as superintending school committee, and was eight years a member of the board of education. He was a member of the state senate in 1871 and 1872, and was given the honorary degree of A.M., by Dartmouth College in 1872. Many years leader of Methodist choir.

CHILDREN

5. Charles Willis, b. Bristol, Aug. 27, 1856; m. June 18, 1878, Abbie Etta, dau. Amos and Jane (Grey) Seavey, b. Alexandria, Oct. 12, 1858. He was clerk and assistant treasurer of Bristol Savings bank, 1884-'90; has been justice of the peace and notary public since 1885. Insurance and legal business. Served on board of education seven years; was town clerk two years; several years a member of the board of health, and is serving his fourth year as fireward. Is a past master of Union Lodge, A. F. and A. M. Democrat. (See under Lawyers.) Children:

    a. Lewis Seavey, b. Bristol, Mar. 8, 1880. Piano salesman in Lowell, Mass. Unm.

    b. Eva, b. B., Feb. 10, 1888.

6. Harry Sleeper, b. B., Feb. 2, 1859; d. Feb. 27, 1861, ae. 2-0-25.

7. Eva Maria, b. B., May 11, 1863; m. Oscar F. Fellows. (See.)

8. Anna Sleeper, b. B., Nov. 4, 1866. She studied music at the New England Conservatory of Music, Boston, and was a teacher of music at Southern Female College, La Grange, Ga., where she m., Aug. 22, 1889, James H. Pitman, a lawyer, of that place. She d. Feb. 18, 1892, ae. 25-3-14. She was a beautiful and talented young woman. Children:

    a. Jim Fling, b. June 14, 1890.

    b. Anna May, b. Jan. 30, 1892.

THE FOGG FAMILIES

1. Oliver B. Fogg, son of Thomas, b. Holderness, Dec. 9, 1825, m. Lucy G. Moore, dau. of Nathan and Sarah (Crosby) Moore, b. Jan. 14, 1821, and d. Boxford, Mass., Dec. 21, 1882, ae. 61-11-7. He d. Pittsfield, Mass., Jan. 15, 1887, ae. 61-1-6. Carriage maker and farmer.

CHILDREN

2. Sarah Maria, b. Alexandria, Jan. 27, 1848; m. Charles M. Musgrove. (See.)

3. Ada Florence, b. A., Mar. 7, 1852; d. Bristol, Apr. 29, 1862, ae. 10-1-22.

    Two children d. in infancy.

Franklin Fogg was b. Hebron, Nov. 2, 1831. He is the son of Dearborn and Mary (Lovejoy) Fogg, and grandson of Samuel Lovejoy, who fought at Bunker Hill. In 1852, he went to California where he remained a year and returned with some of the gold of that state. After spending about twenty

CHARLES W. FLING, ESQ.

years in his native town, he came to Bristol in 1874. For 25 years he has been a guest at Hotel Bristol. Unm. Republican.

THE FOLLANSBEE FAMILIES

1. The Follansbees of Bristol are the descendants of Thomas Follansbee, who came from England with his wife, Abigail, and children, as early as 1677 and settled in Massachusetts. Among his children was

2. Thomas, b. England, 1674 (5). He was the father of

3. William, who was the father of

4. Thomas, b. about 1736. He moved from Hampstead to Weare about 1775. He was twice m. He d. in Hill, Apr. 5, 1818, ae. 82.

CHILDREN

5. Daniel.   6. Abigail.   7. Hannah.   8. Mehitable.

*9. Samuel, b. 1772.

10. William, b. Dec. 20, 1773; was twice m., the second wife being Dolly Colby. He was in Hill as early as 1810. His farmhouse was destroyed by fire on the evening of Dec. 20, 1820, while he and his wife were visiting a neighbor, and in it perished his six children. Four children were b. later.

11. Benjamin, b. June 4, 1775, was in Hill in 1812. He m. (1) Ruth Quimby; (2) Sally Stevens; (3) Lucy Rand. He d. in Hill, Mar. 1835, ae. 59-9-. The *History of Weare* says he had seven children by each wife, and one wife had seven children by a previous husband, so that his home contained 28 children. Among them were

   a. Benjamin, b. Feb. 14, 1799; m. —— Rowell. A dau., Ruth, m. Benjamin Wooster, an engineer on the Bristol branch railroad. Benjamin Follansbee was killed while coupling cars at Bristol station, June 14, 1854, ae. 55-4-0.

   b. Sally, m. Reuben C. Bean. (See.)

   c. David S., b. Hill, Mar. 3, 1818; m. July 14, 1839, Sarah Tirrell, dau. of Samuel (See), b. May 5, 1823. They settled in Bristol in 1852. He was a carpenter and farmer. She d. Feb. 19, 1893, ae. 69-9-14. He d. June 8, 1894, ae. 76-3-5. Republican, Free Baptist. No children.

*12. Jacob M., b. Sept. 17, 1787.

(9) Samuel Follansbee, b. 1772, removed from Weare to Hill about 1799. A soldier in the War of 1812. He m. (1) Shuah Lufkin, b. 1773, and d. July 1, 1797, ae. 24. He m. (2) (Published Nov. 6, 1800) Abigail Hoit, of Salisbury, b. 1771; d. May 28, 1803, ae. 32. He m. (3) Anna Taylor, b. 1769; d. Mar. 10, 1845, ae. 76. He d. Apr. 18, 1847, ae. 75.

CHILDREN

13. Levi, b. Feb. 19, 1794; was a soldier in 1812 from Hill. He m., June 25, 1815, Aseneth Gooding; removed to Dorchester, and there d. Five children.

14. Shuah, b. Sept. 9, 1796; m. Moses Tenney.

*15. John H., b. May 14, 1803.

(12) Jacob M. Follansbee, b. Sept. 17, 1787, m. Sept. 15, 1808, Dorcas Colby, dau. of Jacob A., d. Bristol, Apr. 26, 1860, ae. 80-2-5. He d. Bristol, Dec. 18, 1863, ae. 76-3-1. A soldier in the War of 1812. He succeeded John Ladd in 1846, on the Ezekiel Follansbee farm on west side of lake.

CHILD

*16. Ezekiel, b. Farmington, Me., Apr. 26, 1819.

(15) John H. Follansbee, b. May 14, 1803, m. Mar. 17, 1829, Abigail, dau. of Col. Samuel Martin, b. Alexandria, Jan. 28, 1804 ; d. Hill, Aug. 17, 1860, ae. 56-6-19. He d. Hill, Feb. 19, 1867, ae. 63-9-5.

CHILDREN

17. Abbie Hoyt, b. Hill, May 6, 1832 ; m. Mar. 7, 1858, Amos D. Caswell. Lived in Hill till Oct., 1870, when removed to Afton, N. Y., where he d. Aug. 1, 1897, ae. 71-7-21.
*18. Sam, b. H., Mar. 23, 1837.
19. John Martin, b. H., Sept. 19, 1842 ; d. June 19, 1864, ae. 21-9-0.

(16) Ezekiel Follansbee, b. Apr. 26, 1819, m. Sept., 1841, Sarah M. Howard, dau. of Daniel, b. Manchester, Mar. 18, 1819. He res. on the home farm, 1846-'74, when he removed to the Gustavus Bartlett house on Pleasant street, and here she d. July 11, 1891, ae. 72-3-23. He d. in the family of his daughter, Apr. 13, 1898, ae. 78-11-17. He was a Democrat, farmer, and dealer in furs ; an original character, with little education he was shrewd in business, saving, and accumulated a competency.

CHILDREN, all born in Bristol

20. Helen Moore, b. Mar. 15, 1843 ; d. Sept. 11, 1847, ae. 4-5-26.
21. James Dallas, b. Jan. 15, 1847 ; m. (1) Dec. 13, 1882, Etta P., dau. of David H. Sleeper. (See.) Divorced. He m. (2) Mrs. Ella J. Loverin. He is a fur dealer and speculator. Children :
    a. Emma, b. Bristol, 1884 ; res. in Lowell.
    b. Ada, res. in Lowell, m.
    c. Edgar, b. B., 1896.
22. George Frank, b. Dec. 30, 1848 ; m. Mary Ann, dau. of Asa Drew (See), b. Oct. 31, 1849. For 33 years was an employee and overseer in woolen-mill. Since 1898, farmer in Bridgewater. Democrat, Mason. Children :
    a. Bert George, b. Bristol, Nov. 2, 1871.
    b. Amy L., b. B., July 2, 1873 ; d. May 4, 1894, ae. 20-10-2.
    c. Sarah M., b. B., Jan. 21, 1875.
    d. Rose E., b. B., Aug. 8, 1877 ; m. June 22, 1898, Harry W. T. Norris. (See.)
23. Commodore Perry, b. May 26, 1851. Was for many years meat cook at Hotel Bristol. Unm. Democrat.
24. Martha Etta, b. June 8, 1854 ; m. Charles H. Putney. (See.)
25. Charles Lane, b. Apr. 8, 1857 ; m Aug. 1, 1886, Dora Maud, dau. Sylvester and Anna (Prescott) Bennett (See Prescott Family), b. Nov. 29, 1867. He was for many years barber in Bristol ; landlord Hotel Bristol, 1898-'99, and at Stafford Springs, Conn. Returned to Bristol, Dec., 1901 ; barber. Children :

SAM FOLLANSBEE

HERBERT H. FOLLANSBEE

a. Karl Lawrence, b. Bristol, July 17, 1887.
b. Edna Pearl, b. B., Jan. 4, 1889.
c. Lucille, b. B., June 19, 1891.
d. Ruth, b. B., Oct. 18, 1893.
e. Ermantrude Clytoria, b. Stafford Springs, Conn., Aug. 20, 1899.
f. Reginald Clyde, b. Buffalo, N. Y., Sept. 3, 1901.

(18)   Sam Follansbee, b. Mar. 23, 1837, m. May 20, 1860, Gemima S., dau. of Huron and Jerusha (Stevens) Williams, b. Grafton, June 16, 1840. He was in trade in Danbury. Since 1870, has res. in Bristol on Beech street. For many years, traveled through New England and New York as optician. Is a farmer and has a wide reputation as an auctioneer. Democrat.

CHILD

26.   Herbert Huron, b. Grafton, Aug. 26, 1862 ; m. Apr. 20, 1895, Belle C., dau. of Alonzo B. Gale (See), b. Oct. 25, 1861. He is a speculator and dealer in wool, hides, and furs. A Democrat ; has served one year as selectman ; was postmaster, 1885-'90, and is a Knight Templar Mason. Child :

a.   Reba, b. Bristol, Aug. 1, 1901.

THE FORREST FAMILY

1.   Charles Forrest, son of Sidney, was b. in Portsmouth, Ohio, Apr. 8, 1838. He located in Bristol about 1866, and was for a time in company with James T. Sanborn, as carpenter and builder. He erected several buildings in town, including Hotel Bristol. He m., Jan. 6, 1869, Addie H., dau. of Horace M. Emmons. (See.) In 1877, he removed to Lowell, Mass., where he was a dealer in lumber, and where he d. Aug. 2, 1891, ae. 53-3-24.

CHILDREN

2.   Gertrude Emmons, b. Bristol, Oct. 4, 1869.
3.   Charles Marshall, b. B., Sept. 1, 1873 ; m. Oct. 12, 1897, Ada Ethelyn Buckland, dau. of Gardner, b. Coaticook, P. Q., Oct. 2, 1876 ; dealer in lumber, Lowell. Child :

a.   Charles Gardner, b. Lowell, Oct. 8, 1900.

4.   Mabel Flora, b. Bristol, Dec. 25, 1875 ; m. June 26, 1902, Dr. John H. Lambert, Lowell.

THE FOSS FAMILY

1.   Burton Elwin Foss, son of Frank Elwin and Ella (Bingham) Foss, was b. Hill, May 21, 1875. He m., Sept. 3, 1896, Grace M., dau. of George W. Ballou. (See.) He has been, since 1899, salesman in store of Weymouth, Brown & Co.

THE FOSTER FAMILIES

1.   David Foster, son of David, an early settler in Alexandria from Maine, was b. Nov. 21, 1781. He m., July 14, 1813, Sarah, dau. of Jonathan Huntington (See), b. Dec. 1, 1792. Soon after his m. he succeeded to his father-in-law's farm in the Nelson neighborhood. He removed to Alexandria, where he d. Dec. 8, 1862, ae. 81-0-17 ; she d. Boston, Mass., Jan. 18, 1878, ae. 85-1-17.

CHILDREN

2.   Tryphena, b. Bristol, Dec. 5, 1814 ; m. —— West, and res. Haverhill, Mass., and Providence, R. I. No children.

3.   George W., b. B., Apr. 16, 1816 ; m. June 12, 1844, Martha Wiggin, b. Durham, Mar. 24, 1817. He lived on one farm in Lebanon for over fifty years, where he d. June 10, 1891, ae. 75-1-24 ; she d. Lebanon, Aug. 30, 1893, ae. 76-5-6. Child :

    a.   George W., b. Lebanon, June 16, 1855 ; m. Oct. 1, 1863, Pauline B. Daniels. Farmer in Lebanon.

4.   James C., b. Bristol, Mar. 7, 1818; m. Almira Boothby, of Boothbay, Me. He went to Boston, in 1846, and engaged in teaming. Served on the Boston Watch and, in 1854, was appointed on the police force ; retired Oct. 31, 1885. He d. at Mass. General Hospital, Nov. 1, 1886, ae. 68-7-24. Children :

    a. Fanny, d. at age of 35.   *b.* Minnie, d. at age of 26.

5.   Joshua, b. B., Jan. 8, 1820; m. Oct. 13, 1842, Eliza Sage, dau. Henry Tilton, b. Alexandria, Jan., 1821. A farmer in Bridgewater till 1851, when he went to Boston ; served on the police force till 1881, when retired. His last days were passed on a farm in South Alexandria, where he d. Oct. 25, 1882, ae. 62-9-17. She d. same place, May 24, 1894, ae. 73-2-11. Children :

    a.   Warren Francis, b. Bridgewater, Sept. 11, 1843; m. Maria Ann Kimball, dau. of Samuel, b. Hillsboro, Jan., 1842, and d. Winchester, Mass., May 19, 1883, ae. 41-4-. He m. (2) Sept. 8, 1885, Adelia Weeks, dau. of Washington, b. Jefferson, Me., June 1, 1848. A grocer in Winchester.

    b.   Cordelia V., b. Bridgewater, May 21, 1845 ; d. Dec. 10 (1), 1850, ae. 5-6-19.

    c.   Charles H. S., b. Boston, Dec. 11, 1854; m. June 14, 1876, Florence W. Lawton. Res. Somerville, Mass.

    d.   Maretta (adopted), b. Sept. 9, 1850 ; m. —— Farland. Res. Malden, Mass.

6.   Daniel, b. Bristol, May 15, 1823 ; d. young.

7.   Solomon S., b. B., Apr. 23, 1825 ; m. Aug. 9, 1842, Susan C., dau. John Pattee, b. Alexandria, 1823, d. Boston, Mar. 16, 1876, ae. 53. He was appointed on Boston Watch, 1849, and later, on the police force. At the time of death was sergeant and had been on duty at the city hall since 1878. He d. Boston, Feb. 14, 1882, ae. 56-9-21. Children :

    a.   Ira C., b. Alexandria, Dec. 6, 1843 ; a captain on Boston police.

    b.   Frank M., b. Bristol, Nov. 15, 1846; in wholesale provision business, Boston.

    c.   Helen M., b. Boston, May 20, 1852 ; m. Joseph S. Parker, Boston.

8.   David M., b. Alexandria, Feb. 3, 1827 ; m. Aug. 27, 1847, Lucretia Simonds, b. Alexandria, Dec. 26, 1829, and d. Plympton, Mass., Jan. 22,

1892, ae. 62-0-26. He d. South Boston, Sept. 29, 1881, ae. 54-7-26; was a member of the Boston police force 27 years. Seven children.

9. Sarah, b. A., Jan. 10, 1829; m. Mar. 13, 1855, George Lafayette Wilson, b. Hudson, Nov. 6, 1831. They res. Minneapolis, Minn. Two children.

10. Laura C., b. A., Mar. 29, 1831; m. Feb. 12, 1853, Joseph Verrill. He d. Lebanon, Minn., Mar. 31, 1865. She m. (2) Feb. 19, 1867, James Beatty Gilman. Res. S. E. Minneapolis, Minn.

11. Celestia, b. Alexandria, June 13, 1833; d. July 31, 1851, ae. 18-0-18; unm.

---

1. Wilson Foster is the son of Joseph, one of the first settlers on Foster hill, in Alexandria, and Tryphena (Cawley) Foster. Wilson Foster was b. in Alexandria, Aug. 2, 1822. He m., Oct. 3, 1849, Harriet A., dau. of Alfred Kelley. He res. 12 years on the Calvin H. Martin farm in South Alexandria; since then on the farm originally settled by Cutting Favor, in Hill. A prosperous farmer, Odd Fellow.

CHILDREN

2. Ann M., b. Bristol, Nov. 4, 1851; m. Clarence N. Merrill. (See.)
3. Harriet Emma, b. B., Mar. 1, 1853; m. George W. Ballou. (See.)
4. Ellen F., b. B., Nov. 5, 1856; m. Errol W. Morse, May 11, 1884; res. Concord, Mass.
5. Frank W., b. B., Sept. 20, 1858; m. Cora Bell Call, of Franklin, Oct. 29, 1882. Res. home farm.
6. Hadley J., b. Hill, July 6, 1864; m. Annie Little, of Hill, Sept., 1888. Res. Hill.

---

1. Edwin Scott Foster, M.D., is the son of Jeremiah and Adaline (Rice) Foster. He was b. Henniker, Mar. 22, 1845, and m., Sept. 20, 1868, Elvira Webster, dau. of Col. Walter Favor. (See.) She was a member of the Congregational church and a leading soprano singer in the choir. He located in Bristol in 1865; was clerk in Marshall W. White's drug store two years, in drug store of C. M. Cilley & Co. one year, and succeeded this firm in 1868, continuing the business till April, 1873. Republican; represented Bristol in the legislatures of 1876 and '77. Read law in the office of George A. Emerson, 1877-'79; in the drug business at Haverhill, Mass., seven years from Dec., 1879. Graduated, M.D., from College of Physicians and Surgeons, New York city, in 1887; took course in Post Graduate College and Hospital, New York city. Is a physician at 120 Tremont street, Boston, Mass., making diseases of the eye a specialty. Res. Hyde Park, Mass. No children.

---

1. James Rice Foster, son of James Newton and Sarah Ella (Rice) Foster, was b. Wentworth, Nov. 29, 1851; m. Nov. 23, 1871, Ellen Cordelia, dau. of Ezra W. and Mary M. (Weeks)

Cleasby, b. Warren, Oct. 18, 1854. Came to Bristol from Vermont, 1888 ; farmer at Profile Falls. Affiliates with a sect called the First Fruit Harvesters and occasionally preaches.

CHILDREN

2. Guy Owen, b. Groton, Aug. 19, 1872; m. Aug. 19, 1896, Mary, dau. Ephraim S. Drake. Res. Rumney.
3. Virgil Henry, b. G., Sept. 24, 1874, unm.
4. Ivie Viena, b. Piermont, Jan. 17, 1880.
5. Nellie Grace, b. P., Sept. 25, 1881 ; d. Wentworth, Oct. 14, 1884, ae. 3-0-19.

THE FOWLER FAMILIES

1. Joseph Fowler, the son of David and Susan (Piper) Fowler, was b. in Hopkinton. He m. (published Dec. 21, 1806), Nancy Robinson Leavitt, dau. of Jonathan, of Meredith, who served in the Revolutionary war as private, lieutenant, and captain. Joseph was a harness-maker and learned his trade of John Nash, in New Hampton. He was in Bristol as early as 1808, and resided in the residence on Summer street now owned by Rev. David Calley. His shop was a small building close to Central Square bridge, where is still a harness shop. He was in Bristol as late as 1825. Removed to Andover. Were early Methodists. He d. in Lowell, Mass.; she in West Boxford, Mass., at the age of 91 years.

CHILDREN, all born in Bristol

*2. Oscar Fitzalen, b. Sept. 3, 1808.
3. Amanda M. F., m. (1) Capt. Davis; (2) Edwin Adams, Boxford, Mass.; d. 1888 (?).
*4. Worthen Jonathan, b. 1817.
5. Nancy Leavitt, m. Moses Kelley, of Bristol, and d. DeWitt, Mich., 1877. No children.
6. Joseph Mortimer, b. Sept. 30, 1824 (6) ; d. Madison, Wis., May 13, 1888. He m. Charity Lincoln Winslow, who d. Lowell, Mass., 1865. He m. (2) Apr. 22, 1868, Martha M. Daun, b. in Kent, Eng. He went to Madison, Wis., in 1865. She res. in Madison. Children :
    a. Harry Mortimer, b. Nov. 9, 1850; d. Aug. 23, 1854, ae. 3-9-14.
    b. Frank Alexander, b. Jan. 27, 1856 ; d. Oct. 9, 1857, ae. 1-8-12.
    c. Joseph Haydn, b. Dec. 19, 1869 ; res. Chicago, Ill.
    d. Maud Mary, b. Apr. 10, 1872 ; d. Oct. 16, 1872.
    e. Maria Louise, b. Nov. 12, 1873. Res. Madison, Wis.
7. Caroline Matilda Thayer, m. 1848, in Andover, John B. Norton, a native of Georgia. Children :
    a. Claude Richard, b. Lowell, Mass., Jan. 23, 1851 ; a practicing physician in Philadelphia, Pa.; m. Constanza L. Partz. Children : (1) Ray, b. Dec. 12, 1880. (2) Elsa, b. June 4, 1884.
    b. John Jacob, b. Brooklyn, N. Y., 1854.
    c. Carrie Fowler, b. Madison, Wis., 1856; m. 1877, Dr. Charles H. Hall, Madison.
    d. David Atwood, b. M., Feb. 23, 1869 ; was a D.D.S. ; d. Aug. 20, 1892, in Philadelphia, ae. 23-5-27.

HON. OSCAR F. FOWLER

(2) Col. Oscar F. Fowler, b. Sept. 3, 1808, m. July, 1832, Abigail, dau. of James and Ruth Smith, of Bath. She d. Bristol, June 1, 1833, ae. 27, and he m. Sept., 1834, Louisa M., dau. of Thomas Waterman, b. Lebanon, Feb. 3, 1808. He removed to Andover with his father but returned to Bristol when 18 years of age, and was a harness-maker for many years where his father was in business before him. His fame as an auctioneer extended beyond the borders of the state. He was a gentleman of the old school and was a prominent figure at any gathering, was always a leader in any public enterprise. He was lieut.-colonel of the 34th regiment; was postmaster 17 years, and served as associate justice of the Court of Common Pleas; was prominent in the councils of the Democratic party. Both Col. and Mrs. Fowler were active workers and chief burden bearers of the Methodist church. Their home was always open for the itenerant preachers, and their kitchen was a vestry for social meetings. In the early months of 1874, both were stricken with paralysis, and a year later went to Plymouth and made their home in the family of their daughter, Mrs. John Mason. He d. suddenly while on a visit in Bristol, Aug. 6, 1876, ae. 67-11-3; she d. Plymouth, Sept. 2, 1878, ae. 70-6-29.

CHILDREN, all born Bristol

8. Abby Smith, b. Aug. 12, 1835; m. Jan. 1, 1856, Tristram Rogers, M.D. He has been a practicing physician in Plymouth, where they still reside. Children:

    a. Oscar Fowler, b. New Hampton, Oct. 27, 1856; d. Dec. 10, 1857, ae. 1-1-13.
    b. Hattie Waterman, b. N. H., Mar. 27, 1859; d. Mar. 2, 1881, ae. 21-11-5.

9. Harriet Waterman, b. Oct. 25, 1837; m. May 5, 1858, Prof. Henry Lummis. He is a prominent educator. Taught in the Lynn (Mass.) High school; for five years principal of Tilton Seminary; taught two years at Lasell Seminary, Auburndale, Mass., and since 1886, has been a professor in Lawrence University, Appleton, Wis. She d. Apr. 27, 1861, ae. 23-6-2. Children:

    a. Charles Fletcher, b. Lynn, Mass., Mar. 1, 1859; m. Dorothy Rhoades, at Chilocothe, Ohio, in 1879. Is an author of national fame. (See chapter under Literature.) He now res. Los Angeles, Cal.
    b. Louise Elma, b. L., Dec. 15, 1860. Made her home with Mrs. John Mason, Plymouth. A teacher in Tilton Seminary.

10. Susan Waterman, b. Dec. 9, 1839; m. John Mason. (See.)
11. George Storrs, b. Oct. 11, 1843. In Mar., 1864, located at Fort Wayne, Ind. Dec. 31, 1867, he m. Esther Louise, dau. Joseph Starr and Haddassah (McCullough) Updegraff, b. May 2, 1844, in Sidney, Ohio. He was in the clothing business at Fort Wayne, where he res. Now traveling salesman. Children:

    a. Flay Russell, b. Fort Wayne, Jan. 25. 1869; m. June 20, 1889, Peter Edger Pickard, Fort Wayne. Children: (1) Louise Catherine, b. F. W., May 2, 1890. (2) Margery Esther, b. F. W., Feb. 28, 1893.

13*a*

    b. Harriette Waterman, b. F. W., June 17, 1874.
    c. Clara, b. F. W., Jan. 25, 1883; d. Dec. 29, 1884, ae. 1-11-4.

    12. Rev. Charles J., b. Feb. 6, 1845; m. Feb. 12, 1874, Emily Peavey, dau. Hon. John G. and Tamar (Clark) Sinclair, b. Bethlehem, Aug. 20, 1851. He is a member of the N. H. Methodist conference and a successful evangelist. He was licensed to preach by the Bristol church in 1871; labored as an evangelist, 1872-'83; admitted to N. H. Conference, 1883, and ordained elder by Bishop Simpson at Concord, Apr. 15, 1883; served as pastor at Exeter, 1883; Grace church, Haverhill, Mass., 1884-'86; Great Falls, 1887, and since 1888, has been engaged in evangelistic work. He has labored in many of the large cities from Maine to California with remarkable success, the converts being numbered by the thousands. He is the author of a book —*Back to Pentecost*, published in 1901. Since 1901, he has been editor of the *Christian Witness* published at Boston, Mass., while continuing his evangelistic work. He res. in Haverhill, Mass. Children :

    a. Martha Sinclair, b. Manchester, Oct., 1874; m. Oct. 6, 1898, Andrew S. Woods, of Bath. Child: Margaret Louise, b. Dec. 27, 1900.
    b. Oscar Sinclair, b. Bethlehem, Aug., 1877; d. Sept. 1877.
    c. Louise Waterman, b. B., Feb., 1880; m. Edward Howard Allen, Walpole, Mass., Oct. 6, 1901.
    d. Harriet Rogers, b. B., Apr., 1883.

    (4) Worthen J. Fowler, b. 1817, m. Elizabeth ———, b. Haverhill, Mass., about 1818. She d. Worcester, Mass., 1864; he d. Tilsonburg, Ontario, Canada, 1881, ae. 64.

CHILDREN

    13. Alonzo Constantine, b. Lowell, Mass., Jan., 1837; d. Tewksbury, Mass., 1862, ae. 25.
    14. Frederick Augustus, b. L., 1839; d. Lowell, Mass., 1847, ae. 8 years.
    15. Thadeus Mortimer, b. L., Dec. 21, 1842; m. Mar. 22, 1875, Libbie A. Daun, b. England, Mar. 15, 1851. Served in 21st Regt. N. Y. Vol. Infty., Civil war. Was wounded at Bull Run, Va., Aug. 30, 1861. Res. Morrisville, Pa. Children :

    a. Carrie Mabel, b. Madison, Wis., May 26, 1878.
    b. Gertrude Elizabeth, b. Asbury Park, N. J., Nov. 11, 1881.
    c. Mattie Sadie, b. Lewisburg, Pa., Jan. 3, 1884.
    d. Thaddeus Bertrand, b. Morrisville, Pa., Apr. 28, 188-.
    e. Clarence Paul, b. M., June 15, 1888.

    16. Gustavus Adolphus, b. L., 1844; d. 1847, ae. 3.

----

    1. David Fowler, son of Abner, was b. Sanbornton, June 24, 1783. He m. June 16, 1803, Deborah Blake, b. New Hampton, Jan. 4, 1785. He was a soldier in the War of 1812; went from Sanbornton to Hebron and, about 1846, succeeded his son, Blake, in the lumber business at North Bristol, where he operated a saw-mill. From North Bristol, he removed to Alexandria. He d. Sept. 14, 1866, ae. 83-2-20; she d. Sept. 5, 1871, ae. 86-8-1.

CHILDREN

    *2. Blake, b. Sanbornton, July 29, 1804.
    3. Betsey, b. S., July 17, 1806; d. 1810, ae. 4 years.

REV. CHARLES J. FOWLER

4. Abner, b. S., Jan. 11, 1809; m. Hannah Sanborn, Alexandria, and d. in Minnesota, Mar., 1860; he d. Minn., Oct. 16, 1862, ae. 53-9-5. They had 12 or 13 children.

5. Joseph, b. S., Oct. 2, 1811; d. Jan. 2, 1812.

6. Mary, b. Nov. 15, 1812; m. Hiram Taylor, Oct., 1835, and d. in Warren, Apr. 27, 1874, ae. 61-5-12. Three children.

7. Deborah Jane, b. Hebron, May 7, 1815; m. Rev. Ashley C. Dutton, a Methodist clergyman, and d. Jan. 30, 1869, ae. 53-8-23. He d. Vineland, N. J., Dec. 16, 1897. Two children.

8. Thomas Lord, b. Hebron, Oct. 10, 1823; m. Aug. 20, 1844, Mary Hazelton, who d. Jan. 16, 1848. He m. May 10, 1848, Nancy M. Giles, who d. 1895, and he m. (3) Mrs. Esther Prince. He was a Methodist clergyman. Died at Westport, July 12, 1898, ae. 74-9-2.

(2) Capt. Blake Fowler, b. July 29, 1804, m. Mar. 4, 1824, Ruth, dau. of Daniel Sleeper (See), b. Feb. 10, 1797. Farmer in Bridgewater; in 1835, was operating a saw-mill at No. Bristol; farmer in what is now Adamsville, on the Bristol side of the town line. He recruited 71 men for the Union army in Aug., 1862, and was made captain of Co. C, 12th Regt., and served till May 16, 1863. (See Roll of Honor.) After the war he lived in the residence next south of the Post-office block and there he d. Apr. 28, 1884, ae. 79-8-29. Mrs. Fowler d. Oct. 4, 1889, ae. 92-7-24. Republican, Odd Fellow.

CHILDREN

*9. Hadley Bradley, b. Bridgewater, Mar. 20, 1825.

10. David Sleeper, b. B., Nov. 21, 1827, m. Nov. 25, 1870, Mrs. Mary J. (Sanborn) Eaton, widow of Ebenezer Eaton (See), and dau. of Capt. Moses Sanborn. (See.) She was b. Apr. 1, 1821, and d. July 26, 1887, ae. 66-3-25. He m. Sept. 4, 1891, Anna A., dau. Charles H. Spencer. (See.) He was a druggist in Bristol village for 36 years till his death, Oct. 28, 1894. His age was 66-11-7. No children. She m. (2) George C. Currier. (See.)

11. Hial Lee, b. Alexandria, Nov. 14, 1829; d. in California in 1849.

(9) Hadley B. Fowler, M.D., b. Mar. 20, 1825, m. Nov. 25, 1847, Caroline L. Smith, of Nashua, who d. Apr. 17, 1875. He m. Feb. 19, 1884, Sarah Locke, dau. of Orrin. (See.) He located in Bristol in 1854, coming from Alexandria. He was a distinguished physician and surgeon (See Physicians); served in the Civil war as surgeon of 12th Regt., N. H. Vols., and had charge of hospital at Point of Rocks, Va., for the army of the James, containing 3,500 beds. (See Roll of Honor.) In politics he affiliated with the Democrats and was the Democratic nominee one year for railroad commissioner. He served two years as town clerk and six years on the board of education. He was a man of marked individuality, prominent in society and in Odd Fellow circles. He d. in Bristol, Jan. 13, 1893, ae. 67-9-23.

CHILDREN

12. George Henry, b. Mar. 5, 1849; m. Apr. 24, 1870, Orra Ann, dau. Samuel H. Rollins. (See.) She d. Oct. 26, 1896, ae 51-2-26, and he m.

July 20, 1897, Lauretta D., widow of Elmer V. Pike and dau. Winthrop
R. Fellows. (See.) He first engaged in the drug business in Bristol in
1869, and with the exception of a brief time in New Hampton and
Plymouth, has continued the business in Bristol village till now and for
several years past has had two stores, one on the east side and one on the
west side of Central square. He is an Odd Fellow and a member of the
Knights of Pythias. Children :

    a. George E., b. Bristol, Nov. 14, 1876; m. Apr. 28, 1897, Amelia
M. Johnson, dau. of Oliver. He is a druggist's clerk. Children :
(1) Margaret Ora, b. Bristol, June 24, 1899. (2) Caroline Amelia,
b. Feb. 6, 1901.
    b. Caroline Phoebe, adopted. (Dau. of Charles E. Fowler.)

    14. Charles Edwin, b. Mar. 18, 1850; m. Mar. 22, 1873, Abbie Louise,
dau. David P. Prescott. (See.) She d. Bristol, Sept. 27, 1875, ae. 21-
11-17. He m., Jan. 18, 1879, Ella M. Blaisdell, dau. of Pettingill.
She d. in Franklin, Apr. 19, 1881, ae. 30-8-. He m., Jan. 28, 1884, Addie
C., dau. of B. Frank Brown. He was a dentist at Bristol, Franklin, and
Concord, and a farmer at Lancaster. He d. at Concord, June 20, 1889, ae.
39-3-2.

    a. Nina Abbie, b. Bristol, and d. Sept. 22, 1878, ae. 3 years ; fell
into a pail of scalding water.
    b. Frank Hadley, b. Concord, Oct. 21, 1885.
    c. Edgar Omera, b. Lancaster, Sept. 15, 1886.
    d. Caroline Phoebe, b. L., Sept. 18, 1888.

    15. Edgar Omera, M.D., b. May 7, 1853; m. May 16, 1876, Addie
J., dau. of Otis K. Bucklin. (See.) He graduated at the New Hampton
Literary Institution in 1869; took a medical course at Hanover in 1870;
at Bellevue, New York city, in 1872-'73, and graduated from Dartmouth
Medical College in 1873. He settled in Danvers, Mass., in 1874, and
acquired a large practice. He was of pleasing address, very popular with
all classes, and gave promise of a long life of great usefulness. He
dropped dead in a ballroom from heart disease, May 1, 1884, only three
days after the death of his grandfather, aged 30-11-24. The remains
were interred at Bristol. Masonic services were held at the Methodist
church on Sunday following, and were attended by a large concourse
of people, including 175, who came by special train from Danvers. Mrs.
Fowler m. George H. Calley, M.D. (See.) Children :

    a. Maria Belle, b. June 21, 1882 ; d. Sept. 16, 1882.
    b. Edgar Maude, b. Aug. 28, 1883. She graduated at Tilton
Seminary in June, 1900; and at the Greeley School of Elocution
and Dramatic Art, Boston, in 1903. Is an elocutionist.

------

    1. Abner Fowler, son of Abraham, was b. Hill, Mar. 7,
1827. (Abraham was a brother of David above, b. 1783.) He
m., Dec. 3, 1850, Hannah Favor Dolloff, dau. of Levi L. (See),
b. Jan. 6, 1831. He was a farmer in Bristol from about 1867,
and resided on the silver mine farm at No. Bristol, and later in
the village, where he d. Mar. 31, 1889, ae. 62-0-24. Republican, and an official member of the Methodist church. No
children. Gave a home to a nephew, Ansel G. Dolloff, son of
Gilbert B. She d. Bristol, Mar. 9, 1902, ae. 71-2-3.

    Edgar H. Fowler, son of Handel L. and Elizabeth Kimball, d. Feb.
5, 1888, in family of Abner, ae. 14-9-20.

GEORGE H. FOWLER

THE FRENCH FAMILY

1. Orlando Brooks French, son of Samuel and Anna P. (Stevens) French, was b. in Rumney, July 3, 1850. He m., Feb. 15, 1879, Sarah Evangeline, dau. of Rev. Thomas and Sarah A. (Clark) Wyatt, b. Rumney, Sept. 30, 1853. After five or six years in the tin and stove business in Rumney, he came to Bristol in April, 1885, and continued this business here till his death, Oct. 9, 1902. His age was 52-3-6. Mason, Odd Fellow, Congregationalist, Republican. Represented Bristol in legislature of 1899. No children.

THE FULLER FAMILIES

1. Chase Fuller was a settler in that part of New Chester, now Bristol, as early as August, 1771. At that time he had a cabin just east of the Heath burying-ground, though probably as a young man clearing the land for a home. His wife's name was Lora. In this humble home Chase Fuller and his wife were living with one child when the Revolutionary war commenced. In July, 1776, he first entered the army, leaving his wife and child in the wilderness. Soon after, his wife started on horseback for her old home in Sandown, carrying her two-year-old child in her arms. On reaching Pembroke she gave birth to her second child. The length of his first enlistment is not known, but the family were back to their home here in Feb., 1778, at which time he again enlisted for the expedition against Canada. After the war he resided at what is now known as Moore's Mills, his cabin being nearly opposite the site of the saw-mill.

CHILDREN

2. Hannah, b. Bristol, Apr. 10, 1774; m. —— Shute, and removed to Littleton.

3. Mary Connor, b. Pembroke, July 3, 1776; m. Samuel Clifford. He d. New Hampton, Sept. 24, 1841; she d. Bridgewater, May 17, 1845, ae. 68-10-14. Four children.

4. Anna, b. Bristol, Jan. 13, 1778. Never m.; d. in Littleton.

5. Joseph, b. B., June 14, 1779.

6. Peter, b. B., Oct. 18, 1782. Went to Littleton in 1805; brickmaker. Nine children.

7. Thomas, b. B., May 13, 1787, removed to Littleton 1812, where he d., Mar. 11, 1878, ae. 90-9-28. Brickmaker; m. Jan. 15, 1809, Mary, dau. Sanborn Clay, who d. Jan. 19, 1829. He m. (2) Sept. 10, 1829, Lydia, dau. Sanborn Clay, b. July 15, 1793; d. Dalton, Apr. 10, 1881, ae. 87-8-25. Children, all b. in Littleton:

    a. Luther W., b. Oct. 14, 1810; d. Dec. 15, 1840, ae. 30-2-1.

    b. Edward R., b. Aug. 7, 1812.   *c.* Chase C., b. Nov. 2, 1814.

    d. Robie C., b. Sept. 2, 1817; d. May 15, 1875, ae. 57-8-13.

    e. Lovina A., b. Mar. 2, 1820; d. Feb. 31, 1855, ae. 34-11-29, at Salem, Vt.

    f. Mary G., b. May 2, 1823.   *g.* Mary Jane, b. May, 1830.

    h. George Washington, b. Oct. 23, 1832 ; m. Sept. 19, 1852, Lucy Ann Fisk. Res. Littleton.
    i. Annie Jane, b. Sept. 26, 1838.
    8. Dolly, b. Bristol, July 14, 1789.
    9. Chase, b. B., Oct. 15, 1792 ; m. Hannah Worthen. They res. Bridgewater, where she d. He removed to Danville, and m. (2) —— Bartlett. Children :
        a. Eliza, m. David Sargent. Five children.
        b. Worthen, m. (1) Mary Sawyer, Danville ; (2) —— Sanborn.
        c. Harriet, m. Meservey.
   10. Reuben, b. Bristol, Mar. 9, 1795 ; d. young.
   11. Hulda, b. B. ; m. —— Heath, and removed to Littleton.

---

    1. Josiah Fuller came from Sandown and settled on south slope of Bristol Peak, in 1812. Later, he removed to the east shore of Newfound lake, near foot, to what was afterwards known as the Clark Fuller farm. His first house on this farm was between the shore and the highway. He m. Abigail Locke, dau. of Levi, and sister of Benjamin, b. in Sandown. He d. about 1843. He was a tailor.

CHILDREN

    2. Polly, b. Mar. 21, 1791 ; m. —— Smith, and removed to Boston.
    3. Levi, b. Jan. 6, 1893 ; removed to Exeter when young, m. and d. there.
    4. Rachel, b. Mar. 10, 1795 ; m. Nathan Tirrell. (See.)
    5. Josiah, b. 1802 ; d. Mar. 2, 1849, ae. 47. He m. —— Pike, of Sanbornton. Children :
        a. Merrill.
        b. Julia, b. Bristol, Aug. 5, 1831 ; m. Amasa Drew. (See.)
    6. Clark, m. Comfort Moses, of Bridgewater. He d. May 4, 1875, in Bristol, ae. 67 ; she d. Bristol, Apr. 27, 1875, ae. 77. He succeeded his father on the farm.
    7. Abigail, m. Robert Emmons. (See.)
    8. Russell, d. at about 14.   9. Dorothy, d. unm.; insane.

    Thomas Fuller served several terms in the Revolutionary war from Sandown. He enlisted as early as June 12, 1775, in Capt. Philip Tilton's company, Col. Enoch Poor's regiment. In 1776, he was in Capt. David Quimby's company, Col. Joshua Wingate's regiment. In 1777, he enlisted for three years. He was in the service as late as 1782. He was a brother of Chase Fuller, above. He came to Bristol soon after the war, and in keeping with the customs of the times, was warned out of town for fear he might become a public charge. He lived on the old road on the south side of New Chester mountain. He was familiarly known as "Maj." Fuller. He was a peddler and had a pension. His wife, Sarah, was a great weaver. In 1854, the town, after much opposition on account of the intemperate habits of the old veteran, erected a tablet at their graves in the

Sleeper graveyard on New Chester mountain on which is the following inscription :

Thomas D. Fuller,
A soldier of the Revolution, died Nov. 25, 1819, ae. 73.
His widow, Sarah, died Dec. 13, 1824, ae. 102.
Erected by the town of Bristol.

THE GAGE FAMILY

1. Joseph Gage, son of John, was b. in Manchester, June 7, 1868. He m. Feb. 14, 1893, Alice, dau. of Joseph Decato (See), b. Canaan, Feb. 14, 1874. Res. in Bristol since 1888 ; a workman in paper-mill for 13 years.

CHILD

2. Earl Joseph, b. Bristol, Aug. 18, 1900.

THE GALE FAMILIES

1. Stephen Gale, m. (Published Oct. 18, 1797) Margaret, dau. of Maj. Theophilus Sanborn (See), b. Sept. 30, 1779. He was a farmer in Alexandria and d. about 1836 ; she d. Apr., 1855, ae. 75-7-.

CHILDREN

※2. Sanborn, b. May 19, 1799.
3. Polly, b. Sept. 22, 1800 ; m. May 27, 1819, Nathaniel Woodbury, b. May 4, 1792, d. Nov. 1, 1878, ae. 86-6-27; she d. Jan. 31, 1839, ae. 38-7-27. Ten children.
4. Margaret, b. Oct. 20, 1801 ; d. young.
5. Stephen, b. June 24, 1803, m. Phebe Ingalls, dau. of Lieut. Gilman (See), b. Feb. 8, 1806. Lived and d. in Natick, Mass. Eight children.
6. Ruth, b. Mar. 2, 1805; d. young.
7. Hannah, b. Mar. 28, 1806; m. Franklin Keezer, Woodsville. Three children.
8. Hiram, b. May 27, 1808; m. Elvira Simonds. Nine children.
9. Theophilus, b. Sept. 6, 1809, m. Mary Chase. Nine children.
10. Nancy, b. Jan. 10, 1811; m. Calvin Colby. Two children.
11. Luke, b. Apr. 2, 1812 ; m. Louisa A. Perkins, Nov. 19, 1840. She d. Sept. 4, 1886; he d. Oct. 19, 1888, ae. 76-6-17. Six children.
12. Lavinia, b. Dec. 25, 1813; m. (1) Bradford Bullock ; (2) Elisha Bullock. Nine children.
13. Durinda, b. Apr. 5, 1815; d. ae. about 20.
14. Sally, b. Sept. 28, 1818; m. David Haines. Two children.
15. Frank, b. Nov. 26, 1819; m. (1) Abigail Carleton; (2) Susannah. Nine children.
16. Hezekiah Davis, b. Feb. 28, 1823; m. June 18, 1844, Sarah, dau. Samuel Cole, b. Feb. 9, 1824. He d. May 29, 1877, ae. 54-2-1. Five children.

(2) Sanborn Gale, b. May 19, 1799, m. Nancy, dau. of Col. Samuel Sleeper (See), b. Nov. 30, 1800, and d. Bristol,

Dec. 1, 1877, ae. 77–0–1. He was a farmer on Hemp hill. He was killed June 20, 1862, by a flying piece of rock while witnessing a blast in the construction of Sugar Loaf road, ae. 63–1–1.

CHILDREN, all born Bristol

*17.   John Sleeper, b. Sept. 8, 1826.
18.   Solon, b. Feb. 8, 1829; d. Aug. 30, 1834, ae. 5–6–24.
19.   Miles E., b. July 10, 1832; d. of smallpox, Dec. 21, 1849, ae. 17–5–11.
20.   Emily Lucretia, b. Apr. 9, 1837; m. Mar. 8, 1857, Paschal D. Fitts, of West Upton, Mass. He d. June 16. 1877. Children :
   a.   Emma Estella, b. Bristol, Nov. 26, 1857.
   b.   Addie Etola, b. B., Aug. 31, 1859; d. Nov. 20, 1871, ae. 12–2–19.
   c.   Lillian Gale, b. B., May 28, 1861.
   d.   Annie Lois, b. Manchester, Oct. 17, 1864; m. Oct. 28, 1887, Walter E. Sadler.
   e.   Camillo Urso, b. East Douglas, Mass., June 8, 1874.
   f.   Charles Henry, b. E. D., Nov. 7, 1875.
*21.   Charles G. Atherton, b. May 18, 1840.

(17)   John S. Gale, b. Sept. 8, 1826, m. Apr. 7, 1846, Isabella J., dau. Daniel and Martha (Brown) Simonds, b. Alexandria, Mar. 13, 1824, d. Dec. 29, 1893, in Bristol, while visiting her sister, Mrs. Solon Dolloff, ae. 69–9–16. Blacksmith; d. Jan. 23, 1866, ae. 39–4–15.

CHILDREN

22.   Emma J., b. Bristol, Oct. —, 1856; d. Apr. 7, 1857.
23.   John Sanborn, b. B., July 12, 1858; m. Nov. 23, 1886, Eva J. Jacobs, Manchester. Res. Boston, Mass.

(21)   Charles G. A. Gale, b. May 18, 1840, m. Nov. 27, 1862, Addie A., dau. of Samuel T. W. Sleeper (See), b. Aug. 20, 1841. He succeeded his father on the home farm. Democrat. She d. Dec. 15, 1901, ae. 60–3–25.

CHILDREN

24.   Burt Sleeper, b. Bristol, Dec. 4, 1863; m. June 27, 1888, Hattie Nellie, dau. of Ethan F. and Laura (Hastings) Stickney, b. Lyman, July 12, 1862. Mason. Children :
   a.   Pauline Stickney, b. Manchester, Dec. 3, 1890; d. Mar. 19, 1899, ae. 8–3–16.
   b.   Waldo Wilbur, b. M., July 11, 1893.
25.   Wilbur Fisk, b. B., Feb. 9, 1865; res. at parental home, unm. Democrat. Mason.

1.   Pattee Gale, son of Jacob, was b. in Alexandria. He m. Lydia Ingalls, dau. of Gilman. (See.) He was for 28 years driver of the stage from Bristol to Alexandria. He res. in Alexandria where he d. in 1881 ; she d. in Bristol, Dec. 24, 1884, ae. 80–11–0. Of their twelve children, three settled in Bristol :

CHRISTOPHER C. GARDNER

JOSEPH G. GARDNER, A. M., LL. B.

*2.   Alonzo Bowman, b. Alexandria, Oct. 21, 1836.
  3.   Mary Jane, b. A., Aug. 24, 1841; m. Stephen F. Sanborn. (See.)
  4.   Abbie Frances, b. A., July 10, 1844; m. Alvah Grey. (See.)

(2)   Alonzo B. Gale, b. Oct. 21, 1836, m. June 19, 1858, Harriet Jane, dau. of Daniel F. Wells. (See.) He has been a shoemaker and laborer in Goffstown, Manchester, and since 1870 in Bristol. Was for some years leader of choir at Free Baptist church.

CHILDREN

  5.   Nellie Augusta, b. Goffstown, Nov. 6, 1858; m. May 25, 1892, John O'Neil, of Plymouth, Mass. He d. Boston, Mass., July 14, 1899. She res. Bristol.
  6.   Belle Cora, b. Manchester, Oct. 25, 1861; m. Herbert H. Follansbee. (See.)
  7.   Minnie Emma, b. M., Feb. 20, 1866. Unm. Res. Pittsfield.

THE GARDNER FAMILY

  1.   Thomas Gardner, the first of the name in America, came from Dorsetshire, England, where the name had flourished for more than three hundred years. He settled in Gloucester, Mass., where he was overseer of the plantation. In 1626, he removed to Newbury and Salem, Mass., where some of his descendants still live. Of his children one was
  2.   Thomas, b. England, 1592. He probably came to America with his father. He was a prominent merchant in Salem, and, in 1637, was a member of the general court. He m. Damaris Shattuck. They were the parents of
  3.   Samuel, b. about 1627. He was a member of the general court, 1681-'85. He had a son or nephew
  4.   Samuel. One of his grandchildren was
  5.   Samuel, b. Mar. 6, 1770. He m. (1) Hannah Walker, (2) Mary Walker, a sister of his first wife. He lived in Haverhill and Bradford, Mass. Samuel and Hannah were the parents of
  6.   Samuel Walker, b. Bradford, Apr. 14, 1797. He was a drummer boy in the War of 1812, and later a captain in the militia. He m. Apr. 16, 1818, Sophia, dau. of Joseph and Dorothy (Sargent) Greeley, of Haverhill, Mass., b. Nov. 7, 1798. She was noted for her marked strength of character. They res. for a time in Sutton, for many years in New London, in Danbury, and in Bristol. She d. in Bristol, Aug. 20, 1872, ae. 73-9-13; he. d. in Somersworth, Feb. 28, 1884, ae. 86-10-14.

CHILDREN

  7.   Dolly, b. Sutton, June 14, 1819; m. Jan. 6, 1839, Hezekiah Chase, of Danbury, and d. Jan. 26, 1854, ae. 34-7-12. Four children.
  8.   Joseph Greeley, b. S., Dec. 20, 1822; d. Haverhill, Mass., July 9, 1842, ae. 19-6-19.
  9.   Sophia Greeley, b. Troy, N. Y., Feb. 8, 1825; m. Mar. 8, 1846, Rev. Asa Randlett, New London.

10. George Warren, b. Pomfret, Vt., Oct. 8, 1828; m. Nov. 18, 1852, Celia Lull Hubbard. He was an eminent divine; d. New London, Apr. 27, 1895, ae. 66-6-19.

*11. Christopher Columbus, b. Hudson, May 8, 1833.

(11) Christopher C. Gardner, b. May 8, 1833; m. Apr. 13, 1859, Susan E., dau. of Ezekiel G. and Nancy (Fifield) Bartlett, b. Hill, Nov. 12, 1837. Mr. Gardner res. in New London and Hill and came to Bristol in 1854; was employed by Warren White, making ladies' shoes. He settled in Bristol in 1867, purchasing the residence on School street, where Seymour H. Dodge now res., and succeeded Levi D. Johnson, as photographer. In Nov., 1874, he removed to Somersworth, where he continued the same business, and from there to Biddeford, Me., till Mar., 1893, when he returned to New London, where he now res. He ranks high as a photographer. A Democrat, Baptist, and an Odd Fellow.

CHILDREN

12. Joseph G., b. Mar. 11, 1860; graduated, A.B., Dartmouth College in 1883, receiving later the degree of A.M. He became professor of mathematics and English literature in the Burlington (Iowa) College, and graduated from the Law School of the Iowa State University, at Iowa City, Ia., in 1886, and practiced law at Omaha, Neb. He was later auditor and examiner of titles for the Iowa Deposit and Loan Company, at Des Moines, Ia., and is now comptroller of the Royal Union Mutual Life Insurance Company, at Des Moines. He has been a very successful business man. He is a member of the Episcopal church, a Mason, and a Son of the American Revolution. Politically, he acts with the Republican party. Aug. 8, 1894, he m. Callie Kasson Smith; she d. Mar. 17, 1896. He m. (2) Sept. 27, 1899, Matilda, only dau. of Judge Josiah and Elizabeth A. Given, b. Coshocton, Ohio, Nov. 28, 1860. Judge Given has been for 12 years on the District bench and 13 years on the Supreme bench of Iowa. Child:

a.   Edmond, b. and d. Mar. 17, 1896.

13. Charles C., b. Feb. 28, 1866; received a primary education in the schools of Bristol, and fitted for college in the public schools of Somersworth. He graduated, A.B., from Dartmouth College in 1887, and also fitted for a civil engineer, and later received the degree of A.M. Immediately after graduation he became constructing engineer for the Burlington railroad. In 1888, he accepted the position of cashier of the Custer County bank, at Sargent, Neb., which position he held 14 years. In 1902, having sold his interest in the bank, he removed to Kirkville, Mo., and purchased a half interest in the Farm & Loan business of W. S. Hicks, and the firm became Hicks & Gardner, dealers in farm mortgages and securities. He is a member of the Congregational church, a Mason, and a very popular and influential citizen and business man. Politically, he is a Republican. He m., Dec. 29, 1891, Jennie G., dau. of Henry C. and Mary J. Gilpatrick, cashier of the Somersworth National bank, b. Somersworth, Nov. 24, 1864. Children:

a.   Marion, b. Sargent, Neb., Oct. 30, 1892.
b.   Henry C., b. S., Sept. 30, 1894.
c.   Helen A., b. S., Aug. 6, 1898.
d.   Charles F., b. S., Sept. 1, 1900.

14. George W., b. Nov. 5, 1872; fitted for college in the public

CHARLES C. GARDNER, A. M.

George W. Gardner, A. B., M. D.

schools of Biddeford, Me., and graduated from Brown University, A.B., class of 1894. Six years later he graduated from Harvard Medical school, spending two years in Carney hospital, in Boston, and a year in the Boston Lying-in hospital, receiving a diploma from each of these institutions. He also spent six months in the Children's hospital in Boston. He is now practicing medicine in Providence, R I., popular, and meeting with very flattering success. A member of the First Baptist church, a Democrat. Unm.

THE GATES FAMILY

1. Fred Elton Gates, son of Freedom and Lovina (Luce) Gates, was b. Westmore, Vt., Nov. 13, 1862. He m., Dec. 25, 1882, Lilla, dau. of Peter Rash, b. Holland, Vt., May 7, 1864. He is a mason by trade ; came to Bristol Apr., 1900.

CHILDREN

2. Preston Elton, b. Barton, Vt., Mar. 4, 1887.
3. Homer Harrison, b. B., Oct. 6, 1888.
4. Maynard Henry, b. B., Mar. 6, 1892 ; d. June 10, 1902, ae. 10-3-4.
5. Ethel Lilla, b. B., June 19, 1894.
6. Fred Eugene, b. Cedar Rapids, Neb., Mar. 14, 1897.
7. Julia Ann, b. Bangor, Mich., Oct. 18, 1899.
8. Mary Betsey, b. West Derby, Vt., Mar. 15, 1900.
9. Marguerite Elizabeth, b. Buchanan, Mich., Oct. 16, 1902.

THE GEORGE FAMILIES

1. Arial Huntoon George, son of James and Jane (Fugart) George, was b. Wentworth, Aug. 11, 1814. He m. Louisa, dau. of Daniel and Mary (Walker) Hazelton, b. Hebron, July 17, 1818. He was a miller, in Haverhill ; two years at Moore's Mills ; 20 years in Alexandria grist- and saw-mill ; then in Bristol, till old age compelled him to retire. Res. School street ; he d. Mar. 22, 1895, ae. 80-7-11. Democrat, Odd Fellow. She d. May 25, 1903, ae. 84-10-8.

CHILDREN

2. Adeline Louisa, b. Haverhill, Dec. 14, 1840; m. Feb. 19, 1860, Hudson Gove, and d. Concord, Jan. 1, 1885, ae. 44-0-17. Three children.
3. Mary Hazelton, b. H., Jan. 9, 1843 ; d. June 9, 1846, ae. 3-5-0.
4. Charles Henry, b. H., July 1, 1844 ; m. Ella D. Mahan. He and his brother were in trade in New York city as paper hangers and decorators. He d. June 14, 1889, ae. 44-11-13.
5. Katherine Ferrin, b. Bristol, Mar. 4, 1847. Was teacher in graded school in Bristol 14 years ; later milliner, now in Concord ; unm.
6. Annie Whitmore, b. Alexandria, May 28, 1851 ; m. (1) Henry P. Gale, son of Hezekiah, b. Alexandria, July 6, 1851 ; d. Bristol, Feb. 21, 1881, ae. 29-7-15 ; she m. (2) George H. Hammond. (See.)
7. Wilson Hazelton, b. A., Feb. 8, 1856; m. Alice, dau. of Major Lambert, of Boston. Was in trade with his brother in New York, where he d. Nov. 5, 1888, ae. 32-8-27. She d. Jan. 31, 1903. Children :

    a. Arial Wellington, b. New York city, Nov. 5, 1882. Res. in Bristol.

    b. Katherine Eveline, b. N. Y., Nov. 24, 1884. Res. Bristol.

    8. Laurette Hazelton, b. Alexandria, Feb. 23, 1861; m. Frank C. Buttrick. (See.)

---

    1. Charles Parker George, son of Theodore, a soldier in the War of 1812, was b. in Franklin, July 23, 1829. He came to Bristol in 1852, and Apr. 11, 1854, m. Olive Jane, dau. of Daniel Bennett. (See.) After their m. they res. in Lowell, Mass., and Holderness, returning to Bristol in 1856, and have res. on Merrimack street. She d. Feb. 28, 1897, ae. 65–9–0. He m., Dec. 6, 1899, Alice L., dau. of Thomas H. Wicom. He is a carpenter; a prominent Democrat, and official member of Methodist church.

CHILDREN

    2. Ella Jane, b. Holderness, Sept. 4, 1855; m. Charles E. Davis. (See.)

    3. Flora May, b. Bristol, Dec. 10, 1859; m. Jan. 29, 1879, Hubbard W. Aldrich, son of William, b. Grafton, Dec. 22, 1854. No children. Res. Concord.

    4. Charles Arthur, b. B., Oct. 10, 1867; m. Aug. 15, 1894, Ellen C., dau. of Benjamin L. Wells. (See.) Is a manufacturer of lumber. Children :

    a. Margaret, b. B., July 25, 1896.

    b. Olive Anna, b. B., Apr. 14, 1900; d. Sept. 7, 1900.

    Abbie S. George made her home in the family of her brother, Charles P., and there d. May 2, 1900, ae. 82. Unm.

---

    1. William George is the son of Thomas and Lydia George. He was b. Colombia, Canada, May 29, 1839. He m. Weltha R., dau. of Joseph Braley, b. Northfield, Vt., Sept. 27, 1840. He was 17 years a clerk in millinery store in Manchester; came to Bristol in 1871, succeeding George H. Moore, in the Emerson block, as a dealer in dry goods, boots and shoes; later, he removed to the Rollins block, where he is still in trade. Republican, Mason, Odd Fellow, K. of P.

CHILD

    2. Frank W., b. Bristol, Feb. 27, 1878; was educated at Tilton Seminary, at Wesleyan University, Middletown, Conn., and graduated from Harvard Medical School. Is now in the City Hospital, Worcester, Mass.

---

    1. Frank Henry George, son of David and Elvira (Cheney) George, was b. Plymouth, July 12, 1840. He served in Co. D, 15th N. H. Vols., in the Civil war; res. in Bristol, 1865–'72, a dealer in stoves and tinware. He m., Nov. 5, 1865, Martha Jane, dau. of Trueworthy G. Currier. (See.) They removed to Concord, where he continued same business, and where they now res.

CHILDREN

2. Lena Vira, b. Bristol, Jan. 11, 1870; m. Oct. 2, 1895, Eben M. Willis, Concord. Child:

a. Mary Elisabeth, b. Concord, July 2-, 1899.

3. Roy Elmer, b. B., Sept. 7, 1871; m. Jan. 12, 1898, Mabel Florence, dau. of Ira C., and Helen G. (Rowe) Evans, b. Concord, July 13, 1872. He is manager of the Ira C. Evans Printing Company. Child:

a. Robert Arthur, b. Sept. 13, 1899.

4. Hattie Belle, b. Concord, Dec. 20, 1879; m. Oct. 23, 1901, Daniel B. Donovan. Res. Manchester. Child:

a. Harold, b. St. Johnsbury, Vt., Apr. 2-, 1902.

5. Lawrence Blanchard, b. C., Dec. 15, 1881; d. Feb. 8, 1882.
6. Edward King, b. C., Sept. 7, 1883.

THE GILMAN FAMILIES

1. Edward Stephen Gilman was b. Winchendon, Mass., July 30, 1862. He m., Mar. 18, 1885, Lilla A., dau. of Levi Nelson. (See.) He was a painter; served on the Bristol police force.

CHILD

2. Bertha L., b. Sanbornton, Apr. 2, 1890.

---

1. Frank Nathan Gilman, son of Thomas J. and Lenora E. (Weeks) Gilman, was b. Boscawen, Apr. 28, 1865. He m., Aug. 25, 1887, Melvina Lizzie, dau. of Orrin F. and Dora (Durgin) James, b. Thornton, Feb. 14, 1865. He removed from Woodstock to Bristol in May, 1900; is bookkeeper for Mason-Perkins Paper Company.

CHILDREN

2. Bessie Etta, b. Woodstock, Aug. 30, 1888.
3. Hattie Irene, } b. W., Dec. 11, 1890; {
4. Sadie Weeks, } { d. Feb. 22, 1901.

---

1. John T. Gilman, m. Betsey B., dau. of Jonathan Clark. She was b. Danbury, June 5, 1824. He d. Danbury, Nov. 15, 1851, and she m. Sept. 31, 1854, Ezekiel S. Reed, stone-cutter, who d. soon after. Mrs. Reed removed to Bristol in 1855, and here d. Aug. 15, 1899, ae. 75-2-10.

CHILDREN

2. John Wayland Gilman, b. Danbury, May 8, 1844. Located in Bristol, 1865; machinist and millright. Unm.
3. Maria Betsey, b. D., 1846; m. Charles M. Boyce.

THE GLEASON FAMILY

1. Rev. Salmon Gleason, son of Winsor and Martha (Follett) Gleason, was b. July 9, 1804, and was killed at railroad

14

crossing in Warren, Sept. 9, 1889, ae. 85–2–0.   He m. Dec. 24, 1828, Jerusha Willard, b. July 26, 1803, and d. Jan. 9, 1876, ae. 72–5–13.   He was a Methodist minister ; served on the Bridgewater circuit, 1833–'35.

CHILDREN

2.   William, b. Oct. 29, 1829; d. Dec. 24, 1831, ae. 2–1–25.
3.   Charles, b. Dec. 25, 1830 ; d. Dec. 21, 1831.
4.   Salmon W., b. Dec. 31, 1832 ; m. Feb. 26, 1855, Martha E. Hoit. Six children.
5.   George Leroy, b. Bristol, Feb. 25, 1835 ; m. Oct. 4, 1864, Charlotte Augusta, dau. of Daniel and Charlotte Town Perkins, b. Apr. 27, 1841, at Topsfield, Mass.   He is a Congregational clergyman.   He graduated at Andover Theological Seminary in 1864.   Was ordained at Bristol, Vt., Feb. 1, 1866.   Has filled pastorates at Bristol, Vt., 1864–'67; West Rutland, Vt., 1867–'69; Manchester, Mass., 1869–'81 ; Andover Theological Seminary, 1881–'82 ; South Byfield, Mass., Sept. 20, 1882–'88; Haverhill, Mass., 1888.   Now res. Haverhill.   Children :

a.   Chauncey, b. Bristol, Vt., Jan. 4, 1866 ; graduated from Dartmouth College, 1888 ; m. Oct. 4, 1894, Florence Nichols.   Res. Haverhill, Mass.   Three children.
b.   Alice, b. West Rutland, Vt., Oct. 23, 1868.   Educated Boston University, and is a teacher under the American Board in Guadalajara, Mexico.
c.   Charlotte Lenesa, b. Manchester, Mass., May 5, 1870 ; m. Sept. 25, 1901, Fred Windle, and res. Haverhill, Mass.
d.   Annie Perkins, b. M., Oct. 12, 1872.
e.   George, b. Mar. 8, 1875 ; graduated Harvard University, 1897. Is secretary of the Young Men's Christian Association at Osaka, Japan.
f.   Leroy Willard, b. Andover, Mass., Dec. 18, 1881.   In business at Haverhill, Mass.

6.   Orange Scott, b. July 8, 1837 ; m. Dec. 7, 1858, Ruth Clifford. Three children.
7.   Horace W., b. May 2, 1845.

THE GOLDEN FAMILY

1.   Calvin Golden was b. in Sanbornton, May 30, 1814, and d. Bristol, Sept. 22, 1900, ae. 86–3–22.   He m. Nov., 1840, Elizabeth E., dau. of Osmond and Abigail (Ingalls) Gale, b. Alexandria, Sept. 30, 1820, and d. Bristol, Dec. 26, 1892, ae. 72–2–26.   He was brought up by Dea. Samuel Gurdy.   Shoemaker and farmer.   In Civil war served in 9th Regt., N. H. Vols., June, 1862, till Mar. 15, 1863 ; and in 24th Regt. Veterans Reserve Corps, Sept. 6, 1864, till June 1, 1865.

CHILDREN

2.   Mary Frances, b. Alexandria, Sept. 23, 1842; m. Oct. 31, 1858, Rev. Moses P. Favor.   Res. Hill.   Four children.
3.   Phedora Elizabeth, b. Oct. 3, 1845 ; m. Harrison Sanborn.
4.   Georgia, b. 1846; d. young.
5.   Sarah Lucy, b. Feb. 22, 1848 ; m. Orrin B. Ray (See); m. (2) Ephraim Rand, of Maine.
6.   Nellie Josephine, b. Nov. 21, 1856 ; m. John W. Danforth. (See.)
7.   Osmond Gale, b. June, 1860 ; d. May, 1861.

THE GOODHUE FAMILY

1. Alfred Goodhue, son of Jonathan and Eliza (Goodell) Goodhue, was b. Groton, Aug. 28, 1846. He m. Sept. 8, 1875, Mary Osgood, dau. of Osgood Dale, b. Boxford, Mass., Sept. 28, 1857. Laborer. Came to Bristol from Groton, 1889.

CHILDREN

2. Emma Blanche, b. Groton, Dec. 29, 1876; res. Worcester, Mass.
3. Angie Elizabeth, b. G., Dec. 25, 1881.

Alvin Goodhue, a twin brother of Alfred, above, m. Feb. 16, 1871, Eva E., dau. of Ebenezer B. Butterfield, b. Groton, Nov. 26, 1852. A laborer in Bristol since 1891. Res. Lake street. No children.

THE GOODNOE FAMILY

1. Almon Sylvester Goodnoe, son of George W., was b. Newport, Vt., May 10, 1857. He m. Jan. 12, 1877, Mary Ellen, dau. of Joshua and Sarah Pryor Knight, b. Burlington, Vt., Apr. 5, 1860. Is a mill operative.

CHILDREN

2. Bessie Mae, b. Burlington, Vt., Dec. 6, 1878.
3. Sarah Archer, b. B., July 18, 1881.
4. Almon V., b. Bristol, Nov. 5, 1887.
5. Edwin Ray, b. B., Oct. 9, 1889.

THE GORDON FAMILIES

Stephen Chase Gordon, son of Clark and Susanna (Gordon) Gordon, was b. Sanbornton, Mar. 20, 1811. In 1842, he m. Belinda Knowlton, dau. of Ezekiel, b. Sanbornton, Oct. 19, 1811. They settled in Bristol in 1848; removed to Mansfield, Mass., about 1885, and after ten years returned. She d. Jan. 18, 1898, ae. 86-2-29. He d. Mar. 31, 1900, ae. 89-0-11. No children. He was an expert in laying water pipe and was supposed to be gifted in locating springs by means of the witch-hazel.

George Washington Sherburn Smith Gordon, son of Almon Kimball and Mrs. Hannah (Prescott) (Sanborn) Gordon, was b. New Hampton, Mar. 20, 1824. He m. Dec. 27, 1848, Mary Jane, dau. of John and Polly (Gordon) Kelley, b. New Hampton, July 17, 1824. He was a farmer and blacksmith in his native town. In 1868, he came to Bristol and has since made his home on Summer street. No children. Republican.

1.   Stephen Ladd Gordon, son of William, was b. New Hampton, Mar. 8, 1806. In April, 1841, he m. Betsey Ann, dau. of John H. Sanborn (See), b. June 27, 1819. He was a farmer opposite Pleasant Street cemetery ; later in South Alexandria, where he d., Jan. 24, 1881, ae. 74-10-16 ; she d. Bristol, Dec. 24, 1882, ae. 63-5-27.

CHILDREN

2.   Frank Augustus, b. Bristol, Aug. 9, 1843 ; m Dec. 10, 1863, Ellen Marantha, dau. of Sanders and Susan (Gordon) Simonds, b. Alexandria, Apr. 1, 1845. He is a carpenter and builder, and manufacturer of mill supplies ; is a Congregationalist, superintendent of the Sunday-school, and leader of the choir. Republican ; served in 6th Mass. Vol. Infty. (See Roll of Honor.) Member of the G. A. R., a Mason, and an Odd Fellow. Child :
     a.   Ola Maude, b. Bristol, Jan. 22, 1868; m. Austin H. Roby. (See.)
3.   Martha Bartlett, b. B., Jan. 2, 1849 ; d. 1865, ae. 16.

------

1.   George B. Gordon, son of James and Sally (Smith) Gordon, was b. New Hampton, Oct. 27, 1819. He m., Mar. 7, 1850, Hannah, dau. of Charles and Dolly (Gordon) Flanders, b. New Hampton, Mar. 30, 1829. She d. Bristol, Dec. 31. 1896, ae. 67-9-1. Farmer in New Hampton. Has res. in Bristol with his son since May, 1896, retaining a legal residence in New Hampton.

CHILDREN

2.   Marilla Sarah, b. New Hampton, Jan. 14, 1854 ; m. June 4, 1874, Edwin M. Huckins, New Hampton.
3.   Charles Elmer, } b. Meredith, Apr. 22, 1861 ; { d. at 9 mos.
4.   James Everett, }   { m. Aug. 23, 1897, Mrs. Georgianna, widow of Jonas F. Patten. He succeeded to the Oren Nelson farm in May, 1896. Child :
     a.   Annabelle Hannah, b. Bristol, Aug. 30, 1898 ; d. June 7, 1899.

------

1.   Warren Blake Gordon, son of Benjamin S. and Harriet (Kelley) Gordon, was b. New Hampton, Sept. 10, 1833. He m., Feb. 20, 1851, Mary Ann, dau. of Benjamin and Hannah (Avery) Kelley. Was a farmer in New Hampton till Sept., 1899 ; since in Bristol.

CHILDREN

2.   Clara A., b. Jan. 29, 1855 ; d. May 20, 1876, ae. 21-3-21.
3.   Medora A., b. May 23, 1857 ; d. Apr. 22, 1881, ae. 23-10-29.
4.   Annie J., b. July 19, 1866 ; d. Aug. 16, 1867, ae. 1-0-27.
5.   Ada M., b. Jan. 30, 1871 ; d. Apr. 7, 1871, ae. 0-2-7.

THE GOULD FAMILY

1.   William Gardner Gould, son of James and Rebecca (Gardner) Gould, was b. in 1820, in Vassalboro, Me. He m.,

in 1849, Martha Ann, dau. of Sherburn Wells (See), b. Bristol, Aug. 10, 1829. She d. in Bristol, Sept. 4, 1857, ae. 28-0-24. He was a resident of Bristol, 1847–1859; was in the livery business at St. Paul, Minn., where he d., Feb. 12, 1893, ae. 73 years.

CHILDREN

2. Francis LeRoy, b. Bristol, Jan. 27, 1850. Left Bristol when a young man and res. 811 Washburn Ave., Chicago, Ill., where he is assistant gardener at Douglass Park. He m., Sept. 25, 1876, Mary B., dau. of John and Catherine (McGraw) Slattery, b. Chicago, Ill., Jan. 25, 1858. Children:

a. John Francis, b. Chicago, Ill., Jan. 3, 1878; m. Apr. 11, 1899, Catherine G. Kennedy.
b. Martha Ann, b. C., July 27, 1880; d. Jan. 14, 1890, ae. 9-5-17.
c. James Walter, b. C., Sept. 26, 1881.
d. George Sylvester, b. C., June 22, 1883.
e. Lucy Loretta, b. C., Mar. 22, 1886.
f. William Joseph, b. C., Feb. 20, 1889.
g. Charles Richard, b. C., Jan. 14, 1895; d. Aug. 17, 1896, ae. 1-7-3.
h. Mary Catherine, b. C., Sept. 4, 1896.
i. Helen, b. C., Dec. 7, 1898.

3. George Henry, b. Bristol, Dec. 9, 1853; d. Bristol, Jan. 14, 1857, ae. 3-1-5.

THE GOVE FAMILY

1. Edgar H. Gove was a farmer in Plymouth. He m., Nov., 1855, Mary A. Rogers, b. Oct. 27, 1836. He d. Mar., 1899, ae. 65. She has res. in Bristol since 1900.

CHILDREN

2. Nellie May, b. Plymouth, Dec. 31, 1856; m. George H. Robinson; res. Plymouth.
3. Garrie E., b. P., Oct. 25, 1859; m. Horace H. Kirk. (See.)
4. Charles Warren, b. P., Feb. 27, 1866; m. June, 1890, Martha Webster, who d. Mar., 1898. He m., Dec. 7, 1901, Edith Lucy, dau. of George D. Maclinn. (See.) He has res. in Bristol five years; a machine tender in paper-mill. Child:

a. Marguerite, b. Ashland, Dec. 19, 1892.

GRAHAM

1. Rev. Hugh Finlay Graham, son of James and Mary (MacDonald) Graham, was b. Earltown, Nova Scotia, Mar. 26, 1865. He is a graduate of Bowdoin College, Brunswick, Me., and of Bangor Theological Seminary, Bangor, Me., and studied one year at Andover Theological Seminary, Andover, Mass. Unm. He became acting pastor of the Congregational church in Bristol, in August, 1902.

14a

THE GRAY OR GREY FAMILIES

1. Alvah Gray, son of Jeremiah, was b. Farmington, June 7, 1835. He m., Feb. 27, 1861, Abbie Frances, dau. of Pattee and Lydia (Ingalls) Gale, b. July 10, 1844. He was a farmer in Alexandria, and served in Co. C, 12th Regt., N. H. Vols., in Civil war. He d. in Bristol, Dec. 30, 1897, ae. 62-6-23. She res. Bristol.

CHILDREN

2. Benjamin Clark, b. Alexandria, Jan. 8, 1862 ; m. Oct. 30, 1894, Margaret Jane, dau. of Lucius L., and Sophia A. (Patten) Thomas, b. A., July 4, 1873. No children. He has been a barber in Bristol since 1895.

3. Charles Sepwinner, b. Groton, May 12, 1865; m. Oct. 8, 1891, Jennie May, dau. Aaron and Mary E. (Marston) Clark, b. May 3, 1868. Came to Bristol 1899. Employee in pulp-mill. Children :

    a. Donald Clark, b. Alexandria, July 15, 1892.

    b. Josephine Elizabeth, b. Bristol, Mar. 12, 1902.

4. Albert Hale, b. Bristol, June 5, 1869. Unm.

5. Emma Frances, b. Alexandria, Apr. 16, 1872; d. Jan., 1881, ae. 8-9-.

6. Addie Fidelia, b. A., Dec. 9, 1874; d. Feb. 3, 1881, ae. 6-1-24.

7. Lucius Fred B., b. A., May 19, 1876. Barber in Bristol ; paper-mill operative.

8. Clara Isabelle, b. A., Jan. 23, 1878. Unm.

---

1. Shem Gray was a farmer in Dist. No. 9, from 1844 till his death. He m. Hannah W. Edgerly. He d. Sept. 15, 1871, ae. 66-3- ; she d. Feb. 13, 1898, ae. 89-8-1. They had at least the following

CHILDREN

2. Samuel D., b. Sept. 8, 1828; d. Mar. 16, 1886, ae. 57-6-8.

3. Jenness, m. Jennie Weeks.

*4. Dearborn, b. Aug. 24, 1841.

5. John Augustus, b. Nov. 9, 1840. Died in the army Jan. 28, 1863. (See Roll of Honor.)

(4) Dearborn Gray, b. Alexandria, Aug. 24, 1841, m. Nov., 1855, Eleanor, dau. of Asa Kendall. (See.) She d. Alexandria, Feb. 27, 1901, and he m. Oct. 6, 1901, Kate Lucas. He served in Co. C, 12th Regt., N. H. Vols.; was wounded at Chancellorsville. He d. Alexandria, May 28, 1903, ae. 61-9-4.

CHILDREN

6. Asa Edgar, b. 1856, m. Ellen Bliss ; res. Gilmanton Iron Works. Five children.

7. Nellie Maud, b. 1859 ; m. Warren Wescott ; now res. Franklin. Eleven children.

8. Willie K., b. 1860 ; d. 1874, ae. 14 years.

9. Carrie Lillian, b. May, 1863 ; m. John A. Jones, Grafton. Five children.

10. Hannah Tamson, b. 1867 ; m. David Ford, Grafton. Four children.

11. Jennie Bell, b. 1869 ; m. Frank C. Patten.

12. Minnie Myrtle, b. 1871 ; m. Elwin Hazeltine.

13. Mabel Blanch, b. Mar., 1877; m. Charles Wright, Jr.; res. Concord.

---

1. Benjamin Gray, son of Benjamin and Lydia (Sulloway) Gray, was b. Sheffield, Vt., Nov. 10, 1838. He served two terms in the Union army: three months in the 1st Regt., and from Apr. 11, 1862, till May 14, 1865, in Co. E, 9th Regt., N. H. Vols. He located in Bristol in Nov., 1866, and Dec. 24, 1868, m. Mary E., widow of Augustus B. Drew. Mrs. Gray d. Sept 24, 1895, ae. 54–8–, and he m. Apr. 21, 1897, Henrietta Gray, dau. of William Bispham.

CHILDREN

2. Daniel Hadley, b. Bristol, Sept. 15, 1879. Res. Cambridgeport, Mass.

3. Oscar Robinson, b. B., Jan. 16, 1883; m. June 3, 1903, Evelyn, dau. of Albert Chase.

THE GREEN FAMILY

1. Dr. Peter Green, son of Peter, of Lancaster, Mass., was b. Oct. 1, 1745; graduated from Harvard College in 1766; settled in Concord, 1772, where he was in practice over 50 years. He was a surgeon in the Revolutionary army. He m. Ruth Ayer, had 13 children, and d. Mar. 31, 1828, ae. 82–6–0. His eighth child was

2. William, b. Concord, Dec. 19, 1788. He m., Aug. 10, 1816, Clarissa, dau. of Walter Harris, and widow of Jerrimah Stinson, of Dunbarton, b. June 17, 1790. She d. Apr. 18, 1817, ae. 26–10–1. He m., Mar. 19, 1828, Harriet Kimball, dau. of Benjamin, of Concord, b. Mar. 16, 1799, d. Bristol, Dec. 21, 1881, ae. 82–9–5. He was cashier of Pemigewasset bank at Plymouth, 1828–'45; came to Bristol, 1847, and here d. Aug. 8, 1869, ae. 80–7–19. He was an elegant penman and accurate accountant; was a prominent member of the Congregational church and active in church and temperance work. They succeeded to the Moses Sleeper tavern stand, erected about 1795.

CHILDREN, all born in Plymouth

2. Harriet Eliza, b. Aug. 28, 1830; d. Aug. 9, 1903, ae. 72–11–11; unm. She was active in church and temperance work.

3. Benjamin Kimball, b. Aug. 14, 1832; d. June 16, 1835, ae. 2–10–2.

4. Clarissa Harris, b. July 31, 1834; d. June 19, 1835.

5. Mary, b. May 3, 1836; m. Oct. 19, 1860, Joseph Charles Augustus Wingate, b. Stratham, Nov. 16, 1830; d. Nov. 3, 1876, ae. 40–6–0. No children. He was consul at Swatow, China, for some years.

6. Martha, b. June 7, 1838. Res. Bristol, unm.; d. July 15, 1897, ae. 59–1–8.

7. Annie Douglas, b. Jan. 12, 1842; m. Apr. 11, 1877, Frank W. Robinson; res. Bristol. She is an authoress of note under the *non-de-plume* of Marian Douglas. (See Literature.)

8. Clarissa Harris, b. Feb. 21, 1845; d. May 16, 1846, ae. 1–2–25.

THE GREENOUGH FAMILY

1. Brackett L. Greenough was b. Apr. 22, 1777. He m., 1799, Ruth Stevens, b. 1779, and d. Sept. 16, 1804, ae. 25. He m. (2) Oct. 14, 1808, Abigail Cummings, b. Dec. 17, 1779, and d. Feb. 6, 1846, ae. 66-1-19. He was a resident of Bristol 1829-'46, and the owner of mills and privileges on Newfound river in Bristol village, and the residence corner of Central square and Spring street, which he occupied. He held a prominent place in the affairs of the town, during his stay here.

CHILDREN

2. Brackett L., b. Jan. 15, 1800; m. Amanda Frary, Dec. 23, 1821.
3. Betsey, b. Sept. 18, 1802 ; m. June 1, 1817, Silas Barrows.
4. Mariah Jane, b. July 9, 1810; d. Sept. 28, 1831, ae. 21-2-19.
5. Louisa Ruth, b. Oct. 20, 1812; m. Jan. 23, 1833, William S. Ela.
6. Abigail, b. Nov. 30, 1813; d. Dec. 18, 1813.
7. Solomon C., b. Sept. 1, 1815 ; d. Sept. 22, 1815.
8. Marianne A., b. Apr. 18, 1818 ; m. John Corser. (See.)
9. Norman Cummings, b. Feb. 24, 1820; m. Nov. 23, 1846, Frances D. DeFord, b. Oct. 7, 1816. He d. Aug. 11, 1866, ae. 46-5-17. She d. Feb., 1884, ae. 67-4-.

THE GRIFFITH FAMILY

1. James Wallingford Griffith, son of William, was b. Groveland, Mass., Dec. 29, 1821, and d. Jan. 16, 1891, ae. 69-0-17. He m. July 12, 1843, Adeline Ordway, dau. of Stephen, b. Newburyport, Mass., Apr. 4, 1824. She d. Nov. 11, 1860, ae. 36-7-7, and he m. Jan. 10, 1865, Sarah M., dau. of Dexter Brown. (See.) She d. Jan. 23, 1891, ae. 54-0-18. He was a resident of Bristol from 1854 till his death, with the exception of a few years in Groton. Shoemaker.

CHILDREN

*2. Henry, b. Groveland, Mass., Sept. 1, 1844.
3. George, b. G., Mar. 20, 1847; d. Bristol, July 27, 1862, ae. 15 4-7.
4. Emma, b. G., Sept. 1, 1848; m. (1) Wayland Ballou (See); (2) Amos Truell, Aug., 1887, and res. Nashua.

(2) Henry Griffith, b. Sept. 1, 1844, m. May 27, 1865. Ellen J., dau. Dea. John F. Cass. (See.) She d. June 1, 1893, ae. 48-6-8. He m. Nov. 29, 1899, Mary, widow of Wendell P. Marshall, b. Norwood, Mass., Aug. 1, 1853. He is a miller. Republican.

CHILDREN

5. Linnie Maude, b. Bristol, July 9, 1867; m. Clarence A. Smith. (See.)
6. Nora Viola, b. B., Jan. 31, 1870; m. John A. Favor. (See.)

THE GURDY FAMILY

1. Meshech Gurdy was a resident of Kingston and named as one of the incorporators of Sandown when that town was set off from Kingston in 1756. He was in New Chester as early as 1780, his log cabin being near where the railroad now is, just north of Smith's river. His family consisted of his wife, Judith Eaton, and six children. The wife and three youngest children d. of throat distemper and were buried near their humble home. Some years since, workmen plowed up what was supposed to be an Indian skeleton there, but probably that of one of this family. While living there, the sons cleared land for a farm in the Locke neighborhood, where Meshech Gurdy d.

CHILDREN

2. Mary, b. Sandown, Apr. 20, 1752, was generally known as "Aunt Polly." She was a great weaver and spinner and d., unm., in the Locke neighborhood, Dec. 31, 1846, ae. 94-8-11.
*3. Jacob, b. S.   *4. Samuel, b. S.
5. 6. 7. Judith and two younger as stated.

(3) Jacob Gurdy was an early settler in the Locke neighborhood. He m. May 27, 1782, Mary, dau. Cutting Favor (See), b. Jan. 21, 1764. She d. Apr. 15, 1844, ae. 80-2-24; he d. Mar. 12, 1808. The town clerk of Bridgewater, in recording the death, added these words: "And a great loss to Bridgewater."

CHILDREN, all born Bristol

*8. Jacob, b. Dec. 22, 1782.
9. Dorothy, b. Oct. 7, 1785; m. Amos Drew. (See.)
10. Anne, b. Mar. 11, 1788; m. Benj. Locke. (See.)
11. Joel, b. Mar. 12, 1790; d. Mar. 23, 1790.
*12. Elisha, b. Dec. 2, 1791.
13. Lois, b. June 20, 1794; m. Timothy Chandler. (See.)
14. Huldah, b. Sept. 12, 1796; m. Jonathan Atwood. (See.)
15. Aaron, b. Dec. 15, 1798; d. young.

(4) Samuel Gurdy m., July 12, 1791, Lydia Sanborn, b. Brentwood, Oct. 23, 1762. They were the first settlers on the Otis Sanborn farm in the Locke neighborhood, but later res. on the John F. Merrow farm for many years. He was a man of great physical strength and endurance. He was deacon of the Baptist church in New Hampton. They removed to New Hampton later in life, where they d.

CHILDREN, all born in Bristol

16. Ruth, b. Jan. 9, 1792; m. Amos Drew. (See.)
17. Sophronia; m. and removed to Vermont.
18. Susan, b. Nov. 12, 1794; m. Jacob Hoyt. (See.)
19. Lucy, b. Nov. 12, 1795; m. Moses Morgan Smith. (See.) She was a school teacher and a woman of rare intelligence.
*20. John, b. 1796.

(8)   Jacob Gurdy, b. Dec. 22, 1782, m. Susannah Doton, a descendant of Edward Doton of the Mayflower, b. in Moultonboro, Aug. 30, 1795. Her father, Ephraim Doton, was a Revolutionary soldier. About 1837, Jacob Gurdy settled in Moultonboro, where he d. May 21, 1855, ae. 72-4-29; she d. Apr. 30, 1842, ae. 46-8-0.

CHILDREN

21.   Reuben, b. Bristol, Aug. 23, 1827; d. Aug. 26, 1831, ae. 4-0-3.
22.   Almira, b. B., May 30, 1829; m. Sept. 29, 1850, Charles L. Glines, Moultonboro. She d. in Laconia, June 9, 1892, ae. 63-0-9. Children:
 a.   Sarah L., b. Moultonboro, Mar. 4, 1853; m. W. H. Penniman. Res. Center Sandwich.
 b.   Maria A., b. M., Sept. 2, 1855; m. C. H. Peavey, Laconia.
 c.   Charles W., b. M., May 25, 1864.
 d.   Vesta A., b. M., Jan. 4, 1866.
 e.   Lilla O., b. M., Oct. 14, 1869; m. W. A. Clark, Laconia.
23.   George, b. Bristol, Mar. 24, 1831; m. Mar. 18, 1859, Sarah E. Dale, dau. of Ebenezer, b. Sept., 1836, and d. Feb. 15, 1891, ae. 54-5-. He m., Nov. 1, 1893, Emily Kimball, b. Sandwich, 1825. Child:
 a.   Fred G., b. Sandwich, June 16, 1850; m. Mar. 19, 1883, Mary E. Davis.
24.   Eliza, b. Bristol, Mar. 2, 1833; she m. June 21, 1855, Hazen M. Senter, who d. Center Harbor, 1891. She res. Tilton.
25.   Susan Doton, b. B., June 25, 1834; m. July 10, 1858, Alonzo S. Philbrick. He was a member of 12th Regt., N. H. Vols., and d. of disease at Falmouth, Va., Dec. 21, 1862. She m. (2) Dec. 15, 1865, Alva B. Dockham, Lakeport. Children:
 a.   Albert Addison, b. Center Harbor, Jan. 11, 1860; d. Meredith, July 29, 1861, ae. 1-6-18.
 b.   Edwin Alonzo, b. Meredith, Nov. 6, 1861; m. Lucretia Cole, dau. of Samuel, June 2, 1883. One child.
26.   William Prescott, b. Bristol, Feb. 12, 1836; m. Dec. 24, 1859, Adeline H. Caswell, of Everett, Mass. Child:
 a.   William Caswell, b. Lowell, Mass., Nov. 12, 1860; m. May 12, 1886, Flora Burnham, dau. of Charles. Child: Charles William, b. Ashburnham, Mass., Feb. 25, 1887.
27.   Aramenta D., b. Moultonboro, Aug. 22, 1838; m. Charles L. Cook, May 19, 1855. He d. in Sandwich, Ill., Mar. 26, 1868. She m. (2) Anson Loomis, Sept. 5, 1883, and res. in Peotone, Ill. Children:
 a.   Charles Lyman, b. Sandwich, Ill., Apr. 6, 1862; d. Mar. 30, 1888, ae. 25-11-24.
 b.   William Gurdy, b. S., Apr. 5, 1864; m. Gladious Young, in 1887.

(12)   Elisha Gurdy, b. Dec. 2, 1791; m. Mar. (Nov.) 10, 1814, Abigail Powell, dau. of David (See), b. Jan. 2, 1792. Was the first settler on his farm in the Locke neighborhood; removed to Lake street about 1854, to the home of his son, Levi C. Here she d. Mar. 6, 1871, ae. 79-2-4; he d. Apr. 25, same year, ae. 79-4-23.

CHILDREN, all born in Bristol

28.   Cyrus, b. Jan. 8, 1814; m. (1) Sally Gordon. She d. of consumption and he m. (2) Mar. 28, 1843, Mary, dau. of Seth and Gemima (Batchelder) Glover, b. Plymouth, Dec. 14, 1812. Was a miller in New

Hampton; in 1855, removed West. He d. West Union, Iowa, Aug. 11, 1881, ae. 67-7-3. She d. W. Union, June 7, 1900, ae. 87-5-23.

    a. Seth G., b. New Hampton, Sept. 20, 1845; served three years in Union army; Apr. 10, 1873, m. Miss R. J. Patterson, who d. July 21, 1893. He res. in W. Union. Seven children.

    b. Mary Augusta, b. N. H., May 24, 1852; m. Mar. 21, 1879, George Swale. One child, b. 1894. They res. W. Union.

  29. Adeline Senter, b. Dec. 8, 1816; m. George W. Dow. (See.)

  30. Joel, b. Apr. 27, 1818; m. Nov. 18, 1848, Mary Bean, dau. Sewell Sanborn (See), b. Nov. 18, 1830. She d. Alexandria, Apr. 19, 1868, ae. 37-5-1. He m. (2) Maria Hanson, b. St. Stephen, N. B. Farmer and paper-mill employee in Bristol; d. in Boston, Mass., Dec. 29, 1894, ae. 76-8-2. Children:

    a. Harriette Eliza, b. Bristol, May 25, 1857; m. William G. Crawford. (See.)

    b. Leslie Norris, b. B., Mar. 1, 1859; m. Florence Tryder, and d. Waltham, Mass., Apr. 27, 1887, ae. 28-1-26.

    c. Abbie May, b. B., Aug. 23, 1860; m. Charles L. Jeffroy. (See.)

  31. Benaiah Powell, b. Jan. 13, 1821; m. Dec. 25, 1851, Martha M., dau. of David S. Spaulding, b. Hebron. They went to Hebron, thence to Fairview, Iowa, in 1854, where he d. Apr. 18, 1868, ae. 47-3-5. She returned to Bristol, and here d. Dec. 18, 1896, ae. 69-0-5. Children:

    a. Leonidas Spaulding, b. Hebron, Dec. 30, 1852; m. (1) Sarah Anderson; (2) Mary Hall. Res. Pelham.

    b. Lizzie Lucinda, b. Fairview, Iowa, Apr. 3, 1858; d. Lawrence, Mass., Mar. 22, 1876, ae. 17-11-19.

    c. James Norris, b. Dec. 16, 1861; m. Hattie Olive Colcord, of Lawrence, Mass., June 22, 1881. He is a baker and confectioner in Lawrence. Children: (1) Hattie J., b. July 10, 1882. (2) Myrtie Jane, b. Nov. 1, 1887.

    d. Edward Everett, b. Jan. 9, 1866; d. in Iowa, May 24, 1867, ae. 1-4-15.

  32. Levi Carter, b. Dec. 16, 1824; m. Nov. 24, 1852, Sarah Elizabeth, dau. of Joseph and Sally (Cook) Hastings, b. Waltham, Me., June 10, 1834. He was a moulder and founder in Bristol, 1863-'81, removed to Lawrence, Mass., where he d. Feb. 26, 1889, ae. 64-2-10. Mrs. Gurdy res. Bristol. Children:

    a. Arno Everard, b. Waltham, Me., July 12, 1855; m. Lillian Slagle, at Westfield, Wis.; res. Waupeca, Wis.

    b. Bella Dana, b. Bristol, Sept. 6, 1869; m. Karl G. Cavis. (See.)

  33. Elvira C., b. Sept. 19, 1827; m. David Mason. (See.)

  34. James Norris, b. Dec. 19 (14), 1830. Never married. Killed in mines of California, June 16, 1860, ae. 29-5-27.

  35. Orrin P., b. Mar. 28, 1833; went to Lawrence, Mass., about 1853; m. Dec. 25, 1865, Delia Poole, dau. of Charles. She d. Lawrence, Mar. 16, 1873 He d. in Bristol at residence of David Mason, June 26, 1896, ae. 63-2-28.

    (20) John Gurdy, b. 1796, m. June 23, 1824, Betsey Hoyt, dau. of Samuel (See), b. 1801. He was a farmer next east of the Heath burying-ground. She d. in New Hampton, Aug. 28, 1843, ae. 42; he d. in Burlington, Vt., in 1875, ae. 79.

CHILDREN, all born in Bristol.

  36. Samuel Hoyt, b. Mar. 20, 1825; m. Oct. 7, 1846, Cassandra, dau. of Benjamin Marden, b. Palermo, Me., Nov. 18, 1821. For 25 years or

more he had charge of extensive lime kilns in Rockland, Me., where he d. Nov. 15, 1895, ae. 70-7-25. Children :

 a. Oscar True, b. Aug. 8, 1847 ; d. May 16, 1852, ae. 4-9-8.
 b. Harry Osgood, b. Duxbury, Mass., Jan. 1, 1860; res. in Rockland ; manufacturer of lime and dealer in general merchandise. He m., Jan. 1, 1884, Effie S. Gregory, of Rockland, who d. Jan. 9, 1885, and he m. (2) Apr. 11, 1888, Julia M. Smith, of Brooklyn, N. Y., Children : (1) Ruth C., b. Feb. 6, 1889. (2) Marie W., b. Dec. 25, 1890.
 c. Louise Marden, b. D., Dec. 16, 1865 ; m. Charles F. Ingraham Rockland, May 22, 1889. Children : (1) Hoyt Woods, b. Sept. 4, 1890. (2) Oscar Gurdy, b. Mar. 29, 1892. (3) Edith Louise, b. June 1, 1894.

 37. Harriet, b. about 1829; m. Amasa Witherell, of Duxbury, Mass.
 38. Sophronia Emmons, b. July 6, 1830; m. John P. Flanders, Oct. 25, 1851. He d. in Omaha, Neb., July 29, 1893, ae. 66-4-23. She res. Omaha. Children :

 a. Oscar D., b. Nashua, Sept. 5, 1853 ; m. Dec. 21, 1876, Alice Burns.
 b. Hattie Frances, b. Burlington, Vt., May 28, 1856 ; m. May 28, 1875, George Philemon Tuttle.
 c. John Burton, b. Bristol, Feb 21, 1859 ; m. May 7, 1881, Nettie Beatrice Smith.
 d. Edward Page, b. B., Aug. 3, 1861 ; m. Feb. 10, 1881, Ella Jane Smith.
 e. Frank Emmons, b. B., July 14, 1863 ; m. Aug. 20, 1882, Carrie Utrecht.
 f. Arthur Lansing, b. B., Oct. 31, 1864 ; d. Sept. 10, 1865.
 g. Lillie May, b. B., Dec. 2, 1866 ; m. Nov. 21, 1885, Maitland S. Durfee.
 h. Charles Augustus, b. Vergennes, Vt., Mar. 18, 1869; m. Sept. 23, 1891, Nellie Mabel Lyons.

 39. Moses Newell, b. about 1833 ; a sailor, last heard from in Liverpool, Eng., in 1861.

THE HADLEY FAMILY

 1. Charles Sumner Hadley was a resident of Bristol for a term of years previous to 1888. Painter. He m. Fannie Hasey of Lowell, Mass. He res. in Everett, Mass.

CHILDREN

 2. Charles Addison, b. Lowell, Mass. ; butcher in Everett, Mass.
 3. Herbert Edward, b. L., June 25, 1876; m. Nov. 1, 1899, Blanche E., dau. of William H. and Almira A. (Preston) Welch, b. Canaan, Sept. 1, 1880. He is an employee at the woolen-mill. Child :

 a. Earl William, b. Bristol, Oct. 6, 1900.

 4. Arthur Parker, b. L., Sept. 30, 1877 ; spinner in the woolen-mill.
 5. Edith Amantha Eveline, b. Bristol; m. Edward W. Sanders. (See.)
 6. Nina Belle, b. B.; m. Edward Andrews ; res. Bridgeport, Conn. One child.

 7. Fannie Edwina, b. B.   8. George Henry, b. Lowell.
 9. Una May, b. Bristol.   10. Lillian Leota, b. B.

THE HALEY FAMILY

1. Frank Patrick Haley, son of Patrick and Julia (O'Brien) Haley, was b. Peterboro, Nov. 15, 1857. He came to Bristol about 1874, and here m. June 17, 1877, Lela Ivanette, dau. of Joel C. Adams. (See.) Laborer, Republican.

CHILDREN

2. Frank Joel, b. Bristol, Nov. 9, 1880; d. May 4. 1881.
3. Alice May, (adopted) b. Franklin, May 26, 1885.
4. Myrtie Belle, b. Bristol, Sept. 16, 1887.
5. Timmie Elmer, b. B., May 11, 1890; d. Sept. 11, 1890.

---

1. John Haley, a brother of Frank P., above, was b. Brookline, Oct. 4, 1853. Came to Bristol in 1875. Laborer. Unm.

---

1. Dennis Haley, a brother of above, b. Newport, Nov. 25, 1860, m. Dec. 25, 1882, Addie Etta, dau. of Meshech G. Chandler. (See.) Res. in Bristol since 1880; for 20 years has been a machine tender in paper-mills.

CHILD

1. Bernice Margaret, b. Bristol, June 1, 1895.

THE HALL FAMILY

1. Benjamin Hall was b. Jan. 22, 1790. He m. Nancy Brown, b. Apr. 28, 1791, and d. Bristol, Nov. 2, 1863, ae. 72–6–4. He came to Bristol about 1812, and settled on the Hall farm where he and his son, Oliver S., lived and d. in the Hall neighborhood. He d. May 15, 1855, ae. 65–3–23.

CHILDREN

2. Rufus, b. Candia, Apr. 28, 1809; d. Dec. 4, 1882, ae. 73-7-6.
3. Lyman, b. Mar. 27, 1811; never m.; d. May 1, 1884, ae. 73-1-4.
*4. Oliver Smith, b. Bristol, Apr. 9, 1815.
5. Albon Reuben, b. B., Nov. 28, 1828; d. Dec. 27, 1832, ae. 4-0-29.

(4) Oliver S. Hall, b. Apr. 9, 1815, m. Isabel Chamberlain Morrison. She was b. June 30, 1821, and d. July 8, 1886, ae. 65-0-8. He d. Aug. 10, 1895, ae. 80-4-1. Farmer, Democrat.

CHILDREN

6. Jennie N., b. Bristol, Aug. 16, 1839, m. Uriah H. Kidder. (See.)
7. Adna Morrison, b. B., July 4, 1841; d. in the army Sept. 15, 1863, ae. 22-2-11. (See Roll of Honor.)
8. Oliver Porter, b. B., May 18, 1843. (See Roll of Honor.) He m. Dec. 21, 1889, Della Dicey, dau. James A. Cloutman. Resided on home farm till after his m., then removed to Alexandria, thence to the West.
9. Carrie Brown, b. B., May 13, 1847; m. Otis S. Damon. (See.)

1. Joseph Hall, son of Horatio N. and Mahala (Lee) Hall, was b. Groton, Mar. 2, 1848. He m. Jan. 29, 1868, Myra C., dau. of John C. and Betsey (Hall) Lang, b. Groton, Oct. 6, 1845. They settled in Bristol about 1875. He is a woodworker. Methodist, Republican.

THE HAMMOND FAMILIES

1. Lucius Wilson Hammond, son of John C. and Lydia (Ladd) Hammond, was b. Thetford, Vt., Dec. 21, 1824. He m. June 21, 1847, Elizabeth Jane, dau. of Rev. Liba Conant, b. Nov. 13, 1821. He was a trader in Wentworth, and in Bristol from 1871 till he d., July 23, 1882, ae. 57-7-2. He represented Hebron in legislature of 1856. Democrat. Justice of the peace. She d. Bristol, May 25, 1885, ae. 63-6-12.

CHILDREN

2. Ella Elizabeth, b. Hebron, Mar. 5, 1853; m. Charles H. Calley. (See.)

3. George Henry, b. H., Feb. 7, 1855; m. Mar. 10, 1883, Mrs. Annie W. (George) Gale, dau. Arial H. (See.) He succeeded his father in trade, and d. Apr. 25, 1903, ae. 48-2-18. Child:

    a. Louise Wilson, b. Bristol, Mar. 10, 1885.

---

1. Stephen Frost Hammond is the son of Rodney and Abigail (Frost) Hammond, b. in Bridgewater, Mar. 15, 1852. He m. Apr. 20, 1876, Annie Judson, dau. of Walter H., and Serena Lane (Farrington) Sargent, b. Boscawen, Mar. 21, 1857. (See Literature.) He came to Bristol from Bridgewater, Oct., 1883. Has been salesman for 17 years at the store now owned by Weymouth, Brown & Co.

CHILDREN

2. Arthur Frost, b. Bridgewater, Apr. 27, 1877; m. Aug. 27, 1902, Ella F., dau. Charles F. Dow, b. Londonderry, Apr. 22, 1882. Is a book-keeper for Standard Oil Co., East Boston, Mass.

3. George Walter, b. B., Nov. 26, 1878; m. July 26, 1896, Mamie, dau. Moody S. Cheney. (See.) In boot and shoe business, Bridgewater, Mass. Child:

    a. Cleon C., b. Nov. 9, 1898.

4. Grace Elfleda, b. B., Mar. 6, 1881; m. Sept. 24, 1900, George Hammond Wingate. He is a printer at Beverly, Mass.

5. Serena Belle, b. Bristol, Aug. 14, 1884; m. May 11, 1902, James Barclay Lidstone. He is clerk at Hotel Bristol.

---

1. Elmer Herbert Hammond, son of Nathan D. and Clara (Pike) Hammond, was b. Bridgewater, Sept. 17, 1870. He m. Nov. 4, 1893, Mrs. Lucy Jane Proctor, dau. George W. Keezer. He came to Bristol 1892. Teamster. No children.

THE HANAFORD FAMILY

1. William Foster Hanaford, son of Alfred and Lorana (Smith) Hanaford, was b. Plymouth, Feb. 22, 1841. He enlisted Oct. 4, 1861, from Sanbornton in Co. F, 8th Regt., N. H. Vols., as a private, and served in the department of the Gulf; reenlisted Jan. 4, 1864; appointed corporal Feb. 14, 1864, sergeant Sept. 1, 1864, first sergeant Nov., 1864. He was a volunteer for a forlorn-hope charge on the enemy's works at Port Hudson, in 1863. Was discharged Jan. 1, 1865, at Natchez, Miss. He m. Aug. 11, 1867, Amanda G., dau. of Jeremiah Ward. (See.) He was a farmer in Hill till 1884, when he came to Bristol; here has been a farmer and has operated a milk route. No children. Republican. G. A. R.

Oliver Hanaford, a brother of above, was b. Sanbornton in 1849. He m. Aug. 3, 1894, Julia, dau. James M. Lake, b. England, Aug. 29, 1849. No children. Has been a laborer here.

THE HARLOW FAMILY

William P. Harlow was in Bristol in 1861. He m. Jan. 1, 1862, Octavia, dau. of Nathaniel Moulton, b. Concord, May 21, 1843. Aug. 12, 1862, he enlisted in the 12th Regt., N. H. Vols., and d. of disease at Washington, D. C., Oct. 16, 1862, ae. 23. (See Roll of Honor.) Mrs. Harlow m. (2) John W. Wilbur. (See.)

THE HARRIMAN FAMILY

1. John Harriman, son of John, m. Sally Heath, of Plaistow. They came from Hampstead and settled on the River road in Bridgewater. He was a Free Baptist preacher; d. in Bridgewater; she d. in Stewartstown. Of his nine children, three were as follows:

2. Samuel, b. Feb. 3, 1776; m. Feb. 19, 1798, Chloe, dau. of Simeon Cross. (See.) He is supposed to have been the Samuel Harriman who was post-rider in 1816. They removed to Stewartstown.
*3. John, b. Hampstead, Feb. 11, 1778.
4. Elizabeth, b. Feb. 27, 1786; m. Simeon Cross. (See.)

(3) John Harriman, b. Feb. 11, 1778, lived in what is now the Smith pasture, north of the Locke neighborhood. In 1826, he removed to Plymouth purchasing large farm on Baker's river. He m. in March, 1802, Betsey, dau. of James and Mary (Craig) Aiken, b. Dec. 20, 1785. He d. Plymouth, Jan. 4,

1865, ae. 86-10-23; she d. Mar. 29, 1872, ae. 86-3-9. Of his 13 children, two were

5. Eliza, b. Bridgewater, Aug. 27, 1803; m. Jesse Prescott. (See.)
*6. Hiram, b. B., Dec. 25, 1819.

(6) Hiram Harriman, b. Dec. 25, 1819, was a graduate of the New Hampton Literary Institution. Apr. 1, 1847, he m. Abigail Silvea (or Silver) Preston, b. Rumney, Mar. 6, 1821. Hiram was a prominent man in Plymouth; was selectman and represented his town in the legislature. In April, 1867, removed to Bristol, engaging in the manufacture of buckskin gloves and mittens with Jason C. Draper. He d. Dec. 19, 1871, ae. 51-11-24; she d. Aug. 22, 1887, ae. 66-5-16.

CHILDREN, all born in Plymouth

7. William Edward, b. July 1, 1848; d. B., Nov. 21, 1884, ae. 36-4-20.
8. Alfred Preston, b. Jan. 9, 1850; m. Mar. 14, 1891, Mrs. Minetta M. Norris, widow of William T. Norris, Esq., and dau. of Rufus L. Martin, b. Apr. 30, 1853, in Andover. Was a glove manufacturer and shoe dealer. After his m. res. five years in Danbury, returning to Bristol in 1896, since which time he has been a painter and nurse. Children:

    a. William Martin,   } b. Danbury, Oct. 27, 1891.
    b. John Norris,   }
    c. Fred Rufus, b. Danbury.

9. Moses Franklin, b. Feb. 20, 1855; m. May 3, 1876, Laura Matilda, dau. of Dr. John and Mary Ann Whitmore, b. Hebron, Apr. 2, 1856, and d. Akron, Colo., Apr. 10, 1893, ae. 37-0-8. He m. Dec., 15, 1894, Emily L. Colby, of Warner. He has been connected with glove manufacturing at Warner, Akron, Colo., and at Littleton, where he now res. Children:

    a. Grace Elinor, b. Littleton, Feb. 20, 1881; m. Dec. 25, 1901, Ellsworth Hawkins, of Littleton.
    b. Louise Preston, b. L., Sept. 27, 1884; d. Dec. 6, 1884.
    c. Frederick Whitmore, b. Oskaloosa, Iowa, June 2, 1888.
    d. Laurie, b. Akron, Colo., Mar. 24, 1893; died in infancy.

10. John Fremont, b. May 11, 1857; m. Sept. 9, 1879, Ellen Louise, dau. of Robert L. and Lydia Jane Nelson, b. Bath, and d. Chicago, Ill., Feb. 8, 1894. He m. Dec. 16, 1896, Clara B. Hibbard, b. Piermont, Sept. 11, 1863. No children. Res. Concord.

THE HARRIS FAMILY

1. Simon Harris, son of Job and Helena Harris, was b. in 1770. He was a resident of Bridgewater, and the mail-carrier between Haverhill and Concord, 1817-'20. He was deputy sheriff from 1807 till 1818. He d. in Bridgewater Jan. 13, 1821, ae. 51 years. He m. Sept. 17, 1790, Susanna, dau. of Capt. Jonathan Crawford. She d. July 19, 1850, ae. 77-10-8. They had 13 children, of whom two were

*2. Rufus, b. Bridgewater, Aug. 3, 1805.
3. Phebe, b. B., Jan. 2, 1807; m. (1) Thomas Fogg; (2) Sewell Sanborn.

(2) Rufus Harris, b. Aug. 3, 1805, m., in 1831, Violet Lucy, dau. Solomon Sanborn, b. Rumney, Aug. 30, 1807. He came from Plymouth in 1842; was an employee at Moore's Mills till 1850, when he removed to Ashland. Mrs. Harris d. in Bristol, May 24, 1848, ae. 40-8-24, and he m. in 1853, Elvira Webster. He d. Ashland, Apr. 17, 1886, ae. 80-8-14.

CHILDREN

4. Amanda Melvina, b. Holderness, Jan. 21, 1832; m. 1852, Lucius S. Gordon. She d. New Hampton, June 3, 1865, ae. 33-4-12.
5. Frances Maria, b. Lowell, Mass., Mar. 28, 1834; m. July 30, 1854, Capt. Stephen B. Dow. He followed the sea 38 years visiting nearly all parts of the globe. They res. New Hampton, where he d. Mar. 17, 1871, ae. 52-2-10. Children :

    a. Charles Warren, b. June 22, 1855. At 16 went to Zanzibar, Africa. Was eight years in Africa, India, and Auckland, New Zealand; was U. S. consul at Zanzibar. He m. (1) May 1, 1882, Pauline Avery Whitton ; (2) Louise Caldwell, June 6, 1900. Res. LaCrosse, Wis.
    b. William Henry, b. Jan. 23, 1858; m. Mar. 1, 1893, Mrs. Ellen (Hall) Ellis. Res. New Hampton.
    c. Harriette Simpson, b. June 28, 1860; m. (1) Frank E. Tucker, Dec. 9, 1890; (2) Russell A. Carver, Mar. 26, 1896.
    d. Stephen Webster, b. June 24, 1864; m. Apr. 1, 1888, Carrie Fletcher. Was killed at Newport, Vt., July 31, 1889, while making up a train, ae. 25-1-7.
    e. Walter Raleigh, b. Nov. 11, 1868 ; m. Sarah M. Curtis, Dec. 25, 1893. Was postmaster at New Hampton.
    f. Edward Everett, b. Dec. 4, 1871 ; m. Amy M. Tappan, Oct. 19, 1900 ; res. LaCrosse, Wis.

6. William Franklin, b. Sept. 23, 1836; m. July 19, 1870, Mrs. Electa T., widow of Gustavus Emmons. (See.) Served as musician in Union army; he res. Ashland. Two children.
7. Martha Currier, b. Plymouth, July 27, 1839 ; m. Sept. —, 1859, James L. Cox. She d. Westela, Kan., July 20, 1900, ae. 60-11-23.
8. Angelina Webster, b. P., Aug. —, 1842; d. Aug. —, 1847, in Bristol, ae. 5-0-.
9. Louisa Jane, b. Bristol, Mar. 28, 1844; d. New Hampton, Feb. 27, 1861, ae. 16-10-29.
10. Harriet Lucy, b. B., June 28, 1847 ; m. in 1865, Newton B. Plummer, who served as private in 12th Regt., N. H. Vols., and as captain 32nd U. S. Colored Infty. Res. Meredith Center.

THE HASTINGS FAMILY

1. Asa Hastings was b. Dec. 28, 1752. He m., Mar. 22, 1775, in Mason, Molly Lowell, b. Dec. 30, 1752. They removed from Salem to Alexandria, and about 1779, settled on the Hastings farm in Bristol, where she d. ae. 85. He went to Canada to visit his children and there d., ae. 85. He was a Revolutionary soldier from Alexandria.

CHILDREN

2. Lydia, b. Alexandria, Dec. 3, 1775; m. Daniel McMurphy, Alexandria.

15

*3. Joseph, b. A., May 7, 1777.
*4. Jonas, b. A., Jan. 19, 1779.
   5. Asa, b. Bristol; d. 1781, ae. 16 months.
   6. Phebe, b. B., Dec. 18, 1782; m. Robert Simonds; lived and d. in
Alexandria.
   7. Amos, b. B., Mar. 19, 1785; lived and d. in Canada.
   8. Adnah, b. B., July 7, 1787; m. Blynn (or Ingalls) and removed to
Kentucky. (Bridgewater records say Adnah Hastings m. Jonathan Ingalls, Nov. 25, 1813.)
   9. Simeon, b. B., Mar. 7, 1790; removed to Indiana.
  10. Asa, b. B., Oct. 15, 1792; removed to New York.
  11. Moses, b. B., May 15, 1795; removed to Stewartstown.

(3) Joseph Hastings, b. May 7, 1777, m. Mary (Polly)
Sanborn, dau. of Joseph (See), b. May 4, 1778. They resided
just south of Smith's river in the Borough, and here a family of
children were b. The father and all the children, except John,
went to Canada and there d. The mother d. in Hill, Nov..
1812, ae. 34 years.

CHILD

*12. John, b. Hill, June 17, 1799.

(4) Jonas Hastings, b. Jan. 19, 1779, m. Nov. 28, 1805,
Polly Ordway, of Hebron, who d. Mar. 17, 1811. He m. (2)
Apr. 2, 1812, Nancy Atwood, dau. Moses, b. Aug. 17, 1786, d.
Jan. 18, 1864, ae. 77-5-1. Jonas succeeded his father on the
farm, where he d. Jan. 13, 1869, ae. 89-11-24.

CHILDREN, all born Bristol

*13. John, b. Dec. 19, 1806.
  14. Hannah, b. Jan. 24, 1808; m. Nov. 19, 1828, Joseph Wallace, of
Alexandria, b. Jan. 22, 1808. He was killed by blasting, while at work
building railroad between Lowell and Boston. She m. (2) Caleb Sawyer.
(See.) Children :
        a. Charles, b. Aug. 14, 1829; res. Roxbury, Mass.
        b. Benjamin, b. Nov. 19, 1830; adopted by his uncle, John
Hastings; went to California.
  15. Asa, b. Feb. 20, 1809; d. July 13, 1834, ae. 25-4-23.
  16. Infant, b. Mar. 25, 1810; d. Mar. 28, 1810.
  17. Infant, b. Feb. 27, 1811; d. Feb. 28, 1811.
  18. Polly, b. May 9, 1813; m. Nov. 28, 1837, Benjamin Patten. She
d. B., June 21, 1851, ae. 38-1-12; he d. Alexandria, Oct. 2, 1876, ae. 62-
11-23. Children, all b. in Alexandria :
        a. Emily, b. Aug. 28, 1838; m. Humphrey Pettingill, Alexan-
dria. No children.
        b. Seth G., b. Nov. 16, 1840. Res. unm. in Alexandria.
        c. Amanda, b. Sept. 16, 1843; m. George Martin.
        d. Jonas F., b. Mar. 4, 1845; m. Georgianna, dau. Charles H.
Dicey, b. Alton, Aug. 4, 1864. He d. Bristol, Oct. 8, 1893, ae. 48-
7-4. She m. (2) James E. Gordon. (See.)
        e. Manson B., b. Nov. 4, 1848. (See.)
        f. Polly, b. May 21, 1851; d. June 20, 1851.
  19. Jonas, b. May 28, 1815; m. Oct. 22, 1837, Betsey, dau. Thomas
and Mary (Hemphill) Bailey, b. Bow, Aug. 16, 1813, d. Natick, Mass.,
June 11, 1886, ae. 72-9-25. He d. Natick, June 11, 1888, ae. 73-0-13. He
was a farmer in Bristol till 1840. Children :

a. Asa, b. Bristol, Oct. 10, 1838. Has lived for many years in Honolulu, Sandwich Islands. Unm.

b. Jerome, b. Sanbornton, July 8, 1840; m. May 22, 1867, Lizzie Entwistle, b. England, Oct. 20, 1840; d. Natick, Mass., Nov. 15, 1879, ae. 39-0-25. He res. Natick; is conductor on B. & A. railroad.

20. Nancy, b. Oct. 23, 1817 ; m. Nov. 24, 1842, Samuel C. Harrington. He d. Nov. 19, 1879, in Manchester, ae. 63-0-16. Five children.

21. Sophia, b. Feb. 6, 1820; m. Nov. 25, 1847, Nathaniel Whittier, of Orange, b. June 21, 1825. Child :

a. Julia S., b. Orange, Nov. 17, 1857; m. Nov. 17, 1874, Samuel L. Hoyt, of Orange.

22. Susan, b. Aug. 28, 1823; m. Feb. 13, 1849, Abel Ford, of Orange. Children :

a. Mary Emma, b. Oct. 17, 1853; m. Oct. 17, 1871, Frank H. Dexter, of Danbury.

b. Alice Luella, b. Dec. 31, 1863; m. May 1, 1880, John T. Morrison, of Danbury.

23. Lucy Ann, b. Nov. 30, 1826; m. Sept. 19, 1847, Edwin G. Harrington, b. Jan. 21, 1826. Res. Manchester. Children :

a. Evelyn, b. Manchester, Mar. 7, 1849. Unm.

b. Susan Maria, b. M., Aug. 24, 1850; m. Oct. 24, 1872, Henry Clark.

c. Luther M., b. M., May 8, 1853 ; num.

d. Edward Henry, b. M., Sept. 2, 1855; d. Feb. 11, 1875, ae. 19-5-9.

e. Mary Emma Hastings, b. M., July 29, 1859; d. Feb. 18, 1864, ae. 4-6-19.

f. William Squires, b. M., Oct. 30, 1860; m. Sept. 27, 1884, Lois McIntire; res. Goffstown.

g. James Hastings, b. M., June 1, 1864 ; m. Nov. 2, 1885, May Hunt.

h. Mary Emma, b. M., Mar. 20, 1866. Unm.

i. Lucy Ann, b. M., Apr. 14, 1868; d. May 26, 1873, ae. 5-1-12.

24. Mary Jane, b. Apr. 19, 1829 ; m. David M. Chase. (See.)

(12) **John Hastings,** b. June 17, 1799, m. Sarah, dau. of Robert Morrill. She d. Hill, Sept. 23, 1882, ae. 79-2-6 ; he d. same place, Sept. 20, 1882, ae. 83-3-3. Farmer on south bank of Smith's river in the Borough ; later res. at Profile Falls.

CHILDREN

25. Mary Elizabeth, b. Hill, Dec. —, 1820; m. Pettingill G. Carleton. (See.)

✻26. Robert Smith, b. H., Apr. 14, 1825.

27. Rufus, b. H.; d. at 3 years of age from falling into a tub of scalding water.

28. Sarah Philinda, b. Bristol, Nov. 30, 1831 ; m. Pettingill G. Carleton. (See.)

29. Artemissia, b. Hill, m. Alonzo Addison. Six children. Res. Hill.

(13) **Col. John Hastings,** b. Dec. 19, 1806, m. Apr. 18, 1833, Dorothy S., dau. of Benjamin Emmons. (See.) He spent his life on the farm where his father and grandfather had lived. He was colonel of the 34th Regt., state militia. He d.

Dec. 12, 1890, ae. 83–11–23; she d. Apr. 8, 1891, ae. 77–8–26. Both lifelong Methodists. Republican.

CHILDREN, all born in Bristol

30. Gustavus Adolphus, b. Jan. 25, 1834. He went to Iowa when a young man and never returned. Oct. 31, 1866, he m. Helen, dau. of George and Amanda (Peal) Mentzer, b. Chambersburg, Pa., Mar. 22, 1848. For many years overseer in the iron department of the railroad shops at Oxford Junction, Iowa. Children:

a. George, b. Davenport, Iowa, Feb. 26, 1869.
b. Helen Gertrude, b. D., Dec. 31, 1871.
c. Flora Bell, b. D., Oct. 15, 1873.

31. Eliza Ann, b. July 18, 1836; m. David Batchelder. (See.)
32. Clarinda Jane, b. Jan. 16, 1839; m. Carroll Sanborn. (See.)
33. Laura Maria, b. Apr. 20, 1841; m. Oct. 30, 1880, George Taylor, son of William, b. Derry, June 22, 1839. Res. Franklin Falls. Child:

a. Grace Hastings, b. Derry, Aug. 6, 1881.

34. John Franklin, b. Aug. 9, 1843; m. Jan. 1, 1867, Helen Marzetta, dau. George and Caroline (Danforth) Webster, b. Laconia, June 10, 1843. Since 1875, a harness maker and undertaker at Penacook. Children:

a. Arthur Grant, b. Penacook, Aug. 1, 1868; d. Sept. 26, 1869, ae. 1–1–25.
b. Frank Irving, b. P., Mar. 30, 1871; m. Sept. 14, 1893, Maude May Huggins. Res. Concord.

35. George Henry, b. Jan. 9, 1847; m. Aug. 1, 1872, Laura Jane, dau. Samuel C., and Susan F. Bartlett, b. Campton, June 5, 1847. Is a Methodist clergyman; member of Vermont conference, 1873–'79; New Hampshire conference, 1879–'82; Detroit (Mich.) conference 1882–'87; Northwest Iowa conference, 1887–'91; New England Southern conference since 1891; now at Everett, Mass.

36. Charles Albert, b. Mar. 4, 1849. His last known address was Minneapolis, Minn.

37. Levi W., b. Sept. 1, 1852; m. Apr. 23, 1884, Tillie Esther, dau. of John and Elizabeth McClelland, b. Allegheny, Pa., July 21, 1863. They res. Des Moines, Iowa. No children.

38. Holman Kelley, b. Oct. 15, 1853; m. Apr. 29, 1879, Mary Sophia Rowell, Tunbridge Vt. Graduated Illinois Wesleyan University, Bloomington, Ill., in 1885. A Methodist clergyman. Member of Vermont conference, 1875–'85; Iowa conference, 1885–. Last known address, Ireton, Iowa. He represented Hancock, Vt., in the state legislature, and was superintendent of schools at Hancock.

39. Myron L., b. Sept. 1, 1855. Was living in 1898, at Oxford Junction, Iowa.

40. Almon C., b. Dec. 3, 1859; m. Aug. 21, 1883, Addie M., dau. Lucius L. and Sophia A. Thomas, b. Alexandria, Aug. 5, 1864. He succeeded his father on the home farm. Child:

a. Viola A., b. Aug. 29, 1884.

(26) Robert Smith Hastings, b. Apr. 14, 1825, m. Feb. 17, 1848, Priscilla Straw, of Hill, b. June 30, 1825. She d. Jan. 2, 1854, and he m. June 13, 1855, Julia Ann, dau. of Jeremiah and Betsey (Tenney) Carleton, b. Hill, Apr. 13, 1825. He came to Bristol in 1867; is a surveyor, millwright, and builder, and a man of superior judgment in his lines. Has

Robert S. Hastings

served four years as selectman and two years as supervisor of the checklist. Republican, Odd Fellow.

CHILDREN

41. Ida I., b. Hill, Feb. 27, 1852; m. Isaac C. Ballou. (See.)

42. Cora Agnes, b. H., June 13, 1862; m. Sept. 28, 1884, Lowell I. Hanson. He was b. No. Conway, Dec. 13, 1857; is a farmer in Sanbornton. Children:

    a. Carl Eugene, b. Northfield, Nov. 20, 1885.
    b. Clarissa, b. Sanbornton, Apr. 11, 1888.
    c. Lowell Perley, b. S., Nov. 10, 1890.
    d. Susan Julia, b. S., Mar. 11, 1894.
    e. Robert Louis, b. S., May 7, 1900.

THE HAYNES FAMILY

1. Jeremiah Austin Haynes, son of Stephen and Mary (Foss) Haynes, was b. Northfield, May 4, 1819, and d. in Bristol, Mar. 12, 1893, ae. 73-10-8. He m., Feb. 21, 1843, Sarah C., dau. of Stephen and Hannah (Chase) Long. She d. Bristol, Apr. 10, 1861; he m., Apr. 10, 1868, Mrs. Hattie A. Weaver, of Penacook, widow of William. She d. Bristol, Feb. 28, 1888, ae. 60-10-15, and he m., Jan. 22, 1889, Mrs. Samantha J., widow of Thomas B. Ross, of Hebron. He was one of the founders of the Baptist church at Penacook, and retained his membership there till death. He came to Bristol in 1855; was an active worker in the Congregational church and superintendent of its Sunday-school. A zealous Odd Fellow; a frequent manager of funerals; Republican, represented Bristol in the legislature in 1862 and '63. A blacksmith; in trade a few years.

CHILD

2. Emma Frances, b. Penacook, Mar. 21, 1850; m. Nov. 23, 1871, Frank G. Blake, b. New Hampton, Nov. 2, 1849. He d. Aug. 16, 1891, ae. 41-9-14. She has since res. in Bristol. Children:

    a. Ina Sarah, b. New Hampton, Aug. 2, 1874.
    b. Elwin Austin, b. N. H., Aug. 30, 1879.
    c. Charles Frank, b. N. H., Dec. 18, 1884. Is a printer.
    d. Mary Alice, b. N. H., July 16, 1890.

THE HAYWARD FAMILY

1. Jonas Reed Hayward, son of Josiah and Rebecca, was b. Antrim, Apr. 25, 1805, and d. Alexandria, Jan. 9, 1873, ae. 67-8-14. He m., Oct. 30, 1832, Marcia, dau. of Moses West Sleeper. (See.) She d. Pembroke, Oct. 25, 1854, ae. 44-9-29. He m. (2) Aug., 1855, Mary W. Bodwell. He was a farmer. Res. in Bristol, 1864-'69. Methodist.

15*a*

2. Ruth A., b. Oct. 24, 1833. Unm. Res. Norwood Junction, N. Y.

3. Emma J., b. Oct. 27, 1835; m. John F. Vose, a farmer in Alexandria, where she d., Oct. 4, 1888, ae. 52-11-7.

4. Augusta S., b. May 22, 1840; m. Charles F. Noyes, Franklin, and d. Mar. 5, 1889, ae. 48-9-13.

5. Mary M., b. Alexandria, Mar. 2, 1842; m. Gustavus Roby. (See.)

6. Hattie L., b. A., Oct. 31, 1846; m. Oct. 31, 1867, Lorenzo L. Frost. He is a paper manufacturer, Norwood Junction, N. Y. Children:

    a. Frederic Worthen, b. Franklin, Jan. 8, 1870; graduated from Wesleyan University, Middletown, Conn., 1894. A lawyer in New York city.

    b. Lorena May, b. F., Dec. 21, 1873.

    c. Luther Hayward, b. F., Jan. 17, 1878. Graduated from Wesleyan University, 1903.

THE HEATH FAMILIES

1. The Heaths of Bristol are the descendants of William I., who came from England with his wife, Mary, and five children, on frigate Lyon, landing Sept. 16, 1632. All his children were b. in London. They settled in Roxbury, Mass. He was a member of the first assembly of deputies, May 14, 1634, and for some years subsequently. He d. May 29, 1652; his wife, Mary, d. Dec. 16, 1659. One of his children was

2. Peleg, who m. Susanna. He res. in Roxbury; was freeman in 1652, and d. of wounds Nov. 18, 1671. He had nine children, of whom the sixth was

3. William, b. Jan. 30, 1664. He m. Hannah Weld, Nov. 11, 1685; settled in Roxbury, and d. Nov. 3, 1738, ae. 74-9-3. He had nine children, of whom the seventh was

4. Samuel, b. Dec. 27, 1701. He was a well-to-do farmer in Plaistow. He was probably living with his son, Samuel, in that part of Bridgewater now Bristol, in 1794, as this year it was voted to allow Samuel Heath, Jr., "ten shillings for his father on account of his carrying Molly Clark out of town." He was the father of at least five

5. Stephen. "Stephen Heath m. Anna Peaslee, Nov. 28, 1799."— Bridgewater records.

✳6. Samuel, b. Plaistow, 1754.

✳7. Joshua, b. Sept. 7, 1760.   8. John.

9. Daniel. He was evidently in that part of New Chester now Bristol as early as 1779, as his name appears on the tax-list of that year. In 1785, he was taxed for three acres of tillage land, twelve acres of mowing and twelve of pasturage. The amount of land under cultivation was more than that of any other resident of New Chester, except Cutting Favor and Benjamin Emmons, who had about the same. At the first meeting of the new town of Bridgewater (1788), he served as moderator and was then elected as constable for the collection of taxes. He served as moderator at meetings held Nov. 3 and Dec. 15 of the same

year. At a meeting held Apr. 2, 1789, Samuel Worthen was chosen a collector "to complete the collection of taxes for 1788, committed to Daniel Heath, deceased." By this it would seem that Daniel Heath died between Dec. 15, 1788, and Apr. 2, 1789. He probably d. after the annual meeting in March or the election of a successor would have taken place at that time. He d. "while on a business trip to Coos county." His farm was that now owned by Hiram T. Heath, three miles east of Central square. The buildings were on the opposite side of the road from the present farmhouse. That he had a family is apparent. He had among his children

  a. Daniel. He enlisted in the Revolutionary army from New Chester in June, 1780, when his age was given as 16 years. The marriage of Daniel Heath, Jr., and Joanna Ingalls was recorded as solemnized by Elder Ward, Mar. 8, 1785. A Daniel Heath m. Abigail Ingalls, dau. of Jonathan (See), Nov. 12, 1795, and a Daniel Heath m. Judith George, of Sandwich, June 1, 1797. These three may be identical, but there is nothing to establish the fact.

(6) Samuel Heath, b. 1754, was a Revolutionary soldier from Plaistow. He was a resident of Plymouth 1779 to 1785, when he removed to Bristol. He m., Apr. 11, 1782, Sarah Webster, of Plymouth. Mrs. Lewis Heath, a daughter-in-law, said he bought the Heath farm, in 1794, of his brother, Stephen. If so, it would seem that Stephen succeeded Daniel in the ownership. Samuel was a teamster as well as farmer and made trips to Boston for freight, occupying two weeks for each trip. He d. in Bristol, June 13, 1833, ae. 79. She d. Bristol, July 7, 1839, ae. 76-2-7.

CHILDREN

10. Sarah, b. Plymouth, Sept. 3, 1783. Lived and d. on her father's farm in Bristol. Never m.
  *11. Samuel, b. P., Mar. 22, 1785.
  *12. Robert, b. Bristol, Nov. 14, 1788.
  13. Moses, b. B., Sept. 19, 1791; m. Nancy Norris, Chelsea, Vt., lived and d. in Haverhill.
  14. Elizabeth, b. B., Mar. 15, 1795 (Ballou record says 1793); m. Oct. 12, 1813, Oliver Ballou. (See.)
  15. Hannah, b. B., May 1, 1796; m. Samuel R. Worthen. (See.)
  16. Lucy, b. B., Nov. 3, 1799; d. Aug. 19, 1828, ae. 28-9-16.
  17. Webster, b. B., Dec. 3, 1801; d. Feb. 18, 1830, ae. 28-2-15.
  *18. Lewis, b. B., Aug. 15, 1803.

(7) Joshua Heath, b. Sept. 7, 1760, m. Nov. 7, 1785, Hannah Webster, a sister of the wife of his brother Samuel. He d. Jan. 25, 1832, ae. 71-4-18; she d. Mar. 1, 1842, ae. 75. He was taxed in Plymouth, 1783-'87; removed to Groton. There were among his fourteen

CHILDREN

19. Betsey, b. July 4, 1796; m. Isaac Crosby. (See.)
  20. Willard, b. Groton, Sept. 7, 1807; m. Abigail Spaulding. She was b. Oct. 12, 1812, and d. Apr. 21, 1862, ae. 49-6-9. He m. Nov. 15, 1862, Adeline C., dau. of John C. and Nancy (Ladd) Hammond, b. Hebron, July 6, 1839. He was a farmer and trader. He res. in Bristol from 1874 till he d. Dec. 7, 1884, ae. 77-3-0. Mrs. Heath res. Concord. Children:

a. Willard Russell, b. Groton, Jan. 13, 1868; m. Feb. 7, 1894, Gertrude M., dau. Dr. Alfred and Mary (Moore) Dearborn, b. No. Weare, Mar. 5, 1870. Is a salesman in Fitchburg, Mass.

b. Helen Celia, b. Bristol, Feb. 22, 1880. Is a graduate of Vassar College, Poughkeepsie, N. Y. Is a teacher.

(11)   Samuel Heath, b. Mar. 22, 1785, m. Margaret Fellows, who d. Nov. 22, 1856, ae. 64-4-; he d. June 23, 1874, ae. 89-3-1.   He succeeded his father on the home farm.

CHILDREN, all born in Bristol

21.   Lydia Jane, b. Dec. 30, 1812; m. Isaac C. Tilton. (See.)
22.   Minerva T., b. May 6, 1817; d. in family of her brother, Hiram, Jan. 28, 1892, ae. 74-8-22; unm.
*23.   Hiram, b. Nov. 18, 1820.
24.   David M., b. Aug. 24, 1823; m. Jan. 11, 1853, Susan Emily, dau. Merrill and Ruth (Mooney) Cox, b. Holderness, Oct. 31, 1832; d. Bristol, Oct. 25, 1854, ae. 21-11-24. He m., Dec. 6, 1860, Mary A. Plummer. He was a farmer in Ashland, and there d. Mar. 18, 1865, ae. 41-6-24. Child :

a. Emma Sarah, b. Holderness, Jan. 29, 1854; m. Arthur B. Flanders, Feb. 26, 1874.

25.   Samuel Worthen, b. Aug. 31. 1825; m. May 7, 1850, Hannah N., dau. Eliphalet and Mehitable (Prescott) Lord, b. Northfield, Jan. 9, 1833. He was a shoemaker and removed from Bristol to New Hampton, in 1869, where he d. Mar. 23, 1889, ae. 63-6-22. She res. New Hampton. Children :

a. Annie, b. Bristol, Dec. 4, 1854; m. Charles G. Robinson. (See.)

b. True A., b. B., May, 1856; m., 1882, Rose Willis, of Enfield. Res. Concord.

*26.   Pliney Emmons, b. Aug. 2, 1828.
27.   Webster, b. May 29, 1831; m. Mar. 11, 1866, Angie M., dau. of Levi and Mary (Mathews) Yeaton, b. Epsom, May 20, 1842. Res. Wakefield, Mass. She d. Wakefield, Oct. 20, 1896, ae. 54-5-0. (See Roll of Honor.) Children :

a. Maud Inez, b. Bristol, July 18, 1867; was teacher in Bristol graded schools 4 years; m. Oct. 31, 1893, Lewis E. Carter, M.D., of Wakefield.

b. Myrtland Webster, b. B., May 12, 1872; d. May 17, 1873, ae. 1-0-5.

(12)   Robert Heath, b. Nov. 14, 1788, m. Hannah, dau. of Stephen Nelson (See), b. Feb. 21, 1792. She d. in Bristol, Jan. 6, 1841, ae. 48-10-15, and he m. (2) Mrs. Polly B., widow of Joseph G. Dow. (See.) She d. July 31, 1863, ae. 72-4-9. He d. Oct. 8, 1853, ae. 64-10-24. He was a farmer a half mile from the main highway north of Hiram T. Heath's farmhouse. The buildings long since disappeared and the road has been discontinued.

CHILDREN, all born in Bristol

*28.   Stephen Nelson, b. Feb. 14, 1816.
29.   Sarah Ann, b. Feb. 5, 1817. Married Luther S. Fellows. (See.)
*30.   Samuel P., b. June 18, 1819.
31.   John S., b. July 31, 1821. He went to Vermont, where he m. Abigail Ayer. Two children. He d. Bristol, Sept. 28, 1854, ae. 33-1-27.

HIRAM T. HEATH

*32. Charles B., b. Nov. 5, 1823.
*33. Horace Webster, b. Nov. 14, 1826.
*34. Levi Nelson, b. Mar. 3, 1829.
  35. William P., b. Jan. 23, 1831 ; d. B., Dec. 31, 1847, ae. 16-11-8.
  36. Harriet J., b. Aug. 20, 1833 ; m. John F. Peters, Nov. 3, 1857 ; res. Concord. Children :
      a. Everett F., b. Mar. 12, 1863 ; d. July 28, 1863.
      b. Arthur W., b. Oct. 29, 1867 ; d. Oct. 14, 1872, ae. 4-11-15.
  37. Emily Wells, b. Dec. 14, 1835 ; m. Oliver Ballou. (See.)

(18) Lewis Heath, b. Aug. 15, 1803, m. May 15, 1832, Sarah W., dau. of John Edwards. (See.) A year or two after their m. they removed to Haverhill, Mass., thence to Andover, where he d., Apr. 15, 1858, ae. 54-8-0. Mrs. Heath returned to Haverhill and was there living in 1897, at the age of 95 years.

CHILDREN

  38. Rufus George, b. Bristol, July 11, 1833 ; d. Jan. 2, 1841, ae. 7-5-21.
  39. Charles Edwards, b. Haverhill, Mass., Oct. 16, 1837 ; m. ; res. San Diego, Cal. Child :
      a. Albert Herman, b. Apr. 9, 1867.
  40. Sarah Josephine, b. East Andover, Nov. 25, 1840 ; m. —— Miller. Res. Haverhill, Mass. Children :
      a. Ray.   b. Mabel.
  41. Frank Pierce, b. Andover, July 15, 1846 ; d. San Diego, Cal., Apr. 14, 1897, ae. 50-8-29.
  42. Martha Ellen, b. E. Andover, Oct. 23, 1848 ; m. —— Chandler. Res. Lawrence, Mass.
  43. George Lewis, b. Oct. 6, 1851 ; d. Feb. 15, 1858, ae. 6-4-9.

(23) Hiram Heath, b. Nov. 18, 1820, m. Dorcas Whittemore, dau. of Caleb. She was b. in Bridgewater, July 30, 1826, and d. in Bristol, Sept. 11, 1891, ae. 65-1-11. He d. Feb. 27, 1892, ae. 71-3-9. Farmer ; succeeded his father on the home farm.

CHILDREN, all born in Bristol

  44. Cinda Whittemore, b. Oct. 6, 1850 ; m. Jan. 25, 1876, Thomas O. Taylor, son of Andrew J., b. Sanbornton, July 28, 1851. They res. Sanbornton. Farmers. No children.
  45. Mary E., b. Mar. 1, 1854 ; d. May 22, 1854.
  46. Hiram T., b. Sept. 21, 1856 ; m. July 27, 1881, Ella, dau. of John F. Phillips, b. Alexandria, Aug. 10, 1861, and d. Bristol, Feb. 4, 1892, ae. 30-5-24. He succeeded his father on the home farm. Has served six years as selectman. Is a Republican, Mason, and prominent in Grange circles. Child :
      a. Nellie May, b. Bristol, Apr. 5, 1885 ; d. three days later.
  47. Lilla, b. Nov. 5, 1865 ; m. Jan. 25, 1883, Warren E. Locke. He was a manufacturer of wooden ware in Bristol, 1883-'85 ; since res. in Somerville, Mass., a dealer in real estate, Boston. Children :
      a. Clarence Blaine, b. Somerville, Nov. 27, 1887.
      b. Lilla Marian, b. S., Feb. 26, 1891.

(26) Pliney E. Heath, b. Aug. 2, 1828, m. Jan., 1853, Martha Elizabeth, dau. of Stephen and Abigail Moore (Dimond)

Wells, b. Groton, July 23, 1834. He d. Dec. 30, 1880, in Groton, ae. 52-4-28; she d. Wakefield, Mass., June 22, 1886, ae. 51-10-29. They spent most of their lives in Bristol. Shoemaker.

CHILDREN

48. Joseph Webster, b. Bristol, Mar. 16, 1854; m. Nov. 17, 1879, Sarah Elizabeth, dau. of Frederick E. C. and Elizabeth Hannah (Heath) Greene, b. Boston, Mass., Apr. 4, 1858. He graduated at New Hampton Literary Institution; from Bowdoin Medical College, Brunswick, Me., in 1877, and same year commenced the practice of medicine in Rumney; in 1881, removed to Wakefield, Mass., where he has since been in practice. Children :

    a. Charles Pliney, b. West Rumney, Sept. 7, 1881. Graduated from Harvard College, June, 1903.
    b. Joseph Greene, b. Wakefield, Jan. 6, 1885 ; d. Mar. 3, 1886, ae. 1-1-27.
    c. Harold Luther, b. W., May 14, 1887; d. Aug. 23, 1888, ae. 1-3-9.
    d. Stanley Webster, b. W., Aug. 10, 1892.

(28) Stephen N. Heath, b. Feb. 14, 1816, d. in Bristol, May 9, 1872, ae. 56-2-25. He m. June, 1836, Nancy Taplin, dau. of Jacob and Nancy Farnham, b. Salisbury, June 8, 1816, and d. Bristol, July 16, 1864, ae. 48-1-8. He m. (2) Mary Spencer Brown, Feb., 1871. He was a farmer next east of H. N. Emmons's farm. The buildings have disappeared.

CHILDREN, all born in Bristol

49. Charles Roland, b. Aug. 20, 1837; m. Eliza Spencer, Sept., 1861. He was drowned in Bridgewater, July 7, 1862, ae. 24-10-17; she d. Mar. 6, 1876.
50. Ann Maria, b. Aug. 15, 1839; d. Dec. 15, 1856, ae. 17-4-0.
51. Clara Estelle, b. Mar. 8, 1843; m. Jeremiah G. Atwood, in 1864. He d. 1867, Andover, ae. 29. She m. (2) in 1887, John H. Webster. Res. Franklin. Children :

    a. Hattie Belle, b. Dec. 30, 1864, in Canada. Address Franklin.
    b. Lemuel Greenough, b. Andover, Jan. 7, 1867 ; m. Nov. 9, 1892, Lilla S. Davenport, b. Apr. 5, 1867. Address, Franklin.

52. Lydia Jane, b. July 23, 1845; m. Silas M. Spencer. (See.)
53. Lucy Hannah, b. Sept. 24, 1847. Unm. Res. Concord.
54. George Mansfield, b. Dec. 16, 1850; m. Eliza Page, 1879.
55. Emma Augusta, b. Apr. 24, 1853; m. Horace N. Emmons. (See.)
56. Isabelle Eldora, b. Feb. 23, 1855; m. George S. Tilton. (See.)

(30) Samuel P. Heath, b. June 18, 1819, m. Apr. 13, 1841, Mary Ann, dau. of John and Elizabeth Dunlap, b. Salisbury, May 16, 1820. Farmer in Salisbury; killed by falling from high beam in his barn, Mar. 25, 1847, ae. 27-9-7. She m. (2) Zachariah Scribner, and d. Feb. 7, 1850, ae. 29-8-21.

CHILDREN

57. Eliza,   ⎱ b. Salisbury, Aug. 8, 1845; ⎰ m. Mar. 5, 1867, Jennie N.
58. John C., ⎰   ⎱
Morrill. They res. five years previous to 1876 in California. He d. Laconia, Aug. 12, 1898, ae. 53-0-4. She res. Penacook. Children :

a. Mary Frances, b. Andover, Mar. 23, 1868; m. Samuel M. Clark. (See.)

b. Will Elmer, b. Woodland, Cal., Dec. 23, 1871. Res. Penacook.

c. Ernest S., b. Danbury, Aug. 25, 1881 ; d. Mar. 18, 1897, ae. 15-6-23.

(32) Charles B. Heath, b. Nov. 5, 1823, m. Apr. 6, 1843, Martha C., dau. Joseph G. Dow. (See.) She was b. Dec 20, 1827. He d. in June, 1879, ae. 55-7-. She res. New Hampton.

CHILDREN

59. Henry Ayers, b. Bristol, Apr. 16, 1844 ; m. Feb. 16, 1874, Barbara McEachern, dau. John. She was b. 1849, Prince Edwards Island, and d. Sept. 27, 1885, Healdsburg, Cal. He d. Healdsburg, Cal., Feb. 28, 1900, ae. 55-10-12. (See Roll of Honor.) Child :

a. Herbert M., b. Malden, Mass., Sept. 15, 1876.

60. Hannah Mary, b. B., Apr., 1847 ; d. in New Hampton.

61. William Augustus, b. B., Mar. 7, 1849 ; m. Mary Caroline, dau. of John U. and Caroline (Parker) Dame, b. Oct. 15, 1847, Togus Springs, Me. They res. Shags Springs, Sonoma Co., Cal. Children:

a. Maud Mary, b. Lynn, Mass., Aug. 8, 1869.

b. Ethel Josephine, b. L., June 25, 1871 ; d. Aug. 21, 1871.

c. Julian Barnard, b. L., Nov. 30, 1874 ; d. Healdsburg, Feb. 13, 1877, ae. 2-2-13.

d. Leslie Blanchard, b. Healdsburg, Feb. 16, 1877.

e. Charles Barnard, b. H., Feb. 14, 1880 ; d. Apr. 1, 1880.

f. Roy Wilfred, b. H., June 6, 1881.

62. Olive Jane, b. B., July, 1852 ; d. unm.

63. Josephine Annette, b. B., Oct., 1854 ; d. unm.

(33) Horace W. Heath, b. Nov. 14, 1826, m. Nov. 14, 1850, Unana, dau. Augustus and Sarah Towle (Gove) Atwood, b. Wilmot, Aug. 20, 1832. He was a farmer 34 years in Danbury, where he d., May 10, 1899, ae. 72-5-26. Member of Christian church 38 years.

CHILDREN

64. Lorenzo Merrill, b. Wilmot, Nov. 4, 1851; m. Dec. 25, 1872, Emma Ardella Simons, of Alexandria. Res. Danbury.

65. Leland Edgar, b. W., Mar. 8, 1854; m. June 5, 1901, Emma A. Joy, of Georgetown, O. Res. in Bristol some years on Pleasant street. Residence destroyed by fire.

66. John Henry, b. W., Sept. 5, 1857; m. Apr. —, 1882, Mary E. Thomas, of Barton, Vt.

67. Lurance Jeanette, b. W., Nov. 4, 1862 ; m. Oct. 15, 1878, Fred K. Flanders, of Alexandria. Res. Danbury.

(34) Levi N. Heath, b. Mar. 3, 1829, m. Feb. 20, 1851, Susanna C., dau. of John Gordon, b. New Hampton, June 29, 1832, and d. Bristol, June 11, 1875, ae. 42-11-12. He m. (2) Oct. 11, 1875, Mrs. Julia Seales, dau. Augustus Atwood, Danbury. Farmer on hill near the Locke neighborhood.

CHILDREN, all born in Bristol

68. Annie Abbie, b. Dec. 17, 1851; m. 1873, Henry C. Brown, and res. Lancaster, Mass. He is an inmate insane asylum, Worcester, Mass. Children :

    a.   Mabel Susanna, b. Concord, May 3, 1874.
    b.   Annie Maud, b. C., Dec. 18, 1876; m. June 22, 1897, Elba M.
Carpenter.   Children : (1) Earl, b. Lancaster, June, 1899.   (2)
Ruth Jeanette, b. June 7, 1903.
    69.   Ida Gertrude, b. Dec. 4, 1853; m. Oliver Ballou.   (See.)
    70.   Jennie Naomi, b. May 31, 1856.   For 25 years has been connected
with Best & Co., New York, dealers in clothing.   She is one of the
buyers for the firm, her duties occasionally taking her to Europe.   In
business ability she stands very high and she commands a large salary.
    71.   Edwin Gordon, b. Jan. 31, 1858; m. Anna Eliza, dau. John C.
and Laura A. (Cogswell) Sanborn, b. Canterbury, May 7, 1851.   He is a
farmer and trader in live stock, Canterbury.   Child :
    a.   Chester Earl, b. Mar. 18, 1887.
    72.   Alfred H., b. Mar. 29, 1860; m. Apr. 5, 1888, Elizabeth Herber,
dau. of Christopher John, b. Germany, Feb. 18, 1853.   He is a farmer on
the Moore farm near Pemigewasset bridge.   Children :
    a.   Mary Elizabeth, b. Bristol, Sept. 8, 1889.
    b.   Willie Herber, b. B., Sept. 6, 1891.
    73.   Nellie Emogene, b. May 26, 1863; m. July 4, 1884, Alfred B. Har-
vey, and d. Aug., 1898, ae. 35-3-.   Children :
    a.   Ralph Gordon, b. New York city, June 19, 1885.
    b.   Harold Rolfe, b. N. Y. city, Mar. 5, 1891.
    74.   Carrie Emma, b. June 19, 1865; m. July 16, 1887, Frank A.
Holmes, Sutton, Vt., and d. May 11, 1895, ae. 30-0-27.   No children.
    75.   Levi Bartlett, b. Feb. 23, 1880.   Farmer, Bristol.

———

    1.   Nathaniel (Nathan) W. Heath, the son of James, was
b. Bridgewater, Oct. 7, 1800.   He m., 1822, Esther M. Thomas,
dau. of Jacob.   (See.)   Farmer.   Their last years were passed
in Bristol, where she d. June 16, 1846 ; he dropped dead in the
woods, Dec. 12, 1850, ae. 50-2-5.

CHILDREN

    2.   George W., b. Bridgewater, July 26, 1823.   Served in 6th Vt.
Heavy Artillery, and was a Confederate prisoner.   He d. unm, Stewartstown, Apr. 8, 1896, ae. 72-8-12.
    3.   Ruth Perkins, b. B., Nov. 5, 1825 ; m. Merrill P. Simonds.   (See.)
    4.   Levi Dolloff, b. B., Aug. 13, 1827 ; m. Augusta Harriman, Amos-
keag.   No children.
    5.   Moses Cross, b. B., May 22, 1829 ; m. Nov. 29, 1851, Susan Pettin-
gill.   Served in 5th Regt., N. H. Vols.   (See Roll of Honor.)   Res.
Franklin Falls.   Children :
    a.   Sarah Frances, b. Mar. 24, 1853 ; d. Apr. 5, 1877, ae. 24-0-11.
    b.   George Washington, b. Aug. 3, 1861 ; m. Sept. 21, 1884, Char-
lotte Knight, Stewartstown.
    c.   Esther Mahala, b. Mar. 6, 1866 ; m. Nov. 24, 1881, Thomas H.
Holden, Franklin Falls.
    d.   Hiram Taylor, b. Nov. 7, 1868 ; m. June 26, 1889, Etta Clif-
ford.   Res. Franklin Falls.
    e.   Hattie Belle, b. Feb. 16, 1870 ; m. Wilbur Greenleaf, Belmont.
    6.   Nancy Dolloff, b. B., July 11, 1831 ; m. John F. Rowe, Barrington,
who served in the 7th Regt., N. H. Vols., and d. disease, Nov. 6, 1862,
at St. Augustine, Fla.   Eight children.
    7.   Mary Ann, b. B., July 13, 1833; m. Wesley Haynes.

8.   Lovina Wells, b. B., July 22, 1835; m. Horace G. Kirk.   He d. Nov. 9, 1856, and she m. his brother, Stephen P.   (See.)

9.   Emily Jane, b. B., July 6, 1837; m. Edwin O. Marden.   (See.)

10.   Hiram Taylor, b. Bristol. Aug. 30, 1839; m. Nov. 28, 1867, Ellen F., dau. Charles S. Brown.   (See.)   He served in the 12th Regt., N. H. Vols.   (See Roll of Honor.)   She d. Stewartstown, July 13, 1899.   He res. Stewartstown.   Children :

> *a.*   Levi N., }
> *b.*   George W., } b. Stewartstown, Sept. 8, 1871.
> *c.*   John F., b. S., Aug. 30, 1875.
> John F. and George W., were drowned Aug. 8, 1883.

11.   Laurilla Perkins, b. B., May 13, 1843; m. Frank Cross, of Bridgewater.   He d. and she m. (2) Otis A. Wade, Dec. 18, 1885.   Res. New Hampton.

---

1.   **Charles Brown Heath**, son of Ebenezer and Ruth (Aiken) Heath, was b. Canaan, Aug. 25, 1833.   He m. June 22, 1861, Mary Josephine Adams.   He made two whaling voyages of two years each ; served two years in 42nd Regt., Mass. Vols., Civil war ; came to Bristol, 1868 ; was foreman in bedstead factory.   He d. Mar. 15, 1889, ae. 55-6-20.   Methodist, Odd Fellow, G. A. R.   Mrs. Heath res. Bristol.

CHILDREN

2.   Winnifred May, b. Brookfield, Mass., Feb. 12, 1866 ; m. Oct. 4, 1900, Harry B. Lufkin.   Res. Manchester.

3.   Flora Adams, b. Manchester, Apr. 8, 1868 ; d. Bristol, Oct. 14, 1898, ae. 30-6-6.

4.   Grace Blanche, b. Bristol, May 6, 1870; d. Nov. 12, 1881, ae. 11-6-6.

THE HEMPHILL FAMILY

1.   **Peter Hemphill**, son of James and Ruth (Harthon) Hemphill, was b. in Henniker, Feb. 12, 1800.   His mother d. Sept., 1869, ae. 100-3 .   Farmer.   Came to Bristol from Springfield, about 1872, and here d. Sept. 10, 1888, ae. 88-6-28.   He m. (1) Abigail T. Gilman, b. Nov. 19, 1803 ; (2) Lucy M. Kirk, dau. of John, b. Aug. 16, 1819.   She d. Ashland, Nov. 27, 1900, ae. 81-3-11.

CHILDREN

2.   John, b. Deering, Apr. 14, 1839.   Served in 11th Regt., N. H. Vols., wounded at Spottsylvania, Va., May 16, 1864, and d. of wounds, May 25, ae. 25-1-11.

3.   Horace, b. New London, Dec. 28, 1840; m. (1) Julia, dau. of Calvin D. Sanborn   (See.)   She d. Apr. 8, 1873, ae. 25-11-24, and he m. Nov. 28, 1875, Esther F., dau. of Joseph and Sarah (Kimball) Powers, b. Groton, June 20, 1838.   He came to Bristol about 1872 ; was a carpenter, and here d. July 17, 1895, ae. 54-6-19.   She res. on Spring street.   Her mother, Mrs. Sarah K. Powers, spent her last years with her, and here d. Mar. 31, 1895, ae. 92-6-19.   In her last sickness she gave $300 to the Methodist church of Bristol.

4. Betsey, b. Springfield, Sept. 11, 1842; d. Aug. 6, 1845, ae. 2-10-25.
5. Silas, b. S., Dec. 15, 1844; d. Mar. 23, 1845.
6. Lottie, b. S., Oct.13, 1846; m. Dec. 24, 1881, George W. Miller. He was proprietor for a time of Hotel Bristol livery stable; removed to Henniker, where he d. Jan. 23, 1895.
7. Laura Ann, b. S., Mar. 30, 1849; d. Sept. 21, 1850, ae. 1-5-21.
8. Betsey Ann, b. S., Aug. 3, 1851; d. Sept. 26, 1870, ae. 19-1-23.
9. Joshua Darling, b. S., Feb. 12, 1854; m. Apr. 2, 1878, Finette Eva, dau. Stephen Nelson. (See.) He was in business in Bristol a short time as a machinist, now a hosiery manufacturer and inventor and manufacturer of knitting machines at Central Falls, R. I. Child:

 a. Lucy Louisa, b. Bristol, Sept. 9, 1879; m. Sept. 8, 1897, John Lawson, a machinist in Central Falls. Child: Robert Hemphill, b. Sept. 28, 1900.

10. Robert, b. S., Sept. 6, 1856; d. Sept. 6, 1856.

HENTALL

1. Samuel Hentall, son of Henry and Rebecca (Ewing) Hentall, was b. Uxbridge, England, Dec. 11, 1854. He came to America when 17 years of age and operated a restaurant in Boston 23 years. He came to Bristol in 1895, and has since resided at the foot of the lake on the Luther C. Bailey place. Farmer, and proprietor of two steam launches. He m. Martha Ellis.

THE HIGHT FAMILY

1. Frank Pierce Hight, son of Merrick B. and Hannah (Calley) Hight, was b. New Hampton, Mar. 26, 1853. He m. May 1, 1879, Mary Isabelle, dau. of Rufus B. Hazelton, b. Groton, Oct. 9, 1858. He came to Bristol in 1879; has been a paper-mill workman; foreman of the Train-Smith company's pulp-mill; shoemaker. He enjoys the distinction of being the heaviest man in town, at one time tipping the scales at 330 pounds. No children. Odd Fellow, Democrat.

THE HILANDS FAMILY

1. Samuel Hilands, m. Harriet Harwood. He was a farmer in District No. 8, from 1852 till he d., Feb. 9, 1879, ae. 67. She m. (2) Luther C. Bailey, and d. Aug. 17, 1894, ae. 81-2-21.

CHILD

2. Amasa Smith, (adopted) b. So. Situate, R. I., Dec. 23, 1849; m. July 31, 1869, Laura Elizabeth, dau. of John and Rosetta (Harriman) Nason, b. Bartlett, Dec. 15, 1849. Was an overseer for many years in a mill in Manchester; since 1892, a farmer in District No. 8. Children:

 a. Charles Amasa, b. Manchester, Apr., 1871; d. of cholera infantum, July, 1871.
 b. Willie Henry, b. M., 1875 ('76), d. of cholera infantum.
 c. William, b. M., Apr., 1879; d. of cholera infantum.
 d. Willie Harry (adopted), b. Haverhill, Mass., Feb. 12, 1879.

THE HILL FAMILY

1. Joseph Playston Hill, son of Gideon and Rhoda Hill, of Rumney, was b. Apr. 28, 1841. He m., Jan. 1, 1873, Demis Dale, dau. of Matthias and Priscilla (Davidson) Stone, b. Cabot, Vt., Sept. 29, 1854. A laborer in Bristol since Nov., 1899.

CHILDREN

2. Myrtie Belle, b. Cabot, Vt., Mar. 6, 1874; m. Sept. 8, 1894, George B. Simmons. (See.)
3. Jessie Maud, b. Danville, Vt., Apr. 28, 1877; d. July 12, 1880, ae. 3-2-14.
4. Richard Melverton, b. D., June 27, 1879. Res. Bristol; laborer.
5. Earnest Playston, b. St. Johnsbury, Vt., Mar. 15, 1881. Res. Bristol; laborer.
6. Lottie Blanche, b. Warren, July 6, 1883; m. Willis E. Pray. (See.)
7. Van Clarence, b. Wentworth, June 29, 1886.
8. Leifa Dell, b. West Rumney, Apr. 15, 1894.

THE HOLDEN FAMILY

1. Benjamin Franklin Holden, son of Benjamin Franklin and Harriet (Morse) Holden, was b. West Concord, in 1842. He m., in 1864, Amelia Augusta Crockett. He was the active partner of Dow & Holden and of Holden & Co., manufacturers of shaker flannels, where now is the Dodge-Davis Manufacturing company's mill, 1865-'83, when he went to California, where he was manager of the Napa woolen-mill, and interested in the Sawyer Tanning company. He d. Napa, Cal., Dec. 31, 1899, ae. 57. He was a Republican, represented Bristol in the legislature; official member of the Methodist church.

CHILDREN

2. Mary Genevieve, b. Bristol, Nov. 16, 1866.
3. Clarence, b. B., Nov. 28, 1873.

---

1. Samuel Emery Holden, a brother of Benjamin F., above, was b. West Concord, Feb. 3, 1845. He graduated from Wesleyan University, Middletown, Conn., 1869. Served in Co. D, 16th Regt., N. H. Vols., read law and was admitted to the bar. Res. in Bristol 1867-'75; treasurer of the Bristol Savings bank, a law partner with Judge Samuel K. Mason (See Lawyers), and a member of the firm of Holden & Co. Official member of the Methodist church and superintendent of the Sunday-school. He removed to Napa, Cal., where he was a member of the Sawyer Tanning company, the Napa Woolen-mill company, and acquired a good property. He m., Nov. 18, 1869, Mary Ellen, dau. of Jonathan Taylor, b. Sanbornton, June 6, 1846, and d. Napa, May 4, 1875, ae. 28-10-28. He m., Jan. 8, 1879,

Anna Smyth of Mount Vernon, Iowa. He d. Napa, Dec. 31, 1900, ae. 55-10-28. The family res. in Napa.

CHILDREN

2.   Hattie M., b. Concord, Aug. 28, 1870 ; d. Sept. 25, 1870.
3.   Robert Smyth, b. Napa, May 13, 1880.
4.   Harold Emery, b. N., Apr. 23, 1882.
5.   Grace Edith, b. N., Jan. 8, 1884; d. Oct. 11, 1887, ae. 3-9-3.
6.   Philip Sawyer, b. N., Sept. 25, 1889.

THE HOLMAN FAMILY

1.   Rev. Calvin Holman, son of Calvin and Esther Putney (Bailey) Holman, was b. in Hopkinton, July 17, 1823. He m., Apr. 5, 1842, Lucy T., dau. of Timothy and Lucy Underwood, b. Putney, Vt., Dec. 19, 1816. He commenced his ministerial labors in 1841, and was a member of the New Hampshire conference about 21 years. In 1851 and '52 he was pastor of the Bristol church. Failing health compelled a change of climate, and he went to Kansas and soon after resumed active work, and served six years as presiding elder. Was one year in Tennessee, connected with the Christian Commission during the Civil war. He was a faithful and devoted minister, and occupied a warm place in the hearts of all who knew him. He d. at Topeka, Kan., Feb. 20, 1902, ae. 78-7-3.

CHILDREN

2.   Clara, b. Hopkinton, Apr. 11, 1843 ; res. Topeka, Kansas ; unm.
3.   Hattie Lorraine, b. Putney, Vt., May 26, 1849 ; res. Topeka ; unm.
4.   Merton Calvin, b. Bristol, May 5, 1852 ; m. June 6, 1878, M. Emma, dau. of J. S. and Celia A. (Olmsted) Wright, b. West Barre, N. Y., Sept. 4, 1857. He is a dealer in furniture, carpets, and wall paper at 837-839 No. Kansas Ave., No. Topeka, Kan., and president of the Western Woolen-mill company, Topeka. Children :
   a.   Celia Evelyn, b. Blue Rapids, Kan., Apr. 25, 1879.
   b.   Stella Gencive, b. Topeka, Nov. 12, 1887.
   c.   Leon Wright, b. T., Feb. 16, 1894.
5.   Lura Ella, b. Great Falls, Sept. 26, 1854 ; res. T. ; unm.
6.   Edward Arthur, b. Lawrence, Mass., Sept. 16, 1857 ; m. and has three children.

THE HOLMES FAMILY

1.   Charles Warren Holmes, son of Charles and Caroline E. (Smith) Holmes, was b. Sharon, Mass., Jan. 9, 1841. His parents were of Revolutionary stock. He m., June 10, 1863, Sarah, dau. of James and Mary (LaBounty) Douglass, b. Colton, N. Y., 1840, and d. at Colton, Mar. 17, 1887, ae. 47. He m., Sept. 5, 1889, Mrs. Henrietta Frances, widow of Benjamin F. Johnston, and dau. of Alfred R. Drew (See), b. Nov. 22,

1848. Has res. Bristol since 1890, proprietor of machine shop. Republican, official member of Methodist church ; Mason, Odd Fellow, member of Grange.

CHILDREN

2. Sarah Elizabeth, b. Cambridge, Mass., Jan., 1865 ; m. Alberton B. Howe ; res. Canaan. Children :
    a. Reginald.   *b.* Ralph.   *c.* Jessie.
3. Helen Drew, b. Bristol, Aug. 14, 1891.

CHILD of Mrs. Holmes by first marriage

1. Mabel Frances, b. Boston, Mass., Dec. 5, 1875 ; m. William C. White. (See.)

THE HOMANS FAMILY

1. Henry Clay Homans, the son of James and Ann (Flanders) Homans, was b. Wentworth, Nov. 24, 1830. His grandfather lost a leg in the Revolutionary war. He m., Nov. 6, 1861, Nancy C., dau. of Aaron and Clarissa (George) Stearns, b. Plymouth, Nov. 1, 1828. They removed from Plymouth to the town farm about 1872, thence to Summer street, 1889, where they now res. He is a carpenter and farmer. Republican.

CHILDREN

2. Almer Willis, b. Plymouth, Apr. 13, 1863. A jeweler in Franklin Falls ; unm.
3. Loren Wilbur, b. P., May 22, 1866 ; d. Bristol, Nov. 4, 1893, ae. 27-5-12. A machinist.

THE HORNE FAMILY

1. Noah Horne, the son of Paul, a soldier in the French and Indian war, was b. in Farmington, Jan. 14, 1814. In 1836, he m. Tressa Ann Bellows, b. Sanbornton, March, 1814. They res. in Alexandria till 1853 ; in Bristol till 1871, on farm just below Frederick Kidder's, where she d. 1871. He d. Alexandria, Oct., 1897, ae. 83-9-.

CHILDREN

2. Charles Henry, b. Rochester, July 18, 1838 ; served on quota of Bristol in Civil war. (See Roll of Honor.) He m., 1862, Lizzie, dau. of William Smith, b. Concord, Apr., 1842. Res. Water Village. Nine children.
3. Sarah Ann, b. Alexandria, 1841 ; m. Sylvester Webber ; d. in 1862, ae. 21.
4. Augustus Paul, b. A., Aug. 3, 1845 ; m. July 30, 1867, Frances D. Ricker, dau. Isaiah, b. Monroe, Me., Aug. 2, 1850; d. Manchester, Jan. 5, 1897, ae. 46-5-3. He m., Feb. 8, 1899, Marie Allen Fitzpatrie, dau. Col. Charles E., b. London, Eng., Apr. 15, 1855. He served in 9th Regt., N. H. Vols. (See Roll of Honor.) After the war, was for many years an overseer in a mill in Manchester. Two children.
5. Clarence Archer, res. Exeter.

16

THE HORNER FAMILY

1.   Robert A. Horner, son of John, was b. Apr. 13, 1845, in Thornton.   He m. Frances J. Gilman, who was b. in Thornton, Sept. 5, 1848, and d. in Bristol, June 12, 1885, ae. 36-9-7. He m., Jan. 10, 1889, Belle G., dau. of Russell S. and Elizabeth (Seavey) Gray, b. Hereford, P. Q., Sept. 4, 1866.   Mr. Horner settled in Bristol in 1875, and was for some years in trade in Abel block, later a member of the firm of Dickinson & Horner, dealers in clothing, boots, and shoes.   He was a Mason, a prominent Democrat, and served as selectman of Bristol three years; as county commissioner four years, and as county treasurer four years.   He removed to Woodsville, 1890, where he was treasurer of the Woodsville Guarantee Savings bank and of the Woodsville Loan and Banking Co., and there d. Apr. 16, 1895, ae. 50-0-3.   Mrs. Horner res. Woodsville.

CHILD

2.   Edna Frances, b. in Woodsville, Apr. —, 1893.

THE HOWE FAMILY

1.   Moses B. Howe, son of Lyman C. and Sophronia (Bartlett) Howe, was b. in Bradford, Nov. 16, 1833.   He m., Jan. 31, 1858, Susan E. Boardman, b. Bridgewater, Dec. 4, 1835.   Was the first barber in Bristol.   (See Roll of Honor.) He d. Bristol, Oct. 16, 1877, ae. 43-11-0; she d. Sept. 17, 1881, ae. 45-9-13.

CHILDREN

2.   Frank, d. in infancy.
3.   Elva May, m. in May, 1885, Frank W. Whittier.
4.   Jennie H.

THE HOYT OR HOIT FAMILIES

1.   Samuel Hoyt was b. Aug. 17, 1768, in Newtown or Newbury.   He m. Judith Blaisdell.   They came from Gilford and soon after settled next east of the Heath burying-ground. He d. Feb. 3, 1833, ae. 64-5-16, and she removed to Warren, and there d., Nov., 1858, ae. 85.

CHILDREN

2.   Jacob, m. June 28, 1825, Susan, dau. of Samuel Gurdy (See), b. Nov. 12, 1794.   He went to Alabama, where he d., 1843.   She res. for some years in New Hampton ; d. in Laconia, 1888 or 1890.   Five children.
3.   Betsey, b. Gilford, Nov. 7, 1794 ; drowned, ae. 4.
4.   Mariam, b. G., Dec. 27, 1796; m. Benjamin Fellows.   (See.)
5.   Betsey, b. G., 1801 ; m. John Gurdy.   (See.)
6.   John, b. G., Nov., 1804; m. Abigail, dau. of Samuel and Martha

(Cleveland) Titus, of Colebrook. He came to Bristol from Lowell, Mass., and was here taxed 1848–'53. A stone mason and farmer. He d. Warren, Mar., 1875, ae. 70-4-. She d. Mar., 1874. They had 14 children.

7. Sargent, b. Gilford, 1810; m. Sally Veasey. He was a farmer in Dist. No. 3, where he d. June 19, 1845, ae. 35. She d. June, 1844. Children:

    a. Mariam, m. —— Gault.

    b. Daniel, killed on railroad; unm.   *c.* Anna.

8. Osgood, m. Nancy, dau. of Seth and Elizabeth Dillingham, b. 1812. He d. Charlestown, Mass., Dec. 24, 1841; she d. same place, Aug. 3, 1853, ae. 41.

9. Michael, b. Feb. 20, 1813; m. Nov. 11, 1834, Emily, dau. of Peter Wells. (See.) She d. Bristol, Aug. 23, 1835, ae. 19-5-24. He m. (2) July 2, 1839, Sally M., dau. Hugh and Mary Blaisdell, b. Gilford, May 30, 1817. He d. Bristol, Nov. 9, 1848, ae. 35-8-19. She d. Wilmot Flat, July 27, 1893, ae. 76-1-27. He was a farmer in Dist. No. 4, till his death. Children:

    a. Rosan E., b. Bristol, Apr. 24, 1835; m. Charles W. Chase. (See.)

    b. John B., b. B., Apr. 11, 1840.

    c. Betsey Ann, b. New Hampton, Dec. 9, 1844; m. June 1, 1867, James F. Tilton, b. Wilmot, Apr. 2, 1842. She d. Oct. 23, 1885, ae. 40-10-14. He res. Wilmot. No children.

    d. Frank M., "d. Oct. 23, 1848, ae. 7 mos."

    e. George M., b. Bristol, Mar., 1849; d. Oct., 1849.

———

1. David P. Hoyt is the son of Philip J. and Fannie (Putney) Hoyt. He was b. Wilmot, Aug. 4, 1838, and m. Aug. 5, 1861, Eliza Jane, dau. of Jewell and Mary (Blodgett) Jesseman, b. Hudson, Apr. 5, 1842. Aug. 28, 1862, he enlisted in Co. K, 12th Regt., and served till after the battle of Gettysburg, when he was transferred to Co. D, 1st Regt., Veteran Reserve Corps; discharged at Elmira, N. Y., July 14, 1865. Since October, 1881, has res. on the Solomon French farm at base of Alexandria hill. Farmer.

CHILDREN

2. Fannie Etta, b. Wentworth, Aug. 12, 1866; m. Albon M. Simonds. (See.)

3. Frank Henry, b. W., Apr. 5, 1868; m. Helen M., dau. of Phineas B. Smith, b. Bridgewater, Aug. 8, 1867. Farmer. Res. Bristol. Child:

    a. Vena M., b. Bridgewater, Aug. 23, 1886.

4. David Harvey, b. Wentworth, May 10, 1870; m. July 24 (31), 1888, Abbie C., dau. of Edwin T. Pike. (See.) She d. Bristol, Jan. 31, 1901, ae. 31-8-21. Farmer in Bristol. Children:

    a. Nellie Beatrice, b. Bristol, Apr. 27, 1889; d. Aug. 5, 1894, ae. 5-3-8.

    b. Irving Harvey, b. Bridgewater, Nov. 3, 1891.

    c. Ned Eugene, b. Danbury, Dec. 17, 1892.

THE HUBBARD OR HERBERT FAMILY

1. Jeremiah Hubbard lived on Summer street, near residence of Rufus Eaton. He was a Revolutionary soldier. His

wife was a very decrepit but hard working woman, "bent nearly double." He was a shoemaker and d. in this home. She d. some years later in the home of her daughter, Mrs. Rebecca Danforth.

CHILDREN

*2. Jeremiah.
3. Rebecca, m. (1) John Willard, (2) Abel Danforth.

(2) Jeremiah Hubbard, son of Jeremiah, m. (1) Polly Truell, dau. of David (See), (2) Mrs. Nancy Smart. They lived near Worthen burying-ground. He had nine children by each wife.

CHILDREN

4. Sarah, m. Samuel Eastman.   5. Levi.   6. John.
7. Maria, m. Joshua Stevens.   8. Elizabeth, m. —— Gordon.
*9. Sanders, b. Oct. 10, 1802.   10. Angeline, m. John Jones.
11. Cynthia F., b. Nov. 19, 1811; m. Jeremiah N. Hersey; d. winter 1895-'96.
12. Susan Cilley, twin sister of Cynthia, was the 2d wife of Joab Patterson, Concord. She d. Concord, Jan. 19, 1900, ae. 88-2-0.
13. Sarah Ann.   14. Emeline.   15. Harriet, m. Dearborn Hunt.
16. Almira, }   { m. Stephen Huse. (See.)
17. Alvira, } twins, { m. William Smith.
18. Josiah, m. Almira Caverly.
19. Jeremiah, m. Mrs. Abbie P. Worthen. Certificate issued May 14, 1869; d. Alexandria, Mar. 1, 1893. (See Roll of Honor.)
20. Hannah, m. (3) Isaac Rigg.
21. Died in Maine.

(9) Sanders Herbert, b. Oct. 10, 1802, m. Apr. 2, 1825, Judith Cilley, b. Feb. 14, 1800, d. Dec. 22, 1828, ae. 28-10-8. He m. (2) Jan. 25, 1830, Dorothy Ash, b. May 10, 1804, d. Aug. 30, 1830, ae. 26-3-20. He m. (3) Mar. 3, 1831, Betsey Cilley, b. Sept. 20, 1804, d. Mar. 20, 1838, ae. 33-6-0. He m. (4) July 4, 1839, Mary Gordon Fisk, dau. of Rev. David and Lydia (Morse) Fisk, b. Apr. 6, 1810, d. Nov. 3, 1873, ae. 63-6-27. He was a shoemaker in Bristol. Free Baptist. Died in Hill, June 11, 1880, ae. 77-8-1.

CHILDREN

22. Joseph Cilley, b. Bristol, May 2, 1827; m. Jan., 1853, Mary M. Johnson, dau. of Henry, b. July 24, 1829. Farmer in Bristol and New Hampton; d. New Hampton, May 26, 1878, ae. 51-0-24. She m. (2) Oct. 2, 1884, Joseph A. Swett, and d. Mar. 28, 1903, ae. 73-8-4. Child:
    a. Henry S., b. Bristol; d. May 11, 1861, ae. 5-4-11.
23. Judith W., b. New Hampton, Mar. 2, 1832; d. Bristol, June 29, 1867, ae. 35-3-27.
24. Susan Cilley, b. N. H., Nov. 18, 1833; m. John M. Cilley. (See.)
25. Hiram S., b. N. H., Nov. 13, 1835; d. June 1, 1837, ae. 1-6-18.
26. Hiram S., b. N. H., Oct. 25, 1837; d. Mar. 4, 1842, ae. 4-4-9.
27. Ebenezer Fisk, b. N. H., 1840; d. Nov. 21, 1853, ae. 13.
28. Sarah Frances, b. N. H., Feb. 24, 1842; m. May 1, 1867, Sullivan Ingalls. (See.)
29. Clara Jane, b. Sept. 9, 1845; d. Feb. 2, 1874, ae. 28-4-23.

THE HUCKINS FAMILY

1.   James Henry Huckins, son of Ferdinand A. and Nancy (Jewell) Huckins, was b. Tamworth, Dec. 6, 1843. Sept., 1865, he m. Laura Ann, dau. of Sampson and Sally Pettingill, b. Sandwich, May 1, 1845. Was a farmer in Tamworth. In July, 1900, he removed to Bristol, having purchased the Sylvanus W. Swett farm, where he now lives.

CHILDREN

2.   Charles F., b. Tamworth, Apr. 19, 1868. Farmer. Came to Bristol with his father. He m. Jan. 26, 1898, Sadie V. Burleigh, dau. James W. (See.) Child :

   a. Bessie L., b. Bristol, Aug. 26, 1899.

THE HUNTINGTON FAMILY

1.   Jonathan Huntington, was b. Hopkinton, Feb. 4, 1767. He m. Jan. 27, 1791, Jane Abbott. They came from Hawke to the Nelson neighborhood, his farmhouse being some distance from the highway, just east of the site of the house occupied by Caleb L. Clay. He was noted in early life as a profane, intemperate man, and in later life as very religious though superstitious. His wife was from Chester, and was b. Dec. 17, 1763, and d. Bristol, July 19, 1834, ae. 70-7-2 ; he d. in the family of David Foster, in South Alexandria, Nov. 25, 1842, ae. 75-9-21.

CHILDREN, all born in Bristol

2.   Betsey, b. Bristol, July 1, 1791 ; m. Daniel McMurphy, the son of Alexander, a Revolutionary soldier from Warner. They were farmers in Alexandria, where he d. July 2, 1845, ae. 56-10-17. She d. Mar. 6, 1887, ae. 95-8-5. Children :

   a. Jane H., b. Mar. 6, 1811 ; m. Carlos Swetland ; d. Lebanon, Oct. 10, 1853, ae. 42-7-4. Seven children.
   b. Mary, b. Oct. 15, 1812 ; m. Timothy Tilton. (See.)
   c. Ursula P., b. Aug. 10, 1814 ; m. Mar. 23, 1841, Caleb Wells. She d. Warner, Nov. 13, 1866, ae. 52-3-3. Four children.
   d. Betsey, b. July 5, 1816 ; d. Mar. 7, 1859, ae. 42-8-2.
   e. Hannah J., b. Aug. 20, 1818 ; m. Artemas Simonds.
   f. Sarah Frances, b. Dec. 11, 1820 ; d. Mar. 9, 1822, ae. 1-2-28.
   g. Daniel, b. Dec. 31, 1822 ; m. Sarah E., dau. Silas Rhoades, b. Antrim, June 7, 1822 ; d. Mar. 19, 1902, ae. 79-9-12. Two children.
   h. Almira Palmer, b. Mar. 27, 1825 ; d. Dec. 16, 1857, ae. 32-8-19. Unm.
   i. Sarah F., b. Apr. 27, 1827 ; d. July 24, 1851, ae. 24-2-27.
   j. Alexander, b. Jan. 16, 1830 ; m. (1) Nov. 25, 1851, Mary, dau. of Reuben Kidder, b. Hebron, Oct. 25, 1827 ; d. Feb. 16, 1854, ae. 26-3-21. He m. (2) Dec. 1, 1855, Martha Darling. She d. Feb. 19, 1903, ae. 66-8-11. One child. Res. Plymouth. Farmer.
   k. Caroline K., b. Aug. 11, 1832 ; m. George Downing ; d. Aug. 5, 1859, ae. 26-11-24.

3.   Sarah, b. Dec. 1, 1792 ; m. David Foster. (See.)
4.   Hannah, b. July 1, 1795 ; m. Moses Johnson. (See.)

16*a*

5. Jane, b. May 3, 1797; m. Mar. 12, 1840, Ebenezer Flint, and res. Alexandria, then Franconia, where he d.; she d. Winchester, Mass.
        In Feb., 1835, eight of this family had the smallpox. No fatalities.

THE HUSE FAMILIES

Carr Huse was b. in England in 1740. He emigrated to America, landing in Newburyport, Mass., in 1764. The summer of 1767 and the two succeeding summers, he spent in New Chester clearing land for a farm. His camp was near the Pemigewasset river in what is now the village of Hill. Jonas Minot, who visited New Chester in July, 1771, for the Masonian proprietors, reported that at that time Carr Huse and family had been living in a house in the town one year and four months. (See page 40, Vol. I.) By this it seems he made the second permanent settlement in the town, and at as early a date as the spring of 1770. His cabin stood not far from the cemetery east of the railroad. In 1790, he built a frame house just back of the buildings now occupied by George M. Huse, and in 1824, the present buildings.

Neither Carr Huse nor any of his descendants ever resided within the limits of Bristol but he was so long and so intimately identified with the old town of New Chester, of which the territory of Bristol was a part, that this history would be incomplete without a sketch of this worthy man.

At the first town meeting in New Chester, in 1773, Carr Huse was elected selectman, and he filled this office 18 years; at the second annual town meeting he was elected clerk and served 33 years. In his old age, realizing the importance of a record of the first meeting, he recorded a statement of what was then done, the clerk of that meeting, Joshua Tolford, having failed to make a record. During the Revolutionary war, he was a member of the town committee of safety, and he served as sergeant of a company that marched from Plymouth in September, 1777, to the relief of the northern army under Gen. Gates. He was for many years a justice of the peace ; also served as coroner. He was largely influential in the organization of the First Congregational church of Hill, in 1815, and was elected one of its first deacons. He was a broad-minded, progressive man and his influence is still felt, though he long since ceased to have a voice in the affairs of his town.

Carr Huse m. (1) Sarah Wells, presumed to be the daughter of Lieut. Thomas Wells, four of whose sons were among the earliest settlers in New Chester. She d. July 8, 1773, ae. 33–3–24. He m. (2) in 1775, Joanna Buswell, who d. June 12, 1823, ae. 77. He d. Apr. 10, 1833, ae. 92–9–. He had five children by his first wife and four by his second. The homestead still remains in the family. Carr Huse was succeeded by his son, John, b. 1784. He m. twice, had six children, and d. Feb. 26, 1859, ae. 74. John Huse was succeeded by his son, Carr, b. 1814. He m. (1) Feb. 10, 1842, Arvilla K. Harper, of New Hampton. She d. Oct. 12, 1843, and he m. (2) Dec. 19, 1843, Charlotte W., dau. of Ezekiel Eastman. He d. July 26, 1869, and Mrs. Charlotte W. Huse is the successor to the estate. She is the mother of five children, one of whom, George M., is a resident on the homestead, as is also her grandson, Carr Huse, a son of George M. Huse, and a great-great-grandson of the original settler on this estate.

---

1. Stephen D. Huse, son of Dennison and Mary (Houghton) Huse, was b. Harvard, Mass., July 2, 1823. He m. Almira Hubbard, dau. of Jeremiah. (See.) He was a currier in White's tannery for some years before the Civil war. (See Roll of Honor.) After the war was a whitewasher and paper hanger. She d. Aug. 22, 1881, ae. 51 years; he m. (2); he d. Jan. 12, 1902, ae. 78-6-10.

CHILD

2. Lizzie M., b. Feb. 1, 1849; m. John Colby; d. Bristol, Jan. 11, 1894, ae. 44-11-10.

THE HUTCHINS FAMILY

1. Erastus Thomas Hutchins, son of Thomas and Sarah (Dadman) Hutchins, was. b. Westford, Mass., Apr. 29, 1846. He m. Nov. 27, 1870, Annie, dau. Caleb and Hannah (Keneston) Robie, b. Andover, May 30, 1846. He was a farmer and lumber dealer in Alexandria; came to Bristol, Jan. 1, 1899, and was elected selectman, 1902 and 1903. Republican.

CHILDREN

2. Mabel Augusta, b. Alexandria, Mar. 22, 1872; m. Hial F. Seavey and res. Alexandria.
3. Josie Lila, b. A., Mar. 25, 1874; m. Elmer H. Gordon, of Alexandria.
4. Bert Clarence, b. A., Sept. 14, 1875; m. Ethel, dau. Nathaniel J. Ackerman. Res. Alexandria.
5. Ella May, b. A., Jan. 3, 1878; d. Feb. 13, 1879, ae. 1-1-10.
6. Earl Leon, b. A., July 6, 1882.
7. Allen Erastus, b. A., July 7, 1884.
8. George Chandos, b. A., Jan. 20, 1886.
9. Myrtie Annie, b. A., Jan. 21, 1888.

THE HUTCHINSON FAMILY

1. Alexander Hutchinson, son of Alexander, was b. in Edinburgh, Scotland, June 12, 1790. He came to Bristol

about 1828, and soon after m. Betsey Smith Truell, dau. David
(See), b. May 12, 1801. He was farmer and res. just west of
river on Pleasant street. She d. Oct. 16, 1869, ae. 68-5-4; he
d. May 12, 1870, ae. 79-11-0.

CHILDREN

2. Solomon Jackson, b. Franklin. Left home at 18; was not heard
from till he returned 21 years later. Was a soldier in Mexican war. He
m. Susan O. Hicky. Certificate issued Sept. 9, 1869. No children. Died
at home of his sister, Jane, ae. about 59.

3. Almira Wilson, b. Aug. 27, 1830; m. Feb. 5, 1855, Samuel S. Gale.
Children:

    a. Burleigh Alvin, b. Groton, Apr. 14, 1861.
    b. Flora A., b. Bristol, July 29, 1863; m. —— Barrett.
    c. Alice M., b. Manchester, July 19, 1871, m. —— Dinsmore.
    d. A son died in infancy.

4. Mary, b. Franklin, Nov. 25, 1832; m. Samuel C. Bennett. (See.)
5. Jane, b. Bristol, Mar. 23, 1834; m. George M. Alden. (See.)
6. Alexander, b. B., July 5, 1836; m. Jane Clark, 1862. Killed June
28, 1864, seige of Petersburg. (See Roll of Honor.) Child:

    a. Fred Orlando.

7. Caroline Matilda, b. B., Feb. 28, 1839; m. May 1, 1866, Josiah
Healey; d. Nov. 28, 1882, ae. 43-9-.

8. Susan M., b. B.; m. (1) Jan. 1, 1863, Sumner R. Truell, two
children; m. (2) Bryant E. Crawford, two children.

9. Betsey Ann, b. B., Aug. 5, 1841; m. Oct. 3, 1860, Fred G. Stark,
Manchester. Children:

    a. Charles Alvin, b. Oct. 19, 1861; graduated Dartmouth Medi-
cal school, 1884; m. Oct. 19, 1886, Harriet O. Walker. Was in
practice at Asylum, Concord; in an asylum at Winchendon, Mass.;
and in Louisiana; in Marshfield, Mass., 1887, till he d. 1897, ae. 36.
His widow and one son, Gillis Walker, survive.
    b. Gillis, b. Feb. 9, 1865; graduated at Dartmouth Medical
school, 1889; m. Apr. 9, 1893, Gertrude M. Hall. Is a physician in
Manchester.
    c. Frederick Russell, b. Apr. 21, 1867; m. June 20, 1893, Cora B.
Simmons. Is a dealer in real estate, loans, and insurance, Manchester. Children: (1) Marion Elizabeth. (2) Frederick Norman.
    d. Susan Augusta, b. Sept. 1, 1868; m. Oct. 14, 1896, Charles F.
Smyth, Manchester. Children: (1) Dorothy. (2) Marion Elizabeth.
    e. Maurice Albert, b. July 30, 1874; graduated Dartmouth Med-
ical school, 1896; m. Weltha Ford, June 14, 1900. Is a physician in
Goffstown.

10. Daniel Smith, b. B., Sept. 6, 1842; d. Franklin, Dec. 7, 1891, ae.
49-3-1. Served in 12th Regt., N. H. Vols. (See Roll of Honor.) He m.
Jennie Phelps, dau. Andrew and Johanna. She d. Mar., 1878, and he m.
(2) Oct. 13, 1879, Anna M. Fay, of Spencer, Mass. She d. West Derry,
ae. 46-4-0. Children:

    a. Rose Anna, b. Danbury, Nov. 14, 1867; m. Lariener E. Fay.
Res. Danbury.
    b. Byron Willie, b. Bristol, Nov. 24, 1870.
    c. Charles A., b. Danbury, Apr. 19, 1872.
    d. Elmer E., b. D., June 19, 1874.
    e. Edgbert, b. D., Oct. 14, 1876.
    f. Elias, b. Shirley, Mass., Mar. 12, 1878.
    g. Georgie Hoyt, b. Bristol, Jan. 27, 1881; d. Mar. 9, 1881.

h. Arthur Everett, b. Franklin, May 13, 1886.
i. Flora Bell, b. F., Aug. 30, 1891.
11. Willie, b. B., Sept. 5, 1841 ; d. May, 1847, ae. 5-8-.

---

1. Sullivan Hutchinson, son of Galen and Olive (Flint) Hutchinson, was b. Albany, Me., June 10, 1826. He m. Jan. 2, 1850, Elzina, dau. of Thomas and Naomi (Guernsey) Eastman, b. Whitefield, Nov. 4, 1831. He was a farmer and stationery peddler ; res. in Bristol, 1870-'73, and d. New Hampton, Mar. 4, 1889, ae. 62-8-24. Mason. She res. Bristol.

CHILDREN

2. Orrin, b. Milan, Feb. 13, 1851 ; m. Mary E. Calley, July 4, 1871. Children :

a. Leon Vado, b. Northfield, May 8, 1872 ; m. Aug. 17, 1896, Etta S. Walker, dau. of Walter W. Walker. Res. New Hampton. One son, three dau.

b. Walter Fiske, b. New Hampton, Aug. 7, 1877.

c. Viola Edith b. N. H., Oct. 7, 1881. Res. Tilton.

3. Olive, b. M., Feb. 24, 1853 ; m. George Wells. Children :

a. Carrie Elzina, b. Bristol, Sept. 11, 1873 ; m. Everett C. Cloudman, of Alexandria. Res. Reading, Mass. Four children.

b. Tellis Ruez, b. New Hampton, Dec. 5, 1876. Res. Windham Junction.

c. Frank Bernard, b. Franklin, Mar. 17, 1880.

4. Arthur, b. Contoocook, Feb. 5, 1860. Settled in Bristol, 1879, and m. Jan. 25, 1880, Margaret H., dau. of Merrick B. and Hannah S. (Calley) Hight, b. New Hampton, Feb. 7, 1861. He was a manufacturer and dealer in lumber ; d. Mar. 3, 1898, ae. 38-0-28. She m. (2) Nov. 26, 1902, George A. Gates. He was a mason, b. Westmore, Vt., Oct. 4, 1853, and was drowned in Newfound lake, Apr. 15, 1903, ae. 49-6-11.

5. Homer Harden, b. C., Apr. 13, 1863 ; m. Aug. 27, 1900, Clara J., dau. of William T. Oakley. (See.) He is a manufacturer of lumber in Bristol. No children. Methodist, Republican, Odd Fellow, Mason.

6. Edith S., b. New Hampton, Apr. 13, 1874; d. Sept. 22, 1881, ae. 7-5-9.

THE INGALLS FAMILY

1. Those bearing the name of Ingalls in Bristol are evidently the descendants of Capt. Samuel Ingalls, b. Andover, Mass., May 7, 1683. He settled in Haverhill, Mass., but removed, in 1720, to Chester, where, in 1721, he was granted a mill privilege on agreement to erect a saw-mill within one year. He was a selectman in Chester three years, was one of a committee to erect a church, and, in 1732, erected the first frame house in that town. He d. Oct. 6, 1747, ae. 64-4-29. He had nine children, of whom one was

2. Samuel, b. Sept. 15, 1712. He is supposed to be identical with Samuel, the father of Jonathan and Ebenezer, mentioned below. He was a resident of Sandown and evidently

spent his last days in New Chester. In March, 1782, New Chester voted to exempt him from a poll-tax. Of his children, Ebenezer (No. 3) and Jonathan (No. 4 following) settled in New Chester.

3. Ebenezer was a settler on the Oren Nelson farm west of Danforth brook, while Jonathan settled on the east side of the brook. Both were here as early as 1771, and each served one term in the Revolutionary army from New Chester. Ebenezer served as selectman in 1776, and soon after removed to New Hampton (See p. 252), and Jonathan succeeded to his farm.

4. Jonathan m. Martha Locke, a sister of Thomas Locke (See), probably his second m. The town records say Jonathan Ingalls m. Edna Hastings, Nov. 25, 1813, probably his third m. He removed to Canada with a portion of his family.

CHILDREN

*5. Jonathan, supposed to have been b. about 1765.
6. Joanna, who m. Daniel Heath, Mar. 8, 1785, a dau. probably.
7. Samuel, m. Betsey, dau. of John Clough. (See.)
8. James, b. Bristol, July, 3, 1772; m. Ruth, dau. of David Sleeper (See), b. Mar. 4, 1774. In 1837, they removed to Durham, Lower Canada, where they were farmers. Methodists. Children :

    a. David, b. Bristol, May 31, 1796. Settled in Bristol, Mich.
    b. Jonathan, b. B., Sept. 23, 1798.
    c. Jethro, b. B., Oct. 17, 1801.   *d.* Mary, b. B., Nov. 23, 1803.
    e. Edmond, b. Mar. 26, 1809. Was a Methodist minister.
    f. Orpha, b. June 5, 1811.   *g.* James, b. May 4, 1813.
    h. Elvira, b. Apr. 10, 1815.   *i.* Betsey L., b. Feb. —, 1818.

9. Abigail, b. B., Nov. 26, 1774; m. Daniel Heath, Nov. 12, 1795.
10. Olive, b. B., Aug. 4, 1780; m. William Holt, June 23, 1795.
11. Nanna, b. B., May 2, 1782.   12. Daniel, b. B., June 19, 1784.

(5) Jonathan Ingalls, b. 1765, m. Mar. 8, 1785, Abigail Cleveland, a sister to John Cleveland. They were the first settlers on what was afterward known as the town farm. He became involved financially through the dishonesty of another, and lost his farm. He then purchased what is now the Edwin T. Pike farm, his buildings being on the east side of the highway. Jonathan Ingalls and his wife were of deep religious convictions and were members of the first Methodist class organized in Bristol in 1801. She d. Jan. 10, 1833 ; he went to Michigan with his son, Charles, in 1836, and there d. in 1843, ae. 78.

CHILDREN, all born in Bristol

13. Betsey, b. Oct. 12, 1785 ; m. Aaron Nelson. (See.)
14. Hannah, b. Apr. 3, 1787; m. Ezekiel Smith.
15. Dolly, b. Mar. 12, 1789.
16. Patty, b. Apr. 16, 1791 ; d. at five years of age.
17. Sally, b. July 17, 1793 ; m. John Brown. (See.)
18. Polly, b. Oct. 6, 1795 ; m. John Tirrell. (See.)
19. John, b. Mar. 21, 1798; m. Laura Allen, a niece of Col. Ethan

Allen, removed to Iowa. A son, Timothy, emigrated to California, and became wealthy.

20. Irena, b. Mar. 22, 1800.

21. Susan, b. B., May 19, 1802; m. Nov. 6, 1823, John Fowler, son of Abner, b. Sanbornton, Aug. 3, 1800. He d. 1833, in Hill; she d. in Warner, Apr. 6, 1864, ae. 61-10-17. Children :

    a. Lizzie Ann, b. Sanbornton, July 30, 1825; m. Samuel H. Minard. She d. Mar. 10, 1859, ae. 33-7-10. Four children, all d. He went to California.

    b. Mary Abigail, b. S., Aug. 3, 1826; m. (1) Luther A. Shedd, Penacook. Child : Harriet, d.; he d., she went West and m. (2)—— Clark. She d. Feb. 6, 1880 or '81. Child : Oscar M. Clark, res. Michigan.

    c. Susan Augusta, b. Hill, May 24, 1836; m. Daniel G. S. Davis, and d. Canaan, June 25, 1872, ae. 36-1-1.

    d. Harriet Adeline, b. H., Feb. 19, 1844; m. Jan. 5, 1860, Oscar F. Washburn. He was a corporal 4th Regt., N. H. Vols., and d. Aug. 13, 1864, at Fort Monroe, Va. She m. (2) John D. Webber. (See.)

    e. John Wesley, b. Bristol, Mar. 6, 1848; m. (1) Clara Goodwin, of Warren. Three children ; m. (2) Susan Elliott. He d. Warren, Sept. 14, 1888, ae. 40-6-8. She res. No. Woodstock. Three children.

22. Jonathan, b. B., June 23, 1804; m. Nov. 13, 1828, Eliza M. Harrington, b. Westboro, Mass., Jan. 9, 1806, and d. Aug. 3, 1831, in Waterford, N. Y., ae. 25-6-24. He m., Jan. 1, 1835, Eliza Shepherd, dau. of Harvey and Temperance (Worthington) Spalding, b. Worthington, Mass., Nov. 24, 1808, and d. Green Bay, Wis., Apr. 27, 1877, ae. 68-5-3. He d. Green Bay, Feb. 27, 1875. ae. 70-8-4. He left Bristol about 1830. Res. Waterford ; Lockport, N. Y. ; in 1850 settled in Green Bay, Wis., where he had first shingle-mill in that section ; later operated a large carriage factory. Children :

    a. Frances Augusta, b. Waterford, N. Y., Feb. 20, 1831. She m. Nov. 16, 1853, Myron P. Lindsley. Children: (1) Thales, b. Green Bay, Feb. 23, 1853. (2) Eliza Lelia, b. G. B., Mar. 15, 1859, m. Feb. 9, 1883, Frank B. Desnoyers. (3) Myron P., d. in Madison, Wis., Jan. 16, 1883. She res. Green Bay.

    b. Charles Edward, b. Lockport, N. Y., Jan. 6, 1836. Served through the Civil war as paymaster ; was 20 years in New Orleans custom-house. In 1771, he m. Mrs. Maygie Peters, of New York ; d. Aug. 18, 1893, ae. 57-7-12.

    c. George Albert, b. L., Jan. 24, 1840, and d. July 22, 1840.

    d. George Henry, b. L., Oct. 23, 1841; m. July 6, 1876, Josephine Mojer, of New York. No children.

    e. Mary Eliza, b. L., Oct. 27, 1845 ; m. Feb. 20, 1867, Thomas L. Best. Child : Lavis Freeman, b. Sept 13, 1877. Res. Green Bay.

23. Sherburn Sanborn, b. B., June 2, 1807. He m. at Westville, N. Y., Jan. 1, 1833, Mary Jane Schoff. She was b. in Guildhall, Vt., Feb. 4, 1812, and d. Aug. 4, 1876, at Constable, N. Y., ae. 64-6-0. He d. June 3, 1879. in Chateaugay, N. Y., ae. 72-0-1. Farmer. "They had eight of the handsomest girls in the state." Children :

    a. Charles W., b. Godmanchester, L. C., Nov. 25, 1833; m. Nov. 29, 1859, Lizzie A. Bowers. Res. Boston, Mass.

    b. Marian F., b. G., Apr. 5. 1835; m. Curtis Stevens, Concord, Mass., Nov. 29, 1856.

    c. Sophia S., b. Brasher, N. Y., Jan. 1, 1837; m. Hiram D. Shepherd at Chateaugay, Nov. 29, 1866, and d. Apr. 18, 1872, ae. 35-3-17.

    d. Alzina S., b. B., Jan. 29, 1839; m. Nathan D. Roberts, Feb.

27, 1859, in Huntington, L. C.; m. Feb. 13, 1873, at Bradford, Vt., James C. Stevens.

    e. Susan F., b. Bombay, N. Y., Feb. 4, 1841; m. Bradford S. Wright, May 5, 1861, at Chateaugay.

    f. Lucy J., b. Brasher, May 15, 1842; m. Senaca Marks, May 25, 1862, at Messena, N. Y.

    g. Oscar F., b. B., Mar. 9, 1844; m. Susie C. Dolby, Dec. 3, 1863, at Lowell, Mass., and d. Boston, Mass., Dec. 13, 1865, ae. 21-9-4.

    h. James A., b. Constable, N. Y., Nov. 11, 1846; d. in C., Sept. 27, 1849, ae. 2-10-16.

    i. Martha M., b. C., Apr. 30, 1849; m. Hiram D. Shepherd, Jan. 3, 1874, at Malone, N. Y.

    j. Maria H., b. C., Apr. 10, 1851; m. I. Newton Perkins, at Bradford, Vt., Sept. 3, 1874.

    k. Clara V., b. C., Jan. 11, 1853; m. Julius C. Dennis, Nov. 30, 1871, Malone; m. Jan., 1889, Hyman Carpenter, at Middlebury, Vt.

    l. George A., b. C., Jan. 22, 1858; d. Sept. 9, 1858.

  24. Keziah, b. B., 1810; m. Milton Sawyer. (See.)

  25. Charles Wesley, b. B., Apr. 21, 1812; m. 1834, Catherine, dau. of Hall J. Hamm, b. B., Mar. 21, 1811; d. Harbor Springs, Mich., June 22, 1882, ae. 71-3-1. He d. same place, Feb. 9, 1889, ae. 76-9-18. He went to Boston; about 1836, to Ionia Co., Mich., with his wife, two children, and aged father, where he was one of the first settlers. Went to California by the overland route in 1850. Returned and elected member of the Michigan legislature in 1852. (See Roll of Honor.)

----

    1.   Ebenezer Ingalls (No. 3, of p. 250) was in Bristol as early as 1771. He is supposed to have removed to New Hampton about 1777. One child was

    2.   Gilman, b. Bristol, Feb. 4, 1775. He m. Abigail, dau. of Timothy Emerson, b. Alexandria, Apr. 18, 1778. About 1810, he returned to Bristol and settled on the Chase farm in Dist. No. 8; later res. on Cross street, and still later on the farm first settled by his father, where he d., May. 23, 1855, ae. 80-3-19; she d. Oct. 9, 1860, ae. 82-5-21.

CHILDREN

  *3. Gilman, b. New Hampton, Jan. 29, 1798.

  4. Abigail, b. N. H., Nov. 3, 1799; m. Osman Gale, b. Alexandria, Feb. 13, 1799. Both d. in family of Calvin Golden, Bristol. He d. Aug. 22, 1877, ae. 78-6-9; she d. Aug. 12, 1876, ae. 76-9-9. Children:

    a. Elizabeth F., b. Sept. 30, 1820; m. Calvin Golden. (See.)

    b. Matilda J., b. May 7, 1822; m. Isaac Follansbee; res. Hill.

    c. Emeline H., b. Dec. 15, 1823; m. Hiram Esterbrook, Hill. He d. Bedford, where she res.

    d. Mary M. A., b. Sept. 8, 1825; m. Wells Sargent. He d. Manchester, where she res.

    e. Sarah M., b. July 7, 1827; d. Jan. 27, 1858, ae. 30-6-20; unm.

    f. Gilman E., b. Sept. 12, 1829; m. (1) —— Heath. Res. Manchester.

  *5. Josiah Emerson, b. N. H., Sept. 6, 1802.

  6. Lydia, b. N. H., Jan. 28, 1804; m. Pattee Gale. (See.)

  7. Phebe, b. N. H., Feb. 8, 1806; m. Stephen Gale. (See.)

  8. Mary Jane, b. N. H., July 18, 1807; d. unm., Mar. 6, 1845, ae. 37-7-18.

9. Harvey Nichols, b. N. H., Oct. 1, 1808; m. Sept., 1832, Sarah, dau. of Abigail (Swain) Weeks, b. Sanbornton, Oct. 10, 1811 ; d. Franklin, Jan. 8, 1864, ae. 52-2-28. He m., Dec. 8, 1865, Betsey Gilman Ayer, dau. of John. Was a cabinet maker in Bristol ; in 1847, went to Franklin, and, in 1867, to Manchester, returning to Franklin, April, 1886, where he d., Dec. 22, 1890, ae. 82-2-21. After leaving Bristol, was a farmer. Children :

    a. Horace Sanborn, b. New Hampton, Aug. 29, 1834 ; m. Sarah Ann Hill, Standish Plain, P. Q., Nov. 27, 1859 ; d. Franklin, Dec. 18, 1863, ae. 29-3-19.

    b. Amanda Melvina, b. Sanbornton, July 4, 1836; m. Feb. 14, 1876, Alphonso Crosby, China, Me. Res. on her father's farm at Franklin.

    c. Hiram Berry, b. Bristol, Dec. 29, 1840 ; m. Aug., 1860, Helen Carleton, and d. Manchester, May 5, 1881, ae. 40-4-6. Child : Daughter, b. Aug. 27, 1862 ; m. Oliver F. George, Pittsfield.

    d. Helen Ann, b. B., Jan. 14, 1844 ; d. Franklin, Nov. 29, 1860, ae. 16-10-15.

    e. Narcia Elmira, b. B., Jan. 20, 1847 ; d. unm., Feb. 8, 1870, ae. 23-0-18.

10. Timothy, b. Jan. 19, 1810 ; d. young.

11. Luther, b. Bristol, Nov. 13, 1815 ; m. Eliza Ann Jewell, dau. of John. Succeeded his father on farm. She d. Mar. 6, 1848, ae. 24-0-22. He m., Nov., 1849, Sarah Ann, dau. of Benjamin Emmons, b. Stewartstown, Oct. 27, 1823, and d. in Boston, Mass., Oct. 23, 1891, ae. 67-11-26. He d. Feb. 11, 1852, ae. 36-2-28. Child :

    a. Charles Luther, b. Bristol, Sept. 12, 1851 ; m. Sept 17, 1870. Children : (1) Lillian Maud, b. Lowell, Mass., Feb. 9, 1871 ; m. —— Perkins. (2) Arthur Forrest, b. L., Jan. 19, 1873. (3) Clarence Leland, b. L., Nov. 15, 1881. (4) Milo Luther, b. L., Mar. 21, 1887.

12. George Washington, b. B., Aug. 17, 1817 ; m. Oct. 28, 1840, Mary, dau. of Robert and Betsey (Currier) Lane, a resident of the Borough, b. Aug. 20, 1818, in Crownport, N. Y. He lived on Merrimack street, where he d. Aug. 11, 1853, of cancer, ae. 35-11-24. His widow m. June 9, 1873, Nathaniel Miner, and d. Jerseyville, Ill., May 10, 1894, ae. 75-8-20. Children :

    a. Ellen Maria, b. Bristol, Aug. 6, 1841 ; m. Nov. 6, 1859, Edward Quinn, of Laconia. One child.

    b. Lucy Augusta, b. B., Nov. 30, 1843; m.

    c. Rose Jane, b B., Jan. 11, 1847 ; m. Apr. 3, 1861, Webster Maxfield.

13. Nancy B., b. B., Oct. 25, 1819 ; m. Jan. 10, 1839, John L. Colby, and res. Franklin, where she d. Apr. 3, 1844, ae. 24-5-8. He d. Franklin, 1888. Children:

    a. Georgia Anna, b. Franklin, 1840 ; m. Dec. 14, 1862, Dr. John F. Dodge. She d. Franklin, Mar. 26, 1866, ae. 26. He res. Providence, R. I. Child : (1) Lenora G., b. Aug. 19, 1864; m. Mar. 22, 1887, Charles F. Burnham.

    b. Charles Gilman, b. F., Apr. 8, 1842.

    c. Nancy B., b. F., 1844 ; d. ae. 6. months.

(3) Gilman Ingalls, b. Jan. 29, 1798, m. (1) Nancy Bowen, (2) Oct. 9, 1823, Sarah, dau. of Dr. Thomas Roberts, of Alexandria, b. Nov. 3, 1801. They lived west side of highway on Hemp hill; house destroyed by fire. They removed to Oren Nelson farm to care for his parents, and there he d. July 6, 1862, ae. 64-5-7 ; she d. Jan. 24, 1862, ae. 60-2-21.

CHILDREN

*14. Gustavus Washington, b. Bristol, May 21, 1824.

15. Amanda Jane, b. B., June 11, 1826; m. (1) Joseph Rollins, (2) George W. Dow. (See.)

16. Lucinda Hibbard, b. B., Mar. 6, 1828; m. Andrew J. Waite, a tinsmith in Bristol. No children. She d. Bristol, Feb. 26, 1854, ae. 25-11-20. He d. Lowell, Mass., July 26, 1855, ae. 36.

17. Mahala Plumer, b. B., Feb. 8, 1830; m. Oren Nelson. (See.)

18. George Harvey, b. B., Feb. 5, 1832; m. Helen Louise, dau. of John R. Edmonds, b. Warner, Mar. 25, 1833. He was a superior musician. It is claimed that he was the leader of the Methodist choir at 12 years of age. Was a member of Hilton Head (S. C.) Post band during the Civil war. Res. Concord 1849-'63, when he returned to Bristol; kept restaurant in Abel block and was leader of a cornet band here. He d. Warner, Feb. 8, 1899, ae. 67-0-3. Children:

 a. Alphonso Daniel, b. Dec. 3, 1855; m. Dec. 9, 1882, Mary F. Hardy; she d. and he m., Jan. 1, 1889, Mary Elizabeth Sawyer.

 b. Susie Angie, b. Mar. 8, 1858; m. Dec. 29, 1885, Charles H. Osgood, Warner.

19. Mary Philbrick, b. B., Jan. 3, 1834; m. Lewis F. Pattee. (See.)

20. Ann Maria, b. B., Feb. 16, 1836; d. Sept. 1, 1856, ae. 20-6-15.

21. Horace Langdon, b. B., Aug. 31, 1838; m. Mar. 9, 1869, Mary Pauline, dau. Abel L. and Pauline (Phelps) Crosby, b. Groton, Apr. 21, 1844. They res. Concord, where he is janitor of the state house. Served several terms as door-keeper of house of representatives. (See Roll of Honor.) Is a Republican, Mason, G. A. R. Children:

 a. Linna Augusta, b. Hill, May 13, 1873.

 b. Della Leona, b. Groton, Mar. 22, 1877.

22. John Henry, b. B., Apr. 16, 1841; d. Dec. 5, 1863, of disease contracted in the army, ae. 22-7-19. (See Roll of Honor.)

23. Frances Amelia, b. B., Aug. 13, 1843; m. Capt. George F. Prescott. (See.)

24. Alferetta Augusta, b. B., Oct. 12, 1846; d. Oct. 19, 1868, ae. 22-0-7.

(5) Josiah E. Ingalls, b. Sept. 6, 1802, m. Oct. 23, 1825, Dorothy, dau. of Josiah and Sally (Ladd) Sanborn, b. Alexandria, Sept. 19, 1805. She d. Bristol, Nov. 14, 1831, ae. 26-1-25, and he m., Oct. 18, 1832, Lucy Ferrin, dau. of Jonathan and Hannah (Ball) Ladd, b. Hebron, Mar. 3, 1803, and d. Alexandria, Nov. 24, 1890, ae. 87-8-21. He d. Alexandria, Oct. 28, 1860, ae. 58-1-22. Was a farmer in Alexandria.

CHILDREN

25. Josiah Sanborn, b. Alexandria, Dec. 13, 1827; m July 16, 1851, Laura L., dau. William Mudgett. (See.) They res. Concord, where he is a manufacturer of essences. No children.

26. Sullivan, b. A., Jan. 15, 1831; m. Sept. 19, 1854, Caroline M., dau. of James and Lorana (Fellows) Berry, b. A., July 31, 1835. She d. Jan. 26, 1866, ae. 30-5-25, and he m., May 1, 1867, Sarah F., dau. of Sanders Herbert. (See.) He was a wheelwright in Alexandria and Bristol, where he d., Sept. 14, 1876, ae. 45-7-29. His widow d. Bristol, Oct. 4, 1898, ae. 56-7-10. Children:

 a. Emma Angenette, b. Nov. 7, 1855; d. Feb. 7, 1857, ae. 1-3-0.

 b. Ida Nellie, b. July 4, 1858; d. July 10, 1863, ae. 5-0-6.

 c. Clara Maynette, b. Bristol, Oct. 31, 1868. Has been for three years a teacher in the graded school.

d. Ardena Lougardie, b. B., Aug. 21, 1871. Is a private school teacher.

27. Harriet Elizabeth Brooks, b. Alexandria, Apr. 13, 1837; m. Mar. 17, 1870, Charles L. Dalton, a farmer in Alexandria.

(14) Gustavus W. Ingalls, b. Bristol, May 21, 1824, m. June 20, 1847, Mary C. Sleeper, dau. of David (See), b. Sept. 7, 1827. He was a superior musician. Manufacturer of organ reed boards at Worcester, Mass., where he now res., retired. (See Roll of Honor.) She d. Apr. 21, 1903, ae. 75-7-14.

CHILDREN

28. Mary Susie, b. Concord, Oct. 2, 1849; d. Aug. 3, 1855, ae. 5-10-1.
29. Walter Gustavus, b. C., Aug. 10, 1856; m. Jan. 20, 1879, Mary Gertrude Leland, who d. Worcester, Mass., May 21, 1883, and he m., Oct. 12, 1885, Nettie M. Dunbar. Children :
    a. Lottie Mildred, b. Jan. 31, 1880.
    b. Francis Dunbar, b. Mar. 4, 1887.

THE JEFFERSON FAMILY

1. Rev. Albert Willis Jefferson, son of Rev. Benjamin F. and Anna (Barber) Jefferson, was b. Parishville, N. Y., Aug. 21, 1872. He graduated from Whitefield High school; attended New Hampton Institution, 1893-'94; graduated from Cobb Divinity school, Lewiston, Me., 1897; ordained at Whitefield, June 6, 1897. Was pastor of Free Baptist church, June, 1897– Mar. 1, 1900; since, serving a church in Pawtucket, R. I. He m., June 9, 1897, Lenona L., dau. of Nathan W. Libbey, b. Whitefield, Apr. 9, 1873.

THE JEFFROY FAMILY

1. Charles L. Jeffroy, son of John and Harriet Sherwood Jeffroy, was b. West Chelmsford, Mass., Aug. 13, 1856. He m., Sept. 22, 1892, Abbie May, dau. of Joel Gurdy. (See.) He came to Bristol about 1888, and is employed in weave-room at the woolen-mill.

CHILD

2. Dorothy, b. Bristol, June 22, 1894; d. Oct. 18, 1898, ae. 4-3-26.

THE JESSEMAN FAMILY

1. George Edward Jesseman, son of Jewell and Mary (Blodgett) Jesseman, was b. Dorchester, Feb. 17, 1852. He was one of 16 children. He m., June 30, 1872, Abbie Frances Waldron, one of 13 children, a dau. of Nathaniel and Betsey (Davis) Waldron, b. Dorchester, Nov. 30, 1855. A farmer and lumberman in Bristol since 1888.

2. Bert Henry, b. Dorchester, May 27, 1875; m. Sept. 26, 1896, Alice Marion Remick, dau. of Augustus. Farmer and lumberman. Children :
    a. Bertha Alice, b. Bristol, Dec. 27, 1897 ; d. Nov. 16, 1899, ae. 1-10-19.
    b. Clarence Everett, b. B., Dec. 23, 1900.
3. Eva Lillian, b. D., July 19, 1877; m. Sept. 16, 1896, Thomas E. O'Brien, b. Natick, Mass. Shoemaker. Child :
    a. Helen May, b. Natick, Apr. 13, 1903.
4. Edith Maud, b. D., May 21, 1882; m. Nov. 8, 1898, Fred A. Bean, of Plymouth. Children :
    a. Morris Fred, b. Bristol, Oct. 26, 1899.
    b. Hattie Mildred, b. Laconia, Jan. 29, 1902.
5. Edna Gertrude, b. D., Jan. 29, 1887.

THE JEWELL FAMILY

1. Newton Isaac Jewell, son of William A. and Sarah T. (Kemp) Jewell, was b. Salisbury, Vt., Dec. 22, 1846. He m., Mar. 8, 1871, Lucia A., dau. Samuel W. and Mary A. (Batchelder) Dunbar, b. Orange, Dec. 25, 1852. He came to Bristol from Groton, in 1888, and here d. Mar. 28, 1893, ae. 46-3-6. Carpenter. Mrs. Jewell res. North Bristol.

2. Arthur William, b. Groton, Aug. 25, 1872. Employee in woolen-mill. Member of K. of P.
3. Harry Bert, b. G., Feb. 10, 1878 ; m. Aug. 21, 1897, Bertha F., dau. Joseph Cyr. (See.) An employee in woolen-mill. K. of P. Child :
    a. Maurice Bert, b. Bristol, Dec. 5, 1898; d. Apr. 1, 1899.
4. Clarence Edward, b. G., Mar. 4, 1882. K. of P.
5. Dana Grover, b. G., Apr. 28, 1886.
6. Ernest, b. Bristol, Sept. 16, 1889.
7. Walter Bartlett, b. B., July 24, 1893.

THE JEWETT FAMILY

1. Aaron Jewett, son of Aaron, was b. Dracut, Mass., Mar. 29, 1797. He m., Jan. 27, 1819, Hannah, dau. of Job and Hannah Eaton, b. Dracut, Mar. 15, 1798, and d. Nov. 14, 1849, ae. 51-7-29. He m. (2) Jan. 1, 1852, Lucy J. Hill, and about this time came to Bristol. For a few years was engaged in the manufacture of bedsteads. He d. Feb. 20, 1882, ae. 84-10-21. She d. in Alexandria, Apr. 8, 1898, ae. almost 85 years. Republican.

2. Phebe L., m. Frankie Coburn, May 19, 1844. Res. Westfield, Mass.
3. Hannah M., m. Theodore Hamblet, Feb. 19, 1846. Res. Dracut, Mass.
4. Moses F., served in Union army from Lowell, Mass.; d. Jan. 23, 1865, ae. 37.

1. Alpha C. Jewett, a brother of above, was b. Wentworth, Feb. 28, 1808, and d. Laconia in the home of his son, Alonzo W., Apr. 29, 1887, ae. 79-2-1. He m. Hannah, dau. of Peter Flanders, b. Plymouth, and d. Bristol, Apr. 11, 1877, ae. 57. Carpenter. Republican. Came to Bristol about 1859.

CHILDREN

2. Alonzo W., b. Wentworth, Sept. 27, 1839, came to Bristol with his parents and m. Apr. 23, 1861, Annette Locke, dau. of Levi (See), b. June 27, 1842. (See Roll of Honor.) Was in the meat business in Bristol; a carriage manufacturer in Lowell, Mass., where Mrs. Jewett d. Apr. 29, 1878, ae. 35-10-2. He m. Aug. 5, 1879, Mrs. Celestia Davis Angell, Lowell. Returned to Bristol, and, since about 1882, has been in ice and milk business, Laconia. Republican, Methodist, Mason. Children:

    a. Katie Blanche, b. Bristol, June 5. 1866; d. Nov. 11, 1890, at Laconia, ae. 24-5-6.

    b. Henry Charles, b. B., May 24, 1874; d. Lowell, June 22, 1875, ae. 1-0-28.

    c. Arthur Alonzo W., b. Apr. 18, 1878.

3. Charles Aaron, carriage manufacturer, Lowell, Mass., and Laconia; now living Gilmanton.

4. Martha Woodbury, b. Wentworth, Apr. 8, 1845; m. Timothy Tilton. (See.)

---

1. Jeremiah Jewett, a brother of above, was b. in Wentworth. He m. Mrs. Mary A. (Flanders) Eames, dau. of Moses and Sarah (Bean) Flanders. He was a carpenter and farmer; came to Bristol about 1858; res. Summer street. She d. Nov. 5, 1889, ae. 66-1-5; he d. Feb. 3, 1896, ae. 84-2-.

CHILD

2. Etta, b. Lowell, Apr. 25, 1857; m. Smith D. Fellows. (See.)

THE JOHNSON FAMILIES

1. Moses Johnson, son of Moses and Anna (Morse) Johnson, was b. in Hudson, Dec. 17, 1769. He m. June 6, 1793, Polly, dau. of Rev. William Elliott, b. Mason, Aug. 2, 1773. They settled on a farm in the Nelson neighborhood, as early as 1815. He d. in the family of his son, Jonathan, in Bridgewater, Aug. 5, 1860, ae. 90-7-18; she d. in Plymouth in same family, May 22, 1866, ae. 92-9-20.

CHILDREN

2. William, b. July 7, 1794; killed at Salisbury, May 22, 1802, ae. 7-10-15.

3. Moses, b. Aug. 11, 1796; m. Hannah, dau. of Jonathan Huntington, Jan. 21, 1816. (See.) He d. Apr. 26, 1881, ae. 84-8-15. Had eight children.

4. Polly, b. Aug. 16, 1798; d. of spotted fever, Nov. 22, 1815, ae. 17-3-6.

5. Dolly M., b. Warner, Mar. 23, 1800; m. May 11, 1822, John Fletcher, b. Chelmsford, Mass., Dec. 11, 1794; d. May 1, 1842, ae. 47-4-20.

17

She m. (2) Mar. 28, 1846, Maj. Jesse Colburn, who d. 1860. She d. Tyngsboro, Mass., Jan. 4, 1883, ae. 82-9-11. Children:

    a. Laura M., b. Lowell, Mass., Apr. 1, 1823; m. July 3, 1847, James Harris. He d. Tyngsboro, Apr. 20, 1883. She res. Tyngsboro.

    b. John E., b. L., Oct. 1, 1824; m., Oct. 1, 1847, Ruth Stearns. and d. California, in 1851, without issue.

    c. Josiah M., b. Halifax, Mass., Jan. 14, 1828; m. Jan. 23, 1851. Adaline J. Eastman, of Rumney. Res. Nashua. Six children, all deceased.

  6. Hannah U., b. Aug. 31, 1802; m. Edmond Cheney. (See.)
  7. Moody, ⎫ b. May 23, 1805; ⎰ d. 1815.
*8. Merrill, ⎭ ⎱
  9. Eliza, b. Jan. 1, 1808; m. Kimball Whitney. (See.)
  10. Sarah, b. Apr. 18, 1810; m. Edmond Cheney. (See.)
  11. Jonathan Huntington, b. June 25, 1812; m. Eliza A., dau. Rufus and Eliza (Murray) Wiggin, b. Wolfeboro, Nov. 4, 1816; d. Lynn, Mass., Dec. 23, 1895, ae. 79-1-19. Jonathan H. Johnson was a farmer, a member of the Congregational church, a great worker in the Sunday-school, and a lover of debate. He was for many summers superintendent of a Sunday-school held in a schoolhouse near Ariel Pike's in Bridgewater. He settled, in 1843, on the farm which embraced site of the state fish hatchery in 1862, removed to Plymouth, returning to Bridgewater, in 1873, where he d. Jan. 28, 1887, ae. 74-7-3. No children. He was emphatically a peacemaker.
  12. Elliott Andrew, b. Bristol, Feb. 15, 1815; m. Apr., 1840, Mary S. Caneley, dau. of Samuel and Phebe Howe, b. New Hampton, and d. Abington, Mass., Jan. (Apr.) 14, 1891. In 1836, went to Haverhill, Mass., and to Lowell, Mass., in 1863; in 1879, to Bridgewater, thence to Chelmsford, Mass., where he has since been in the mercantile business. Children:

    a. Laura, b. Bridgewater; m. Sept. 25, 1858, George S. Adams.
    b. Caroline H., b. Haverhill, Mass.; m. Apr., 1861, John Hobbs.
    c. Jennie S., b. H.; m. George Sinclair.
    d. Medora, b. H.; m. Eldorus Smith, Bridgewater.

  13. Joseph Varnum, b. Jan. 8, 1819; d. young.

(8) Merrill Johnson, b. May 23, 1805, m. Hannah, dau. of Melvin and Hannah (Wade) Holmes, in 1828. She was b. Bridgewater, Mass., 1803, and d. Dec. 11, 1835, ae. 32; he d. Dec. 1, 1835, ae. 30-6-8, both in Goffstown of typhus fever.

CHILDREN

  14. Eliza Ann, b. Sept. 28, 1828; m. James Monroe.
  15. Daughter, d. in infancy.
  16. Melvin, b. Campton, Jan. 14, 1833; m. Aug. 7, 1856, Maria H. Elliott. She was the dau. of Daniel, and was b. Rumney, Jan. 23, 1836. Was a blacksmith and livery keeper in Bristol for some years. Children:

    a. Perley Melvin, b. Bridgewater, Sept. 30, 1857; m. Mary A. Bayley, b. Plymouth, Apr. 23, 1857. He res. Bristol, 1880-'90. now Plymouth. Child: Harry Perley, b. Holderness, Dec. 7, 1877.
    b. Frank Merrill, b. Bristol, May 12, 1862; m. Mar. 22, 1891, Elsie M., dau. Joshua Rowen, b. Dorchester, Jan. 4, 1870. Children: (1) Ernest Melvin, b. Bridgewater, Mar. 14, 1892. (2) Hattie Maria, b. B., July 1, 1897. (3) Charles Karl, b. Bristol, May 20, 1899.

  17. Israel Franklin, b. Goffstown, May, 1835. At 21 years of age went West. No further information.

1.   Jeremiah Johnson, son of Jeremiah and Olive (Shepard)
Johnson, was b. Epping, May 9, 1797. He m. (1) Polly
Edgerly, of Northwood; (2) Sept. 1, 1830, Elizabeth, dau. of
Daniel Sleeper. (See.) He was a farmer, in District No. 7,
1832-'35, when he removed to Bridgewater, where he d. Dec.
21, 1867, ae. 70-7-12. She d. Everett, Mass., Jan. 8, 1893, ae.
87-5-20. Methodists.

CHILDREN

2.   Melinda Morgan ; m. Charles M. Barnard
3.   Elizabeth Olive, m. Morrison P. Haynes, Tilton.
4.   Levi Dolloff, b. Bridgewater, Jan. 19, 1832; m. 1860, Ellen Caroline, dau. Samuel H. Rollins. (See.) She d. Dec. 31, 1864, ae. 24-6-, and
he m. Aug. 3, 1865, Abbie J. Hanchett. He was a photographer in Bristol ;
town clerk, 1864-'66; removed to Vineland, N. J., where he has been a
photographer. Children :
  a.   Nellie Florence, b. Bristol, Feb. 2, 1863 ; m. Frank D. Dolloff.
  (See.)
  b.   Alice R., b. Vineland, June 21, 1876.

5.   John Edgerly, b. Bristol, Mar. 24, 1834; m. June 8, 1858, Ellen
Maria, dau. of Eben and Betsey Cummings, b. Thetford, Vt., Aug. 26,
1833. He d. in Everett, Mass., Nov. 25, 1896, ae. 62-8-1. He was a
Methodist, active in church work. Mrs. Johnson res. Everett. Children :
  a.   Mary Elizabeth, b. Hodgdon, Me., Apr. 26, 1861 ; m. Charles
  M. Scoville, June 19, 1888.
  b.   Alice Luella, b. Vineland, N. J., June 1, 1869; d. July 19,
  1869.
  c.   Ellen Louise, b. V., Sept. 5, 1870.
  d.   Gertrude Florence, b. Glassboro, N. J., Jan. 6, 1872.

6.   Daniel Sleeper, b. Bridgewater, Mar. 28, 1836; m. Mary Noyes,
dau. of Rodney Hammond, b. Bridgewater, Mar. 14, 1840. He d. in
Boston as the result of a surgical operation, Dec. 21, 1875, ae. 39-8-23.
He was a farmer in Bridgewater. Methodist. Children :
  a.   Ora Paul, b. Hartford, Vt., Feb. 5, 1863.
  b.   Ula May, b. Bridgewater, Jan. 8, 1865 ; d. young.
  c.   Herman Fisher, b. B., July 12, 1870.

7.   Warren Marshall, b. B., July 9, 1838. He emigrated to Utah, and
became an elder of the Mormon church. He was a good man — evidently
a devoted and sincere adherent of that church. In sending the genealogy of his families for this history, he wrote : "I am a member of the
Church of Jesus Christ of Latter Day Saints, and I fully believe in every
principle of this church." He was for many years postmaster at Lee's
Ferry, Arizona. He d. at Byron, Wyoming, in Mar., 1902, ae. 63-8-. He
had two families :
  He m. Oct. 4, 1869, Permelia Jane, dau. of Jonathan Smith, b. July
12, 1850, in Farmington, Utah. Children :
  a.   Mary Eveleth, b. Glendale, Utah, May 6, 1872.
  b.   Warren Marshall, b. G., Oct. 5, 1874 ; d. Oct. 5, 1874.
  c.   Melinda, b. G., Dec. 3, 1875 ; d. July 5, 1891, ae. 15-7-2.
  d.   Polly Abigail, b. Harrisville, Utah, Oct. 27, 1877.
  e.   Nancy, b. Lees Ferry, Arizona, Nov. 8, 1879.
  f.   Permelia, b. L. F., July 18, 1881 ; d. June 15, 1891, ae. 9-10-27.
  g.   Laura Alice, b. L. F., Sept. 25, 1883; d. June 11, 1891, ae.
  7-8-16.
  h.   Jonathan Smith, b. L. F., Oct. 30, 1885; d. May 19, 1891, ae.
  5-6-19.

    i. Leroy Sunderland, b. L. F., June 12, 1888.
    j. Joseph Smith, b. L. F., Mar. 28, 1891.

    Oct. 28, 1872, he m. Samantha, dau. of Price W. Nelson, b. Oct. 28, 1853, at San Bernardino, Cal.   Children:

    a. Elizabeth, b. Glendale, Apr. 26, 1874.
    b. Jeremiah, b. G., Feb. 24, 1876.
    c. Frank Tilton, b. Lees Ferry, Aug. 3, 1878.
    d. Lydia Ann, b. L. F., Apr. 3, 1880.
    e. Samantha, b. L. F., Apr. 5, 1882.
    f. Lucy, b. L. F., Mar. 30, 1884.
    g. Price Williams, b. L. F., Feb. 2, 1886.
    h. Estella, b. L. F., Dec. 25, 1887.
    i. Warren Elmer, b. L. F., Apr. 27, 1890.

    8.   Leroy Sunderland, b. B., Jan. 11, 1841; m. Apr. 14, 1868, Jerusha Dyer, dau. Seth N. Covell, b. Wellfleet, Mass., June 21, 1844. He is a manufacturer of lumber and veneers, Boston, Mass. Res. Malden, Mass. Children:

    a. Everett Leroy, b. Boston, Mass., Mar. 28, 1869; m. Oct. 19, 1898, Mabel Annie Hayes. Two children.
    b. Frank Wallace, b. Malden, Mar. 28, 1872.
    c. Gilbert Haven, b. M., Mar. 5, 1876.
    d. Ethel May, b. M., Oct. 30, 1878; m. June 3, 1902, Richard B. Hopkins, Jamaica, W. I.

    9.   Charles Wesley, b. B., Nov. 18, 1843; m. Nov. 18, 1869, Ellen Eunice, dau. of William G. and Clarissa H. Fisher, b. Brookfield, Vt., Mar. 2, 1843. Since a young man, has been engaged in the fancy woods business in Boston, with exception of a few years in Grand Rapids, Mich., in same business. Methodist; many years superintendent of Sunday-schools in Everett and Wollaston, Mass.; in 1894, president of Boston Methodist Social Union. Now res. Dorchester, Mass. Children:

    a. Grace Elizabeth, }
    b. Helen Clara,   } b. Everett, Nov. 29, 1875.

    10.   Mary Ann, b. B., Apr. 22, 1846; m. Herman B. Fisher; d. Everett, Jan. 24, 1871, ae. 24-9-2.

---

    1.   **Joseph William Johnson,** son of Charles White and Lizzie L. (Wheet) Johnson, was b. Campton, Jan. 7, 1876. He m., Nov. 8, 1901, Flora Polly, dau. of Cyrus B. and Ellen M. (Couch) Dow, b. Warner, Aug. 1, 1872. He has res. in Bristol since October, 1898; a machinist, Republican, Methodist, Granger.

THE JONES FAMILY

    1.   John Jones was b. in Enfield, Nov. 23, 1812. He m., Dec. 28, 1839, Susan B. Greeley, b. Canaan, Mar. 15, 1815. He d., Apr. 22, 1880, ae. 67-4-29. In 1885, Mrs. Jones made her home in Bristol, where she d., Dec. 26, 1899, ae. 84-9-11.

CHILD

    2.   Lizzie Arabell, b. Enfield, Sept. 25, 1860. She came to Bristol in 1885. Has been an employee in woolen-mill; taught one year in Union district.

THE JUDKINS FAMILY

1. Rev. George Janvrin Judkins, the son of William and Anne Judkins, was b. Kingston, Dec. 21, 1830. He was educated at Kingston Academy, Tilton Seminary, and Wesleyan University, where he graduated 1860. He taught at Kingston Academy five years, and was principal of Tilton Seminary six years. Was ordained as a Methodist Episcopal clergyman at Bristol in 1872, and was stationed at Methuen, Mass., 1872-'75; Newmarket, 1875-'77; was presiding elder of Claremont district, 1877-'81; of Dover district, 1881-'85, when his health failed and he settled on a farm in Bristol village. He was a dairy farmer for several years and then operated a milk route. He has been for a long term of years treasurer of the board of trustees of the New Hampshire Methodist Conference. Republican. He m., Aug. 16, 1860, Almira S. Dolloff, dau. of Abram. (See.) After her m., she was teacher at the Kingston Academy. She has been prominent in the Woman's Foreign Missionary society and church work.

CHILDREN

2. George Dolloff, b. Kingston, Dec. 24, 1864; m. Sept. 4, 1886, Helen A. Ferrin, adopted daughter of Augustus J. Ferrin. (See.) He was associated with his father in business, and d. May 26, 1899, ae. 34-5-2. Methodist, Republican, Granger. Children :

    a. Morris Ferrin, b. Mar. 28, 1888.
    b. A twin brother, d. same day as born.

3. Charles Otis, b. Bristol, Oct. 2, 1868. Is a Methodist clergyman. Educated at Tilton Seminary, East Greenwich Academy, Wesleyan University, Boston University Theological School, graduating in 1895. Ordained deacon, Springfield, Vt., 1898, by Bishop Vincent; elder, at Bellows Falls, Vt., 1900, by Bishop Merrill. Has filled pastorates at Windsor, Vt., Montpelier, Vt., and now at Glens Falls, N. Y. He m., Mar. 30, 1898, Eva Viola, dau. of Abram and Mary (Odell) Austin, b. Yonkers, N. Y., Feb. 26, 1874. Child :

    a. Ruth Elizabeth, b. Jan. 5, 1899.

4. Anne Lydia, b. Methuen, Mass., Sept. 16, 1873; graduated from Wesleyan Academy, Wilbraham, Mass. ; m. Jan. 17, 1901, Rev. Leon K. Willman, a Methodist clergyman, now pastor M. E. church at Montpelier, Vt.

THE KELLY OR KELLEY FAMILIES

1. John Kelly, the son of Richard, of Exeter, Devon, England, who arrived in Boston on the ship "Hector" in 1633, was the progenitor of the Kellys of Bristol and vicinity. In 1634, he and his associates settled Newbury, Mass. He d. Dec. 28, 1644. He was the father of two children, of whom the second was

17*a*

2. John, b. Newbury, 1642 ; m. Sarah, dau. of Dea. Richard Knight, May 20, 1663. He d. Mar. 21, 1718, ae. 76. He had 11 children, one of whom was

3. Jonathan, b. Newbury, Mar. 20, 1687. He m., July 6, 1702, Esther Morse, dau. of Dea. Benjamin, of Newbury. He removed to Merrimac, Mass., in 1727. He had eight children, the third being

4. Jonathan, b. Oct. 10, 1709. He m. Hannah Blaisdell, dau. of John, of Amesbury, Mass., May 22, 1733, and removed to Hampstead, where he d. Jan., 1780, ae. 70-3-. Of his nine children, the third was

5. Jonathan, b. Amesbury, Dec. 24, 1736; m. Nov. 22, 1760, Sarah Foote Whicher, dau. of Capt. John Foote ; m. (2) Judith Eastman, of Hopkinton, Sept. 12, 1778. Jonathan Kelly served in the Colonial wars, and was one of 24 from Amesbury who "went in the alarm when Fort William and Henry was taken." In 1795, he was in Rochester, Vt., and later in Bristol, probably being a member of Dr. Timothy Kelly's family.

CHILDREN

*6. Timothy, b. Dec. 12, 1761. (1762—tombstone.)
7. Enoch, b. June 25, 1764; m. Betsey Kidder and res. Wolfeboro.
8. Abigail, b. Apr. 11, 1766; m. —— Bowen, Dunbarton; d. 1854, ae. 88.
*9. Ebenezer, b. Amesbury, Sept. 9, 1768.

(6) Timothy Kelly, M.D., was b. Amesbury, Mass., Dec. 12, 1761. Dec. 28, 1783, he m. Joanna Newcomb, b. Cape Ann, Mass., in June, 1762. Dr. Kelly was a soldier of the Revolutionary war, and removed from Amesbury to Candia, where he practiced medicine a few years. He was in Bristol as early as 1790, and was the first settler on Lot 60, First Division, a part of which was recently owned and occupied by William G. Kelley, on Summer street. Here he res. till 1799, practicing medicine (See Physicians), and teaching school. He was a prominent member of Rev. David Fisk's Free Baptist church on the New Hampton side of the Pemigewasset river, and occasionally preached. In 1799, he sold to David Cheney, and removed to the base of Alexandria hill, thence to the George Price farm, a mile south of Bristol village, and later to Hill village, where he d. Feb. 12 (19 — tombstone), 1845, ae. 83-2-0. She d. Hill, Oct. 14, 1845, ae. 83-4-.

CHILDREN

10. Charlotte, b. Oct. 29, 1784; m. Greenleaf Blake. (See.)
11. Horatio, b. Candia, Feb. 5, 1787 ; m. Dec. 3, 1818, Priscilla Doton, of Moultonboro. He learned the blacksmith's trade of Edmond Brown, the first blacksmith of the town, and removed to Boscawen, but returned and opened a shop at North Bristol. He was a lieutenant in the 34th Regt., state militia. He d. Grafton, June 26, 1865, ae. 78-4-21. She d. July 18, 1877. Children :

EBENEZER KELLY

    a. Elizabeth Hardy, b. Hill, Dec. 11, 1819; m. June 4, 1842, True Healy, of Raymond. He d. Feb. 29, 1852, and she m. (2) 1852, James Dearborn, of Danville, who d. June 10, 1876, in Raymond.

    b. John Solon, b. H., Sept. 15, 1821; served in Co. C, 10th Regt., N. H. Vols., in the Civil war. Res. Sandown.

    c. Joanna, b. June 30, 1823.

    d. Alfred S., b. Pembroke, Mar. 20, 1825; m. Mary Jane, dau. Jonathan Sargent, Apr. 4, 1849.

    e. Laura Angelina, b. May 21, 1827; m. Thomas Holt, Penacook.

    f. Edward Doton, b. June 8, 1829; m. Nov. 22, 1851, Mary A. Keen; d. Apr. 23, 1879, ae. 49-10-15. Children: (1) Edward Lowell, b. Mar. 28, 1854. (2) Elmer Frederick, b. Nov. 6, 1862.

    g. Mary Charlotte, b. May 1, 1831; m. Josiah Blaisdell, Newburyport, Mass.

    h. Ellen Mariah, b. June 9, 1833; d. Aug. 15, 1835, ae. 2-2-6.

  12. Clarissa, b. Feb. 17, 1789; lived in the family of Albert Blake, and d. in Hill, unm., Feb. 26, 1846, ae. 57-0-9.

  13. Amelia, b. Bristol, Apr. 1, 1791; d. Feb. 26, 1792.

  14. Drucilla, twin sister of Amelia, b. B., Apr. 1, 1791; lived in the family of William C. Kelley, and there d. Sept. 16, 1882, unm., ae. 91-5-15.

  15. Amelia, b. B., Aug. 18, 1793; d. Dec., 1796, ae. 3-4-.

  ✳16. Alfred, b. B., Nov. 13, 1795.

  17. Launcellot, b. B., Apr. 9, 1797; went to Louisiana and never heard from afterward; unm.

  18. .Joanna, b. B., May 3, 1800; m. J. L. Haines and went to New York. She was living in Morrisana, N. J., 1878.

  19. Mary Ann, b. B., Jan. 7, 1803; d. in Hill, May 27, 1853, unm., ae. 50-4-20.

  20. Harriet, b. B., Apr. 27, 1807; d. Sept., 1809, ae. 2-5-.

    (9) Ebenezer Kelly, b. Amesbury, Mass., Sept. 9, 1768, m. Apr. 16, 1789, Elizabeth Cheney. She was the dau. of Daniel, of West Newbury, Mass. He was a farmer in Newbury, and came to Bristol about 1793. A little later, he built what is now known as the Fisk house, corner of Central square and Summer street. Here he kept tavern for some years, and later kept a store. He was also associated with Col. Moses Lewis in the manufacture of custom cloth on Central street, probably the first to engage in this industry where is now the grist-mill. The last five years of his residence here, he served as selectman of Bridgewater. He removed to Haverhill about 1809, and to Geneva, N. Y., about 1810. He d. Marion, N. Y., Mar. 13, 1829, ae. 60-6-4. She d. Marion, in 1858, ae. 85.

CHILDREN

  21. Elizabeth, b. Newbury, Mass., June 12, 1791; m. 1809, Joseph Ives. He d. in 1812, and she m. (2) Caleb Jackson, 1814. She d. Feb. 5, 1850, ae. 58-7-23.

  22. Sally, b. Bristol, Mar. 6, 1794; m. Apr. 2, 1810, Capt. Francis J. Tay, of Bristol. He d. Concord, Jan. 23, 1826; she d. in Charlestown, Mass., Apr. 26, 1855, ae. 61-1-20. Children:

    a. Hiram K., b. 1810; d. Mar. 17, 1841, ae. 31.

    b. Albert J., } b. 1814.
    c. Rufus Lewis, }

    d. Harriet Elizabeth, b. 1822; m. Thomas F. Johnson.

e. Noah Hinkley, b. Farmington, N. Y., 1824. Now living (1903) in Shortsville, N. Y. A successful farmer.

23. Harriet, b. B., Aug. 26, 1797; d. Geneva, N. Y., 1817, ae. 20.

24. Sophronia, b. B., Mar. 1, 1800 (Bridgewater records say Aug. 29, 1796), m. Jeremiah Mooers, 1820; d. Apr. 30, 1881, ae. 81-1-29. Children :

> *a.* Cyrus F., b. 1821.   *b.* Henry C., b. 1828.
> *c.* Laura F., b. 1831.

*25. Luther, b. B., Oct. 13, 1803. (Bridgewater records say 1802.)

26. Caroline, b. B., Nov. 6, 1805; d. Aug. 30, 1821, ae. 15-9-24.

27. Almira, b. B., Apr. 21, 1808 (Bridgewater records, Apr. 27, 1807); m. Joseph Jackson, West Ogden, Mich; d. July 2, 1832, ae. 24-2-11. One dau.

> *a.* Elizabeth.

28. Louise, b. June 9, 1810; m. 1837, John W. Frye, West Ogden Mich. Children :

> *a.* James H., b. 1838.
> *b.* Elizabeth A., b. 1841 ; m. Edward W. Lapham, now resides in Clayton, Del. Two sons.
> *c.* Luther E., b. 1843.   *d.* Carrie, b. 1847.

29. Laura, b. Mar. 28, 1813; m. Dec. 17, 1840, William R. Hawley ; (2) Apr. 1, 1858, James Requa. One child, d. 1867.

30. Susan, b. May 29, 1816; m. 1841, Lewis H. Danford, in Williamstown, Mich. Six children.

(16) Alfred Kelly, b. Bristol, Nov. 13, 1795, m. June 30, 1829, Mary, dau. of Daniel and Molly (Smith) Currier, b. Aug. 27, 1805, in Plymouth, and d. in Hill, Nov. 20, 1893, ae. 88-2-23. He was a farmer in Hill, where he d. Sept. 28, 1845, ae. 49-9-15.

CHILDREN, all born in Hill

31. Harriet Augusta, b. Apr. 19, 1830 ; m. Oct. 3, 1849, Wilson Foster. (See.)

32. Mary Emeline, b. Aug. 16, 1832 ; m. Samuel Carleton. (See.)

33. William Currier, b. June 6, 1834 ; m. May 28, 1867, Anna Ruth, dau. of Clark Merrill. (See.) He served in Co. D, 12th Regt., N. H. Vols., Civil war, and was present at all its engagements, except Cold Harbor. Is a farmer in Hill. Children :

> *a.* Alfred Merrill, b. Jan. 29, 1869.
> *b.* Minie Jane, b. Jan. 4, 1873 ; m. Harry F. Prescott. (See.)
> *c.* Elizabeth Mary, b. Apr. 20, 1881; m. George H. Ballou. (See.)
> *d.* Arthur William, b. Apr. 11, 1883; killed Jan. 19, 1901, at a road crossing in Franklin — struck by an engine, ae. 17-9-8.

34. Martha Jane, b. May 22, 1841 ; d. Nov. 12, 1858, ae. 17-5-20.

(25) Luther Kelly was b. in Bristol, Oct. 13, 1803. He m., Apr. 26, 1842, Jeannette Eliza, dau. of Col. Hezekiah Sage, of Madison County, N. Y. He was for many years a merchant at Geneva, N. Y.; was president of the board of trustees of the village and filled other positions of public trust. Was prominent in the Methodist church and Masonic circles, a man of high character, positive in his convictions. He d. Geneva, Feb. 14, 1857, ae. 53-4-1.

LUTHER KELLY

CHILDREN

35. Luther Sage, b. Geneva, N. Y., July 27, 1849; m. Sept. 23, 1885, Alice M. Morrison, Detroit, Mich. He served in the 10th U. S. Infty., in the Army of the Potomac, during the Civil war, and later on the northwestern frontier. He was chief of scouts under General Miles in the Yellowstone district during the campaign of 1876-'78, after Sitting Bull and Bull Eagle. He was chief scout at the catonment on White river, Colo., 1880-'83, captain of the 7th U. S. Vols. in the Spanish war, and captain in 40th M. S. V. in Philippine Islands. Is now (1903) treasurer of Province of Sarigao, Island of Mindaneo, Philippines; a man of culture and frequent contributor to journals of the day.

36. William Dunham, b. G., June 14, 1852; m. Oct. 9, 1877, Charlotte L., dau. of George Cook, of Waterloo, N. Y. He res. Germantown, Pa., and is a railroad director; president of the Clearfield Bituminous Coal corporation, of Philadelphia, Pa., and Tygarts River Coal company; member of Union League of Philadelphia, Historical Society of Pennsylvania, Sons of American Revolution, New England Society, etc. Children:

    a. Gregory Cook, b. Aug. 27, 1879.
    b. Jeanette Sage, b. May 28, 1882.
    c. Anna Louise, b. July 12, 1884; d. Nov. 30, 1890, ae. 6-4-18.
    d. William Dunham, } b. May 27, 1891.
    e. Cornelia Clarke, }
    f. Luther Wrentmore, b. Apr. 14, 1896.

37. Anna J., b. Dec. 24, 1855. Res. in Germantown, Philadelphia, Pa. Is a writer and Browning scholar.

38. Albert F., b. Oct. 29, 1857; m. Mary King, Stauchfield, Pa., Oct. 27, 1896. Is treasurer and manager of Empire Coal Mining company, of Philadelphia; member of New England Society in Pennsylvania; Academy of Social and Political Science, and is interested in hospital work.

------

1. Eliphalet Gordon Kelley, son of Jonathan D. and Polly C. (Gordon) Kelley, was b. in New Hampton, Aug. 24, 1833. He m. in California, Nov. 10, 1857, Sarah, dau. of Robert and Harriet (Fisher) Noble, b. Philadelphia, Pa., July 4, 1841. He was 16 years a resident of California, three years of which time he was postmaster at Dutch Flat. He was salesman four years in New Hampton; for Hon. Cyrus Taylor, in Bristol, 1876 till he d., Oct. 24, 1886, ae. 53-2-0. Mrs. Kelley res. Bristol.

CHILDREN

2. Florence Dustin, b. California, Sept. 17, 1861; m. Harry W. Tilton. (See.)

3. Alvah Bugbee, b. New Hampton, Sept. 22, 1865. He m., Sept. 29, 1888, Maria Ida Bishop, dau. of John, b. Presque Isle, Me., May 14, 1865. Was shipper for Lowell Machine company, Lowell, Mass., 1882 till June, 1902; since, a farmer at Presque Isle. Children:

    a. Lloyd Bishop, b. Lowell, Mass., Aug. 7, 1890.
    b. Sarah Hazel, b. Presque Isle, June 20, 1894.
    c. Alvah Bugbee, b. P. I., Apr. 13, 1903.

------

1. William Gordon Kelley, son of John and Polly (Gordon) Kelley, was b. New Hampton, Nov. 12, 1820. He m. in

June, 1844, Eliza Ann, dau. David Dearborn, b. New Hampton, Aug. 26, 1824. They were farmers in New Hampton till 1871, when they removed to Bristol and took possession of a residence on Summer street that he erected the year before, where she d. May 21, 1888, ae. 63-8-25. He d. Oct. 3, 1902, ae. 81-10-21. His will made the town of Bristol residuary legatee of his estate, from which about $15,000 is expected to be realized for the purchase of a public park as stipulated in the will.

1. Daniel Kelley, brother of William G., above, was b. New Hampton, June 26, 1816. He m. June 19, 1842, Julia M., dau. of Gen. David Sanborn, b. Mar. 3, 1822. They were farmers in their native town till 1874, when they located on Summer street in Bristol, where he d. Oct. 18, 1885, ae. 69-3-22. She d. New Hampton, Feb. 11, 1896,, ae. 73-11-8. No children.

1. Joseph Dearborn Kelley, son of Joseph and Mary (Crawford) Kelley, was b. Rumney, May 28, 1826 (May 30, 1828 — Crawford record). His mother d. when he was young and he was given a home in the family of Abbott Lovejoy. He was for 18 years a member of the firm of Lovejoy & Kelley, carriage makers. He m. (1) Dec. 17, 1855, Sarah E., dau. of Jacob and Sally Tilton, b. New Hampton, Apr. 8, 1835. She d. Aug. 29, 1859, ae. 24-4-21, and he m. Dec. 17, 1862, Laurana, widow of Nathaniel Keniston, b. July, 1815. She d. Jan. 21, 1888, ae. 72-6-; he d. Odd Fellows' Home, Concord, Nov. 2, 1892, ae. 66-5-4. Democrat. Served as captain of the fire company several years, and seven years as fireward.

CHILDREN

2. Charles Roscoe, b. Bristol, Apr. 1, 1858.
3. Sarah S., d. Sept. 8, 1859, ae. 1 month.

Laura Augusta Keniston, dau. of Mrs. Kelley, b. Jan. 1, 1853, made her home in Mr. Kelley's family.

THE KEEZER FAMILY

1. William Keezer was a resident of Bristol village for about 20 years, previous to 1836. He res. on the B. Q. Fellows place on No. Main street and a part of the time was an employee of Reuben Hosmer, hatter. He came to Bristol from Salisbury. Of his ten children, eight are said to have been born in Bristol.

CHILDREN

*2. Joseph.	3. Sally, m. Joshua Harriman.
4. Clarissa, m. John Gage.	5. Samuel, m. Esther Brown.
6. William, m. Hannah Bray.	7. John, m. Abigail Holt.
8. Eliza, m. Joseph Johnson.	9. Susan, m. Rufus Abbott.
10. Cynthia, m. Daniel Davis.	11. Amos.

(2) Joseph Keezer, m. Betsey Kemp. He was a farmer in Alexandria, and d. in Groton. He had ten children, among whom were:

12. Nathaniel Plumer, b. Alexandria, May 9, 1824. He m., Dec. 30, 1844, Lucy Buck Tilton, and she d. Dec. 1, 1890, ae. 64-8-3. He is a farmer in Alexandria. Seven children, one of whom is

    a. Warren Foster, b. Alexandria, Feb. 18, 1863; is a farmer in A. Has served as selectman of his town. He m., Apr. 28, 1894, Nellie M., dau. of Andrew J. Burpee. (See.) Child: Neil, b. A., Apr. 10, 1898.

*13. George Washington, b. A., Apr. 27, 1826.

(13) George W. Keezer, b. Apr. 27, 1826. He m., in 1849, Mary, dau. of Nathan and Sallie C. Moore, b. Hanover, 1824, and d. in Bristol, Mar. 23, 1901, ae. 77. He was a farmer in Groton; in Bristol since 1888.

CHILDREN

14. Mary E., b. Groton; m. Alonzo Cross, Groton.
15. Nellie Adelaide, b. G., Apr. 9, 1852; m. George F. Cass. (See.)
16. Charles Russell, b. G., June 9, 1859; m. May 8, 1886, Sarah Abbie, dau. Taylor and Laura (Butterfield) Reed, b. Dorchester, Oct. 31, 1855. Teamster. Res. Bristol since 1878. Republican, Odd Fellow, Free Baptist. Children:

    a. Lewis Merville, b. Bristol, Mar. 30, 1887.
    b. Carl Russell, b. B., Jan. 8, 1891.
    c. Edna Marguerite, b. B., June 23, 1894.

17. Lucy Jane, b. G., m. (1) —— Holt; (2) Fred H. Proctor. (3) Elmer H. Hammond. (See.)
18. Frank Edwin, b. G., Apr. 2, 1864; m. Feb. 3, 1895, Minnie Eva, dau. Henry W. Drake (See), b. Bristol, Oct. 8, 1870.
19. Addie Caroline, d. young.
20. Everett, res. Montpelier, Vt., m. Annie Herbert.

THE KEMP FAMILY

1. Charles Edward Kemp, son of Asa and Catherine (West) Kemp, was b. Hooksett, Sept. 5, 1848. He m., May 8, 1871, Clara Eudora, dau. of William H. Perkins (See), b. Aug. 10, 1853. Res. in Bristol since 1882; overseer in spinning-room of the woolen-mill.

CHILDREN

2. Mabel Frances, b. Londonderry, Dec. 17, 1872; m. Everett Wicom. (See.)
3. Grace May, b. L., June 20, 1874; d. June 24, 1895, ae. 21-0-4.
4. Nettie Maud, b. Orange, July 5, 1879.
5. Edmond Cheney, } b. Bristol, Sept. 28, 1885, { d. Oct. 11, 1886.
6. Edwin Worth, } { d. Oct. 19, 1886.

THE KENDALL FAMILIES

1. The Kendalls of Bristol were the descendants of Francis Kendall, who settled in Woburn, Mass., about 1640. He m.,

Dec. 24, 1644, Mary, dau. of John Tidd, and had a large family. He was selectman of Woburn for nineteen years. His eighth child was

2. Jacob, b. Jan. 25, 1661. He m., Jan. 2, 1684, Persis Hayward. She d. and he m., Jan. 10, 1695, Alice Temple. He d. Billerica, Mass. He had children by both wives, one being

3. Ebenezer, b. Woburn, Apr. 5, 1710; m. in 1733, Hannah Hasey, of Rumney Marsh, Boston, b. Dec. 11, 1716, and d. Dunstable, Mass., Feb. 10, 1761, ae. 44-1-29. He probably m., Nov. 14, 1761, Lucy Cummings, of Dunstable. He d. Dec. 20, 1774, ae. 64-8-15. Hannah Hasey was dau. of Asa and Mary (Walton) Hasey. Asa was son of Lieut. John Hasey, and grandson of Lieut. William Hasey, an ensign in the Ancient and Honorable Artillery company of Boston in 1652, and later a lieutenant in King Philip's war. Ebenezer was the father of

4. Ebenezer, b. Oct. 5, 1736, in Revere or Dunstable. He m, Feb. 23, 1762, Martha, dau. of John Walton, b. Reading, Mass., Nov. 16, 1735. Ebenezer settled in Hollis, but later removed to that part of Plymouth, now Hebron, where he d. Nov. 2, 1802, ae. 66-0-27. She d. Oct. 13, 1817, ae. 81-10-27. They had four or more children, two of whom were

*5.　Ebenezer, b. Hollis, May 11, 1765.
*6.　Hasey, b. June 2, 1772.

(5)　Ebenezer Kendall, b. May 11, 1765, m. Jan. 20, 1793, Susanna Dow, of Hanover, b. Coventry, Conn., Apr. 10, 1759. She was a dau. of Samuel and Anna (Mellington) Dow, and a cousin of Rev. Lorenzo Dow. Ebenezer lived in Hebron, and here d. Feb. 15 (16), 1837, ae. 71-9 4. She d. at the home of her dau., Mary Morse, in Haverhill, Nov. 28, 1837, ae. 78-7-18.

CHILDREN

7.　Anna, b. Hebron, Apr. 12, 1794; m. Jonathan Powers. (See.)
*8.　Ebenezer, b. H., Dec. 10, 1795.
9.　Lydia, b. H., Oct. 22, 1797; d. Sept. 22, 1800, ae. 2-11-0.
10.　Lemuel, b. H., Mar. 3, 1799; d. Sept. 18, 1800, ae. 1-6-15.
11.　Mary, b. H., Oct. 4, 1800; m. Isaac Morse, of Haverhill.
12.　Lemuel, b. H., Mar. 6, 1803; m. Aug. 31, 1824, Philinda Hastings. Children :

　　a.　Aurilla, m. Ebenezer B. Butterfield, res. Groton, where he d. She removed to Bristol and here d.

　　b.　Oscar Rensselaer, b. Hebron, Dec. 1, 1827; m. Dec. 19, 1868, Rachel Elmira, dau. Josiah R. Plumer. He d. Groton, Feb. 21, 1893, ae. 65-2-20. She res. Bristol. Children : (1) Oscar Prescott, b. Groton, Sept. 6, 1872; d. G., Dec. 20, 1899, ae. 27-3-14. (2) Josiah Chester, b. Groton, June 7, 1881.

　　c.　Caroline Eliza, b. Hebron, May 12, 1836; m. Nathaniel Bartlett. (See.)

　　d.　Lemuel C., res. East Boston, Mass.

(6)　Hasey Kendall, b. June 2, 1772,˙res. Hebron. He m. Elsa Flanders.

*13. Asa, b. Hebron, Jan. —, 1803.
*14. Jesse F., b. H., Feb. 15, 1809.
15. Joshua T., b. H., 1819; came to Bristol when a boy; m. Oct. 9, 1839, Mary Ann, dau. of Dr. Daniel Favor (See), b. Apr. 18, 1817. He was a dealer in lumber here till 1857, when he removed to Concord, where he d. Jan. 4, 1882, ae. 63; she d. June 9, 1899, ae. 82-1-21. No children.
16. Joseph, b. H., June 20, 1817, killed by lightning on his 21st birthday.
17. Elsie.

(8) Ebenezer Kendall, b. Dec. 10, 1795, m. Dec. 16, 1821, Susan A., dau. of Reuben Allen, of Ellsworth, b. Sept. 9, 1804. He removed from Hebron to North Bristol in 1821, and there built saw-mill, grist-mill, and woolen-mill. Removed to Bristol village in 1846 or '47. He was a millwright and manufacturer, and was considered a genius in that he could do anything and do it well. Republican. He believed in an overruling power, but not in creeds; and yet he was active in the construction of the Congregational church, and purchased eight pews, while no other person purchased more than three. He d. May 9, 1867, ae. 71-4-29. She d. Bristol, Oct. 15, 1871, ae. 67-1-6.

*18. Hiram Woods, b. Bristol, June 21, 1828.

(13) Asa Kendall, b. Jan., 1803, m. Mar. 23, 1830, Sarah Emmons, dau. of Joseph. (See.) He d. Alexandria, Dec. 3, 1854, ae. 51-11-; she d. Orange, 1875, ae. 67.

19. Lenora, b. Hebron, 1832; m. 1849, David Morse, Francestown. Lived in Alexandria, and there she d. May, 1860. Four children.
20. Eleanor, b. H., May 7, 1836; m. Dearborn Gray. (See.)
21. Marinda, b. H., 1840; d. Nov., 1854, ae. 14.
22. Elsie Mariah, b. H., Aug. 23, 1842; m. George Ebenezer Place, and d. Newmarket, 1885. Three children.
23. Asa Wayland, b. Alexandria, Aug. 26, 1845; m. in Ohio, Mary M. Reed, and res. Santa Cruz, Cal. No children.
24. Henry Clay, b. A., Dec. 25, 1851; m. May 25, 1877, Francelia Medora Hoyt, dau. of Enos. Four children. Res. 30 Prescott street, Hyde Park, Mass.

(14) Jesse F. Kendall, b. Feb. 15, 1809, m. Jan. 11, 1832, Louisa F., dau. of Josiah Fellows. (See.) He removed from Hebron to the silver mine farm, and later operated grist- and saw-mill at No. Bristol. Removed to Woodstock in 1851, and in the 60's to Thornton, thence to Campton, where he d. from the effects of a fall, Oct. 1, 1877, ae. 68-7-16. Mrs. Kendall d. Thornton, May 11, 1888, ae. 76-10-15.

25. Albon H., b. Hebron, Mar. 1, 1833; m. Nov. 28, 1861, Elizabeth N., dau. of Walter H. and Sarah A. (Fifield) Sawyer, b. Woodstock, July

28, 1840. He is now a station agent at West Thornton. Children:
    a. Milton Howard, b. Woodstock, Jan. 26, 1865; m. July 28, 1888, Charlotte Smith.
    b. Joseph Morey, b. Thornton, Jan. 21, 1868; m. Jan. 26, 1897, Ada W. Wilkinson.
    c. Gertrude Elsie, b. T., Jan. 2, 1873.
    d. Jesse Albon, b. T., June 8, 1874; m. June 19, 1897, Mabel R. Willey.
    e. Anna Lizzie, b. T., Mar. 4, 1884.

  26. Elsey Susan, b. Bristol, Apr. 8, 1838; m. Sept., 1866, Alfred Webster, and d. Campton, Oct. 9, 1868, ae. 30-6-1.
  27. Josiah Fellows, b. B., Nov. 23, 1844; m. Eliza Smith, and res. Chicago, Ill.

  (18) Hiram W. Kendall, b. June 21, 1828, was a tinsmith and manufacturer of bedsteads in Bristol. He m., June 6, 1852, Lydia Morse, of Francestown, b. Whitefield, Apr. 26, 1831, and d. Bristol, Apr. 24, 1853, ae. 21-11-28. He m., Dec. 17, 1853, Lucy A., dau. Timothy D. Hinman, of Dorset, Vt., b. Oct. 4, 1831. He was an invalid for many years before his death, which occurred in Bristol, Feb. 29, 1896, ae. 67-8-8. She res. Woodsville.

CHILDREN

  28. Edward Frank, b. Bristol, Dec. 30, 1858; m. Sept. 28, 1885, Emma M., dau. of Daniel K. Cummings. (See.) He has been a wood-worker and mechanic at Bristol, Lisbon, and now at Woodsville. Child:
    a. Fred Edward, b. Bristol, Aug. 15, 1889.
  29. George Henry, b. B., June 23, 1865, m. Kate I., dau. George W. Hadley, b. Manchester, Sept. 9, 1869, and d. Nov. 1, 1894, ae. 25-1-22. He m., May 16, 1896, at Woodsville, Louise Amelia, dau. Joseph and Abbey (Stevens) Willis, b. June 16, 1874. He commenced trade in Bristol when 13 years of age and continued till elected register of deeds in 1894. He served as register eight years, retiring in 1903. While in Bristol, served two years as deputy sheriff. Now res. in Woodsville. Children:
    a. Nellie Alice, b. Bristol, Oct. 13, 1887.
    b. Georgia Isabel, b. B., Oct. 14, 1889.
    c. Rupert Hiram, b. B., Sept. 4, 1891; d. Woodsville, June 29, 1898, from the effects of a fall from a wagon, ae. 6-9-25.

THE KENNEY FAMILIES

  1. James Kenney was b. in Ireland in 1836. He m., 1854, Mary Ellen McPard, b. Ireland, 1834. Res. in Quebec and Gaspe Basin till 1882, when they came to Bristol. Farmers; removed to Franklin Falls, 1890.

CHILDREN, all born in Canada.

  2. George, b. Nov. 15, 1855; m. Catherine Gonie, Nov. 1, 1881; res. Lowell, Mass.
  3. James, b. Nov. 1, 1857; m. Mary Ann Kenney, 1882; res. Hill. Children:
    a. Minnie, b. July, 1884.   *b.* Harold, b. 1891.

GEORGE H. KENDALL, ESQ.

4. Patrick Henry, b. Nov. 29, 1859; m. Nov. 27, 1884, Mattie Belle Veasey, of Hill. Res. Franklin Falls.

5. Michael John, b. Feb. 28, 1861; m. 1885, Abbie Evans, of Hill; res. New Hampton.

6. Margaret Ellen, b. Feb. 29, 1863; m. Charles T. Smith. (See.)

7. Mary, b. May 4, 1865; m. 1883, Hiland Ballou; res. Bristol.

8. Christina, b. June 4, 1867; m. William Smith; res. Hebron.

*9. Frank Parker, b. Nov. 11, 1870.

10. William, b. Oct. 29, 1871; m. 1896, Jennie Hanaford; res. Franklin Falls.

11. Louise, b. Aug. 12, 1873; d. 1881, ae. 8.

12. Rebecca, b. Mar. 4, 1875; d. 1881, ae. 6.

13. Thomas Edmond, b. 1880; res. Franklin Falls.

(9) Frank P. Kenney, b. Nov. 11, 1870, m. Nov. 28, 1894, Lizzie A., dau. of James P. and Mary (Charwood) Dugdale, b. Providence, R. I., June 28, 1876. Has been a resident of Bristol since 1880. Blacksmith, Republican, Methodist.

CHILDREN

14. Hulda Mary, b. Bristol, Apr. 22, 1896.

15. Helen Gertrude, b. B., Aug. 23, 1898.

16. Mae, b. B., Oct. 1, 1900; d. same day.

17. Frank Proctor, b. B., Nov. 30, 1901.

---

1. Patrick M. Kenney, son of Oney McKenney, was b. County Waxley, Ireland, Mar. 16, 1843. He m., Feb. 15, 1866, Agnes, dau. of Felix Adams. (See.) He came to Bristol about 1872, and has res. Profile Falls. Mill operative.

CHILDREN

2. Mary Ann, b. Gaspe, P. Q., Sept. 28, 1868; m. James Kenney. (See.)

3. Arthur L., b. G., Feb. 25, 1871. A mill operative in Bristol; unm.

4. Katherine, b. Haverhill, Apr. 15, 1873; m. 1889, William G. Tilton; res. Alexandria. Child:

    a. Fremont, b. 1891.

5. Oney, b. Bristol, June 6, 1875. A wood-worker in Bristol.

6. Lawrence, b. Hill, Sept. 30, 1877; m. Mary Handerson. An employee at crutch factory. Child:

    a. Arline May, b. Bristol, Aug. 30, 1902.

7. Felix, b. H., Nov. 22, 1883; is an operative in paper-mill; unm.

THE KETCHUM FAMILY

1. Rev. Silas Ketchum was the son of Silas and Cynthia (Doty) Ketchum. He was b. Barre, Vt., Dec. 4, 1835, and m. Apr. 4, 1860, Georgia Cenitia, dau. of Elbridge and Sarah (Stickney) Hardy, b. Amherst, July 1, 1843. He was pastor of the Congregational church in Bristol, Nov., 1866–May, 1875. (See Congregational Church.) He d. at Boston, Mass., Apr. 24, 1880, ae. 44-4-20, and his remains were interred at Contoocook. Mrs. Ketchum res. Brookline, Mass.

2. George Crowell, b. Bangor, Me., May 16, 1862 ; m. Oct. 29, 1890, Annie, dau. of Dexter Taylor, of Woburn, Mass. He is a druggist at Brookline, Mass.

3. Edmond, b. Bristol, Sept. 17, 1871. He is a graduate of the Normal Art School of Boston, in art and nature studies. Res. 677 Washington street, Brookline, Mass. Unm. He is a talented painter in oil and water colors. His marine views especially have attracted much attention.

THE KIDDER FAMILIES

1. The Kidders are of ancient British, Danish, and Saxon stock. The name as first written was Kyddwr ; in 1500, it was written Kydder. James Kidder, b. East Grinstead, Sussex, England, in 1626, was the ancestor of the Kidders of New England. He was in Cambridge, Mass., as early as 1650.

2. John Kidder, a descendant of James, was b. in Bedford, Mass., in 1736. He m. Jenny Lynn, b. Bedford, Aug. 2, 1740 (1737), and came to Bristol in 1769, for the purpose of tending the grist-mill just erected for the proprietors of the township by Maj. John Tolford, where the Train-Smith Co. pulp-mill now stands. He moved into a log house at the corner of Central square and Spring street, where now stands Emerson's block. After tending this mill three years he bought the farm now owned by Fred Kidder, and moved his family into a log house he erected on the east side of the highway, a little distance above the schoolhouse near Solon Dolloff's. In time, a frame house succeeded the log structure, but both have succumbed to the ravages of time, and the site is now marked only by the partially filled cellar and the lilac and rose bushes that stand sentries over the spot. Here he cleared the land that gave him and several succeeding generations a home. He was a Revolutionary soldier. (See.) At one time when out of provisions he walked to Haverhill corner, bought a bushel of corn, had it ground at Bristol, and got back home on the evening of the second day. The family were entirely out of food when he reached home. He d. in Bristol, Sept. 7 (3), 1828, ae. 92. She d. Aug. 3, 1833, ae. 93-0-1.

3. Sarah, b. Bedford, Aug. 16, 1764 ; m. Moses Cleveland. (See.)
*4. Benjamin, b. B., Mar. 27, 1766.
5. Mary, b. June 6, 1768 ; d. at Albion, N. Y.; unm.
*6. James, b. Bristol, Apr. 30, 1771.
*7. John, b. B., May 29, 1773.
8. Hannah, b. B., May 9, 1775 ; m. James Fuller, who came to Bristol when a young man. They removed to Albion, N. Y. Children, all b. in Bristol :

a.	Daniel Dean, b. Mar. 6, 1796.	b.	Holland, b. Feb. 10, 1798.
c.	Hibbard, b. May 30, 1800.	d.	Joel, b. Sept. 23, 1802.
e.	Amelia, b. Feb. 2, 1805.	f.	John, b. Apr. 6, 1807.
g.	James, b. Oct. 8, 1809.	h.	Mary, b. Feb. 8, 1812.

9. Reuben, b. B., Nov. 21, 1777. He m., June 13, 1805, Sally, dau. of David and Mary Straw, b. Dec. 24, 1779, and d. Bristol, Feb. 1, 1852, ae. 72-1-7. He was a farmer at the base of Bristol Peak ; house destroyed by fire, Dec. 14, 1857. He d. in New Hampton, Feb. 16, 1856, ae. 78-2-25. They had no children but brought up Alonzo Cheney.

10. Betsey, b. B., May 25, 1781 ; m. Enoch Cheney. (See.)

(4) Lieut. Benjamin Kidder, b. Mar. 27, 1766, came to Bristol 1769, with his father's family. Feb. 14, 1788, he m. Molly Heath, b. 1769, and d. in Bristol, Mar. 15, 1804, ae. 35. (Feb. 16, 1803 — tombstone.) He m. (2) Sally, dau. of John Wiggin, of Candia, b. 1777, and d. May 22, 1839, ae. 62. He m. (3) Nov. 10, 1839, Widow Sarah (Cross) Willey, of Northfield. She d. of malignant smallpox, July 6, 1860, ae. 74. He settled on the farm next above his father, where Fred Kidder now lives, where he d. Mar. 11, 1853, ae. 86-11-14. A member of the Methodist church more than 50 years before his death.

CHILDREN, all born Bristol

*11. Daniel Heath, b. Aug. 22, 1788.
12. Dorothy, b. Aug. 17, 1790; m. Oliver Ballou. (See.)
*13. John, b. Jan. 7, 1793.   *14. Benjamin, b. June 13, 1795.
15. Jane, b. July 30, 1797 ; m. Joseph H. Brown. (See.)
16. Mary, b. Sept. 3, 1799 ; d. at 20.
17. Hannah, b. Nov. 29, 1801 ; m. Benjamin Q. Fellows. (See.)
*18. Joshua, b. June 8, 1805.
19. Aaron, b. Sept. 3, 1806 ; m. (1) Dec. 31, 1832, Mary, dau. of Oliver Ballou (See), b. June, 1808. She d. May 4, 1846, in Alexandria, ae. 37-11--. He m. (2) July, 1847, Mary Jane, dau. of Samuel Cole, b. Alexandria, Jan. 11, 1815, and d. Jan. 26, 1855, ae. 40-0-15. He m. (3) Jan. 1, 1856, Mariam, dau. of James Eastman, b. Enfield, June 24, 1811, and d. Apr. 24, 1865, ae. 53-10-0. Aug. 28, 1870, (?) he m. (4) Rhoda S., dau. of John and Rhoda Tucker, b. Hill, Nov. 10, 1822. He res. in Bristol, Plainfield, Hanover, where he lived seven or eight years, and then returned to Bristol, and a year later removed to Hill, where he d. Nov. 10, 1898, ae. 92-2-7. She d. Hill, Mar. 21, 1901, ae. 78-4-11. He was for years a member of the Methodist church and a class leader. Republican. Children :

a. Sarah, b. Hill, Mar. 21, 1833 ; d. Apr. 10, 1841, ae. 8-0-19.
b. Jephthah P., b. Bristol, Feb. 18, 1837 ; m. Mar., 1863, Melvina, dau. Levi Cary. Was superintendent of knitting-mill at Philmont, N. Y., where he d. July, 1898, ae. 61-5-.
c. Hannah, b. Alexandria, Sept. 17, 1839 ; d. Aug. 24, 1840.

*20. Joseph, b. Aug. 2, 1809.
21. Nancy, b. June 24, 1812 ; d. at nine years of age.
22. Polly, d. young.

(6) James Kidder, b. Apr. 30, 1771, m. Mary, dau. of Oliver Smith and Deborah (Ingalls) Blake, b. Aug. 16, 1775, and d. May 10, 1843, in Enosburgh, Vt., ae. 67-8-24. He was a farmer in Hebron ; removed to Enosburgh, where they resided in the family of his son, James. He d. Oct. 30, 1833, ae. 62-6-0.

CHILDREN

23. Oliver Blake, b. Hebron, Aug. 19, 1796; d. in Plymouth, July 2, 1854, ae. 57-10-13. He m. Betsey Dodge, dau. of John, b. Nov. 6, 1794, and d. Orland, Me., Jan. 9, 1875, ae. 80-2-3.

18

24. Reuben, b. H., Aug. 9, 1798; m. Nov. 6, 1825, Sally Powell, dau. of David (See), b. Mar. 3, 1800; d. Plymouth, Apr., 1859, ae. 59-1-. He d. in Montague, Mass., Apr. 30, 1875, ae. 76-8-21. Children:

    a. Mary, b. Hebron, Oct. 25, 1827; m. Alexander McMurphy, of So. Alexandria, and d. in Jan., 1852, ae. 24-3-.

    b. Almira, b. H., Apr. 27, 1830; m. Warren Glover of Bridgewater, and emigrated to California, where he d. Jan. 16, 1891.

    c. Orpha, b. H., Dec. 30, 1834; d. July 18, 1835.

    d. David Smith, b. H., Dec. 9, 1838. He m., Sept. 3, 1861, Augusta Anne, dau. of John and Phoebe (Batchelder) Boynton, b. Bridgewater, Apr. 25, 1836. He was for a time in trade in Bristol, as dealer in stoves and tinware, left Bristol 1868, and now res. in Vineland, N. J. Children: (1) Fred Smith, b. Bristol, Mar. 4, 1863. (2) Cora Augusta, b. Turners Falls, Mass., Mar. 23, 1873. (3) Minnie Belle, b. Feb. 13, 1876; unm. Res. Chicopee Falls. (4) Infant son, b. Aug. 13, 1871; d. Sept. 22, 1871.

25. Mary, b. H., June 20, 1800; m. her cousin, Moses Kidder, son of John, Jan. 16, 1823. Res. Enosburgh and Montgomery, Vt., and Norfolk, Neb., where she d. Mar. 22, 1886, ae. 85-9-2.

26. James, b. H., Oct. 9, 1802, and d. in Enosburgh, Vt., Oct. 13, 1852, ae. 50-0-4. He m., Oct. 31, 1831, Lura, dau. Allen Adams, who was b. May 8, 1807, in Charlotte, Vt., and d. Dec. 1, 1891, in Enosburgh, ae. 84-6-23. Nine children.

27. Sherburn, b. Dec. 21, 1804; m., and d. in Canada, Jan. 15, 1857. ae. 52-0-24.

(7) John Kidder, son of John, b. Bristol, May 29, 1773, m. Nov. 17, 1796, Mehitable Blake, dau. of Oliver Smith and Deborah (Ingalls) Blake, b. in Sandown, Jan. 17, 1773, and d. in Holland, Vt., Mar. 24, 1863, ae. 90-2-7. He settled on the John Smith farm in Bridgewater, and here he res. till 1811, when his property was swept away through signing a note with Moses Lewis, and he removed to Hebron. In March, 1815, he purchased a farm in Enosburg, Vt., and removed his family thither on an ox sled, and there he resided till his death, Feb. 8, 1856, ae. 82-8-9. He was a strong man physically and spiritually ; a member of the Congregational church.

CHILDREN

28. Lynn, b. Feb. 8, 1798; m. widow Abigail Pease, and d. in Michigan. Was a Congregational minister.

29. Moses, b. Bridgewater, Mar. 5, 1800; m. his cousin, Mary Kidder. Res. in Enosburg and Montgomery, Vt., then near Pawpaw, Mich., and Norfolk, Neb., where he d. Aug. 21, 1888, ae. 88-5-16.

30. Sarah, b. B., Mar. 31, 1802; d. unm., in Holland, Vt., Nov. 6, 1861, ae. 59-7-5.

31. John, b. B., Apr. 6, 1804; was twice m., and d. in West Kendall, N. Y., Aug. 6, 1850, ae. 46-4-0.

32. Mehitable, b. B., July 5, 1806, and d. unm., in Enosburg, Vt., Apr. 5, 1855, ae. 48-9-0.

33. Lucy, b. B., Mar. 22, 1809; m. Luke Gilbert, and res. Vermont, New York, Michigan, and Nebraska, and d. at Oakdale, Neb., Dec. 18, 1894, ae. 85-8-26.

34. Amasa, b. B., Sept. 24, 1811; m. Feb. 19, 1835, Esther Brewer, b. Sept. 3, 1815. She d. Holland, Vt., Dec. 16, 1889, ae. 74-3-13. He d. Holland, Feb. 7, 1888, ae. 76-4-13. Five children.

35. Mary, b. Enosburg, Vt., June 17, 1815; m. Sept. 24, 1861, Enoch Huggins. Res. Holland.

(11) Daniel H. Kidder, son of Benjamin, b. Aug. 22, 1788, m. Nov. 22, 1810, Eliza Chandler, dau. of Abial. (See.) In the fall of 1822, they removed to Stewartstown, where he d. Oct. 16, 1864, ae. 76-1-24: she d. same place, Sept. 10, 1891, at the advanced age of 102-1-12. They both d. in family of their son, James Monroe. Their children were all b. in Bristol, except the last.

CHILDREN

36. Leonard Cummings, b. June 22, 1811; m. Aug. 5, 1832, in Clarksville, Susanna Fellows, dau. of Isaiah, b. Lisbon, Aug. 13, 1811, and d. Stewartstown, June 18, 1881, ae. 69-10-5. He res. in Clarksville. Children:

    a. Benjamin W., b. Jan. 11, 1834; d. Sept. 21, 1876, ae. 42-8-10.
    b. Eben Perry, b. Dec. 26, 1835; m. Sarah Chase, Mar. 26, 1861. She was b. Jan. 24, 1840. Two children.
    c. Alvin, b. Nov. 16, 1837; unm.
    d. Malona, b. Nov. 8, 1839; unm.
    e. Bertha, b. Mar. 4, 1842; d. Aug. 5, 1860, ae. 18-5-1.
    f. Martha, b. Mar. 6, 1844; d. Nov. 11, 1861, ae. 17-8-5.
    g. Persis, b. Nov. 16, 1848; unm.
    h. Noah F., b. Feb. 20, 1851; m. Una Brooks, Apr. 24, 1878. Child: (1) Susan E., b. Jan. 24, 1884.

37. Almira Jane, b. Feb. 4, 1813; m. Mar. 13, 1837, Noah Cummings and d. Dec. 16, 1896, ae. 83-10-12. He d. Colebrook, Feb. 6, 1860. They res. Colebrook. Children:

    a. Daniel E., b. Colebrook, July 1, 1840; m. July 13, 1874, Lucy A. Egleston. Res. Colebrook.
    b. Elvira, b. C., June 1841; m. Nov. 9, 1882, Milton Harriman, of Colebrook.

38. Abial Chandler, b. Sept. 10, 1814; m. Jan. 28, 1839, Julia A. Johnson, dau. of Moses, b. Apr. 25, 1818; d. in Colebrook, July 18, 1865, ae. 47-2-23. He d. in Colebrook, June 23, 1866, ae. 51-9-13. Abial was a farmer, and operated a saw-mill. Children:

    a. Aurilla, b. July 6, 1840; m. July 18. 1866, Martin B. Noyes, of Colebrook. One child.
    b. Lee M., b. Dec. 4, 1858; d. Sept. 7, 1863, ae. 4-9-3.

39. Daniel Erskine, b. June 15, 1815. He m. (1) 1843, Jane Bonney, in Lowell; m. (2) 1857, Mary E. Ellas, in Nebraska. Was a soldier in Co. A, 1st Neb. Inf. (See Roll of Honor.) He d. in Nebraska, June 17, 1864, ae. 49-0-2. Children:

    a. Albert Edward, b. Jan. 12, 1844. Was a soldier in Union army, Co. A, 1st Neb. Regt. He m. Sept. 14, 1867, Mary S. Powers, b. Jan. 15, 1849. Res. Norton, Kansas. Ten children, all b. in Kansas.
    b. Thomas O., b. 1858.   *c.* Amanda, b. 1860.

40. Julia Ann Locke, b. July 2, 1816; m. Feb. 15, 1844, Orrin Covell, Farmer. He d. Stewartstown, Dec. 18, 1891, ae. 73-5-15; she d. June 2, 1883, ae. 66-11-0. Children:

    a. Murcilva, b. Jan. 26, 1846; m. Aug. 4, 1862, Benjamin F. Crawford.
    b. Miranda, b. Mar. 25, 1849; m. Benjamin C. Young.
    c. Celon E., b. June 28, 1852; m. Nov. 10, 1880, Susie Brooks, and d. Apr. 23, 1889, ae. 36-9-25.

41. Lydia Ann Barnard, twin sister of Julia Ann Locke, d. young.

42. Jonathan Thomas, b. Feb. 6, 1820 ; m. Polly Carter. (See Roll of Honor.) He d. Carleton, Vt. Family res. there.

43. James Monroe, b. Aug. 22, 1822 ; m. Jan. 1, 1848, Mary Ann, dau. of Thomas R. Holden, b. in Stewartstown, Aug. 17, 1827. (See Roll of Honor.) Was selectman of Stewartstown, 1857-'58, and represented his town in the legislature 1883-'84. They res. Stewartstown. Children :

    a. Murrilla, b. July 24, 1848 ; d. Mar. 10, 1864, ae. 15-7-16.

    b. Almira, b. June 6, 1850; m. Josiah Young, and d. Sept. 16, 1877, ae. 27-3-10. Children: (1) Eleanor S., b. July 24, 1868. (2) Murrilla K., b. Sept. 11, 1870. (3) John F., b. Dec. 22, 1872 ; d. Dec. 28, 1872. (4) James A., b. Feb. 28, 1874. (5) Bessie I., b. Apr. 3, 1876.

    c. Augusta A., b. May 12, 1853; m. 1870, Charles D. Young, at Stewartstown.

    d. Eliza A., b. Jan. 4, 1857; m. Jan. 1, 1874, John H. Haynes at Stewartstown. Child: (1) Chloe, b. Jan. 29, 1880.

44. Benjamin Wiggin, b. Stewartstown, Dec. 3, 1827; d. at 3 years of age.

(13) John Kidder, son of Benjamin, b. Jan. 7, 1793, m. Dec. 25, 1820, Ruth, dau. of Josiah Fellows (See), b. Feb. 9, 1795, and d. Apr. 9, 1879, ae. 84-2-0. He was a farmer in the Kidder neighborhood. He d. Mar. 25, 1848, ae. 55-2-18.

CHILDREN, all born in Bristol

45. Frederick Kidder, b. Apr. 8, 1822 ; m. Jan. 15, 1845, Samantha, dau. of Timothy Chandler (See), b. July 4, 1822. He is a farmer where his great-gandfather settled. Children, all born in Bristol:

    a. Ellen Georgianna, b. May 29, 1849. Unm.

    b. Dennis Herman, b. June 8, 1851; d. Sept. 4, 1854, ae. 3-2-26.

    c. Cora Augusta, b. Mar. 5, 1857 ; m. Orrin J. Muzzey. (See.)

    d. Hiram Dana, b. Jan. 5, 1861. Farmer on home farm. Unm.

46. John W., b. Apr. 15, 1831 ; d. unm., Nov. 19, 1855, ae. 24-7-4.

47. Charles, b. May 25, 1836; m. Mar. 13, 1862, Susan E., dau. of Moses and Mary (Putney) Johnson, of Weare, b. Feb. 14, 1839. He lived on the Kidder farm till about middle life then removed to the village, where he now res. Democrat, laborer, Methodist. Children, all b. in Bristol :

    a. Hattie A., b. Dec. 22, 1863 ; mill operative.

    b. John H., b. May 6, 1867. Unm. Official member Methodist church. Odd Fellow. Democrat.

    c. Lurie A., b. July 9, 1869.

    d. Ellen I., b. May 7, 1872 ; m. June 2, 1897, David H. Goodhue, locomotive fireman. (His second wife.) She d. Oct. 7, 1900, ae. 28-5-. Children: (1) Son, b. Nov. 3, 1898; d. same day. (2) Lucia May, b. Jan. 6, 1900.

48. Arianna, b. Aug. 29, 1838 ; m. Richard K. Sawyer, and d. Bristol, Jan. 12, 1863, ae. 24-3-13. He d. diphtheria, Mar. 20, 1869, ae. 29-5-. Child :

    a. Lurie Ann, b. Bristol, Dec. 12, 1862 ; d. Plymouth, diphtheria, Mar. 15, 1869, ae. 6-3-3.

(14) Benjamin Kidder, son of Benjamin, b. June 13, 1795, first settled on the Frank Sanborn farm. About 1827, he moved

BENJAMIN KIDDER

to farm now owned and occupied by Levi N. Heath. Jan., 1856, he removed to Illinois. He m. Mar. 4, 1824, Sarah Dodge, b. in Irasburg, Vt., Nov. 24, 1801, and d. in Bristol, Oct. 15, 1831, ae. 29-10-21. He m. June 5, 1832, Mary Doton, b. Moultonboro', Jan. 16, 1807, dau. of Ephraim and Susanna Doton, and sister of Dr. Isaac Doton, of New Hampton. She d. at Woosung, Ill., Apr. 3, 1892, ae. 85-2-17. He d. same place, Aug. 6, 1883, ae. 88-1-23.

CHILDREN, all born in Bristol

49. Adoniram, b. May 8, 1825. He m. Apr. 10, 1846 (June 13, 1846 — Records Cong. church), Lydia Ann, dau. Smith Powell (See), b. June 29, 1830. Res. Bristol, New Hampton, Dixon, Ill.; Helena, Mont.; Utah; Evanston, Wyoming; thence to Sanborn, Iowa, in 1882, where she d. Mar. 19, 1894, ae. 63-8-20. He res. Sanborn. Children:

a. Malvenah S., b. Bristol, Feb. 1, 1847; m. Nov. 30, 1869, William C. Green, of Dixon, Ill. Res. Sanborn, Iowa. Children: (1) Lulu, m. Charles Anderson, at Sanborn, Nov. 30, 1894. (2) Edna.

b. Ella D., b. B., May 5. 1854; m. Dec. 9, 1872, Allen E. Bradbury, of South Pass, Wyo. Res. Red Canon, Wyo. Children: (1) Silas N. (2) Velorus. (3) Earl.

c. Jennie L., b. New Hampton, May 5, 1856; m. July 21, 1873. Peter A. McPhee, of Green River, Wyo. Res. Kaslo, B. C.

50. Levi Nelson, b. Mar. 13, 1827. Left Bristol in 1851; was in Georgia two years and in the West; was a railroad contractor in Pennsylvania, and d. of consumption at Dixon, Ill., July 17, 1865, unm., ae. 38-4-4.

51. Sarah Ann, b. May 18, 1829; m. Apr. 6, 1856, James W. Taylor, Sandwich; she d. Jordan, Ill., Aug. 1, 1861, ae. 32-2-13. Children:

a. George Almond, b. Jordan, Ill., Dec. 30, 1857. Res. in Pueblo, Colo.

b. Nellie Dodge, b. Mar. 15, 1859; m. Dec. 21, 1875, S. H. Todd; res. Millidgeville, Ill.

c. Lizzie Florence, b. Jordan, July 15, 1860.

52. Nelson B., b. Jan. 16, 1834; m. Dec. 30, 1862, Amanda Mingle, dau. of Joseph H. and Catherine Mingle, b. Dec. 26, 1841, in Bradford, Co., Penn. He left Bristol for Illinois in Jan., 1855; res. in Polo, Ill. Children:

a. Aldanah C., b. Jordan, Ill., Oct. 12, 1863; d. June 29, 1868, ae. 4-8-17.

b. Irvin M., b. J., July 18, 1869; m. Feb. 11, 1891, Maggie Maxwell, who d. Feb. 28, 1895; he m. (2) Janette Allison, of Chickasaw Co., Iowa.

c. Fred J., b. J., Feb. 11, 1874. Res. Polo.

53. Electa H., b. Nov. 15, 1837; m. Jan. 1, 1855, Harrison J. Taylor, of Sandwich; d. in Iowa, June 9, 1878, ae. 40-6-24. Children:

a. William.   b. Merrow.   c. Charles.   d. Frank.
e. Emma.   f. Sherman.   g. Levi.

54. Marcellus, b. Sept. 8, 1840; m. Apr. 22, 1871, Ella J. Annan, dau. John G. and Hannah Annan, b. Sept. 2, 1849. He went West in 1854, and res. Penrose, Ill. Children:

a. Ida Luella, b. Jordan, Ill., May 9, 1875.

b. Royce Annan, b. J., July 8, 1878.

18a

(18) Joshua Kidder, son of Benjamin, b. June 8, 1805, m. Dec. 28 (31), 1832, Mary Jane, dau. Ezekiel and Sarah (Cross) Willey, b. Dec. 19, 1808, in Canterbury, and d. in Bristol, May 11, 1889, ae. 80-4-22. He was a farmer and settled on his grandfather's farm but in middle life removed to Merrimack street, and conducted the saw-mill on the south side of the river. He d. Apr. 20, 1863, ae. 57-10-12.

CHILDREN, all born in Bristol

55. Nancy Jane, b. May 7, 1835; m. Benjamin E. Blackstone. (See.)
56. Helen Augusta, b. Aug. 13, 1837; m. (1) Apr. 1, 1854, Lyman R. Roberts, of Orford. She m. (2) Thomas Ryan, of Franklin. Children:
    a. Mary Jane, b. Sept. 18, 1855; m. Oct., 1878, George W. Ryan, of Franklin.
    b. Nellie, b. Feb. 23, 1858; d. Mar. 16, 1859, ae. 1-0-23.
    c. Joshua, b. Mar. 11, 1860; m. Mary E. Williams, Boston, 1882.
    d. Ira Lyman, b. Nov. 28, 1862; m. Mary Gilman, Portsmouth, 1884.
    e. Nellie Etta, b. July 19, 1865; m. Dec. 3, 1885, Bert Orton, of Fairfax, Vt.
    f. Minnie Bell, b. Nov. 14, 1868; m. Sept., 19, 1889, Frank C. Kittridge.
57. Francena, b. Apr. 22, 1841; m. Daniel Cass. (See.)
58. Laura Augusta, b. Aug. 11, 1842; m. Etna A. Ferrin Concord. She d. May 31, 1900, ae. 57-9-20.
59. Cornelia, b. Jan. 2, 1849; m. Nov., 1866, Charles A. Bond, a captain in the Union army. She d. in Concord, Nov. 17, 1889, from a surgical operation the day previous, ae. 40-10-15.

(20) Joseph Kidder, son of Benjamin, b. Aug. 2, 1809, m. Dec. 25, 1834, Dorcas, dau. of Levi Nelson (See), b. Nov. 6, 1814. Divorced. She d. in Bristol, Apr. 7, 1878, ae. 63-5-1. He m. (2) Louisa Lavina, widow of Orrin Gordon, and dau. of David Batchelder. (See.) She d. Concord, Oct. 3, 1891, ae. 69-0-13. He was a farmer on North Main street, at the base of Sugar hill. He carried on his farm and at odd hours with one horse did all the job teaming required in the village at that time. He d. Nov. 17, 1873, ae. 64-3-15.

CHILDREN, all born in Bristol

60. Jessie M., b. Nov. 16, 1835; d. Jan. 27, 1837 ae. 1-2-11.
61. Uriah H., b. June 26, 1836; m. Mar. 29, 1881, Nancy Jane, dau. of Oliver S. Hall. (See.) He was a carpenter and farmer, res. on Hall farm. (See Roll of Honor.) He d. Mar. 29, 1903, ae. 66-9-3. No children.
62. Albert Harvey, b. July 16, 1838; m. Aug. 26, 1861, Emeline, dau. Josiah M. Healey, b. Alexandria, Oct. 15, 1837. He has res. 359 Pearl street, Manchester, since Mar., 1871. Carpenter. Children:
    a. Rosetta, b. Bristol, Feb. 27, 1862.
    b. Annie M., b. B., July 25, 1869; m. May 20, 1896, Rufus H. Perkins. He d. Mar. 11, 1900. She res. Manchester.
    c. Alma Dean, b. Manchester, Mar. 3, 1873; m. Oct. 8, 1894, George A. Hoyt, res. North Londonderry.
63. Henry R., b. Apr. 13, 1841. Killed at battle of Chancellorsville, May 3, 1863, ae. 22-0-20. (See Roll of Honor.)

64. Frank M., was a salesman in St. Louis, Mo.; m. Feb. 10, 1885, Ann McDonald. Present residence unknown.

---

1.   Francis Kidder, son of Francis and Abigail (Russell) Kidder, was b. Littleton, Mass., Feb. 11, 1785. He. m. Jan. 18, 1810, Nancy Hartwell, of Littleton. Francis Kidder was a merchant in Andover, Mass. He was taxed in Bristol, 1839–'52, and d. in Bristol, Nov. 7, 1852, ae. 67–8–26. Mrs. Kidder removed to Cambridge, Mass., and there d.

CHILDREN

2.   Frances Ann, b. June 18, 1811 ; d. Apr. 11, 1830, ae. 18–9–23.

3.   Martha Jane, b. Feb. 1, 1813 ; m. Oct. 10, 1832, Nathaniel Swift, of Andover, Mass., merchant, partner of Francis Kidder. Was President Andover Savings bank 25 years. She d. Nov. 28, 1843, ae. 30–9–27. Four children.

4.   Mary Elizabeth, b. Feb. 4, 1815 ; m. Sept. 2, 1835, Samuel Prentiss Cobb, Andover ; d. Sept. 30, 1836, ae. 21–7–26. No children.

5.   William, b. Mar. 29, 1817, settled in Newburyport, Mass., and never res. in Bristol.

6.   Francis Henry, b. July 20, 1819, merchant, came to Bristol, 1840. Was identified with first woolen-mill near railroad station ; was first conductor on Franklin & Bristol railroad ; was badly injured on road ; resigned, and engaged in horse trade ; d. from kick of horse in old stable once connected with tavern on South Main street in May, 1853, ae. 43–10–.

7.   Ellen Caroline, b. Andover, Mass., Mar. 20, 1823 ; m. Solomon S. Sleeper. (See.)

8.   Sarah Dix, b. Andover, July 6, 1825 ; m. Sherburn S. Merrill. (See.)

9.   Susan Hayward, b. Nov. 3, 1829 ; m. Nov. 7, 1848, Israel Lombard, of Boston ; d. Oct. 29, 1851, ae. 21–11–26. One dau. d.

THE KIMBALL FAMILIES

1.   Arthur Lamprey Kimball, son of John A. and Sarah (Nudd) Kimball, was b. Gilford, Apr. 11, 1875. He m. Sept. 1, 1894, Ida May, dau. of Francis L. and Elmira Blake, b. New Hampton, Oct. 4, 1877. Employee of pulp-mill most of the time for past 12 years.

CHILDREN

2.   Minnie Maria, b. New Hampton, Jan. 13, 1895.

3.   Eva Maud, b. Bristol, Aug. 8, 1898 ; d. Sanbornton, Oct. 20, 1901.

---

1.   Charles Edward Kimball is the son of Daniel S. and Martha A. (Bennett) Kimball. He was b. Franklin June 10, 1867, and m. May 2, 1891, Hattie Etta, dau. Henry Decato. (See.) He is a farmer in the Kidder neighborhood. A Catholic, and a member of the grange.

2. Sadie Belle, b. Bristol, Mar. 20, 1892.
3. Hervie Charles, b. B., Nov. 26, 1895.
4. Florence Della, b. B., June 24, 1901.

THE KING FAMILIES

1. Edward Franklin King is the son of Benjamin Franklin and Mary Ann (Waterman) King. He was b. White River Junction, Vt., Jan. 19, 1847, and m. Oct. 10, 1885, Adelaide Victoria, dau. of Joseph and Matilda (Burnham) Huntoon, b. at Enfield, July 5, 1848. He came from Enfield in 1885, and has had charge of the finishing room of the woolen-mill 17 years. No children.

---

1. Fred Louis King, son of Oliver A. and Lucy A. (Hall) King, was b. in New York city, June 9, 1865. He m. Belle N., dau. of George H. and Jane Simonds, b. Alexandria, Mar. 15, 1868. He has been a laborer in Bristol since Mar., 1885.

2. Perley G., b. Bristol, June 3, 1889.
3. Fred Louis, b. B., Nov. 11, 1892.

THE KIRK FAMILIES

1. Robert Moore Kirk was the son of John D. Kirk, of Alexandria. He was b. in Alexandria, May 26, 1824; m. Sarah Jane, dau. of John B. Straw, b. Feb. 1, 1819. Farmer in Alexandria till 1866; then a laborer in Bristol till he d., May 2, 1883, ae. 58-11-6. She d. Mar. 11, 1896, ae. 77-1-10.

2. John D., b. Alexandria, Aug. 20, 1843; m. Oct. 5, 1871, Frances, dau. of Jacob S. Hall, b. Georgetown, Mass., June 12, 1847. He was station agent at Franklin; later in trade there; d. Sept. 24, 1900, ae. 57-1-4. Deacon Congregational church, Mason, Odd Fellow. Child:

    a. Charles Almont, b. Oct. 22, 1873; m. June 11, 1902, Minnie Dell Jellison.

3. Lizzie A., b. A., Apr. 25, 1845; m. George H. Spiller. (See.)
4. Frank Samuel, b. A., Jan. 18, 1849; m. May 7, 1866, Julia Ann, dau. of Benjamin and Adeline (Roberts) Spiller, b. Bridgewater, May 5, 1842; d. Bristol, Nov. 25, 1901, ae. 59-6-20. She was two years a member of the board of education. He m. (2) Apr. 22, 1902, Emma Frances, dau. of Joseph A. and Lois A. (Cummings) Judkins. Has res. in Bristol since Jan., 1869. Was an employee at woolen-mill three years; since 1872, salesman at the grist-mill on Central street. Served one year as selectman. Republican, Free Baptist, Odd Fellow, K. of P., Granger. Children:

a. Ellis Leslie, b. Bridgewater, June 20, 1867; graduated in the classical and commercial courses at New Hampton, 1885. Res. in Melrose, Mass., since Sept., 1886. Is a cutter in a manufactory of gent's furnishing goods, Boston. He m., Mar. 7, 1895, Alice M., dau. of Solomon L. Howes, b. Melrose, Mass., May 5, 1872, and d. June 7, 1896, ae. 24-1-2. He m., Sept. 19, 1899, Lillian Frances, dau. of Enoch and Naomi (Moore) Bird, b. Malden, Mass., June 24, 1872. Child : Alice May, b. May 25, 1896.

b. Harry Raymond, b. Bristol, June 13, 1876; d. Sept. 11, 1876.

c. Harland Frank, b. B., Sept. 4, 1883; drowned July 1, 1896, ae. 12-9-27.

5. Daniel G., b. A., Jan. 6, 1851; d. Bristol, Oct. 24, 1869, ae. 18-9-18.

6. Horace Herbert, b. A., Aug. 10, 1855; m. Aug. 17, 1903, Garrie E., dau. of Edwin H. Gove. (See.) He has been for 23 years superintendent of the pulp-mill near railroad station. Republican, Odd Fellow, K. of P.

7. Mary Jane, b. A., Aug. 10, 1856; d. scarlet fever, July 10, 1861, ae. 4-11-0.

8. George Elmont, b. A., Jan. 16, 1861; d. scarlet fever, July 20, 1861.

---

1. Stephen Peaslee Kirk, son of Daniel, and grandson of John D. Kirk, was b. Alexandria, Dec. 5, 1836. He m., Jan. 27, 1857, Mrs. Lovina Wells (Heath) Kirk (See), widow of his brother, Horace G. He located in Bristol, 1873. Is a carpenter. Republican. Has been janitor of town hall 20 years.

CHILDREN

2. Cora Eva, b. Alexandria, Feb. 16, 1860; d. Mar. 28, 1860.

3. Addie Lunette, b. A., Apr. 19, 1861; d. Mar. 29, 1863, ae. 1-11-10.

4. Frank Newell Cross, b. Bristol, Jan. 9, 1881; m. Mar. 25, 1901, Anna, dau. Eddie and Delia (Bennett) Billivao, b. Canaan. Is a woodworker. Republican.

THE KITTRELL FAMILY

1. William H. Kittrell is the son of Solomon H. and Harriet A. (Orcutt) Kittrell. He was b. Randolph, Mass., Oct. 16, 1851. He m., Nov. 21, 1885, Georgiana P., dau. of Newell and Elizabeth A. (Pease) Avery, b. Ellsworth, Aug. 2, 1861. They have res. in Bristol since October, 1886. He is an employee of Mason-Perkins Paper Co.

THE KNIGHT FAMILY

1. George Henry Knight, son of John and Juliette Knight, was b. Concord, Apr. 14, 1850. Sept. 19, 1874, he m. Amanda R., dau. of Jonas Call. (See.) He was a painter in Bristol, 1872, till he emigrated to Cambridge, Neb., 1886, where they now reside.

CHILD

2. William Call, b. June 5, 1888.

THE LADD FAMILIES

1. The Ladds of Bristol were the descendants of Daniel Ladd, who came from England in ship "Mary and John" in 1633 or '34. He settled in Ipswich, Mass., and was one of the original settlers of Haverhill, Mass.

2. Peter Ladd, son of Jeremiah, was a descendant of Daniel, of the fifth generation. He was a farmer in Bristol in 1801, and probably for some years previous. In 1804, he was town clerk of Alexandria. He m., May 27, 1789, Rhoda Quimby, and d. Jan. 19, 1818.

CHILDREN

3. Nancy, b. Nov. 22, 1790; m. Samuel Tay.
4. Lydia, b. Nov. 2, 1791; m. Peter Fellows. (See.)
5. Priscilla, b. July 14, 1793; never m.
6. Polly, b. July 4, 1795; m. John Simonds.
7. Betsey Sleeper, b. July 9, 1797; d. unm., May 12, 1889, ae. 91-10-3.
8. Peter, b. May 21, 1799; d. Sept. 9, 1800, ae. 1-3-18.
*9. David Chandler, b. Bristol, Aug. 6, 1801.
10. Ruth, b. Dec. 13, 1803; m. Eben Corliss, Concord.
11. Jeremiah Quimby, b. July 25, 1805. He m. Abigail Collins. He was a tax-payer in District No. 9, 1828-'32. He res. in a house that stood 20 or more rods east of the highway opposite the Ezekiel Follansbee farmhouse.

(9) David C. Ladd, b. Aug. 6, 1801, m. Aug. 1, 1823, Judith Atwood, dau. of Moses (See), b. Aug. 26, 1805. He was a farmer and hewer of ship timber on the Ezekiel Follansbee farm, near Sugar Loaf mountain, from 1829 till he d., June 17, 1840, ae. 38-10-11. She m. (2) Abel Ford, and res. in Orange.

CHILDREN

12. James Minard, b. May 24, 1824; d. June 14, 1839, ae. 15-0-20.
13. Gustavus Bartlett, b. Jan. 29, 1829; d. May 12, 1854, ae. 25-3-13.
14. Rhoda F., b. Bristol, Apr. 2, 1831; m. Feb. 26, 1849, Elisha Whittier, and d. Sept. 24, 1852, ae. 21-5-22.
15. David Newell, b. B., Mar. 17, 1834; m. Apr. 1, 1857, Sarah B. Poole. He served in the 6th Regt., N. H. Vols., Civil war. (See Roll of Honor.) Res. Enfield. Children:

　　a. David Marshall, b. Enfield, Nov. 5, 1859.
　　b. Mabel Jennie, b. E., Feb. 5, 1867.

16. Melissa Jane, b. B., Aug. 7, 1836; m. Elisha Whittier, Apr. 24, 1853; d. Jan. 1854, ae. 17-5-.
17. Leroy Sunderland, b. B., Dec. 7, 1839. Died of wounds July 1, 1862, ae. 22-6-24. (See Roll of Honor.)

---

1. John Ladd, son of Jeremiah, was b. Alexandria, Mar. 26, 1804. He m. (1) June, 1828 (May 5, 1828 — town records), Fannie G., dau. of Nathaniel Collins, b. Sanbornton, Feb. 27,

1807. She d. in Bristol, Feb. 29, 1851, ae. 44-0-2. He m. (2) June 26, 1852, Sarah Fellows Collins, a sister of his first wife, who d. Apr. 22, 1892. John Ladd was a farmer in what is now called Adamsville, near the lake, till 1842, when he removed to Alexandria. A year later returned to his old farm, where he remained till spring of 1850, when he went to California. After two years he returned and settled in Alexandria village, where he d. Mar. 28, 1876, ae. 72-0-2.

CHILDREN

2. George Lovering, b. Bristol, Aug. 29, 1829; d. Feb. 1, 1830.

3. Mahala Williams, b. B., Dec. 7, 1830; m. Jeremiah F. Dow, Oct. 21, 1858, and res. Shirley, Mass. He d. and she m. (2) Henry Orange. She d. Jan. 29, 1901, ae. 70-1-22.

4. Emily Jane, b. B., Sept. 28, 1832; m. Dugal H. Barr, Lawrence, Mass., and d. Sept. 25, 1850, ae. 17-11-27.

5. Esther Ann, b. B., Nov. 30, 1834; m. 1866, Dr. John Pray, Rochester. He d. 1871. She d. Franklin, Mar. 7, 1895, ae. 60-3-7.

6. Tirzah Harvey, b. B., Aug. 29, 1836; m. Walter F. Simonds in 1858. She d. May 26, 1860, ae. 23-8-27. He d. Campton.

7. Sylvester Sleeper, b. B., July, 25, 1838; d. Dec. 9, 1839, ae. 1-4-14.

8. Charles Wesley, b. B., July 1, 1840; d. Aug. 18, 1843, ae. 3-1-17.

9. Mary Augusta, b. Alexandria, May 12, 1842; m. Jan. 4, 1865, Edwin Judkins. He d. in Franklin, 1888, ae. 55. She res. Franklin.

10. Luther Crawford, b. Bristol, Dec. 22, 1843. This man was the first to fall in defense of the Union in the Civil war, being killed by the mob in Baltimore, Md., Apr. 19, 1861, at the age of 17-3-27. (See Roll of Honor.)

11. Ella Frances, b. Oct. 2, 1850; m. William H. Stevens; d. Dec. 5, 1893, ae. 43-2-3.

---

1. Joseph Warren Ladd, son of James M. and Emily T. (Clough) Ladd, was b. Gilford, Aug. 16, 1871. He m. Feb. 1, 1895, Mabel D., dau. of Albert M. and Dorothy J. (Moses) Marden, b. July 28, 1872. Both graduated from New Hampton Literary Institution, 1894. Came to Bristol and erected residence in 1897. Piano tuner and musician. Odd Fellow, K. of P.

CHILDREN

2. Harold Marden, b. New Hampton, Oct. 1, 1896.

3. Bernard Gordon, b. Bristol, Jan. 31, 1903.

LAMPREY

1. Frank Lamprey is the son of Daniel Lamprey, who served in the 8th Regt., N. H. Vols., and d. of wounds received at the battle of Port Hudson. His mother was Mary M. (Coffin) Lamprey. He was b. Lyman, May 3, 1852, and became a resident of Bristol, 1882. Is a workman at crutch factory. Is a Republican, Odd Fellow, and K. of P.; unm.

THE LANEY FAMILY

1.   John Laney was b. in Rumney, Mar. 12, 1791, and m. Oct. 18, 1816, Nancy, dau. of Daniel Sleeper (See), b. Mar. 12, 1794.   He was a farmer in Alexandria and Bridgewater, and d. June 8, 1860, ae. 69-2-26 ; she d. Aug. 23, 1881, ae. 87-5-11.

CHILDREN

2.   Daniel, b. Alexandria, Sept. 16, 1817 ; d. Feb. 21, 1818.
3.   Louise P., b. A., Dec. 3, 1818 ; m. May 29, 1847, Harrison P. Nelson. He d. in Mitchell, Iowa, Sept. 1, 1859, ae. 39-5-4.   Later she res. for some years in Bristol; now in Franklin.   Children :

  a. Luella Lucy, b. Antioch, Ill., Apr. 28, 1848 ; d. Apr. 17, 1849.
  b. Luella Louisa, b. A., Apr. 2, 1851. Res. Franklin.
  c. Elizabeth Ann, b. A., Jan. 30, 1854. She was two years a teacher in Union district in Bristol. Is a proof-reader in Concord.
  d. Lucy Nancy, b. Mitchell, Iowa, Nov. 13, 1856. Res. Franklin. Taught one year in Union district in Bristol. Is a teacher of art in Franklin and Tilton.
  e. William Harrison, b. M., May 25, 1859. Is a merchant in Franklin.

4.   John, b. A., Aug. 17, 1820 ; d. in California.
5.   Gilman Dodge, b. A., Mar. 1, 1823 ; m. Apr. 11, 1852, Eliza Ann, dau. of Nathan and Caroline (Bryant) Burnham, b. Corinth, Me., Nov. 14, 1830. He was a farmer at Profile Falls, 1861-'66 ; thence moved to Hill, where he d. Sept. 3, 1877, ae. 54-6-2. She m. (2) James Patten. (See.) Children :

  a. Kate Madora, b. Antioch, Ill., Apr. 15, 1855 ; d. Oct. 18, 1856, ae. 1-6-3.
  b. Dora Mae, b. A., Oct. 8, 1857 ; m. Frank E. Clifford. (See.)

6.   Isaac H., b. A., Oct. 6, 1825, res. Methuen, Mass. He m. (1) Betsey Sargent, Methuen, who d. 1882. He m. (2) Sarah Dowen, who d. 1898. He d. Malden, Mass., June 10, 1903, ae. 77-8-4. No children.
7.   Levi Bartlett, b. Bridgewater, Aug. 16, 1828 ; m. Oct. 8, 1851, Elizabeth Brown, dau. of Moses Smith, b. Bridgewater, June 20, 1825, and d. in Alexandria, May 8, 1852, ae. 26-10-18. He m. (2) Nov. 3, 1858, Margaret A., dau. of Benjamin Huntington, of Weare, b. Feb. 11, 1831. She d. July 22, 1893, ae. 62-5-11. He was a resident of Bristol 1861-'67 ; removed to East Weare and still res. there. He served in 12th Regt., N. H. Vols. (See Roll of Honor.) Democrat, Methodist, Granger. Child :

  a. Infant son, "given and taken June 3, 1873."

8.   Francis E., b. Hebron, May 29, 1831. Went to California in 1852. Was last heard from directly in 1860, when he was a teacher in a Catholic school ; is supposed to be a Catholic priest on the Pacific coast.

THE LEWIS FAMILY

1.   Col. Moses Lewis, son of Benjamin and Mary (Brown) Lewis, was b. Billerica, Mass., Apr. 17, 1770. He settled in Bridgewater village as early as 1794, and Aug. 15, of that year, he m. in Alexandria, Sally, dau. of William and Jane (McDonald) Martin, b. Pembroke, July 21, 1776. (Records of Rev. Enoch Whipple, pastor of the First Congregational church in

LEVI B. LANEY

Alexandria, say that he married this couple Dec. 10, 1795.)
He was the first merchant in what is now Bristol village, opening a store soon after he came here in a building that stood
where is now Fowler's block. He did a large business for those
times, and all his goods, including a liberal supply of West
India rum, was brought from Boston by teams. In 1795, he
built at the corner of Central square and Spring street a two-
story frame house which was remodeled in 1879 by George G.
Brown into the present four-story structure and used for a hotel.
Col. Lewis owned Lot No. 61, First Division, containing the
grist-mill and saw-mill, and all the privileges on the falls of
the river. He converted the mills named into a tannery, and
erected a saw-mill and a grist-mill on the south side of the river.
The depression of business previous to the War of 1812 caused
his failure. He was owing largely through the community,
and the distress caused by his failure was widespread. Suits
were bought for as small sums as one dollar, after the custom of
those days, and the sheriff levied on all the household goods.
In the Fisk block, at the corner of Central square and Summer
street, lived friends who watched for the coming to town of the
sheriff, and notified the family of his arrival, when some of the
cooking utensils were hid, and in this way such articles were
saved from his relentless grasp. The "Lewis Letter" printed
in Connecticut, says Col. Lewis was imprisoned for debts he
could not pay. Col. Lewis was a prominent man in this section
in the days of his prosperity. He served four years as selectman, represented Bridgewater nine times in the general court,
and was the commanding officer in the 34th Regt., state militia.
He removed to Alabama, being last taxed here in 1815. He d.
in Gainesville, Ala., Oct. 7, 1836, ae. 66–5–20. His widow d.
same place, Jan. 10, 1853, ae. 76–5–19.

CHILDREN, all born in Bristol

   2. Mary, b. Oct. 14, 1796; d. of consumption, Nov. 6, 1827; ae. 31–
0–22.
  *3. William Martin, b. Aug. 29, 1798.
  *4. Rufus Graves, b. Sept. 14, 1800.
   5. Hiram, b. Aug. 14. 1802 ; d. Mar. 14, 1803.
   6. Eliza Webster, b. June 26, 1804 ; d. Kemper Springs, Miss., Oct.
1, 1843, ae. 39–3–5 ; unm.
   7. Sarah, b. Sept. 1, 1807 ; m. May 28, 1835, in Springfield, Ala., Dr.
Samuel Smith, a former practicing physician in Bridgewater, and d.
Loudonville, Ohio, Aug. 29, 1844, ae. 36–11–28.

    (3) William M. Lewis, b. Aug. 29, 1798, was a school
teacher. He was associated with Nathaniel S. Berry and Jonathan Emmons, in 1824, in establishing Sunday-schools in Bristol. He followed his father to the South, being last taxed here
in 1824. Four years later, however, he made a trip to Bristol,
and m., Sept. 25, 1828, Mary, dau. of Ichabod C. Bartlett
(See), b. June 7, 1802. She d. Gainesville, May 28, 1831, ae.

28–11–21.   He m. (2) May 2, 1836, at Columbus, Miss., Aurelia Hiley Axtell, b. Windsor, Mass., Oct. 6, 1811, and d. at Gainesville, July 15, 1861, ae. 49–9–9.   He d. Feb. 13, 1881, ae. 82–5–14.   He was a Presbyterian elder ; a merchant, and a man of large means till the Civil war swept most of his property away.

CHILDREN

8.   William Frederick, b. May 2, 1831 ; d. Hickory, Miss., about 1891.   His widow res. Hickory.   Several children.

9.   Eliza Jane, b. Aug. 10, 1837 ; m. 1858, Croget C. Converse, LL.D., Res. Highwood, Bergen Co., N. J.   Children :

    a.   Charles Henry, b. 1863 ; d. Elmira N. Y., 1864.

    b.   Clarence, b. Brooklyn, N. Y. ; m. June 8, 1897, Mary Elisabeth Manard.

10.   Sylvester Creswell, b. Aug. 8, 1839 ; res. Webster Grove, St. Louis Co., Mo.   He has a family.

11.   Moses Boardman, b. Apr. 6, 1842 ; d. Jan. 15, 1844, ae. 1–9–9.

12.   Laura Aurelia, b. Apr. 6, 1844 ; d. Apr. 16, 1847, ae. 3–0–10.

13.   Maria Creswell, b. May 14, 1846 ; d. Oct. 29, 1862, ae. 16–5–15.

14.   Mary Russell, b. Oct. 30, 1848 ; d. Aug. 16, 1850, ae. 1–9–16.

15.   Charles Carrington, b. Sept. 26, 1850 ; d. Feb. 11, 1873, at Brooklyn, N. Y., ae. 22–4–15.

16.   Sally Martin, b. Mar. 28, 1854 ; d. 1887, at Tuscaloosa, Ala., ae. 33.

(4)   Col. Rufus G. Lewis, b. Sept. 14, 1800, m. Oct. 29, 1828, Sally, dau. of Daniel Smith, b. in New Hampton, Apr. 4, 1806.   Col. Lewis res. in New Hampton, in what is now called the Mansion.   In connection with his residence he supported a fine conservatory and grounds.   He also had large estates in Alabama and Mississippi.   He was a liberal supporter of New Hampton Literary Institution.   Dartmouth college conferred upon him the degree of Master of Arts.   He d. Sept. 27, 1869, ae. 69–0–13 ; she d. Oct. 15, 1878, ae. 72–6–11.

CHILDREN

17.   Son, b. New Hampton, June, 1831 ; d. in infancy.

18.   Rufus Smith, b. N. H., June 14, 1833 ; married July 14, 1856, Eliza Bean Hilton.   He was in business in Lowell, Mass.; was register of deeds of Belknap county for some years.   He d. Laconia, May 22, 1887, ae. 53–11–8.   His widow m. his brother, Edwin C. Lewis.   Child :

    a.   Winnifreda Wallace, b. Feb. 3, 1858 ; m. Chas. H. Turner.

19.   Edwin Creswell, b. N. H., Nov. 28, 1836.   Graduated from New Hampton Institution, 1854 ; Harvard college, 1859 ; read law in Lowell, Mass., and settled in New Hampton, where he was trustee of the literary institution, secretary and member of the executive committee ; was town treasurer and moderator.   Removed to Laconia where he was editor and part proprietor of the *Laconia Democrat*, 1878–'97 ; was county treasurer two years, and member of the governor's council, 1891–'93.   He m. July 24, 1890, Mrs. Eliza Bean (Hilton) Lewis.   She d. Apr 15, 1899.

20.   Sarah Eliza, b. Sept. 4, 1839 ; m. F. C. Jordan, June 12, 1866 ; res. Biddeford, Me.   Children :

    a.   Ellen Bell.   *b.*   Benjamin.   *c.*   Sally.

21.   James Pickering, b. Feb. 10, 1842 ; m. Molly Winne.   He was a clerk in the post-office department at Washington, D. C.   He d. at Washington, Dec. 22, 1901, ae. 59–10–12.   Child :

    a.   James.

THE LOCKE FAMILIES

The Lockes of Bristol are the descendants of John Locke,
b. England, Sept. 16, 1627. He settled in Portsmouth or Rye
about 1640, m. Elizabeth Berry in 1652, and was a prosperous
farmer and noted Indian fighter. While at work in his field,
Aug. 26, 1696, he was ambushed and killed by the Indians.
The line of descent appears to have been as follows:

1. Capt. John Locke, b. England, Sept. 16, 1627, was the
father of
2. Edward. He was the father of
3. Thomas Locke, b. Rye, 1713. He was the father of

   4. Benjamin.
*5. Levi, b. Kingston, 1745.
*6. Thomas, b. Oct. 14, 1751.

(5) Levi Locke, b. 1745, m. Rachel Fuller.

CHILDREN

*7. Benjamin, b. Sandown, Apr. 10, 1770.
  8. Rachel, b. Rye, Oct. 15, 1772; m. Abraham Dolloff. (See.)
  9. Abigail, b. Sandown; m. Josiah Fuller. (See.)

(6) Thomas Locke was b. Oct. 14, 1751. He m. Martha
Worthen, b. 1745. She is supposed to have been a sister of
Lieut. Samuel Worthen. They were in Bristol as early as
the summer of 1771, on the farm where Solon Dolloff now lives.
The road or path in those days was higher up on the hillside
than now and their log cabin was beside this road directly back
of the present farmhouse. "Tom" Locke was a great bear
hunter, and one fall trapped or killed sixteen bears on Briar
hill, near by. This family removed to Stanstead, Canada, some
time previous to 1800, where he d. Apr. 14, 1816, ae. 64-6-0.
She d. same place, Mar. 17, 1826, ae. 81.

CHILDREN, all born Bristol

10. Moses, b. May 3, 1773; m. Margaret Durgan.
11. Sarah, b. Jan. 28, 1776; m. —— Converse; lived and d. in Wilmot.
12. Abigail, b. Sept. 22, 1778; m. Obadiah Belknap; settled in Barnston, Canada, 1807. He was b. Lisbon, 1774, and d. 1834, ae. 60. She d.
Apr. 3, 1861, ae. 82-6-11. Children:
    a. Mitchell, b. Jan. 21, 1800.
    b. Sally, b. Dec. 21, 1801; m. Nicholas Davis.
    c. Thomas, b. Aug. 10, 1803; m. Sally Dearborn.
    d. William, b. Sept. 20, 1805; m. Roxanna Taylor.
    e. Martha, b. Apr. —, 1807; m. James Felden.
    f. Hannah, b. 1810; m. Joseph Bailey.
13. Levi, b Dec. 22, 1780; m. Sally Clement, Sept. 30, 1804. She was
b. Penacook, Feb. 27, 1787. Settled in Barnston, Canada. Children:
    a. Betsey, b. Nov. 23, 1805; m. John M. Mosher.
    b. Levi, b. Jan. 19, 1814; d. unm.
    c. Chloe, b. Jan. 16, 1816; m. Guy Aldrich, b. Barston, Can.,
    Apr. 30, 1813. Had nine children.

    d. Louisa, b. Nov. 8, 1819; m. William Burroughs.

    e. Amanda, b. Feb. 13, 1822; m. Thomas Cooper.

    f. Thomas, b. June 16, 1824; m. Lydia E. Howard, b. Lisbon, Feb. 22, 1825. Res. Barnston. Five children.

    g. Sally, b. Apr. 20, 1826; m. Walter S. Baldwin; d. Jan. 15, 1855, ae. 28-8-25.

    h. Lucy, b. May 27, 1829; m. John Sheerar.

  14. Ward, b. Aug. 12, 1784.

  15. Mary, b. Mar. 28, 1787; m. Levi Hill, b. Portsmouth.

(7) Benjamin Locke, b. Apr. 10, 1770, came to Bristol in 1785, when he was 15 years of age, and made his home with his uncle, Thomas Locke. Three years later, he shouldered a pack of provisions, and with ax in hand penetrated the wilderness seven miles on Bridgewater hill, built a hut and cleared land for a home. After spending a year or two in this lonely retreat, during which time he was constantly annoyed by bears and other wild animals, he sold, and located in the neighborhood that was destined to take his name. He m. (1) Mar. 17, 1796, Hannah, dau. Cutting Favor (See), b. Aug. 6, 1776. They commenced life in a log cabin of two rooms near where the schoolhouse now stands. Later, he erected a more commodious house near where Stephen Staples lately resided, and here nearly all of his children were born. May 27, 1822, during the absence of the family, this home, with all the comforts and conveniences of the day, was destroyed by fire. With characteristic energy, he erected another house, though comparatively poor, for the shelter of his family. Mr. Locke was a man of marked individuality, a leader in thought and influence in the town. He and his wives were prominent Methodists, and their home was always open to the itinerant preacher. He was a man of great piety and great strength of lungs, and at a meeting in the schoolhouse when thirteen were converted his shouts were heard more than a mile distant. His wife, Hannah, d. Nov. 15, 1825, ae. 49-3-9, and he m. (2) July 23, 1826, Nancy, dau. of Jacob Gurdy (See), b. Mar. 11, 1788, and d. Apr. 15, 1866, ae. 78-1-4. He. d. Apr. 9, 1858, ae. 87-11-29.

CHILDREN, all born in Bristol

  *16. Favor, b. Aug. 21, 1797.

  17. Roxy, b. Dec. 3, 1798; m. Levi Dolloff. (See.)

  *18. Sherburn, b. Apr. 10, 1801.

  19. Lavina, b. June 29, 1805; m. Henry Wells. (See.)

  20. Joanna, b. Apr. 6, 1807. She m., Mar. 23, 1825, Jacob Webster, b. New Hampton, Aug. 29, 1805. They removed to New York, and, in 1853, to Caledonia, Minn., where he d. Oct. 26, 1873, ae. 68-1-27; she d. same place Nov. 1, 1892, ae. 85-6-25. Children:

    a. Hannah, b. Bristol, Oct. 25, 1826; d. Lowell, Mass., Sept. 19, 1842, ae. 15-10-24.

    b. Elizabeth Amanda, b. New Hampton, July 13, 1828; m. Washington F. Robinson. She d. Caledonia, Feb. 15, 1855, ae. 26-7-2; he d. Redwood Falls, Minn.

c. Benjamin Bailey, b. Alexandria, Apr. 22, 1841; m. Sally Ann Wheaton, Dec. 25, 1864. They res. Caledonia.

21. Philena, b. Mar. 1, 1809; m. May 20, 1857, Timothy Wiggin, Bridgewater, b. Mar. 1, 1809. He d. Bridgewater, Mar. 31, 1890, ae. 81-0-30; she d. Bristol, May 20, 1898, ae. 89-2-19. No children.

22. Benjamin, b. Apr. 17, 1810. He m. Apr. 18, 1835, Harriet, dau. David and Esther (Moore) Mason. He d. May 30, 1840, ae. 30-1-13, and she m. (2) Nicholas Dolloff. (See.) Children:

a. Mary, b. Bristol, July 19, 1837; m. Oct. 11, 1855, Thomas Knight, b. Franconia, Sept. 28, 1828, and removed to St. Johnsbury, Vt. One child, Grace.

b. Esther M., b. B., Apr. 28, 1839; m. Warner Huntoon, Jan. 8, 1858; d. Boston, Mass., Dec. 9, 1880, ae. 41-7-11.

23. Hannah, b. June 2, 1812; m. Kiah Wells. (See.)
24. Sally D., b. Sept. 4, 1814; m. Winthrop R. Fellows. (See.)
*25. Levi, b. May 15, 1817.
26. Dorothy Sargent, b. Mar. 25, 1819; m. Mitchel H. Page. (See.)
27. Harriet, b. Jan. 14, 1822; m. Philip S. Drake. (See.)
28. Susan, b. Feb. 11, 1828; m. Milo Fellows. (See.)

(16) Favor Locke, b. Aug. 21, 1797, m. Jan. 30, 1821, Sally Clough, dau. Abraham Dolloff (See), b. May 30, 1798. He commenced life on the Abraham Dolloff farm, thence moved to the Edwin T. Pike farm. Here he res. till 1852, when he removed to North Main street. He d. July 10, 1882, ae. 84-10-19. She d. in family of her son, Favor, May 29, 1894, ae. 96, lacking one day. He was a deacon of the Free Baptist church.

CHILDREN, all born in Bristol

29. Jane, b. Aug. 22, 1823; m. John F. Cass. (See.)
30. Orrin, b. Jan. 13, 1826; d. Bristol, Feb. 5, 1898, ae. 72-0-22. He m. Apr. 19, 1849, Nancy Jane, dau. Daniel Favor, M.D., b. Hill, Feb. 26, 1825. He was a carpenter and workman in paper-mill, and res. Lake street. Odd Fellow, Free Baptist, Republican. She d. Bristol, May 16, 1900, ae. 75-2-20. Children, all born Bristol:

a. Mary Ann, b. Sept. 21, 1850; m. Burley M. Ames. (See.)
b. Sarah, b. Dec. 31, 1857; m. Hadley B. Fowler, M.D. (See.)

31. Abram Dolloff, b. May 21, 1828; m. Jan. 16, 1853, Sarah A., dau. of Daniel Sleeper. (See.) She d. June 1, 1901, ae. 71-0-4. He m. (2) Jan. 16, 1902, Augusta A. Locke, of Concord. They res. Concord. No children.

32. Favor, b. July 5, 1831. Was a boot-maker for some years, later a farmer west of New Chester mountain. He m. Nov. 27, 1862, Adeline White, dau. of Andrew Crocket and Eliza (Perkins) Thompson, b. Franklin, June 11, 1838. Child:

a. Ada Maria, b. Bristol, Aug. 13, 1869; m. Jan. 1, 1891, Rev. Frank D. George, a Free Baptist clergyman, now at Ashland.

(18) Sherburn Locke, b. Apr. 10, 1801, m. 1820, Sally, dau. of Daniel and Sally (Young) Hill, b. Northfield, Nov. 26, 1800. He d. Mar. 23, 1874, in Faribault, Minn., ae. 72-11-13; she d. Mar. 19, 1863, ae. 62-3-23.

CHILDREN

33. Hannah Favor, b. Bristol, June 26, 1826; m. Samuel Little, May 7, 1854. He d. Austin, Minn., Nov. 23, 1881. She res. Austin.

34. Sarah Jane, b. Cayuga, N. Y., Feb. 15, 1833; m. Oct. 30, 1855, Henry Roberts, b. Cambridge, Eng., July 19, 1832. They res. Austin, Minn.

35. Levi, b. Chautauqua, N. Y., Mar. 23, 1835, and d. in Des Moines, Iowa, Apr. 3, 1892, ae. 57-0-10. He m., Jan. 8, 1863, Elizabeth, dau. of Andrew Hodges, b. Aug. 2, 1841. Res. Des Moines. Children:

    a. Wilfred D., b. Cedar Falls, Ia., Mar. 4, 1865; m. June 30, 1891, Mary McLeon.

    b. Fred Leroy, b. C. F., Mar. 27, 1868; d. at Des Moines, May 10, 1891, ae. 23-1-13.

    c. John Earl, b. C. F., Apr. 23, 1870.

    d. Walter, b. Des Moines, Aug. 23, 1875.

    e. Carl, b. D. M., Mar. 14, 1881; d. Apr. 14, 1890, ae. 9-1-0.

(25) Levi Locke, b. May 15, 1817, m. July 18, 1839, Susan Gilman, b. in Dorchester, Oct. 10, 1819. She d. Jan. 7, 1881, ae. 61-2-27, and he m. Feb. 13, 1884, Mrs. Sarah P., widow of Andrew J. Robinson, of New Hampton. He d. May 14, 1898, ae. 81, lacking one day. She d. May 31, 1901, ae. 79-9-10. He was a farmer on Summer street, and kept a meat market for many years in the village. For nearly 50 years an official member of the Methodist church. Mason, Republican. Member of legislature 1866 and 1867.

CHILDREN, all born in Bristol

36. Roxy Dolloff, b. Apr. 19, 1840; m. George H. White. (See.)

37. Annette, b. June 27, 1842; m. Alonzo W. Jewett. (See.)

38. Benjamin, b. June 23, 1847; m. Mrs. Mattie J. Colbath, dau. of Smith C. Place, b. Gilmanton. He d. Stratham, Nov. 24, 1879, ae. 32-5-1. She res. Exeter.

39. Levi Manson, b. Dec. 9, 1854; m. Fannie Martha, dau. of Henry Anson and Sarah (Pike) Smith, b. Haverhill, Apr. 8, 1858. In meat business at East Weymouth, Mass., now in Lebanon. Odd Fellow. Children:

    a. Ethel Maude, b. Bristol, Nov. 13, 1877.

    b. Hazel Maria, b. E. Weymouth, Mass., Aug. 12, 1892.

40. Charles E., b. July 5, 1858. Unm. Is a painter in Bristol.

---

1. Reuben Blake Locke, son of Samuel B. and Betsey (Philbrick) Locke, was b. Concord, May 23, 1821. He was the sixth generation from John Locke, of Rye, b. England, Sept. 16, 1627. Jan. 9, 1848, he m. Sarah H., dau. of Benjamin Cass, b. Andover, Aug. 24, 1828. He was a blacksmith in Bristol in 1851; and later a miller and dealer in grain and flour. Removed to Tilton, Mar., 1884, where he d. Feb. 3, 1903, ae. 81-8-10.

CHILDREN

2. Martha E., b. Alexandria, Oct. 14, 1848; d. Concord, Dec. 5, 1865, ae. 17-1-21.

3. Hannah Lucina, b. Bristol, May 5, 1851; d. Plymouth, May 31, 1854, ae. 3-0-26.

4. Francis Asbury, b. Concord, Mar. 3, 1855; d. Concord, Feb. 7, 1866, ae. 10-11-4.

5. Helen Sarah, b. C., Jan. 10, 1859; d. B., Jan. 10, 1877, ae. 18-0-0.

6. George Reuben, b. East Concord, Jan. 1, 1851; m. June 23, 1887, Fannie S., dau. of Savory and Margaret (Cobleigh) Gordon, b. Landaff, Jan. 11, 1851. Educated in schools of Bristol and at Tilton Seminary. Is a Methodist clergyman, member of N. H. conference. Ordained deacon at Rochester by Bishop Goodsell, Apr. 23, 1893; ordained elder at Concord, by Bishop Merrill, Apr. 14, 1895. Has filled pastorates at Chichester, Moultonboro, East Haverhill, East Colebrook, Henniker and Sanbornville; now res. at Tilton. Children:

    a. Margaret Sarah, b. Tilton, Aug. 10, 1888.

    b. Helen Frances, b. T., Apr. 8, 1893.

7. William Benjamin, b. Bristol, Oct. 10, 1867; m. Aug. 16, 1893, Mary Frances, dau. of Charles E. and Judith (Gile) Rowell, b. Merrimac, Mass., June 16, 1870. Is a Methodist clergyman, and member of N. H. conference. Educated in public schools of Bristol, at Tilton Seminary, and at Boston University, receiving degrees of A.B. from latter institution, June 4, 1890. Ordained deacon at Rochester, Apr. 23, 1893, by Bishop Goodsell; and elder at Concord, Apr. 14, 1895, by Bishop Merrill. He has filled pastorates at Landaff, Merrimacport, Mass., Rumney, Smithtown, Newfields, and now, 1903, at Colebrook. Children:

    a. Judith May, b. Seabrook, May 24, 1896.

    b. Mildred Sarah, b. S., June 10, 1897; d. at S., Sept. 27, 1897.

THE LOTHROP FAMILY

1. Rev. Nathan C. Lothrop, son of Solomon and Fanny (Chase) Lothrop, was b. in Norton, Mass., June 19, 1839. He m., Nov. 16, 1865, Sarah J., dau. of Stephen and Belinda (Fogg) Lovejoy, b. Meredith, Nov. 19, 1843. He is a clergyman of the Free Baptist denomination. Was pastor of Free Baptist church in Bristol, 1877-'81. (See Free Baptist church.) He now res. Contoocook.

CHILDREN

2. Ormsby A., b. Milton, Sept. 17, 1867; m. Nov. 4, 1886, Della A., dau. of Green L. Tilton (See), b. June 21, 1867. He was clerk in store at Center Harbor and Concord, later messenger for American Express company with residence at Concord. She d. of consumption at Bristol, Mar. 6, 1889, ae. 21-8-15. He was killed by falling from train at Tyngsboro, Mass., Jan. 1, 1890, ae. 22-3-14. Interment at Bristol. No children. He was a young man of much promise.

3. Fannie B., b. Strafford, May 29, 1870. Teacher. Res. Concord.

THE LOUGEE FAMILY

1. Elwood Simpson Lougee, son of Rev. Samuel F. and Hattie S. (Robinson) Lougee, was b. in Chichester, May 8, 1867. He m. (1) Dec. 25, 1888, Julia Ann Atwood, dau. of George Keniston. She d. in Alexandria, and he m. (2) Apr. 25, 1897, Mrs. Fannie Etta Simonds, dau. of David P. Hoyt. (See.)

2. Bernice Maud, b. Hill, Dec. 24, 1889; d. Bristol, Sept. 13, 1890.
3. Donald Elwood, b. Bristol, Nov. 8, 1891.

THE LOVEJOY FAMILIES

1. Abbott Lovejoy was b. in Milford, July 17, 1800. He was the son of Samuel, who fought at Bunker Hill at the age of 15, and the grandson of Nathan, who came from Scotland and settled in Pepperell, Mass. When Abbott was 17 years old he went to Hebron and learned the blacksmith's trade of his brother. In 1821, he commenced business for himself in Alexandria, and two years later succeeded to the ownership of the blacksmith shop that stood where Cavis Brothers' store now is. After doing business there a few years he erected a shop near the west end of the carriage shop, corner of Central and Water streets, and here he continued his trade for nearly or quite 40 years. In 1826, he erected the residence on Pleasant street now owned by Mrs. Aldonna Bingham. Nov. 29, 1824, he m. Sarah, dau. of William Crawford (See), b. Alexandria, July 29, 1801. He d. Aug. 14 1879, ae. 79-0-27. Mrs. Lovejoy lived alone for 20 years previous to her death, which occurred Feb. 9, 1900, at the age of 98-6-10. She was a great lover of birds and flowers and every room in her home was adorned with curios from all parts of the world.

2. William Crawford, b. Bristol, Sept. 28, 1828; m. Oct., 1850, Ellen Preston, dau. of Michael, b. in Hill, and d. in Bristol, Oct. 3, 1852, ae. 21. He m. (2) May 12, 1853, Ann Maria. dau. of John L. Blake, b. Mar. 12, 1828. From 1849 till 1872 he was in the carriage business on Central street, most of the time with Joseph D. Kelley. He d. May 6, 1901, ae. 72-7-8. Democrat. Children:
>   a. Aldonna, b. Bristol, Nov. 29, 1854; m. Frank W. Bingham. (See.)
>   b. Mary Ellen, b. B., Dec. 9, 1863; d. unm., Nov. 8, 1898, ae. 34-10-29.

3. James, b. B., Aug. 19, 1831. He was a jeweler in Manchester for many years. Retiring from business, he removed to Kansas, where he has children and grandchildren living.

Abbott Lovejoy adopted or gave homes to:

4. Joseph D. Kelley, b. May 30, 1828. (See.)
5. William Bruce, went to sea and was never heard from.
6. Sarah Jane, dau. of Benjamin Tilton, of Plymouth. She m. a Prescott, went West, and soon after d. of consumption.
7. Sarah Wyatt, dau. of Richard and Lavina Merrill, was adopted when eight years old. She d. Jan. 7, 1865, ae. 23 years.

----

1. John Lovejoy, the son of Artemas and Mehitable (Wetherbee) Lovejoy, was b. in Lancaster, Nov. 11, 1828. He m.

Helen Maria, dau. of Larkin Dodge and Sarah (Sheldon) Herrick, b. Nashua, Sept. 7, 1829. He was a locomotive engineer on the Northern road from the age of 20. He took the first passenger train into Bristol; was engineer of the free train that was run from Bristol to Concord, July 4, 1848, and operated the first engine that was run from New Hampshire into Vermont. He continued as engineer 20 years; was foreman of the round house at West Lebanon 28 years; retired from business and located in Bristol in 1895, and erected a residence on Beech street where he now res. A Democrat, Mason, and Congregationalist.

CHILD

2. Frank Herrick, b. West Lebanon, Mar. 11, 1856; m. Feb. 13, 1884, Hattie Louise, dau. of Otis K. Bucklin. (See.) He has been conductor on trains between Bristol and Concord since July, 1882. Children:

　　a. John Otis, b. Bristol, July 3, 1887.
　　b. Clifton Royal, b. B., Aug. 27, 1893.

LOVERIN

1. Ora Howard Loverin is the son of Prescott and Betsey (Sawyer) Loverin. He was b. in Springfield, July 3, 1853. Since about 1871, has been an employee at Hotel Bristol. Unm.

THE LOWELL FAMILIES

1. Wayland Ervin Lowell, son of Daniel Greeley and Louise Helen (Wescott) Lowell, b. Canaan, Sept. 24, 1869. He m., July 1, 1893, Nora Agnes, dau. of Nathan E. and Mary Elsie (Gray) Hopkins, b. Bristol, Nov. 11, 1873. They came to Bristol in September, 1894. He is a laborer in Mason-Perkins Co.'s pulp-mill. Built a house one-half mile south of Central square.

CHILD

2. Elnora Elsie, b. Boston, Mass., Aug. 9, 1894.

Allen Lowell, brother of above, b. Canaan, Apr. 18, 1867. Came to Bristol in September, 1900. Unm. Laborer in pulp-mill.

---

1. Burton Winford Lowell, a brother of above, was b. Canada, Jan. 29, 1873. He m. Etta, dau. of Charles G. and Aurelia (Wood) Lord, b. Canada, July 8, 1877. He has been a laborer in Bristol since January, 1898.

19a

2. Ernest James, b. Canada, Dec. 10, 1895.
3. Charles Burton, b. Feb. 15, 1899.
4. Raymond Ervin, b. Bristol, May 2, 1903.

---

1. Wallace Harry Lowell, brother of above, was b. Canaan, Aug. 29, 1877. He m., May 11, 1901, Isabel Addie, dau. of Jonathan J. and Cora B. (Ford) Smith. He came to Bristol, September, 1900. Is a laborer in Train-Smith Co.'s pulp-mill.

2. Helen Cora, b. Bristol, Aug. 16, 1902.

THE LUCAS FAMILY

1. Charles Alvin Lucas, son of Henry and Jane (Henderson) Lucas, was b. Westminster, Mass., Sept. 12, 1849. He m., June 7, 1876, Ida May, dau. of H. J. and Mary M. Leland, b. Westminster, 1856, and d. Boston, Mass., Apr. 7, 1891, ae. 35. He m., Apr. 1, 1901, Mrs. Lizzie Etta (Gray) Webster. He has been superintendent of the Train-Smith Co.'s mills in Bristol since they were put in operation in 1885. Democrat, a Knight Templar Mason.

2. Maude Katharine Clark, b. Westminster, June 7, 1877; m. Nov., 1898, George Merrick Bigelow. Res. Worcester, Mass.
3. Bernice Leotine, b. Pepperell, Mass., Jan. 4, 1879. Res. Boston, Mass.

THE McCLARY FAMILY

1. John McClary came to Bristol in 1821 or '22, and became a partner of N. S. Berry in the tanning business. He was a soldier in the War of 1812, serving as sergeant-major, 45th Regt., through the war and was wounded. He was b. Newburyport, Mass., June 12, 1792, and in 1819, m. Rebecca Dodge, dau. of Thomas, b. Ipswich, Mass., June 10, 1795; d. Bristol, Mar. 8, 1828, ae. 32-8-28. He m. (2) Nov. 30, 1830, Hannah, sister of first wife, who d. Haverhill, July 23, 1867. He removed to Haverhill in 1832; represented town in legislatures 1834-'36, register of deeds five years, selectman and town clerk. Died Haverhill, Sept. 24, 1868, ae. 76-3-12.

2. Ellen Dodge, b. Lisbon, Apr. 5, 1820; m. Apr. 5, 1842, Sylvester Redding, of Portsmouth. She d. Kansas City, Mo., Nov. 17, 1893, ae. 73-7-12; he d. July, 1882. Children:

    a. Mary Rebecca, b. Apr. 4, 1843; m. G. F. Putnam; res. Kansas City.

CHARLES A. LUCAS

b. John, b. Apr. 12, 1845; wholesale hat dealer in Boston, Mass.
c. Ellen McClary, b. Mar. 12, 1848; m. G. W. Butler, Portsmouth.
d. William, b. Dec. 12, 1850; res. Boston.

  3. Julia Minot, b. Bristol, Mar. 18, 1824; d. unm., Jan. 16, 1862 (1865), ae. 37-9-28.
  4. Caroline D., b. B.; d. Sept. 2, 1826, ae. 17 months.

THE McCURDY FAMILY

  1. Rev. Converse Lilly McCurdy was b. Hallowell, Me., in 1809. He m., in 1828, Elizabeth, dau. of Stephen Reynolds, who d. in Bristol, Oct. 12, 1848, ae. 38. He m. (2) in 1849, Eveline Bradford. He was a Methodist clergyman 42 years and was pastor of the Bristol church two years from the spring of 1847. He d. at Wakefield, Mass., Nov. 22, 1876, ae. 67 years. She d. in 1877.

CHILDREN

  2. Elizabeth Reynolds, b. Somersworth, Mar. 14, 1830; m. Marshall W. White. (See.)
  3. George Sumner, b. S., 1831.
  4. Charles Wesley, b. S., Feb. 26, 1835; m. Sept. 30, 1866, Eva Sabrina, dau. of John and Mary Ann Hall, b. Dowagiac, Mich., May 6, 1844, and d. in Ogden, Utah, Feb. 6, 1876, ae. 31-9-0. He m., Mar. 4, 1877, Laura, dau. of John and Bertha Berg, b. Norway, Ill., Feb. 25, 1855. Res. Basalt, Idaho. Children :

    a. Ray Weston, b. Yorkville, Ill., Aug. 2, 1870. Res. Ulysses, Idaho. Unm.
    b. Bert Marshall, b. Ogden, Utah, Apr. 9, 1878. He m., June 3, 1902, Belle, dau. Charles and Mary Cockrell. Res. Basalt.
    c. Winn Ward, b. Ovid, Idaho, Dec. 12, 1880. Res. Basalt.
    d. Nellie Louise, b. O., June 27, 1882.
    e. Maud Fidelia, b. O., Oct. 12, 1883; d. in Iona, Idaho, Oct. 10, 1893, ae. 9-11-28.
    f. Gena Emeline, b. O., Aug. 7, 1885.
    g. Earl Edward, b. O., July 18, 1887.
    h. Frank Logan, b. O., Mar. 9, 1889.
    i. Mabel Edith, b. O., Aug. 11, 1891.
    j. Charles Berg, b. Iona, Idaho, Feb. 9, 1894.
    k. Fred Duboise, b. Basalt, July 15, 1896.

  5. Harriet Newell, b. Kingston, May 8, 1836.
  6. Hannah Nason, b. May 6, 1838; m. Edward B. Kinsley. He d. She res. 36 C Vinal Ave., Somerville, Mass. Two children.
  7. Mariamne, b. Lebanon, Nov. 13, 1844; d. Dec. 20, 1852, ae. 8-1-7 .
  8. Eva Griggs, b. Palmer, Mass., 1849; m. Dr. George H. Pierce, and d. Aug., 1900, ae. 51. Five children.

THE McDANIEL FAMILY

  1. Charles W. McDaniel, son of Charles S. and Sarah F. (Frost) McDaniel, was b. South Berwick, Me., May 5, 1852. He m., June 26, 1879, Ida Frances, dau. of Benjamin Saunders (See), b. in Lowell, Mass., June 30, 1854. He was a machinist

in Bristol, June, 1878, till Oct., 1888, when he removed to Lakeport; inspector of steamboats, 1896–'99; now in equipment department, Portsmouth navy yard.

2. Harry Sewal, b. Bristol, Apr. 18, 1880. Is a druggist's clerk in Laconia.

3. Jessa Saunders, b. B., May 23, 1881; graduated from Laconia High school.

4. Charles Stanley, b. Lakeport, Jan. 17, 1890.

THE McINTIRE FAMILY

1. John William McIntire, son of Amos and Harriet McIntire, was b. Berwick, Me., Mar. 6, 1861. He is of the 6th generation from Micum McIntire, a settler on the Maine coast in 1640. He m. Mar. 6, 1889, Minnie Adelaide, dau. of John H. Ferguson, b. Eliot, Me., Aug. 25, 1862. He was a merchant tailor in Bristol, 1896–1902, when he removed to Somersworth. Methodist, Republican, Mason.

2. Pauline, b. Somersworth, June 20, 1890.
3. Scott Ferguson, b. S., June 9, 1892.
4. Lenora, b. No. Berwick, Me., May 24, 1894.
5. Son, b. Somersworth, Aug., 1903.

THE MACLINN FAMILY

1. George Darling Maclinn is the son of Alexander and Hannah (Darling) Maclinn. He was b. in Danville, Vt., Mar. 25, 1839. At six years of age he came to Bristol and made his home with his great-uncle, Ebenezer Darling. (See Roll of Honor.) Oct. 1, 1865, he m. Mary Elizabeth, dau. of Daniel and Mary (Frye) Hobart, b. Hebron, July 4, 1842. He was a farmer and engineer in Hebron and Groton till 1894, when he returned to Bristol. Republican, Methodist, G. A. R.

2. Daniel Horace, b. Groton, July 29, 1868; m. June 5, 1893, Emily Belle, dau. Hiram B. Farnum, b. Plymouth. No children. Res. Woodsville.

3. Etta Mina, b. Hebron, Mar. 7, 1871; m. Aug. — 1890, Will Woodward. Res. Amesbury, Mass. Two children.

4. Walter Edward, b. Concord, Oct. 28, 1873; d. Mar. 22, 1892, in Groton, ae. 18-4-24.

5. Edith Lucy, b. Groton, Sept. 19, 1876; m. Dec. 7, 1901, Charles W. Gove. (See.)

6. Lilla Hannah, b. G., Feb. 13, 1880; m. June 25, 1902, George E. Randell. Res. Amesbury, Mass. No children.

7. Leston Hobart, b. G., Aug. 3, 1883; m. June 7, 1902, Mabel E., dau. Arthur and Belle (Wadleigh) Dow, b. Sanbornton, July 18, 1883. Res. Bristol.

THE MALVERN FAMILY

1. Rev. Lewis Malvern is the son of Thomas and Elizabeth (Lewis) Malvern. He was b. in Cheltenham, Eng., June 9, 1846. He m. Aug. 13, 1874, Mary, dau. of William Brindley, b. Derby, Eng., May 8, 1846. He was pastor of the Free Baptist church, 1873-'76. (See Ecclesiastical History.) Is now pastor of a church in Portland, Me.

CHILD

2. Mary Elizabeth Adelaide, b. Bristol, Apr. 6, 1876.

THE MANCHESTER FAMILY

1. Elijah C. Manchester, son of Timothy and Maria (Sawyer) Manchester, was b. Charlestown, Vt., Apr., 1835. He m. Nov. 12, 1865, Olive Ann, dau. of James and Lorana (Fellows) Berry, b. Alexandria, Feb. 1, 1846. He located in Bristol in 1863, and here d. of typhoid fever, Sept. 16, 1871, ae. 36-5-. She m. (2) Apr. 28, 1874, Milton G. Bailey, and res. Concord.

CHILDREN

2. Wilbur Berry, b. Bristol, Apr. 25, 1867.
3. Amy Lunette, b. B., May 4, 1869.
4. Lorana Fellows, b. B., Apr. 29, 1872 ; d. Mar. 28, 1880, ae. 7-10-29.

THE MANSON FAMILY

1. Rev. Albert Charles Manson, son of Capt. William and Katherine Manson, was b. in Limerick, Me., Mar. 12, 1802. He m. Apr. 15, 1831, Mary Jane, dau. of John and Hannah Brown, b. Ipswich, Mass., Sept. 27, 1812. He was in the active work of the Methodist ministry 1845-'84, and pastor of the Methodist church in Bristol 1849-'50. Mrs. Manson was distinguished for her robust form, her great personal beauty, her cheerful spirit, her sympathetic interest in the welfare of others, and her melodious voice. He d. Suncook, June 2, 1886, ae. 84-2-20. She d. New York, June 14, 1891, ae. 78-8-17.

CHILDREN

2. Charles Albert, m. Helen F. Wadleigh. He was a physician; d. Apr. 14, 1883.
3. Maria Lucretia, m. Is now Mrs. O. B. Douglas, Concord.

THE MARDEN FAMILY

1. Edwin Oscar Marden is the son of Albert Alonzo and Phebe (Wright) Marden. He was b. Grafton, Dec. 11, 1833, and m. Jan. 31, 1854, Emily Jane, dau. of Nathaniel Heath

(See), b. July 6, 1837 ; m. (2) Feb. 26, 1880, Jennie (Hawes) Cornock, b. Williston, Vt., Mar. 20, 1848. He has been a lumber manufacturer and farmer in Bristol since 1854. In 1863, was drafted into the army and served in the 5th Regt., N. H. Vols. (See Roll of Honor.)

CHILDREN

2. Walter, b. Hill, Jan. 31, 1855; d. ae. 2 weeks.
3. Nellie L., b. H., Oct. 5, 1857 ; m. (1) Orrison Ballou, of Alexandria ; m. (2) Oct., 1888, William Gormon ; d. Oct. 19, 1897, ae. 40-0-14.
4. Elvie, b. H., Aug. 25, 1859; m. George Patten and res. Fitchburg, Mass.
5. Carrie Belle, b. Bristol, July 31, 1861 ; m.; res. California.
6. Lurie Clyde, b. B., Sept. 14, 1863; res. Fitchburg.

THE MARSHALL FAMILY

1. Rev. Moody P. Marshall, the son of Abel and Martha (Pierce) Marshall, was b. Alexandria, Mar. 2, 1812. He m. May 6, 1841, Liberty, dau. of Samuel and Judith (Lewis) Smith, b. Sandwich, Feb. 11, 1817. She d. Sandwich, Apr. 10, 1845, ae. 28-1-29. He m. Mar. 15, 1846, Rebecca L., dau. of Benjamin Adams, b. Lancaster, Sept. 17, 1813, and d. Lancaster, Jan. 24, 1887, ae. 73-4-7. He was pastor of the Methodist church 1838-'39. He located and passed his last years in Lancaster, where he d., May 3, 1902, ae. 90-2-1.

CHILDREN

2. Ellen L., b. Sandwich, Apr. 9, 1845; m. 1867, John W. Savage.
3. Ruth A., b. Apr. 15, 1848 ; d.
4. Martha J., b. Cornish, Dec. 12, 1849 ; m. Mar., 1870, Edson Hartford.
5. Gilbert A., b. Columbia, June 27, 1851 ; m. Jan. 21, 1879, Myrtie L. Griswold.
6. Charles M., b. C., Mar. 26, 1853 ; m. Dec. 25, 1880, Mary E. Griswold.

MARSTON

1. William H. Marston is the son of Charles H. and Nellie E. (Elmer) Marston. He was b. in Oakland, Me., Aug. 18, 1876. Since 1898, has been teller of the Bristol Savings bank and of the First National Bank of Bristol. Republican, Mason.

THE MARTIN FAMILIES

1. Calvin H. Martin is the son of Jonathan H. and Mary Ann (Richards) Martin. He was b. Grafton, June 6, 1839, and m., June 29, 1870, Addie R., dau. of Ezra P. and Almira K. (Kimball) Gifford, b. Grafton, May 4, 1847, and d. Bristol, Dec. 14, 1898, ae. 51-7-10. Is a dairy farmer in the southwestern part of the town. Has res. in Bristol since 1866. No children.

2. Addie L., dau. of Ezra Lewis and Helen L. (Braley) Gifford, b. Alexandria, Nov. 1, 1881, has made her home in the family since girlhood. Parents both d.

---

1. Calvin Martin, son of Francis B. and Betsey B. (Hadley) Martin, was b. Goffstown, Aug. 15, 1833. He m. Nov. 19, 1857, Minda J., dau. of George and Lucinda (Gile) Tucker, b. Grafton, Nov. 20, 1836. He is a laborer in Bristol.

CHILDREN

2. Walter C., b. Grafton, Aug. 20, 1858; m. June 16, 1883, Cora E., dau. of James Garland and Amy Tenney, b. Sept. 17, 1862. He was a laborer in Bristol; res. Franklin Falls and again in Bristol.
3. Ida A., b. G., Apr. 10, 1860; m. Dec. 24, 1880, John Hazen; res. Mont Vernon.
4. Emily A., b. Dunbarton, May 2, 1862; m. Apr., 1884, Alonzo J. Gove. She d. Apr. 22, 1887, ae. 24-11-20.
5. Mortimer, b. D., July 29, 1869. Res. Burlington, Vt.

---

1. Asa Martin, son of Sylvester, was b. Grafton, Mar. 14, 1803. About 1821, he m. Amy Flag, dau. of Jacob (?) and Hannah Flag, b. Grafton, Feb. 11, 1800. He removed to Bristol with his family in 1849. He was a painter in Bristol till about 1853, when he removed to Haverhill, and in 1860, returned to Grafton, where he d. Apr. 11, 1876, ae. 73-0-27. She d. Grafton, Jan. 8, 1892, ae. 91-10-27.

CHILDREN, all born in Grafton

2. Richard W., b. Nov. 21, 1823; m. Mamie H. Crow, and d. Manchester, Aug. 17, 1885, ae. 61-8-26.
*3. Jacob W., b. Apr. 27, 1825.
4. Hannah, b. Nov. 25, 1826; m. Edwin Litchfield, and d. Danbury, June 23, 1882, ae. 55-6-28.
5. Gilford, b. Apr. 15, 1828; m. Judith, dau. of John Hoyt, b. Bethlehem, Sept. 24, 1834. He d. Grafton, Feb. 9, 1869, ae. 40-9-24. She d. Danbury, June 2, 1901, ae. 66-8-8. He had at least one son :
  a. Charles Albie, b. Manchester, Apr. 5, 1861; m. Nov. 26, 1881, Ella V. Bates, b. Sanbornton, Mar. 3, 1864. They res. Danbury.
6. Alba, b. June 26, 1830; d. Haverhill, Oct. 15, 1858, ae. 28-3-19. He m. Rispah Kimball, Grafton.
7. Mary E., b. Oct. 22, 1832; d. Grafton, Nov. 17, 1834, ae. 2-0-25.
8. Sylvester, b. Sept. 30, 1838 (1837); m. Apr. 7, 1861, Mary Emily, dau. Isaac and Ann Clark, b. Newbury, Vt., June 3, 1843; d. Manchester, Dec. 13, 1872, ae. 29-6-10. He m. (2) Elvira Jane Goss and d. Grafton, Jan. 2, 1879, ae. 40-3-2. His widow res. W. Manchester. He served as first lieutenant in Co. F, 15th N. H. Vols., on quota of Grafton. Children :
  a. Ida Ann, b. Grafton, Sept. 6, 1862; m. Sept. 6, 1883, Charles P. Nelson.
  b. Gertrude Maud, b. Manchester, May 19, 1875; m. Lewis W. Crockett. Res. 475 Amherst street, Manchester.
9. Charles H., b. Mar. 10, 1842; m. May 16, 1867, Lida C., dau. John W. Clark, b. Allen, N. Y., July 17, 1844; d. Concord, Mar. 2, 1891, ae. 46-7-15. He has been in the drug business, Concord, since 1863. Children.

a. Amy C., b. Concord, June 10, 1871; m. Feb. 22, 1899, Richard C. Goodell, Antrim.

b. Charles E., b. C., Sept. 14, 1877.

(3) Jacob W. Martin, was b. Grafton, Apr. 27, 1825. He was a carriage painter and came to Bristol in 1847, and Nov. 25, 1848, m. Jane Moffet Sanborn, dau. of Maj. Daniel. (See.) In 1853, he left his family in Bristol and went to California, but returned previous to the death of his wife, which occurred at Haverhill, Aug. 7, 1859. He m. (2) and res. Yreka, Cal., where he d. Feb. 4, 1898, ae. 72-9-7.

CHILDREN

10. Clara Jane, b. Bristol, Aug., 1850; m. Charles H. O'Neil, June 6, 1872, who d. Chicago, Ill., Feb., 1892. She res. 3,500 Grand Ave., Milwaukee, Wis. Children:

a. George Edwin, b. Milwaukee, Mar. 29, 1873; m. Nov. 28, 1900, Ethel Virgin, Plattsville, Wis. Res. 374 33d street, Milwaukee.

b. Charles Houston, b. M., Aug. 21, 1875.

c. Harry Martin, b. M., Mar. 19, 1877.

d. Robert Layfield, b. M., Dec. 7, 1879.

e. Stanley Sanborn, b. M., Mar. 22, 1881.

f. Frederick, b. M., Nov. 6, 1886; d. Nov. 27, 1886.

11. Luther Edwin, b. B., July 30, 1852; m. Sept. 28, 1876, Cora Louise, dau. of Wicom and Louise Savory. b. Georgetown, Mass., June 2, 1855. They res. many years Haverhill, Mass.; later Langdon Hotel, Boston, Mass. No children.

---

1. Ira Martin is the son of James. He was b. Grafton, Aug. 15, 1832, and m. Hannah Elizabeth, dau. of Hoyt Martin, b. Grafton, Oct. 6, 1841, and d. New Hampton, Nov. 26, 1900, ae. 59-1-20. He was a farmer in Alexandria till 1875; farmer and watchman in Bristol till 1882, since in New Hampton.

CHILDREN

2. Ara Hoyt, b. Alexandria, Nov. 17, 1868; m. Aug. 11, 1893, Rose May, dau. of Edward Kirk, b. Grafton, May 11, 1873. A jeweler in Enfield, and since 1902, in Bristol. Child:

a. Doris May, b. Wilton, May 7, 1897.

3. Hadley Bert, b. A., Dec. 11, 1873.

THE MASON FAMILY

1. The earliest known ancestor of the Masons of Bristol was Edward Mason, an early resident of Stratham. Ward Mason, a son, m. Jerusha Burley and settled in Sanbornton soon after 1786. There his wife d. Jan. 2, 1795. He returned to Stratham and there d. Of his eight children, one was

2. David, b. Sanbornton, Nov. 13, 1788. When about 21 he settled in the Moore's Mills neighborhood. There he m., 1808, Esther Moore, dau. of Robert (See), b. Oct. 5, 1790.

DAVID MASON

Farmer. He d. Aug. 20, 1853, ae. 64-9-7; she d. Dec. 11, 1852, ae. 62-2-6.

CHILDREN, all born in Bristol

\#3. Daniel Smith, b. Apr. 2, 1809.

4. Mary Jane, b. Sept., 1811; m. Dea. Levi Carter (his third wife) and d. New Hampton, Apr. 19, 1890, ae. 78-7.

5. Harriet, b. July 22, 1814; m. (1) Benjamin Locke. (See.) (2) Nicholas Dolloff. (See.)

6. Jerusha, b. Apr. 3, 1817; m. Joseph D. Robinson, Apr., 1854. He was b. New Hampton, May 12, 1816. Farmer in New Hampton till 1882; res. in Bristol, 1882-'90; returned to New Hampton, where he d. Dec. 16, 1896, ae. 80-7-4. She d. New Hampton, Oct. 10, 1890, ae. 73-6-7. Children:

    a. Child, d. in infancy.

    b. Antha Emerson (adopted or brought up), b. Oct. 29, 1855; m. Lincoln A. Gray.

    c. Jerome Giles Wells (brought up), b. Sanbornton, Jan. 27, 1859.

7. David, b. June 27, 1820; m. Nov. 7, 1854, Elvira C., dau. of Elisha Gurdy (See), b. Sept. 9, 1827. In early life he was engaged in farming, at work in the mills at Moore's Mills, or running spars and lumber down the river in rafts to market. In his first trip down the river and subsequently, he was pilot. He "run" the river 17 years, twice with logs. In 1852, he came to Bristol village and engaged in the manufacture of straw-board in company with George W. Dow, on the site of the pulp-mill on Willow street, under the firm name of Dow & Mason. Mr. Dow retired during the Civil war and Mr. Mason continued the business. He was later interested in a paper-mill, where is now the woolen-mill of the Dodge-Davis Manufacturing company, under the name of D. & D. S. Mason & Co. In January, 1871, he became the head of a new firm — Mason, Perkins & Co., which erected the brick paper-mill, now at the North End, and absorbed the strawboard-mill. He continued in this position till his death, assuming the presidency of the Mason-Perkins Paper company, when the above named company was incorporated, July 7, 1886. He was also engaged in the manufacture of pulp, near the railroad station with R. D. Mossman and William A. Berry, from 1878 till this business was also absorbed by the Mason-Perkins Paper company in February, 1891. In his business transactions he was sagacious and successful and at his death was considered the wealthiest man in town. By his will he left $1,000 to the Methodist church and $1,000 to the Bristol Cemetery association. He was for ten years vice-president of Bristol Savings bank, and represented his town three years in the legislature. Republican; an official member of the Methodist church. He resided on Lake street till about 1884, when he erected a residence on South Main street, where he d. June 26, 1899, ae. 78-11-29. Child:

    a. Addie Jane (adopted), b. Mar. 18, 1867; m. Charles E. Mason. (See.)

8. Robert Moore, b. May 21, 1823; m. Jan. 8, 1856, Hennie, dau. of Samuel and Eliza (Warren) Emmons, b. Newport, Feb. 25, 1839. Resided on the Mason farm, and "run" the river 17 years. In Apr., 1872, removed to the village and engaged in the manufacture of strawboard with George M. Wooster on site of the Train-Smith Co.'s paper-mill. He d. Feb. 6, 1894, ae. 70-8-15. She d. Bristol, Jan. 9, 1899, ae. 59-10-14. Children:

    a. Charles Emmons, b. Bristol, June 13, 1862; m. Nov. 1, 1894, Addie J., adopted dau. of David Mason (See), b. Mar. 18, 1867. She d. Jan. 20, 1899, ae. 31-10-2. He m. (2) Feb. 15, 1900, Catherine A., dau. of Charles Handerson, b. Sept. 11, 1878. He d. Nov. 20, 1900, ae. 38-5-7. She m. (2) May 29, 1902, William J. Decato.

(See.) Charles E. Mason was a Knight Templar Mason, a past master of Union Lodge, No. 79, A. F. and A. M.; was a Democrat, and served two years as selectman. Was agent at the Bristol railroad station, Dec., 1890 to Apr., 1893. He succeeded David Mason as a stockholder of the Mason-Perkins Paper company. By his will he left the income of this stock to his widow during her life; at her decease the stock is to be sold and the avails thereof paid to the town of Bristol for a town hall.

b. Elsie, b. B., June 13, 1869; d. Nov. 22, 1871, ae. 2-5-9.

9. Joseph Moore, b. Feb. 1, 1828; m. Dec. 23, 1862, Olive Jane Cheney, dau. Alonzo (See), b. Jan. 1, 1835. No children. He d. Mar. 31, 1891, ae. 63-2-0.   Farmer.   She res. Bristol.

10. John A., b. June, 1831; d. Sept. 15, 1834, ae. 3-3-.

(3)   Capt. Daniel S. Mason, son of David, b. Apr. 2, 1809, m. Dec. 1, 1835, Angelina W., dau. Walter and Elizabeth (Pingree) Webster, b. Bridgewater. She d. Plymouth, 1848, and he m. (2) Jan. 31, 1849, Anna C., dau. Nicholas M. and Sally (Eastman) Taylor, b. New Hampton, Apr. 27, 1817. He was a farmer and lumber manufacturer in early manhood. In company with Nicholas Dolloff and Joseph Moore, he run the first raft of lumber down the Pemigewasset. On this occasion the raft was wrecked on Worthen's rock and he was swept down stream and narrowly escaped drowning. In 1835, he purchased the saw-mill at Moore's Mills and manufactured lumber some years. In 1858, he removed to Bristol village and engaged in the manufacture of paper with David Mason, Calvin Swett, and George W. Dow, at the site of Dodge-Davis Manufacturing Co. till 1863, when the mill was destroyed by fire. He served ten years as selectman. Republican, Congregationalist. He d. Oct. 15, 1885, ae. 76-6-13. She d. Sept. 13, 1859, ae. 78-4-16.

CHILDREN

11. John Mason, b. Bristol, Oct. 22, 1836; m. June 16, 1864, Susan Waterman, dau. of Oscar F. Fowler (See), b. Dec. 9, 1839. He was elected town clerk in 1859, but resigned and removed to Plymouth, where he spent his life. She d. June 21, 1895, ae. 55-6-12. He d. Sept. 9, 1898, ae. 61-10-17. He was an extensive merchant; a prominent Republican, Mason, official member of the Methodist church. She was active in church work and a leading soprano in the choir. Children, all born in Plymouth :

a. Harry, b. June 22, 1865; m. Dec. 31, 1889, Arabella L. Roberts, of Dover.

b. Walter Webster, b. July 25, 1867; unm. Is now serving as postmaster of Plymouth.

c. Susie Elizabeth, b. Nov. 7, 1869; d. July 30, 1888, ae. 18-8-23.

12. Elizabeth Webster, b. Nov. 20, 1838. She was a brilliant young lady. Graduated at New Hampton Literary Institution with high honors before she was 18; taught the classics at Fort Atkinson, Wis., several years; m. Dec. 6, 1865, Rev. J. K. Warner, a Congregational clergyman of Wyoming Co., N. Y., and d. June 19, 1870, at Jacksonville, Fla., ae. 31-6-29. He d. Burdett, N. Y., Feb. 12, 1885. No children.

13. Ann Maria, b. Nov., 1840; d. Feb. 19, 1871, ae. 30-3-.

14. Louisa Angelina, b. Bristol, Mar. 30, 1845; m. Albert Blake. (See.)

CHARLES E. MASON

1. Hon. Samuel K. Mason, son of David B. and Eunice R. (Kelley) Mason, was b. New Hampton, May 17, 1832. He m. Sept. 27, 1858, Helen Mar, dau. of Andrew J. Smith (See), b. July 22, 1838. He was a practicing lawyer in Bristol. (See Lawyers.) He represented Bristol in the legislature three years; was postmaster seven years; judge of probate two years; county commissioner, three years; and was the candidate for governor of the Liberal Republicans in 1874. He was a trustee and president of the Bristol Savings bank ten years. He d. June 13, 1882, ae. 50-0-26. Mrs. Mason and dau. res. Second street.

CHILDREN

2. Smith Weston, b. Bristol, May 30, 1859; d. Oct. 2, 1859.
3. Helen Alice Maud, b. B., Oct. 15, 1860; d. July 17, 1861.
4. Ethel Sophia, b. B., Sept. 7, 1867. Res. B., unm.
5. Hattie, b. B., 1869; d. ae. 4 days.

THE MAYHEW FAMILY

1. Lieut. William Mayhew was a son of Peter Mayhew, one of the moving spirits in the construction of the Mayhew turnpike. During its construction, Lieut. William resided on the east side of the turnpike opposite the present farmhouse of Edwin T. Pike. The following

CHILDREN, were evidently born in Bristol

2. Orpha, b. Apr. 30, 1804.
3. Thompson, b. Sept. 23, 1805.
4. Franklin, b. Jan. 17, 1807.
5. St. Ialiar, b. Nov. 14, 1808.

THE MENG FAMILY

1. Christian Meng is the son of D. Sebastian and Annie Maria (Weenmen) Meng. He was b. Trimmis, Switzerland, Apr. 23, 1858. He m. Jan. 9, 1888, Etta Pierce, dau. of David H. Sleeper. (See.) Since 1890, has been a farmer and employee at the woolen-mill. No children.

THE MERRILL FAMILIES

1. The Merrills are of French origin. Being Huguenots they fled to England at the time of the massacre of St. Bartholomew in 1552, and settled in Salisbury, County of Wiltshire. Sir Peter Merrill, of the British army, was knighted in 1634. John and Nathaniel, brothers, came to this country in 1635 and settled in Newbury, Mass. John had no son but one daughter. Nathaniel is the father of the Merrills of New England. Of his five sons, one

2. Nathaniel, was b. in England about 1610, settled in Newbury, 1635, and d. 1655. He had five sons, of whom the second was

3. Nathaniel, b. Newbury, 1635, and d. 1683. Of his children

4. John was b. Newbury, 1663, and d. Haverhill, Mass., 1705. Of his children

5. John was b. Haverhill, Mass., Apr. 3, 1696, settled in Concord about 1728, where he was a deacon of the Congregational church, and where he d. He was the father of

6. Jonathan, b. Concord, Feb. 10, 1733, and m. Mary Farnham, b. Concord, Aug. 8, 1737. He settled on the Harvey Locke farm in Alexandria, and was said to have been the first man in that town to own a cow. About 1782, he removed to New Chester to the Meshech Gurdy farm north of Smith's river at Profile Falls. He d. Apr. 2, 1794, ae. 61-1-22. She d. Feb. 14, 1805, ae. 67-6-6.

CHILDREN

*7. John, b. Mar. 9, 1769.
8. Polly, settled in Vermont.
9. Susan, settled in Vermont.
10. Lydia, d. ae. 20.
11. Stephen Merrill, b. Apr. 25, 1776, removed from Concord about 1795, to that part of Sanbornton now Tilton, where he did a large business as a tanner, currier, and shoemaker. He m. June 3, 1803, Ruth, dau. of Dea. Benjamin Darling, b. July 4, 1774. She d. Dec. 29, 1835, ae. 61-5-25. He removed to Bristol and made his home with his son-in-law, Jonathan, about one mile south of Central square, where he d. Jan. 5, 1860, ae. 83-8-10. Children:

    a. Anna S., b. Apr. 15, 1804; m. Jonathan Merrill. (See.)
    b. Farnham, b. Mar. 25, 1806; m. Elizabeth Remington; d. Lowell, Mass., Mar. 27, 1872, ae. 66-0-2. Five children.
    c. Abigail, b. Aug. 29, 1811; m. Samuel Condon. He was b. Dec. 15, 1795. Was a printer in Boston, Mass.; served in War of 1812, and was a prisoner of war at Dartmoor prison, England, several months. He d. Boston, May 23, 1881, ae. 85-5-8; she d. Tilton, Jan. 17, 1900, ae. 88-4-18. Child: Samuel, b. Nov. 26, 1843; m. Nov. 17, 1869, Mary C. Lang. Res. Tilton.
    d. Mary Ann, b. July 8, 1814; d. Boston, unm.
    e. Stephen, b. Feb. 20, 1817; m. July, 1840. Res. Charlestown, Mass. Five children.
    f. Jonathan, b. Jan. 1, 1820; d. Sept. 30, 1826, ae. 6-8-29.
12. Jonathan, b. 1777; m. Mary Barnard, dau. of Ezekiel, b. Warner, Dec. 30, 1779. He succeeded his father on the farm and there d. Jan. 20, 1820, in his 43rd year. She m. (2) Ezekiel Moore, who res. at Profile Falls, and d. in the family of George M. Wooster, Oct. 1, 1875, ae. 95-9-1. Children:

    a. Rosanna, b. Bristol, Dec. 6, 1812; m. Nov. 13, 1832, Eleazer Wooster, and res. in Campton. She d. Jan. 29, 1834, in Campton, ae. 21-1-23. Child: George M. Wooster. (See.)
    b. Chauncey, b. B.; d. Mar. 11, 1818, ae. 2 years.

13. Sally, b. Apr. 14, 1778; m. —— Harding and removed to Ohio.
*14. Ephraim, b. Concord, Oct. 26, 1779.
15. Abigail, b. Mar. 13, 1782; d. ae. 24, unm.
*16. Moses W.

(7) John Merrill, son of Jonathan, b. Mar. 9, 1769, m. Nov. 12, 1794, Betsey, dau. of Benjamin Darling, b. Sanbornton, Apr. 27, 1771. He was a tanner and shoemaker in Sanbornton; removed to Bristol to the Peaslee farm at Profile Falls about 1801. He had a tannery west of the road below the falls which was first taxed 1810. What is now a very small brook furnished power to grind the bark. He operated this mill till he d., May 18, 1830, ae. 61-2-9. She d. Oct. 8, 1834, ae. 63-5-11.

CHILDREN

*17. Jonathan, b. Dec. 5, 1795.

18. Susanna, b. Dec. 24, 1797, res. on Lake street, and d. in family of Jonathan Merrill, unm., Mar. 25, 1869, ae. 71-3-1.

19. Mary Ann, b. Jan. 23, 1800; m. Apr. 20, 1851, Joseph Chadwick, Boscawen. He d. and she returned to Bristol; res. Lake street; d. in family of Clark Merrill, Mar. 19, 1873, ae. 73-1-26. (Jan. 20, 1874—Cong. church record.)

20. John, b. Bristol, Apr. 10, 1802; m. 1824, Rhoda Cilley, dau. of Nathan B., b. Hill, June 12, 1807. They settled on Periwig mountain; moved to Andover; thence to Dorchester in 1840, and to Wisconsin in 1867. He spent his summers for nearly forty years at the Franconia mountains, where he was on duty at the Pool. He was termed the "Mountain Philosopher." He was in great demand among tourists, never tiring of talking and lecturing on what he termed the scientific construction of the earth, arguing that the earth was hollow and inhabited inside and that the sun shone half the time inside, and explaining the relation of this state of affairs with the tides. With the exception of this delusion he was a well balanced man. She d. Pardeeville, Wis., May, 1883, ae. 75-11-. He d. Wisconsin, Jan. 13, 1892, ae. 89-9-3. Children:

    a. Abby B., m. (1) Luther J. Elliott, Dorchester. He d. and she m. (2) Oct. 17, 1858, Quintus Sanborn, and res. Pardeeville, Wis. Three children.

    b. Charles C., killed in Civil war.

    c. Willard C.   *d.* William C.

    e. John, res. Cheever. (See Roll of Honor.)

    f. Peter H., res. Pardeeville, Wis.

*21. Clark, b. B., Dec. 16, 1804.

22. Moses, b. Apr. 13, 1807; m. Sally Bennett, and d. Mar. 4, 1868, ae. 60-10-21. She d. Dec. 15, 1881, ae. 70-8-. Farmer, one mile south of Central square, east side of highway. Free Baptist. Child:

    a. John William, d. May 21, 1862, ae. 22-6-.

(14) Ephraim Merrill, son of Jonathan, b. Oct. 26, 1779, settled on the river north of Pemigewasset bridge. He m. Apr., 1808, Sally, dau. of Samuel Drew (See), b. Sept. 28, 1791. He d. Oct. 16, 1844, ae. 64-11-20. She d. Lawrence, Mass., Sept. 21, 1885, ae. 93-11-23. He was a farmer and tanner.

CHILDREN, all born in Bristol

23. Rufus, b. Apr. 27, 1809; m. July 4, 1839, Betsey J. Bartlett, Tunbridge, Vt.; d. Lowell, Mass., Jan., 1847, ae. 37-9-. Children:

    a. George W., served in 4th Mass. Battery; d. Ship Island, 1863.

    b. Carrie Elizabeth.

24. Calvin Clark, b. June 24, 1814; m. Oct., 1845, Eliza Parker; d. Cambridge, Mass., Dec. 16, 1853, ae. 39-5-22. No children.

25. Eliza Webber, b. June 22, 1816; m. Apr. 10, 1838, Dudley Leavitt Stokes, son of Jeremiah, b. Northwood, Mar. 13, 1812 They res. Lawrence, Mass., where she d. Mar. 15, 1863, ae. 46-8-23. Children :

   a. Stephen D., b. Bristol, Mar. 15, 1839; m. Oct. 16, 1860, Martha Ellen Rowe, b. Plymouth, July 15, 1839. He d. Utah, Nov. 21, 1866, ae. 27-8-6. Children: (1) Carrie May, b. Dubuque, Iowa, Sept. 26, 1864. (2) George Warren, b. Chicago, Ill., Oct. 20, 1866.
   b. Mary Ellen, b. B., May 18, 1841; m. Jan. 1, 1866, Augustine R. Hardy. He d. Lawrence, Mass., Feb. 19, 1889, ae. 54-3-18. She res. Lawrence. Child : Georgia Etta, b. Nov. 21, 1866.
   c. Sarah Ann, b. Freedom, Sept. 5, 1843; m. Dec. 10, 1860, William W. Wallace. He d. June 29, 1864, ae. 27-10-. She m. (2) July 15, 1874, Francis E. Towle, b. Feb. 27, 1834. Res. Worcester, Mass. No children.
   d. George Walter, b. Aug. 20, 1856; d. Dec. 10, 1856.

26. David Mason, b. Nov. 21, 1819; m. Dec. 17, 1845, Clarissa Cass, dau. of John, b. Bridgewater, Jan. 16, 1829, and d. Bristol, Aug. 4, 1870, ae. 41-6-18. He m. (2) June 11, 1871, Mrs. Belinda Donavan, of North Sandwich, who d. Sandwich, June, 1893. He was farmer in Bridgewater, Bristol, and Sandwich. Methodist. His last years were passed in Ashland in home of his daughter and granddaughter, where he d. May 21, 1901, ae. 81-6-0. Children :

   a. Sarah Jane, b. Bridgewater, Sept. 11, 1848; m. Louis Rowe. (See.)
   b. Laura Etta, b. B., Jan. 31, 1852, and d. Bristol, Mar. 15, 1869, ae. 17-1-14.
   c. Augusta M., b. Nov. 11, 1859; d. June, 1860.

27. Sarah Hardy, b. Jan. 10, 1821; m. Nov., 1845, Levi J. Gilbert, Lowell, Mass., and d. Lawrence, Mass., July 28, 1874, ae. 53-6-18. Children :

   a. Chandler, d. Lawrence.   *b.* Charles, d. L.

28. Judith Cross, b. Sept. 11, 1823; m. Mar., 1848, Levi B. Owen, and d. Leeds, Me., May 24, 1864, ae. 40-8-13. Children :

   a. Sarah, b. Leeds, Me. ; d. Monmouth, Me.   *b.* Etta, b. L.

29. Mary Lucia, b. July 21, 1825; m. Apr., 1843, Timothy Foster, and d. Curtis Corner, Me., Apr. 2, 1892, ae. 66-8-11. No children.

30. Almira E., b. Nov. 27, 1827; m. Sept., 1848, Samuel Edgerly, Lowell, Mass., and d. East Otisfield, Me., Jan. 28, 1859, ae. 31-2-1. Children :

   a. Emma.   *b.* Lucia.   *c.* Annie.

31. John Farnham, b. Nov. 19, 1829; d. Dec., 1844, ae. 15-1-.
32. Stephen M., b. Sept. 5, 1831 ; d. Sept., 1836, ae. 5-0-.

(16) Moses W. Merrill, son of Jonathan, m. Mariam Barnard, sister to wife of his brother, Jonathan. She d., and he m. (2) Mrs. Sally (Worthen) Sanborn, widow of Sherburn. (See.) He was a farmer at South Alexandria. Methodist.

CHILDREN, all born in Alexandria

33. Harum, b. Feb. 3, 1811. Was general ticket agent of Milwaukee & Mississippi railroad, Milwaukee, Wis.; m., had a large family, and d. Boston, Oct. 29, 1890, ae. 79-8-26.
34. Sherburn Sanborn, b. July 28, 1818; m. Nov. 14, 1847, Sarah Dix Kidder, dau. of Francis (See), b. July 6, 1825, and d. in Milwaukee, Mar.

26, 1855, ae. 29-8-20. He m. (2) May 6, 1858, Mary Ellen Freeman. She was b. Knox, Albany Co., N. Y., Mar. 13, 1831. He d. Milwaukee, Feb. 8, 1885, ae. 66-6-10. Mr. Merrill received only the meager education of the district school at South Alexandria. At sixteen years of age he went to Concord and worked one year in a hotel ; then was clerk in a store in Boston for six years. At the end of this time he came to Bristol and took charge of the Bristol House, and in November, 1850, went to Milwaukee. When he reached that place he had but five dollars in his pocket. He obtained a position as foreman of a gang of graders for the Chicago, Milwaukee & St. Paul railroad. His ability marked him for promotion and he was soon made brakeman, then conductor of a freight train, then of a passenger train. Soon after, he became paymaster, then assistant general manager, and finally, in 1865, general manager. Under his management the road increased in mileage till it embraced 6,000 miles, and had in its employ over 30,000 men. He was also largely interested in the Milwaukee street railway and other enterprises. Children :

 a. Sarah Worthing, b. Bristol, June 7, 1850; m. Washington Becker, June 22, 1875. Res. Milwaukee, where he is largely interested in street railways. Child : (1) Sherburn Merrill, b. Milwaukee.

 b. Susan Kidder, b. Milwaukee, Dec. 3, 1854; d. Aug. 3, 1871, ae. 16-8-0.

 c. Sherburn Freeman, b. July 17, 1859; d. Feb. 8, 1861, ae. 1-6-21.

 d. Marion, b. Dec. 19, 1861; m. Dec. 31, 1884, Grant A. Smith, who d. May 23, 1887. She m. July 22, 1889, Rev. William Chester. Children : (1) Sherburn Merrill, b. Jan. 11, 1886. (2) William Merrill, b. Nov. 4, 1890.

 e. Frederick Freeman, b. Aug. 1, 1864.

 f. Richard, b. Dec. 27, 1868.

 35. Mariam, b. Oct. 9, 1820; d. Apr. 17, 1822, ae. 1-6-8.

 36. Narcissa S., b. Aug. 8, 1822; m. Galustia Heath ; res. Concord, Mass. No children.

 37. Chastina, b. June 18, 1827; m. Bradley Walker ; d. Concord, Mass.

 38. Moses Worthing, b. Jan. 6, 1829; m. Ann Elizabeth Blackmore, b. Nov. 28, 1832. Both are living (1903) in Newton Center, Mass. Children :

 a. Sarah Letitia, b. Mar. 26, 1856; d. Aug 9, 1856.

 b. Emma Elizabeth, b. Nov. 7, 1857; m. Philip H. Butler; res. Newton Center, Mass.

 c. Alice Chastina, b. Oct. 20, 1860 ; m. W. F. Pillsbury, and res. Chicago, Ill.

 d. William Blackmore, b. Aug. 8, 1862; m. Jessie Muer, Milwaukee. Is a manufacturer of metalic packing. Res. Newton Center, Mass.

 e. Mabel Worthing, b. Dec. 22, 1866 ; m. Dr. George L. West. Res. Newton Center.

 f. Sherburn Moses, b. Dec. 12, 1871. Graduated from Harvard College ; is treasurer and manager of the Morley Button company. Res. Newton Center.

(17) Jonathan Merrill, son of John, b. Dec. 5, 1795, m. Nov. 11, 1824, Anna S. Merrill, dau. of Stephen, b. Apr. 15, 1804. (See.) He was a tanner and farmer one mile south of Central square. His tan yard was in ravine on west side of road. She d. Nov. 17, 1862, ae. 58-7-2 ; he d. Feb. 19, 1868, ae. 72-2-14.

CHILD

39. John Morris, b. Bristol, Oct. 3, 1825; m. Aug. 21, 1849, Mary F., dau. Jeremeak C. and Ruth (Fifield) Martin, b. Bridgewater, Aug. 11, 1827. He was a farmer and manufacturer of pocket-books and wallets, on Curtice place, opposite his father's. He d. Penacook, July 1, 1871, ae. 45-8-28; she d. Rochester, N. Y., Apr. 28, 1897, ae. 69-8-17. Children :

    a. Annie Maria, b. Bristol, June 5, 1851; m. June 5, 1869, George Henry Royce, and res. Boscawen. Child : Lillian May, b. Boscawen, Feb. 23, 1871; res. Boston, Mass.; unm.

    b. Frank S., b. B., Nov. 28, 1857; d. Jan. 2, 1858.

(21) Clark Merrill, son of John, b. Dec. 16, 1804, m. Mar. 26, 1827, Elizabeth Crowell, dau. of Newman and Harriet Crowell, b. in Andover, May 31, 1808. They commenced life on the Elijah Sanborn place at Profile Falls ; a few years later purchased a farm in the Borough where they resided till he was 80 years of age, when he made his home with his daughter, Mrs. Kelley, in Hill, where he d. Apr. 2, 1887, ae. 82-3-16. She d. in family of her son, Edwin C. Merrill, Mar. 26, 1893, ae. 84-9-25. He was a life-long Methodist ; a class leader. Republican.

CHILDREN

40. Hannah C., b. Bristol, Oct. 23, 1827; m. Mar. 16, 1854, Benjamin B. Southmayd, son of Levi, b. Campton, June 12, 1820; d. Campton, June 6, 1893, ae. 72-11-24. She d. Rumney, Mar. 4, 1903, ae. 75-4-11. Children :

    a. Benjamin Franklin, b. May 17, 1855; d. Aug. 1, 1856, ae. 1-2-14.

    b. Merrill Clark, b. Nov. 25, 1856; m. Nov. 25, 1877, Augusta A., dau. of Joseph H. Moulton, b. Ellsworth, Feb. 1, 1860. They res. West Campton. Children: (1) Leon Frank, b. Dec. 1, 1878. (2) Joseph Benjamin, b. Aug. 11, 1881. (3) William Baker, b. July 20, 1894. (4) Raymond, b. and d. July 17, 1901.

41. Mary Elizabeth, b. Hill, Oct. 19, 1831; m. Nov. 10, 1864, Merrill Greeley, son of Nathaniel, b. Waterville, July 2, 1832, and d. Plymouth, Oct. 6, 1894, ae. 62-3-4. He had a summer hotel in Waterville; was in livery business in Plymouth. She res. Plymouth. Children :

    a. Nannie Wyman, b. Waterville, May 4, 1868; d. Aug. 6, 1869, ae. 1-3-2.

    b. Mabel Lillian, b. W., Feb. 3, 1871; unm.

    c. George Henry, b. W., Nov. 3, 1872.

42. Rose W., b. H., Apr. 13, 1834; m. Eben K. Blodgett. (See.)

43. Moses W., b. H., Oct. 19, 1837; m. June 15, 1865, Almira H., dau. of Levi and Mercy (Smith) Southmayd, b. Campton, Aug. 2, 1835. Res. Campton. No children.

44. George S., b. H., Nov. 28, 1839; m. May 5, 1861, Agnes J. Sleeper, dau. of Nathan. (See.) They went West in November, 1864. He was for more than 20 years baggage master at Portage City, Wis. Now farmer at Clear Lake, Iowa. No children.

45. Edwin C., b. H., Mar. 27, 1842; m. June 13, 1864, Sophronia C. Abbott, who d. Jan. 28, 1867, ae. 23. He m. (2) Mrs. Lydia Davis, of Grafton. Is a farmer in Alexandria.

46. Anna Ruth, b. H., July 9, 1844; m. William C. Kelley. (See.)

47. Albert L., b. H., June 17, 1847; m. Oct. 7, 1865, Mary, dau. of

CLARENCE N. MERRILL

Hiram and Hannah C. (Elliott) Webster, b. Nov. 25, 1845. He is a farmer in Rumney. Children:

    a. Marietta, b. Mar. 18, 1867; m. J. Warren Pulsifer, Holderness.

    b. Jennie Edna, b. Mar. 9, 1885.

48. Clarence N., b. H., Dec. 31, 1850; m. Mar. 14, 1872, Ann M., dau. of Wilson Foster (See), b. Nov. 15, 1851. In 1869, he went West and was a brakeman on the Chicago, Milwaukee & St. Paul railroad for a year; returned; spent a year on his father's farm, and was an employee for a year in a bedstead shop in Bristol. In 1872, he entered the employ of Taylor & Shaw at their grist-mill on Central street, and in July, 1884, purchased Mr. Shaw's interest, the firm becoming Taylor & Merrill. In 1896, Mr. Taylor retired, and the business was conducted by Mr. Merrill till May 7, 1903, when the firm name became C. N. Merrill & Son. Besides doing a large business in grain, Mr. Merrill has been an extensive dealer in farming machinery, coal, and fertilizers, and a large manufacturer of lumber. He has a saw-mill at Groton that he operates most of the year, giving employment at the mill and in the woods to from 25 to 50 hands. He is also a large holder of real estate, owning in Bristol and neighboring towns over 2,000 acres of land. He is a Democrat; an official member of the Methodist church; a Knight Templar Mason, and a director of the First National Bank of Bristol. Child:

    a. Everett Clarence, b. Bristol, Nov. 11, 1876; m. Nov. 12, 1900, Ethel M., dau. of Sylvester and Mary Elizabeth (Merrill) Wheet, b. 1881, and d. Sept. 29, 1901, of consumption, ae. 20. He m. (2) Oct. 26, 1902, Ella, dau. of Wallace Smith, of Hill. He is associated with his father in business. Mason, Republican.

THE MINOT FAMILY

1. All by the name of Minot in New England are supposed to be the descendants of George Minot, Esq., son of Thomas, of Seffron, Essex, England, b. 1592. George emigrated to America in 1630, and settled in Dorchester, Mass.

2. Capt. Jonas Minot, b. Apr. 25, 1735, was fourth in descent from George Minot, Esq. He m. Mary, dau. of Rev. Willard Hall, of Westford, Mass., and settled in Concord, Mass. He was a soldier of the Revolutionary war, and a prominent man in his day. That vast tract of land now embraced in the towns of Alexandria, Danbury, and New London was granted to him and his associates, and he was interested in other large land transactions in this state. He was the father of

3. Capt. James Minot, b. Concord, Mass., July 4, 1779. He m., Feb. 9, 1804, Sally, dau. of Archelaus and Sarah (Morse) Wilson, b. Nelson, July 19, 1783. At the time of his m. he was a resident of New London, having taken possession of a part of his father's estate in that town three years before. In 1807, he removed to South Sutton, and engaged in trade. Feb. 13, 1813, while residing at South Sutton, he enlisted in Capt. Thomas Currier's company, War of 1812, and was made adjutant of the regiment, with the rank of first lieutenant. Six of his grandsons served in the Union army during the Civil war. He settled in that part of Bridgewater now Bristol, in 1813, and here

he spent the remainder of his life, with the exception of one year (1836) in Newport, and 14 years in Lebanon, returning to Bristol in 1851. He was a man of means, of superior intelligence and ability, and easily ranked among the most influential in this section of the state. He represented Bridgewater in the legislature of 1819, and Bristol in 1820 and 1826, and the senatorial district in 1827. He resided, on coming to town, in a house that stood on the site of Hotel Bristol. He d. Feb. 29, 1864, ae. 84-7-25. She d. Aug. 19, 1853, ae. 70-1-0.

CHILDREN

4. Almira, b. New London, Nov. 23, 1804; m. Solomon Cavis. (See.)

5. George, b. N. L., Aug. 10, 1806; m. May 1, 1838, Selina Walker, dau. of George Lewis and Charlotte (Turner) Clark, b. Portsmouth, Dec. 22, 1817. He graduated from Dartmouth College in 1828; was admitted to the bar in 1831, and practiced in Bristol till 1834, when he was chosen cashier of the Mechanick's bank at Concord, and removed to that city, remaining with that institution till his death. He was chosen its president in 1854. He was a member of the state constitutional convention of 1850; was U. S. pension agent, and was treasurer of the Boston, Concord & Montreal railroad. (See under Lawyers.) He d. at Concord, Mar. 8, 1861, ae. 54-6-28. Children, all b. in Concord :

　　　a. Julia Maria Barrett, b. June 13, 1842; m. Aug. 10, 1871, George Henry Twiss, and res. 108 Hamilton Ave., Columbus, Ohio. Three children.

　　　b. Henry Carroll, b. Oct. 30, 1845.

　　　c. George Edward, b. Feb. 16, 1851; m. Apr. 8, 1872, Mary J. Floyd, who d. Feb. 7, 1881. Three children.

　　　d. Edith Parker, b. Oct. 14, 1853.

6. Julia Maria, b. Sutton, Jan. 1, 1808; d. Bristol during the typhoid fever epidemic, Dec. 28, 1822, ae. 14-11-27.

7. Sally, b. S., June 19, 1809; m. William M. Chase. (See.)

8. Abigail, b. S., May 17, 1811; d. Oct. 18, 1811.

＊9. Jonas, b. S., Sept. 17, 1812.

＊10. Charles, b. Bristol, Sept. 19, 1814.

11. James Miller, b. B., May 23, 1816; m. 1856, Elizabeth Hoit, who d. in Concord, Oct. 31, 1865. He d. Concord, Aug. 8, 1872, ae. 56-2-15.

＊12. Josiah, b. B., Sept. 17, 1818.

13. Abigail, b. B., Apr. 7, 1821. She res. at Bristol and Concord; d. at Concord, while on the train to Bristol, Oct. 1, 1888, ae. 67-5-24. Unm.

14. Martha, b. B., Sept. 29, 1822; m. Cyrus Taylor. (See.)

15. Harriet Maria, b. B., Apr. 27, 1825. She m., Aug. 1, 1848, Arthur Fletcher. He was the son of Nathan Fletcher, and was b. in Bridgewater, Oct. 1, 1811. He graduated from Yale College in 1837, read law with his uncle, Samuel Fletcher, and practiced his profession in Concord till within a few years of his death. He d. Concord, Feb. 19, 1885, ae. 73-4-18. She d. Apr. 9, 1900, ae. 74-11-12. Children :

　　　a. Sarah M., b. Aug. 31, 1851; d. Aug. 7, 1853, ae. 1-11-6.

　　　b. Julia Minot, b. Mar. 13, 1855; d. May 12, 1870, ae. 15-1-29.

　　　c. Almira Minot, b. June 16, 1859.

(9) Jonas Minot, b. Sept. 17, 1812, m. Oct. 12, 1835, Anne, dau. of Ichabod C. Bartlett (See), b. Dec. 14, 1813. She d. Clarkson, N. Y., Nov. 18, 1848, ae. 34-11-4, and he m. (2) May 7, 1849, Electa Frary, dau. of Rev. Daniel O. Morton

(See), b. May 28, 1820. He d. Oct. 27, 1891, ae. 79-1-10. She d. Brockport, N. Y., July 13, 1897, ae. 77-1-15.

16. Mary Maria, b. Aug. 1, 1840; d. Feb. 1, 1841.

17. James, b. Clarkson, N. Y., Apr. 12, 1843; m. May 13, 1874, Fanny E., dau. of Hazen Pickering, of Concord, b. Barnstead, Sept. 27, 1847. In August, 1862, he enlisted in the 140th N. Y. Vols, and served in the same regiment with Gen. Otis, of Philippine Islands fame. Was wounded at the Battle of the Wilderness, May 5, 1864 — foot shattered. Was captured and held a prisoner four months at Lynchburg, Va. After the war was for many years cashier of the Mechanicks National bank, Concord, where he res. Both Mr. and Mrs. Minot have been prominent in Grand Army circles. He served four years as adjutant general of the department of New Hampshire, and one year as department commander. She has served as department president of the Woman's Relief Corps.

18. Bartlett, b. Oct. 2, 1845; served in the Union army; m. about 1867, Harriet Murphy. She d. and he m. (2) Orpha O. Hill. Children:

    a. Harriet A., b. Feb. 2, 1875.
    b. Jonas J. E., b. Nov. 14, 1879.

19. Ann Bartlett, b. Mar. 22, 1850; d. Apr. 29, 1895, ae. 45-1-7.
20. Electa Morton, b. July 23, 1851.
21. Jonas, b. June 18, 1853.   22. Morton, b. Dec. 5, 1855.
23. Mary Maria, b. Nov. 16, 1859.

(10) **Charles Minot**, b. Sept. 19, 1814, m. May 11, 1841, Sarah, dau. of Samuel and Myra (Ames) Tilton, b. Sanbornton, Oct. 23, 1819. He was a merchant in New York, cashier of Citizen's bank, Tilton, and of Mechanick's bank, Concord, and when state banks went out of existence, he formed with his brother, Josiah, the private banking house of Minot & Co., Concord, where he remained till he d., Aug. 25, 1879, at the age of 64-11-6. She d. Feb. 25, 1882, ae. 62-4-2.

24. Charles Alfred, b. Clarkson, N. Y., June 16, 1842; m. at Rockfort, Ill., Feb. 14, 1870, Christianna Vanston, and d. at New York city, June 18, 1889, ae. 47-0-2. He served in the Union army during the Civil war. Children:

    a. Sarah Tilton, b. Marion, Ill., May 28, 1871.
    b. Charles, b. M., Aug. 27, 1876; d. Nov. 13, 1876.

25. Sarah Louise, b. Tilton, Dec. 25, 1855; m. June 8, 1880, at Concord, Thomas C. Bethune. Children:

    a. Maud Eastman, b. Mar. 13, 1881.
    b. Minot Chauncey, b. July 28, 1882.

26. Anne Bartlett, b. Concord, Feb. 13, 1860; m. Oct. 30, 1883, Harry H. Dudley. Children:

    a. Dorothea Minot, b. Mar. 7, 1889; d. Dec. 17, 1902, ae. 13-9-10.
    b. Charles Hubbard, b. June 26, 1892.
    c. Thomas Minot, b. Nov. 29, 1897.

(12) **Judge Josiah Minot**, b. Sept. 17, 1818, m. Aug. 24, 1843, Abbie Pickering, dan. of Stephen and Mary (Pickering) Haines, b. Canterbury, July 6, 1819. He graduated from

Dartmouth College in 1837, and was a lawyer of high standing (See Lawyers) and a superior financier. He was one of the donors of the Minot-Sleeper library to the town. (See Libraries.) He d. Concord, Dec. 14, 1891, ae. 73-2-27. She d. Sept. 2, 1902, ae. 83-1-26.

CHILDREN

27. Isabel, b. Concord, Sept. 24, 1846; m. Apr. 24, 1873, Judge George R. Fowler, son of Judge Asa Fowler. He was a practicing lawyer in Boston, and at time of his death was senior justice of the West Roxbury district court. He d. suddenly at Philadelphia, Apr. 11, 1897. Children:

    a. Ethel Walker, b. Dec. 24, 1875; d.
    b. Mary Pickering, b. Jan. 25, 1877.
    c. Josiah Minot, b. May 17, 1880.
    d. Robert, b. July 11, 1884.

28. Grace Melville, b. Concord, Apr. 28, 1851; m. Oct. 14, 1878, Ferdinand A. Stillings, M.D., a practicing physician of Concord. Children:

    a. Mary Walker,   } b. Aug. 3, 1879.
    b. Charlotte Melville, }

29. Frances, b. Concord, Nov. 7, 1855. Res. Concord.

THE MITCHELL FAMILY

1. Alpheus C. Mitchell, son of Daniel M. Mitchell, was b. June 30, 1835. He m., Apr. 2, 1856, Laura R., dau. of Samuel and Sally (Beede) Smith, b. Bridgewater, Jan. 8, 1835. After three years' residence with her parents, they settled on the Seth Spencer farm in Dist. No. 7, Bristol, and there he d. Feb. 5, 1865, ae. 29-7-5. Mrs. Mitchell carried on the farm till May, 1895, when she m. Stephen S. Brock, son of John, b. Alexandria, 1835. They removed to the Moses Worthley farm in Hebron, where they now reside.

CHILDREN

2. Beede Morse, b. Bristol, June 22, 1857; d. June 18, '1864, ae. 6-11-26.
3. Sarah Beede, b. B., July 23, 1862; m. William T. Woodward. (See.)

THE MOORE FAMILIES

1. The Moores of Bristol are descendants of John and Janet Moore, Scotch Irish emigrants to Londonderry in 1723. He d. Jan. 24, 1774; she d. Mar. 8, 1776. Of their four children, one was Col. Robert Moore, b. Londonderry, 1727. He was a member of Capt. John Mitchell's troopers in 1744, in the French and Indian war, and he was a conspicuous commander at the battle of Bunker Hill. He d. 1778. Of his children, one was

2. Capt. Robert Moore, b. Londonderry, Sept. 20, 1769. He m. Jenny (Jane) Rolfe, b. Newburyport, Mass., Sept. 22,

JAMES G. MOORE

1771. They res. on Shirley hill in Goffstown, where five children were b., and their buildings destroyed by fire. They removed to Bristol in 1805, and settled near Pemigewasset bridge. He erected a large two-story house where he kept tavern for some years, and where he d. Aug. 10, 1813, ae. 43-10-20. She d. Feb. 6, 1852, ae. 80-4-14. He was called the strongest man in the county and was a man of great intelligence.

CHILDREN

3. Esther, b. Goffstown, Oct. 5, 1790; m. David Mason. (See.)
4. Jane W., b. G., Sept. 20, 1792; d. Mar. 1, 1794, ae. 1-5-11.
, 5. Robert W., b. G., Feb. 3, 1795; m. June 29, 1826, Abigail, dau. of Levi and Abigail (Godfrey) Dow, b. New Hampton, Nov. 26, 1799. He succeeded his father on the farm. He was a man of intelligence, an advocate of temperance and anti-slavery; when a mere boy united with the Methodist church. Represented Bristol in the legislature and served as selectman six years. He d. Oct. 15, 1848, ae. 53-8-12. She d. New Hampton, Apr. 21, 1884, ae. 84-4-25. No children.
6. Jane, b. G., July 16 (15), 1797; m. Daniel Shirley of Goffstown, and d. Apr., 1881, ae. 83-9-.
*7. Joseph R., b. G., Jan. 16, 1800.
*8. Jonathan H., b. G., June 18, 1802.
*9. William, b. Bristol, Apr. 6, 1806.
10. Mary, b. B., Sept., 1808; m. (1) Ovid Dearborn, Plymouth; (2) Washington Mooney, New Hampton.

(7) Joseph R. Moore, son of Robert, b. Goffstown, Jan. 16, 1800, m. Dec. 15, 1825, Mary, dau. of Abraham Dolloff. (See.) He succeeded his brother Robert on the farm. He was a great lover of fruit culture and fine gardening, and bordered his farm with fruit and shade trees. Was interested in the manufacture of lumber at Moore's Mills, and furnished the floor beams for the first factory in Lawrence, Mass. He was a man of great energy of character, of literary and scientific taste, and an upright man. Served as selectman ten years and represented Bristol in the legislature three terms. He d. Bristol, Apr. 30 (28), 1880, ae. 80-3-14. She d. New Hampton, Feb. 15, 1887, ae. 81-8-6.

CHILDREN, all born in Bristol

11. Jane Ralph, b. Aug. 8, 1826; d., unm., June 4, 1884, ae. 57-9-26.
12. James G., b. Jan. 27, 1828; m. Nov. 4, 1856, Christiana C., dau. of Rev. Isaiah H. and Charlotte R. Shipman, b. North Springfield, Vt., Sept. 25, 1836. Moved to Franconia, 1849, to Lisbon, 1870, where he now res.; manufacturer of lumber, bobbins, shoe pegs and pulp. He has invented machines for grinding pulp and making excelsior. Is a great mathematician.
13. Ovid D., b. Aug. 6, 1829; m. Aug. 28, 1854, Harriet Irene, dau. of Russel and Lorena (Spooner) Howland, b. Franconia, Aug. 31, 1832; d. Franconia, Mar. 20, 1871, ae. 38 6-19; m. (2) Feb. 1, 1877, Hattie A., dau. of Steven and Elsie (Drury) Howland, b. Oct. 10, 1850. He left Bristol 1859, lived in Littleton and Franconia, and located in Lisbon, 1875, manufacturer of wood pulp and shoe pegs. Children:
    a. Genevieve, b. Bristol, Nov. 10, 1856; m. July 3, 1886, William S. Nelson, a peg manufacturer, Lisbon.

b. Fred Joseph, b. Mar. 10, 1865; m. Dec. 18, 1886, Jennie E. Harris, of Warren. Associated with his father, Lisbon. Child: Hattie Irena, b. May 31, 1889.

14. Rachel Locke, b. Aug. 1, 1831; m. Oct. 25, 1854, Denison Taft, b. Barre, Vt., June 6, 1819; d. Montpelier, Vt., Sept. 22, 1897, ae. 78-3-16. She res. Montpelier. Children:

a. Alice Rachella, b. Montpelier, Sept. 22, 1866.

b. Edna Moore, b. M., June 30, 1870; m. June 9, 1892, Charles A. Gay, of Boston.

15. Mary, b. July 14, 1836; m. Dec. 22, 1862, John Daily, of Lebanon, Pa., b. Cornwall, Pa., July 7, 1832; d. Philadelphia, Pa., Aug., 1897, ae. 65. She was a teacher; is now a successful landscape painter. Children:

a. Grace Moore, b. Lebanon, Pa., Dec. 16, 1863. A music teacher in Philadelphia.

b. Claude Lorraine, b. L., Jan. 9, 1866. Was an expert pistol shot in Buffalo Bill's Wild West show. Went to Europe in 1889, and gave exhibitions of his skill before the nobility and received many gifts and medals of honor. "Acknowledged to be the best shot in the world." Died of cholera in Brussels, Nov. 29, 1892, ae. 26-10-20.

c. Lillian Blanch, b. L., Oct. 7, 1869. An actress. Has played in Europe and through the states; since 1901, an osteopath physician in Rochester, N. Y.

d. Paul Maurice, b. Altoona, Pa., Aug. 11, 1871. Clerk in employ of the Pennsylvania railroad, Philadelphia, Pa.

16. Sarah Clough, b. Dec. 26, 1837; was a teacher in Pennsylvania; d. unm., Feb. 8, 1873, ae. 35-1-12.

17. Josephine, b. May 22, 1841; was a teacher in New York state; m. Oct. 15, 1872, Methusalem DuBois, of New York; d. Aug. 28, 1874, ae. 33-3-6. Child:

a. Rachel, b. Oct., 1873. Is a stenographer in Boston, Mass.

18. Joseph West, b. May 22, 1841; m. Nov. 8, 1863, Harriet Ellen, dau. of John M. and Harriet Lincoln (Kelley) Flanders, b. New Hampton, Apr. 9, 1844. Res. New Hampton and Bristol. For many years owned stage route from New Hampton to Bristol and was brakeman on trains between Bristol and Concord 13 years, till Feb., 1883. He d. Bristol, June 20, 1892, ae. 51-0-28; she res. No. Main street. Children:

a. Eugene Flanders, b. Bristol, May 8, 1866; m. Mar. 4, 1888, Alice Blanch Howard, dau. Samuel A., b. New Hampton, Nov. 6, 1869. Concrete contractor at Burlington, Vt. Children: (1) James Howard, b. Burlington, May 15, 1892. (2) Arthur Howard, b. B., May 16, 1900.

b. Robert Flanders, b. B., May 24, 1867; m. June 27, 1894, Annie B. Rice, dau. of Isreal T. (See.) Veterinary surgeon, Laconia. Children: (1) Otis Rice, b. Laconia, June 18, 1895. (2) Nellie Josephine, b. L., Jan. 4, 1899.

c. Mary Dolloff, b. B., Oct. 27, 1868; d. New Hampton, Jan. 8, 1879, ae. 10-2-11.

d. Harriet Kelley, b. New Hampton, Oct. 22, 1870; m. May 2, 1889, Charles H. Gordon, a horse trainer. Children: (1) Ida May, b. New Hampton, July 2, 1891. (2) Maud Moore, b. N. H., Nov. 29, 1892. (3) John B., b. Manchester, July 21, 1895; d. Jan. 12, 1896. (4) Eugene Robert, b. Bristol, Mar. 16, 1899; d. Feb. 25, 1903, ae. 3-11-9.

e. Joseph Flanders, b. N. H., Oct. 22, 1881; a machinist in Hyde Park, Mass.; unm.

f. Josephine DuBois, b. N. H., Sept. 8, 1883.

(8) Jonathan H. Moore, son of Robert, b. Goffstown, June 18, 1802, m. Hannah Van, dau. of Capt. Moses W. Sleeper (See), b. July 26, 1805. She d. Manchester, Aug. 3, 1858, ae. 53-0-7. He d. Nov. 12, 1869, ae. 67-4-24.

CHILDREN

19. Frederic Adolphus, b. Bristol, Feb. 11, 1826 ; m. Aug. 12, 1855, Cornelia Heiywin, of Springfield, Ill.; (2) Emily Hewith Bugbee, La Cross, Wis.; (3) Nellie Warner, of Michigan. He read law at Manchester, but gave his attention to journalism. (See chapter on Literature, Vol. 1.) He d. Nashua, Dec. 7, 1888, ae. 62-9-26. Son :

    a. Leland, res. Brooklyn, N. Y.

20. William Hart, b. Apr. 17, 1827; d. Dec., 1858, ae. 31-8-.
21. Lucie Van, b. Sept. 10, 1829 ; m. Feb. 1, 1854, George W. Mitchell ; and d. July 21, 1855, ae. 25-10-11.
22. Jonathan B., b. Feb. 8, 1831 ; m. (1) Abbie F. Brown ; (2) Eliza Humphrey. He d. Manchester, 1888, ae. 57.
23. Hannah Jane, b. Jan. 20, 1832 ; m. Feb. 22, 1872, Merritt Parsons, Buckfield, Me.
24. Robert Frames, b. Dec. 12, 1833 ; m. Susan E. Dinsmore, of Derry, and d. Apr. 29, 1876, ae. 42-4-17.
25. Orren Augustus, b. Oct. 25, 1835 ; d. 1837, ae. 2.
26. Joseph Rolfe, b. Feb. 17, 1837. Killed at Battle of Cold Harbor, June 3, 1864, ae. 27-3-16.
27. Orren Cheney, b. Aug. 10, 1839; m. Nov. 29, 1860, Nancy W. Thompson, of Ashland ; d. at Nashua, May 12, 1893, ae. 53-9-2. He was a leader in the Republican party of the state; represented his ward in the legislature; his district in the N. H. senate was railroad commissioner ; member of congress from the 2d N. H. District, editor of the *Nashua Telegraph*, and a popular and eloquent platform political speaker.
28. James Mendon, b. Hebron, Aug. 24, 1841 ; m. Nov. 20, 1867, Mary O. Preston. Children :

    a. Myron Van, b. Manchester, May 21, 1875.
    b. Mendon Preston, b. M., Aug. 31, 1877.

29. Julia Fletcher, b. Dec. 3, 1844 ; m. Jan. 16, 1868, William O. Clough, of Meredith.

(9) William Moore, son of Robert, b. Bristol, Apr. 6, 1806, m. Jan. 18, 1831, Abigail D., dau. of Josiah and Susannah (Dow) Robinson, b. New Hampton, Aug. 12, 1808 ; d. New Hampton, Feb. 11, 1898, ae. 89-5-29. He d. Bristol, Oct. 28, 1868, ae. 62-6-22. In 1835, he settled on the John F. Merrow farm ; from 1844 to 1861, kept hotel at New Hampton village, and the last named year returned to his farm.

CHILDREN

30. Harriet R., b. Bristol, Dec. 17, 1831 ; d. Feb. 29, 1852, ae. 20-2-12.
31. Emily M., b. B., Sept. 22, 1834 ; m. June 20, 1858, George B. Mac-Lellan, and emigrated to Mississippi; after ten years returned. She d. Feb. 12, 1892, ae. 57-4-20.
32. Laura D., b. B., Oct. 11, 1839. Res. in New Hampton.
33. William Andrew, b. New Hampton, May 28, 1845 ; d. New Hampton, Feb. 10, 1855, ae. 9-8-12.

THE MORSE FAMILY

1. The Morses of Bristol and vicinity are the descendants of Anthony Morse, b. in England, settled in Newbury, Mass., in 1635, and d. Oct. 12, 1686. The line of descent is through

2. Benjamin, b. Mar. 28, 1640, m. Ruth Sawyer, and lived in West Newbury.

3. Benjamin, b. Aug. 24, 1668, m. Susannah Merrill, res. Newbury.

4. Capt. Abel, b. Oct. 5, 1692, m. Grace Parker, and res. Chester.

5. Stephen, b. Feb. 15, 1733 or '34, m. Abigail, dau. of Capt. Samuel Ingalls, of Chester, supposed to be identical with Capt. Samuel Ingalls mentioned on page 249, a descendant of Edmond Ingalls, of Lynn, Mass.

6. Dea. Jonathan, b. Mar. 3, 1757, m. in Chester, June 8, 1786, Abiah, dau. of Edmond Worth. He was a Revolutionary soldier, settled in Hebron, and d. in Haverhill, Mar. 3, 1840, ae. 83. They had nine children, of whom the fourth was

7. Jonathan, b. Hebron, Feb. 21, 1793. He m., Feb. 24, 1820, Jerusha Gilson, of Dunstable, Mass. One son was

8. Oscar Fitzallen, b. Hebron, June 12, 1826. He m. (1) Sept. 17, 1848, Eliza Ann, dau. of Capt. Moses Sanborn (See), b. June 14, 1831. She d. Bristol, Mar. 18, 1886, ae. 54-9-4, and he m. (2) Dec. 28, 1886, Mrs. Lavinia S. Drake. He located in Bristol when 21 years of age (1847). In 1849, he became a brakeman on the old Northern railroad; in 1855, conductor, continuing 21 years. In 1858, he also assumed the duties of express messenger, and on retiring as conductor, became local express agent and completed 41 years continuous service for the Express company, Oct. 1, 1899, when he was retired on a pension. He is a Democrat and a Mason.

    a. Elizabeth Lucy, b. Bristol, Apr. 12, 1853; m. Fred W. Bingham. (See.)

    b. Irvin DeWitt, b. B., Oct. 7, 1856; d. Sept. 4, 1881, ae. 24-10-27.

    c. Ona Amelia, b. B., Sept., 1862; d. June 14, 1869, ae. 6-9-.

THE MORTON FAMILY

1. Rev. Daniel Oliver Morton, A.M., was the eldest son of Livy and Hannah (Dailey) Morton, and was b. in Winthrop, Me., Dec. 21, 1788. He was a descendant of George Morton, who came to this country in the ship Ann, in 1623. He m., Aug. 30, 1814, Lucretia Parsons, b. at Goshen, July 26, 1789, dau. of Rev. Justin and Electa (Frary) Parsons. She d. at Philadelphia, Pa., Jan. 11, 1862, ae. 72-5-15; he d. at Bristol, Mar. 25, 1852, ae. 63-3-4, and both are interred in the Bristol cemetery. Was pastor of Congregational church 1842 till his death. (See Ecclesiastical History.)

HON. LEVI P. MORTON

CHILDREN, all born in Shoreham, Vt.

2. Daniel Oliver, b. Nov. 8, 1815; m. 1839, Elizabeth A. Tyler; d. at Toledo, Ohio, Dec. 5, 1859, ae. 44-0-27.

3. Lucretia Parsons, b. Jan. 20, 1817; m. Sept. 7, 1842, Rev. Myron W. Safford.

4. Electa Frary, b. May 28, 1820; m. Jonas Minot. (See.)

5. Levi Parsons, b. May 16, 1824; m. Oct. 15, 1856, at Flatlands, Long Island, Lucy Kimball, dau. of Elijah H. and Sarah Wetmore (Hinsdale) Kimball, of Flatlands, b. July 22, 1836. She d. July 11, 1871, ae. 34-11-19, and he m., Feb. 12, 1873, Anna Livingston Read, dau. of William Ingraham Street, Esq., b. May 18, 1836. He began life as a clerk in a country store at Enfield, Mass., when 14 years of age, but soon after was a clerk in Hanover. From Hanover he came to Bristol, where he remained a few months, and then went to Concord as a clerk in a dry goods store, but at the age of 21 commenced business there for himself. In 1849, he entered the house of James M. Beede & Co., in Boston, Mass., and three years later became a member of the firm. In 1854, he went to New York and founded the dry goods commission house of Morton & Grinnell. In 1863, he engaged in the banking business in Wall street as L. P. Morton & Co., which later became Morton, Bliss & Co., with a branch office in London. This firm took part in some of the largest transactions in the history of American finance. It headed the syndicate in 1871 to float a five per cent. loan to aid in the resumption of specie payments and saved the government $70,000,000 in interest. The payments of the Geneva award of $15,-500,000, and of the Fishery award of $5,500,000, were through his house. In 1878, he was elected a member of Congress; President Garfield appointed him minister to France, and in 1888, he was elected vice-president of the United States, and in 1894, elected governor of the state of New York. Children:

  a. Edith Livingston, b. Newport, R. I., June 20, 1874.
  b. Lena Kearney, b. N., May 20, 1875.
  c. Helen Stuyvesant, b. N., Aug. 2, 1876. She m. in London, Eng., Oct. 5, 1901, Talleyand de Perigord, Duke de Valencay, France.
  d. Lewis Parsons, b. London, Eng., Sept. 21, 1877; d. there Jan. 10, 1878.
  e. Alice, b. New York, Mar. 23, 1879.
  f. Mary, b. June 11, 1881.

6. Mary, b. May 5, 1829; m. Feb. 27, 1856, Hon. William F. Grinnell.

7. Martha, b. May 5, 1829; m. Aug. 8, 1852, Rev. Alanson Hartpence.

THE MOSHIER FAMILY

1. Ira Cornelius Moshier is the son of Harvey and Mary Jane (Merrill) Moshier. He was b. Barnston, P. Q., Feb. 22, 1857, and m. May 16, 1877, Mary Frances, dau. of Nathan O. and Harriet (Lucas) Phelps, b. Groton, Dec. 30, 1860. He was a farmer in Groton and Dorchester till 1895; since, a laborer in Bristol.

CHILDREN

2. Mary Grace, b. Groton, Aug. 22, 1878; m. Aug. 20, 1898, Frank W. Morrison, and res. Penacook.

3. Harvey Chester, b. G., Aug. 4, 1880; laborer in Bristol.

4. Myron Herbert, b. G., Oct. 29, 1882; m. Apr. 15, 1900, Angie, dau. of William W. Benton. (See.) A teamster. Children:

    a. Unice Velma, b. Bristol, Dec. 13, 1900.
    b. Verne Benton, b. B., Dec. 5, 1901.
  5. Harold Earl, b. Dorchester, Nov. 29, 1886.
  6. Ray Otis, b. D., Mar. 11, 1890.
  7. Sarah Ethel, b. D., Apr. 10, 1892.

THE MOSSMAN FAMILY

    1. Robert D. Mossman is the son of William and Janet Mossman. He was b. Edinburgh, Scotland, Jan. 25, 1841. He m., 1866, Sarah, dau. of Mark and Emily Jane (Hobbs) Knight, b. Windham, Me., July 19, 1841. He was superintendent of the Mason-Perkins Paper company 1873-'79; since, a member of the firm of Tileston & Hollingsworth Paper company, Mattapan, Mass. He is a Mason; a member of the Massachusetts Charitable Mechanics Association, and a director of the Dorchester Co-operative bank. Res. 1,616 Blue Hill Ave., Boston, Mass.

CHILDREN

  2. Mary.
  3. William, b. Westbrook, Me.; graduated at the Mass. Institute of Technology; is assistant superintendent of the Tileston & Hollingsworth Paper company.

THE MOULTON FAMILY

    1. Jonathan Moulton was the son of Edward Brown Moulton, a Revolutionary soldier, and Ann Smith Moulton, his wife. Jonathan was b. Apr. 1, 1781, and m. (2) Mary Morse. He was first taxed in Bristol in 1839. He res. on Central street and operated the clothing-mill opposite his residence. He removed to Meredith about 1850, where he d. in 1860, ae. about 79.

CHILDREN

  2. Ann, b. 1823; d. 1901, ae. 78.
  3. Albert A., b. Oct. 6, 1829; studied medicine with Dr. Moody C. Sawyer. He m., in May, 1850, Ann Maria, dau. of Richard H. Sawyer (See), b. June 23, 1823. He practiced medicine in Laconia; was surgeon of the 3d Regt., N. H. Vols. After war, practiced in Tilton. She d. Concord, June, 1872, ae. 49. He d. Soldiers' Home, Tilton, Apr. 26, 1890, ae. 60-6-20. Children:
    a. Harry, infant, d. Apr. 16, 1851.
    b. Arthur Channing, b. Meredith, Apr. 24, 1855; m. Nov. 30, 1887, Ada, dau. David R. and Mahala Castiday, b. Canada, Dec. 30, 1863. He has res. Colorado since 1876, now in trade in Meeker, Colo. Children: (1) Victor Channing, b. Rawlins, Wyo., Mar. 14, 1889. (2) Ada Katharine, b. Sept. 27, 1890; d. Nov. 1, 1894. (3) Mary Sawyer, b. Meeker, May 9, 1896.

THE MUDGETT FAMILY

    1. William Mudgett, b. Nov. 29, 1786, was the son of Joseph, who settled in New Hampton previous to 1790, going

there from Poplin. William came to Bristol in March, 1815, and settled on the Mudgett farm on Fowler's river near the lake, and here he spent his life. He m., Mar. 9, 1815, Eunice Huckins, dau. of Joseph, b. Parsonsfield, Me., Dec. 31, 1792 ; d. Bristol, Aug. 30, 1847, ae. 54-7-29. He m. (2) Mar. 20, 1850, Mary Cheney, dau. of David (See), b. July 24, 1804. He d. Bristol, Nov. 13, 1876, ae. 89-11-14. His widow d. in family of E. W. Locke, in Alexandria, Jan. 22, 1892, ae. 87-5-28.

CHILDREN

2   Mary Mooney Smith, b. Bristol, Feb. 20, 1816; m. James H. Brown. (See.)

3.   Hannah Huckins, b. B., Apr. 21, 1819; d. Mar. 10, 1836, ae. 16-10-19.

4.   John Philander, b. B., Sept. 15, 1821 ; d. Oct. 17, 1842, ae. 21-1-2.

5.   Calvin Huckins, b. B., Aug. 1, 1823 ; m. (1) July 15, 1851, Julia, dau. of Ellis and Hannah (Noyes) Fisher, b. Northfield, Vt., Apr. 19, 1827, and d. Bristol, Dec. 18, 1886, ae. 59-7-29.   He m. (2) Oct. 29, 1887, Mrs. Clara Lamprey, sister of his first wife, and widow of Reuben Lamprey, of New Hampton, b. Canada, July 11, 1824, d. at Hopkinton, Sept. 12, 1891, ae. 67-2-1. He m. (3) Sept. 7, 1892, Mary Jane (Perry) Dow, widow of J. French Dow of Hopkinton. He res. on the home farm till 1853; in Northfield till 1858; returned to Bristol; removed to Hopkinton 1887. Republican. Represented Bristol in the legislature. Children :

   a.   William Ellis, b. Northfield, Vt., Sept. 16, 1854; m. Saloma B. Chase. A farmer in Contoocook.

   b.   Amy Florence, b. Bristol ; d. in infancy.

   c.   Ellen Fisher, b. B., Feb. 26, 1866 ; m. Henry Chase Eastman, of Hopkinton. He d. a few months after their m. and she m. (2) George Blood. They res. Contoocook. No children.

6.   Orinda Mehitable, b. B., Apr. 17, 1827 ; m. June 29, 1848, Curtis Smith, b. Nov. 8, 1822. She d. Ashland, June 19, 1884, ae. 57-2-2 ; he d. Ashland, Dec. 9, 1872, ae. 50-1-1. Children :

   a.   Clara Ella, b. New Hampton, Apr. 7, 1856 ; d. Apr. 11, 1856.

   b.   Albert Linvill, b. N. H., Apr. 17, 1858 ; m. Oct. 25, 1886, Ella M. Smith, of New Hampton. Res. Ashland.

   c.   Mary Alice, b. N. H., Nov. 6, 1860 ; m. Apr. 30, 1891, Henry E. Fones. Res. Warwick, R. I.

   d.   Ederie Oregon, b. N. H., Oct. 30, 1863 ; m. May 30, 1889, Kate G. Eastman. He d. Plymouth, Apr. 28, 1893, ae. 29-5-28.

   e.   Martha Susan, b. N. H., Oct. 26, 1865 ; m. Oct. 26, 1886, Dana W. Carey. Res. Ashland.

   f.   William Leonett, b. Ashland, Dec. 8, 1869; m. Feb. 29, 1892, Mabelle Maud Steele, of Fall River, Mass. Res. Boston, Mass.

7.   Laura Lettice, b. B., Jan. 21, 1829; m. Josiah S. Ingalls. (See.)

8.   Sarah Ann Baker, b. B., July 22, 1833; m. Jan. 20, 1855, Hosea F. Hawkins, Meredith. She d. while visiting in Ashland, Sept. 13, 1874, ae. 41-1-21. He res. Meredith. Children, all born in Meredith :

   a.   Laura E., b. Nov. 29, 1856 ; m. Fred Rollins, Meredith, and res. East Concord.

   b.   Arthur Stanley, b. Mar. 7, 1859 ; d. Dec. 16, 1880, ae. 21-9-9.

   c.   Fred Alliston, b. Apr. 11, 1862 ; m. Ella Atwood, Alexandria. Res. Meredith.

   d.   Amy Eunice, b. Oct. 30, 1868 ; d. June 6, 1885, ae. 16-7-6.

   e.   Herman Curtis, b. Sept. 26, 1872. Res. Meredith.

THE MUSGROVE FAMILY

1. James Musgrove, a son of James and Sarah (Hacket) Musgrove, was b. in London, Eng., Dec. 13, 1798. His father was a custom house officer of the East India company at Calcutta, India. From eight till seventeen years of age, he was a cabin boy in the British navy; served four years as tailor's apprentice at St. John's, N. B., whence he sailed for Boston, Mass. Was shipwrecked at the mouth of the Penobscot river, from which point he walked to Boston; there he finished a seven years' apprenticeship, then required to learn most trades, and returned to London. He was m. in Bethnel Green church, London, Dec. 29, 1827, to Ann, dau. of Isaac and Mary (Ship) Donker, b. in Spittalsfield, London, Sept. 3, 1802. They emigrated to America in September, 1832, and res. Boston, Charlestown, and Lynn, Mass. In the financial panic of 1837, he was thrown out of work and advertised for a place in which to establish himself in business. Replies came from Hon. Nathaniel S. Berry, of Bristol, and other places. To visit the places where he was asked to locate he walked from Lynn to Vermont, thence to Haverhill Corner and Bristol. Here he located and conducted the tailoring business till incapacitated by age. He was a great reader and a well informed man, an abolitionist, and both were lifelong active workers in the Methodist church. He d. May 13, 1878, ae. 79-5-0; she d. Mar. 20, 1879, ae. 76-6-17.

CHILDREN

2. James, b. London, Dec. 24, 1828; d. Nov. 13, 1829.

3. Ann, b. L., Nov. 10, 1830; d. Bristol, of scarlet fever, Mar. 21, 1846, ae. 15-4-11.

4. Susan, b. L., Nov. 24, 1831. Res. Concord. Unm.

5. Mary Donker, b. Charlestown, Mass., Sept. 5, 1833; d. Nov. 23, 1851, ae. 18-2-18.

6. William Isaac, b. Lynn, Mass., July 13, 1835; m. May 29, 1859, at Cohoes, N. Y., Cornelia Emma, dau. of Miron and Elvira Potter, b. Troy, N. Y., June 27, 1840; d. Cohoes, Dec. 7, 1872, ae. 32-5-10. He was for several years an overseer in a knitting-mill at Cohoes; in trade 20 years at Cohoes; superintendent of the Medlecott-Morgan knitting-mill at Springfield, Mass., till he d., Dec. 26, 1900, ae. 65-5-13. Republican, Methodist. Children:

    a. Charles Watson, b. Cohoes, Oct. 3, 1865; m. May 17, 1886, Mary Ellen, dau. of Martin Lewis and Mary Elizabeth Pattee, b. New York city, Apr. 12, 1865. He is a letter carrier in Springfield, Mass. Children: (1) Mary Clara, b. Cohoes, Mar. 25, 1887. (2) Charles William, b. C., Oct. 12, 1888. (3) Grace Frances, b. Springfield, Sept. 10, 1890.

    b. Clara Belle, b. C., Aug. 27, 1867. Res. Springfield. Unm.

7. John Henry, b. L., May 7, 1837; m. Apr. 8, 1866, Carrie Sophia, dau. of Rev. Newell Culver (See), b. May 5, 1841. She d. Pittsfield, Mass., Oct. 27, 1883, ae. 42-5-22. He m. (2) June 11, 1888, Mary L., dau. of Rev. James C. and Sarah Ann (Chase) Aspinwall, b. Weathersfield, Vt., Nov. 10, 1848. She graduated from Tilton Seminary 1871, and was a school

teacher. He has been a knit goods manufacturer at Bristol, Enosburg
Falls, Vt., Cohoes, N. Y., Stillwater, N. Y., and for 16 years superintendent of the Berkshire Knitting-mills at Pittsfield, Mass. Now president and manager of the Musgrove Knitting-mills, at Pittsfield. Children :

    a. Nellie Mabel, b. Bristol, Mar. 18, 1868 ; m. Apr. 27, 1889,
Charles W. Mink, of Pittsfield. He d. Jan. 12, 1896, and she m.
(2) Sept. 18, 1896, George Corwin, of Glenfield, N. Y. Children :
(1) Caroline Elizabeth, b. Pittsfield, June 11, 1890 ; d. Aug. 26,
1891, ae. 1-2-15. (2) Reuben Raymond, b. Aug. 26, 1891. (3)
John Harold, b. June 22, 1897. (4) Charles Lester, b. Aug. 21, 1898.
(5) Laura Gertrude, b. Sept. 13, 1900 ; d. Oct., 1900.

    b. Carrie Gertrude, b. B., Apr. 7, 1870. Is a school teacher in
Edgerton, Wis.

    c. Newell Culver, b. B., Feb. 7, 1873 ; d. Cohoes, N. Y., July 26,
1873.

    d. John Culver, b. Cohoes, Mar. 7, 1880; graduated as electrical
engineer at Cornel University, Ithaca, N. Y., 1903.

    e. Sophie Donker, b. Pittsfield, Mass., Oct. 26, 1890.

    8. Sara Minot Chase, b. Bristol, Mar. 10, 1839. Graduated from Til-
ton Seminary, 1865. Was teacher in the public schools, and at Poultney,
(Vt.) Seminary ; was in city missionary work at Troy, N. Y., for the
Second Street Presbyterian church ; and, since 1887, has maintained a
mission home at 3,337 6th Ave., Troy. Was formerly a Methodist, now
connected with the Christian Alliance. Unm.

    9. Richard Watson, b. B., Nov. 21, 1840. Served nearly four years
in the Union army. (See Roll of Honor.) Was two or three years in
the wool business, and in December, 1870, opened a printing-office in
town, and in June, 1878, established the *Bristol Weekly Enterprise*,
which are continued by him. Was six years on board of education
of Union School district, six years town clerk, represented the town in
legislature of 1885; was author of the bill to provide for the publication
of the *Register of New Hampshire Soldiers and Sailors, War of the
Rebellion;* represented the Fourth Senatorial district in the senate of
1891-'92, and has been for 33 years recording steward of the official board
of the Methodist church, and chairman of trustees of Minot-Sleeper
library since its organization. Republican, Mason, Odd Fellow, G. A. R.
He m., Dec. 23, 1869, Henrietta Maria, dau. of Ebenezer and Sarah Maria
(Brown) Guild, b. Walpole, Sept. 14, 1843. She has been from girlhood
a music teacher and church organist; successful in training children for
chorus singing; with her children has given concerts throughout the
state as the "Musgrove Family." Active in church and temperance
work. Children, all born in Bristol :

    a. Isadore Maria, b. Dec. 24, 1870 ; graduated from New Hamp-
ton Literary Inititution 1893 ; was a public reader ; m. Nov. 17, 1896,
Prof. Charles W. Cutts, a teacher at New Hampton Institution,
now principal of High school and superintendent of schools at
Merrimac, Mass. She d. Merrimac, Sept. 22, 1902, ae. 31-8-28.
Child : Mary Elisabeth, b. Bristol, Oct. 4, 1897.

    b. Frank Abbott, b. July 19, 1872. Graduated from New Hamp-
ton Literary Institution, 1892; Dartmouth College, 1899 ; now proprietor Dartmouth Press, and editor *Hanover Gazette*, Hanover.

    c. Carrie Etta, b. Jan. 24, 1874 ; pursued classical course at New
Hampton Literary Institution ; m. Sept. 11, 1900, Pierce J. Little,
foreman in shoe factory at Exeter. Child : Margaret Musgrove, b.
Exeter, Jan. 23, 1903.

    d. Mary Donker, b. Oct. 22, 1875 ; graduated at New Hampton,
1896 ; is associate editor of *Bristol Enterprise;* member of Methodist choir.

21

e. Anna Belle, b. Jan. 7, 1878. Since 1898, a student and teacher of music in Boston.

f. Eugene Richard, b. Aug. 20, 1879. Graduated from Tilton Seminary, 1900; now a student at Dartmouth College.

10. Adam Clark, b. B., Aug. 22, 1842. In 1862, was employed in a knitting-mill at Cohoes, N. Y., where he changed his first name to Abbott, and under this name enlisted in Co. H, 115th Regt., N. Y. Vols. Killed in action at Deep Bottom, Va., Aug. 16, 1864, ae. 21-11-24. (See Roll of Honor.)

11. George Gustavus Sanborn, b. B., Dec. 27, 1845; d. Apr. 15, 1846.

12. Charles Marston, b. B., Feb. 2, 1848; m. Dec. 21, 1867, Sarah Maria, dau. of Oliver B. Fogg. (See.) A farmer in Bristol till about 1880; an overseer in knitting-mills in Cohoes, N. Y., and Pittsfield, Mass., for 19 years. Has taken out several patents for improvements in knitting machinery; now manufacturer of knit goods, Pittsfield. Children:

a. Addie Viola, b. Bristol, May 24, 1868; m. Feb. 5, 1891, Perry E. Miller, of Pittsfield. They res. Pawtucket, R. I., where he is a knit goods manufacturer. Children: (1) Florence, b. Coventry, R. I., Nov. 3, 1891. (2) Clarence McArthur, b. Pittsfield, Nov. 15, 1893. (3) Lester Arthur, b. Pawtucket, Nov. 23, 1896.

b. William Abbott, b. B., Sept. 11, 1871; m. Nov. 23, 1892, Nellie W., dau. of Nelson and Nettie (Tayer) Parker, b. Pittsfield, Mass., Nov. 23, 1872. He is in the meat business at Pittsfield. Child: Nelson Parker, b. Dec. 12, 1894.

c. Clara Elizabeth, b. B., Mar. 11, 1874; m. Dec. 2, 1896, Elmon R. Johnson, M.D., an ear, nose and throat specialist in Boston, Mass. Children: (1) Charles Musgrove, b. Wollaston, Feb. 2, 1898. (2) Elmon Reuben, b. W., Aug. 16, 1901.

d. George Egbert, b. B., Sept. 26, 1876; took a three years' scientific course at Dartmouth College, 1899-'02; now electrical engineer at Schenectady, N. Y.

e. Arthur Sylvanus, b. B., Mar. 3, 1879.

f. Grace Cole, b. Pittsfield, Jan. 7, 1883.

g. Alberta, b. P., Nov. 13, 1885.

THE MUZZEY FAMILY

1. Samuel Muzzey, son of Joseph and Jane (Bartlett) Muzzey, was b. Boscawen, Jan. 28, 1810. He m. Sept. 13, 1834, Sally G., dau. of William and Nancy (Gove) Blake, b. Andover, June 28, 1815. They came to Bristol from Northfield in March, 1844, and settled in the Locke neighborhood, where he d. July 5, 1886, ae. 76-5-7; she d. same place, Dec. 17, 1898, ae. 83-5-19. Farmer, Methodist, Republican.

CHILDREN

2. Ann A., b. Canterbury, Nov. 6, 1835. Res. on home farm. Unm.

3. John B., b. Northfield, Feb. 5, 1838. Was machinist in Penacook. Served in 2nd Regt., N. H. Vols., private, Co. E; killed at battle of Bull Run, Va., Aug. 29, 1862, ae. 24-6-24.

4. Hannah H., b. N., Mar. 13, 1840; m. Charles H. Phipps. (See.)

5. Sarah, b. N., June 30, 1842; d. May 19, 1903, ae. 60-10-19.

6. William Joseph, b. Bristol, June 6, 1844; m. Oct. 15, 1872, Helen Ann, dau. of Thomas T. and Nancy B. (Clesby) Moore, b. Concord, Mar. 10, 1855. Was a machinist in Concord till 1892; a farmer in Bristol; now res. Tilton. Mrs. Nancy B. Moore d. in this family in Bristol, Oct. 4, 1888, ae. 70-0-24. Children:

WILLIAM I. MUSGROVE.   JOHN H. MUSGROVE

CHARLES M. MUSGROVE

SARA M. C. MUSGROVE   HENRIETTA (GUILD) MUSGROVE

    a. Frankie William, b. Bristol, Jan. 31, 1880; d. Sept. 16, 1881, ae. 1-7-15.

    b. Bertha Helen, b. Penacook, July 18, 1890.

  7. Orrin Jacob, b. B., Oct. 21, 1846; m. Dec. 30, 1875, Emma Jane Avery, dau. John F., b. Apr. 6, 1854; d. Bristol, July 2, 1880, ae. 26-2-26. He m. (2) Oct. 18, 1882, Cora Augusta, dau. Frederick Kidder. (See.) They res. Warner. Children :

    a. Fred Charles, b. Franklin, Feb. 27, 1877. Res. Bristol.

    b. Ralph Kidder, b. Bristol, Mar. 5, 1884.

    c. Roy Chandler, b. Concord, June 22, 1890.

    d. Carl, b. C., Aug. 9, 1892.

    e. Marion E., b. Warner, Apr. 20, 1899.

    f. Son, b. Warner, Apr. 20, 1899; d. May 3, 1899.

  8. Walter Scott, b. B., July 13, 1849; m. Nov. 26, 1873, Ellen Catherine, dau. of David Abbott, Concord, b. Sept. 17, 1852. In meat business at Tilton. Children :

    a. Harry Walter, b. Franklin, Apr. 20, 1876; m. Oct. 17, 1898, Emma Jennie, dau. of Frank Lovell, b. Lawrence, Mass., July 3, 1877. In meat business, Tilton. Children : (1) Merle Ellen, b. Apr. 25, 1899. (2) Miriam Lovell, b. Dec. 13, 1900.

    b. Arthur Phipps, b. July 23, 1883 ; d. Apr. 17, 1884.

  9. Albert Collis, b. B., July 6, 1851 ; m. July 20, 1880, Mary A., dau. Richard Thomas, b. Lawrence, Mass. In the meat business, Tilton. Child :

    a. Herbert Thomas, b. Tilton, Jan. 2, 1887.

THE NEALY FAMILY

  1. Rev. William Alson Nealy was the son of John and Sarah (Cooper) Nealy. He was b. West Bolton, Vt., Nov. 3, 1845, and m. Sept. 3, 1873, Martha M., dau. of Thomas and Roxy (Shaw) Brill, b. St. Armands, P. Q., Jan. 9, 1850. He was pastor of the Free Baptist church in Bristol, 1888-'90, and here d. June 28, 1890, ae. 44-7-25. She res. 39 Church street, Malden, Mass.

CHILDREN

  2. Walter Alson, b. Putnam, N. Y., Nov. 17, 1876. Is a chemist in Norwood, Mass.

  3. Milo Arthur, b. Tiverton, R. I., Oct. 26, 1879; m. June 3, 1903, Harriet O., dau. of Charles B. and Harriet M. (Dale) Glover, b. Chelsea, Mass., Sept. 3, 1881. He is clerk in freight office, Malden, Mass.

  4. Martha Alice, b. Adamsville, R. I., Dec. 9, 1886.

THE NELSON FAMILIES

  1. The Nelsons of Bristol are descendants of Thomas Nelson, the ancestor of most of the Nelsons of New England. Thomas and his wife, Joan, emigrated to this country with twenty families from Rowley, Yorkshire, England, in 1638. They arrived in Salem, Mass., in December, and in the spring following removed to a place named, a year later, Rowley, after their old town in England. Thomas d. in England, August

1648, where he had gone on business. They had five children, of whom the eldest, was

2. Philip, b. England, 1636. He graduated from Harvard college in 1654, the only one in that class. He was a captain in Sir William Phipps's expedition against Quebec in 1690. He d. Aug. 19, 1691, ae. 55. He m. (1) Sarah Jewett, June 24, 1657. She had two children and d. Feb. 14, 1665. He m. (2) Nov. 1, 1666, Elizabeth, dau. John Lowell, by whom he had eleven children. The ninth child was

3. Joseph, b. Nov. 28, 1682. He m. in 1706, Hannah, dau. of Capt. Samuel Brocklebank. She d. June 5, 1732, ae. 48. They had ten children, the second of whom was

4. Joseph, b. Mar. 10, 1709, and res. in Rowley. He m. Lydia, dau. of Aaron and Elizabeth (Pearson) Pingree, Nov. 7, 1734. Joseph, d. Mar. 6, 1769, ae. 59-11-26; she d. Mar. 8, 1786. They had eight children, of whom the youngest was

5. Stephen, b. Apr. 5, 1752. He was a farmer in Sutton, and sold his farm during the Revolutionary war for $800 in Continental scrip. A year or two later he purchased another farm in Salisbury, when he found his $800 had depreciated to $8. He m. Abigail Page in Salisbury. He spent the last 12 years of his life in the family of his son, Levi, in Bristol, where he d. Dec. 15, 1847, ae. 95-8-10. He was the father of 11 children, four of whom were :

6. Aaron, m. Jan. 20, 1807, Betsey, dau. of Jonathan Ingalls (See), b. Bristol, Oct. 12, 1785. They erected a farmhouse near where is now Raymond Cavis's cottage on east shore of lake, and there res. till they removed to No. Faystown, Vt. Later in life, they removed to Massena, N. Y., where they d. Children :

    a. Charles, m. Sophronia Ingalls.
    b. Luther W.
    c. Betsey, m. Walter Wheeler and d. at Raymondville, N. Y., Aug. 9, 1881; he d. Apr. 15, 1903.
    d. Eliza, m. Horace Ingalls.

7. Affa, b. Aug., 1779; made her home in the family of her brother, Levi, in Bristol, and d. Oct. 25, 1838, ae. 59-2-.

*8. Levi, b. Sutton, Aug. 12, 1789.

9. Hannah, b. Salisbury, Feb. 21, 1792 ; m. Robert Heath. (See.)

(8) Levi Nelson, son of Stephen, b. Aug. 12, 1789, m. May 28, 1809, Sara Evans, b. Salisbury, June 3, 1788. They removed to Bristol in 1812, and purchased the Nelson farm. The first dwelling on this farm stood higher up on the hillside and some distance west of the present highway, near the schoolhouse destroyed by fire in 1816. Here he resided for some years, and then built a house just above the present farmhouse on this farm. He d. Jan. 18, 1875, ae. 85-5-6 ; she d. Dec. 14, 1877, ae. 89-6-11. The Nelsons of Bristol have been noted for their sterling character, physically and mentally.

teacher. He has been a knit goods manufacturer at Bristol, Enosburg
Falls, Vt., Cohoes, N. Y., Stillwater, N. Y., and for 16 years superintendent of the Berkshire Knitting-mills at Pittsfield, Mass. Now president and manager of the Musgrove Knitting-mills, at Pittsfield. Children:

    a. Nellie Mabel, b. Bristol, Mar. 18, 1868; m. Apr. 27, 1889,
Charles W. Mink, of Pittsfield. He d. Jan. 12, 1896, and she m.
(2) Sept. 18, 1896, George Corwin, of Glenfield, N. Y. Children:
(1) Caroline Elizabeth, b. Pittsfield, June 11, 1890; d. Aug. 26,
1891, ae. 1-2-15. (2) Reuben Raymond, b. Aug. 26, 1891. (3)
John Harold, b. June 22, 1897. (4) Charles Lester, b. Aug. 21, 1898.
(5) Laura Gertrude, b. Sept. 13, 1900; d. Oct., 1900.

    b. Carrie Gertrude, b. B., Apr. 7, 1870. Is a school teacher in
Edgerton, Wis.

    c. Newell Culver, b. B., Feb. 7, 1873; d. Cohoes, N. Y., July 26,
1873.

    d. John Culver, b. Cohoes, Mar. 7, 1880; graduated as electrical
engineer at Cornel University, Ithaca, N. Y., 1903.

    e. Sophie Donker, b. Pittsfield, Mass., Oct. 26, 1890.

    8. Sara Minot Chase, b. Bristol, Mar. 10, 1839. Graduated from Til-
ton Seminary, 1865. Was teacher in the public schools, and at Poultney,
(Vt.) Seminary; was in city missionary work at Troy, N. Y., for the
Second Street Presbyterian church; and, since 1887, has maintained a
mission home at 3,337 6th Ave., Troy. Was formerly a Methodist, now
connected with the Christian Alliance. Unm.

    9. Richard Watson, b. B., Nov. 21, 1840. Served nearly four years
in the Union army. (See Roll of Honor.) Was two or three years in
the wool business, and in December, 1870, opened a printing-office in
town, and in June, 1878, established the *Bristol Weekly Enterprise,*
which are continued by him. Was six years on board of education
of Union School district, six years town clerk, represented the town in
legislature of 1885; was author of the bill to provide for the publication
of the *Register of New Hampshire Soldiers and Sailors, War of the
Rebellion;* represented the Fourth Senatorial district in the senate of
1891-'92, and has been for 33 years recording steward of the official board
of the Methodist church, and chairman of trustees of Minot-Sleeper
library since its organization. Republican, Mason, Odd Fellow, G. A. R.
He m., Dec. 23, 1869, Henrietta Maria, dau. of Ebenezer and Sarah Maria
(Brown) Guild, b. Walpole, Sept. 14, 1843. She has been from girlhood
a music teacher and church organist; successful in training children for
chorus singing; with her children has given concerts throughout the
state as the "Musgrove Family." Active in church and temperance
work. Children, all born in Bristol:

    a. Isadore Maria, b. Dec. 24, 1870; graduated from New Hamp-
ton Literary Inititution 1893; was a public reader; m. Nov. 17, 1896,
Prof. Charles W. Cutts, a teacher at New Hampton Institution,
now principal of High school and superintendent of schools at
Merrimac, Mass. She d. Merrimac, Sept. 22, 1902, ae. 31-8-28.
Child: Mary Elisabeth, b. Bristol, Oct. 4, 1897.

    b. Frank Abbott, b. July 19, 1872. Graduated from New Hamp-
ton Literary Institution, 1892; Dartmouth College, 1899; now proprietor Dartmouth Press, and editor *Hanover Gazette,* Hanover.

    c. Carrie Etta, b. Jan. 24, 1874; pursued classical course at New
Hampton Literary Institution; m. Sept. 11, 1900, Pierce J. Little,
foreman in shoe factory at Exeter. Child: Margaret Musgrove, b.
Exeter, Jan. 23, 1903.

    d. Mary Donker, b. Oct. 22, 1875; graduated at New Hampton,
1896; is associate editor of *Bristol Enterprise;* member of Methodist choir.

21

e. Anna Belle, b. Jan. 7, 1878. Since 1898, a student and teacher of music in Boston.

f. Eugene Richard, b. Aug. 20, 1879. Graduated from Tilton Seminary, 1900; now a student at Dartmouth College.

10. Adam Clark, b. B., Aug. 22, 1842. In 1862, was employed in a knitting-mill at Cohoes, N. Y., where he changed his first name to Abbott, and under this name enlisted in Co. H, 115th Regt., N. Y. Vols. Killed in action at Deep Bottom, Va., Aug. 16, 1864, ae. 21-11-24. (See Roll of Honor.)

11. George Gustavus Sanborn, b. B., Dec. 27, 1845 ; d. Apr. 15, 1846.

12. Charles Marston, b. B., Feb. 2, 1848; m. Dec. 21, 1867, Sarah Maria, dau. of Oliver B. Fogg. (See.) A farmer in Bristol till about 1880; an overseer in knitting-mills in Cohoes, N. Y., and Pittsfield, Mass., for 19 years. Has taken out several patents for improvements in knitting machinery; now manufacturer of knit goods, Pittsfield. Children :

a. Addie Viola, b. Bristol, May 24, 1868 ; m. Feb. 5, 1891, Perry E. Miller, of Pittsfield. They res. Pawtucket, R. I., where he is a knit goods manufacturer. Children : (1) Florence, b. Coventry, R. I., Nov. 3, 1891. (2) Clarence McArthur, b. Pittsfield, Nov. 15, 1893. (3) Lester Arthur, b. Pawtucket, Nov. 23, 1896.

b. William Abbott, b. B., Sept. 11, 1871 ; m. Nov. 23, 1892, Nellie W., dau. of Nelson and Nettie (Tayer) Parker, b. Pittsfield, Mass., Nov. 23, 1872. He is in the meat business at Pittsfield. Child : Nelson Parker, b. Dec. 12, 1894.

c. Clara Elizabeth, b. B., Mar. 11, 1874; m. Dec. 2, 1896, Elmon R. Johnson, M.D., an ear, nose and throat specialist in Boston, Mass. Children : (1) Charles Musgrove, b. Wollaston, Feb. 2, 1898. (2) Elmon Reuben, b. W., Aug. 16, 1901.

d. George Egbert, b. B., Sept. 26, 1876; took a three years' scientific course at Dartmouth College, 1899-'02 ; now electrical engineer at Schenectady, N. Y.

e. Arthur Sylvanus, b. B., Mar. 3, 1879.

f. Grace Cole, b. Pittsfield, Jan. 7, 1883.

g. Alberta, b. P., Nov. 13, 1885.

THE MUZZEY FAMILY

1. Samuel Muzzey, son of Joseph and Jane (Bartlett) Muzzey, was b. Boscawen, Jan. 28, 1810. He m. Sept. 13, 1834, Sally G., dau. of William and Nancy (Gove) Blake, b. Andover, June 28, 1815. They came to Bristol from Northfield in March, 1844, and settled in the Locke neighborhood, where he d. July 5, 1886, ae. 76-5-7 ; she d. same place, Dec. 17, 1898, ae. 83-5-19. Farmer, Methodist, Republican.

CHILDREN

2. Ann A., b. Canterbury, Nov. 6, 1835. Res. on home farm. Unm.

3. John B., b. Northfield, Feb. 5, 1838. Was machinist in Penacook. Served in 2nd Regt., N. H. Vols., private, Co. E ; killed at battle of Bull Run, Va., Aug. 29, 1862, ae. 24-6-24.

4. Hannah H., b. N., Mar. 13, 1840; m. Charles H. Phipps. (See.)

5. Sarah, b. N., June 30, 1842; d. May 19, 1903, ae. 60-10-19.

6. William Joseph, b. Bristol, June 6, 1844; m. Oct. 15, 1872, Helen Ann, dau. of Thomas T. and Nancy B. (Clesby) Moore, b. Concord, Mar. 10, 1855. Was a machinist in Concord till 1892 ; a farmer in Bristol ; now res. Tilton. Mrs. Nancy B. Moore d. in this family in Bristol, Oct. 4, 1888, ae. 70-0-24. Children :

STEPHEN NELSON

a. Frankie William, b. Bristol, Jan. 31, 1880; d. Sept. 16, 1881, ae. 1-7-15.

b. Bertha Helen, b. Penacook, July 18, 1890.

7. Orrin Jacob, b. B., Oct. 21, 1846; m. Dec. 30, 1875, Emma Jane Avery, dau. John F., b. Apr. 6, 1854; d. Bristol, July 2, 1880, ae. 26-2-26. He m. (2) Oct. 18, 1882, Cora Augusta, dau. Frederick Kidder. (See.) They res. Warner. Children :

a. Fred Charles, b. Franklin, Feb. 27, 1877. Res. Bristol.

b. Ralph Kidder, b. Bristol, Mar. 5, 1884.

c. Roy Chandler, b. Concord, June 22, 1890.

d. Carl, b. C., Aug. 9, 1892.

e. Marion E., b. Warner, Apr. 20, 1899.

f. Son, b. Warner, Apr. 20, 1899; d. May 3, 1899.

8. Walter Scott, b. B., July 13, 1849; m. Nov. 26, 1873, Ellen Catherine, dau. of David Abbott, Concord, b. Sept. 17, 1852. In meat business at Tilton. Children :

a. Harry Walter, b. Franklin, Apr. 20, 1876; m. Oct. 17, 1898, Emma Jennie, dau. of Frank Lovell, b. Lawrence, Mass., July 3, 1877. In meat business, Tilton. Children : (1) Merle Ellen, b. Apr. 25, 1899. (2) Miriam Lovell, b. Dec. 13, 1900.

b. Arthur Phipps, b. July 23, 1883 ; d. Apr. 17, 1884.

9. Albert Collis, b. B., July 6, 1851 ; m. July 20, 1880, Mary A., dau. Richard Thomas, b. Lawrence, Mass. In the meat business, Tilton. Child :

a. Herbert Thomas, b. Tilton, Jan. 2, 1887.

THE NEALY FAMILY

1. Rev. William Alson Nealy was the son of John and Sarah (Cooper) Nealy. He was b. West Bolton, Vt., Nov. 3, 1845, and m. Sept. 3, 1873, Martha M., dau. of Thomas and Roxy (Shaw) Brill, b. St. Armands, P. Q., Jan. 9, 1850. He was pastor of the Free Baptist church in Bristol, 1888–'90, and here d. June 28, 1890, ae. 44-7-25. She res. 39 Church street, Malden, Mass.

CHILDREN

2. Walter Alson, b. Putnam, N. Y., Nov. 17, 1876. Is a chemist in Norwood, Mass.

3. Milo Arthur, b. Tiverton, R. I., Oct. 26, 1879; m. June 3, 1903, Harriet O., dau. of Charles B. and Harriet M. (Dale) Glover, b. Chelsea, Mass., Sept. 3, 1881. He is clerk in freight office, Malden, Mass.

4. Martha Alice, b. Adamsville, R. I., Dec. 9, 1886.

THE NELSON FAMILIES

1. The Nelsons of Bristol are descendants of Thomas Nelson, the ancestor of most of the Nelsons of New England. Thomas and his wife, Joan, emigrated to this country with twenty families from Rowley, Yorkshire, England, in 1638. They arrived in Salem, Mass., in December, and in the spring following removed to a place named, a year later, Rowley, after their old town in England. Thomas d. in England, August

1648, where he had gone on business. They had five children, of whom the eldest, was

2. Philip, b. England, 1636. He graduated from Harvard college in 1654, the only one in that class. He was a captain in Sir William Phipps's expedition against Quebec in 1690. He d. Aug. 19, 1691, ae. 55. He m. (1) Sarah Jewett, June 24, 1657. She had two children and d. Feb. 14, 1665. He m. (2) Nov. 1, 1666, Elizabeth, dau. John Lowell, by whom he had eleven children. The ninth child was

3. Joseph, b. Nov. 28, 1682. He m. in 1706, Hannah, dau. of Capt. Samuel Brocklebank. She d. June 5, 1732, ae. 48. They had ten children, the second of whom was

4. Joseph, b. Mar. 10, 1709, and res. in Rowley. He m. Lydia, dau. of Aaron and Elizabeth (Pearson) Pingree, Nov. 7, 1734. Joseph, d. Mar. 6, 1769, ae. 59-11-26; she d. Mar. 8, 1786. They had eight children, of whom the youngest was

5. Stephen, b. Apr. 5, 1752. He was a farmer in Sutton, and sold his farm during the Revolutionary war for $800 in Continental scrip. A year or two later he purchased another farm in Salisbury, when he found his $800 had depreciated to $8. He m. Abigail Page in Salisbury. He spent the last 12 years of his life in the family of his son, Levi, in Bristol, where he d. Dec. 15, 1847, ae. 95-8-10. He was the father of 11 children, four of whom were :

6. Aaron, m. Jan. 20, 1807, Betsey, dau. of Jonathan Ingalls (See), b. Bristol, Oct. 12, 1785. They erected a farmhouse near where is now Raymond Cavis's cottage on east shore of lake, and there res. till they removed to No. Faystown, Vt. Later in life, they removed to Massena, N. Y., where they d. Children :

    a. Charles, m. Sophronia Ingalls.
    b. Luther W.
    c. Betsey, m. Walter Wheeler and d. at Raymondville, N. Y., Aug. 9, 1881; he d. Apr. 15, 1903.
    d. Eliza, m. Horace Ingalls.

7. Affa, b. Aug., 1779; made her home in the family of her brother, Levi, in Bristol, and d. Oct. 25, 1838, ae. 59-2-.
*8. Levi, b. Sutton, Aug. 12, 1789.
9. Hannah, b. Salisbury, Feb. 21, 1792 ; m. Robert Heath. (See.)

(8)   Levi Nelson, son of Stephen, b. Aug. 12, 1789, m. May 28, 1809, Sara Evans, b. Salisbury, June 3, 1788. They removed to Bristol in 1812, and purchased the Nelson farm. The first dwelling on this farm stood higher up on the hillside and some distance west of the present highway, near the schoolhouse destroyed by fire in 1816. Here he resided for some years, and then built a house just above the present farmhouse on this farm. He d. Jan. 18, 1875, ae. 85-5-6 ; she d. Dec. 14, 1877, ae. 89-6-11. The Nelsons of Bristol have been noted for their sterling character, physically and mentally.

CHILDREN, all except first born Bristol

10. Cyrus, b. Salisbury, Oct. 3, 1810; d. Nov. 30, 1820, ae. 10-1-27.
*11. Stephen, b. Aug. 2, 1812.
12. Dorcas, b. Nov. 6, 1814; m. Joseph Kidder. (See.)
*13. Levi, b. Dec. 7, 1816.
14. Lydia, b. Dec. 4, 1818; m. Abram Dolloff. (See.)
15. Hannah, b. July 26, 1820; d. June 23, 1829, ae. 8-10-27.
16. Hiram, b. Jan. 24, 1822; m. Oct. 15, 1843, Sally M., dau. James and Lydia Randall, b. Barnstead, Feb. 15, 1820. When a young man he went to Texas; returned and settled in Meredith in 1833. He served in the 12th Regt., N. H. Vols. (See Roll of Honor.) His last years were passed on a farm in Belmont, where he d. Sept. 1, 1894, ae. 72-7-7. Children:

    a. Ann R., b. Bristol, Nov. 9, 1844; m. Sept. 6, 1865, Charles E. Whitney, Lake Village, d. June 25, 1891, ae. 46-7-16.
    b. Electa M., b. B., Feb. 20, 1847; m. Oct. 28, 1865, John F. Davis, b. Lakeport, Apr. 22, 1843. No children.
    c. Clara Belle, b. B., Dec. 15, 1850; d. Meredith, Aug. 22, 1855, ae. 4-8-7.

17. John S., b. Sept. 16, 1823; m. Nov. 23, 1843, Belinda, dau. of Silas B. and Abbie (Sanborn) Tilton, b. Andover, Aug. 6, 1820, and d. Canterbury, Jan. 2, 1855, ae. 34-4-26. He m. (2) Jan. 21, 1886, Jennie B., dau. John L. and Julia A. (Grant) Clement, b. Groton, Feb. 9, 1846. He was in California three years in the fifties, and was wagon master of the 2nd Regt., N. H. Vols., in the Civil war, the first year of its service. Res. Canterbury. Children:

    a. Son, d. Aug. 13, 1844.
    b. Winfield Scott, b. Rumney, May 11, 1846; m. July 4, 1865, Hattie S. Glidden.
    c. Clara P., b. Hebron, Nov. 20, 1848; m. Mar. 6, 1878, Charles H. Lovejoy.
    d. Clora E., b. Groton, Nov. 28, 1850; m. Oct. 23, 1877, Solon S. Southard. (See.)
    e. Nellie B., b. Bristol, Jan. 31, 1860; d. Jan. 21, 1881, in Canterbury, ae. 20-11-20.

18. Henry Darius, b. Sept. 30, 1825; m. July 4, 1847, Elizabeth G. Merrill, of Gilmanton. He was a blacksmith. Was killed in Lawrence, Mass., Oct. 5, 1852, while firing a salute in the political campaign of that year, ae. 27-0-5. Children:

    a. Emma, b. Manchester.
    b. Ellen E., b. Lawrence; d. Feb. 12, 1855, ae. 4-9-0.

19. Cyrus Weeks, b. July 10, 1827; m. Jan. 31, 1852, Mary Augusta b. Gilmanton, Mar. 18, 1830, dau. of John and Hannah (Osborne) Merrill. He left Bristol 1850; was watchman in Stark mills at Manchester; located on a farm on the turnpike in Plymouth in 1855, where he still continues. His wife d. Oct. 3, 1900, ae. 70-6-15. He m. (2) Oct. 7, 1901, Sarah A. (Leavitt) Hartford, who d. Jan. 30, 1902, ae. 67; he m. (3) Nov. 26, 1902, Lucretia C. (Lufkin) Flanders. Children:

    a. Ina Affa, b. Manchester, July 26, 1853; m. Oscar J. Piper, and res. Meredith Center.
    b. Ida Augusta, b. Plymouth, Apr. 27, 1856; m. Feb. 24, 1873, Robert Dustin, of Hebron; (2) Dec. 26, 1891, Sherman Woodbury. Res. Plymouth.
    c. Ai Henry, b. P., July 19, 1857; m. Jennie L. Couch, Salisbury; merchant, Littleton Center, Mass.
    d. May Ellen, b. P., Jan. 4, 1859; m. Marcus T. Day, Pittsburg, Oct. 25, 1893. Res. Pittsburg.
    e. Carrie Helen, b. P., Oct. 2, 1863; m. Bennie A. Cass, Plymouth.

21*a*

f. Minnie Georgiana, b. P., May 19, 1865; m. Alfred E. Hartford, Hebron. Res. 12 Monument street, Somerville, Mass.

g. Marcia Lillian, b. P. Apr. 6, 1868; m. Aug. 17, 1887, C. W. Prescott, Tilton.

h. Miles Grant, b. P., July 29, 1870; m. Jan. 11, 1892, Nellie G. Tucker, Penacook. He is a clergyman and pastor of a church at Springfield, Mass.

20. Relief, b. May 10, 1829; m. Jan. 6, 1853, Benjamin F. Shaw, b. Salisbury, Feb. 3, 1826, and d. Salisbury, Mar. 4, 1890, ae. 64-1-1. She and her children res. Salisbury. Children :

a. Adoniram J., b. Dec. 9, 1853; d. Jan. 15, 1857, ae. 3-1-6.
b. Charles, b. June 22, 1855.
c. Naomi A., b. Nov. 8, 1858.
d. Oscar F., b. Dec. 20, 1862.
e. Sarah E., b. Dec. 16, 1864.

21. Oren, b. Apr. 25, 1831; m. Dec. 1, 1853, Mahala P., dau. of Gilman Ingalls (See), b. Feb. 8, 1830. He was a farmer and res. on a farm near Danforth brook, on road to New Hampton, where he d. Nov. 8, 1887, ae. 56-6-13. Republican. Free Baptist. She d. Bristol, Jan. 29, 1902, ae. 71-11-21. Children :

a. Arthur Vale, b. Bristol, Aug. 21, 1854; m. Eva Adeline Hall, and d. Minneapolis, Minn., Oct. 27, 1884, ae. 30-2-6.
b. Alvin Sumner, b. B., Apr. 4, 1859; d. Sept. 29, 1859.
c. Winnie Augusta, b. B., Dec. 21, 1864; d. Mar. 15, 1865.
d. Augusta Ingalls, b. B., Apr. 20, 1869; m. (1) Everett H. Emmons. (See.) She m. (2) Scott Tirrell. (See.)

22. Norman G., b. Dec. 4, 1832; m. May 20, 1854, Frances, dau. of Ansel and Elisabeth (Vickery) Weeks, b. Merrimack, Feb. 22, 1831. Was a blacksmith and millwright. Went to Lawrence, Mass., in 1851. Has been for many years superintendent of the U. S. Tubular Bell company's works at Methuen, Mass. Res. Lawrence. She d. Aug. 23, 1900, ae. 69-6-1, and he m. Sept. 16, 1902, Mrs. Martha (George) Baxter. Children :

a. Lindsey A., b. Meredith, Apr. 29, 1857; m. Nov., 1885, Lonie W. Chandler, and res. Lawrence.
b. Leo G., b. M., July 6, 1859. Res. Lawrence. Unm.

(11) Stephen Nelson, son of Levi, b. Bristol, Aug. 2, 1812, m. Mar. 15, 1838, Louisa, dau. of Joseph and Lydia (Worthen) Prescott, b. Bridgewater, Feb. 5, 1813, and d. Bristol, Mar. 16, 1893, ae. 80-1-11. He was a farmer on the home farm and a teamster, making frequent trips to Boston with a six-horse freight wagon, carrying country produce and returning with goods for the farmers or country traders. He was a Republican, and member of the Free Baptist church. He d. Feb. 17, 1892, ae. 79-6-15.

CHILDREN, all born in Bristol

23. Dan Prescott, b. Nov. 12, 1838; killed at battle of Chancellorsville, May 3, 1863, ae. 24-5-21. (See Roll of Honor.)

24. Albert Day, b. Jan. 28, 1840; d. Feb. 10, 1865, of disease contracted in the army, ae. 25-0-12. (See Roll of Honor.)

25. Major Jesse, b. Mar. 14, 1841; m. July 19, 1867, Susie Mary, dau. William H. and Susan Samler, b. Albany, N. Y., Jan. 21, 1850. He served in Co. D, 12th Regt., N. H. Vols. (See Roll of Honor.) Farmer; has res. in Norwood, Mass., since about 1880. Children:

    a. William Samler, b. Hammonton, N. J., Apr. 15, 1858.
    b. Flora Louise, b. Salem, Mass., Nov. 15, 1870; d. Aug. 14, 1871.
    c. Albert Stephen, b. S., June 22, 1872; d. Oct. 21, 1872.
    d. Jesse Edwin, b. S., Apr. 11, 1875; d. Apr. 23, 1881, ae. 6-0-12.

26. Daughter, b. 1843.
27. Harriet M., b. June 9, 1845; d. May 26, 1867, ae. 21-11-17.
28. Sarah E., b. Nov. 18, 1846; m. George A. Robie. (See.)
29. Martha Smith, b. Aug. 8, 1850; m. (1) Jan. 3, 1871, George Carrol Mason, who d. Hill, Nov. 4, 1875. She m. (2) May 15, 1877, Luther L. Mason, and res. Hill. Children:

    a. Harry Ruric, b. Hill, Apr. 20, 1872; m. June 22, 1892, Sadie J. Lindsey. Res. Dorchester, Mass. Child: (1) Harold Lindsey, b. Mar. 3, 1894.
    b. Lillian Blanch, b. Feb. 28, 1878.
    c. Martha Belle, b. Aug. 11, 1879.

30. Finette Eva, b. Apr. 6, 1853; m. Joshua D. Hemphill. (See.)
31. Levi Joseph, b. Nov. 19, 1856; m. Sept. 28, 1881, Mrs. Zoa O. Dow, dau. Stephen P. and Elizabeth (Roberts) Wiggin, b. Ashland, June 10, 1858. He is a farmer on the farm occupied by his father and grandfather. Republican. Children:

    a. Ralph Waldo, b. Mar. 27, 1883.
    b. Orea Prescott, }
    c. Oral Stephen, } b. June 20, 1885.

(13) Levi Nelson, son of Levi, b. Bristol, Dec. 7, 1816, m. Apr. 21, 1846, Lucinda Thompson, dau. of David Batchelder (See), b. Bridgewater, Apr. 5, 1826, and d. Bristol, Apr. 7, 1895, ae. 69-0-2. He was a farmer and shoemaker. He built a farmhouse on the site of the Huntington house, on east side of highway from the Clay farmhouse, which he removed later to Summer street, the house now occupied by Charles H. Phipps. He d. Bristol, May 18, 1899, ae. 82-5-11.

CHILDREN

32. Cynthia, d. in infancy.
33. Hattie, b. Hebron, May 7, 1856; m. Nov. 4, 1872, Clark O. Braley. Res. Alexandria. Children:
    a. Christie Allen.   *b*. George Edmonds.   *c*. Iola.
34. Lilla Arrimetta, b. Hill, June 8, 1858; m. Edward S. Gilman. (See.)
35. Stephen, b. Nov. 3, 1859; d. May 21, 1869, ae. 9-6-18.

THE NICHOLS FAMILY

    1. Charles Frederick Barron Darrell Nichols, the son of Luther Washington and Sarah Jane Talbot (Darrell) Nichols, was b. Boston, Mass., May 26, 1846. He m., Sept. 19, 1872, Alice L., dau. of John Adams and Jane Woodbury (Roberts) Lang, b. Meredith, Oct. 20, 1852. He early entered the employ of the Northern railroad, serving as clerk, and passenger conductor for 20 years. In July, 1875, he succeeded Oscar F. Morse as conductor on the Bristol branch, continuing till September, 1883, when he resigned. On leaving Bristol, he engaged

with his father-in-law in the manufacture of piano cases at
Meredith; was proprietor of cafe at Nashua Junction railroad
station. In March, 1902, purchased the "Corner Book and Art
store," Concord, where he is now in trade.

CHILD

2.   Joseph Percival, b. Concord, Apr. 22, 1885.

THE NORRIS FAMILIES

1.   Rev. George Washington Norris is the son of Benjamin and Zaphira (Ross) Norris, b. Dorchester, July 7, 1837.
He m., Sept. 26, 1863, Martha F., dau. of Henry and Martha
(French) Sanders, b. Wilmot, May 9, 1835, and d. Dover, Mar.
6, 1895, ae. 59-9-27. He m. (2) Nov. 23, 1896, Mary Augusta
Hamilton, who had been for 26 years a teacher in the public
schools of Lawrence, Mass.; b. Lawrence, Sept. 21, 1848, dau.
of Oliver B. and Mary Hamilton. He has been a Methodist
clergyman and member of the New Hampshire conference since
1864, 14 years as presiding elder. Was pastor of the M. E.
church in Bristol three years from 1871. Res. in Lawrence.

CHILD

2.   George Channing (adopted), b. about Sept., 1866. Was eight
months on a whaling cruise on the Atlantic; served in the 1st N. H.
Regt., Spanish war. Now employed by Concord Axle company at Penacook. He m., in Concord, Mary Abbie Plummer, of Boscawen. Children :
    a.   Irving F.   b.   Howard C.
    c.   Charlotte Abbie, b. June 30, 1902.

----

1.   Harry William Taylor Norris is the son of William T.
and Mennetta (Martin) Norris. He was b. Danbury, Mar. 9,
1877, and m. June 22, 1898, Rose E., dau. of George F. Follansbee. (See.) He was a boot and shoe dealer in Emerson block
for five years, till Oct., 1899. Is now head waiter Hotel Rockingham, Portsmouth.

THE NOYES FAMILY

1.   Fred Eugene Noyes is a son of Fred Page and Anna
(Johnson) Noyes. He was b. in Landaff, Oct. 17, 1869, and m.
Jan. 19, 1897, Lill Ethel, dau. of Will A. Shaw (See), b. Brooklyn, N. Y., Dec. 23, 1872. Since June 1, 1900, has been proprietor of the North End store.

CHILDREN

2.   Helen Ardele, b. Tilton, Mar. 12, 1900; d. Bristol, Nov. 21, 1901,
ae. 1-8-9.
3.   Harold Arthur, b. Bristol, Mar. 12, 1902.

THE NUDD FAMILY

1.   Andrew Taylor Nudd, son of Benjamin, was b. in Loudon, May 8, 1849.   He served as a private in Co. H, 18th Regt., N. H. Vols., Civil war, and came to Bristol soon after the war. He m., Aug. 8, 1869, Abra Ann, dau. of Philip S. Drake (See), b. Jan. 13, 1851.   He d. in Bristol, Jan. 10, 1882, ae. 32-8-2. She d. Laconia, Sept. 4, 1892, ae. 41-7-21.

THE OAKLEY FAMILIES

1.   Stephen A. Oakley was a son of David and Charity Oakley.   He was b. Yonkers, N. Y., Sept. 19, 1813, and m. Sarah Louise, dau. of Greenleaf Blake (See), b. Jan. 29, 1814. He spent the greater portion of his life in New York, and came to Bristol about 1873.   Here he d., June 26, 1880, ae. 66-9-7. She d. Randolph, Vt., in Jan., 1897, ae. 83.   No children.

---

1.   William Thatcher Oakley, a brother of the above, was b. Yonkers, N. Y., Dec. 30, 1828.   He m. Mar. 22, 1865, A. Elizabeth, dau. of Robert and Elizabeth (Hardham) Tharp, b. New York city, Jan. 8, 1836.   He was an expressman in New York; located in Bristol, 1875, and here d. Mar. 13, 1884, ae. 55-2-13.   She res. Bristol.   Methodists.

CHILDREN

2.   Minnie L., b. New York city, Dec. 24, 1865; d. Mar. 29, 1876, ae. 10-3-5.
3.   Clara J., b. N. Y., Mar. 9, 1873; m. (1) Arthur T. Chase; (2) Homer H. Hutchinson.   (See.)   Methodist, member of choir.
4.   Charles T., b. Bristol, May 29, 1880; d. Mar. 6, 1881.

THE O'LEARY FAMILY

1.   Arthur O'Leary, son of Arthur and Julia (O'Brien) O'Leary, was b. Nashua, Nov. 19, 1847.   He m. Oct. 13, 1872, Ida Lizzie, dau. of Joel C. Adams.   (See.)   She d. July 12, 1888, ae. 33-9-, and he m. July 12, 1889, Ella A., dau. of Henry W., and Margaret (Frizzell) Stoddard, b. Canaan, Vt., Nov. 24, 1851.   He came to Bristol 1869.   Laborer.   Republican.

2.   Arthur, b. Bristol, Aug. 15, 1874; d. Oct. 19, 1874.
3.   Bert Elmer, b. B., Aug. 9, 1876.   Res. Montpelier, Vt.
4.   Arthur Leslie, b. B., July 27, 1892.
5.   Elbon Stoddard, b. B., Mar. 7, 1895.

THE ORDWAY FAMILY

1.   Col. Giles W. Ordway, the son of Giles and Elizabeth (Webster) Ordway, was b. in Haverhill, Mass., Aug. 27, 1811.

He was of the fifth generation from James Ordway, who came to this country from England or Wales between 1635 and 1640; settled in Dover in 1641, and m. Anne Emery in 1648. The grandfather of Col. Giles was Edward, Jr., who served in the Colonial wars and was with Wolfe at the capture of Quebec. He settled in Sutton and there d. at great age; his wife d. the same day. Col. Ordway went to Concord with his parents in 1821. He was a brick and stone mason and had charge of laying the stone work for the extension of the U. S. General Post-office building, and of the brick work for the extension of the U. S. Patent Office building, Washington. He superintended the stone work for six bridges on the river between Manchester and Bridgewater. He was captain of a company of infantry in the militia in Concord, 1834-'39, and Division inspector general on Gen. Wm. R. Parker's staff in 1849, with rank of colonel. In 1853, was member of common council, of Concord. He m. (1) Feb. 22, 1837, Jane Morrison, of Pembroke. She was b. Mar. 24, 1807, and d. Mar. 18, 1852, ae. 44-11-24. He m. (2) Nov. 29, 1853, Betsey Abbott, of Hooksett, b. Jan. 12, 1824, and now res. in Manchester. He came to Bristol, Dec. 27, 1864, and lived on the David H. Sleeper farm near foot of the lake, where he d. Mar. 26, 1873, ae. 61-6-29.

CHILDREN

2. Isaac Henry, b. Dec. 2, 1838; a stone mason, res. Concord, unm.
3. George Renton, d. in infancy.
4. Jennie, b. Washington, D. C., Aug. 2, 1858; m. Nov. 25, 1886, Joshua F. Martin of Weare. Res. Manchester. Children:

    a. Giles Ordway, b. Oct. 19, 1894.
    b. Richard Hadley, b. Oct. 3, 1896.
    c. Philip Abbott, b. June 2, 1899.

THE OSGOOD FAMILIES

1. Thomas Emerton Osgood was a son of Timothy and Deborah (Pierce) Osgood. He was b. in Hebron, June 26, 1814, and m. Nov. 16, 1846, Sylvia, dau. of Jacob and Betsey (Scales) Lovejoy, b. Rehoboth, Mass., Oct. 16, 1828. He was a carpenter and joiner in Hebron till fall of 1856 or '57; after which his legal home was in Bristol. She d. Bristol, Dec. 13, 1858, ae. 30-1-27. He served in the 12th Regt., N. H. Vols. (See Roll of Honor.) After the war, spent a portion of his time at Woonsocket, R. I., and Hopedale, Mass. Republican, Odd Fellow, Universalist. He d. Bristol, Oct. 16, 1896, ae. 82-3-20; death was hastened by his being struck by a runaway horse. The sunshine of his life was conspicuous in his old age, and he died in perfect contentment and in a firm trust in God.

CHILDREN

2. Timothy, b. Hebron, Sept. 8, 1849; m. Sept. 28, 1876, Sarah E., dau. of Dearborn and Margaret (Haines) French, b. Barnstead, Dec. 29, 1848.

She d. Hopedale, Mass., Jan. 17, 1895, ae. 46-0-18. He res. Hopedale. Machinist. Children :

> *a.* Paul, b. and d. July 4, 1878.
> *b.* Harry, b. and d. May 24, 1879.

3. Betsey Jane, b. H., Feb. 3, 1851; m. John R. Bennett. Res. Medfield.

4. Clara Sylvia, b. H., Oct. 28, 1854; m. July 2, 1876, Frank H. French.

5. Deborah Pierce, b. H., Nov. 28, 1856; m. Dec. 2, 1899, Charles A. Palmer.

6. Joseph Lovejoy, b. Bristol, Dec. 8, 1858; m. Aug. 30, 1879, Mary E. Cline. Res. Ansonia, Conn. Four children.

---

1. Reuben Osgood was b. in Sanbornton June 7, 1778. He m. Ann Clifford, Sept. 30, 1783. They settled in Bristol about 1838, and here he d., Jan. 17, 1865, ae. 86-7-10. She d. Mar. 1, 1854, ae. 70-5-1. He was a tailor and res. Lake street.

CHILDREN

2. Mahala Rollins, b. Sanbornton, Sept. 21, 1805; m. Moses G. Edgerly. (See.)

3. Edward Mudgett, b. June 29, 1813; m. Susan A. Taylor and came to Bristol about 1840 from Amoskeag, and here they d.: she, May 1, 1848; he, July 6, 1849, ae. 36-0-7. Children :

> *a.* Edward F., b. Mar., 1835; d. Bristol, Sept. 29, 1853, ae. 18-6-.
> *b.* Lydia, b. Bristol, res. Boston, Mass.
> *c.* Frank, b. B.; was a merchant tailor in Boston.

THE PADDLEFORD FAMILY

1. John Blake Paddleford is a son of Joseph B. and Mehitable (Walker) Paddleford. He was b. Hanover, Feb. 1, 1860, and m. Sept. 1, 1892, Edith Josephine, dau. of Robert B. and Josephine (Kellogg) Lillie, b. Yellow Springs, Ohio, Oct. 21, 1872. He was a farmer in Hanover till 1892; since then, a job teamster in Bristol. Odd Fellow, Republican.

CHILDREN

2. Robert Dean, b. Bristol, Apr. 4, 1894.
3. John Clifton, b. B., Oct. 9, 1896.

THE PAGE FAMILIES

1. Onesiphorus Page was a resident of that part of New Chester now Hill as early as 1808; in the early twenties, he occupied the Fisk block in Bristol village. He was evidently a prominent man in his day, being one of the incorporators of the New Chester and Danbury pike in 1808 and of the Central bridge in 1820. He d. Jan. 27, 1827, ae. 50. The name of his wife was Jane.

CHILDREN

2. Onesiphorus J., b. 1815; d. Dec. 11, 1824, ae. 9 years.
3. Mary Ann, b. Nov., 1818; d. Aug. 16, 1821, ae. 2-9.

1.   Isaac Page and his wife, Dolly Cilley, were residents of Bristol for some years previous to their death, their home being on Merrimack street, and there she d. Aug. 19, 1856, ae. 72-7-. He d. July 9, 1865, ae. 79-6-.   A son,

2.   Samuel, was b. Andover, June 16, 1818. He m. (1) Mary Wells who d. in Bristol, Jan. 15, 1858, ae. 39.   He m. (2) Aug. 23, 1858, Abby E., dau. of Nathaniel and Abigail M. (Williams) Moulton, b. Emden, Me., Dec. 25, 1833.   He settled in Bristol, 1847, was a cabinet maker, and here d. Dec. 22, 1879, ae. 61-6-6. She res. Lawrence, Mass.

CHILDREN

3.   Mamie E., b. Bristol, Aug. 23, 1860; d. Nov. 7, 1862, ae. 2-2-14.
4.   John Wadleigh, b. B., Jan. 23, 1862; m. July 28, 1894, May Florena Witham, b. Rockport, Mass., June 9, 1862.   He is a conductor on Western Division of Boston & Maine railroad.   Res. Lawrence, Mass. Children :

    a.   Emma Witham, b. Lawrence, Aug. 12, 1895.
    b.   Kenneth Allen, b. L., Mar. 28, 1902.

———

1.   Mitchell Hibbard Page, son of John and Dorcas (Hibbard) Page, was b. in Ryegate, Vt., Apr. 11, 1810.   He settled in Bristol about 1834, and m. July 18, 1837, Dorothy S., dau. of Benjamin Locke (See), b. Mar. 25, 1819. Later he res. in Sanbornton, Hebron, Groton, Bridgewater, and again in Bristol, where he d. Aug. 16, 1890, ae. 80-4-5.   Carpenter. Methodist. She res. Bristol.

CHILDREN

2.   Martin Van Buren, b. Bristol, Jan. 15, 1838.   Went West in 1856; has res. many years in Eau Claire, Wis. He m. (1) Katherine Kendricks; (2) Lavina Thompson. Four children ; two d.
3.   Levi Locke, b. B., Sept. 6, 1839 ; m. Dec., 1861, Hannah W., dau. of Asa Drew.   (See.) He served in the 7th Regt., N. H. Vols., and d. at Fort Jefferson, Fla., Mar. 21, 1862, ae. 22-6-15.   (See Roll of Honor.) She m. (2) Lorenzo Flanders, Bridgewater.
4.   Lizzie A., b. Hebron, May 21, 1841 ; m. Harvey W. Drew.   (See.)
5.   John C., b. Groton, May 28, 1843 ; m. Georgianna Hall.   Served in 7th Regt., N. H. Vols., and d. at Fort Jefferson, Fla., Apr. 16, 1862, ae. 18-10-18.
6.   Andrew J., b. Hebron, June 2, 1845.   He served as private in Co. B, 9th Regt., N. H. Vols.; was captured at Poplar Grove Church, Va., Sept. 30, 1864, and was confined in Salisbury (N. C.) prison; escaped therefrom ; re-captured, and d. in prison, Dec. 25, 1864, ae. 19-6-23.
7.   Nathaniel Springer, b. H., Sept. 6, 1846 ; m. July 4, 1866, Mary Jane, dau. of Samuel Hollon.   He served in the 9th and 6th Regts., N. H. Vols.   Res. Leominster, Mass.   Child :

    a.   Lillian A., b. Bridgewater, Apr. 15, 1867; m. (1) Feb. 26, 1885, Arthur L. Adams; (2) Jan. 11, 1894, Lewis O. Hawkins. Three children.   Res. Meredith.

8.   Ruth B., b. H., Sept. 8, 1849 ; m. Nov. 22, 1866, John Smith.
9.   James H., b. Bristol, May 8, 1851 ; d. Oct. 4, 1870, ae. 19-4-26.
10.   Lavina J., b. B., Sept. 20, 1854; m. (1) Henry W. Drake; m. (2) Oscar F. Morse.   (See.)

THE PAIGE FAMILY

1. Cyrus Paige, son of Jonathan and Judith (Coburn) Paige, was b. in Deering, in 1811. He m. Maribah, dau. of Josiah Mason, b. Hill, in 1809. He was of the 9th generation from John Paige, of Dedham, who came to this country in 163–. He came to Bristol from Hill in 1840; res. Profile Falls; built a house near base of Alexandria hill, about opposite David P. Hoyt's residence, moved in while in process of building and d. before it was completed, Aug. 11, 1848, ae. 37. He was a carpenter. She res. later on Summer street, till fall of 1859, then removed to So. Boston, where she d. May 16, 1866, ae. 57.

CHILDREN

2. Hiram Lemuel, b. Hill, Feb. 22, 1836; m. 1870, Leavie Rebecca, dau. of Joseph Paget, b. South Boston, Mass., Mar. 12, 1848. He left Bristol when 21 years of age and has been for many years a machinist in the employ of the Michigan Central railroad at Jackson, Mich. Children:

    a. Albert, b. Mar. 7, 1873; d. Aug. 24, 1873.
    b. Cora Ella, b. Dec. 27, 1874.

3. Susan Marium, b. H., Sept. 9, 1842. Res. Lowell, Mass.; unm.
4. Mary Barnard, b. Bristol, Aug. 28, 1844; m. July 30, 1881, William Gelston, and res. 200 Hale street, Lowell, Mass. Child:

    a. George S., b. Manchester, Oct. 30, 1885; d. Dec. 19, 1889, ae. 4-1-19.

THE PATTEE FAMILIES

1. Lewis F. Pattee is a son of Moses and Jane (Gordon) Pattee. He was b. Alexandria, Mar. 23, 1834. He m., Jan. 25, 1861, Mary Philbrick Ingalls, dau. of Gilman (See), b. Jan. 3, 1834. He has been a farmer and stone mason in Alexandria and Bristol. Is a Republican and a Methodist.

CHILDREN

2. Fred Lewis, b. Bristol, Mar. 22, 1863; m. Mar. 9, 1889, Anna L., dau. of Charles N. and Louisa (Simons) Plumer, b. in Alexandria, Dec. 9, 1859. He graduated from New Hampton Literary Institution, 1884; Dartmouth College, 1888. Is professor of English and rhetoric at Pennsylvania State College. (See Chapter on Literature, Vol. 1.) Child:

    a. Sara Lewis, b. State College, Pa., May 13, 1895.

3. Charles Henry, b. B., Oct. 26, 1864; graduated from New Hampton Literary Institution, 1886; m. Dec. 25, 1889, Sadie W. Morey, b. Wilmot; res. Ashland. Child:

    a. Charles Walter, b. Dec. 12, 1890.

4. Mary Lou, b. Alexandria, Mar. 4, 1872.

---

1. Henry H. Pattee is a son of Moses and Jane (Gordon)

Pattee.   He was b. Alexandria, June 12, 1839. He m., Feb. 1, 1868, Ellen Frances, dau. of Hezekiah D. and Sarah (Cole) Gale, b. Alexandria, Mar. 3, 1846. She d. Bristol, Feb. 13, 1896, ae. 49-11-10.   Farmer and stone mason in Alexandria, and since 1885, in Bristol. Methodist, Republican, G. A. R.

CHILDREN

2. Ida Florence, b. Alexandria, Sept. 27, 1875. Was graduated from State Normal School, Plymouth. Is a school teacher in Minnesota.
3. George Kynett, b. A., Sept. 5, 1879. Graduated from New Hampton Literary Institution, 1898; Dartmouth College, 1902; took one year post-graduate course, receiving the degree of A.M. in 1903. Teacher of Latin and Greek at Pensacola, Fla.

---

1.   James Monroe Pattee, is a son of Moses and Jane (Gordon) Pattee. He was b. Alexandria, Dec. 1, 1845, and has been a laborer in Bristol since 1888. Unm. Republican, Methodist.

THE PATTEN FAMILIES

1.   James Patten, son of John and Jane (Abbott) Patten was b. Alexandria, July 7, 1817. He m., Mar. 8, 1840, Emeline, dau. of Daniel Mills, b. Corinth, Vt.; d. Alexandria, Sept. 5, 1865. He m., Mar. 8, 1866, Phebe, dau. of Moses Burns. She d. Alexandria, Nov. 11, 1877. He m. May 25, 1878, Mrs. Eliza Ann, widow of Gilman D. Laney. (See.) James Patten was a carpenter and farmer. Came to Bristol about 1854, later lived on Burns's hill in Alexandria ; back to Bristol about 1882, on the Levi Locke farm, Summer street. Republican. No children. Has been confined to his bed for nearly 11 years.

---

1.   Manson B. Patten is a son of Benjamin and Polly (Hastings) Patten, b. Alexandria, Nov. 4, 1848, m. June 22, 1870, Nellie, dau. of Uriah and Laura (Bailey) Pearson. He is a farmer just north of Smith's river.

CHILDREN, all born in Bristol

2. Mabel, b. Feb. 3, 1872.
3. Fred B., b. June 27, 1874 ; d. Aug. 14, 1875, ae. 1-1-17.
4. Fred H., b. May 6, 1877.   5.   Anna L., b. Oct. 21, 1887.

---

1.   Frank C. Patten, a son of Hadley B. and Nellie E. Patten, was b. Alexandria, Apr. 29, 1874, and m. June 16, 1894, Mrs. Jennie B. Doe, dau. of Dearborn Gray (See), b. Apr. 3, 1870. He is a farmer near Alexandria line, and stage driver.

THE PEARSON FAMILY

1. Willard J. Pearson, son of William and Mary (Jones) Pearson, was b. Tewksbury, Mass., July 29, 1799, and d. Danbury, Jan. 22, 1875, ae. 75–5–23. In 1819, he m. Harriet Avery, dau. of Ebenezer, b. Gilmanton, Feb. 16, 1802, and d. Danbury, July 22, 1874, ae. 72–5–6. He was a carpenter and stone mason; came from Hill, 1836; res. in Bristol on north bank of Smith's river. After six years removed to Alexandria.

CHILDREN

2. Mary J., b. Hill, Jan. 25, 1820; d. 1862, ae. 42.
3. John, b. H., Oct. 29, 1822; d. when 2 years old.
4. Sherburn, b. H., Aug. 13, 1824; twice m.; d. in Orange, 1877, ae. 53.
5. Cyrus J., b. H., Feb. 2, 1826; m. Freelove King; d. Attleboro, Mass., 1893, ae. 67. Widow res. Attleboro. Two children.
6. Esther B., b. H., Aug. 11, 1828; m. William Currier, res. Iowa.
7. Horace B., b. H., Apr. 27, 1830; m. Lovey J. Gray, Alexandria. Res. Farmington. Five children.
8. Joseph S., b. H., Jan. 19, 1832. Unm.
9. Eliza J., b. H., Mar. 6, 1835; m. Samuel A. Patten; res. Alexandria. Five children.
10. Arvilla A., b. Bristol, Jan. 12, 1838; m. William H. Currier. He d. Warren, 1894. She d.
11. Willard A., b. B., Aug. 12, 1840; m. Sarah Gray; d. Alexandria, May 15, 1876, ae. 35–9–3. His widow res. Hill. Two children.
12. Harriet M., b. Hill, Jan. 8, 1845; m. Josiah H. Welton and res. Central Falls, R. I. One child, m. John Danforth.
*13. Charles Avery, b. Alexandria, May 27, 1847.
14. George W., b. A., Aug. 25, 1850; m. (1) Augusta Braley; (2) Mary Whitcher. Res. Bristol. No children.

(13) Charles A. Pearson, b. May 27, 1847, m. Sept. 25, 1867, Irena G., dau. of Heman J. Welton, b. Alexandria, 1845, d. Grafton, July 25, 1874, ae. 29. He m. Dec. 5, 1875, Ella A., dau. Lorenzo and Elizabeth (Briggs) Braley, b. Danbury, 1856, d. Bristol, Feb. 15, 1884, ae. 28. He m., Dec. 12, 1884, Francelia, dau. of Cyrus and Rectyna (Roe) Ladd and widow of Charles M. Rollins, b. Mar. —, 1839. He was a blacksmith in Alexandria; in Bristol from Nov., 1879, till Oct., 1891; in Hinsdale and now a farmer in Winchester.

CHILDREN

15. Bert Haskins, b. Grafton, July 4, 1868. Was clerk for some years at Revere House, Boston, Mass.; now keeping a riding school at North Hampton, Mass. Unm.
16. Will Leston, b. G., June 27, 1873. Now employed in Winter Place hotel, Boston.
17. Edith Elizabeth, b. G., May 27, 1881.

Ruby Mable Rollins, dau. of Mrs. Pearson, was b. in Alexandria, Apr. 20, 1867; m. Oct. 13, 1892, Charles H. Pearson, of Hinsdale.

THE PEASLEE FAMILY

1. "Dr." Peter Peaslee and his wife, Hannah, were settlers south of Smith's river as early as 1810. They came from Epsom. He d. 1839, ae. 89 years.

CHILDREN

2. Anne, b. Nov. 10, 1800; m. Oct. 10, 1826, Ira Ash, of New Chester; (2) David Eaton. (See.)
3. Rachel, b. Nov. 11, 1801.
4. Peter, b. Feb. 24, 1803. Hung himself on the Peaslee place in Bristol.
5. Hannah, b. Nov. 3, 1806; m. May 3, 1836, John Austin.
6. Elizabeth, b. July 10, 1808; m. Elijah Ballou. (See.)
7. Samuel, b. Sept. 10, 1809; m. and d. in Dorchester.
*8. John P., b. July 31, 1812.
9. James, b. June 8, 1814; m. —— Batchelder and res. Alexandria.

(8) John P. Peaslee, b. July 31, 1812, m. Nov., 1833, Cynthia, dau. of Oliver Ballou. (See.) He was a farmer in Hill and at Profile Falls. Committed suicide in Bristol, Sept. 19, 1873, ae. 61-1-18. She d. Aug. 7, 1870, ae. 77-11-.

CHILDREN

10. Sarah Jane, b. June 9, 1837; d. Aug. 23, 1862, unm., ae. 25-2-14.
11. Aaron, a twin brother of Sarah Jane, is a farmer at Profile Falls. Unm.
12. Cynthia A., b. Jan. 28, 1848; d. Feb. 6, 1868, ae. 20-0-8.

THE PERKINS FAMILIES

1. Benjamin Franklin Perkins was b. in Center Harbor, Jan. 7, 1831. His father was Benjamin, b. Haverhill, Mass., July 13, 1791, and d. New Hampton, Jan. 24, 1862, ae. 70-6-11. His mother was Mary (Drake) Perkins, b. New Hampton, June 24, 1800, and educated at the old institution in that town and res. in Bristol from 1865, till she d., Jan. 30, 1890, ae. 89-7-6. Benjamin F. attended the high school at Ashland; left home when 16 years of age and learned the bricklayer's trade in Boston, Mass. He worked at his trade summers and attended a commercial school at Lowell, Mass., winters, and in this way completed his education. In Sept., 1854, he m. Susan M., dau. of Otis and Mary (Magoon) Perry, b. Mar. 7, 1831. He m. (2) Jan. 13, 1890, Mrs. Flora A. Ford. In 1856, he removed to New Hampton, where he was selectman six years and town treasurer. As first selectman, he was town agent to fill the town's quota for the army during the Civil war, and at the same time acted as government agent for the enlistment of men. He was drafted for the army; rejected on examination, but put in a substitute at the cost of $200. He represented New Hampton in the legislature two years. He came to Bristol in 1866,

and, in company with George Z. Collins, of Boston, bought the saw-mill where is now the paper-mill of the Train-Smith company, and engaged in the manufacture of strawboard under the firm name of B. F. Perkins & Co. One year later he and Burley M. Ames purchased Mr. Collins's interest, and the business was continued under the old name. In Jan., 1872, the firm of Mason, Perkins & Co. was formed. Mr. Ames sold his interest to the new firm and they erected the present brick mill in 1872, and sold the old mill to Mason & Ames. The brick mill was completed and the manufacture of paper commenced about Jan., 1873. (See Manufacturing Industries in Vol. I.) Mr. Perkins was the managing member of the firm. The company was incorporated July 7, 1886, under the name of the Mason-Perkins Paper Company, and Mr. Perkins continued as manager and treasurer till 1897, when ill health compelled him to retire from active service. Mr. Perkins is a Mason, an Odd Fellow, and a Free Baptist, an influential member of society and an active Republican. He has served six years as moderator at the annual town meetings, and, in 1883, was elected senator from the fourth senatorial district. Since 1875, has been a trustee of the Bristol Savings bank, and served as its president six years; is a director and the vice-president of the First National Bank of Bristol.

CHILD

2. Clara Bean, b. Bristol, May 14, 1858. She graduated in both Classical and English courses at New Hampton Literary Institution; d. Bristol, May 22, 1879, ae. 21-0-8.

---

1. William Harrison Perkins, a son of Abel and Jane (Miller) Perkins, was b. in New Lisbon, N. Y., Nov. 21, 1817, and m. June 19, 1839, Susan Hoyt, dau. of Amos W. Drew (See), b. June 21, 1820. He was a shoemaker and farmer at Bartlett, Londonderry, Manchester, and many years at Goffs Falls and Orange. He spent his last years in Bristol in the family of Charles E. Kemp, where he d., Aug. 30, 1896, ae. 78-9-9; she d. Sept. 11, 1896, ae. 76-2-20.

CHILDREN

2. Susan Jane, d. young.
3. William Henry, b. Bartlett, July 25, 1852; was a machinist at Goffs Falls. Three children.
4. Clara Eudora, b. Londonderry, Aug. 10, 1853; m. Charles E. Kemp. (See.)
5. Frank Herbert, b. Manchester, Sept. 17, 1859. He is a clergyman; m. Fanny Sanborn.

---

1. Daniel Perkins, b. in Boston, Mass., Sept. 8, 1751, m. (1) Lois Adams, b. Rowley, Mass., Nov. 1755; (2) Mehitable,

22

b. Rowley, Feb. 23, 1750.   He had four children by his first
wife and one by his second.   The youngest child was

2.   Paul, b. Rowley, Jan. 31, 1790.   He m. Betsey Brown,
b. Candia, Feb. 14, 1791, and settled in Bridgewater ; was an
ordained elder of the Free Baptist denomination and for many
years at the head of the First Free Baptist church of Bridgewater.   She d. and he. m. (2) Aug. 20, 1835, Sally Thompson,
dau. of Moses T. Willard and widow of Dea. David Batchelder.
(See.)   He d. Apr. 3, 1843, ae. 53-2-2.   He was the father of
four children, one of whom was

3.   David Brocklebank, b. Bridgewater, July 8, 1816, m.
Apr. 13, 1838, Mehitable Chandler, b. May 29, 1818.   He was
a farmer in Hebron, and there d. Jan. 29, 1894, ae. 77-6-21.
Since his death she has made her home in the family of her son,
David, in Bristol.   Of their three children, one was

4.   David, b. Hebron, Sept. 21, 1840.   He m. July 12,
1862, Ann Elisa, dau. of Lyman G. and Elisabeth Cummings
Huckins, b. New Hampton, Aug. 13, 1840.   He was a carpenter in Hebron till 1889 ; since in Bristol.   Served several years
as selectman of Hebron.   Is a Democrat, Odd Fellow, Free
Baptist.

CHILDREN

5.   Norman Frost, b. Hebron, Oct. 7, 1871 ; m. Oct. 3, 1894, Jennie M.,
dau. of David M. Chase.   (See.)   He is a carpenter in Greenwood, Mass.
Children :
    a.   David Norman, b. Worcester, Mass., Aug. 8, 1897.
    b.   Donald Frost, b. W., July 13, 1898.
    c.   Dorris Eliza, b. W., Apr. 27, 1900.
    d.   Norma Emmaetta, b. Dorchester, Mass., Dec. 30, 1901.

6.   Fred Lyman, b. H., Dec. 22, 1875; m. June 6, 1897, Emma Elizabeth, dau. of John I. Brown, b. Sept. 7, 1876.   He is a carpenter in
Holderness.   No children.

THE PHILBROOK FAMILY

1.   Fred Aubrey Philbrook is the son of Thomas P. and
Minnie R. (Jones) Philbrook.   He was b. Sandown, Feb. 3,
1859, and m. June 27, 1889, Emma Hannah, dau. of Benjamin
S. and Sarah Ann (Smith) Gordon, b. New Hampton, May
26, 1859.   He came to Bristol from New Hampton in 1890, and
is a teamster.   Democrat, Odd Fellow, Methodist.

CHILDREN

2.   Walter Aubrey, b. Bristol, May 13, 1891.
3.   Arthur Fred, b. B., Sept. 20, 1893.
4.   Roy Smith, b. B., Apr. 25, 1899.

THE PHILLIPS FAMILY

1.   Dexter Fairbanks Phillips, son of Ebenezer and Hannah (Hagar) Phillips, was b. in Henniker, July 16, 1819.   He

m., about 1850, Catherine Joselyn, dau. of Mead Case, b. Groton, 1820, and d. Groton, fall of 1869, ae. 49. He settled on the Philip Bean farm in Dist. No. 7, in 1870, and there d. June, 1897, ae. 77-11-.

CHILDREN

2. Ebenezer Mead, b. Dorchester, Apr. 2, 1851 ; a farmer in Bristol, 1870-'82 ; since, in Hebron. Unm.
3. Betsey, b. D. ; d. ae. 5-6-.
4. Mary Ann, b. D., Apr. 5, 1857 ; m. Charles H. Tenney. Res. New Hampton. Four children.

THE PHIPPS FAMILY

1. Charles Henry Phipps, son of William and Abia Swan Phipps, was b. Charlestown, Mass., Jan. 18, 1829. He m., Nov. 29, 1866, Hannah H. Muzzey, dau. of Samuel. (See.) He was an expert jig sawyer, at Charlestown, and 17 years at Concord. Since 1883, has been a farmer in Bristol. Republican, Methodist.

CHILDREN

2. Albert Charles, b. Bristol, Apr. 19, 1871. Graduated from New Hampton Literary Institution, class of '92. In trade gents' furnishing goods, Bristol. Member official board M. E. church. Republican.
3. Willie Muzzey, b. Concord, Oct. 24, 1875 ; d. July 23, 1877, ae. 1-8-29.

THE PIKE FAMILIES

1. Edwin Trull Pike, the son of Moses and Clara (Phelps) Pike, was b. Groton, Oct. 27, 1842. Apr. 27, 1866, he m. Sarah Jane, dau. of Bradford and Lavina (Gale) Bullock, b. Alexandria, Nov. 30, 1844, d. Bristol, Feb. 27, 1888, ae. 43-2-27. He m. (2) Mary Ryan, May 15, 1892. He has been a farmer on east side of Newfound lake near foot, since 1882. Served in Co. D, 12th N. H. Vols., on quota of Groton. Republican.

CHILDREN

2. Abbie Clara, b. Groton, May 10, 1869 ; m. David H. Hoyt. (See.)
3. Harry Otis, b. Hebron, Mar. 11, 1874 ; m. July 1, 1902, Margaret J., dau. of George Price. (See.) A farmer in Bridgewater.
4. Alonzo Clinton, b. Bristol, Oct. 9, 1885.

1. Rev. James Pike, D.D., was a son of Caleb and Mary Pike. He was b. in Salisbury, Mass., Nov. 10, 1818. He m., Apr. 19, 1840, Mary Rebecca, dau. of John and Mary (Dodge) Brodhead, b. Newfields, Sept. 11, 1816. He d. Newfields, July 26, 1895, ae. 76-8-16. She res. Newfields. He was a Methodist clergyman, and pastor of the Bristol church 1882-'83.

2. James Thurston, m. Oct. 29, 1867, Augusta M. White. Res. Newfields. One child.

3. Anna G., m. Nov. 18, 1868, Charles B. Kendall. Res. Boston, Mass. Three children.

THE PILLSBURY FAMILY

1. Rev. Hervey Gorham Pillsbury is a son of Gorham and Fannie Knapp (Cutter) Pillsbury. He was b. Newburyport, Mass., Oct. 9, 1851, and m. Oct. 21, 1872, Hannah, dau. of George and Sophia Hargrave, b. Geneva, N. Y., Jan. 26, 1850. He is a Congregational clergyman. Was graduated from Andover Theological Seminary, 1882; ordained pastor of the Congregational church Bristol, Sept. 28, 1882, where he served till 1887; Vergennes, Vt., 1887-'91; Chicopee Falls, Mass., since 1895.

2. Berton Hargrave, b. June 17, 1875; d. of accidental gunshot wounds, 1892, ae. 17.

3. Fannie Belle, b. May 21, 1882; d. June 29, 1884, ae. 2-1-8.

4. Maude Alice, b. Oct. 15, 1888.

THE PLANKEY FAMILY

1. Chris Plankey is the son of John and Zoe (Roberts) Plankey. He was b. Redford, N. Y., May 16, 1852, and m. Jan. 19, 1885, Adell F., dau. of Clark A. and Lucy Hilliard Gray, b. Holderness, Aug. 6, 1866. He has been a mica miner in Bristol and neighboring towns for 30 years; res. last seven years in Bristol. Republican.

2. Ivy Ethelyn, b. Alexandria, July 30, 1886.

3. Charles Morton, b. A., Oct. 20, 1888.

4. Leo Chandos, b. A., Oct. 26, 1891.

5. Elmer Clark, b. A., Aug. 16, 1893.

THE POLLARD FAMILY

1. Arthur Clarence Pollard was a son of Horace and Elsa (Dunham) Pollard. He was b. Lyme, Dec. 26, 1853, and m. Nov. 21, 1882, Mrs. Josephine Strickford, widow of Joseph, and dau. of John D. and Mehitable (Fisk) Wheeler, b. Hebron, Jan. 16, 1858. He was a laborer in Bristol from 1900 till he d., Aug. 28, 1903, ae. 49-8-2. She res. Lake street.

2. Sidney Strickford, son of Mrs. Pollard by her first husband, b. Groton, Mar. 18, 1880; res. Barre, Vt.

3. Elsa May, b. G., Feb. 22, 1885.

4. Lee Adrian, b. G., May 13, 1893.

THE POPE FAMILY

1. The Popes of Bristol trace their descent from John Pope, who was in Dorchester, Mass., as early as 1634. Albert Pope, of the seventh generation from John, was a son of David and Susanna (Emerson) Pope. He was b. Sept. 13, 1822, in Henniker, and m. Feb. 12, 1856, Alma, dau. of Dr. Sewell and Judith Stearns Seavey, b. Tunbridge, Vt., Dec. 1, 1825. He was a painter in Bristol from 1867 till he d. Sept. 10, 1887, ae. 64-11-27. She d. Apr. 7, 1902, ae. 76-4-6.

CHILDREN

2. Bert David, b. Bradford, Jan. 20, 1859; m. Jan. 10, 1882, Eliza, dau. of Joseph and Mary D. (Leeman) Brown, b. Franklin, May 31, 1862. He was a jeweler in Tilton, and d. of blood poison, June 17, 1895, ae. 36-4-27. She m. (2) Charles H. Thomas. Children :
   a. Bernice Alma, b. Mar. 8, 1887.
   b. Edith May, b. Oct. 15, 1894.

3. Charles William Wilson, b. Hebron, Nov. 10, 1864. Located in Bristol, 1869. Painter till 1892; since, a salesman in store of Cavis Brothers. He m. Dec. 25, 1888, Alice Maria, dau. of Joseph F. and Flora A. Hadley) Ford, b. Gloucester, Mass., Mar. 14, 1870, and d. Bristol, Dec. 8, 1895, ae. 25-8-24. He m. (2) Jan. 5, 1897, Mary Jane, dau. of Lyman G. and Sarah J. Thompson, b. Franklin, Mar. 10, 1872, and d. Bristol, Mar. 31, 1900, ae. 28-0-21. Children :
   a. Ralph Perkins, b. Bristol, Sept. 17, 1890.
   b. Florence Alma, b. B., June 15, 1893.
   c. Alice May, b. B., Dec. 31, 1898.

THE POWELL FAMILIES

1. David Powell, the son of Jonathan, was b. Mar. 12, 1768. He m. Theodate Smith, b. New Hampton, Aug. 3, 1771, and d. Bristol, Sept. 28, 1852, ae. 81-1-25. He d. (found dead in his bed) Mar. 12, 1828, aged exactly 60 years. He was a farmer, resided most of his life north of the Locke neighborhood, but was in Stewartstown a few years.

CHILDREN, all probably born in Bristol

2. Abigail, b. Jan. 2, 1792; m. Elisha Gurdy. (See.)
3. Smith, b. Oct. 12, 1794; m. Nov. 30, 1815, Anna, dau. of Benia Sanborn, b. 1791. He went to Alabama in company with Jacob Hoyt, Damon Y. Emmons, and Thomas R. Emmons, and there d. of yellow fever. His name was last on the tax-list in 1833. She d. in the family of her dau., Mrs. Andoniram Kidder, in Illinois, in 1862, ae. 71. Children :
   a. Osmond, b. Bristol ; m. Dec. 5, 1845, Sally C., dau. Ebenezer Darling (See), b. Aug. 13, 1822. He d. B., Mar. 16, 1883, ae. 65-9-. She res. Summer street.
   b. Lydia Ann, b. B., June 29, 1830; m. Andoniram Kidder. (See.) Was a student at the Baptist school in New Hampton.
   c. Comfort.
   d. Rufus, d. Nov. 30, 1819, ae. 7 weeks.
   e. Susan, d. Jan. 25, 1820, ae. 4 months.

    f. Lavina, d. Sept. 15, 1825, ae. 2-6-.
    g. Rufus, d. Sept. 5, 1826, ae. 2-3-.
    h. Comfort, d. June 3 (8), 1832, ae. 4-6-.
  4. Betsey, b. June 24, 1797 ; m. Dec., 1835, Joshua Willard. Child :
    a. Elvira Ann, b. Bristol, Sept., 1836; res. Bristol, unm.
  5. Sally, b. Mar. 3, 1800; m. Reuben Kidder. (See.)
  6. Mary, b. Aug. 2, 1802; m. Benjamin Emmons. (See.)
  7. Benaiah, b. May 20, 1806; d. at Stewartstown, of lockjaw at about 16 years of age.
  8. David, b. Aug. 11, 1808. He was a farmer and a Methodist local preacher. He m. Apr. 9, 1828, Lydia H., dau. Jonathan Fellows. (See.) He res. Bristol, Danbury where he was in trade, and in Alexandria, where he d. Oct. 6, 1865, ae. 57-1-25. His widow m. (2) Alonzo Cheney. (See.) Children :
    a. Jonathan G., d. May 22, 1830, ae. 1-0-10.
    b. Olive J., d. Sept. 19, 1832, ae. 2-2-.
    c. Levi S., d. Nov. 14, 1856, ae. 24.
  9. Orpha, b. May 26, 1811 ; m. Jonathan B. Sawyer and res. Alexandria. He d. Mar. 20, 1848, ae. 43, and she returned to Bristol where she m. (2) Capt. Daniel Sleeper. (See.) She m. (3) Perrin Prescott, who removed to Minnesota. She d. Bristol, Apr. 20, 1888, ae. 76-10-24. Children :
    a. Lois Ann (Sawyer), d. Aug. 28, 1843, ae. 1-3-.
    b. Richard K. (Sawyer), m. Arianna Kidder, dau. of John. (See.)
  10. Theodate, b. Nov. 25, 1814 ; m. Alonzo Cheney. (See.)

---

  1. William Powell was a settler on south side of Bristol Peak in the Locke neighborhood as early as 1780. How long he remained there is unknown.

CHILDREN

  2. Benjamin, b. Apr. 26, 1771.
  3. Anne, b. Mar. 25, 1773.
  4. Daniel, b. Mar. 23, 1775.
  5. William, b. Sept. 24, 1777.
  6. Comfort, b. Apr. 19, 1781 ; m. Theophilus Tilton. (See.)

---

  1. Joseph Powell was a farmer in the Locke neighborhood about 1800. His wife was Ruth Trumbull, whom he m. Jan. 30, 1798.

CHILDREN

  2. Jared, b. Feb. 11, 1799.
  3. Betsey, b. Oct. 29, 1800.

THE POWERS FAMILY

  1. Jonathan Powers, son of William and Mary (Thompson) Powers, was b. Groton, June 30, 1795. He m. Oct. 3, 1819, Anna, dau. of Ebenezer Kendall (See), b. Apr. 12, 1794. In 1817, Jonathan was a clothier on Central street.

About 1827, he removed to Lansingburg, N. Y., where Mrs. Powers d. Aug. 16, 1833, ae. 39-4-14. He m. (2) Feb. 4, 1841, Esther Jane Heath, b. Exeter, Nov. 9, 1817, d. Grand Rapids, Mich., July 26, 1881, ae. 63-8-17. He d. Grand Rapids, Oct. 16, 1864, ae. 69-3-16.

CHILDREN

2. William Thompson, b. Bristol, July 8, 1820; m. Dec. 11, 1838, Louisa, dau. of Charles J. and Sara (Gaskin) Hall, b. London, England, Dec. 3, 1823. At 27 years of age he went to Grand Rapids, Mich., where he became largely interested in timber lands and manufacturing lumber and furniture. He put in operation the first circular saw-mill in Michigan and the first furniture factory in Grand Rapids, and helped largely to make that city a noted furniture center. He built the canal on the west side of Grand river and the larger part of the manufacturing buildings in that district and also on the east side, and erected some of the best business blocks, including the opera house block. "There is no one man more identified with the growth and prosperity of the city than Mr. Powers."

3. Mary Ann, b. B., Dec. 12, 1821; m. Sept. 1, 1851, Edward Augustus Filley, b. Lansingburg, N. Y., Mar. 14, 1818. He was an importing merchant in St. Louis; res. Hebron some years; d. Haverhill, Sept. 12, 1901, ae. 83-5-28. Mrs. Filley has been identified with the Woman's Suffrage movement and other reforms. In 1879, she purchased the farm of her deceased uncle, Joseph Powers, at North Haverhill, stocked it with a choice herd of Jerseys and has since been engaged in farming. In one year she made with her own hands 4,000 pounds of butter. Children :

    a. Frances Amelia, b. St. Louis, Aug. 4, 1852; m. Oct. 29, 1878, Darwin E. Kithredge, of St. Louis.

    b. Chloe, b. St. L., Feb. 26, 1856; d. July 5, 1858, ae. 2-4-9.

    c. Augustus, b. St. L., July 26, 1858.

    d. Anna Kendall, b. St. L., Aug. 22, 1861.

4. Deborah Ball, b. B., Apr. 2, 1823; m. May 1, 1843, in Troy, N. Y., Alfred Osgood Currier, son Sylvanus, b. Haverhill, Apr. 9, 1817, and d. Grand Rapids, Mich., May 24, 1881, ae. 64-1-15. She d. same place Apr. 21, 1881, ae. 58-0-19. Children :

    a. Arthur Webster, b. Troy, N. Y., Apr. 11, 1844; m. Oct. 30, 1867, Amelia Mary Snyder, of Grand Rapids. Children : (1) Maggie Amelia, b. Grand Rapids, May 24, 1869; m. Horace V. Ward, June 30, 1892. (2) Julia Deborah, b. G. R., Aug. 24, 1873. (3) Edith Anna, b. G. R., Sept. 20, 1882. (4) Arthur Webster, b. G. R., Nov. 24, 1884. (5) George Leonard, b. G. R., Mar. 3, 1887.

    b. Anna, b. T., June 27, 1847; m. Mar. 4, 1868, Theodore Chandler Putnam, of Grand Rapids, b. Nov. 4, 1840, at Warwick, Mass. Children : (1) Theodore Franklin, b. Grand Rapids, June 26, 1869. (2) William Powers, b. G. R., Oct. 23, 1873.

    c. Alfred, b. Grand Rapids, May 29, 1851.

    d. Adeline, b. G. R., Aug. 5, 1858.

5. Susan Dow, b. Hebron, Nov. 3, 1826; m. May 24, 1843, Caleb C. Heath, son of Daniel, b. Springfield, Feb. 14, 1822; d. Plainfield, Mich., Jan. 8, 1867, ae. 44-10-24. She res. Mill Creek, Mich. Children :

    a. Jonathan, b. Rensselaer Co., N. Y., Apr. 27, 1844; m. Sept. 14, 1872, Ellen Minerva Zareba, b. Cuyahoga Co., Ohio, July 27, 1848. Res. Bijou Hills, Brule Co., South Dakota. Two children.

    b. Daniel, b. Troy, N. Y., Feb. 25, 1846; m. June 21, 1873, Elizabeth Obrion, b. Ireland, Jan. 27, 1855; d. Sept. 26, 1876, ae. 21-7-29. He m. (2) Apr. 20, 1886, Sarah Kate Brown, b. England, June 7, 1854. Six children.

    c. Phebe Ann, b. T., Dec. 5, 1847; m. in Plainfield, Mar. 20,

1868, Augustus Richmyre, b. Cleveland, June 25, 1838. She d. Mack's Creek, Camden Co., Mo., May 18, 1891, ae. 43-5-13. Six children.

d. Caleb, b. T., July 18, 1850; m. Oct. 21, 1871, Euphema Isabelle Norton, b. Grand Rapids, Dec. 16, 1850. Seven children.

6. Eben, d.   7. Jonathan, d.   8. Daniel.

THE PRAY FAMILIES

1.   Ebenezer K. Pray, son of Ira and Nancy P. (Keezer) Pray, was b. Parsonsfield, Me., Nov. 19, 1829, and m. Aug. 1, 1852, Ruth F., dau. of Sewall and Mary S. (Goss) Smith, b. Wentworth, Nov. 5, 1833.   He was a blacksmith and hosiery manufacturer in Ashland ; located in Bristol in 1868, and engaged in the manufacture of leather at tannery then on Lake street. Later in the cultivation of oranges in Florida.   Residence, No. Main street, near Union.   Was selectman four years and a trustee of the Bristol Savings Bank eighteen years.   Republican, Mason.   He d. Bristol, Feb. 16, 1902, ae. 72-2-27 ; she d. Ashland, May 2, 1903, ae. 69-5-27.

CHILD

2.   Anson Burlingame (adopted), son of Aaron Burnham and Harriet (Gordon) Cate, b. Holderness, Nov. 7, 1857.   He came to Bristol in 1868. He m. July 3, 1890, Martha B., dau. of Rev. David Calley.   (See.)   He was a jeweler and assistant postmaster in Bristol 1879-1902.   Res. Summer street.   Child :

a.   Frances Mary, b. Bristol, July 15, 1891.

---

1.   Martin Bradeen Pray, brother of Ebenezer K., above, was b. South Tamworth, Nov. 1, 1845.   He m. Marcia Ann, dau. of Jeremiah M. Calley, b. Holderness, July 3, 1840.   They came to Bristol in March, 1878, and own and occupy the George T. Crawford residence, Winter street.   He is a job teamster. Has served as road agent.   Republican.

CHILDREN

2.   Bertha, b. Ashland, Aug. 7, 1870 ; d. Bristol, Jan. 18, 1889, ae. 18-5-11.

3.   Lela Mae, b. A., Aug. 14, 1872 ; m. June 28, 1899, William A. Moore, son of Robert, b. Canada, May 30, 1869.   He was in trade at Hardwick, Vt., in Pomona, Cal., and now at Ludlow, Vt.   Child :

a.   George Anthony, b. Hardwick, Vt., May 9, 1901.

4.   Willis Everett, b. A., Feb. 29, 1876 ; m. Nov. 9, 1902, Lottie B., dau. of Joseph P. Hill.   (See.)   Child :

a.   Son, b. Sept. 28, 1903.

5.   Elwyn Lawrence, b. Nov. 10, 1884.

THE PRESCOTT FAMILIES

1.   James Prescott, the ancestor of the Bristol Prescotts, came from Dryby, in the county of Lincolnshire, England, in

1665, and settled in Hampton. In 1668, he m. Mary, dau. of Nathaniel and Grace Boulter, b. Exeter, May 15, 1648. In 1694, the town of Kingston was granted to James Prescott and others, and in 1725 he settled there, and there d. Nov. 25, 1728, aged about 85 ; Mary, his widow, d. Kingston, Oct. 4, 1735, ae. 87–4–19. They were the parents of nine children, of whom the first was

2. Joshua Prescott, b. Mar. 1, 1669; removed to Kingston as early as 1725. He was the father of eleven children, of whom the second was

3. Joshua Prescott, b. about 1713, m. (1) Abigail Ambrose. They had four sons and two daughters. She d. and he m. (2) Mary Moulton, about 1763, and removed to Chester, where he d. July 12, 1785, ae. about 72. By his second wife he had five sons. He served six months in the expedition against Crown Point in 1758, and signed the association test in Chester in 1776. One son was

4. Joseph Prescott, b. June 8, 1767 ; m. in 1790, Lydia Worthen, b. Aug. 28, 1772. After the birth of their first child in Chester, they removed to Bridgewater and first settled near the site of the meeting-house, but soon after located on what is still known as the Prescott farm, and here he d. Nov. 7, 1861, ae. 94–4–29. She d. Apr. 25, 1852, ae. 79–7–27. He was one of seven who organized the first Methodist class in Bristol. Was a prominent and respected man in the community ; represented Bridgewater several years in the legislature.

CHILDREN

5. Elizabeth, b. Chester, Feb. 23, 1791. She m. (1) Abner Fellows. (See.) She m. (2) July 15, 1834, Joseph Goss, of New Hampton.

6. Josiah Worthen, b. Bridgewater, Feb. 9, 1793; m. 1817, Dorothy Leavitt, and settled in Hooksett.

7. Abigail Bartlett, b. B., Oct. 11, 1795 ; m. July 29, 1821, Elisha Worthen, and d. Oct. 1, 1851, ae. 55–11–20. Two children.

8. Jesse, b. B., Nov. 29, 1797; d. Sept. 6, 1799, ae. 1–9–7.

*9. Jesse, b. B., Apr. 24, 1800.

10. Mary, b. B., Apr. 20, 1802; m. Nov. 24, 1825, Samuel Worthen. (See.)

11. Lydia, b. B., Apr. 4, 1804 ; m. Gilman Fletcher, b. Aug. 27, 1804. She d. Feb. 18, 1828, ae. 23–10–14.

12. Dorothy, b. B., Mar. 9, 1806 ; m. June 21, 1830, Gilman Fletcher (his second wife). She d. Nov. 10, 1853, ae. 47–8–1.

13. Joseph, b. B., Mar. 23, 1808; m. Oct. 2, 1833, Harriet Marshall, b. July 16, 1810, and d. Sept. 15, 1848, ae. 38–1–29. He m. (2) Mar. 14, 1850, Lucy Frost, b. Feb. 13, 1833. He was a shoe manufacturer in Natick, Mass., where he d. July 26, 1852, ae. 44–4–3.

14. Almira, b. B., May 5, 1810 ; m. Jan. 12, 1836, Joseph Huckins.

15. Louisa, b. B., Feb. 5, 1813 ; m. Stephen Nelson. (See.)

16. Ruth Ann, b. B., Oct. 7, 1815 ; m. Apr. 12, 1853, Simon Batchelder, b. Aug. 29, 1797.

17. Harriet Newell, b. B., Feb. 23, 1819 ; d. June, 1821, ae. 2–4–.

(9) Jesse Prescott, b. Apr. 24, 1800; m. Jan. 8, 1827,

Eliza Harriman, dau. of John (See), b. Aug. 27, 1803. He succeeded his father on the home farm, where he d. Mar. 17, 1871, ae. 70-10-23 ; she res. some years in Bristol and here d., Nov. 24, 1889, ae. 86-2-27. Members of the Bristol Methodist church.

CHILDREN

18. Aaron Charles, b. Bridgewater, June 18, 1829 ; m. Mar. 17, 1858, Marinda, dau. of William and Laura (Harriman) Webster, b. Plymouth, Dec. 20, 1836. He was a farmer on the Prescott farm till 1874 ; res. Bristol, 1874-1901, since in Montpelier, Vt., employee in pulp-mill, and a meat-cutter. Republican, Odd Fellow, official member of Methodist church. Child :

    a. Arthur Webster, b. Bridgewater, May 4, 1861 ; m. Nov. 1, 1882, Helen M. White, dau. Marshall W. (See), b. Bristol, Oct. 12, 1863. He m. (2). Was auditor in railroad offices at Plymouth and Concord ; now cashier Montpelier & Wells River railroad, at Montpelier, Vt. Child : Lawrence Hayward, b. Bristol, Dec. 14, 1883.

19. Lucian William, b. Sept. 23, 1831 ; m. Aug. 12, 1857, Julia Platt French, dau. Abijah, b. Stratford, June 1, 1832. He was granted a license to preach by the Bristol Methodist church ; graduated from the Methodist Biblical Institute, Concord, in 1855, joined N. H. Methodist Conference same year, and filled pastorates till 1881 ; has since res. in Warren. Children :

    a. Willie Andrew, b. Stratford, Aug. 28, 1858 ; d. Nov. 13, 1861, ae. 3-2-15.

    b. Ettie Lucia, b. Haverhill, Oct. 9, 1865 ; m. Sept. 1, 1892, Fred C. Gleason. Res. Warren. Child : Kenneth Prescott, b. July 19, 1900.

    c. Frank Jesse, b. Somersworth, May 9, 1869 ; d. Sept., 1869.

    d. Gracie Bell, b. Rumney, July 13, 1874 ; graduated from Bates College, Lewiston, Me., 1896. Teacher in High school, South Portland, Me.

20. Amanda Ann, b. Apr. 11, 1837 ; m. Mar. 23, 1868, Daniel W. Spencer, a lawyer, Berwick, Me. Two children.

21. Orpha Jane, b. May 4, 1839 ; m. May 4, 1861, Herbert A. Shaw, who d. May, 1874. She d. Feb. 9, 1875, ae. 35-9-5. Children :

    a. Jessie Amanda, b. June 4, 1864 ; burned to death 1883, ae. 19.

    b. Hattie Jane, b. Aug. 15, 1866 ; m. Benjamin Jones, 221 Lowell street, Arlington Heights, Mass. Two children.

    c. Ruth Belle,   }
    d. Susie Dell,   } b. Sept. 11, 1871.

Another branch of the Prescott family is as follows :

1. James Prescott, who came from England in 1665. (See p. 344.) His second child was

2. James Prescott, b. Sept. 1, 1671. He m. Mar. 1, 1695, Maria Marston, dau. of William, b. May 16, 1672. She d. and he m. June 17, 1746, Abigail, widow of Dea. Benjamin Sanborn. He had eight children, of whom the second was

3. Samuel Prescott, b. Mar. 14, 1697, m. Dec. 17, 1717, Mary, dau. of Joseph Sanborn, b. July 28, 1697. He was a farmer at Hampton Falls, where he d. June 12, 1759, ae. 62-2-28. He had five sons, the youngest of whom was

Rev. Lucian W. Prescott

4. Jeremiah Prescott, b. Sept. 29, 1718, m. Jan. 15, 1741, Mary Hayes. Served in the French war 1755-'56. She d. and he m., Feb. 10, 1780, Mary, widow of Lemuel Towle. Of his nine children, the first was

5. Jeremiah Prescott, b. Dec. 22, 1741, m. Jan., 1764, Jane Sherburne, b. Oct., 1745. Served in Revolutionary war as lieutenant. Was a farmer in Epsom; d. Apr. 25, 1817, ae. 75-4-3; she d. Sept., 1828, ae. 82-11-. The first of his eight children was

6. John Prescott, b. Dec. 17, 1764, m. June 11, 1792, Deborah, dau. of Benjamin and Betsey (Dudley) Hill, of Northwood, b. June 17, 1757. She d. Bristol at the home of her son, Jeremiah, Nov. 25, 1843, ae. 86-5-8. He was a carpenter and millwright in Epsom. He spent his last years in Bristol and celebrated his 92nd birthday by walking from Bristol village to New Hampton village, and the next day continued his walk to New Hampton Center. He d. Bristol, May 20, 1857, ae. 92-5-3. He was the father of thirteen children. Of these, two settled in Bristol, viz.:

*7. Jeremiah Hill, b. Epsom, Feb. 24, 1800.
*8. Jonathan Leavitt, b. E., May 29, 1806.

(7) Jeremiah H. Prescott, b. Feb. 24, 1800, m. Nov. 25, 1820, Sally Drake, b. May 23, 1803. Res. Chichester and Wentworth till 1834, when he settled in Bristol. She d. Nov. 20, 1832, ae. 29-5-27, and he m., June, 1833, Lucinda Berry, b. Feb. 26, 1812. In Bristol, at intervals for seventeen years, he kept the tavern on east side of South Main street. He was deputy sheriff for ten years, and served as selectman two years. In 1851, he removed to Babcock's Grove, Ill., where he kept a restaurant, and where he d. Feb. 6, 1852, ae. 51-11-12. She returned to Bristol and here d. Dec. 12, 1896, ae. 84-9-16.

CHILDREN

*9. Josiah Drake, b. Wentworth, June 15, 1822.
10. James Harriman, b. W., Aug. 6, 1824; m. May 2, 1851, Catherine Webster, b. Mar. 13, 1829, and d. Freeport, Ill., Dec. 26, 1868, ae. 39-9-13. He kept hotel a few years at Newmarket; taught music and was proprietor of a dining saloon at Freeport, where he res. Children:
    a. Frank Pierce, b. Laconia, May 17, 1852.
    b. Hetta May, b. Freeport, Ill., Dec. 12, 1858; d. Oct. 8, 1859.
    c. Willie Walker, b. F., Mar. 29, 1862; d. May, 1869, ae. 7-2-.
    d. Carrie Francena, b. F., Mar. 28, 1865.
11. Francena M., b. W., Aug. 16, 1826; m. Aug. 17, 1847, Samuel F. Taylor, b. June 5, 1821. They res. Freeport, Ill., where he had a livery stable. Children:
    a. Nellie F., b. Haverhill, Mass., July 28, 1848.
    b. George E., b. Amesbury, Mass., May 11, 1850; d. May 5, 1851.
    c. Julia M., b. Rockport, Dec. 31, 1852.
12. David Porter, b. Chichester, July 14, 1828; m. July 22, 1852, Anna Maria, dau. of Warren White (See), b. June 22, 1833. She d. Aug. 28,

1869, ae. 36-2-6. He was for several years in the boot and shoe trade in White's block and res. on Beech street. Was ten years deputy sheriff. He was a sweet singer, having a tenor voice of great purity, compass, and strength, and he ranked high as a musician. Was leader of the Methodist choir and of the Congregational choir for twenty-five years before his death, which occurred Jan. 3, 1895, ae. 66-5-19.

    a. Abbie Louise, b. Bristol, Oct. 10, 1853; m. Charles E. Fowler. (See.)

    b. Ida May, b. B., Nov. 2, 1855; d. Mar. 15, 1856.

    c. Katherine White, b. B., Aug. 19, 1865; m. June 17, 1895, William H. Crafts, son of William G., b. Melrose, Mass., Oct. 10, 1866. She received a musical education in Boston and New York and ranks high as soprano singer and teacher of vocal music in Boston.

13. Sarah M., b. W., Oct. 27, 1830; m. Feb. 5, 1852, Rev. Samuel McKeen, b. Saratoga, N. Y., May 19, 1826. He was a leading member of the Troy (Methodist) Conference. "Mrs. McKeen was an amiable and lovely woman, distinguished for her acquirements and many virtues." She d. Aug. 23, 1867, ae. 36-9-26. Children:

    a. Carrie, b. Vergennes, Vt., Apr. 18, 1854.

    b. Willard Prescott, b. Saratoga, N. Y., Apr. 29, 1862.

14. Mary P., b. W., Aug. 8, 1832; d. Mar. 13, 1833.

15. Jeremiah Hill, b. Bristol, Dec. 5, 1834; m. in 1852, Hannah Sargent, of Franklin. He d. in Texas, 1879, ae. 45; she d. Bristol. Children:

    a. Frank H., b. 1853; m. 1881, Lizzie Shields, of Jamestown, N. Y. Res. 122 Walnut street, Philadelphia, Pa. Children: (1) Estelle. (2) Ethel. (3) Ruth.

    b. Ida, d. unm., at Haverhill, Dec. 18, 1888.   *c.* Nettie.

    d. Fred, b. 1864; res. New York.   *e.* George, d.

16. Charles Henry, b. B., Sept. 12, 1836; m. 1865, Laura Davis Pinkham, of Mayville, N. Y., and d. Meadville, Pa., 1882, ae. 46.

17. Anna, b. B., June 3, 1839; m. July 28, 1866, Sylvester Bennett, b. Jan. 4, 1842. He was a machinist in Concord, and d. Meadville, Pa., May 15, 1885, ae. 43-4-11. She res. Bristol. Child:

    a. Dora Maud, b. Hartford, Conn., Nov. 29, 1867; m. Charles L. Follansbee. (See.)

18. Horace M., b. B., Apr. 11, 1841. Served in Union Army. (See Roll of Honor.)

19. Frederick William, b. B., Aug. 10, 1844. Served in Union army. (See Roll of Honor.) He m. June 6, 1868, Eldora A., dau. of Samuel H. Rollins. (See.) Kept hotel at Pit Hole, Pa., till 1869; since then, at 210 Upper 1st street, Evansville, Ind. Child:

    a. Dora M., b. Bristol, Mar. 10, 1869; m. Edward E. Wheet. (See.)

20. George F., b. B., Nov. 5, 1845; m. Feb., 1869, Frances Amelia Ingalls, dau. of Gilman Ingalls (See) b. Aug. 13, 1843. She d. Franklin, May 21, 1898, ae. 54-9-8. He was a captain in the militia. Is a superior house carpenter at Franklin. Child:

    a. Lillian Blanche, d. Franklin, Nov. 12, 1878, ae. 5-18-9.

    b. Carl Henry, } b. Franklin, Nov., 1882.
    c. Bertha May, }

21. Hattie Louise, b. B., Dec. 15, 1847; d. Sept., 1851, ae. 3-9-.

22. Susan M., b. B., May 15, 1850. Unm. Legal home, Bristol.

(8) Jonathan L. Prescott, b. May 29, 1806, m. May 1, 1834, Helen M. Mansur, b. Aug. 11, 1809. He came to Bristol, about 1840, from Claremont. Kept hotel on South Main street four years, removed to Wentworth and after four years

returned and took charge of Bristol House ; removed to Milwaukee, Wis., about 1855, and d. Palatine, Ill., in Aug., 1865, ae.
59-3-.

CHILDREN

23. George Crombie, b. Nashua, Mar. 14, 1835. Was a conductor on
the Milwaukee and Prairie du Chien railroad.
24. Helen Frances, b. Claremont, Apr. 9, 1836. Res., unm., 539 63rd
street, West Chicago, Ill.
25. Ann Maria, b. C., Aug. 19, 1837 ; m. Moody A. Sawyer. (See.)
26. Abby Emma, b. Bristol, Dec. 14, 1843 ; m. Dec. 19, 1863, Joseph
Strong, b. Wheeling, Ill., Oct. 20, 1842, and d. Wheeling, Nov. 20, 1869,
ae. 27-1-. She res. 539 63rd street, West Chicago. Children :
    a. George William, b. Athens, Pa., Jan. 28, 1865 ; m. May 24,
    1888, Hattie B. Allen, of Chicago, who d. June 6, 1891, and he m.
    Mar. 10, 1894, Fannie E. Allen, of Chicago. Child : (1) Ethel.
    b. Helen Maria, b. Sept. 13, 1866. Res. Chicago, unm.
    c. Joseph Leavitt, b. May 20, 1869 ; m. Sept. 1, 1891, Estella W.
    Cresap, of Uhrichsville, Ohio. Res. Chicago. Child : (1) Don-
    ald Cresap.

(9) Josiah D. Prescott, b. June 15, 1822, m. Jan. 11, 1843,
Elizabeth, dau. of Col. Isaac Crosby, b. Hebron, Dec. 11, 1823,
and d. Bristol, May 23, 1854, ae. 30-5-12. He m. Dec. 5, 1864,
Mary Frances, dau. of Samuel S. Fellows (See), b. Aug. 26,
1842. He was landlord of the Bristol House for twenty-two
years, and there d. Dec. 12, 1866, ae. 44-5-27. His widow d.
Apr. 9, 1900, ae. 57-7-13.

CHILDREN

27. Ellen Elizabeth, b. Bristol, Jan. 29, 1844 ; m. George G. Brown.
(See.)
28. Josiah Everett, b. B., Apr. 10, 1846 ; m. July 28, 1869, Sarah
Lavina, dau. of Lorenzo D. Day (See), b. Feb. 6, 1846, and d. Merrimac,
Mass., Aug. 18, 1887, ae. 41-6-12. He was associated with his father in
hotel business ; a traveling optician ; landlord of hotel in Merrimac. He
d. at home of his dau. at Amesbury, Mass., Apr. 1, 1903, ae. 56-11-21.
Child :
    a. Donna Elizabeth, b. Bristol, Feb. 20, 1873 ; m. Nov. 27, 1894,
    G. L. Batchelder, 54 Sparhawk street, Amesbury, Mass.
29. Anna Donna, b. B., Mar. 5, 1852 ; d. Bristol.
30. Harry Fellows, b. B., Aug. 14, 1865 ; m. Feb. 15, 1898, Minie
Jane, dau. William C. Kelley. (See.) Farmer. Republican. Children :
    a. Frances Anna, b. Bristol, Jan. 10, 1899.
    b. Harry William, b. B., Aug. 24, 1900.

———

1. Charles Henry Prescott is a son of Joseph and Persis
Felton (Thompson) Prescott, and was b. Newfame, Vt., Jan. 21,
1853. Is of the 8th generation from John Prescott, who landed
in Boston from England in 1640. He m., June 18, 1901, Mrs.
Alice Ann Knight, widow of Frank, and dau. of Nelson and
Elizabeth (Miller) Willard, b. Dummerstown, Vt. He was a
dry goods merchant in Brattleboro, Vt., till spring of 1901, when
he became proprietor of Hotel Bristol and has since been its
landlord. Republican. No children.

THE PRESTON FAMILY

1. Nelson Sylvanus Preston is the son of Alpheus and Almira (Tucker) Preston, and was b. Tunbridge, Vt., Dec. 14, 1834. July 4, 1857, he m. Paulina, dau. of Daniel and Abbie (Reed) Lowell, b. No. Hatley, P. Q., Apr. 27, 1838. She d. Bristol, June 29, 1897, ae. 59-2-2. He m., Oct. 26, 1899, Mrs. Annie Jones, b. Ireland, Feb. 26, 1852, dau. of John Doren and widow (1) of Charles Green, (2) of Carleton Jones. He has been a paper-mill employee most of the time since coming to town about 1882. Democrat, Free Baptist, G. A. R. He served as corporal in Co. B, 6th Regt., N. H. Vols., from Aug. 6, 1862, to June 4, 1865. On his discharge is the following endorsement:

He was engaged in the following battles : Fredericksburg, Va., Dec. 13, 1862 ; Seige of Vicksburg and Battle of Jackson, Miss., June and July, 1863 ; Wilderness, May 6, 1864 ; Spottsylvania Court House, May 12, 1864 ; North Anna, May 24 ; Totopotomy Creek, May 31 ; Bethesda Church, June 3 ; Cold Harbor, June 9 ; Petersburg, June 16-18 ; Cemetery Hill, July 30 ; Weldon Railroad, Aug. 22 ; Poplar Grove Church, Sept. 30, 1864 ; Capture of Petersburg, Apr. 2, 1865. He has ever been a brave and faithful soldier.   CHARLES L. CLARK, Lt. Com'd'g Co. B.

CHILDREN

2. Florence J., b. North Hatley, P. Q., May 19, 1858 ; d. Aug. 7, 1858.
3. Almira A., b. Orange, Oct. 8, 1859 ; m. Nov. 18, 1876, William H. Welch. She d. Feb. 22, 1897, ae. 37-4-14. He m. (2) Mrs. Alice (Adams) Rice. Child :

    a. Jessie May, b. Canaan ; m. Robert L. Annis. (See.)
    b. Blanche E., b. C., Sept. 1, 1880 ; m. Herbert E. Hadley. (See.)

4. George Nelson, b. West Lebanon, June 12, 1862 ; m. Aug. 10, 1881, Emma Wescott. Was brakeman on railroad and was killed by falling from a moving train at East Andover, Feb. 19, 1888, ae. 25-8-7.
5. Wesley Monroe, b. Canaan, Nov. 20, 1866 ; m. Nov. 15, 1892, Julia O'Leary. He is a shoemaker at Berlin.
6. Frank Martin, b. C., Sept. 1, 1875. A painter in Somerville, Mass.
7. William, b. Grafton, Oct. 12, 1877 ; d. Grafton, Mar. 23, 1878.

THE PRICE FAMILY

1. George Price, the son of Frederick and Katherine (MacKenzie) Price, was b. in Little Gaspe, P. Q., Jan. 1, 1840. He m., Nov. 19, 1866, Jane, dau. of Alexander and Jane (Porter Simpson, b. Little Gaspe, June 3, 1847. They emigrated to Bristol in October, 1888 ; he has been a farmer and laborer ; res. a mile south of Central square. Methodists.

CHILDREN, all except last born in Little Gaspe.

2. Elizabeth Amelia, b. July 4, 1868 ; d. Bristol, Mar. 29, 1894, of consumption, ae. 25-8-25.
3. William Henry, b. Aug. 19, 1870 ; m. Dec. 4, 1900, Lura Patten, of Alexandria. Child :

    a. Cleora, b. Jan. 14, 1902.

HARRY W. PROCTOR
(Died May 17, 1904)

4. Alfred Alexander, b. Nov. 19, 1872. He went to Granite Creek, British Columbia, in February, 1897, where he now res.

5. Margaret Jane, b. Apr. 15, 1875; m. Harry O. Pike. (See.)

6. George Edwin, b. Sept. 5, 1877; a laborer in Bristol.

7. Emma Reta, b. Dec. 28, 1879; res. Boston, Mass.

8. Laura Mary, b. Jan. 19, 1882; m. June 24, 1903, Chester S. Patten, of Alexandria. He is a carpenter and builder in Wollaston, Mass.

9. Florence Maud, b. Apr. 15, 1884. A compositor in *Enterprise* office.

10. Robert Sydney, b. June 24, 1886.

11. Ethel Kate, b. Bristol, Feb. 24, 1889.

THE PROCTOR FAMILY

1. Charles Hall Proctor is the son of Amos Batchelder and Liddy Jane (Edwards) Proctor. He was b. in Enfield, Apr. 9, 1838, and m. (1) Abbie Hayes, dau. of William and Rhoda Meade. She d. in Bristol, Dec. 12, 1874, ae. 34-2-. He m. (2) Feb. 24, 1876, Abbie F., dau. of Israel T. Rice. (See.) He enlisted in Co. C, 15th Regt., N. H. Vols., Sept. 13, 1862, and served with his regiment on the lower Mississippi, participating in the seige of Port Hudson. Discharged Aug. 13, 1863. He came to Bristol in May, 1869, and worked two years in E. K. Pray's tannery. Has been for twenty-five years in North End woolen-mill as overseer and superintendent. Was postmaster at Bristol four years. Democrat, Mason, Odd Fellow, G. A. R. Official member of the Methodist church.

CHILDREN

2. Fred Lewis, b. May 25, 1861; m. (1) Mar. 27, 1886, Mrs. Lucy Holt; (2) Sept. 27, 1894, Isabel, dau. of William and Margaret (Sinclair) Ward, b. St. Margaret's Hope, Scotland, Sept. 22, 1869. A machinist in Bristol, Chicago, and Alabama, now in Philadelphia. No children.

3. Harry Weston, b. Dec. 5, 1874. Is a jeweler in Bristol.

THE PUTNEY FAMILIES

1. Charles Henry Putney, son of Alfred S. and Hannah (Hobart) Putney, was b. in Hebron, May 26, 1844. He m., Apr. 11, 1875, Martha Etta, dau. of Ezekiel Follansbee (See), b. June 8, 1854. He was a wood turner in Bristol from 1885, and here d. Apr. 19, 1900, ae. 55-10-23.

CHILDREN

2. Josephine M., b. Aug. 24, 1876.

3. William Everett, b. Dec. 26, 1879.

---

1. Rufus Wright Putney is a son of Alfred S. and Hannah (Hobart) Putney. He was b. Hebron, May 18, 1847, and m. Dec. 2, 1872, Emma F., dau. of Eldridge F. and Samantha

Farrington Perry. Res. Natick, Mass., 1870-'84; Bristol, 1884-'96, where he was a wood worker; returned to Natick, where he has since been an electrical engineer.

CHILDREN

2. Arthur Farrington, b. Natick, Oct. 8, 1875. In Bristol, was clerk in George H. Hammond's store; while studying pharmacy in Natick, lost his eyesight, was partially blind five years till 1900; since, totally blind; devotes his time to the poultry industry.

3. Harry Elbridge, b. N.; d. Jan. 25, 1879, ae. 22 months.

THE QUIMBY FAMILIES

1. Jacob Quimby, son of Jeremiah and Olive (Saunders) Quimby, was b. Hill, Feb. 28, 1796. He m. Martha Orr Smith, dau. of John, b. Chelmsford, Mass., May 12, 1797. He was a farmer in Hill, and in Bristol, 1824-'27. He d. Hill, Dec. 9, 1860, ae. 64-9-11. She d. Sanbornton, Feb. 11, 1868, ae. 70-8-29.

CHILDREN

2. Martha J., b. Hill, Nov. 20, 1820.
3. Daniel, b. H., Mar. 17, 1823.
4. Jacob, b. H., Mar. 5, 1825; d. Apr. 8, 1894, ae. 69-1-3.
5. Frederic W., b. Bristol, Jan. 17, 1827; m. (1) Almira M. Wiggin, dau. Jesse, b. Hill, May 13, 1833, and d. Apr. 15, 1851 (1853), ae. 17-11-2. He m. (2) Mary Josephine, dau. Eliphalet and Mary (Trumbull) Kenson, b. East Boston, Mass., May 29, 1843. He has been a farmer in Hill, Sanbornton, and in Bristol, near the engine-house of the B. & M. railroad since 1868. Is a noted fox and bee hunter. Republican. Children :
     a. Asceneath, b. Hill, Dec. 20, 1850; m. John B. Sanborn, Apr. 5, 1877, and d. Sanbornton, 1896 (?). He res. East Tilton. Child : Maynard Ray, b. July 6, 1878.
     b. Fred Herbert, b. Sanbornton, Jan. 6, 1867. Unm.
     c. Maurice Burden, b. Bristol, Apr. 10, 1870. Unm.
     d. Charles Russell, b. B., June 24, 1876; m. July 13, 1899, Inez, dau. Edwin and Lucy (King) Rogers, b. Milton, Vt., Jan. 10, 1884. Children : (1) Leslie Charles, b. Bristol, Feb. 19, 1900. (2) Ray Russell, b. B., Dec. 25, 1901.
6. Parker C., b. Hill, Nov. 25, 1828; m. May 25, 1862, Mary, dau. of Charles and Sarah (Calley) Emerson, b. Sanbornton, May 10, 1836. Farmer and blacksmith in Sanbornton. Child : George Emerson, b. July 1, 1865. Res. Gaza.
7. Hannah A., b. H., Dec. 26, 1830; d. New Whatcom, Wash., Mar. 17, 1901, ae. 70-2-21.

1. Ephraim Quimby, b. Hill, Sept. 28, 1773; supposed to be the son of Jeremiah, m. Hannah, dau. of Reuben Wells (See), b. Jan. 16, 1777. They were farmers west part of Hill.

CHILDREN

2. Sarah, b. Sept. 19, 1796; m. Daniel F. Rowell.
3. Reuben, b. Sept. 6, 1800; taken sick 11 a. m., Jan. 19; d. Jan. 20, 1816, 1 a. m., ae. 15-4-14.
4. John, b. Sept. 16, 1802; taken sick 9 a. m., Jan. 21; d. Jan. 25, 1816, at 11 a. m., ae. 13-4-9.

5. Henry, b. Oct. 4, 1804; taken sick Jan. 20, 3 p. m.; d. Jan. 21, 1816, at 3 p. m., ae. 11-3-17.

6. Ephraim, b. Sept. 9, 1808; stricken 10 a. m., Jan. 20; d. 7. a. m., Jan. 22, 1816, ae. 7-4-13.

7. Polly, b. Oct. 16, 1810; stricken 6 a. m., Jan. 21; d. 10 a. m., Jan. 22, 1816, ae. 5-3-6.

8. Joanna, b. Nov. 26, 1812; stricken 6 p. m., Jan. 19; d. 10 a. m., Jan. 20, 1816, ae. 3-1-24.

9. Reuben, b. Feb. 22, 1818.

The above-named six children all d. of spotted fever and were buried in two graves.

THE QUINT FAMILIES

1. Sebastian Streeter Quint, son of Silas and Rhoda (Gray) Quint, was b. in Grafton, Jan. 8, 1857. He m. Jan. 7, 1877, Ida, dau. of Alanson and Laura (Straw) Blake, b. Plymouth, Aug. 9, 1859. Has been a painter and paper-hanger in Bristol since 1872. Democrat, K. of P.

CHILDREN, all born in Bristol

2. Beulah Florence, b. Jan. 8, 1878; m. Arthur Robie. (See.)
3. George Marvin, b. Mar. 20, 1880; d. Oct. 23, 1883, ae. 3-7-3.
4. Silas Alanson, b. Aug. 20, 1882; a painter in Bristol.
5. Linnell Jasper, b. Nov. 18, 1884.
6. Lorin Blake, b. Jan. 12, 1887.
7. Glacie Marguerite, b. May 17, 1895.
8. O'Rilla Gertrude, b. Dec. 3, 1897.
9. Franka, b. Mar. 12, 1899; d. June 23, 1899.

---

1. Hosea B. Quint, a brother of above, was a painter in Bristol, 1874-'81, when he removed to Concord, where he now res. He m. Jan. 13, 1872, Ida F. Haines, b. Oct. 8, 1854, dau. of J. Wesley Haines.

CHILDREN

2. Edgar M., b. Bristol, May 7, 1873.
3. Erdine M., b. B., Aug. 3, 1874.
4. Ida V., b. B., Sept. 16, 1876; d. Oct. 1, 1881, ae. 5-0-15.

THE RANDOLPH FAMILIES

1. Henry A. Randolph was a son of Samuel and Anna Flude, and was b. Northampton, Eng., June 9 (11), 1821. He changed his name from Flude to Randolph. At 17 he enlisted in the British army, served in the West Indies four years, and in Canada, where he deserted and came to the United States. He m. Martha J. French, b. Feb. 27, 1823, and settled in Bristol about 1859. Was a merchant tailor on west side of Central square; burned out by the fire of July 4, 1861. (See Roll of Honor.) After the war re-entered business. Last four years of

23

his life was reading law and a pension agent ; committed suicide Aug. 17, 1884, ae. 63-2-8. Was a Methodist, Odd Fellow, G. A. R. She d. Nov. 18, 1891, ae. 68-1-21. In her will she made the Methodist church of Bristol residuary legatee, from which the church received $700.

CHILD

2. Annie May, b. Bristol, Oct. 29, 1860 ; d. Mar. 14, 1879, ae. 18-4-15.

Anna French, an insane sister of Mrs. Randolph, made her home with Mrs. Randolph. She was b. Dec. 31, 1810, and d. Feb. 25, 1885, ae. 74-1-24.

---

1. William F. Randolph was a son of Samuel and Anna Flude. He was b. Northampton, Eng., Aug. 14, 1817, and m. May 28, 1844, Lucia Sharp, dau. of William and Martha Sharp, b. Cranford, England, Dec. 22, 1818. He came from England to Bristol in August, 1869, and changed his name from Flude to Randolph after reaching Bristol. His family followed in April, 1870. He was an expert landscape gardener. A Methodist. She d. Bristol, May 10, 1878, ae. 59-4-18 ; he d. Aug. 14, 1898, ae. 81 years.

CHILDREN, all born in England

2. Anna E., b. June 22, 1849; d. ae. 28 months.
3. Martha Marie, b. June 30, 1851; m. Aug. 9, 1873, Charles W. Casely. He was b. Northamptonshire, Eng., Nov. 18, 1853, and came to Bristol from England with the Randolph family. He is a Methodist clergyman, a member of the Illinois conference. Children :
   a. Herbert William, b. Bristol, Jan. 6, 1875.
   b. Lucy Elizabeth, b. Bristow, Kansas, Jan. 13, 1880.
   c. Cyrus Warren, b. Minneapolis, Kansas, Oct. 13, 1885.
   d. Charlotte Willard, b. Lincoln, Kansas, Aug. 16, 1888.
4. John R., b. Sept. 4, 1864; d. ae. 3 months.
5. Lizzie M., b. Oct. 29, 1855 ; m. John M. Dow. (See.)
6. John, b. Aug. 3, 1857 ; d. ae. 5 years.
7. William John, b. June 15, 1859 ; m. Nov. 30, 1885, Lizzie A., dau. of Timothy E. and Susan (Cochran) Bayley, b. Plymouth, June 18, 1861. He res. Plymouth, where he is clerk, and correspondent *Boston Globe*. Two children, d. in infancy.

THE RAY FAMILY

1. John Ray, son of Nathaniel, was b. Apr. 16, 1805. He m. (1) Ann, dau. of Josiah and Sally (Ladd) Sanborn, b. Alexandria, June 29, 1803, and d. Apr. 1, 1848, ae. 44-9-2. He m. (2) Dec. 9, 1851, Eliza Ann (Sanborn) Roby, sister of first wife, b. Jan. 5, 1816. He was a carpenter and builder in Lowell, Mass., Alexandria and Bristol. He d. Concord, Dec. 3, 1878, ae. 73-7-17, (75—tombstone); she d. in Bristol, in the family of her dau., Mrs. Sarah A. (Roby) Taylor, Mar. 17, 1903, ae. 87-2-12.

CHILDREN

2. Orrin B., b. Lowell, Mass., Sept. 22, 1846; m. (1)(certificate June 27, 1868) Lucy Sarah, dau. of Calvin Golden (See), b. Feb. 22, 1848. He m. (2) Mar. 7, 1882, Mary Antoinette, dau. of Milo H. Crosby (See), b. Mar. 19, 1853. He was a merchant tailor in Bristol, now farmer. Republican. Was captain of Train Rifles. Children:

    a. Walter, b. Bristol, Apr. 17, 1869; m. Mar. 14, 1892, Mary E. Irving, dau. of William and Julia Irving, b. Plymouth. They res. Worcester, Mass. Child: Florence Gertrude, b. Franklin Falls, July 22, 1893.

    b. Everett, b. B. Set fire to his father's buildings while playing with matches in the barn, and perished in the flames, Mar. 31, 1875, ae. 4 years.

    c. Malvern, b. B., Dec. 10, 1874; m. May 30, 1901, Sarah Etta, dau. of Richard and Sarah Marsden, b. Wrentham, Mass., Sept. 10, 1881. They res. Worcester, Mass. Children: (1) Eva Elizabeth, b. Burrillville, R. I., Apr. 6, 1902; d. Jan. 21, 1903. (2) Walter, b. July, 1903.

    d. Florence Putnam, b. B., June 16, 1883; d. Aug. 3, 1892, ae. 9-1-17.

    e. John Crosby, b. B., Apr. 6, 1891.

3. Eudora Marcelia, b. L., Dec. 9, 1840; m. Israel Putnam; res. Minneapolis, Minn.; he d. and she m. (2) his brother, William, fall of 1881. She res. Lesueur, Minn.; d. Bristol, Feb. 14, 1895, ae. 54-2-5.

4. Mary Etta, b. Alexandria, Feb. 24, 1855; m. 1881, Frank W. Fellows; res. Collinsville, Conn. Child:

    a. Ethel, b. Scytheville, May 6, 1883.

THE REED FAMILY

1. Ervin Huntoon Reed, son of Hiram and Hannah (Moore) Reed, was b. Dorchester, Sept. 6, 1869. He m. Dec. 25, 1894, Effie A., dau. of Abel Bailey, Jr. (See.) He came to Bristol in Apr., 1895, and is a finisher of flannel at mill of Dodge–Davis Manufacturing company.

CHILDREN

2. Maud Bailey, b. Bristol, Mar. 17, 1896.
3. Ethel Dewey, b. B., June 3, 1898.
4. Ralph Ervin, b. B., Oct. 12, 1900.

THE REID FAMILY

1. Samuel Reid is a son of Joseph Nelson and Mary Ann (Smith) Reid. He was b. AuSable, N. Y., Jan. 7, 1870, and m. Nov. 23, 1892, Alice May, dau. of Ira F. and Jane L. (Hutchins) Varney, b. Rumney, July 8, 1876. A farmer in Bristol, from Nov., 1890.

CHILDREN

2. Pearl Ira, b. Groton, Apr. 24, 1893.
3. Eva May, b. Bristol, Dec. 8, 1896.
4. Dora Maud, b. B., Dec. 15, 1898.
5. Norman Nelson, b. Alexandria, June 22, 1901.

THE REMICK FAMILY

1.　Willard Spaulding Heath Remick is a son of Augustus and Eliza Ann (Prior) Remick. He was b. Natick, Mass., July 20, 1861, and m. (1) May 9, 1881, Ida A., dau. of Edson and Elizabeth Drake. She d. in Groton, Dec. 1, 1886. He m. (2) June 26, 1887, Isabel, dau. of Isaac B. and Martha J. Gove, who d. in Groton, Feb. 15, 1888. He m. (3) Dec. 21, 1895, Lucy M., dau. of John Seavey (See), b. Aug. 19, 1877. He has been a carpenter in Groton, and in Bristol since Dec., 1892, res. on Turnpike.

CHILDREN

2.　Edwin S., b. Groton, July 27, 1882.
3.　Lewis F., b. G., Mar. 22, 1886.
4.　Eleanor Charlotte, b. Bristol, June 28, 1902.

THE RICE FAMILIES

1.　Israel Thomas Rice, son of Israel Thomas and Jemima (Osgood) Rice, was b. in Eaton, P. Q., Apr. 23, 1822. He m. in Nov., 1848, Abbie P., dau. of Leander Badger (See), b. Nov. 14, 1827. He came to Bristol about 1857, and was an employee at tannery and paper-mill; d. June 4, 1889, ae. 67-1-11. She d. Jan. 26, 1896, ae. 68-2-12.

CHILDREN

2.　Abbie Frances, b. Nashua, Oct. 28, 1849; m. Charles H. Proctor. (See.)
3.　Martha Jane, b. Ham, Canada, Sept. 6, 1851; m. A. Sylvester Smith, Apr. 5, 1871; res. in Hubbardton, Vt. Two daughters.
4.　Lock Willard, b. H., Aug. 7, 1853; m. Nov. 25, 1882, Emma Wallace; d. Nov. 10, 1891, ae. 38-3-3. Was an auctioneer. Republican.
5.　Edgar Augustus, b. H., May 18, 1856; d. June 20, 1872, ae. 16-1-2.
6.　Albertine Lora, b. Bristol, May 29, 1859; res. Boston, Mass.
7.　Oscar Warren, b. B., July 6, 1862; m. May 11, 1887, Inez Florence, dau. Horace and Hannah (Chellis) Saunders, b. Alexandria, 1866. He was for some years a salesman in store of Charles H. Dickinson. One year in California, now bookkeeper in Chelsea, Mass.
8.　Nellie Florence, b. B., Oct. 26, 1865; m. Sept. 16, 1897, Clinton A. Borden, West Somerville, Mass.; d. Apr. 1, 1898, ae. 32-5-5. Child, b. and d. Apr. 1, 1898.
9.　Eva Mabel, b. B., Feb. 19, 1867; d. Apr. 21, 1868, ae. 1-2-2.
10.　Annie Blandena, b. B., Aug. 31, 1869; m. Robert F. Moore. (See.)
11.　Charles Proctor, b. B., May 9, 1872; m. Alice Adams, dau. of Felix. (See.) She m. (2) William H. Welch. Child:
　　a.　Edgar Harold, b. Bristol, Dec. 1, 1895.

————

1.　David Henry Rice, son of Col. David and Maria (Garron) Rice, was b. Andover, Mass., Sept. 9, 1825, and m., Apr. 16, 1852, Laura A., dau. of John F. Coleman, b. Gilford, Aug. 5, 1833. He went to California in 1849; was in stove business

in Lynn, Mass., 1855-'60; in the hosiery business at South
Canton, Mass.; came to Bristol in 1865, as superintendent of the
Merrimack Hosiery company, which did business for a few
years in the mill near the railroad station. In 1891, was super-
intendent of a mining company at Cannon City, Colo., where
he d., Apr. 6, 1892, ae. 66-6-27. Interment at Bristol. Mrs.
Rice was engaged for some years in the millinery business in
Bristol. She now res. with her son, Cecil C., in Concord.

CHILDREN

2.   Edward Henry, b. July 16, 1853; m. Apr. 10, 1871, Mary A., dau.
Henry C. Dubia, b. Warner, Feb. 18, 1853. He was a machinist in Belmont; since May, 1885, in Laconia. Children:
    a.   Laura Bessie, b. Bristol, Aug. 2, 1872; m. Dec. 25, 1888,
Joseph N. Neal, and d. Oct. 10, 1890, ae. 18-2-8.
    b.   Harry David, b. Belmont, Jan. 10, 1877; machinist in Shel-
ton, Conn.
    c.   Edith May, b. B., Mar. 2, 1883. Graduated from Laconia
High school. Is a stenographer, Laconia.
    d.   Charles Edward, b. Laconia, July 5, 1885; d. Aug. 10, 1885.
    e.   Pearl Lucile, b. L., Apr. 22, 1894.
3.   John Blaisdell, b. Lynn, May, 1855; d. Aug., 1855.
4.   Cecil Coleman, b. South Canton, Mass., Mar. 22, 1865; m. Dec.
18, 1897, Jennie Gertrude, dau. Charles M. and Maria (Davis) Colby, b.
in Warner, Aug. 30, 1873. Since December, 1897, he has been baggage-
master Boston & Maine railroad, running between Concord and White
River Junction. Res. Concord. Mason, Republican.

------

1.   William A. Rice, son of Col. David and Maria (Garron) Rice, was b. Andover, Mass., July 16, 1828. He m. Jan.
13, 1852, Margaret A., dau. of Abiel and Betsey (Rogers) Messer, b. Lowell, Vt., May 29, 1833. He came to Bristol 1865,
was a manufacturer of hosiery, and later a speculator in mines
and mining lands. He d. Bristol, Oct. 8, 1891, ae. 63-2-22.
His widow res. Bristol.

CHILD

2.   Mabel Nellie, b. Dedham, Mass., July 23, 1864; m. Elbridge S.
Bickford. (See.)

------

1.   William Rice is the son of Andrew and Ann (Good)
Rice. He was b. in Province of New Brunswick, Mar. 5, 1850,
and m. Oct., 1873, Mary, dau. of Thomas Mitchell. She d.
July, 1882, and he m. (2) Oct. 14, 1885, Harriet Clark. He
located in Bristol, July, 1900, and is an employee at the Mason-
Perkins paper-mill.

CHILDREN

2.   William A., b. Sept. 1, 1874.
3.   Sarah, b. Feb. 3, 1879; m. June 4, 1902, Roscoe Tenney. (See.)
4.   Andrew, b. Jan., 1881; m. May, 1903, Alice Maude Mitchell,
removed to New Brunswick.
5.   Pearl, b. 1887.   6.   Charlie, b. 1890.

23a

7. Nellie, b. 1894.　　　　　　　8. Frank, b. 1896.
9. Grace, b. 1898.　　　　　　10. Robert, b. Bristol, Aug. 2, 1900.
11. Leona May, b. B., May 14, 1903.

THE ROBBINS FAMILY

1. William Gilbert Robbins, son of Benjamin Franklin Curtis and Sarah (Hazelton) Robbins, was b. Hill, Dec. 7, 1869. He m., 1887, Elvira Ruth, dau. of Jonathan S. and Mary Elizabeth (Marden) Chapman, b. Alexandria, July 14, 1869. He has been a paper-mill and woolen-mill employee and laborer in town for fifteen years.

CHILDREN

2. Lizzie Lena, b. Dover, Sept. 26, 1888.
3. Shirley Rex, b. Bristol, Sept. 22, 1891.

THE ROBIE FAMILIES

1. George Alvin Robie is the son of Jeremiah S. and Mary (Green) Robie, b. Plymouth, Sept. 3, 1842. He came to Bristol in fall of 1861, and m., July 31, 1864, Sarah E. Nelson, dau. of Stephen (See), b. Nov. 18, 1846. He was a carpenter, manufacturer of bedsteads, machinist, carriage-maker, and for forty-two years, has been undertaker and dealer in furniture. Is also owner of telephone exchange. Republican, Odd Fellow, Mason ; business in Robie's block of which he is the owner.

CHILDREN, all born in Bristol

2. Albert George, b. Sept. 14, 1865 ; m. Mar. 10, 1886, Georgia Nellie, dau. of William Evans and Abbie Hannah (Staples) Roberts, b. Lynn, Mass., Aug. 3, 1869. Farmer. Children :
 a. Frank Albert, b. July 2, 1888.
 b. Warren George, b. June 23, 1890.
 c. Ervin William, b. Oct. 14, 1892.
 d. Harold Bernard, b. Oct. 6, 1903.

3. Harriet Ann, b. May 12, 1867 ; m. Albro Wells. (See.)
4. William Green, b. Jan. 29, 1869 ; m. Dec. 1, 1897, Lottie Belle, dau. of Orrin W. and Mary Ann (Ray) Shattuck, b. Canaan, Aug. 14, 1877. Farmer in Bristol. Children :
 a. Isabel Mary, b. Bristol, Oct. 20, 1898.
 b. Lawrence William, b. B., Mar. 24, 1901.

5. Louis Stephen, b. Jan. 30, 1870 ; m. Feb. 12, 1894, Lettie E., dau. Isaac N. and Etta E. (McGrath) Ford, b. Groton, June 23, 1873. Was in grain business, North End grist-mill, July, 1895, till fall, 1903, when he removed to Hardwick, Vt. Children :
 a. Gladys, b. Bristol, July 8, 1897.
 b. Ethel Marguerite, b. B., Sept. 22, 1899.

6. Mabelle, b. Mar. 25, 1873 ; m. June 17, 1896, William S. Lougee. They res. Rochester, where he is superintendent of Bell telephone lines. Children :
 a. Katherine Robie, b. Rochester, Dec. 23, 1900.
 b. Robert William, b. R., Aug. 20, 1903.

7.   Arthur, b. Nov. 22, 1875 ; m. Feb. 1, 1894, Beulah F. Quint, dau. of Sebastian S. (See.) Child :
    a.   Marian Frances, b. Bristol, Mar. 20, 1895.

---

1.   Frank Robie, son of John W. L. and Caroline W. (Titcomb) Robie, was b. Raymond, July 20, 1872. He m., Apr. 9, 1896, Minnie L., dau. of Alfred A. and Mary J. (Austin) Lewis, b. Meriden, Conn., Aug. 12, 1872. He came to Bristol from Raymond in 1887. Electrician.

CHILDREN

2.   Raymond L., b. Bristol, Sept. 21, 1898.
3.   Harry A., b. B., Apr. 28, 1901.

THE ROBINSON FAMILIES

1.   Luther Robinson, son of Benjamin and Polly (Glines) Robinson, was b. New Hampton, Nov. 9, 1806, and m. Betsey, dau. of Daniel and Polly (Nichols) Kelley, b. New Hampton, Sept. 4, 1809. He was a farmer in New Hampton and Bristol, where he d., Oct. 7, 1880, ae. 73–10–28. She d. New Hampton, Aug. 29, 1880, ae. 70–11–25.

CHILDREN

2.   Elizabeth, b. Jan., 1833 ; m. John B. Gordon, and d. Oct. 30, 1875, ae. 42–9–.
3.   Frank Warren, b. Bristol, Aug. 20, 1839 ; m. Apr. 11, 1877, Annie Douglas, dau. of William Green (See), b. Jan. 12, 1842. They res. Bristol. He is a farmer. Republican. No children.

---

1.   George Howe Robinson, son of Andrew J. and Sally Piper (Carter) Robinson, was b. in Allenstown, Dec. 8, 1851. He m. Dec. 20, 1883, Lizzie Kathleen, dau. John Roby (See), b. Apr. 11, 1853. For many years he resided at New Hampton, drove stage to Bristol and then run to Concord as brakeman each day. Sold his stage line, and removed to Bristol, Nov., 1896, and continues as brakeman.

CHILDREN, all born in New Hampton

2.   Son, b. Jan. 24, 1885 ; d. Jan. 26, 1885.
3.   Myra Kathleen, b. Apr. 1, 1886.
4.   John Gustavus, b. Sept. 8, 1889 ; d. Dec. 3, 1898, ae. 9–2–25.
5.   Levi Carter, b. Sept. 23, 1891.
6.   Fred Carl, b. Dec. 4, 1894 ; d. Nov. 15, 1899, ae. 4–11–11.

---

1.   Charles Green Robinson, brother of George H., above, was b. Nov. 12, 1852. He m. Dec. 25, 1875, Annie, dau. of Samuel W. Heath (See), b. Dec. 4, 1854. He was a stonecutter in New Hampton ; has res. since 1896 in Bristol; is a laborer at railroad station.

CHILDREN, all born in New Hampton

2. Arthur Jackson, b. Nov. 11, 1876; brakeman on railroad. Res. Concord.
3. Sarah Hannah, b. Oct. 31, 1878. Res. New Hampton.
4. Mabel Perkins, b. Mar. 10, 1880.
5. Nellie Carter, b. Aug. 26, 1882.
6. George Eugene, b. Sept. 22, 1885.
7. Maud Alice, b. Mar. 9, 1887.
8. Ruth Louise, b. Sept. 8, 1893.

THE ROBY FAMILY

1. Ichabod Roby came from Scotland about 1727, and settled in that part of Chester now Candia.

2. Lowell Roby, a descendant of Ichabod, was in Weare, evidently, as late as 1807. He removed to Fifield hill in Bridgewater, and, about 1823, to Alexandria. He was a great bear hunter and trapper. He used a steel trap that Ichabod brought from Scotland, which is now in the possession of the family. At one time he set his trap on Tenney hill, in Hebron, and caught a troublesome bear that weighed 450 pounds. At another time he caught a bear near where is now the stable of John W. Wilbur & Co. in Bristol village. In all, he killed or trapped 49 bears. He m. Margaret Kinson, and d. Alexandria, Sept. 28, 1858. She d. May 11, 1861.

CHILDREN

3. Sarah, b. Weare, Mar. 10, 1806; d. young.
4. Olive, b. W., July 20, 1807; m. Timothy Taylor.
*5. John, b. Bridgewater, June 20, 1809.
*6. Levi, b. B., Sept. 28, 1813.
7. Eldred, b. B., 1818; m. July 13, 1844, Eliza A., dau. of Josiah Sanborn, b. Alexandria, Jan. 5, 1816. He d. "Nov. 9, 1847, ae. 29." She m. (2) John Ray. (See.) Children:
    a. Sarah Alma, b. Alexandria, June 12, 1845; m. William T. Taylor. (See.)
    b. Clara Albertine, b. Lowell, Mass., Feb. 19, 1847; m. Joseph N. Dickinson. (See.)
8. Lowell Rufus, b. B., Aug. 28, 1821; m. Jan. 29, 1848, Nancy Stickney Flanders. He d. Hebron, Jan. 2, 1902, ae. 80-4-4. She res. Hebron. Eight children.
9. Charles.

(5) John Roby, b. June 20, 1809, m. Feb. 14, 1832, Elmira Smith, dau. of Abraham Dolloff (See), b. Dec. 14, 1810. He was a farmer in Alexandria, New Hampton, Moore's Mills, in Bristol, where he d. Feb. 23, 1892, ae. 82-8-3. She d. in in the family of Augustus J. Ferrin, New Hampton, Feb. 24, 1902, ae. 91-2-10.

CHILDREN

*10. Gustavus, b. Bristol, Dec. 1, 1832.
11. Olive, b. B., Feb. 8, 1835; m. Augustus J. Ferrin. (See.)

Austin H. Roby

Maude (Gordon) Roby

12. Nicholas Dolloff, b. B., Nov. 6, 1838 ; d. June 26, 1846, ae. 7-7-20.
13. Sarah M., b. B., Apr. 15, 1843 ; m. Augustus J. Ferrin. (See.)
14. Lizzie Kathleen, b. B., Apr. 11, 1853 ; was a school teacher ; m. George H. Robinson. (See.)

(6) Levi Roby, b. Sept. 28, 1813, m. Susan Sumner, dau. of Capt. Ebenezer and Mehitable (Lawrence) Thompson, b. Thomaston, Me., Feb. 22, 1817. He res. Concord, Manchester, Nashua, Lowell, Mass., and Bristol. He was for 20 years connected with the Mass. Cotton Corp., Lowell, having charge of its buildings, grounds, and the construction of foundations for new mills. He d. Bristol, Feb. 9, 1889, ae. 75-4-11 ; she d. Boston, Mass., Dec. 20, 1891, ae. 74-9-28.

CHILDREN

15. Solon, b. Alexandria, Nov. 2, 1843 ; d. Concord, Dec. 13, 1875, ae. 32-1-11.
16. Homer, b. Lowell, Mass., Oct. 5, 1848; m. Sept. 10, 1870, Clara DeAlba, dau. Marshall W. White (See), b. Aug. 21, 1850. She d. Bristol, Apr. 7, 1872, ae. 21-7-16. He m. Oct. 5, 1875, Sarah Comfort, dau. O. K. and Mary J. (Ackerman) Gray, b. Alexandria, Dec. 28, 1854. He was an employee at Calley & Currier's crutch factory for some years. Served as fireward 6 years ; as selectman two years. In 1899, removed to Hollis, where he is in trade. Democrat, Odd Fellow. Children :
  a. Bertie, b. Bristol, Feb. 11, 1872; d. Oct. 31, 1872.
  b. Levi Bertrand, b. B., Sept. 24, 1877; m. Dec. 13, 1898, Mabelle L., dau. Moses F. Wilbur. (See.) He was a hotel clerk, Bristol. Now res. Hollis. Child : Wilbur Homer, b. Lexington, Mass., Oct. 27, 1902.
  c. Ralph Homer, b. B., July 26, 1887.
17. Fred Forrest, b. Nashua, Sept. 17, 1855; m. Dec. 8, 1881, Ella, dau. Capt. Ahira and Sabra (Rogers) Kelley, b. South Dennis, Mass., Dec. 28, 1855, and d. Boston, Mass., Feb. 20, 1895, ae. 39-1-22. From Apr., 1881, till 1901, practiced dentistry in Boston ; then became member firm of John S. Doane & Co., wholesale liquor dealers, Boston.
18. Frank Lowell, b. Bridgewater, Dec. 26, 1860; d. Concord, Apr. 25, 1880, ae. 19-3-29.

(10) Gustavus Roby, b. Dec. 1, 1832, m. Nov. 21, 1861, Mary Marcia, dau. of Jonas R. Hayward, b. Alexandria, Mar. 1, 1842, and d. Bristol, June 20, 1894, ae. 52-3-19. Has spent most of his life as a paper maker ; has been for 24 years superintendent of Mason-Perkins Paper company's mill. Republican. Represented Bristol in constitutional convention of 1889.

CHILDREN

19. Austin Hayward, b. Bristol, June 17, 1867 ; m. July 28, 1888, Ola Maude, dau. of Frank A. Gordon (See), b. Jan. 22, 1868. He was in the shoe trade in Bristol ; town clerk two years till 1891, when he removed to Boston where he was actuary in a banking house ; was for a few years secretary of Y. M. C. A., in Nashua ; state secretary for New Hampshire and Vermont ; since 1900, in wholesale coal business ; now connected with the Anderson Coal Mining company as director and secretary, with office in Boston. Republican. Methodist. Res. Malden, Mass. Mrs. Roby is a superior vocalist. Child :
  a. Donald Gordon, b. Bristol, Oct. 22, 1889.

20. John Elwyn, b. B., Jan. 3, 1876; m. Oct. 16, 1897, Mary Annie, dau. Frank and Ellen Maria George, b. Chester, Vt., June 10, 1877. Child:

    a. Leslie Milton, b. Bristol, May 16, 1898.

---

1. Oscar Samuel Roby is a son of Lowell Rufus (See), b. Alexandria, Mar. 27, 1862. He m. Apr. 22, 1903, Emily, dau. of Felix Adams. (See.) He has been a hostler in Bristol since about 1896.

THE ROLLINS FAMILY

1. Reuben Rollins was of the sixth generation from James Rawlius, who migrated to America, in 1632, with the settlers of Ipswich, Mass., and afterwards settled in Dover. Reuben was b. in Epping, Nov. 15, 1751; was a soldier in the Revolutionary army, serving two years in Col. Stark's regiment, and was at the battles of Trenton and Princeton. In 1778, he m. Elizabeth, dau. of Reuben Smith, and in 1784, removed to Sanbornton. He d. in Sanbornton, June 18, 1808, ae. 56-7-3; she d. after a long widowhood, Aug. 28, 1853, ae. 93-7-. They had thirteen children, of whom two removed to Bridgewater.

    ＊2. Joshua, b. Mar. 19, 1779.
    ＊3. Joseph, b. Sanbornton, Apr. 8, 1789.

(2) Joshua, b. Mar. 19, 1779, m. Lydia, dau. Simeon Rollins, of Andover. He removed to Bridgewater about 1810, where he d. Dec. 9, 1858, ae. 79-8-20. She was living in Bridgewater in 1868, ae. 85.

CHILDREN

    ＊4. Reuben, b. Sanbornton, Feb. 10, 1809.
    5. Mary, b. Bridgewater, June 5, 1811; m. June 5, 1837, David B. Clement, of Thornton, who afterward res. in Bridgewater.
    6. Harriet, b. B., Jan. 31, 1821; d. Aug. 19, 1825, ae. 4-6-18.

(3) Joseph Rollins, b. Apr. 8, 1789; in early life removed to the Richard Brown farm in Bridgewater, where he had made for himself a home. He m., Dec. 6, 1812, Mary, dau. Samuel Huckins, of New Hampton. She d. Mar. 23, 1876, ae. 75, and he m. (2) the widow of Rev. Paul Perkins. He was ordained a "ruling elder" in the Free Baptist church in Bridgewater, in 1829. About 1832, he located at No. Bristol. In company with Ebenezer Kendall, he built the saw-mill where is now the electric light plant, and in company with his son, Samuel, operated this mill for twenty-eight years. Was deacon of Free Baptist church in Bristol. He d. in Bristol village, Aug. 9, 1877, ae. 88-4-1. She d. in Bristol.

CHILDREN

7. Eliza, b. Bridgewater, Sept. 13, 1813; m. May 5, 1833, Putnam Spaulding, of Bridgewater, later a merchant in Chelsea, Mass. She d. Sept. 28, 1848, ae. 35-0-15. He m. (2) Mary Cutler. Children :

    a. Putnam Frost, d. young.   *b.* Joseph, d. young.

*8. Samuel H., b. B., June 30, 1815.
  9. Sarah J., b. B., Oct. 14, 1817 ; m. John F. Tilton. (See.)
 10. Mary S., b. B., Apr. 20, 1821 ; m. Samuel S. Fellows. (See.)
*11. Joseph Flanders, b. B., Nov. 6, 1824.
*12. Richard B., b. B., Jan. 13, 1829.
 13. Harriet, b. B., Feb. 16, 1831 ; d. May 9, 1842, ae. 11-2-23.
*14. Lyman, b. Bristol, Nov. 22, 1832.

(4) Reuben Rollins, b. Feb. 10, 1809, m. (1) Apr. 27, 1834, Laura, dau. of Samuel Sleeper (See), b. Feb. 24, 1808, and d. Jan. 24, 1835, in Bristol, ae. 26-11-. He m. (2) Aug. 31, 1835, Lavinia, sister of his first wife, b. June 29, 1803, and d. Jan. 27, 1859, ae. 55-6-28. He m. (3) Mrs. Rosilla D. Evans, Oct. 23, 1864. He removed from Bridgewater to Bristol about 1836, owned and operated the woolen-mill on Willow street. Farmer and school teacher. In 1855, removed to Caledonia, Minn., where he d. in the family of his son, Henry M., May 9, 1903, ae. 94-2-29.

CHILDREN

*15. Samuel Sleeper, b. Bridgewater, May 1, 1836.
*16. Joshua, b. B., May 21, 1838.
 17. Henry Morse, b. B., Feb. 4, 1844 ; m. Ellen Lenora, dau. Lyman B. and Rosilla D. Evans, b. Jan. 13, 1850, in Tilton. He is a railway postal clerk ; res. Caledonia. Children :

    a. Fred Herbert, b. Caledonia, Sept. 30, 1867.
    b. George Lee, b. C., Jan. 3, 1870.
    c. Charles Albert, b. C., Mar. 29, 1872.
    d. Lulu Mabel, b. C., Jan. 19, 1883.

(8) Col. Samuel H. Rollins, b. June 30, 1815, came to Bristol with his parents when a young man. Was a farmer and manufacturer of lumber, and res. near No. Bristol cemetery, west side of highway. He m., Oct. 17, 1838, Irene Whipple, of Hebron, who d. Oct. 30, 1875, ae. 57-10-. He m. (2) Feb. 27, 1876, Mrs. Huldah D. Walker, and d. May 12, 1895, ae. 79-10-12. Republican. Served four years as selectman ; was colonel of 34th Regiment militia. Odd Fellow, Free Baptist.

CHILDREN, all supposed to have been born in Bristol

 18. Ellen Caroline, b. Mar. 6, 1840 ; m. Levi D. Johnson. (See.)
 19. Harriet Augusta, b. Sept. 9, 1842 ; m. Charles N. Drake. (See.)
 20. William Henry Harrison, b. Nov. 29, 1843 ; d. June 8, 1863, ae. 19-6-9.
 21. Ora A., b. July 28, 1845 ; m. George H. Fowler. (See.)
 22. Eldora A., b. June 10, 1848 ; m. Fred W. Prescott. (See.)
 23. Samuel Dinsmore, b. Aug. 17, 1849 ; m. Mar. 20, 1871, Clara M.,

dau. of Amos Damon. (See.) Divorced. He m. (2) Mary Bartlett.
Children :

> *a.* Willie Weston, b. Bristol, Jan. 16, 1872. Res. Hyde Park,
> Mass.
> *b.* Harold Bertrand, b. B., May 21, 1875.

(11) Joseph F. Rollins, b. Nov. 6, 1824, m. Oct. 29, 1848,
Amanda J. Ingalls, dau. of Gilman. (See.) Was the first
fireman and later engineer on Bristol branch railroad for ten
years, and subsequently in trade where is now Rollins's block.
Represented town in legislature. Republican, Free Baptist.
He d. July 13, 1864, ae. 39-8-7. She m. (2) Capt. George W.
Dow. (See.)

CHILDREN

24. Leston Laforest, b. Bristol, Feb. 3, 1850; m. Dec. 1, 1878, Addie
M., dau. Nicholas T. Chase (See), b. July 2, 1858. He built Rollins's
block in Central square. Mill operative. Republican, Mason. Child :

> *a.* Edith Mae, b. Bristol, May 24, 1882. Is a compositor in
> *Enterprise* office.

25. Daniel Webster, b. B., Dec. 8, 1852; d. Dec. 21, 1855, ae. 3-0-13.

(12) Richard B. Rollins, b. Jan. 13, 1829, m. Martha
Gray, b. Sheffield, Vt., Nov. 22, 1829. He was a farmer at No.
Bristol, where he d. Apr. 2, 1886, ae. 57-2-19. She res. Lake-
port.

CHILDREN

26. Franklin Leroy, b. Bristol, Oct. 31, 1853; m. Dec. 16, 1875, Mary
E. Colby, dau. of Wilson, b. Hill, Dec. 27, 1851. Was a stone mason
and contractor at Bristol, and after 1887, at Lakeport, where he d. Aug.
2, 1896, ae. 42-9-1. Children :

> *a.* Charles Albert, b. Bristol, Sept. 21, 1877; d. 1878.
> *b.* Bert Wilson, b. B., Jan. 12, 1879.
> *c.* George Parker, b. B., Apr. 21, 1882.

27. George Gray, b. B., Dec. 11, 1854; m. Nov. 26, 1890, Nellie M.,
dau. of Abel H. and Emily M. (Coburn) Stone, b. Lowell, Mass., Apr.
3, 1861. No children. He left Bristol 1871; since 1879, has been foreman
for "Lake company," Lakeport.

28. Mary Eliza, b. B., Feb. 28, 1859; m. Oct. 28, 1878, Orvis Thomas
Muzzey, b. Hebron, Mar. 18, 1854. Res. Lakeport. Children :

> *a.* Gertrude Estelle, b. Lakeport, Sept. 17, 1879; d. Nov. 9, 1885,
> ae. 6-1-22.
> *b.* Victor Gray, b. L., July 10, 1897.

(14) Lyman Rollins, b. Nov. 22, 1832, m. July 4, 1854,
Caroline Augusta, dau. Timothy P., and Mary Jane Flanders,
b. Hopkinton, Apr. 5, 1837. Was engineer on Northern road,
and for four years previous to May, 1859, engineer on road
from Milwaukee to LaCrosse, Wis. Served in 6th Regt., N. H.
Vols. (See Roll of Honor.) Went to California in 1866, where
he was engineer. Died in New Orleans, Sept., 1885, ae. 52-10-.
Mrs. Rollins was divorced in June, 1867, and is now Mrs. A. A.
Young, 4 Fuller street, Concord. She is the founder of the
Pythian Sisterhood.

CHILD

29. Lyman J. T., b. Concord, July 6, 1855; m. Oct. 13, 1880, Ellen Lucy Carter. He d. Concord, Nov. 11, 1892, ae. 37-4-5. Mrs. Rollins res. Concord. Children:

 a. Lyman, b. Apr. 21, 1881.
 b. Harry Lewis, b. Apr. 27, 1883.
 c. William Manly, b. Jan. 26, 1885.

(15) Samuel S. Rollins, b. Bridgewater, May 1, 1836. He removed to Minnesota with his father in 1855, and m., Nov. 8, 1860, Martha Melissa Elmore, b. Farmington, Me., Oct. 31, 1843. Res. Alma City, Minn.

CHILDREN

30. Martha Lavina, b. Aug. 16, 1861; d. Caledonia, Minn., Jan. 18, 1864, ae. 2-5-2.
31. Edith Augusta, b. May 22, 1865; m. Mar. 24, 1887, John Harmon.
32. Henry C., b. Dec. 1, 1866; m. July 28, 1892, Ella A. Runnels.
33. Lilian Grace, b. Dec. 5, 1871; m. Mar. 18, 1890, Frank Vanderwaka.
34. Nora May, b. July 21, 1876.
35. Ruby, b. Mar. 25, 1889.

(16) Joshua Rollins, b. May 21, 1838, went West with his father, and m., Nov. 5, 1876, Emma J., dau. of William R. and Charlotte (Crow) Reynolds, b. Clarington, Pa., Feb. 17, 1860. They res. Caledonia, Minn., where he d., Apr. 2, 1884, ae. 45-10-11.

CHILDREN

36. William Sleeper, b. Caledonia, Nov. 21, 1877.
37. Reuben, b. C., June 4, 1879.
38. Pearl, b. C., Sept. 10, 1881.
39. Ruby, b. C., Apr. 18, 1885.
40. Ralph Harold, b. C., Nov. 7, 1888.

THE ROUNDS FAMILY

1. Charles Edgar Rounds is the son of William and Lucretia (Manchester) Rounds. He was b. West Buxton, Me., Oct. 25, 1864, and m. July 11, 1895, Katherine Belle Wilbur, dau. of George H. and Elizabeth Augusta Spiller, b. Hill, May 27, 1866. He was in the wholesale dry goods business as traveling salesman, 1880 till Dec., 1894; since in retail dry goods trade in Bristol. Republican, Mason.

THE ROWE FAMILY

1. Louis Rowe (spelled Rhault in Canada) was b. Gentilly, Canada, Feb. 14, 1838; came to Bristol in 1858, and by his good nature, ability, and desire to learn, made many friends. He served in Co. D, 12th Regt., N. H. Vols. (See Roll of

Honor.) He m., 1867, Phebe, dau. of Sewell Sanborn (See), b. May 21, 1851, and d. of consumption, June 30, 1869, ae. 18-1-9. He m. (2) Aug. 31, 1872, Sarah Jane, dau. of David M. Merrill (See), b. Sept. 11, 1848. He was a carriage-maker in the employ of Lovejoy & Kelley. He d. of wounds received in the service, June 27, 1882, ae. 44-4-13. Methodist, Republican. She removed to Ashland, and d. in Boston, Oct. 27, 1894, as the result of a surgical operation, ae. 46-1-16.

CHILDREN

2. Nellie Edwidge, b. Bristol, Mar. 2, 1869 ; d. June 5, 1869.
3. Ellie Etta, b. B., June 6, 1873; res. Ashland. Unm.
4. Louis Elmer, b. B., Nov. 5, 1874; concreter; res. Malone, N. Y.
5. Annie Leoza, b. B., July 9, 1877 ; d. Aug. 25, 1879, ae. 2-1-16.
6. Charles David, b. B., May 21, 1879 ; employed in train dispatcher's office at Woodsville.

THE SANBORN FAMILIES

The Sanborns of America are the descendants of the Sambornes or Sambournes of England. These names appear on the records of England from the middle of the 12th century. The ancestor of a large part at least of the Sanborns of New England was John Samborne, b. in England, a few years previous to 1600. He m. a dau. of Rev. Stephen Bachiler, and d. in England in 1632, leaving three sons : John, b. 1620 ; William, b. 1622 ; Stephen, b. 1624. Rev. Stephen Bachiler came to America in the ship William and Francis, and landed in Boston June 5, 1632, in company with the three sons named above. They all settled in Lynn, and here Mr. Bachiler, though over seventy years of age, was pastor of a church. Difficulties arose and he removed to Ipswich, and, in 1638, to Hampton, where he was installed as first pastor of the Congregational church there. The Sanborns of Bristol are the descendants of the first two of the three sons named. In the early years of New Chester all spelled the name Sandborn.

1. Lieut. John Samborne, b. England, 1620, m. (1) Mary Tuck, dau. of Robert. She d. Dec. 30, 1668, and he m. (2) Margaret Moulton, a widow, dau. of Robert Page. She d. July 13, 1699. He d. Oct. 20, 1692, ae. 72. He was the father of twelve children, of whom the sixth was

2. Joseph, b. Mar. 13, 1659. He m., Dec. 28, 1682, Mary Gove, dau. of Capt. Edward, of Hampton. He was a farmer at Hampton, and there d. between 1722 and 1724. He had eight children of whom the fifth was

3. Abraham, b. Mar. 10, 1696. He m., Jan. 22, 1718, Dorothy, dau. of John Smith, who d. Jan. 11, 1788. He d. Sept. 2, 1757, ae. 61-5-22. He had ten children, of whom the fifth was

4. Daniel, b. Kensington, May 28, 1728. He m. (1) July 27, 1748, Anna, dau. of Sherburne Tilton. She d. June 8, 1759, and he m. (2) July 9, 1760, Mary Collins. He res. Kensington, Chester, and Franklin, where he d., May 25, 1812, ae. 83-11-27. His remains rest in the old, neglected burying-ground near the track of the Bristol branch railroad in Franklin. He had nine children. Of these, Abraham, b. 1762, m. Deborah Scribner, and removed to Bridgewater. Daniel, b. Nov. 21, 1763, m. Molly Smith, and settled in Hill. The following settled in Bristol :

    5.   Mary, b. Kensington, Sept. 24, 1751 ; m. Peter Sleeper. (See.)
    *6.   Theophilus, b. Oct. 24, 1753.
    *7.   Sherburn, b. July 10, 1756.
    *8.   Elijah, b. Sept. 22, 1761.

THEOPHILUS SANBORN AND HIS DESCENDANTS

(6) Theophilus Sanborn, son of Daniel, b. Oct. 24, 1753, m. in 1779, Mary Sleeper, dau. of David (See), b. Sept. 22, 1758. Before he m. he came to Bristol, and built a log cabin just above the present residence of Mrs. J. W. Sanborn, on the east side of the highway, on north slope of New Chester mountain. In the spring of 1779, he brought his young wife here and such household goods as could be brought on a pack horse. They occupied the cabin for some years, when a two-story frame house took its place. Mr. Sanborn was the first shoemaker and tanner in town and had his tan pits near his house. He was a soldier in the Revolutionary army, being a sergeant in Capt. Page's company, and served in Rhode Island in Sept., 1777. He was also a member of Capt. Moses Leavitt's company and Col. Moses Nichols's regiment in expedition to Rhode Island, Aug., 1778. Another account says he was a drum-major. He d. in the family of his son, Daniel, in Bristol, Mar. 4, 1839, ae. 85-4-10. She d. in Bristol, May 2, 1845, ae. 86-7-10. Methodists, Democrat.

CHILDREN, all born in Bristol

    9.   Margaret, b. Sept. 30, 1779 ; m. Stephen Gale. (See.)
    *10.   Sherburn, b. Dec. 8, 1780.
    11.   Daniel, b. Feb. 10, 1783 ; d. 1783.
    12.   Polly, b. Mar. 30, 1785. Lived in the family of her brother, Daniel, where she d. unm., Sept. 19, 1851, ae. 66-5-19.
    13.   Ruth, b. Mar. 6, 1786 ; m. Aaron Favor. (See.)
    14.   Nancy, b. Nov. 18, 1788 ; m. Moses Worthen. (See.)
    *15.   Theophilus, b. Jan. 8, 1791.
    16.   Sally, b. Sept. 17, 1793 ; m. Rev. Hezekiah Davis. (See.)
    17.   Catherine, b. Nov. 11, 1795 ; d. Apr. 2, 1797, ae. 1-4-21.
    *18.   Daniel, b. Aug. 23, 1797.
    19.   David, b. July 21, 1800 ; d. July 10, 1802, ae. 1-11-19.
    20.   Catherine, b. Aug. 6, 1803 ; m. Sept. 5, 1827, Nathan Davis, of Canaan. They res. Canaan till three children were b., and then removed to Ohio. She d. East Trumbull, Ashtabula Co., Ohio, Jan. 9, 1863, ae. 59-5-3 ; he d. same place, June 27, 1882. Children :

a. Mary Jane, b. Aug. 30, 1828; d., unm., in Ohio, Mar. 4, 1894, ae. 65-6-4.

b. Almira, b. July 7, 1831; m. Feb. 16, 1846, William Young, Hartsgrove, O., where he d. Jan. 10, 1881, ae. 61-1-10. Two children : (1) Elbert William, b. June 20, 1849; m. Lucy Fenton and res. Hartsgrove. (2) Irena E., b. Sept. 28, 1850; m. William Rice, Dec. 19, 1871. Three children. Res. Hartsgrove.

c. Elvira, twin sister of Almira; m. June 2, 1852, Elhanan W. Adams. Res. East Trumbull, O. Children : (1) Edmond U., b. June 26, 1854; m. 1878, Ella Brown. (2) Laura O., b. July 11, 1857; d. May 4, 1862, ae. 4-9-23. (3) Georgia S., b. Aug. 14, 1871.

d. Sarah, b. Mar. 25, 1836; m. Jan. 17, 1853, Samuel T. Adams. Child : Lucy C., b. Apr. 5, 1857; m. Arthur J. White. Res. Boistfort, Louis Co., Wash.

e. George Washington, b. May 25, 1838; m. Mar. 20, 1863, Mary Elizabeth Brooks. Res. Piper City, Ford Co., Ill.

(10)   Sherburn Sanborn, son of Maj. Theophilus, b. Dec. 8, 1780, m. June 24, 1802, Sarah Worthen, dau. of Samuel. (See.) He was a farmer and was drowned while driving logs down the Newfound river, June 29, 1807, ae. 26-6-21. She m. (2) Moses W. Merrill. (See.)

CHILDREN

*21.   Martin Luther, b. Bristol, Jan. 1, 1803.

22.   Laura Worthen, b. B., Sept. 5, 1804; m. Rev. William D. Cass, Mar. 11, 1824, and d. Plymouth, Dec. 5, 1830, ae. 26-3-0.

(15)   Theophilus Sanborn, son of Maj. Theophilus, b. Jan. 8, 1791, m. Sept. 15, 1815, Fanny Cross, dau. of Jonathan, b. New Salem, Mar. 6, 1794, and d. Hartsgrove, Ashtabula Co., Ohio, Aug. 23, 1866, ae. 72-5-17.   He d. Ford Co., Ill., Aug. 25, 1872, ae. 81-7-17.

CHILDREN

23.   Hannah Dustin, b. Bristol, Oct. 5, 1816; m. Joseph Brooks in 1840, and d. Mar. 16, 1890, ae. 73-5-11.   Children :

a. Mary Elizabeth, m. Rev. George Davis.

b. Emily Phebe, m. John Baer, and had two children.

c. Caroline Rebecca, m. Henry Pepper.

d. Olive Estella, m. John Baer.

24.   Jonathan Cross, b. B., Feb. 13, 1819; went to Indiana when 20 years of age, and m. Ophelia Porter. They res. in Michigan City, Ind. They had one daughter who d. of consumption at 22. The mother d. of same disease four years before. He d. Dec. 3, 1892, ae. 73-9-20.

25.   Rebecca Dustin, b. Canaan, July 30, 1824; m. June 8, 1848, Fitch Andrews, of Trumbull, Ohio.

26.   Mary, b. Bristol, Dec. 13, 1825; d. Apr. 14, 1836, in Bath, ae. 10-4-1.

27.   Lorain H., b. B., Oct. 6, 1829; d. unm., in Trumbull, Ohio, Feb. 11, 1865, ae. 35-4-5.

(18)   Maj. Daniel Sanborn, son of Maj. Theophilus, b. Aug. 23, 1797, m. Oct. 22, 1818, Hannah Worthen, dau. Lieut. Samuel (See), b. July 17, 1796.   She d. Mar. 9, 1831, ae. 34-7-22, and he m. (2) Jemima (Edwards) Blake, widow of John, and dau. of John Edwards (See), b. Apr. 29, 1799, and d. Dec.

24, 1882, ae. 83-7-25. He was a farmer on the Favor Locke farm, west of New Chester mountain, where he d. July 19, 1854, ae. 56-10-26.

CHILDREN, all born in Bristol

28. Plummer Worthing, b. Feb. 15, 1821 ; m. May 30, 1844, Sarah F., dau. of Jonathan Dearborn, b. North Danville, Feb. 9, 1819, and d. in Candia, May 28, 1880, ae. 61-3-19. He d. in Hartford, Wis., Jan. 24, 1893, ae. 71-11-9. He was postmaster of Candia many years, and justice of the peace. He removed to Wisconsin eight years before his death. Child :

    a. Clarence, b. Bristol, May 27, 1847 ; d. Mar. 5, 1850, ae. 2-9-8.
    b. Abbie Lowell (adopted), m. William H. Benson.

*29. Charles Heading, b. Feb. 23, 1824.
  30. Jane Moffet, b. Dec. 10, 1826 ; m. Jacob W. Martin. (See.)
*31. Luther B., b. Mar. 16, 1829.
  32. Hannah Worthing, b. Mar. 1, 1831 ; m. Dec. 3, 1854, Lewis Burnham Rock, b. Drummondville, Canada, Aug. 13, 1825. In March, 1844, being then nineteen years of age, he left his home with $2.50 in his pocket, and his wardrobe in a small bundle, and walked 200 miles to Bristol. Here he met one with whom his fortune was to be closely linked, Sherburn S. Merrill, then proprietor of the village hotel, but later, general superintendent of the Chicago, Milwaukee & St. Paul railroad. He was given employment at the hotel by Mr. Merrill, remaining four years, then went to Lowell, Mass., and one year later to California, sailing December, 1849. In July, 1854, he went to Milwaukee, and became train baggagemaster on the Milwaukee and Prairie du Chien railroad. In 1856, was made passenger conductor, and in 1865, assistant superintendent, and in November, 1867, superintendent of the Northern Division of the Chicago, Milwaukee & St. Paul railroad, which position he held till his death, May 28, 1888. His age was 62-9-15. His widow res. in Milwaukee. Children :

    a. Lewis F., b. Milwaukee, July 29, 1857 ; m. Nov. 17, 1885, Minnie Johnson, at Aberdeen, So. Dakota.
    b. Charles Frederick, b. M., Dec. 18, 1867. Res. Milwaukee.
    c. Frank Daniel, b. M., Mar. 24, 1871. Res. Milwaukee.

(21) Martin Luther Sanborn, son of Sherburn, b. Jan. 1, 1803, m. Dec. 17, 1829, Emeline S., dau. of James and Ruth (Weeks) Smith, b. Oct. 23, 1811, in Bath. He was a farmer in Bath, but late in life removed to the West and d. Waukesha, Wis., June 19, 1885, ae. 82-5-18. She d. Milwaukee, Oct. 8, 1900, ae. 88-11-15.

CHILDREN

33. George Washington, b. Bath, Sept. 25, 1832 ; m. Eliza Etta Richards, Oct. 2, 1859, at Monroe, Wis. He commenced his life work as "yard man" at Boston, for the Fitchburg railroad. In September, 1854, with his brother Sherburn, he located at Milwaukee, Wis., and became brakeman on the Milwaukee & Mississippi railroad ; soon after, passenger conductor. From 1868 to 1870, he was assistant superintendent of the Northern division of the Chicago, Milwaukee & St. Paul railroad. Was superintendent of the Iowa and Dakota division till 1885, when impaired health compelled him to rest for two years. He then accepted the superintendency of the Southern California railroad. In 1889, he settled in Mason City, Iowa, where he still res. Children :

    a. Harry Richards, b. July 6, 1862 ; res. Huron, S. D.
    b. George L., b. Jan. 21, 1865 ; res. Edgemont, S. D.

24

    c. James S., b. Mar. 21, 1867; res. Pukwana, S. D.
    d. Bonnie Anna, b. Dec. 1, 1869; res. Mason City.

  34. Sherburn, b. B., Sept. 15, 1834; m. (1) Nov. 10, 1864, Laura L. Moss, of Fort Wayne, Ind., b. July 8, 1840, and d. May 6, 1866, ae. 25-9-28. He m. (2) June 1, 1870, Eliza V. Cary, of Milwaukee, b. May 10, 1845. Sherburn went to Milwaukee in 1854 with his brother, and secured a position with the American Express company on the Milwaukee & Mississippi railroad. In 1863, he entered the employ of the Chicago and Northwestern railroad, and was for many years general superintendent of this great corporation, with its 6,000 miles of track, ranking among the best railroad men in the country. Now retired. Res. Milwaukee. Children :

    a. Edwin Cary, b. June 25, 1873; d. 1874.
    b. Mabel, b. July 17, 1875.
    c. Jesse E., b. June 15, 1877.

  35. James Smith, b. B., Nov. 14, 1837; m. June 12, 1872, Anna E. Esterbrook, of Portage, Wis., b. Aug. 13, 1847. He was a resident of Bristol for some years previous to 1870, being in the employ of Draper & Berry, glove manufacturers. Soon after this he went to Milwaukee, Wis., where he has accumulated a competency in the ice business. Children :

    a. Ellen Dunlap, b. May 7, 1873.
    b. Dwight Alexander, b. Sept. 12, 1874; a chemist in Milwaukee.
    c. Anna Louise, b. July 6, 1876.
    d. Ralph Sherburn, b. Sept. 8, 1882.

  36. Frank Luther, b. B., Aug 27, 1848; m. Ellen Barker, of Lisbon, Mar. 10, 1875. A successful manufacturer at Portage, Wis. Children :

    a. Edith Emeline, b. Apr. 14, 1876.
    b. Elizabeth Turner, b. Nov. 6, 1877.
    c. Raymond Parker, b. Nov. 22, 1884.

  37. Frederick Augustus, b. Apr. 12, 1852; m. Ida Baker. No children. Res. South Bend, Ind.

  (29) Charles H. Sanborn, son of Maj. Daniel, b. Feb. 23, 1824, m. (1) May, 1850, Parmelia O., b. Mar. 1, 1832; d. Feb. 27, 1857, ae. 24-11-26; (2) Sarah Jane, b. Feb. 11, 1830, d. July 24, 1885, ae. 55-5-13; both were daughters of John M. Bowen. He went to Milwaukee in 1835; was engineer on the Milwaukee & LaCrosse railroad, and later on the Milwaukee & Watertown railroad. In 1863, he was promoted to passenger conductor on the Chicago, Milwaukee & St. Paul railroad, and was killed while coupling cars at Oconomowoc, Wis., Sept. 7, 1865, ae. 41-6-14.

CHILDREN

  38. Charles H., b. Aug. 5, 1851; d. Bristol, Sept. 3, 1854, ae. 3-0-28.
  39. Hannah J., b. Nov. 30, 1853; d. B., Sept. 7, 1854.
  40. Lewis Henry, b. Sept. 26, 1856; d. at San Bernardino, Cal., Feb. 1. 1890, ae. 33-4-5.
  41. Sarah Parmelia, b. Watertown, Wis., Feb. 6, 1860; d. San Bernardino, Apr. 17, 1879, ae. 19-2-11.

  (31) Luther B. Sanborn, son of Maj. Daniel, b. Mar. 16, 1829, m. Aug. 17, 1856, Sarah E., dau. of Joshua and Polly Norris, b. Wayne, Me., Aug. 16, 1829. They res. Freeport, Ill., where he is foreman of the Chicago, Milwaukee & St. Paul shops.

CHILDREN

42. Joshua Norris, b. Milwaukee, Wis., July 19, 1858; m. Sept. 7, 1885, Charlie Talley. He is master mechanic of the Brainard & Northern Minn. railway. Children:

    a. Minnie, b. 1886.   *b.* Sarah, b. 1889.

43. Laura Bell, b. Mar. 4, 1860; d. Apr. 25, 1860.

44. Alice Jane, b. Nov. 22, 1861; m. Jan. 30, 1889, George Irving Brown. Res. Watertown, Wis.

45. Anna Maude, b. Nov. 25, 1868; m. Sept. 9, 1891, Frank A. Stoltze.

SHERBURN SANBORN AND HIS DESCENDANTS

(7) Sherburn Sanborn, son of Daniel, was b. July 10, 1756. He was a soldier of the Revolutionary army, from Kensington. In 1775, he was serving at Portsmouth, in company with Moses Sleeper, who later settled in Bristol, and Abram Hook, who settled on the Gilbert B. Dolloff farm in Bridgewater. In 1777, he served in Rhode Island, and, in 1780, was in Colonel Bartlett's regiment at West Point. In one enlistment his occupation is given as a cordwainer. He m. Molly Hoyt, dau. of John, of South Hampton, b. Jan. 26, 1764. He came to Bristol about 1780, and built a log cabin on the site of the present farmhouse of Mrs. J. W. Sanborn, and to this humble home he brought his bride. Besides his household goods he brought a pig and cow, but the bears carried off his pig and nearly killed his cow. Some years later he built a frame house where he kept tavern. He removed to Chester to care for his father-in-law, and there d. May 8, 1836, ae. 79-9-28.

CHILDREN, all born in Bristol

*46. Moses Hoyt, b. Sept. 22, 1783.

*47. John Hoyt, b. Apr. 2, 1789.

48. Dolly, b. Aug. 17, 1791; m. Ebenezer Poor, and was the mother of eight children: Climena, Boardman, Sarah Ann, Hannah, Polly, Sherburn, Octave, Orren B.

49. Nancy, b. Oct. 17, 1793; m. Nathaniel Brown, of Fremont.

50. Lucretia, d. in Bristol.

*51. Simon Merrill, b. Dec. 15, 1796.

(46) Moses H. Sanborn, son of Sherburn, b. Sept. 22, 1783, m. in Fremont, Sept. 20, 1801, Susanna, dau. of Jonathan and Sarah (Moulton) Brown, b. Fremont, Feb. 10, 1785, and there d. May 15, 1850, ae. 65-3-5. He was a farmer in Fremont till about 1807, when he returned to Bristol, occupied his father's farm for a few years, and here a part of his children were b., when he again went to Fremont to care for his wife's parents, and there d., Apr. 21, 1867, ae. 83-6-29.

CHILDREN

52. Sarah, b. Oct. 14, 1801; m. Ariel Sanborn.

53. Asa, b. Jan. 30, 1803; m. (1) Dec. 31, 1825, Farrena Gilman, who d. Mar. 20, 1841, (2) Oct. 27, 1841, Abigail Sanborn. Res. and d. in Fremont.

54.   Rena, b. July 15, 1804; m. James Sawyer, of Danville; d. June 13, 1887, ae. 82-10-28.

55.   Moses Nelson, b. Jan. 9, 1806; m. Dec. 13, 1827, Cyrene Tucker, dau. Benjamin, b. 1806.   He d. June 4, 1873, ae. 67-4-25.   She d.

56.   True Glidden, b. Bristol, Jan. 8, 1808; m. Nov. 25, 1830, Rachel, dau. David Sleeper, of Sandown, b. July 12, 1811; d. July 20, 1885, ae. 74-0-8. He d. Apr. 19, 1886, ae. 78-3-11.   Farmer in Sandown.   Children :

    a.   Charles, b. July 27, 1832; m.; no issue; res. Fremont.

    b.   Harrison, b. Oct. 12, 1836; m. Nov. 24, 1881, Sylvia H. Beede. of Fremont.   He was a lumber merchant in Epping.   Daughter, Sylvia, b. May 26, 1883.

    c.   Francellus Burton, b. Apr. 3, 1844; unm.; res. Sandown.

57.   John L., b. B., Mar. 8, 1810; m. 1828, Hannah, dau. of David Sanborn (See), b. Jan. 31, 1809.   He was a farmer in Fremont, where he d. Mar. 8, 1845, ae. 35-0-0.   She m. (2) Oren Poore, of Fremont, and d. Fremont, Mar. 4, 1897, ae. 88-1-3.   Children :

    a.   David, b. Sept. 25, 1828; m. Nov., 1847, Elizabeth Branscomb. Children :   (1) Elizabeth Ann, b. June, 1848.   (2) John, b. Nov., 1850.   (3) Arabella, b. Sept., 1852.   (4) —— b. 1856.

    b.   Sarah Ann, b. Fremont, June 26, 1832; m. Warren W. Wilbur. (See.)

    c.   Otis Frank, b. Aug. 4, 1835; d. unm., about 1886, ae. 51.

    d.   William Foote, b. May 11, 1839; m. (1) Frank Morey, d. 1864; (2) Emma Smith, d. 1871; (3) Kate Flanders.   He d.; she res. in Massachusetts.

58.   Jonathan Brown, b. Oct. 12, 1811 : m., Sept. 17, 1837, Rachel S. Tilton.   He was a farmer in Sandown; d. Aug. 30, 1884, ae. 72-10-18. She d. Dec., 1887.   Seven children.

59.   Nancy, b. July 13, 1813; d. Mar. 5, 1814.

60.   Sherburn, b. Dec. 18, 1814; m. Dec. 12, 1839, Elizabeth Sanborn, and d. Apr. 27, 1889, ae. 74-4-9.   She d. May 29, 1880.

61.   Nancy, b. May 2, 1816; d. Sept. 20, 1824, ae. 8-4-18.

62.   Lewis, b. July 18, 1819; m. Oct. 18, 1842, Abigail F. York.   He d. in Fremont, April, 1891, ae. 71-9-.   She d.

63.   Alvah, b. Mar. 6, 1822; d. June 3, 1823, ae. 1-2-27.

64.   Alvah, b. Dec. 31, 1823; a prosperous farmer in Fremont.   He m., Sept. 26, 1843, Nancy, dau. John Page, of Sandown.   Children :

    a.   John Page.   *b.*   Susan Emily.

    c.   Alden F.   *d.*   Eugene Dana.

65.   Nancy, b. Sept. 14, 1825 ; d. Jan. 27, 1843, unm., ae. 17-4-13.

(47) John H. Sanborn, son of Sherburn, b. Apr. 2, 1789, went to Fremont, where he m., Mar. 21, 1810, Olive Sawyer, of Danville, b. Hawke, Nov. 25, 1790.   He was a farmer and brick mason in Fremont till about 1817, when he returned to Bristol and took possession of his father's farm.   He erected the farmhouse now standing, and there he res. till 1832, when he removed to the farm now occupied by George Price, on the road to Hill, where he d. May 17, 1849, ae. 60-1-15.   She d. in Fremont.

CHILDREN

66.   Adeline, b. Fremont, Oct. 22, 1812 ; m. Sept. 19, 1833, Parker P. Roberts, and d. in Lawrence, Mass.

67.   Luella Bartlett, b. F., Sept. 30, 1814; d. unm., Jan. 22, 1836, ae. 21-3-22.

68.   John Washington, b. F., Apr. 21, 1816; m. June 24, 1841, Mary C.,

dau. Daniel Bennett (See), b. Oct. 5, 1824. He spent his life in Bristol. He built and occupied for years the farmhouse now occupied by Benjamin Gray, on the Hill road. Was a brick mason as well as a farmer. He d. Jan. 9, 1885, ae. 68-8-18. She res. on the farm originally settled by Sherburn Sanborn on north slope of New Chester mountain. No children.

69. Sherburn Sawyer, b. Bristol, Mar. 31, 1818; d. Apr. 21, 1818.
70. Betsey Ann, b. B., June 27, 1819; m. Stephen L. Gordon. (See.)
*71. Sherburn Sawyer, b. B., Mar. 29, 1821.
72. Mary H., b. B., July 6, 1823; m. (1) Oct. 24, 1844, Daniel M. Elliott. He went to California in 1849, and was never heard from later. She m. (2) June 1, 1857, Capt. Isaiah Sanborn. Child :
    a. Helen Elliott, m. —— Colston ; res. Fremont.

73. James Templeton, b. B., June 28, 1825; m. Sarah W., dau. of Nathaniel and Abigail M. (Williams) Moulton, b. Oct. 24, 1818. He was a carpenter and builder. Was selectman five years, deputy sheriff three years, and served as town recruiting agent during Civil war. He d. Bristol, Sept. 26, 1884, ae. 59-2-28. She res. with her daughter, Mrs. M. F. Wilbur, in Lexington, Mass. Children, all b. in Bristol :
    a. John Hoyt, b. May 10, 1846 ; d. Feb. 16, 1851, ae. 4-9-6.
    b. John Hoyt, b. Oct. 16, 1851 ; d. July 14, 1852.
    c. Kate E., b. Nov. 16, 1855 ; m. Moses F. Wilbur. (See.)
    d. Alla Betsey, b. Feb. 9, 1858 ; m. June 23, 1877, James S. Roberts, b. Barton, Vt., Jan. 26, 1836, his second wife. Res. Medford, Mass. Children : (1) Alla Bessie, b. Exeter, May 24, 1878. (2) James Levi, b. E., May 4, 1880. (3) Ivaloo, b. Medford. Apr. 12. 1887.

74. Sarah Jane, b. B., July 12, 1827; m. Feb. 3, 1846, Augustus S. Bunker, Durham ; d. Lawrence, Mass., Apr. 24, 1850, ae. 22-9-12. Children :
    a. Franz, b. Lawrence, Jan. 4, 1847 ; d. Oct. 11, 1848, ae. 1-9-7.
    b. Dion Cammillo, b. L., Mar. 9, 1850. Res. Lawrence.

75. Abram Jackson, b. B., Aug. 6, 1829; d. Bristol, Aug. 1, 1846, ae. 16-11-25.
76. Caroline Matilda, b. B., Aug. 27, 1831; m. Sept. 21, 1850, Augustus S. Bunker, his second wife. She d. Lawrence, Mass., Oct. 17, 1868, ae. 37-1-20; he d. L., Aug. 19, 1896, ae. 73-0-28. Children :
    a. Flora Annielka, b. Gilford, June 30, 1851 ; m. Jesse Moulton, Oct. 3, 1876. Res. Dorchester, Mass.
    b. George Augustus, b. Lawrence, Apr. 12, 1853 ; d. July 16, 1853.
    c. Fred Clinton, b. L., June 18, 1854 ; d. Oct. 19, 1893, ae. 39-4-1.
    d. Arthur Lovell, b. L., Aug. 15, 1857 ; d. June 2, 1858.
    e. Carrie Addie, b. L., Aug. 20, 1860 ; d. Sept. 11, 1860.

77. George W. L., b. B., Apr. 13, 1834 ; d. Bristol, Nov. 3, 1853, ae. 19-6-20.

(51) Simon M. Sanborn, son of Sherburn, b. Dec. 15, 1796, m. Roxana Mills, b. Oct. 11, 1796, d. Aug. 20, 1846 ; divorced, and m. (2) Belinda West, b. Oct. 20, 1817, and d. Aug. 11, 1857, ae. 39-9-21 ; m, (3) Mary West. He was a cooper and farmer in Chester, where he d.

CHILDREN

78. Mary A., b. Dec. 10, 1819 ; d. 1824, ae. 5.
79. Isaiah, b. Jan. 24, 1821 ; m. (1) May 21, 1848, Lydia A. Swain, of Candia; (2) June 1, 1857, Mary H. (Sanborn) Elliott. Children :
    a. Madison M. b. Nov. 7, 1849. *b.* Loretta E., b. Nov. 21, 1853.

80.   Horace, b. Nov. 9, 1822; m. Mar. 19, 1850, Chastina M. Sanborn. res. in Chester, and there d. without issue, June 19, 1852, ae. 29-7-10.

81.   Luther M., b. Jan. 15, 1824; m. Dec. 16, 1845, Nancy J. Sanborn. He d. Oct. 27, 1851, ae. 27-9-12.   His widow m. Henry W. Quimby.

82.   Mary A., b. Oct. 10, 1825; m. Sept. 23, 1846, David T. Sleeper, of Sandown.

83.   Sarah J., b. Jan. 16, 1827 ; d. May 7, 1847, ae. 20-3-21.

84.   John Collins, b. Apr. 20, 1828 ; m. 1863, Mary A. B. Hook, of Fremont.   He is a house carpenter in Fremont.   Children :

  a.   Bert S., b. Sept. 30, 1863 ; m. and res. No. Uxbridge, Mass.
  b.   Ruth Grace, b. Mar. 10, 1865 ; m. —— Bartlett, of Kingston.

85.   Sylvester, b. July 13, 1829 ; a wheelwright in Amesbury, Mass.; m. June 5, 1855, Mrs. Chastina M. Sanborn, widow of Horace, above ; she d. Jan. 23, 1856 ; m. (2) Nov. 16, 1856, Almira Fassett, of Kingston.   No issue.

86.   Alvira, b. Apr. 23, 1831 ; m. 1851, Elijah Sanborn.   She d. Sept., 1855, ae. 24-5-.

87.   Clarissa, b. Dec. 18, 1832 ; m. Aug., 1856, Elijah Sanborn.

88.   Laura, b. Sept. 4, 1834 ; d. 1838, ae. 4.

89.   Harriet, b. Mar. 26, 1836; m. John S. Kelly, of Sandown.

90.   Mark, b. Oct. 21, 1839; m. June 20, 1889, Martha J. Marden, of Chester.

91.   Harrison, b. July 2, 1843; d. New York, a member of Co. D, 7th Regt., N. H. Vols., Feb. 19, 1862, ae. 18-7-17.

92.   Frank, b. Nov. 17, 1846; d. 1852, ae. 6.

93.   Laura J., b. Mar. 14, 1848; m. John M. Haines, of Sandown.

94.   Daniel, b. Jan. 12, 1850 ; m. Jan. 1, 1876, Abigail C. Elkins, of Kingston.   A carpenter at Danville.   Children :

  a.   Eva C., b. Sept. 26, 1877.
  b.   Herman Elkins, b. May 11, 1879.
  c.   Lillian Louise, b. Oct. 19, 1882 ; d. 1886, ae. 4.
  d.   Clifton, b. Aug. 24, 1885 ; d. 1889, ae. 4.

95.   Maria Ellen, b. July 27, 1851 ; m. S. S. West, Raymond.

96.   Lucinda, b. Feb. 13, 1853; d. 1854.

97.   Frank, b. Aug. 8, 1854; d. 1854.

(71)   Sherburn S. Sanborn, son of John H., b. Mar. 29, 1821, m. Aug. 22, 1843, Nancy K., dau. of Jonathan Fellows (See), b. Apr. 26, 1821.   He was a farmer and brick mason, and d. Bristol, Mar. 24, 1891, ae. 69-11-25.   She res. with her daughter, in Waltham, Mass.

CHILDREN

98.   Malina J., b. Wentworth, Oct. 8, 1844; m., Jan. 6, 1861, John W. Marden.   He is master car builder for the Fitchburg railroad, at Waltham, Mass.

99.   Charles W., b. Thornton, Jan. 20, 1846; m. Aug. 12, 1875, Abbie M., dau. of Moses Emmons (See), b. Apr. 20, 1851.   He is a mason and woodworker in Bristol.   Mason, Odd Fellow.

100.   Frank S., b. Bristol, Feb. 21, 1853; m. Nov. 29, 1876, Ella J. Swallow.   Res. 45 Columbus Ave., Somerville, Mass.   Since 1881, in the employ of Fitchburg railroad, now general foreman and general wrecker of that road.

101.   Maron J., b. B., Apr. 23, 1857; m. Dec. 25, 1880, Helen M. Nowell. Res. Cambridge, Mass.

ELIJAH SANBORN AND HIS DESCENDANTS

(8) Elijah Sanborn, son of Daniel, b. Sept. 22, 1761, m. Sept. 7, 1779, Elizabeth Tilton, of Danville. He saw service in the Revolutionary army; came to Bristol with his family as early as 1794, and was a farmer and miller. At one time he lived on High street and had charge of the first grist-mill in town. At another time he res. on the Solon Dolloff farm. After the death of his first wife he m., Apr. 21, 1799, Sarah Gordon, and removed to Burroak, Mich., where he d. He had two children by his second wife, whose names are unknown.

CHILDREN

102. Elijah, went West with his father.
103. Eben, b. Jan. 20, 1780; d. June 20, 1780.
*104. David, b. Danville, July 26, 1783.
105. Mercy, b. Sept. 1, 1785; m. Sherburn Tilton, of Sandown; d. Sept. 20, 1855, ae. 70-0-19.
106. Elizabeth T., b. Dec. 27, 1787; m. Caleb Atwood, of Enfield.

(104) David Sanborn, son of Elijah, b. July 26, 1783, was a resident of Bristol from the time his father came here till about 1812, when he removed to the Sanborn farm on the New Hampton side of the Pemigewasset river. He had charge of Ichabod C. Bartlett's potash for some years. He m., Feb. 11, 1806, Sally Foot, dau. of Samuel and Sally (Lowell) Foot, b. Amesbury, Mass., May 14, 1784; d. in New Hampton, Oct. 3, 1864, ae. 80-4-19. He d. New Hampton, Apr. 24, 1862, ae. 78-8-28.

CHILDREN

107. Elizabeth, b. Bristol, Mar. 16, 1807; m. Oct. 28, 1856, Morrill Dickerson, of Hill, who d. spring of 1882. She d. at home of her brother David, Oct. 16, 1881, ae. 74-7-0.
108. Hannah, b. B., Jan. 31, 1809; m. John L. Sanborn. (See.)
109. William Foot, b. B., Mar. 23, 1811; drowned June 3, 1837, while rafting lumber down the Pemigewasset, ae. 26-2-10. (See Stories and Incidents.)
110. Nancy, b. New Hampton, Jan. 29, 1814; m. July 12, 1832, Jacob Heath, of Franklin. They settled in New Hampton, where he was a farmer, and d. Dec. 14, 1872; she d. New Hampton, May 18, 1885, ae. 71-3-19. Children:
    a. Sarah A., b. Mar. 25, 1836; m. Hiram P. Ballou. (See.)
    b. Annette, b. Jan. 4, 1839; m. Edgar A. F. Hammond, Jan. 10, 1858; d. Aug. 5, 1893, ae. 54-7-1. He res. New Hampton. Children: (1) Frank W., b. Oct. 10, 1859; res. New Hampton. (2) Edgar A. F., b. June 11, 1865; d. Nov. 16, 1866, ae. 1-5-5. (3) Henry A., b. Aug. 4, 1871.
    c. Maria S., b. June 7, 1842; m. John R. Swain, Apr. 5, 1860; d. Sept. 14, 1879, ae. 37-3-7. Seven children.
    d. Gustavus S., b Jan. 2, 1848; d. Nov. 1, 1871, ae. 23-9-29.
    e. Julia K., b. June 1, 1852; res. unm., New Hampton.
*111. Otis, b. N. H., Aug. 20, 1816.
112. Gustavus Bartlett, b. N. H., Jan. 12, 1819; m. July 4, 1842, Sophronia Maria, dau. of Moses M. Smith (See), b. May 9, 1822. He

was a farmer in Hill, and there d. May 10, 1845, ae. 26-3-28. She m. (2 William P. Ballou. (See.) Child:

a. Henrietta Newell, b. Hill, Oct. 10, 1843; m. Everett Chandler. and d. Minneapolis, Minn., Jan. 2, 1899, ae. 55-2-22. Child: George Brinton, m.; one child; res. 922 Ave. D, Bayonne, N. J.

113. Julia M. M., b. N. H., Mar. 3, 1822; m. Daniel Kelley. (See.)

114. Elijah, b. N. H., June 21, 1824; m. Nov. 15, 1849, Mahala K., dau. of James and Sally (Gordon) Hight, b. New Hampton, Apr. 1, 1824. He was a farmer, lumber manufacturer, and brick maker at Profile Falls; d. No. Main street, Dec. 16, 1900, ae. 76-5-25. She res. No. Main street. No children.

115. David, b. N. H., Nov. 11, 1829; m. June 1, 1852, Aramentha, dau. of Benjamin and Harnel (Kelley) Gordon, b. New Hampton, Nov. 6, 1830, and d. June 10, 1883, ae. 52-7-4. He succeeded his father on the home farm. Children:

a. Sarah Hattie, b. New Hampton, Dec. 2, 1855. Res. with her father, unm. Two sisters d. in infancy.

(111) Otis Sanborn, son of David, b. Aug. 20, 1816, m. Aug. 22, 1840, Lucy Ann Tilton, dau. of Jonathan, b. Sandown, Nov. 11, 1822, and d. Laconia, June 15, 1898, ae. 75-7-4. He was a farmer and brick mason, and spent most of his life in Bristol. For thirty-eight years he res. in the Locke neighborhood, where he d. Oct. 19, 1895, ae. 79-1-29. When a young man, for ten years he run rafts of lumber down the river from Moore's Mills to market.

CHILDREN

116. William Jewett, b. Fremont, Mar. 11, 1841; m. (1) in 1865, Maria. dau. of Isaac Healey. He m. (2) Cornelia Arabella Grant. In company with his father-in-law, he kept the hotel known as Boars Head on Lake street in the sixties, and res. many years in Plymouth. He served in the 5th Regt., N. H. Vols., in the Civil war and was twice wounded. Discharged for disability, and later served in 2d Mass. Heavy Artillery. He d. at Soldiers' Home, Tilton, Dec. 25, 1901, ae. 60-9-14. Children, all born in Plymouth:

a. Jewett Perley.   b. George Tilden.   c. Edna.
d. Frank.   e. Lewis.

117. Julia Maria, b. New Hampton, July 17, 1842; d. 1844, ae. 2.

118. Lizzie Harriet, b. N. H., Dec. 4, 1846; m. Oct. 25, 1871, Joseph C. N. Davis. Res. 16 Spring street, Laconia.

119. Daniel Kelley, b. N. H., Dec. 31, 1849; m. Ada Shaddock, b. Canaan. He was for 30 years steward at Eagle Hotel in Concord. He d. Concord, Jan. 3, 1903, ae. 53-0-2.

120. Frank E., b. Plymouth, Sept. 23, 1852; m. 1898, Jennie Jay Cox. Is a brick mason in Hartford, Vt. Child:

a. Harry June, b. Hartford, Vt., Mar. 17, 1900.

121. Roscoe Elijah, b. Bristol, June 2, 1860; m. June 3, 1886, Mary Susan, dau. Joseph and Harriet (Beckford) Clough, b. Dorchester, Jan. 7, 1863. He is a brick mason. Res. Hanover. Child:

a. Channing, b. Laconia, Jan. 25, 1890.

122. Elmer Tilton, b. B., Nov. 9, 1862; m. Jan. 14, 1887, Emma Archibault, dau. of John, b. Enosburg Falls, Vt. He is a farmer in Bristol. Child:

a. Otis, b. New Hampton, Nov. 21, 1898.

1. Joseph Sanborn, b. Kensington, Sept. 9, 1751, was of the fourth generation from Lieut. John, b. England, 1620; through Nathaniel, b. Hampton, Jan. 27, 1766; Richard, b. Hampton Falls, Feb. 27, 1793; Moses, b. Kensington, July 12, 1717. Joseph, m. Mary Clough, of Danville. They came from Sandown and settled on lot 75 in New Chester, about one mile south of Smith's river, in 1773, and here they rounded out seventy years of wedded life. He d. Mar. 14, 1841, ae. 89-6-5.

CHILDREN, all born in Hill

2. Priscilla, b. Jan. 11, 1772; m. —— Corless, and d. in Alexandria.
3. Sarah, b. Feb. 18, 1773.
4. Obediah, b. Mar. 7, 1775; m. Sally Moore; lived in Hill a farmer, and there d., Mar. 31, 1805, ae. 30-0-24. He was the father of Tappan, Moses, and Obediah.
5. Polly, b. May 4, 1778; m. Joseph Hastings. (See.)
6. Judith, b. Nov. 16, 1780; m. Nathaniel Collins; d. Webster.
*7. Joseph, b. May 24, 1784.
8. Elizabeth, b. July 29, 1786; d. 1797, ae. 11.
9. Reuben, b. June 27, 1791; d. Hill, Apr., 1812, ae. 20-10-.
*10. Moses, b. July 24, 1795.

(7) Joseph Sanborn, son of Joseph, b. May 24, 1784, m. Sally Pearson, dau. of William and Sarah (Jones) Pearson, of Tewksbury, Mass.; b. Sept. 7, 1784, and d. in Bristol, at the residence of her son Gilman, Feb. 9, 1864, ae. 79-5-2. He d. same place, Mar. 24, 1861, ae. 76-10-0. At m., they settled on a farm in the Borough, about one-half mile south of Smith's river, and here their children were b.

CHILDREN

11. Cynthia, b. Hill, June 19, 1807; m. Hosea Ballou. (See.)
12. Mary, b. New Hampton, Apr. 10, 1809; m. (1) Alexander Simon Wolcott, who d. New York city, Nov. 10, 1844. She m. (2) James Meeker, who d. 1886; she d. at her home on the New Hampton side of the Pemigewasset river, July 20, 1895, ae. 86-3-10.
13. William, b. Hill, Mar. 20, 1811; m. Aug., 1833, Joanna Wells. He d. in Bristol, June 10, 1865, ae. 54-2-20. She d. Mar. 15, 1877. Two children.
14. Reuben, b. H., Dec. 29, 1813; lived in Bristol, unm., where he d. Jan. 3, 1840, ae. 26-0-4.
*15. Gilman, b. H., Apr. 5, 1816.

(10) Moses Sanborn, son of Joseph, b. July 24, 1795, m. Mar. 2, 1815, Lucy Wells, dau. of Reuben and Priscilla, b. Nov. 8, 1797, and d. Oct. 3, 1843, ae. 45-10-25. He m. (2) Betsey Stevens. He was a carpenter and farmer and spent his last years in the family of his daughter, Mrs. O. F. Morse, in Bristol, where he d. Nov. 27, 1888, ae. 93-4-3. He was a captain in the artillery, state militia.

CHILDREN

16. Cyrus, b. Sept. 20, 1816; d. Nov. 22, 1822, ae. 6-2-2.
17. Mary Jane, b. Hill, Apr. 1, 1821; m. Eben Eaton. (See.)

18.   Rozilla, b. Mar. 2, 1825 ; d. May, 1839, ae. 14-3-.
19.   Eliza Ann, b. June 14, 1831 ; m. Oscar F. Morse. (See.)
20.   Catherine, b. Mar. 17, 1834; d. in the family of Eben Eaton in Bristol, Mar., 1848, ae. 14-0-.

(15)   Gilman Sanborn, son of Joseph, b. Apr. 5, 1816, m. (1) Apr. 9, 1835, Mary Elizabeth Badger, dau. of Daniel, b. Malden, Mass., Mar. 8, 1816, and d. May 9, 1859, ae. 43-2-1. He m. (2) Widow Morrill, of Bridgewater. She d. Apr. 30, 1866, and he m. (3) Dec. 14, 1868, Rubie Hayward. He was a carpenter and farmer in Alexandria, and, for many years before his death, on the west side of the lake in Bristol, where he d., Mar. 20, 1883, as the result of having one leg nearly severed from his body three days before. He walked on a revolving saw in a saw-mill while snow blind. His age was 66-11-15.

CHILDREN

21.   Carroll, b. Alexandria, Mar. 5, 1836 ; m. Clarinda J. Hastings, July 5, 1859. She was dau. of John Hastings (See), b. Jan. 16, 1839. He was a soldier in the 9th Regt., N. H. Vols., and was wounded at Antietam and again at Fredericksburg. Died at Lowell, Mass., of gunshot wound. Children :
      a.   Fred, d.   b.   Lola, b. before war.   c.   Ada E., b. during war.
22.   James, b. A.; killed when 18, by accidental discharge of gun while hunting in Lowell, Mass.
23.   Mary Elizabeth, killed while young, by the accidental discharge of a gun in the hands of a brother.
24.   Charles, d. in infancy.
25.   John Gilman, d. in infancy.
26.   Henry Augustus, b. Alexandria, Apr. 16, 1847 ; m. 1872, Elvira Straw ; divorced ; m. (2) Dec. 12, 1887, Ida May, dau. of Capt. James W. Saunders. (See.) Child :
      a.   Elmer Earl, b. Franklin Falls, May 12, 1896.
27.   Julia, b. Bristol, Oct. 26, 1849. Res. Tilton. Unm.
28.   Henrietta, b. Alexandria, Sept. 25, 1854 ; m. Samuel Scott Fellows. (See.)
29.   A daughter, b. Bristol ; d. infancy.
30.   Anna Donna, b. B., Feb. 16, 1857 ; d. Feb. 26, 1873, ae. 16-0-10.

-----

1.   Benia Sanborn, son of Zadok, b. Brentwood, Jan. 14, 1759, was of the fourth generation from William, b. England, 1622, through Stephen, b. Hampton, 1671 : Zadok, b. Hampton, 1707 ; and Zadok, his father, b. Brentwood, 1733. Benia, m. Lydia Powell and settled in New Hampton, but later came to Bristol and settled in the Locke neighborhood, on the farm where Otis Sanborn lived for many years. She d., Aug. 18, 1845, ae. 79.

CHILDREN

2.   William, b. New Hampton, about 1786 ; m., and had one daughter. He was a school teacher for many years.
3.   Susanna, b. 1789 ; m. Josiah Fellows. (See.)
4.   Anna, b. 1791 ; m. Smith Powell. (See.)

5. Ruth, b. 1793; m. Nathaniel Smith. She came in possession of her father's farm well stocked; signed notes to cover her husband's debts contracted before marriage, and d. in poor-house at New Hampton.

---

1. Benjamin Franklin Sanborn, son of Jacob B., was of the sixth generation from William, b. England, 1622, through Stephen, b. Hampton, 1671; Zadok, b. Hampton, 1707; Zadok, b. Brentwood, 1733; Nathaniel, b. Brentwood, 1768, who lived in New Hampton and Alexandria, and Jacob B., b. New Hampton, Feb. 19, 1801. Benjamin F. is supposed to have been born in Alexandria, Oct. 11, 1826. He m., Feb. 20, 1850, Joanna L. Darling, dau. of Ebenezer (See), b. July 20, 1825, and d. Bristol, Sept. 19, 1891, ae. 66-1-29. He was a farmer on the road to the Locke neighborhood, till after the death of his wife. He d. Alexandria, Apr. 8, 1898, ae. 71-5-27.

CHILDREN

2. Infant son, d. Oct. 5, 1851, ae. 6 weeks.
3. Charles E., d. Sept. 24, 1853, ae. 14 months.
4. Orrin D., b. Bristol, 1854.
5. George Selden, b. B., Aug. 2, 1861; is a farmer on his father's farm; unm.

---

1. Sewell Sanborn was b. in Salisbury, Oct. 16, 1801. He was of the sixth generation from John, b. England, 1620, through John, b. about 1649; Tristram, b. 1684; Abraham, b. Kingston, 1717; John, b. Kingston, 1741, and Capt. Abraham, his father, b. Sandown, 1759. Sewell m. (1) Nov., 1829, Harriet Bean, who d. Mar. 17, 1847; (2) Dec. 5, 1847, Mrs. Phebe Fogg, widow of Thomas, who d. May 7, 1882, ae. 75-4-5. He came to Bristol, 1863, and d. Oct. 30, 1866, ae. 65-0-14.

CHILDREN

2. Mary Bean, b. Salisbury, Nov. 18, 1830; m. Joel Gurdy. (See.)
3. Harriet, b. May 19, 1833; m. Eben Trask, Salem, Mass.; d. Apr. 21, 1868, ae. 34-11-2.
4. George W., d. at Alexandria, July 28, 1858, ae. 21.
5. William Henry Harrison, b. Sept. 15, 1839; m. Apr. 21, 1869, Phedora Elizabeth, dau. of Calvin Golden; d; she res. New Hampton. (See.) Children:
    a. Herman H., b. Alexandria, July 25, 1874; res. New Hampton.
    b. Raymond, b. Hill, Apr. 29, 1876; m. Alice Hammond. One child: Katherine.
6. Ira Chase, b. July 29, 1841; m. Alberta S. Crowell, and d. in Albany, Vt.
7. Sylvanus, b. June 12, 1843; d. unm.
8. Horace, b. May 10, 1845; m.; res. at Franklin; one son.
9. Gustavus B., b. Sept. 4, 1848; m. Susan Ford, Groton. Divorced. He was a manufacturer of waterproof blacking, babbit metal and rules in Bristol, removed to Ballard, Wash., where he accumulated a property through the rise of real estate, and d. in Dec., 1902, ae. 54-3-. They had two children.
10. Phebe, b. May 21, 1851; m. Louis Rowe. (See.)

1.   Daniel H. Sanborn, son of Jonathan, was b. Andover,
Aug. 7, 1825.   He m. (1) Amanda, dau. of Elijah Prescott, of
Danbury.   He m. (2) Nov. 30, 1871, Mrs. Eliza Ellen Weeks,
widow of George W. Weeks and dau. of Joseph Farnham, of
Sanbornton, b. Oct. 7, 1837.   He was a farmer in Danbury,
came to Bristol, October, 1880, and here d. Sept. 28, 1891, ae.
66-1-21.

———

1.   Calvin D. Sanborn, son of Nathaniel, was of the sixth
generation from William, b. in England, 1622, through Stephen,
b. Hampton, 1671 ; Zadok, b. Hampton, 1707 ; Zadok, b. Brentwood, 1733 ; Nathaniel, b. Brentwood, 1768.   Calvin D. was b.
in New Hampton, Sept. 30, 1814.   He m. (1) July 15, 1838,
Maria Flint, who d. June 19, 1856.   He m. (2) Mar. 3, 1860,
Octavia F. Pattee.   He was a farmer in Alexandria till 1884,
when he purchased the Samuel Page residence on Pleasant
street, and there res. till he d. Aug. 15, 1891, ae. 76-10-15.

CHILDREN

2.   Mary E., b. Alexandria, Sept. 15, 1841 ; m. May 31, 1863, Calvin
Brown, Alexandria.
3.   George Francis, b. A., Oct. 7, 1844 ; m. Aug. 29, 1868, Ellen A.,
dau. of James and Octavia F. (Townsend) Pattee, b. Alexandria, Feb. 16,
1848.   Came from Alexandria, Jan., 1884.   Laborer.   Child :
    a.   Julia Octavia, b. Alexandria, July 9, 1876.
4.   Julia M., b. A., Apr. 14, 1847 ; m. Horace Hemphill.   (See.)

———

1.   William Sanborn was b. Meredith, Apr. 8, 1799.   He
was of the fifth generation from Lieut. John, b. England, 1620,
through Nathaniel, b. Hampton, 1666 ; Nathan, b. Hampton
Falls, 1709 ; Nathaniel, b. Hampton Falls, 1737 ; Stephen, b.
Epping, 1772.   William m. (1) Rachel Swain, who d. in Bristol about 1844.   He m. (2) Mary Gordon ; (3) —— Brown,
dau. of Josiah.   He res. Meredith, New Hampton, in the Locke
neighborhood, and in Hill, where he d. about 1875.   His last
wife d. in Hill.

CHILDREN

2.   William C., b. 1825 (?) ; d. in Errol.
3.   Noah R., b. 1827(?) ; left home before the Civil war and was never
heard from.
4.   Betsey Jane.
5.   Stephen Frank, b. Meredith, Nov. 25, 1834 ; m. Oct. 30, 1859,
Mary Jane, dau. of Pattee Gale (See), b. Aug. 24, 1841.   They settled in
Bristol about 1870 ; farmer on Lake street and Profile Falls.   No children.
6.   Emeline C., m. Richard Calley.
7.   Abby, m. Horatio Chase.

———

1.   George Weston Sanborn, son of Laurentine and Laura

(Robinson) Sanborn, was b. Belmont, Nov. 27, 1870. He m.,
Feb. 5, 1887, Mertie Colby, dau. of John H. and Lizzie M.
(Huse) Colby, b. Bristol, Dec. 1, 1870. He came to Bristol
in 1887, and is an employee at Calley & Currier's crutch manufactory. No children.

THE SANDERS FAMILY

1. Warren Albert Sanders, son of Charles G. and Abigail
(Ayer) Sanders, was b. Chichester, July 5, 1852. He m., June
4, 1870, Mary Ida, dau. of Edward and Nancy L. (Goss)
Edmonds, b. Chichester, Apr. 27, 1853. They came to Bristol
from Franklin, in July, 1887. He was master mechanic in the
employ of the Train-Smith company twelve years ; at Middletown, Ohio, till Apr., 1901 ; now employed by Champton Coated
Paper company, Hamilton, Ohio. Republican, Mason.

CHILDREN

2. Olin Bert, b. Epsom, Oct. 20, 1871 ; m. Jan., 1893, Florence J. Gray.
Was an employee at paper-mill. Left Bristol Sept., 1896. Now at Hamilton, O.
3. Minnie E., b. Chichester, Nov. 30, 1873 ; m. Jan. 18, 1895, Robert
H. Butterworth. He was clerk in Hotel Bristol ; removed to Pinehurst,
N. C.
4. Edward Warren, b. Chichester, Dec. 4, 1875 ; m. Sept. 5, 1896,
Edith A. E. Hadley, dau. of Charles S. (See), b. July 13, 1879. He is a
paper-mill employee, Hamilton, O. Children :

   a. Edward Warren, b. Chichester, Jan. 25, 1897 ; d. Jan. 30, 1897.
   b. Robert Arthur, b. Bristol, June 18, 1900.
   c. Frank Edwin, b. Hamilton, June 14, 1903.

5. Rena, b. Franklin, June 30, 1881 ; m. Oct. 15, 1899, Benjamin
Davis, and res. Sound Beach, Conn.

THE SARSONS FAMILY

1. Adelbert E. Sarsons, son of Eleazer L. and Emeline
(Campbell) Sarsons, was b. Nashua, Sept. 30, 1859, and m.
Liller, dau. of Frank W. Mathews, b. Natick, Mass., Jan. 3,
1865. He was a tinsmith in Bristol, Apr., 1898, till Aug.,
1903, when he removed to Swampscott, Mass.

THE SAUNDERS FAMILIES

1. Benjamin Saunders was b. in Lisbon, Feb., 1822. He
m., June 18, 1851, Priscilla R., dau. of Royal and Mary (Prescott) Blake, b. Sanbornton, July 29, 1818. He settled in Bristol 1858, and was a workman in tannery. He served in 12th
Regt., N. H. Vols., and 1st N. H. Cavalry ; was wounded and

captured, and d. in prison at Florence, S. C., Nov. 1, 1864, ae. 42-9-. (See Roll of Honor.) She d. Bristol, Dec. 21, 1885, ae. 67-4-22. Methodist, Republican.

CHILDREN

2. Emma Jane, b. Lowell, Mass., Nov. 1, 1852; d. Bristol. Sept. 14, 1875, ae. 22-10-13.
3. Ida Frances, b. L., June 30, 1854; m. Charles W. McDaniel. (See.)

---

1. Capt. James William Saunders, son of Joel and Phebe (Scott) Saunders, was b. in Strafford, Jan. 17, 1833, and m. Nov. 7, 1857, Mary Jane, dau. of John and Abigail (Gray) Ackerman, b. Alexandria, Nov. 30, 1834. She d. Bristol, Jan. 29, 1903, ae. 68-1-29. Capt. Saunders was a farmer and lumber manufacturer in Alexandria till 1889, when he purchased the saw-mill where is now the Electric Light plant, and removed to Bristol, and operated same till 1896. He has served six years as supervisor of the checklist, and is now serving his third year as first selectman. Capt. Saunders served in the 12th Regt., N. H. Vols., from Aug. 11, 1862, till May 19, 1865, as sergeant, first sergeant, second lieutenant, first lieutenant and captain, and was a brave and capable officer. He was in every engagement in which his regiment took part and escaped unscathed, and was never in a hospital a day. At the battle of Drury's Bluff, a Rhode Island battery that had position near the 12th Regt. was silenced by the sharpshooters of the enemy. Lieut. Saunders, seeing the situation, took a half dozen of his men, and, assisted by Lieut. E. E. Beede, worked one of the guns and did good execution till the ammunition was exhausted. Two of Lieut. Saunders's men were wounded. For this bravery Capt. Saunders was complimented in General Orders by Gen. B. F. Butler.

CHILDREN

2. Alice, b. Methuen, Mass., Feb. 7, 1859; m. Edward M. Perkins; res. Franklin Falls. Child:
    a. Fred, b. Aug. 18, 1887.
3. Horace William, b. Alexandria, Nov. 18, 1862; m., 1892, Estella, dau. of Alonzo H. and Emeline (Wescott) Twombly, b. Rumney, Dec. 14, 1874. Children:
    a. Beatrice Florence, b. Bristol, Nov. 30, 1893.
    b. Mildred Therease, b. Danbury, May 11, 1896.
4. Ida May, b. A., Mar. 1, 1866; m. Henry A. Sanborn. (See.)

THE SAVAGE FAMILY

1. Rev. John W. Savage, son of Lorenzo D. and Lucretia Ann (Bates) Savage, was b. Somers, N. Y., Feb. 3, 1837. He m. Georgine Adelaide, dau. of Capt. Tristram and Abigail

(Lambert) Luce, b. Vineyard Haven, Mass., Oct. 25, 1847. He was pastor of the Congregational church in Bristol, Nov., 1890, till Aug. 2, 1902, since which date he has been pastor of a church at Greenfield. (See sketch under Congregational church.)

CHILD

2. Ross Eliot, b. Dover, Apr. 6, 1874. He graduated from Bowdoin Medical College in June, 1897. He was three years on medical staff of the Connecticut General Hospital at Middletown, Conn.; six months at Strong's Sanitarium, Saratoga Springs, N. Y., and since, in general practice at Attleboro, Mass.

THE SAWYER FAMILIES

1. Caleb Sawyer came to Bristol from Boscawen in 1816, and res. for many years in the Andrew J. Crocket house on Pleasant street. He was b. June 1, 1767, and d. Bristol, Aug. 13, 1837, ae. 70-2-12. He m., Jan. 27, 1790, Susanna Hall, dau. Lieut. Richard Hall. She was b. May 25, 1773, and d. Bristol, Jan. 26, 1843, ae. 69-8-1. She was one of the first members of the Congregational church.

CHILDREN

2. Sarah Hall, b. Dracut, Mass., Aug. 7, 1790; m. Robert Smith. (See.)
3. Richard Hall, b. Pelham, Mass., Nov. 1, 1792; m. in 1819, Relief, dau. Robert Brown (See), b. Aug. 11, 1804, and d. in Bristol, Dec. 17, 1861, ae. 57-4-6. He was a blacksmith for many years where is now Post-office block, and a farmer on New Chester mountain. Was a prominent man in town and a member of the Congregational church. He d. Bristol, Feb. 26, 1877, ae. 84-3-25. Children:

   a. Ann Maria, b. Bristol, June 24, 1829; m. Albert A. Moulton, M.D. (See.)

   b. Edward Payson, b. B., July 15, 1840; m. Feb. 2, 1859, Mary, dau. of William R. Blodgett (See), b. July 5, 1842. They res. Bristol. Child: (1) Harry Edward, b. Feb. 22, 1866; d. Oct. 19, 1874, ae. 8-7-27.

   c. Susan Hall (adopted), dau. of Alvah Sawyer. She m. Benjamin F. Flanders. (See.)

4. Alvah, b. Feb. 7, 1795. He m., Feb. 13, 1826, Elizabeth McMurphy. They removed to Bergen, New York. During a prevailing epidemic the father, mother, and one child died and were all buried in one grave. Two children survived, Susan, b. Buffalo, N. Y., and Catherine. Robert Smith made a journey to New York state by carriage and brought the surviving children to Bristol, and adopted Catherine. She never m.; d. in the family of Robert S. Hastings, in Bristol, Nov. 5, 1884. Susan Hall was adopted by Richard H. Sawyer, as above.

5. Caleb, b. Dracut, Mass., Feb. 12, 1797; m. Nov. 5, 1843, Hannah, widow of Joseph Wallace, and dau. Jonas Hastings (See), b. Jan. 24, 1808. He d. Alexandria, July 11, 1871, ae. 74-4-29; she d. same place, Sept. 5, 1853, ae. 45-7-11. Child:

   a. Mary Frances, b. Alexandria, Apr. 11, 1845; m. George M. Bean. (See.)

6. Putnam, b. May 4, 1799. He settled in Canada, where he d. unm-

7. Henry I., b. May 13, 1801; d. Boscawen, July 18, 1817, ae. 16-2-5.
8. Mary, b. July 2, 1803; d. at Cambridge, Mass., unm., May 17, 1832, ae. 28-10-15.
9. Milton, b. Hopkinton, July 27, 1805, and d. Portland, Mich., Aug. 4, 1884, ae. 79-0-7. He m., July 8, 1832, Kesiah Ingalls, dau. of Jonathan (See), b. 1810. She d. Portland, Mich., 1882, ae. 72. No children.
10. Moody Currier, b. H., Oct. 2, 1807. He m., June 15, 1835, Sarah, dau. Robert Brown (See), b. Nov. 1, 1809, and d. in Bristol, Feb. 10, 1853, ae. 43-3-9. He practiced medicine in Bristol for a time and then opened a drug store where is now Fowler's east-side drug store. He was a public spirited citizen. He d. Bristol, July 24, 1854, ae. 46-9-22. (See Physicians.) Children:

    a. Moody A., b. Concord, Vt., Apr. 30, 1836. He succeeded his father in the drug business. Served one year as hospital steward in the 3rd Regt., N. H. Vols., at Hilton Head, S. C. He m., at Milwaukee, Wis., July 2, 1865, Annie Maria, dau. of Jonathan L. Prescott (See), b. Aug. 19, 1837. He located at Boscobel, Wis., where he was in the drug business till his death, Mar. 26, 1895, ae. 58-10-26. His wife preceded him only three weeks, dying Feb. 3, 1895, ae. 57-5-14. He was for many years connected with the public schools, was treasurer of school board at time of death. Child: Annie Ellen, b. Dec. 19, 1869.

    b. Helen Augusta, b. Bristol, Oct. 20, 1843; m. Ichabod C. Bartlett. (See.)

11. Emily, b. Feb. 2, 1810; m. Peter A. Sleeper. (See.)
12. Charlotte Augusta, b. Boscawen, Apr. 5, 1812; d. Boscawen, Oct. 2, 1813, ae. 1-5-27.

---

1. Frank Ropes Sawyer is a son of Walter Harris and Sarah Ann (Fifield) Sawyer. He was b. in Woodstock, Jan. 19, 1842, and m., Jan. 1, 1870, Olive Melinda, dau. of Albert W. and Hannah Dodge (Felch) Browne, b. Newport, Jan. 22, 1850. He was a foreman in tannery, at Bristol, 1868–'81; Enfield, 1881–'87, and Salem, Mass., till 1902. Now res. West Somerville, Mass. Republican, Odd Fellow. Official member of Methodist church.

CHILDREN

2. Myra Clair, b. Bristol, Apr. 16, 1871; a school teacher in Salem; m. Sept. 4, 1895, Everett W. Durgin, paying teller North End Savings bank, Boston, and president of Lynn District Epworth League. He d. Dec. 26, 1901, ae. 30-4-1. Children:

    a. Dorothy, b. Oct. 31, 1896.
    b. Eleanor, } b. Mar. 19, 1899.
    c. Olive, }
    d. Lura, b. Jan. 1, 1901.

3. Mae Frances, b. B., Dec. 7, 1873; m. Nov. 15, 1894, Eugene L. Pack. Children:

    a. E. Paul, b. Sept. 23, 1897.
    b. Norman Sawyer, b. Aug. 29, 1900.

4. Frank Roy, b. B., May 25, 1878; is discount clerk and note teller in United States Trust Co., 28 Court street, Boston, Mass.
5. Olive Maud, b. Enfield, June 8, 1885; is a music teacher and soprano soloist.

1. Charles H. Sawyer, son of Thomas W. and Mary (Danforth) Sawyer (See page 131) was b. Hill, June 4, 1862; m. Feb. 9, 1882, Cora Estelle, dau. of Lieut. George W. Hall, b. Tilton, Sept. 6, 1858. Left an orphan, he made his home with his grandfather, Benaiah Danforth. (See.) He learned the printer's art in the office of the *Bristol Enterprise*, and has worked at his trade at Concord, and in the Government printing-office at Washington, D. C., where he has been for twelve years, four as compositor and eight as proof-reader. Is a Royal Arch Mason and Knight Templar.

CHILD

2. Estelle May, b. Concord, Nov. 7, 1884.

THE SCRIBNER FAMILY

1. George Henry Scribner, son of Lowell and Charlotte (Bean) Scribner, was b. Salisbury, Sept. 17, 1843. He m. Feb. 7, 1873, Olive, dau. of Samuel and Caroline (Sanborn) Sanborn, b. Apr. 10, 1853. Res. in Salisbury, where he was a farmer; a woolen-mill operative in Franklin seventeen years; paper maker in Newport five years, and since 1893 in Bristol. Methodist, Republican.

CHILD

2. George Lowell, b. Jan. 7, 1874; d. Nov., 1877, ae. 3-10-.

THE SEAVER FAMILY

1. Eben Seaver, son of John L. and Fannie (Cone) Seaver, was b. Cornish, July 2, 1849. He m., Dec. 26, 1874, Sarah, dau. of Job A. and Mary E. (Knowles) Gray, b. Jan. 5, 1848, in Alexandria. They came from Franklin in May, 1883. He was a manufacturer and repairer of carriages. He d. Mar. 6, 1898, ae. 48-8-4. Served ten years on Bristol police force.

CHILDREN

2. Edgar Eben, b. Franklin, Oct. 21, 1875; m. Dec. 5, 1898, Eva Rebecca, dau. of Frank D. Sanborn, b. New Hampton, Aug. 6, 1877. Child :
   a. William Harrington, b. Jan. 13, 1900.

3. Fred Eugene, b. F., July 1, 1877; m. Jan. 1, 1899, Ella May, dau. of Samuel A. and Abigail H. (Pike) Howard, b. New Hampton, Oct. 4, 1878. Was salesman in store of Weymouth, Brown & Co., now in insurance business in Burlington, Vt. Child :
   a. Ruth, Ernstone, b. Bristol, Feb. 9, 1902.
   Clarence Leon, b. Alexandria, June 10. 1870; is a spinner in woolen-mill.

THE SEAVEY FAMILIES

1. John Seavey, son of Samuel P. and Judith (Jenness) Seavey, was b. Farmington, Jan. 15. 1832, and m. Feb. 11.

25

1856, Rebecca J., dau. of Stephen and Betsey (Jenness) Nutter. b. Sandwich, July 8, 1833. He was a farmer in Alexandria till 1881; since in Bristol; in trade on Lake street till 1884. She d. Mar. 5, 1900, ae. 66-9-27.

CHILDREN

2.   Charles R., b. Alexandria, June 15, 1858; m. Feb. 19, 1896, Ida May, dau. Quincy S. Dustin (See), b. Dec. 25, 1879; clerk in his father's store, operative in woolen-mill 15 years; in North Carolina six months; laborer in Bristol. Children.

    a.   Clinton Herbert, b. Bristol, Dec. 17, 1896.
    b.   Leslie Walter, b. B., Nov. 13, 1899.
    c.   Agnes Mildred, b. B., Jan. 21, 1902.

3.   Edgar A., b. A., May 9, 1862; m. Jan. 6, 1883, May E. Nash; res. Rochester.

4.   Arthur W., b. Penacook, Sept. 1, 1870; m. June 26, 1895, Minnie Ella, dau. of Hiram P. Ballou (See), b. Dec. 18, 1876. He is an electrician in Providence, R. I. Children:

    a.   Mona, b. Bristol, Jan. 25, 1896.
    b.   Marian, b. B., May 12, 1897.

5.   S. Emma, b. Alexandria, Dec. 22, 1874; m. William J. Sullivan. (See.)

6.   Lucy M., b. A., Aug. 19, 1877; m. Willard S. H. Remick. (See.)

---

1.   Roscoe J. Seavey, son of Amos and Jane (Gray) Seavey, was b. Alexandria, Mar. 27, 1856; m. July 19, 1877, Esther H., dau. Job and Mary E. Gray, b. Alexandria, June 4, 1857; d. Bristol, Apr. 25, 1897, ae. 39-10-21. He was clerk in employ of Charles Boardman, later of Cyrus Taylor, afterwards in office of Dodge Davis Manufacturing Company, and d. Jan. 4, 1890, ae. 33-9-7.

---

1.   Allen Jenness Seavey is a son of Andrew Jackson and Aurilla Lovina (Pierce) Seavey. He was b. Andover, July 9, 1857, and m. June 27, 1880, Mary Hannah, dau. of Silas H. and Anna B. Chase, b. Groton, Oct. 16, 1862. He was a laborer in saw-mill in Andover; since 1884, in Bristol, a printer and laborer.

CHILDREN

2.   Eva Blanche, b. Andover, June 30, 1881; m. May 5, 1902, Ethan A. Day. Child:

    a.   Harry Ralph, b. Bristol, May 11, 1903.

3.   Vivia I., b. Bristol, Sept. 29, 1885; d. Jan. 29, 1887, ae. 1-4-0.

4.   Howard Lawrence, b. B., Dec. 28, 1887.

5.   Infant, b. and d. July 13, 1890.

THE SHATTUCK FAMILY

1.   Orrin Varnum Shattuck, son of Eliab Bennett and Indiana (Spaulding) Shattuck, was b. Brookline, June 30, 1845. He m., Jan. 6, 1872, Mary Ann, dau. of Benjamin and Isabella

(Miller) Ray, b. Canada, May 31, 1843. He was a farmer in Canaan; from 1886, an operative in woolen-mill in Bristol till he d., Dec. 26, 1890, ae. 45-5-26. She res. Bristol.

CHILDREN

2. Charles, b. Canaan, July 9, 1874; d. July 18, 1875, ae. 1-0-9.
3. Arthur, b. C., Jan. 23, 1876; d. Enfield, July 14, 1880, ae. 4-5-21.
4. Lottie Belle, b. C., Aug. 14, 1877; m. William G. Robie. (See.)

THE SHAW FAMILY

1. Ebenezer Gerry Shaw, son of John and Edna (Straw) Shaw, was b. in Sanbornton, Jan. 3, 1830. His grandfather was John, b. 1764, and his great-grandfather, Edward Shaw, one of the original grantees of the town of Hampton, where he was living in 1748. Ebenezer G. m. Dec. 6, 1849, Mary Ann, dau. of Jedediah and Permelia Cole, b. Hill, June 3, 1827. He was a resident of Bristol, 1850-'54; was station agent. He d. Sanbornton, Jan. 21, 1859, ae. 29-0-18. She res. Tilton.

CHILDREN

2. Willis Arthur, b. Bristol, Oct. 22, 1850; m. Dec. 23, 1871, Alice M., dau. of John C. Leavitt, b. Andover, June 22, 1853. He res. East Andover. Children :
   a. Lill Ethel, b. Manchester, Dec. 23, 1872; m. Fred E. Noyes. (See.)
   b. Gladys Abbie, b. Andover, Sept. 12, 1889.
3. Edward Everett, b. B., Mar. 24, 1853. A traveling optician; m. Dec. 2, 1878, Etta Frances, dau. of J. William Johnson. She m. (2) George G. Brown. (See.) He m. (2), and res. East Tilton.

THE SIMONDS FAMILIES

1. Daniel Simonds, son of John, m. Martha Brown, dau. of Stephen T. (See.) He was a farmer in Bristol and Alexandria, and d. Alexandria, of smallpox, Feb. 16, 1850. She made her home for many years in the family of her daughter, Nancy, in Bristol, and there d. Nov. 14, 1894, ae. 94-5-29.

CHILDREN

2. Isabella J., b. Alexandria, Mar. 13, 1824; m. John S. Gale. (See.)
3. John Wesley, d. in infancy.
4. Nancy, b. A., Mar. 1, 1829; m. Solon Dolloff. (See.)
5. Frank L., res. in Tilton.
6. Rebecca, m. Thomas P. Frost, and d. in Manchester.
7. Parker, res. in Tilton.

1. Artemas Simonds, b. Alexandria, May 14, 1817; m. Hannah McMurphy, dau. of Daniel, b. Alexandria, Aug. 20, 1818. He was a farmer in Bristol and Alexandria, and d. latter place, June 25, 1867, ae. 50-1-11. She has res. many years with her son, Fred W., on Central street.

2. George Hannibal, b. Alexandria, Dec. 17, 1842; res. in Hill.
3. Charles Henry, b. A., June 4, 1844; res. Saint Francis, Minn.
4. Fred Warren, b. Bristol, July 5, 1846. Has been a painter and paper-hanger in Bristol for many years. Unm.
5. Ellen Augusta, b. Alexandria, Mar. 13, 1851; d. unm., Apr. 14, 1875, ae. 24-1-1.
6. Laura Belle, b. A., June 17, 1859; d. Nov. 14, 1863, ae. 4-4-27.

---

1. Merrill P. Simonds, son of Thomas and Rhoda (Merrill) Simonds, was b. in Alexandria, July 16, 1822. He m. July 21, 1846, Ruth P., dau. of Nathaniel Heath (See), b. Nov. 5, 1825. He d. June 26, 1864, in the army, ae. 41-11-10. (See Roll of Honor.) She m. (2) Charles S. Brown. (See.)

CHILDREN, all born in Bristol

2. Annette A., b. May 23, 1847; d. Aug. 29, 1848, ae. 1-3-6.
3. Charles F., b. Mar. 29, 1849. Since 1871, has res. Gold, Cal., where he m., Dec. 15, 1890. One child.
4. Lucina F., b. Sept. 19, 1850; m. Nathaniel N. Walker, and d. Concord, May 5, 1893, ae. 42-7-16.
5. George O., b. Nov. 9, 1856. Since 1876 has res. Gold, Cal.
6. Orrin Alba, b. July 10, 1859; d. Oct. 5, 1863, ae. 4-2-25.
7. Flora E., b. Nov. 9, 1861; m. Albert F. Cate. (See.)
8. Albon M., b. Apr. 24, 1864; m. Aug. 8, 1883, Fannie Etta, dau. of David P. Hoyt. (See.) He res. Bristol. She m. (2) Elwood S. Lougee. (See.) Children:
    a. Ora Frank, b. Bristol, May 3, 1885.
    b. Ethel Estella, b. B., Dec. 24, 1888.

THE SIMMONS FAMILY

1. George Burton Simmons is the son of George A. and Abby (Piper) Simmons. He was b. Lyme, Apr. 22, 1863, and m. Alice L. (Whicher) Robbins, dau. of John A. Whicher, b. Wentworth, 1854, and d. Wentworth, Aug. 2, 1891, ae. 37. He m. (2) Mertie Belle, dau. of Joseph P. Hill (See), b. Mar. 6, 1874. Came to Bristol from Plymouth in Nov., 1895; fireman and watchman at paper-mill of Train-Smith company. Removed to Lincoln, 1902.

THE SINCLAIR FAMILY

1. Noah L. Sinclair is a son of Noah and Hannah (Cotton) Sinclair. He was b. Meredith, Nov. 2, 1842, and m. Nov. 16, 1867, Etta, dau. of James S. and Hannah Lawrence, b. Tamworth, Mar. 19, 1845. He has been in Bristol since May, 1894: a teamster. Deacon Free Baptist church. Republican.

CHILD

2. Minnie Iva, b. Meredith, Jan. 21, 1875; d. in Bristol, July 18, 1898, ae. 23-5-27.

THE SLEEPER FAMILIES

The Sleepers made the first settlements within the limits of Bristol village, and in the early days of the town were very numerous here. Though the name is not as common now as formerly, Sleeper blood flows in the veins of a very large number of her people, and the sons and daughters of Bristol bearing this name and their descendants are now worthy citizens of many states in the Union.

1. The Sleepers of Bristol are the descendants of Thomas Sleeper, b. in England about 1607. He emigrated to this country when a young man, and was in Hampton in 1640, where he probably resided till his death, which occurred July 30, 1696, at the age of 89 years. His widow, Joanna, d. in Kingston, Feb. 5, 1703, ae. 80. They had eight children, of whom the sixth was

2. Aaron, b. Hampton, Feb. 20, 1661. He m. (1) Elizabeth Shaw, May 23, 1682; (2) Sarah. He d. in Kingston, May 9, 1732, ae. 71-2-19. He had seventeen children by his first wife and two by his second, of whom the second was

3. Moses, b. Kingston, Feb. 22, 1685. He m., Jan. 9, 1714, Margaret, dau. Capt. Jonathan Sanborn. She was b. Mar. 20, 1698. He d. in Kingston, Jan. 13, 1754, ae. 68-10-21. They had fifteen children, of whom the fourth was

4. David, b. Kingston, Nov. 16, 1721. He m. (1) Nov. 24, 1743, Margaret Scribner, and soon after became one of the first settlers in Sandown. He was a farmer and amassed a large fortune for those days, dividing it among his children as they commenced life for themselves. Though not one of the proprietors of New Chester, he became a large owner of real estate in the town, much of which he deeded to his children as they settled here. "His firm and unshaken government over his numerous family, and his established principle in educating them in virtuous and useful habits was not surpassed by any of his age." He was a prominent member of the Baptist church, and held numerous town offices. "As a military officer he was bold and enterprising, and when the news of the battle of Lexington reached Sandown he called his company of militia and the cavalry to arms and immediately repaired to Boston to defend his country." He m. (2) Ruth Jenness (James), who was b. Mar. 29, 1735, and d. July 6, 1823, ae. 88-3-7. He d. Oct. 18, 1780, ae. 58-11-2.

CHILDREN, all supposed to have been born in Sandown

*5. Gideon, b. July 25, 1744.
*6. Peter, b. May 28, 1746. (Another record says May 27; another April.) [For (6) see p. 394.]
7. David, b. Sept. 8, 1748; took charge of his father's estate, and gave a home to his mother. Removed to Vershire, Vt., where he res.

till the death of his mother, then returned to Sandown. He m. Rachel Tilton, and had four children.

8.   Edmond, b. Mar. 17, 1753; was a tailor, m. (1) Mrs. Lydia Colby, (2) Elizabeth Worthen.   Res. Chester, and d. June 10, 1838, ae. 85-2-23. One child.

9.   Nathan, b. Apr. 12, 1754.   Supposed to have commenced a home in Bristol, and d. Sept. 11, 1775, ae. 21-4-29.   (See chapter on "First Settlements in New Chester.")

  *10.   Moses, b. Sept. 4, 1755.   [For (10) see p. 401.]
    11.   Margaret, b. Feb. 5, 1757; d. Jan. 13, 1777, ae. 19-11-8.
    12.   Mary, b. Sept. 22 (29), 1758; m. Theophilus Sanborn.   (See.)
  *13.   John, b. Apr. 15, 1760.   [For (13) see p. 402.]
  *14.   Daniel, b. Feb. 22; 1762.   [For (14) see p. 405.]
  *15.   Samuel, b. Feb. 14, 1764.   [For (15) see p. 407.]
    16.   David, Nov. 23, 1766; d. Aug. 25, 1846, ae. 79-9-2.
    17.   Jethro, b. Sept. 18, 1767; shoemaker, lived in Corinth, Vt.; d. Oct. 4, 1843, ae. 76-0-16.
    18.   Jonathan, b. Feb. 6, 1769; d. Nov. 20, 1775, ae. 6-9-14.
    19.   Benjamin, b. Jan. 17, 1771; m. Betsey Hill, and removed to Compton, Lower Canada, where she d., and he m. Anna Harriman, of Plymouth.   He d. Apr. 7, 1838, ae. 67-2-20.
    20.   Josiah, b. July 14, 1772; d. Apr. 22, 1835, ae. 62-9-8.
    21.   Ruth, b. Mar. 4 (14), 1774; m. James Ingalls.   (See.)
    22.   Nathan, b. Aug. 13, 1777.   Carpenter; settled in Maine.   Twelve children.
    23.   Jonathan, b. Aug. 8, 1780; d. May 29, 1805, ae. 24-9-21.

Of the above, Gideon, Peter, Nathan (probably), Moses, John, Daniel, Samuel, Mary, and Ruth settled in Bristol.

GIDEON SLEEPER AND HIS DESCENDANTS

(5)   Gideon Sleeper, son of David, b. July 25, 1744, settled in Bristol in 1769, next north of his brother Peter.   His log cabin was near where is now the dwelling of F. H. Briggs on High street, and there he remained till 1784, when he moved to Grafton; thence to Kirk hill in Alexandria, where he d. Feb. 27, 1829, ae. 84-7-2.   He m. Sarah Hoyt, of Grafton.   An inscription on a tombstone in the Burns cemetery, near his home in Alexandria, reads "Elizabeth, wife of Gideon Sleeper, died Feb. 3, 1815, aged about 65 years."   This may have been his second wife; he m. Aug. 22, 1815, Anna Phillips.

CHILDREN

  24.   Sarah, b. Bristol, Apr. 10, 1770; m. —— Stevens, in Grafton.
*25.   David, b. B., Dec. 28, 1771.
*26.   Jonathan, b. B., Oct. 10, 1776.
  27.   Joseph Hoyt, b. B., Jan. 12, 1778, settled in Grafton, where all his children were b. and where he d. in 1850, ae. 72.   Children:

    a.   Benjamin.   b.   Joseph.   c.   John.   d.   Arnold.
    e.   Dexter.   f.   Molly.   g.   Matilda.   h.   Amy.
    i.   Lizzie.   j.   Diantha.   k.   Lettier.

  28.   Molly, b. B., Mar. 5, 1781.   *29.   Peter, b. B., Mar. 7, 1784.
*30.   Gideon, b. Grafton, 1786.

(25)   David, son of Gideon, b. Dec. 28, 1771, m. Mary Williams, of Grafton, (2) Mar. 19, 1815, Elizabeth Simonds,

widow of Jonathan Simonds, who was killed at Battle of Lundy's
Lane, War of 1812. She was dau. of John Bailey, and was b.
Apr. 8, 1791.

31. Lydia, b. in Grafton and d. in Woburn, Mass., Nov. 23, 1853.
She m. William Prince, Oct. 18, 1827. He was b. in Woburn, Mass., and
there d. Jan. 10, 1880. Children:

    a. Sullivan, b. June 18, 1828, d. at 31.
    b. Lydia J., b. Sept. 26, 1829; d. May 10, 1831, ae. 1-7-14.
    c. Anna U., b. June 10, 1831; d. May 31, 1890, ae. 58-11-21.
    d. William H., b. Dec. 10, 1832; d. in infancy.
    e. Eliza J., b. Mar. 4, 1835; m. May 29, 1872, Lowell W. Chamberlin, Charlestown, Mass.
    f. Ellen F., b. May 1, 1836; m. George Ware, Waltham, Mass.
    g. Mariette Williams, b. Nov. 18, 1843; m. John H. Simonds, Boston. She is a writer of ability.
    h. William E., b. Dec. 17, 1847, and d. in infancy.

32. Eliza, b. Jan. 18, 1816, and d. Nov. 25, 1819, ae. 3-10-7.

33. John B., b. Oct. 1, 1818, and d. Oct. 22, 1846, ae. 28-0-21, unm. A
stonecutter.

34. Jane Caroline, b. Grafton, Jan. 21, 1821; m. Aug. 22, 1839, Luther
C. Bailey, b. Alexandria, Apr. 13, 1811. He was a farmer in Alexandria
till 1871, when he removed to Bristol and res. foot of the lake, and here
d. Mar. 4, 1892, ae. 80-10-21. She d. Bristol, Sept. 8, 1874, ae. 53-7-17.
Children, all b. in Alexandria:

    a. Rosilla Simonds, b. Sept. 6, 1841; m. Oct. 8, 1859, Charles
W. Gould, Manchester, who d. Plymouth, 1886. She m. (2) John
Breck; (3) Apr. 5, 1888, Henry J. Young. She res. Bristol. Child:
(1) Florence Julia, b. Manchester, Nov. 26, 1861; m. Nov. 26, 1890,
Norman L. Hobart; res. Medford, Mass.
    b. Caroline Elizabeth, b. July 19, 1844; m. Jan. 22, 1861, Henry
H. Bailey, of Alexandria. Children: (1) Carrie Jennie, d. May
6, 1887. (2) Luther Henry, b. Jan. 27, 1870; m. June 20, 1892,
Flora D. Cass, dau. Daniel. (See.) Farmer in Alexandria. Child:
Harry Hobart, b. Apr. 4, 1893.
    c. Mary Jane, b. May 25, 1846; d. June 9, 1857, ae. 11-0-14.
    d. Martha Ann, b. Oct. 23, 1848; m. 1868, Marcellus Bailey; d.
Manchester, Jan. 23, 1881, ae. 32-3-0.

✳35. David H., b. Alexandria, Mar. 18, 1823.

36. Mary Elizabeth, b. Feb. 25, 1826; m. Sept. 24, 1843, Charles
Williams, Pepperell, Mass.

37. Gideon C., b. Aug. 3, 1828; m. June 21, 1850. He m. (2). Killed
by a fall down stairs, breaking his neck. Children:

    a. John Cummings, b. Concord, Mass., June 13, 1851.
    b. Henry Lovell, b. C., Feb. 14, 1853.
    c. Rosilla Elizabeth, b. Roxbury, Mass., July 18, 1855.

✳38. Jonathan Randall, b. Jan. 2, 1833.

(26) Jonathan Sleeper, son of Gideon, b. Oct. 10, 1776,
removed with his parents to Grafton, where he m. Mary Weare,
b. Dec. 5, 1785. She d. Grafton, Mar. 26, 1864, ae. 78-3-21.
He is reported to have d. same month.

39. Jonathan Weare, b. Grafton, Mar. 6, 1805; m. Hannah Hoyt Mc-
Murphy, dau. of John T., b. Alexandria, Mar. 7, 1803; d. in Alexandria,

Mar. 22, 1874, ae. 71-0-15. He d. No. Chelmsford, Mass., Oct. 10, 1886, ae. 81-7-4. Child :

  a. Daniel W., b. Ipswich, Mass., Feb. 16, 1838; m. Nov., 1862, Hannah H. Johnson, of Alexandria. She was b. Pennsylvania, Nov. 22, 1842; d. Boston, Apr. 19, 1869, ae. 26-4-27. He m. (2) Nov., 1872, Sophia Douglass, b. New Brunswick, Nov. 12, 1848. He was a policeman in Boston sixteen years. Res. in No. Chelmsford, Mass., twenty-two years, where he d. Aug. 2, 1901, ae. 63-5-16. Children : (1) Arthur T., b. Boston, Apr. 20, 1864 ; d. Apr. 28, 1869. ae. 5-0-8. (2) Laura A., b. B., Nov. 23, 1865. (3) Abbie F., b B., June 24, 1867 (4) May D., b. Alexandria, May 24, 1874. (5) Hannah H., b. No Chelmsford, Mass., Apr. 15, 1879.

  40. Solomon Sayles, b. Grafton, Aug. 23, 1811; m. Dec. 27, 1832, Abbie Hoyt McMurphy, dau. John T., b. Alexandria, and d. No. Chelmsford, Mass., Feb. 14, 1898. He d. same place, Dec. 24, 1892, ae. 81-4-1. Children :

  a. James Foster, b. Alexandria, Sept. 18, 1837 ; d. Danvers, Mass., June 6, 1893, ae. 55-8-18. He m., Jan., 1859, Betsey S. Perham, who d. June 6, 1881. Children : (1) Irving Foster, b. Aug. 27, 1860; m. Anna S. Gilman, Exeter, May, 1885. (2) Kate, b. Haverhill, Mass., Aug. 28, 1865.

  b. Hannah Foster, b. Sept. 20, 1841 ; m. Jan. 1, 1869, John H. Butterfield, Tyngsboro, Mass., b. July 27, 1847; d. Apr. 18, 1897. ae. 49-8-21. Res. No. Chelmsford, Mass. Children : (1) Abbie Blanche, b. Feb. 18, 1879. (2) May Grace, b. Jan. 27, 1882 ; d. Mar. 13, 1882.

(29) Peter Sleeper, son of Gideon, b. Mar. 7, 1784, m. Apr. 24, 1806, Sally Atwood, dau. David, b. Alexandria, Dec., 1788, d. in Alexandria, Dec., 1885, ae. 97-0-. He d. Apr. 9, 1870, ae. 86-1-2. A farmer in Alexandria.

CHILDREN, all born in Alexandria

*41. Caleb, b. Jan. 10, 1807.
  42. Ruth, b. Feb. 3, 1809 ; m. Alva Phillips ; d. July 29, 1885, ae. 76-5-26.
  43. Peter, b. Aug. 22, 1811 ; m. Weltha Bowen Corliss, dau. John, b. Alexandria, Aug. 17, 1817. He d. Alexandria, May 11, 1883, ae. 71-8-19. Was selectman and twice represented his town in legislature. Children :

  a. James M., m. Lettie A. Harriman ; res. in Chicago, Ill.
  b. John Marshall, m. Clara S. Merrill, and res. Newbury, Vt.
  c. Marcus Olando ; m. Minnie E. Vose ; res. Norwood Junction, N. Y.

  44. James M., b. July 3, 1815; d. Lowell, Mass., Mar. 10, 1838, ae. 22-8-7.
  45. Joanna C., b. Aug. 14, 1818; d. Jan. 27, 1832, ae. 13-5-13.
  46. Isaac N., b. Mar. 6, 1822, enlisted in the United States army about 1852, and supposed to have been killed by Indians in Oregon.
  47. Sarah B., b. Dec. 8, 1825 ; m. Apr. 7, 1852, Miles Hodgdon. She d. June 26, 1885, ae. 59-6-18. Children :

  a. Charles G., b. Apr. 7, 1853; m. Mar. 10, 1878, Abbie N. Sparks, b. Philadelphia, Pa., Sept. 17, 1859. Res. Council Bluffs, Iowa. He is general agent Walter A. Woods M. & R. M. Co. Two children.

  b. George S., b. Nov. 20, 1854 ; settled in Boise City, Idaho.

  48. Sylvester B., b. July 28, 1828; m. Oct. 10, 1858, Mary L. Verrill, dau. Joseph, b. Alexandria, Sept. 28, 1832, and d. Aug. 12, 1889, ae. 56-10-14. No children.

(30) Gideon Sleeper, son of Gideon, b. 1786, m. in 1823 (1824), Mrs. Margaret Stribling, b. Georgia, Jan. 2, 1793, d. Liberty, Miss., Jan. 21, 1864. He was a trader and farmer in Liberty, where he d. Sept. 17, 1838, ae. 52.

CHILDREN

49. Martha, b. Liberty, Nov. 23, 1825; m. Van F. Swearingen, and d. Dec. 27, 1883, ae. 58-1-4. Two children.

50. Clorinda B., b. L., Aug. 27, 1827; m. Robert Torrence, by whom she had three children. He d. and she m. (2) John Morgan, by whom she had four children. He d.; she res. in Waco, Texas.

51. Gardner Southworth, b. L., Jan. 17, 1829; m. Nancy Daniels. Children: Gideon, Emma and Hoyt. He m. (2) Isadore Cansey. He d. She and children res. Waco.

52. Fabens Hoyt, b. L., May 20, 1830; m. 1850 or '51, Clara, dau. Rev. J. C. Chamberlainn, president of Oakland College. She d. 1856, leaving three children, and he m. (2) 1858, Pattie Markham, by whom he had three children. He graduated with distinction from Oakland College in 1848; at the age of twenty-one was elected to the Mississippi legislature, and there distinguished himself. An old line Whig he opposed vigorously the secession of his state, but when she voted to go with her sister states, all his means and talents were used in the service of the South. In 1868, he removed to Waco, Texas, where he was elected judge, and where he d. June 19, 1881, ae. 51-0-29. His family res. Waco. Children :

 a. Jerry C., b. Jan. 24, 1853; a farmer in Waco; m. 1881, ——— Shaw. Six children.

 b. John, b. Dec. 12, 1854; in boot and shoe trade, Waco, for twenty-five years ; m. 1881, ——— McMuller. No children.

 c. Clara, b. 1856; m. 1881, John Norris, and d. 1886, ae. 30. No children.

 d. Susie M., a teacher in city schools, Waco.

 e. William Markham, b. Liberty, Oct. 9, 1859; m. Apr. 26, 1892, Laura Risher. Children: (1) Benjamin Risher, b. Waco, Dec. 11, 1894. (2) Martha Margaret, b. W., May, 1896. (3) Alethia Holbert, b. W., Nov. 26, 1898. (4) William Markham, b. W., Nov. 30, 1900.

 f. Lucy, m. R. F. Gribble, cashier First National Bank, Waco. Three children.

 g. Thomas M., m. Miss Lockard, of Clarksville, Tenn. He is a grain merchant in Waxahachie, Texas. Four children.

 h. Van, d. young.

53. Julia, b. Nazoo Co., Miss., Aug. 18, 1832; m. Dec. 25, 1851, William P. Anderson. Res. Liberty, Miss., till 1885, then removed to Gloster, Miss. Nine children, three deceased.

54. Lewis Gideon, b. Liberty, May 16, 1835 ; m. Imogene Eggleston. He served in Southern army, and was wounded in head. After his return home had a minie-ball and a piece of his hat taken from the wound. He d. three years later, Dec. 2, 1866, ae. 31-6-16. No children.

55. Arminda, b. Jan. 8, 1837; m. Stephen Barbie. She d. Jan., 1870, ae. 43-0-. He deceased. Children, living in Merrick, La.: Mrs. W. T. Coyle, Mrs. Frank Tessier, Eugene Henry.

(35) David H. Sleeper, son of David, b. Mar. 18, 1823, m. May 20, 1850, Sarah Cloutman, b. Alexandria, Oct. 26, 1832. He res. in Alexandria till about 1870, when he purchased

a farm on the old Turnpike near the foot of the lake. Farmer and speculator. Now res. No. Bristol.

CHILDREN

56. Etta Pierce, b. Mar. 31, 1851; m. (1) James D. Follansbee, (2) Wm. H. Folsom, (3) Chris Meng. (See.)

57. John Franklin, b. Dec. 3, 1852; d. Nov. 8, 1863, ae. 10-11-5.

(38) Jonathan R. Sleeper, son of David, b. Jan. 2, 1833, m. Jan. 20, 1858, Emma Bailey, dau. Daniel, b. Alexandria, Nov. 2, 1843, and d. Bristol, Mar. 17, 1889, ae. 45-4-15. He was foreman of tannery many years; a farmer and had charge of the Bristol Water Power Company's dam at outlet of the lake, residing in its house, and had charge of the state fish hatchery; now farmer in Bridgewater.

CHILDREN

58. Oscar Fowler, b. Alexandria, Apr. 25, 1860; m. Oct., 1883, Alma, dau. Roswell Blake. (See.) Farmer in Bridgewater. She m. (2) Albion A. Veasey. (See.) Child:

a. Oscar Blake, b. Sept. 18, 1884; d. Dec. 23, 1884.

59. Susan Ivanette, b. Bristol, Mar. 6, 1868; m. Dec. 24, 1896, Orrin S. Gray. She was school teacher ten years. Res. Bridgewater. Children:

a. Sarah Emeline, b. Bristol, June 16, 1899.

b. Helen Belle, b. Bridgewater, Aug. 6, 1901.

(41) Caleb Sleeper, son of Peter, b. Jan. 10, 1807, m. Oct. 26, 1828, Eliza Smith, dau. Christopher, b. in Grafton. Farmer in Alexandria, where he d. July 13, 1854, ae. 47-6-3.

CHILDREN

60. George W., b. Alexandria, Mar. 12, 1831; m. Sept. 6, 1848, Emeline, dau. Roby Prescott, b. Grafton, Mar. 4, 1829. He went to California about 1855, was there two or three years, and then started for home across the plains with a few companions, and never was heard of after. Supposed to have been killed by Indians. Children:

a. Isabelle, b. Danbury, Nov. 22, 1849; m. Mar. 19, 1865, Augustus G. Russell, b. Springfield, Feb. 11, 1842. Three children.

b. Francis M., b. Danbury, May 10, 1852; m. Aug. 18, 1873, Flotila, dau. Alonzo Barden, b. Springfield, Dec. 14, 1858. Res. Grafton. Four children:

PETER SLEEPER AND HIS DESCENDANTS

(6) Col. Peter Sleeper, son of David, b. May 28, 1746, evidently first came to Bristol in 1768, and commenced to clear land for a farm. On the 29th day of May, 1769, his father gave him a deed of Lot 63, First Division, where he had been making improvements. He built a log cabin directly in front of the present residence of Mrs. Solon S. Southard on High street, on the west side of the highway. Tradition says he was m. about 1770, and in the fall of 1771, brought his wife here who rode from Sandown, horseback, carrying in her arms her firstborn.

He was the first settler within the limits of Bristol village. He was a justice of the peace, and for fifty years was prominent in town affairs. In 1800, he was in command of the 14th Regiment of militia, with the rank of lieutenant-colonel. At some time previous to 1800, he erected a commodious frame house and here for many years he kept tavern. At his house, during the Revolutionary war, were held several town meetings, to act on matters of importance connected with that struggle. Col. Sleeper served at least one enlistment in the Continental army. (See New Chester in the Revolutionary War.) He was a man of fine presence, stout, erect and every inch a gentleman. He m. Mary, dau. of Daniel Sanborn, b. Kensington, Sept. 23, 1751, and d. Bristol, Oct. 27, 1834, ae. 83-1-4. He d. Bristol, Sept. 11, 1826, ae. 80-3-13.

CHILDREN, all except first born in Bristol

*61. Peter, b. Sandown, July 29, 1771.
62. Daniel, b. Mar. 17, 1773; m. Ruth Tilton, and settled in Vermont.
*63. Nathan, b. Sept. 27, 1775.
*64. Moses West, b. Dec. 24, 1777.
65. Sherburn Tilton, b. Oct. 11, 1779; m. Elizabeth Cummings, of Hebron. Pub. July 3, 1802. He was last taxed in New Chester in 1809. Tradition says that he had a family, but deserted them and went South ; was supposed to have d. in Louisiana. The family had name changed to Montgomery, and res. in New York state. One son, Romanzo Warwick, went to New Orleans. A daughter m. —— Evans, and lived in Belmont. She had two children ; one, a son, was adopted by Romanzo on condition that he change his name to Sleeper, which he did.
*66. Sanborn, b. Dec. 1, 1781.
67. Anna, b. Aug. 12, 1783; m. Ichabod C. Bartlett. (See.)
*68. David, b. June. 16, 1785.
69. Abraham, b. June 16, 1787; m. —— Tolford ; removed to Elba, N. Y., and there d. No children.
*70. Jonathan E., b. Aug. 6, 1789.
71. Mary, b. Mar. 25, 1793; m. Dr. Daniel Favor. (See.)

(61) Peter Sleeper, son of Col. Peter, b. July 29, 1771, m. Molly Burpee. He was a farmer on Bridgewater hill, in Orford, and in Bristol.

CHILDREN

72. Jonathan, b. Mar. 11, 1800; d. young.
73. Molly, b. June 2, 1802; d. at Orford, unm.
74. Hannah, b. May 2, 1805; d. Bristol, July 9, 1837, unm., ae. 32-2-7.
75. Thomas Christie, went to Millport, N. Y., where he m. and had a family, and where he and his wife both d.
76. Nancy, b. Bristol, May 10, 1809; m. Sherburn S. Worthen. (See.)
77. Peter A., b. Apr. 20, 1811 ; m. Oct. 14, 1834, Emily S. Sawyer, dau. Caleb. (See.) He was in business as a blacksmith, with Richard H. Sawyer in building standing on site of Post-office block ; in Oct., 1850, emigrated to Grand Rapids, Mich. He d. Apr. 21, 1880, at Sparta, Mich., ae. 69-0-1, and she made her home with her only living dau., Mrs. Wylie. Children :

    a. Emily Henrietta, b. Meredith, Apr. 18, 1836; m. Nov. 27, 1860, Kent Seaman, Newaygo, Mich.; d. Sparta, Mich., Sept. 27, 1873, ae. 37-5-9.

b. Clara Belle, b. Piermont, Apr. 9, 1840; d. Piermont, May 4, 1842, ae. 2-0-25.

c. Susan Claribel, b. Bristol, May 5, 1844; d. Feb. 10, 1846, ae. 1-9-5.

d. Annie Maria, b. B., Feb. 14, 1846; m. Mar. 4, 1866, William Delancy Wylie, b. Madison Co., N. Y., Sept. 30, 1845. They res. Elmira, Otsego Co., Mich. Children: (1) Ernest Sleeper, b. Sparta, June 1, 1867. (2) Ira Clark, b. S., June 29, 1872. (3) Clyde Avery, b. S., Sept. 10, 1876. (4) Mary Emily, b. S., Apr. 21, 1879.

e. Milton Henrie, b. B., Oct. 21, 1849; m. in Sparta, 1876, Fidelia Snyder, and settled in Grand Rapids, Mich.

78. Benjamin, m. and settled in Orford.
79. Jonathan, m. and settled in Orford.
80. Nathan, m. and settled in Nashua.

(63) Nathan Sleeper, son of Col. Peter, b. Sept. 27, 1775, m. 1799, Fanny or Frances Jones, of Portsmouth. They res. on New Chester mountain, where he d. July 22, 1855, ae. 79-9-25. She d. Feb. 28 (18), 1848, ae. 74-3-5.

CHILDREN, all born in Bristol

81. Sherburn Tilton, b. Sept. 27, 1799; d. Nov. 11, 1841, unm., ae. 42-1-14.

*82. Sanborn, b. Aug. 13, 1801.

*83. Nathan, b. June 18, 1803.

84. Elizabeth, b. July 6, 1805; m. Jan. 13, 1825, Gideon D. Wheeler. She d. Boston and was interred in Sleeper burying-ground on New Chester mountain. Children given a home in family of Nathan Sleeper:

a. Harriet D., b. June 5, 1825; d. Lowell, Mass., Aug. 17, 1850, ae. 25-2-12.   *b.* Ai, d. in Boston.

85. Son, b. Oct. 1, 1807; d. same day.
86. Olive, d. Aug. 9, 1809, ae. seven months.
87. Polly, b. Nov. 10, 1811; d. Sept. 14, 1818, ae. 6-10-4.
*88. Jonathan Emerson, b. Feb. 16, 1813 (14).
89. Daughter, b. May 16, 1816; d. May 17, 1816.
90. Mary, b. June 1, 1819; m. Oct. 16, 1842, Thomas Shepard Shaw, b. Holderness, Apr. 3, 1821, and res. Lowell, Mass. She d. Manchester, May 31, 1896, in family of Sherburn Sleeper, ae. 76-11-30. Children:

a. Thomas Pierpont, b. Holderness, Sept. 27, 1843; m. Apr. 5, 1876, Carrie Maria Stephenson, dau. Rev. William S., b. Montville, Me., Sept. 20, 1850; d. Sept. 11, 1895, in Lowell, where he is a practicing physician. Children: (1) Frederick Pierpont, b. Lowell, June 13, 1877. (2) Annie, b. L., Feb. 23, 1880.

b. Harriet Letina, d. Aug. 29, 1848, ae. 0-6-21.

c. Mary Lizzie, d. Sept. 4, 1850, ae. 1-4-21.

(64) Moses W. Sleeper, son of Col. Peter, b. Dec. 24, 1777, m. Mar. 16, 1802, Ruth, dau. Lieut. Samuel Worthen (See), b. Feb. 14, 1783. He settled on a farm near the Danforth brook in the Hall neighborhood; was a soldier in the War of 1812; resided a short time in Alexandria and about 1832, removed to Hermon, Me., where he d. Dec. 25, 1845, ae. 68-0-1. She d. Nov. 17, 1840, ae. 57-9-3.

CHILDREN, all born in Bristol

*91. Levi H., b. Mar. 10, 1803.
92. Hannah Van, b. July 26, 1805; m. Jonathan H. Moore. (See.)

93. Sally, b. Feb. 27, 1807; m. (1) Isaiah Emerson, (2) Jonathan Emmons. (See.)

94. Marcia, b. Dec. 26, 1809; m. Jonas R. Hayward. (See.)

95. Mary Lucia, b. May 5, 1812; m. (1) Dec. 4, 1835, Cyrus Fletcher, (2) Fletcher, both of Bridgewater, and d. in Bridgewater, Apr. 11, 1878, ae. 65-11-6

96. Francis M., b. June 24, 1815; m. Jane Clark, of Hermon, Me., and had five sons and two daughters. He d. in Bangor, Me., 1885, ae. 70.

97. Anna B., b. Dec. 26, 1819; m. (1) James Clark, of Hermon, Me. One son, Lauren. She m. (2) Nathaniel Eaton, of Hermon. Three children, one son and two daughters. She d. in Hermon, May 13, 1854, ae. 34-4-17.

98. Augusta Jane, b. Oct. 27, 1823. She m. Capt. William Gordon, Oct. 5, 1843. He was b. in Holderness, Apr. 11, 1821, and was the son of Simeon L. and Ruth (Cheney) Gordon, and grandson of Capt. William Gordon of the Revolutionary army. He served as captain in the 14th Regt., N. H. Vols., Civil war. She d. Canaan, Mar. 21, 1897, ae. 73-4-24. He res. with his son, Hon. George H. Gordon, Canaan. Children :

    a. Charles Sleeper, b. Holderness, Nov. 8, 1844.

    b. Frank L., b. H., Jan. 3, 1846; d. Aug. 9, 1847, ae. 1-7-6.

    c. Clemma A., b. Suncook, Oct. 5, 1847.

    d. Frank L., b. Holderness, May 10, 1849.

    e. Willie, b. H., Mar. 10, 1853.

    f. Mary Ella, b. H., Oct. 27, 1855; d. Apr. 8, 1876, ae. 20-5-11.

    g. Ella A., b. H., May 2, 1857; d. Aug. 28, 1859, ae. 2-3-26.

    h. George H., b. Sept. 27, 1859; res. Canaan ; was member of N. H. senate in 1899.

(66) **Sanborn Sleeper,** son of Col. Peter, b. Dec. 1, 1781, m. (1) Sally McKean, pub. June 1, 1802. She d. Nov. 6, 1803, and he m. (2) Polly McKean, who d. Oct. 7, 1807.

CHILDREN

99. Hiram, b. Bristol, Feb. 17, 1803; m. June 16, 1831, Mary, dau. of Dudley Leavitt, b. Grantham, July 12, 1804; d. Plainfield, June 20, 1881, ae. 76-11-8. He d. Plainfield, Dec. 2, 1870, ae. 67-9-15. Children :

    a. Hiram Lewis, b. Grantham, July 1, 1832. He graduated from Dartmouth College, 1857, read law and settled in New York city ; d. May 31, 1864, ae. 31-10-30.

    b. Hubert, b. G., Jan. 13, 1835; graduated from Dartmouth Medical School in 1859, and located Grantham. Was assistant surgeon in 16th Regt., N. H. Vols. After the war removed to Meriden, where he practiced till 1890, when he retired. Never m.

    c. Hannah Leavitt, b. Aug. 31, 1839; m. Aug. 26, 1873, Edgar A. Conant, son of Nathan, and res. Dorchester.

    d. Mary Elizabeth, b. G., June 22, 1844. Unm.

100. John McKean, b. B., Jan. 8, 1805. Res. Elba, N. Y. One son, settled in Kansas.

(68) **David Sleeper,** son of Col. Peter, b. June 16, 1785, m. Susan Harriman, who d. Bristol, May 11, 1849, ae. 61-7-21. He was last taxed in Bristol, 1818 ; d. Canaan, Sept. 12, 1863, ae. 78-2-26.

CHILDREN, all born in Bristol

101. Walter Harriman, b. Feb. 10, 1808. He went South, was in trade in Mississippi in 1836. During the war lost all his property by a Union raid. Was m., had several children, and d. during the war.

102. Nehemiah Snow, b. June 18, 1810; m. in 1835, Julia McConnell, dau. of Hon. David Moulton, b. Floyd, N. Y., May 15, 1818. He d. Floyd, Feb. 3, 1886, ae. 75-7-15. Children:

    a. Cesarine Metz, b. Feb. 5, 1837; m. Hon. Eaton J. Richardson, a lawyer of Utica, N. Y.; d. July 28, 1869, ae. 32-5-23. A son, Everett Sleeper Richardson, res. New Orleans, La.

    b. David Moulton, b. May 12, 1839; m. Apr., 1871, Annie Thayer, of Amsterdam, N. Y. Children: (1) Walter Thayer, b. Amsterdam, May 12, 1872. (2) William Ernest, b. Aug., 1875. (3) Mary Ingalls, b. June, 1882.

    c. Prudence Moulton, b. Rome, N. Y., Aug. 11, 1843; m. Nov. 24, 1870, William A. Davies, merchant, now of New York. Child: (1) William Everett, b. Jan. 11, 1872.

103. Jane Bartlett, b. July 30, 1813; m. Simeon H. Wadleigh. (See.)
104. John Weston, b. Feb. 10, 1815; went to New York state and m. Charlotte Spriggs, dau. of John, b. England. Children:

    a. William, was drowned in the Tennessee river during the Civil war.

    b. Hannibal, is supposed to be living in the South.

    c. Maria.

105. Charlotte Pearson, b. Sept. 8, 1820; m. June 29, 1840, James M. Davis, b. Concord, Jan. 31, 1820, and d. Canaan, Sept. 28, 1872, ae. 52-7-27. She d. Canaan, Feb. 24, 1901, ae. 80-5-16.

    a. Horace Lyman, b. Holderness, Feb. 16, 1841.

    b. Walter Sleeper, b. Bristol, Feb. 2, 1843; res. Canaan Street.

    c. Frank Weston, b. Sanbornton, Dec. 27, 1844. Res. Minneapolis, Minn.

    d. James Scott, b. Boscawen, Mar. 11, 1847. Res. Providence, R. I.

    e. Charles Edward, b. Concord, Apr. 27, 1849, and res. Canaan Street.

    f. George Henry, b. Nov. 9, 1851.

    g. Ellen Caroline, b. Hartford, Vt., May 5, 1854.

106. Jonathan Knight, b. Apr. 20, 1823; went to New York, thence to Canada, where he d., leaving one son, David.

107. Mary Crawford, b. Sept. 7, 1827; m. Gustavus W. Ingalls. (See.)

(70) Jonathan E. Sleeper, son of Col. Peter, b. Aug. 6, 1789, m. Adelia Aurelia Sweep, Apr. 24, 1826, in Bellville, C. W., whither he went at the age of 17. He d. in the family of his son, William, in Concord, Jan. 24, 1873, ae. 83-5-18; she d. in New Jersey, July, 1887.

CHILDREN

108. Mary Ann, b. Bellville, Jan. 10, 1828.
109. Jonathan W., b. B., Jan. 7, 1831; d. Nov. 11, 1834, ae. 3-10-4.
110. Abraham F., b. Apr. 22, 1833; res. in Partello, Mich.
111. Adelia A., b. Jan. 31, 1835; m. Charles Littlefield. Res. Eatontown, N. J.
112. William A., b. Bellville, Mar. 31, 1837; m. Nov. 22, 1860, Laura E., dau. of Ephraim and Sarah Lamprey, b. Alexandria, June 19, 1843. Res. in Concord. Children:

    a. Carrie Idella, b. in Concord, Aug. 20, 1862; m. Dec. 2, 1885, Fred N. Ladd.

    b. Etta Frances, b. C., Mar. 18, 1869.

113. Letitia M., b. B., June 19, 1839; d. young.

114. Josephine Victoria, b. June 4, 1841; m. —— Griffith, and res. Three Rivers, Mich.

115. Jonathan W., b. Oct. 14, 1842; m. Anna T. Hurd, and d. in Wolfeboro.

116. Charles Wellington, b. Feb. 28, 1846; m Oct. 20, 1868, Clementine Thompson, b. Ashland, June 14, 1846. Res. Franklin. Children:

    a. Alvah Guy, b. Oct. 23, 1872.
    b. Fred Asa, b. May 14, 1876.

117. Andrew A , b. Bellville, Jan. 12, 1848. Res. Nickerson, Kan.
118. Peter, b. B., Oct. 10, 1851; d. June 26, 1852.

(82) Sanborn Sleeper, son of Nathan, b. Aug. 13, 1801, d. in Manchester, Mar. 17, 1866, ae. 64-7-4. He m. Hannah Gillis, Jan. 17, 1833. She was b. in Bedford, Apr. 25, 1810, and d. in Merrimack, Mar. 15, 1892, ae. 81-10-20.

CHILDREN

119. Son, b. and d. Oct. 18, 1834, Nashua.
120. Ellen, b. N., Jan. 26, 1836; m. John P. Wheeler, and res. at Reeds Ferry.
121. Cornelia, b. Hudson, Jan. 3, 1838; d. Apr. 26, 1842, ae. 4-3-23.
122. Edwin, b. H., Jan. 12, 1840; m. and res. in Chester, Pa. Children:

    a. Lottie.   *b.* Josiah.   *c.* Elmer.

123. Josiah Graves, b. H., Jan. 26, 1842; d. Manchester, Jan. 25, 1862, from swallowing a cent 12 or 15 years before, ae. 19-11-29.
124. Nathaniel B., b. Hooksett, Apr. 13, 1844; m. Fannie Allen, of Lowell. Child:

    a. Gertie. Res. in Fitchburg, Mass.

125. Sherburn Tilton, b. H., May 7, 1846; m. Ellen M. Taber, Alleghany City, Pa. Child:

    a. Lillian M. Res. Manchester.

126. Nathan Allen, b. H., Dec. 9, 1850; m. Helen Chase, of Vermont. Children:

    a. Flora.   *b.* Fanny.   *c.* Edna. Res. Manchester.

127. Arthur L., b. H., Jan. 3, 1852; d. Manchester, Sept. 10, 1855, ae. 3-8-7.

(83) Nathan Sleeper, son of Nathan, b. June 18, 1803, m. Jane W., dau of John and Hannah (Wheeler) Evans, of Hill, b. Unity, July 1, 1816. He settled in Alexandria and carried on the George mills till about 1845, when he removed to Bristol and settled on a farm on New Chester mountain, where he d. Feb. 28, 1854, ae. 50-8-10; she spent her last years with her daughter, Mrs. George S. Merrill, in Iowa, and d. June 27, 1892, ae. 75-11-26.

CHILDREN

128. Twin daughters, b. Alexandria, Jan. 15, 1840; d. Feb. 1840.
129. Mary Frances, b. A., Feb. 15, 1841; d. in Bristol, May 17, 1860, ae. 19-3-2.
130. Agnes J., b. A., Sept. 21, 1844; m. George S. Merrill. (See.)
131. Eri, d. Aug. 15, 1846.
132. Curtis, b. Jan. 1, 1847; d. Feb. 12, 1847.
133. Sylvanus I., b. Bristol, May 22, 1848; m. Mar. 29, 1869, Lilla

Viola, dau. of Anson H. and Jane H. Sutton, of Chickasaw Co., Iowa, who was b. Sept. 15, 1852, in Ontario, N. Y. He went to Iowa in 1863, and engaged in the sale of farming implements and now res. Canova, South Dakota. Child :

 a. Daisy Alice, b. Watertown, Wis., Sept. 9, 1875 ; d. Aug. 28, 1894, ae. 18–11–19.

 134. Eugene W., b. B., Mar. 10, 1850. He went to Iowa in 1864, and Feb. 19, 1880, m. Belle, dau. of William and Catherine Ijams, b. Mar. 7, 1859, in Logan, Iowa. Locomotive engineer on St. Paul and Sault St. Marie Ry. Res. Minneapolis, Minn. Child :

 a. George Merrill, b. Minneapolis, Dec. 6, 1884.

 135. Milan E., b. B., Feb. 20, 1852 ; m. June 15, 1879, Jennie L. Hatcher, dau. George and Amelia I. (Phillips) Hatcher, b. Oct. 15, 1855, in Portage, Minn. He left Bristol in June, 1868; has been for 19 years superintendent of sewers in Minneapolis, Minn. Res. 2,205 17th Ave., A. L. Children :

 a. Paul Emmons, b. Nov. 30, 1888.
 b. Agnes Jane, b. Aug. 31, 1889.

(88) Jonathan E. Sleeper, son of Nathan, b. Feb. 16, 1813 (14), m. Hannah O., dau. of Peter and Bessie (Cate) Ackerman, b. Dover, May 28, 1824, who d. in Bristol, May 12, 1855, ae. 30–11–14. He m. (2) Rachel C. Ackerman, sister of first wife. He d. in Bristol, May 10, 1868, ae. 55–2–24. She m. (2) Dimond G. Wells, of Rumney.

CHILDREN

 136. Loring Curtis, b. Apr. 9, 1847. He m. Emma Hadley, and d. in Lowell, Sept. 6, 1876, ae. 29–4–27. Children :

 a. Ethel Enna.   *b.* Grace.

 137. Enna Annette, b Bristol, Nov. 5, 1849 ; m. Nov. 5, 1868, Joseph Emery Hastings, and res. in Boston, Mass. She d. Boston, Mar. 23, 1898, ae. 48–4–18.

 138. Hannah Otis, d. July 18, 1855, ae. 2 mos., 24 days.

(91) Levi H. Sleeper, son of Moses W., b. Mar. 10, 1803. He m., Oct. 4, 1827, Lydia A., dau. of Nathaniel and Anna (Wilkins) Merrill, b. Deering, Oct. 13, 1809. At m. he settled in Alexandria ; was in Bristol 1839–'40 ; returned to Alexandria ; removed to Manchester in 1843, where he had charge of a department on a corporation ; was member of city council two years and of the legislature two years ; was a class-leader in Methodist church thirty years. "He was an exemplary man and had the respect and esteem of the people." He d. Jan. 30, 1877, ae. 73–10–20. She d. Dec. 4, 1900, ae. 91–1–21. "Her long life was a continuous career of usefulness."

CHILDREN

 139. Mary L., b. Alexandria, July 2, 1828 ; was 24 years a teacher in the public schools of Manchester, where she now res.

 140. Harriet K., b. A., Dec. 8, 1829 ; m. 1854, Edward Prime, of Manchester, who d. in 1870. Children :

 a. George E., b. 1857 ; res. Manchester.
 b. Arthur M., b. 1880 ; res. Watertown, Wis.

141. William F., b. A., May 20, 1832. He m. Nov. 15, 1855, Hannah Stark, dau. of Thomas and Sarah (Stevens) Pollard. She was b. Manchester, in 1834, and there d. Nov. 20, 1890, ae. 56. Was in the grocery business thirty years. Was member legislature in 1870 and '71, and served two terms in city council. He d. Mar. 10, 1899, ae. 66-9-20. Children :

    a. Frank S., b. Manchester, Apr. 6, 1857; in mercantile business in Duluth, Minn.

    b. Walter J., b. M., June 15, 1860; m. 1886, Emma Chadwich, of Manchester. Graduate of Dartmouth Medical College ; since 1887, a physician in Westford, Mass.

142. Levi H., b. Plymouth, 1837; m. 1870, Susan Sampson, of Whitefield. Is an iron monger in Manchester.

143. Jonas H., b. Bristol, 1839; went to Watertown, Wis., in 1860, where he m., Sept. 3, 1863, Sally Ann, dau. of Joseph and Mary Hamlin. She was b. Middletown, Vt., Oct. 12, 1843. He d. in Watertown, July 16, 1888. He was station agent of the C., M. & St. Paul Ry., president of a gas company, and connected with other business interests. Children :

    a. Mamie. d. at 6 years.   *b.* Veina.

144. Silas R., b. Alexandria, Mar. 21, 1840; m. (1) Oct. 8, 1874, Asineth Anderson. She was b. Jan. 19, 1856, and d. in Watertown, Wis., Nov. 15, 1884, ae. 28-9-26. He m. (2) Mrs. Carrie Taylor, Mar. 10, 1886. He was in the elevator business with his brother, Jonas H., and proprietor of stone works. He d. in Biloxi, Miss., Mar. 3, 1895, ae. 54-11-12. She res. Watertown. Children :

    a. Lydia May, b. Manchester, July 19, 1875.

    b. Fred Levi, b. M., Feb. 4, 1878, and d. Watertown, Nov. 20, 1884, ae. 6-9-16.

MOSES SLEEPER AND HIS DESCENDANTS

(10) Moses Sleeper, son of David, b. Sept. 4, 1755, m. Dec. 17, 1778, Mrs. Betty Colby, b. Mar. 8, 1759. Moses Sleeper was a Revolutionary soldier from Sandown. In September, 1775, he was at Portsmouth, and had among his companions Sherburn Sanborn, who afterward settled in Bristol, and Abraham Hook, who later settled on the Gilbert B. Dolloff farm in Bridgewater. In August, 1776, his brother John enlisted for one year and served till fall, when his company received orders to prepare to go to Ticonderoga. John was reported as unable to make the march, and Moses took his place, going to Ticonderoga, where he remained till the evacuation of that post. Moses again enlisted in a company that marched from Sandown, in September, 1777, and joined the northern army at Saratoga. In this company he ranked as corporal. In 1818, he was granted a pension of $96 a year. Moses Sleeper and his bride arrived in Bristol, Mar. 2, 1779, and spent a short time with his brothers, Peter and Gideon. He went to the north side of Newfound river on snow shoes, and first occupied the mill-house at the corner of Central square and Spring street, while building a log cabin where the town house now stands. This in readiness, they commenced to clear the land; his wife, Betsey, assisting in all the laborious work of those days. After a few years they built the frame house occupied for many years by

26

William Green, and now by his daughter, Mrs. Frank W. Robinson, and here for 22 years he kept tavern. In 1816, he returned to Sandown and eleven years later settled in Alexandria, where he d., May 14, 1838, ae. 82-8-10. She came to her death, same place, by falling into the open fireplace, Nov. 25, 1846, ae. 87-8-17.

CHILDREN, all born in Bristol

145. Betsey, b. Mar. 6, 1780; m. Reuben Emmons. (See.)
146. Ruth, b. Dec. 6, 1782; m. Joseph Emmons. (See.)
147. Mary Merrill, b. July 18, 1786; m. (Pub. Oct. 25, 1809), David Atwood, Esq., and d., ae. 30.
148. Benjamin Colby, b. Jan. 25 (29), 1795. He m. Sally Sanborn, dau. of Josiah, Alexandria; (2) Mary Pickering. He res. in Alexandria, where he d. Feb. 10, 1881, ae. 86-0-15. He had one child.
149. Moses, b. Sept. 25, 1798. He went to sea at the age of 17, and was never heard from afterward.
150. Joanna, b. Oct. 5, 1801; m. Mar. 24, 1824, Col. William Crawford. (See.)

JOHN SLEEPER AND HIS DESCENDANTS

(13) John Sleeper, son of David, b. Apr. 15, 1760, served in the Revolutionary army from Sandown. He settled in Bristol when about twenty years old, and erected a log cabin near where the Uriah H. Kidder farmhouse stands on North Main street, on the west slope of Sugar hill. His farm included a strip of land extending from top of Sugar hill across Newfound river to the Alexandria line. He m., May 9, 1785, Elizabeth Tilton, dau. of Sherburn, b. June 26, 1765. In 1800, he erected the frame house at the junction of Lake and Willow streets, called for many years the "tannery house," and here she d. Dec. 10, 1814, ae. 49-5-14; he d. Feb. 4, 1818, ae. 57-9-19.

CHILDREN, all born in Bristol

151. Dorothy, b. Aug., 1786; d. at 26 years.
*152. Edmond, b. Feb. 3, 1788.
*153. Walter, b. Jan. 20, 1790.
154. Sherburn, b. Aug. 31 (3), 1792; m. Betsey Towle, pub. Aug. 13, 1815, and settled on that part of his father's land now constituting the farm of Zerah E. Tilton. He came to his death by having a fit and falling into a spring of water and thus drowning, his head only being in the water. They had at least one child, Sylvester Bradley, who res. Charlestown, and there Betsey T. d. Aug., 1865.
155. Rebecca, b. Mar. 12, 1797; d. young.
156. Nancy, b. Feb. 22, 1802; m. Dec. 31, 1838, Alexander Marshall, b. Hudson, Dec. 3, 1805. (His second wife.) He d. Hudson, Mar. 11, 1844, ae. 38-3-8. She d. Warner, Apr. 28, 1873, ae. 71-2-6. Child:
  a. Mary Alcinda, b. Hudson, Feb. 10, 1844; m. June 13, 1861, Joseph F. Keniston, Andover. He d. Jan. 18, 1890. Mrs. Keniston m. (2) Sept. 9, 1891, John R. Farnum, of Salisbury. Child: (1) Frank Elbridge, b. July 30, 1863; d. Apr. 5, 1889, ae. 25-8-5.
*157. John, b. Oct. 3, 1804.
158. Eliza, b. Jan. 13, 1811; m. Dec. 25, 1835, Alexander Marshall.

She d. Dec. 12, 1837, ae. 26-10-29, and he m. her sister, Nancy, as above.
Child :

    a. Eliza Ann, b. Hudson, Dec. 6, 1837; d. Andover, July 2, 1888, unm., ae. 50-6-26.

(152) Edmond Sleeper, son of John, b. Feb. 2, 1788, m. (Pub. Feb. 21, 1813) Betsey, dau. of Archippus W. and Polly (Sanborn) Wheelock, of Sanbornton. They evidently removed to Littleton, immediately after their m., where they took up eighty acres of wild land. In 1825, they removed to Newport, Vt., where they passed the remainder of their days. He d. July 4, 1866, ae. 78-5-2 ; she d. in June, 1871.

CHILDREN

159. Dorothy, b. Littleton, Apr., 1814; m. —— Baker, and settled in Newport Center, Vt.

160. Sarah, b. L., 1817; m. Loren Cutts, and d. 1868, ae. 51. A dau.. Mrs. Briggs Waite, res. Boynton, P. Q.

161. George L., b. L., 1819; m. Eliza G. Blake. He went to Newport with his parents. Is called the father of Newport Center. He built a hotel here of which he was landlord for 16 years ; had a grocery store for 12 years ; was selectman five years ; was founder of the Methodist church and served as a steward for 40 years. Mrs. Sleeper was proprietor of a millinery store for 23 years. Both were living in summer of 1903, retired from business. Children :

    a. Carlos G., is a manufacturer of ladies' straw and felt hats, 90 Blackstone street, Boston, Mass.
    b. William E., in same business as Carlos ; res. Boston.
    c. George L., res. Boston.
    d. Nye T., in a wholesale house, Cincinnati, O.
    e. Ella, m. Dr. C. L. Erwin, and res. Newport Center.
    f. Nettie, m. Rev. C. W. Morse, Newport Center.
    g. Carrie, m. J. F. Buzzell, and res. Topeka, Kan., 113 West 10th street.

162. Elizabeth, b. L., 1821 ; m. Eyery Sias, res. Newport Center.

163. Alice, b. Newport, Vt., 1829; m. Lewis Harris ; d. 1872, ae. 43. A son, A. C. Harris, res. Barton Landing, Vt.

164. Mary, b. N., 1831 ; m. Fred Shaw ; d. 1875, ae. 44.

165. Asa C., b. N., 1839 ; m. Harriet Corse, and res. Newport, Vt.

(153) Rev. Walter Sleeper, son of John, b. Jan. 20, 1790, m. in Apr., 1814, Nancy Plaisted, of New Hampton, b. July 3, 1790. He was one of the very early members of the Methodist Episcopal church in Bristol, and became an ordained clergyman of this denomination. He was admitted to the New England Conference on trial in 1812 ; was ordained deacon by Bishops McKendricks and Roberts at Bristol, R. I., June 25, 1816 ; and elder, by Bishop George at Barre, Vt., June 24, 1821. He served on the Tuftonboro circuit in 1812 ; Bridgewater circuit, 1813; Canaan circuit, 1814-'15 ; Landaff, 1816, and located in 1817 to care for his father. After his father's death, he occupied for a time what later became the town farm ; operated a grist-mill at North Bristol ; was gate-keeper at the Mayhew Turnpike tollgate on North Main street, and in 1841 erected

the house on North Main street, lately owned by Orrison G. Cass. He was seven years selectman of the town, and twice represented his town in the legislature. She d. Jan. 3, 1862, ae. 71-6-0. He d. in the home of Robert S. Hastings, May 1, 1875, respected and beloved by all, having rounded out a long and useful life, ae. 85-3-11.

CHILDREN

*166. Solomon Sias, b. Bristol, Mar. 18, 1815.

167. Horace Lyman, b. B., Apr. 7, 1820; m. Jan. 5, 1851, Martha W. Haynes, of Danbury. He m. (2) Susan A. Burnham, of Winchester, Mass. He res. in Winchester, and was in the wholesale grocery business in Boston, in company with his brother, Solomon S., for more than twenty years. He d. Nov. 23, 1884, ae. 64-7-16. Children :

 a. Ida L., b. Woburn, Mass., May 25, 1852; m. July 15, 1875, George Woodward, a merchant in New London, b. July 31, 1843 ; d. Mar. 1, 1894, ae. 50-7-. She res. Bristol. Child : Florence Edna, b. New London, Apr. 20, 1883. Graduated from Colby Academy, 1900, m. Nov. 18, 1903, Leo J. Richardson, of Worcester, Mass.

 b. Charles H., b. Mar., 1860, res. Winchester.

168. Margaret Hall, b. B., Nov. 20, 1828; m. Hon. Lewis W. Fling. (See.)

(157) John Sleeper, son of John, was b. Oct. 3, 1804. When a young man, he went to Union Springs, N. Y., and became a clerk in the dry goods store of Philip Winegar, and in 1835 became his partner. Sept. 14, 1836, he m. Sarah Mosher Winegar, a dau. of his partner, b. Galway, N. Y., Apr. 16, 1813. While a resident of Union Springs, he filled many offices of trust and honor. In 1842, he and his father-in-law emigrated to Comstock, Mich., where he became supervisor of the town and filled other offices. In 1848, he was elected probate judge and removed to Kalamazoo where he was trustee of the village and served twelve years as judge. Returned to Comstock became county superintendent of the poor, county drain commissioner, and again supervisor. "He was a man of large experience in the affairs of the world, of decided ability and great industry ; in social life refined, unselfish and courteous, attracting the warm friendship of the intelligent and cultivated ; in business just and honorable." He d. Comstock, May 19, 1865, ae. 60-7-16. She d. Kalamazoo, Mar. 9, 1888, ae. 74-10-23.

CHILDREN

169. Lewis Philip, b. Union Springs, N. Y., July 14, 1837; was killed by a run-away horse at Kalamazoo, May 19, 1855, ae. 17-10-5.

170. Eliza, b. U. S., Sept. 8, 1839; m. July 20, 1876, Charles Lewis Rounds, of Kalamazoo. Children :

 a. Mary Elmira, b. Kalamazoo, May 30, 1877.

 b. Walter, b. K., Oct. 31, 1878, and res. K.

171. Henry Sias, b. U. S., Aug. 8, 1841 ; m. Dec. 26, 1872, Jennie Conrad. He was a farmer and real estate agent; was assistant secretary and secretary of state senate, 1863-'71 ; clerk of county, 1872-'78 ; deputy

commissioner, state land office, 1879-'91. He. d. Lansing, Mich., June 15, 1892, ae. 50-10-7. Children :

   a. Lewis Conrad, b. Kalamazoo, Mar. 31, 1874; graduated Michigan University, 1897, teacher in Portland, Mich.
   b. Alice, b. Lansing, Mich., Nov. 3, 1879.

172. Esek Winegar, b. Comstock, Nov. 6, 1843; m. June 5 ,1872, Emma Conrad, a sister to Jennie. He res. in Milwaukee, Oregon. Children :

   a. John Story, b. Kalamazoo, Mar. 22, 1875 ; a printer in Portland, Mich.
   b. Sarah, b. K., Nov. 14, 1876 ; a teacher in Portland.

173. Frank Story, b. C., June 5, 1847 ; d. Mar. 25, 1884, ae. 36-9-20.

(166) Hon. Solomon S. Sleeper, son of Rev. Walter, b. Bristol, Mar. 18, 1815, m. July 30, 1844, Ellen Caroline, dau. of Francis Kidder. (See.) He was commonly addressed as colonel, having attained this rank in the 34th Regiment of N. H. militia when a young man. When a boy he entered the store of Ichabod C. Bartlett, as a clerk, and later became a partner. In April, 1842, he sold his interest to Cyrus Taylor, and went to Boston and purchased an interest in the firm of E. Raymond & Co., wholesale grocers. Fifteen years later the firm became Sleeper & Dickinson. In 1861, he formed the firm of S. S. Sleeper & Co., his brother, Horace L., being his partner, where he continued till his death. He did an extensive business and accumulated a fortune. He served on the board of aldermen of Cambridge six years, and was four years in the Massachusetts legislature. The S. S. Sleeper Camp, Sons of Veterans, Cambridge, was named in his honor. He was interested in charitable work and was a liberal giver. Was one of the donors of the Minot-Sleeper Library to Bristol. (See.) His home was in Cambridge, where he d. Jan. 6, 1895, ae. 79-9-18.

CHILDREN

174. Ella Frances, b. Dec. 1, 1850; d. Jan. 23, 1861, ae. 10-1-22.
175. Frank Henry, b. Oct. 11, 1853 ; m. July 30, 1878, Carrie M. Hyde. He was a member of the firm of S. S. Sleeper & Co., residing in Cambridge, where he d. Feb. 25, 1898, ae. 44-4-14, leaving a widow and two daughters.
176. Florence, b. Aug. 18, 1859 ; d. Feb. 6, 1867, ae. 7-5-18.

DANIEL SLEEPER AND HIS DESCENDANTS

(14) Daniel Sleeper, son of David, was b. Sandown, Feb. 22, 1762, where he was selectman soon after coming to his majority. He probably came to Bristol in 1790, and, in December of that year, m. Anna, dau. of Sherburn Tilton (See), b. Aug. 11, 1763. They resided for a time in the family of her father on the east side of South Main street, where their first child was b. He settled on the farm on the hillside to the east of Newfound lake, recently occupied by Mrs. Laura R. Mitchell. At that time the route to Bristol village was by a path over the base of Bristol Peak to the Locke neighborhood, where a road leading to the village was reached. He was a shoemaker, probably the

26a

first in town. He taught his sons this trade and they used to go from house to house to work. He was one of the movers in the erection of the church on Bridgewater hill. Mr. Sleeper passed his life on this farm, and here he d. Feb. 28, 1838, ae. 76-0-6. His widow d. in the family of her son, Capt. Daniel, in May, 1856, ae. 92-9-.

CHILDREN

*177. Amos, b. July 24, 1791.
178. Nancy, b. Mar. 12, 1794; m. John Laney. (See.)
179. Ruth, b. Feb. 10, 1797; m. Capt. Blake Fowler. (See.)
* 180. Daniel, b. June 10, 1799.
181. Odlin, b. Oct. 18, 1801. He was a shoemaker, carpenter and builder, and erected a great many buildings in Bridgewater and adjoining towns. When a young man, he spent four or five years in New York state surveying and one year in Michigan. He d. unm. in Bridgewater, Mar. 22, 1894, ae. 92-5-4.
182. Elizabeth, b. July 19, 1905; m. Jeremiah Johnson. (See.)

(177) Amos Sleeper, son of Capt. Daniel, b. July 24, 1791, m. Sept., 1812, Phebe Mussey Clough, dau. of John (See), b. Sept. 18, 1794. He was a farmer in Bristol, moved to Bridgewater in 1823, and to East Concord in 1836, where he d. June 9, 1871, ae. 79-10-15. She d. East Concord, July 3, 1842, ae. 47-9-15.

CHILDREN

183. Mary Ann, b. Bristol, Mar. 23, 1814; d. Dec. 9, 1846, unm., ae. 32-8-16.
184. Charlotte Wood, b. B., June 21, 1816, and res. Malden, Mass. Never m. She d. Nov. —, 1901, ae. 85-5-.
185. Oren Clough, b. B., Mar. 26, 1818; m. Jane Vittum, Concord, Me., and d. Malden Mass., June 28, 1887, ae. 69-3-2. He was a milliner and later in the real estate business in Boston, Mass. Nine children.
*186. Jonathan Clough, b. B., Jan. 3, 1820.
187. John Kilburn Clough, b. Bridgewater, Feb. 7, 1828; m. Hannah M. Shaw, of Exeter, Me., dau. Asa and Mary T. Shaw, b. Exeter, Dec. 9, 1824. He was wholesale milliner of firm of John K. C. Sleeper & Co., Boston He was twice a member of Massachusetts house of representatives. He res. Malden, Mass., where he d. Apr. 18, 1893, ae. 65-2-11. Children :
a. Charles Frederick, b. Somerville, Mass., June 25, 1852; m. Jan., 1875, Ella P. Fogue, and d. Malden, Apr. 9, 1886, ae. 33-9-14.
b. Mary Emma, b. Exeter, Me., Dec. 5, 1859; m. Dec. 12, 1893, Sidney S. Horton. Res. Malden.

(180) Capt. Daniel Sleeper, son of Daniel, b. June 10, 1799, m. Apr. 18, 1824, Dorothy R. Tilton, dau. of Jonathan (See), b. Oct. 7, 1802. She d. June 3, 1854, ae. 51-7-26, and he m., Apr. 2, 1855, Orpha (Powell) Sawyer, widow of Jonathan. He was a farmer and shoemaker, and succeeded his father on the home farm, later res. on east shore of lake, where Edwin T. Pike now lives, but spent his last years in Bristol village, where he d. Mar. 13, 1872, ae. 72-9-3; she m. (3) Perrin Prescott, and d. Bristol, Apr. 20, 1888, ae. 76-10-24. He was a captain in the militia. Methodist.

CHILDREN, all born in Bristol

188. Soloman Cavis, b. June 20, 1825; m. Feb. 28, 1850, Fanny A. Leach. He went to Lowell, Mass., in 1850, where he was a mill operative eight years, was a railroad employee in the West fifteen years, then an officer in the New Hampshire state prison. In the Civil war served in the 1st Massachusetts Sharp-shooters. (See Roll of Honor.) He d. Concord, Feb. 2, 1900, ae. 74-7-12.

189. Sarah A., b. May 10, 1830; m. Abram D. Locke. (See.)

190. Isaac T., b. July 10, 1832; d. May 21, 1833.

191. Ellen F., b. Apr. 12, 1846; m. Mar. 21, 1872, John Coffin, and lived in Mason City, Iowa, where she d. May 24, 1890, ae. 44-1-12. Children :

    a. Lura, b. Mar. 25, 1873.

    b. George Henry, b. Dec. 10, 1875 ; res. Mason City.

    c. Frank Joseph, b. Dec. 27, 1879; res. Mason City.

(186) **Jonathan C. Sleeper**, son of Amos, b. Jan. 3, 1820, m. Oct. 19, 1842, Sally, dau. James and Elsie (Bailey) Martin, b. Epsom, Dec. 25, 1822. They res. No. Acton, Mass.

CHILDREN

192. James Amos, b. Chelsea, Mass., June 22, 1845 ; m. May 16, 1867, Flora Lillian, dau. Ivory White and Abigail (Greely) Richardson, b. Chester, Vt., June 4, 1846. Res. Hollis. Children :

    a. Charles Henry, b. Malden, Mass., May 3, 1868 ; m. June 8, 1892, Charlotte Matilda Reeves, of Chicago, Ill. They res. Pueblo, Colo. Child : Harold Reeves, b. Pueblo, Mar. 18, 1893.

    b. James Edwin, b. M., Aug. 30, 1869 ; m. Sept. 12, 1891, Annie Lucinda Fowler, of Epsom. Res. West Somerville, Mass. Child : Arthur, b. Oct. 9, 1894.

    c. Herbert Alwyn, b. Chelsea, Jan. 28, 1873.

    d. Lila Ethel, b. C., Dec. 23, 1875 ; d. Nov. 13, 1883, ae. 7-10-20.

    e. Lillie Martin, b. Malden, May 3, 1877.

193. John Wesley, b. Boston, Mass., Oct. 19, 1849 ; m. Dec., 1873, Caroline Harwood Cox, of Malden, and res. Denver, Colo. Children :

    a. Elsie Elizabeth, b. Malden, Apr. 19, 1875 ; m. June 6, 1894, A. Herbert Johnson, Denver.

    b. John Harold, b. M., July 4, 1883.

194. George Albert, b. Malden, June 25, 1855 ; m. Sept., 1883, Emma L. Pettengill. Res. No. Acton, Mass.

195. Samuel Martin, b. M., Aug. 12, 1857. Res. Salida, Colo.

SAMUEL SLEEPER AND HIS DESCENDANTS

(15) **Samuel Sleeper**, son of David, b. Feb. 14, 1764, m. Elizabeth Sanborn, of Chester. They were in Bristol as early as 1790, and settled on the Aaron Sleeper farm on the hill west of this village, when there was only a path beyond Lake street. He built a log cabin in which he lived seven years, when he erected the present frame house, and here he spent his life and here d. Jan. 23, 1837, ae. 72-11-9 ; she d. May 14, 1846, ae. 77-9-. Samuel owned two lots of land of 144 acres each.

CHILDREN, all born in Bristol

196. Sally, b. Mar. 13, 1791 ; m. Benjamin Emmons. (See.)

✱197. Moses, b. Apr. 24, 1793.

＊198. John, b. Jan. 23, 1795.

＊199. Samuel, b. June 20, 1796. Name afterwards changed to Samuel Thomas Worthington Sleeper.

200. Elizabeth, b. Nov. 23, 1798; m. Nov. 6, 1823, Elder Moses Wallace. He was b. Feb. 12, 1803, in Fairfield, Vt., and d. in Waterbury, Vt., May 16, 1880, ae. 77-3-4. She d. in Waterbury, Feb. 6, 1885, ae. 86-2-13. Children:

    a. William Clinton, b. Alexandria, May 16, 1824, and d. Nov. 14, 1825, ae. 1-5-28.

    b. Elizabeth Sleeper, b. A., May 9, 1829; m. July 27, 1848, Myron Francis Morse, who d. July 4, 1852, in Boston, Mass. She m. (2) Jonathan Church, Vershire, Vt. Four children.

    c. Lavinia Sleeper, b. Thetford, Vt., July 1, 1832. She m., Mar. 19, 1848, Sidney Wallace. They had three sons and three dau. who lived to maturity, two dau. who d. young of consumption. One son was burned to death in Everett, Mass., Dec. 21, 1892.

    d. Samuel Sleeper, b. West Fairlee, Vt., Apr. 13, 1837; d. Mar. 13, 1838.

    e. Son, b. W. F., Oct., 1839; d. in infancy.

＊201. Aaron, b. Apr. 6, 1801.

202. Lavinia, b. June 29, 1803; m. Reuben Rollins. (See.)

203. Laura, b. Feb. 24, 1808; m. Reuben Rollins. (See.)

204. David V., b. May 3, 1810; m. Jan. 22, 1835; Maria Ferrin, of Alexandria, and went to Vermont, where he d. No children.

(197) Moses Sleeper, son of Samuel, b. Apr. 24, 1793, m. Dec., 1817, Mary, dau. of John Harriman, of Plymouth, b. 1799. He joined the Osgoodites and moved to Moultonboro. He later "went West and was never heard of after." The family removed to Ashland, thence to Springfield, Mass., "while the children were young." The mother d. Springfield, June, 1876, ae. 77.

CHILDREN

205. Augustus Merrill, b. Hebron, Oct. 6, 1818. He m. May, 1848, Maribah Humphrey, dau. of Bela, b. Sept., 1826, in Sutton, Vt. He d. Springfield, May 26, 1895, ae. 76-7-20. Children:

    a. Frank Augustus, b. 1849; d. 1850.

    b. Ida Rebecca, b. 1852; d. 1858, ae. 6.

206. Mary Bartlett, b. Bristol, 1832; res. Springfield.

207. Valeria McQuestion, b. B., 1832; d. Ashland, 1848, ae. 16.

208. Joseph Dean, b. B., 1836; d. unm., Springfield, 1865, ae. 29.

209. Marcellus Dearborn, b. B., 1838; dealer in real estate, Springfield. Unm.

(198) John Sleeper, son of Samuel, b. Jan. 23, 1795, m. June 3, 1824, Sally, dau. Jeremiah Bean (See), b. May 6, 1805. She d. Bristol, Apr. 19, 1828, ae. 22-11-13, and he m. Apr. 1, 1829, Polly Huckins, b. Parsonsfield, Me., Jan. 5, 1797; d. Alexandria, Jan. 30, 1883, ae. 86-0-25. He was the first settler on the John Olin Tilton farm, west of Newfound lake, and built the house now standing there, and there he d. Sept. 10, 1862, ae. 67-7-17.

CHILDREN, all born in Bristol

210. Belinda, b. Mar. 3, 1825; m. Samuel Worthen. (See.)

211. Lucinda, b. Mar. 3, 1825; d. June 4, 1828, ae. 3-3-1.

212. Matilda, b. Mar. 19, 1827; m. Thomas H. Marston, and res. Belmont, Mass.

213. Daughter, d in infancy, Feb, 1830.

214. Son, d. in infancy, June, 1832.

215. John Franklin, b. July 13, 1834; d. Sept. 27, 1841. ae. 7-2-14.

216. David Calvin, b. Mar. 23, 1837; m. Nov. 30, 1864, Jane Eliza Batherick, dau. Thomas K., b. Nov. 4, 1836, at Leominster, Mass. He left Bristol in 1864, and res. Fitchburg, Mass. Children:

    a. Althea Villa, b. Westminster, Mass., May 20, 1866. Res. Fitchburg, Mass.

    b. Flora Etta, b. Fitchburg, Dec. 20, 1868, where she now res.

217. Woodbury, b. June 1, 1839; m. May 17, 1863, Annie, dau. of William Crawford (See), b. May 22, 1837. He was a farmer; served two years as selectman; was for a time in the grain business; removed to Alexandria about 1878, where he d. Nov. 24, 1900, ae. 61-5-23. Republican, Odd Fellow. She res. Manchester. Children:

    a. Lura Mabel, b. Bristol, June 3, 1864; m. June 1, 1893, George G. Hoitt, an extensive farmer in Durham. Children: (1) Carrie Elizabeth, b. Mar. 17, 1894. (2) Alice Joanna, b. Apr. 28, 1895. (3) Martha Luena, b. Sept. 2, 1896. (4) Ellen Crawford, b. Sept. 1, 1898.

    b. Perley Howell, b B., Dec. 1. 1866; m. May 30, 1896, Annie Bertha, dau. Timothy P. and Mary (Murphy) Collins, b. Cork, Ireland, July 29, 1869. A farmer in Alexandria.

    c. Harry Lubert, b. B., Dec. 15, 1870; a farmer in Alexandria.

    d. Wilbert Artelle, b. B., Sept. 20, 1874. Is a carpenter in Manchester; res 196 Sagamore street.

(199) Samuel T. W. Sleeper, son of Samuel, b. June 20, 1796, was a school teacher and farmer and a man of superior intelligence. He was a justice of the peace for forty years and hundreds of cases were heard by him, but not in one case was his decision reversed by the higher court. He was three years selectman and five years superintending school committee. He represented his town in the state legislature two years and was the nominee of his party for member of congress. He m. Bethana Seavey, and settled on the farm later occupied by his son, Justin Martin Sleeper, in Dist. No. 9, and there he d. Jan. 15, 1868, ae. 71-6-25. She d. Dec. 28, 1876, ae. 80-6-. Democrat, Methodist.

CHILDREN, all born in Bristol

218. Albertus, b. Dec. 9, 1817; d. unm., July 16, 1839. ae. 21-7-7.

219. Jane F., b. Mar. 25, 1819; m. Albert Simpson, and d. Sept. 24, 1893, ae. 74-5-29.

220. Julia Maria Minot, b. Dec. 24, 1820; d. Mar. 7, 1843, ae. 22-2-13.

221. Lucina, b. Sept. 9, 1822; m. Silas Rhodes, and d. Mar. 7, 1847, ae. 24-5-28. No children.

222. Philotes, b. Sept. 1, 1824; d. Oct. 23, 1825, ae. 1-1-22.

223. Hanson Murray, b. Jan. 21, 1827, was twice m., and d. in California.

224. Laura Lovertia, b. Nov. 18, 1828; m. Sept. 18, 1856, Asa Woodbury Berry, b. Moultonboro, Sept. 4, 1826. They res. Somerville, Mass. She d. Aug. 27, 1900, ae. 71-9-9. He d. Dec. 22, 1901, ae. 75-3-18. Children:

    a. Mary Estelle, b. Somerville, May 16, 1858. Res. 29 Kidder street, West Somerville.

    b. Willis Woodbury, b. S., May 24, 1869, and d. June 2, 1869.

225. Justin Martin, b. Mar. 4, 1831; m. Nov. 27, 1857, Louisa Berry, dau. John, b. Moultonboro, Nov. 2, 1830. He succeeded his father on the home farm. Was a Democrat, and for many years a trustee of the Methodist Episcopal church. Removed with his children to Hudson about 1890, where he is still a farmer. Child :

    a. Eve Ducille, b. Bristol, Sept. 24, 1858; m. Nov. 13, 1883, Joseph H. LeGalle.

226. Wilbur Fisk, b. Mar. 5, 1833; m. May 8, 1855, Sarah Strate, dau. Asa, b. Enfield, Apr. 25, 1831, and d. Aug. 2, 1876, ae. 45-3-7. He res. Fitchburg, Mass. ; a car builder.

227. Timothy DeMerritt, b. May 18, 1837 ; m. Mar. 7, 1869, Cynthia A., dau. Nathan and Ann (Robinson) Gove, b. Bridgewater, Feb. 2, 1845. They res. East Cambridge, Mass. Was in grocery business; now retired. Children :

    a. Fred Woodbury, b. Rumney, Sept. 4, 1870. Res. East Cambridge.

    b. Frank Nathan, b. Rumney, Aug. 11, 1871 ; d. Sept. 2, 1871.

    c. Mary Lena (Rogers), adopted, b. in Ashland, Apr. 4, 1873. Res. East Cambridge.

    d. Wilbur Fisk, b. R., Nov. 18, 1873; d. Oct. 9, 1874.

    e. Bertha Ann, b. Lexington, Mass., July 23, 1877 ; d. Nov. 8, 1878, ae. 1-3-15.

228. Addie A., b. Aug. 20, 1841 ; m. Charles A. Gale. (See.)

(201) Aaron Sleeper, son of Samuel, b. Apr. 6, 1801, m. Polly P., dau. of Nathaniel Plumer, of Meredith, b. June 11, 1800, and d. in Bristol, Nov. 3, 1859, ae. 59-4-22. He succeeded to his father's farm, and there d. Oct. 28, 1888, ae. 87-6-22.

CHILDREN

229. Mary Ann, dau. of Matilda Pike, was adopted. She was b. Oct. 11, 1831; m. Charles Stewart, had five sons and two daughters, and d. Jan. 23, 1894, at Durand, Wis., ae. 62-3-12.

230. George Washington, b. Bristol, Aug. 21, 1833. Was a member of Co. G, 16th Mass. Vols.; severely wounded at battle of Fair Oaks, May 31, 1862, and d. of his wounds June 25, 1862; ae. 28-10-4. (See Roll of Honor.)

---

1. Col. Samuel Sleeper came to Bristol from Sandown about 1790 (?) and settled on the hill nearly opposite the residence of Charles A. Gale. His relation to the other Sleepers of the town was not known. The story is told that, to make a distinction between the two Samuel Sleepers in town, it was proposed that the one who would furnish the most rum on a certain occasion should be called colonel, and the other captain. Samuel Sleeper, 2nd, furnished the largest quantity and thereafter ranked as colonel. Col. Samuel d. Nov. 27, 1838, ae. 73-7- ; his wife, Phebe, d. Jan. 20, 1850, ae. 85 years.

CHILDREN

2. Reuben, d. Mar. 16, 1791, ae. 8 mos., 13 days.
3. "John, d. Nov. 6, 1798, in the 6th year of his age."—Tombstone.
4. "Hannah, d. Aug. 18, 1796, ae. 2 mos., 23 days."—Tombstone.
5. Nancy, b. Nov. 30, 1800; m. Sanborn Gale. (See.)

6. "Moses, d. Feb. 11, 1824, in 21st year of his age."—Tombstone.
7. Polly, m. James Martin, went to Lowell, Mass. Children :
    a. Sarah, d. about 1890.
    b. Clementia, d.   *c.* Eastman.
8. A dau., m. —— Dimond, and removed to New York state.

THE SMILEY FAMILIES

1. David Smiley, son of William and Sarah (Robinson) Smiley, was b. Jaffrey, Mar. 26, 1769. He m., Dec. 23, 1802, Mary, dau. of Thomas and Elizabeth (Putnam) Harkness, b. Lunenburg, Mass., Oct. 25, 1771, and d. Grafton, Jan. 25, 1858, ae. 86-3-0. He settled in Bristol in 1807, and was the first practicing lawyer in town. (See Lawyers.) He removed to Plymouth about 1818, and two years later to Grafton. He d. at Plymouth of lung fever while attending court May 19, 1845, ae. 76-1-23.

CHILDREN

2. Sarah, b. Jaffrey, June 7, 1804 ; d. June 16, 1804.
3. Mary Harkness, b. J., July 5, 1806 ; m. Oct 9, 1834, Dea. David Fosdick, Charlestown, Mass. ; d. June 25, 1864, in Groton, Mass., ae. 57-11-20. Children :
    a. Parmelia Tarbelle, d. in infancy.
    b. James Smiley.   *c.* Elizabeth Harkness.
    d. Adelaide Lane.   *e.* James Smiley.
*4. James Robinson, b. Bristol, June 17, 1808.
5. Daughter, b. and d. B., Jan. 21, 1811.
6. Elizabeth H., b. B., Apr. 30, 1813 ; d. June 28, 1813.

(4) James R. Smiley, M.D., b. June 17, 1808, m. Jan. 26, 1837, Elizabeth, dau. Robert and Mary (Kelsey) Lane, b. Newport, Nov. 14, 1807 : d. Sutton, Dec. 20, 1891, ae. 84-1-6. He removed from town with his father's family about 1818 ; graduated from Dartmouth Medical School in 1833 ; settled in Grafton, where he practiced for nearly thirty years and had a large and lucrative practice. Was also justice of the peace and superintendent of schools. He was a skilful physician, a broad-minded man, consistent Christian, and active worker in the temperance cause. Removed to Sutton where he spent the rest of his life in practice and farming, and there he d. Oct. 15, 1886, ae. 78-3-28.

CHILDREN, all born in Grafton

7. Adelaide Lane, b. Oct. 10, 1837. Res. No. Sutton.
8. Mary Elizabeth, b. Nov. 9, 1839 ; d. Sept. 9, 1856, ae. 16-10-0.
9. Frances Farley, b. July 8, 1841. Res. No. Sutton.
10. Susan Ela, b. Aug. 11, 1843 ; m. July 30, 1885, Chas. LeRoy Pulsifer ; d. Apr. 2, 1890, at Lakeport, ae. 46-7-21.
11. Parmelia Tarbelle, b. Jan. 19, 1846 ; m. Aug. 18, 1874, Benjamin O. True. Res. 7 Portsmouth Terrace, Rochester, N. Y. Children :
    a. Susan E., d. in infancy.   *b.* Edward Harold.
    c. Helen Elizabeth.   *d.* Ruth.
12. Robert Lane, b. Apr. 10, 1849 ; m. Feb. 29, 1892, Hattie E. Keyser, Sutton. Child, b. Feb. 10, 1894. Res. Harriman, Tenn.

THE SMITH FAMILIES

1.   John Smith was of Scottish birth or descent.   He was
b. about 1746, and in 1778 was a resident of Bedford.   That
year he purchased lot No. 58 in the 4th Div. in New Chester,
containing 105 acres.   In 1780, he was the owner of the mills on
Smith's river, and res. in a small 4-roofed house on the north
bank of this stream at the head of the falls opposite the mills as
they then were.   He continued to own and operate these mills
through life.   He d. Mar. 25, 1826, ae. 80.   His wife, Margaret Dinsmore, d. May 27, 1829, ae. 79.   Congregationalists.

CHILDREN

2.   Kate, b. Dec. 11, 1778; m. Robert McMurphy, of Alexandria,
pub. June 18, 1796; d. Apr. 1, 1812, ae. 33-3-20.
3.   Daniel D., b. Bristol, Aug. 30, 1782.   He was a saddler, had shop
in his father's house.   He went to Illinois and acquired large tracts of
land, and was killed by his partner in a business dispute.
4.   John Dinsmore, b. B., July 30, 1784; went to Pennsylvania.
5.   Samuel, b. B., July 16, 1788; was Indian agent in Tennessee.
6.   James, b. B., Feb. 16, 1790; went to Canada; m., and had a large
family.
*7.   Robert, b. B., June 11, 1791.
8.   "Elizabeth, d. Apr. 23, 1801, ae. 21."—Tombstone.

(7)   Robert Smith, b. June 11, 1791, m. Oct. 14, 1823,
Sarah Hall, dau. of Caleb Sawyer (See), b. Aug. 7, 1790.
She d. Dec. 29, 1838, ae. 48-4-22, and he m. (2) Hannah S.,
dau. of Rev. Christopher Sargent, who "d. May 10, 1868, ae.
73."   He succeeded his father in the ownership of the mills and
other real estate on Smith's river.   He erected a new dwelling
on the site of the old.   The new house was destroyed by fire
about 1875.   His home was the abode of culture and one of the
focal points of Bristol society.   He possessed original and well
defined traits of character, an unbending will being prominent.
He was a school teacher and for many years a justice of the
peace and a land surveyor.   He had political aspirations but his
opinions vigorously expressed did not make votes, though his
abilities secured him an election six times as moderator of the
annual town meeting. [1]   When 50 years of age he united with
the Congregational church and continued the practice of standing during the opening prayer long after all others had abandoned the practice.

----

[1] On one occasion he was nominated for representative.   When about
to leave home for town meeting, feeling sure of election, he said to his
wife, "You will have the privilege of sleeping with the representative
to-night."   He was defeated by Joseph Moore.   That night, in ill humor,
he retired early, but not to sleep.   Finally he said to Mrs. Smith, "Why
don't you come to bed?"   "Oh," said she, "I am waiting for Esq. Moore
to come."

9. Catherine Sawyer (adopted), was dau. of Alvah Sawyer. (See p. 383.) She d. in the family of Robert S. Hastings, Nov. 5, 1884, ae. about 57.

---

1. Moses Morgan Smith, son of Benjamin, was b. in Poplin, Feb. 18, 1794. When he was three years old his father settled in Bridgewater. He m., Nov. 29, 1819, Lucy, dau. of Dea. Samuel Gurdy (See), b. Nov. 12, 1795. She d. Bridgewater, Oct. 28, 1851, ae. 55-11-16, and he m. Oct. 17, 1855, Mary Buswell, of Grantham. He d. Bridgewater, Sept. 30, 1864, ae. 70-7-12.

CHILDREN, all born in Bridgewater

2. Eveline Hall, b. Aug. 13, 1820; m. Dec. 21, 1852, Joshua P. Smith. Res. Grantham, Bristol 1868-'70, Warren. He d. Warren, June 29, 1891, ae. 74-3-16. She d. Warren, Mar. 2, 1901, ae. 80-6-19.
3. Sophronia Maria, b. May 9, 1822; m. Gustavus B. Sanborn. (See.) 2) William P. Ballou. (See.)
4. Lucy, b. June 12, 1823; d. Aug. 26, 1825, ae. 2-2-14.
5. Elizabeth Brown, b. June 20, 1825; m. Levi B. Laney. (See.)
6. Moses Newell, b. May 4, 1831; d. Apr. 11, 1832.
7. Sylvester Jameson, b. and d. Apr. 24, 1834.

---

1. Ezekiel Smith was b. Andover, July 20, 1770, and m. Jan. 16, 1807, Hannah Ingalls, dau. of Jonathan (See), b. Apr. 3, 1787. He was a farmer in Bristol, as early as the date of his m. He removed to Peacham, Vt., where he remained twenty years; thence to Piermont, where he d. Dec. 17, 1857, ae. 87-4-27; she d. Jan. 3, 1877, ae. 89-9-0.

CHILDREN, all except last born in Bristol

2. Daniel, b. Oct. 16, 1807; m. May 17, 1829, Mary Jane Dearborn, of Plymouth, and emigrated to Illinois, where he d. Oct. 28, 1865, ae. 58-0-12. Four children.
3. Anson Coult, b. Dec. 20, 1810; was a Methodist clergyman; admitted to the New Hampshire conference 1835; ordained deacon by Bishop Hedding at Great Falls, July 9, 1837, and elder by same at Sandwich, July 7, 1839. He labored chiefly in Vermont till he d. at Hardwick, Apr. 23, 1862, ae. 51-4-3. He m. July 20, 1838, Mary Bartlett, of Sutton. Two children.
4. Ezekiel D., b. July 23, 1813; m. Mehitable Pike, Bradford, Vt. Both d. 1885, in Waterbury, Vt., same hour, of pneumonia, and both buried in same grave. Six children.
5. John C., b. Oct. 3, 1815; m. May 7, 1838, Mary Jane, dau. John Tirrell, b. May, 1819. They emigrated to Portland, Mich., where he d. May, 1883, ae. 67-5-. She d. Westville, Mich., Oct. 4, ——. Children:

a. Hial W., b. Jamestown, N. Y., Nov. 7, 1839; m. July, 1860, Maria Sutherland, of Portland, Mich. He served in 1st Mich. Engineers in Civil war; d. June 17, 1875, ae. 37-7-10.

b. Devine B., b. Portland, Jan. 16, 1847; m. Mar., 1876, Hattie Culver. Served in Civil war, in 2nd Mich. Infty. Res. North Evanston, Ill.

  c. W. R., b. P., July 24, 1850; m. July 4, 1876, Julia Dunning. Res. Lake View, Mich.

  d. Adelman, b. P., Mar. 4, 1857; m. Clara Westfall. Res. Allegan, Mich.

  e. J. C., b. P., Sept. 30, 1860; m. Kittie Fisher. Res. Mecosta, Mich.

 6. James D., b. Oct. 21, 1818; d. Oct., 1822, ae. 4.

 7. Luther, b. May 18, 1821 ; d. Nov. 14, 1882, ae. 61-5-26.

 8. Cyrus F., b. Oct. 12, 1825 ; m. Abbie Harris, of Mattapoiset, Mass. He was connected with the C., R. I., and P. railroad, and d. in Chicago, Ill., July 16, 1895, ae. 69-9-4. Children :

  a. Elgin C.   *b.* Edwin.

  c. Marcellus E., m. Sheldon Leavitt; res. 148 37th street, Chicago.

  d. Abbie R., d.   *e.* Clara A., d.

 9. Charles W., b. Oct. 28, 1827; m. Cordelia Durgin, Cabot, Vt., and d. at St. Louis, Mo., Feb. 16, 1895, ae. 67-3-18.

 10. George H., b. Peacham, Vt., Sept. 10, 1830; m. June, 1851, Arvilla Hill, dau. Samuel, b. Canada, Mar. 19, 1828. Res. Piermont. Children :

  a. Anson C., b. May 6, 1853; m. Apr., 1873, Annie Colby, of Warren, and d. Milford, May, 1893, ae. 40-0-.

  b. Loren G., b. Piermont, Nov. 11, 1855. Unm.

  c. Willie B., b. Sept. 2, 1862; m. Mar., 1886, Rose Farrell. Res. Hartford, Conn.

---

  1. **Daniel S. Smith,** a son of Jonathan and Seraphina (Putnam) Smith, was b. Oct. 27, 1800, in Lancaster. He m., Jan. 30, 1823, Nancy, dau. of Col. Aaron Hibbard, b. Bath, June 27, 1804. She d. Hill, Sept. 13, 1857, ae. 53-2-16; and he m., 1858, Mary Pinkham, of New York city. He d. Thornton, June 8, 1877, ae. 76-7-11. He came to Bristol from Wentworth in 1829 ; was landlord of hotel on South Main street for two years or more, when he sold to Jeremiah Prescott. The hall and shed connected with hotel he moved across the street and remodeled into a dwelling, now the double tenement house owned by Frank W. Calley, and later kept a store in the building at the corner of South Main and Beech streets. His farm consisted of the territory between the river and Prospect street. He removed to Woodstock about 1840, where he was in trade till 1847, when he returned to Bristol and removed to Hill, 1856, thence to Franklin and Thornton.

CHILDREN

  2. Jane Eliza Southerland, b. Orford, Mar. 12, 1824; m. Frederick Bartlett, Esq. (See.)

  3. Martha Amelia, b. Wentworth, Mar. 5, 1826; d. Hill, Aug. 8, 1859, unm., ae. 33-5-3. She was a superior school teacher.

  4. George P., b. Dec. 5, 1828; m. Jan. 1, 1852, Laura Elizabeth A. Taylor, dau. of Nicholas M. (See), b. Sanbornton, Aug. 31, 1830. He was freight agent of Milwaukee & St. Paul Railroad company, at St. Paul, Minn., where he d. Feb. 25, 1895, ae. 66-2-20. Five children.

  5. Angeline D., b. Bristol, Apr. 7, 1832; m. Jan. 2, 1853, Joseph M. Fellows, b. Andover, Nov. 2, 1831, a farmer and mill man at Franklin, where she d. Dec. 3, 1898, ae. 66-7-26. Four children :

CLARENCE A. SMITH

1. Andrew Jackson Smith, son of Jonathan and Seraphina (Putnam) Smith, was b. Oct. 8, 1816, and d. in Bristol, June 9, 1880, ae. 63-8-1 In 1837, he m. Sophia Weston, dau. of Wentworth Downes, of Bath, b. Dec. 30, 1817, and d. Bristol, Aug. 24, 1863, ae. 45-7-24. He m. (2), Dec. 15, 1864, Mary J. Hight, who d. June 17, 1875, ae 37. He m. (3) Elizabeth Taylor, of Woodstock, who d. in Georgia. He came to Bristol about 1838, and here he spent his life. He was a watchmaker and jeweler, and gathered a competency.

CHILDREN

2. Helen Mar, b. Bristol, July 22, 1838; m. Samuel K. Mason. (See.)
3. Howard M., b. B., May 24, 1866; m. Oct. 1, 1887, Ellen A. Drake; d. St. Paul, Minn., Mar. 1, 1892, ae. 25-9-7.
4. Homer Van Ness, b. B., May 22, 1872; drowned at Franklin, June 20, 1896, ae. 24-0-28.

---

1. Clarence Alvin Smith, son of Richard Ransom and Sarah Emeline (Eastman) Smith, was b. Orange, Feb. 18, 1861. He m., Jan. 20, 1884, Linnie Maude, dau. of Henry Griffith, (See), b. Bristol, July 9, 1867. He learned the blacksmith trade at Canaan; settled in Bristol in June, 1880, and had charge for one year of repairs of depots and bridges for Northern railroad; has carried on since Sept., 1880, the blacksmith shop on Lake street, near Willow, and since 1897, one on Water street. Is a Republican; has served as health officer over twenty years; as supervisor of the checklist since 1898; seven years as fireward, one year as selectman, and has been deputy sheriff since 1895.

CHILD

2. Roy Raymond, b. Bristol, Oct. 24, 1884. Graduated Tilton Seminary, 1903; now student in engineer course, Brown University.

---

1. Nathan P. Smith, son of Phineas B. and Sophronia P. (Covell) Smith, was b. July 5, 1863. He m., Aug. 30, 1888, Aletea Elira, dau. of Burley M. Ames (See), b. Feb. 27, 1872. Farmer in Bridgewater till 1892; in Bristol till April, 1903; now in Plymouth.

CHILD

2. Abbie Sophronia, b. Bridgewater, May 12, 1889.

---

1. Ai Bowen Smith is the son of Isaiah and Caroline P. (Bowen) Smith. He was b. in Ashland, Oct. 30, 1853, and m. Feb. 16, 1890, Flora I., dau. of Bainbridge W. Richardson, b. Mount Desert, Me., 1871. Divorced May 14, 1896. Has been a resident of Bristol since 1881; employee at crutch factory.

1.   Willie Herbert Smith is a son of Daniel T. and Sarah
Elizabeth (Drake) Smith.   He was b. New Hampton, Feb. 24,
1856, and m. Oct. 11, 1879, Mary Emma, dau. of John H. and
Polly (Dow) Harper, b. New Hampton, Oct. 17, 1858.   Has
res. Bristol since July, 1893, millwright and machinist.

---

1.   Charles Thomas Smith is the son of Jonathan J. and
Diantha R. (Cross) Smith.   He was b. Orange, Apr. 9, 1853,
and m. Dec. 23, 1883, Margaret Ellen, dau. of James Kenney
(See), b. Feb. 29, 1863.   He came to Bristol from Orange, 1887,
and is a section hand on the railroad.

CHILDREN

2.   Angie Abbie, b. Orange, Nov. 10, 1885.
3.   Otis James, b. Bristol, Oct. 25, 1887.
4.   Earle Frank, b. New Hampton, May 24, 1890.
5.   Grover Colby, b. Bristol, Mar. 23, 1893.
6.   Alice Maude, b. B., July 9, 1894.
7.   Wesley Charles, b. B., Jan. 30, 1900.

---

1.   Mrs. Cora Bell (Ford) Smith was b. Dec. 12, 1865.
She m., Nov. 12, 1881, Jonathan C. Smith, b. Apr., 1855, and
d. Mar. 5, 1899, ae. 43–11–.   She settled in Bristol, Apr., 1900.

CHILDREN

2.   Sumner P., b. Orange, Mar. 16, 1883.
3.   Isabel Addie, b. O., July 17, 1888; m. Wallace W. Lowell. (See.)
4.   Nellie Augusta, b. Groton, Sept. 16, 1889.
5.   Julia Ford, b. Orange, Apr. 20, 1894.
6.   Violet Gladys, b. O., May 18, 1896.

---

1.   Albie E. Smith, son of Samuel Newell and Sally (Richardson) Smith, was b. No. Charleston, Vt., Feb. 25, 1853.   He
m. (1) Mary Driver, who d. No. Charleston, Oct., 1886.   He
m., July 15, 1888, Gracie A., dau. of David and Ruth Bartlett
(Nutting) Royce, b West Charleston, Vt., Oct. 14, 1861.   He
has been a farmer on the Homans or town farm in Bristol since
Nov., 1900.

CHILD

2.   Ruth May, b. Deland, Fla., Aug. 28, 1892.

THE SOUTHARD FAMILY

1.   Solon S. Southard was a son of Moses and Nancy (King)
Southard, of Acworth.   He was b. May 28, 1813; m. Dec. 22,
1841, Berentha, dau. of David Morrill, b. Mar. 4, 1817, and d.
Haverhill, Jan. 17, 1854, ae. 36–10–13.   He m. (2) Sept. 14,
1854, Melissa, dau. of Moses and Sally (Smith) Eastman, b.

July 25, 1817. He was an extensive farmer in Haverhill till 1867, when he located on a farm on High street, Bristol, where he d. Dec. 21, 1870, ae. 57-6-23.

CHILDREN

2. George, b. Haverhill, May 14, 1843. Served in Co. G, 11th Regt. N. H. Vols., and d. of disease at Cincinnati, Apr. 17, 1863, ae. 19-11-3.

3. Frank, b. H., Apr. 21, 1845; d. Apr. 13, 1879, unm., ae. 33-11-22.

4. Solon Sumner, b. H., Sept. 17, 1855; m. Oct. 23, 1877, Clora E., dau. of John S. Nelson (See), b. Nov. 28, 1850, and d. Canterbury, Apr. 1, 1894, ae. 43-4-3. He m. (2) Ellen M. Parshley, b. Canterbury, Apr. 7, 1855. He was a farmer in Haverhill; since Nov., 1898, a manufacturer of excelsior at Profile Falls.

5. Moses Eastman, b. H., June 26, 1857; m. Feb. 16, 1880, Nellie A., dau. of William A. Beckford. (See.) He m. (2) Aug. 27, 1893, Clara, dau. of Russell Tirrell, b. Hebron, Sept. 11, 1864. He is a farmer at the parental home. Republican. Odd Fellow. Children:

    a. William, b. Bristol Oct. 15, 1881.

    b. Vera Belle, b. B., Nov. 19, 1894; d. Dec. 9, 1894.

    c. Ethel, b. B., May 26, 1897.

6. Charles Aaron, b. H., Feb. 14, 1861; m. Dec. 12, 1887, Cora, dau. of Stephen W. and Maria (Chapman) Knowles. Carpenter and farmer in Bristol till 1902, when he removed to Franklin; killed in a paper-mill at Bellows Falls, Vt., Oct. 28, 1903, ae. 42-8-14. Republican, Odd Fellow, K. of P. Children:

    a. Zilla, b. July 17, 1889.   *b.* Harry, b. May 29, 1892.

    c. Abbie Maria, b. July 31, 1896.

Sally (Smith) Eastman passed her last years in the family of her daughter, Mrs. Solon S. Southard. She was b. Bath, Feb. 18, 1795, and m. Moses Eastman. She was the sister of Hannah, who m. John Woolson; Abigail, who m. Oscar F. Fowler, and Ruth, who m. Nathaniel S. Berry, all of whom became residents of Bristol. She d. Dec. 1, 1886, ae. 91-9-13.

THE SPENCER FAMILIES

1. Seth Spencer was an early resident of Bridgewater. He m. Nancy Crawford.

CHILDREN

2. Lydia, b. Nov. 5, 1793.   3. Charles, b. Feb. 11, 1796.

4. John, b. Apr. 19, 1798.   *5. Seth, b. Nov. 1, 1800.

6. Simeon Dana, b. July 30, 1805.

(5) Seth Spencer, b. Nov. 1, 1800, m. in 1832, Mary Potter, dau. of Henry Brown (See), b. Sept. 12, 1816. He was a farmer in Bridgewater; in Bristol in Dist. No. 7, 1853-'59, and in Plymouth, where he d. Feb. 1, 1876, ae. 75-3-0. She d. Plymouth, Jan. 14, 1892, ae. 75-4-2.

7. Charles Henry, b. Bridgewater, May 20, 1834; m. Mar., 1857, Emily Jane, dau. of Cyrus W. Eaton. (See.) He was a farmer in Bridgewater; in Bristol, 1856-'58, and Plymouth, where he d. Oct. 5, 1865, ae. 31-4-15. She m. (2) Gilbert B. Dolloff. (See.) Children:

    a. Fred E., b. Plymouth, Jan. 30, 1858; res. Sioux City, Iowa.

    b. Anna A., b. P., Apr. 29, 1860; m. Sept. 4, 1891, David S. Fowler. (See.) (2) George C. Currier. (See.)

27

c. Charles E., b. P., Sept. 20, 1865; m. Jan. 19, 1895, Ethel W., dau. Burley M. Ames. (See.) He was engaged in ice business in Bristol; now farmer in Bridgewater.

8. Silas Montgomery, b. B., Jan. 20, 1836; m. Dec. 11, 1862, Lydia Jane, dau. of Stephen N. Heath (See), b. Bristol, July 23, 1845. Children:

a. Fannie Maria, b. Plymouth, Dec. 25, 1863; m. Nov. 1, 1890, Henry Greeley; res. Rumney. Four children: Mildred B., Winnifred B., Freida E., and Zena B.

b. Louis Allen, b. P., Sept. 13, 1867; m. Nov. 6, 1895, Mabel A. McQuesten; res. Plymouth. Three children: Archie M., Marion E., and Harry H.

c. Harry Wesley, b. P., Oct. 30, 1871; d. Apr. 13, 1876, ae. 4-5-13.

d. Eva Lillian, b. P., Feb. 6, 1878; m. Sept. 27, 1897, Jerry W. Tewksbury; res. Plymouth. Child: Bethrenee D.

9. Hannah Eliza, b. B., Jan. 30, 1839; m. 1861, Charles R. Heath: d. Mar. 6, 1876, ae. 37-1-6. Child: Cora L.

10. Laura Ann, b. B., Jan. 31, 1844; m. Eugene Harriman; d. Feb. 6, 1869, ae. 25-0-5. No children.

11. Sarah Louisa, b. B., 1847; d. 1865, ae. 18.

12. Lucian Scott, b. Bristol, Nov. 4, 1856; m. Mar. 23, 1885, Emma J., dau. of Gideon Boardman. (See.) Res. Sloane, Iowa, dealer in lumber. Three children.

---

1. Fred Ashton Spencer is a son of Joseph Gates and Angeline Boynton (Clough) Spencer. He was b. in Enfield, May 25, 1862. He m., Feb. 9, 1887, Grace Leone, dau. of Horace Burns and Emeline Almeda (Gates) Stanley, b. Enfield, Jan. 27, 1862. He came to Bristol in April, 1885; is assistant treasurer and salesman of the Dodge-Davis Manufacturing company, and a director of the First National Bank of Bristol. A Democrat, past master of Union Lodge, A. F. and A. M., and a Knight Templar.

CHILD

2. Stanley Ashton, b. Bristol, May 11, 1891.

THE SPILLER FAMILY

1. George H. Spiller is the son of Benjamin Spiller, and was b. Bridgewater. He m., May, 1865, Lizzie, dau. of Robert M. Kirk. (See.) He was clerk at the Bristol house; has been for many years traveling optician.

CHILD

2. Katherine Belle, b. Bristol, May 27, 1866; m. (1) Frank W. Wilbur, (2) Charles E. Rounds. (See.)

THE STEVENS FAMILY

1. Samuel Hubbard Stevens, Esq., was a son of John and Rhuhamah (Fifield) Stevens. He was b. in Kingston, Nov. 20, 1802, and m. July 27, 1840, Seraphina, dau. of Moses

and Seraphina (Stevens) Sanborn. He graduated from Dartmouth college in 1830; read law with Stephen C. Lyford, Meredith Bridge, now Laconia; was admitted to the bar and opened an office in Bristol about 1834. He represented Bristol in the legislature 1845 and 1846, and served eight years as superintending school committee. He removed 1846 to Lawrence, thence to Exeter, where he was cashier of the Granite State bank. From Exeter he removed to Kingston, thence to Concord, where he d. in 1876, ae. 74. She d. Concord.

CHILD

2. Seraphina Elizabeth, b. Bristol, about 1842; supposed to be living in Washington, D. C., unm., in 1903.

THE STOLWORTHY FAMILY

1. Charles Stolworthy is a son of Walter and Ellen (Hilloury) Stolworthy. He was b. Franklin July 11, 1866, and m. Mar. 15, 1890, Celia Riel, dau. of George and Delia (Lampron) Riel, b. Penacook, July 9, 1874. He has been a wool sorter at the Dodge-Davis Manufacturing company's mill since about 1893.

CHILDREN

2. Ralph, b. Franklin, Mar. 20, 1891.
3. Arthur, b. Laconia, June 27, 1893.

THE SULLIVAN FAMILY

1. William J. Sullivan was b. St. Johns, N. B., in 1872. He came to Bristol in 1887 and was for ten years wet finisher in the woolen-mill. Aug. 1, 1891, he m. S. Emma, dau. of John Seavey. (See.) In Dec., 1902, he removed to Charlestown, Mass., where he is freight brakeman. K. of P.

CHILDREN

2. Bertha May, b. Bristol, Jan. 14, 1892.
3. Ella Beatrice, b. B., July 25, 1893.
4. Karl Rupert, b. B., May 22, 1898.

THE SUMNER FAMILY

1 Luke Sumner was a son of George; was b. in Antrim, Mar. 5, 1805, and m. Sarah Ross. He came from Hillsboro to Bristol in 1837, and was a farmer here till he d. Feb. 10, 1872, ae. 66-11-5. She d. Alexandria, Aug. 14, 1860, ae. 55-5-9. They united with the Congregational church in 1843.

CHILDREN

2. George Washington, b. Alexandria, Aug. 31, 1833; m. Mar. 17 1858, Eva N., dau. of Edward and Lydia Haselton, b. Manchester, Oct., 1833,

and d. Alexandria, Jan. 3, 1861, ae. 27-3-. He m. (2) June 13, 1861, Mary N., a sister of his first wife, b. Aug. 28, 18.8 and d. Bristol, June 14, 1900, ae. 71-9-16. He came to Bristol, 1864; was a farmer in the northeast part of the town five years, since then on High street; Democrat, deacon of Congregational church since April, 1879. Child :

> *a.* Frank R., b. B. Dec. 22, 185- ; d. July 10, 1879, ae. 20-6-18.

3   John Ross, b A.. Jan 15, 1837; m. Sept. 22, 1864, Harriet, dau. of Simon and Lucinda Cunningham, b. Boston, Mass., Sept. 22, 1837, and d. Boston, Mar., 1873, ae. 35-5-9. He m. (2) Dec. 16, 1876, Lucy, dau. Aaron Hawthorne, . Cushing, Me., Jan. 1, 1844. He was in trade in Rollins's block with George F. Buttrick, 1864-'67 ; in Boston, boarding and sale stables, till 1902, when he returned to Bristol. Res. High street. Methodist. Children :

> *a.* Edith Houghton, b. Bristol, Oct. 9, 1866; d. Sept. 2, 1887, ae. 20-10-23
> *b.* Clara Davis, b. Concord, Mass., Aug. 13, 1868; m. Sept. 11, 1888, Thomas C. Newcomb, res. South Boston. Nine children.
> *c.* Walter Dickerson. b. East Weymouth, Mass., Aug. 1, 1870 ; d. Feb. 11, 1875, ae. 4-6-10.
> *d.* Herbert Ross, b. E. W., Dec. 9, 1871 ; m. Sept. 13, 1900, Grace Wi son, Boston.
> *e.* George, b. and d. Aug. 13, 1877.
> *f.* Alice Faith, b. June 9, 1879.

4.   Lydia, b. Apr. 24, 1829; m. Jan. 28, 1852, James Dickerson.
5.   Mary Ann, d. ae. 2 years.

THE SWETT FAMILIES

1.   Isaac Swett was a son of Benjamin and Hannah (Merrill) Swett. He was b. in Orange, Dec. 22, 1784, and m. in Oct., 1817, Nancy (Anne), dau. of Stephen T. Brown (See), b. May 27 (28), 1791. They commenced life on the Thomas H. Wicom farm in Bristol, east of the lake and here he d. Jan. 19, 1873, ae. 88-0-27. She d. June 7, 1887, ae. 96-0-10.

CHILDREN, all born in Bristol

2.   Lucinda, b. Nov. 13, 1818; d. an infant.
3.   Benjamin, b. Nov. 9, 1820 (1819), m. in Manchester, Mar. 13, 1854, Sarah E., dau. of Henry and Sarah (Russ) Todd, b. Pembroke, Oct. 2, 1829. He served in the 15th Regt. N. H. Vols. (See Roll of Honor.) Was a farmer and d. at Soldiers' Home, Tilton, Sept. 12, 1901, ae. 80-10-3. She has been unable to walk for 21 years by reason of a fall; given a home by the Shakers at Canterbury, where she still resides, 1903. She is an expert in making toy animals for sale. Children :

> *a.* Ida Jane, b. Bristol, Dec. 18, 1859 ; d. Aug. 13, 1874, ae. 14-7-25.
> *b.* Henry Todd, b. B., June 25, 1862 ; res. Clarksville, unm.
> *c.* Ella Anne, b. B., Nov. 5, 1867 ; d. Nov. 17, 1867.

4.   Roswell D., b. Oct. 12, 1823 ; d. at Boston, while *en route* home from the army, Oct. 12, 1863 ae. 40-0-. (See Roll of Honor.)
5.   Mary, b. Feb. 16, 1826 ; d. Haverhill.
6.   Sylvester, b. Apr. 29, 1831. He m. (1) Ermine E., dau. of John Jaqueth. She d. while he was in the army, leaving one dau. two years old. He m. (2) Sept. 24, 1865, Marcia Ann, dau. of Benjamin H. Smith, of Rumney. He is a farmer in Plymouth, nearly incapacitated

from labor by reason of wounds received at the battle of Gettysburg.
(See Roll of Honor.) Children :

    a. Mynetta Jane, b. Bristol, July 23, 1860.
    b. George Francis, b. B., Jan. 20, 1867; d. Mar. 26, 1867.
    c. Elinor Josephine, b. Plymouth, Feb. 20, 1868.
    d. Andrew Francis, b. P., Dec. 22, 1872.
    e. Elvira Mabel, b. P., July 5, 1874; d. Sept. 20, 1881, ae. 7-2-15.
    f. Wesley Sylvester, b. P., Mar. 3, 1876.

  7. Marinda Nelson, b. July 4, 1836; m. Thomas H. Wicom. (See.)

———

  1. **Calvin Swett** was b. in Warner in 1812, and came to
Bristol about 1832. He was a school teacher and farmer in the
Moore's Mills neighborhood. He m. Mar. 11, 1834, Rachel L.,
dau. of Abraham Dolloff (See), b. Apr. 24, 1814. She d. Bristol, Aug 2, 1865, ae. 51-3-8. After 1866, he res. in Campton
and Ashland. He m. (2) Mrs. Shepherd, of Ashland. He was
a Republican and twice represented Bristol in the legislature,
and served five years as selectman of the town. He was a
farmer, a dealer in lumber, and for a time interested in the
manufacture of paper. He served one year as selectman of
Campton, and was filling the same office in Ashland when he d.
Oct. 28, 1882, ae. 70-10-.

CHILDREN

  2. Sylvanus W., b. Wentworth, Dec. 4, 1834; m. Dec. 17, 1857,
Susan A., dau. of William R. Blodgett (See), b. Nov. 9, 1837. He was an
extensive and well-to-do farmer on the Pemigewasset river in district No.
5. Was a Republican, Odd Fellow, and a Granger. He d. Apr. 23, 1900,
ae. 65-4-19. Children :

    a. Sara Moore, b. Bristol, Apr. 27, 1861; graduated from New
    Hampton Institution.
    b. Son, b. Feb. 11, 1873; d. in infancy.

  3. Orrison, b. Bristol; drowned May 1, 1847. ae. 5-9-22.

THE TAYLOR FAMILIES

  1. **Edward Taylor**, of Stratham, was one of the first
settlers of Sanbornton, and there he d. Mar. 11, 1784, ae. 88.
He had four children, one of whom was

  2. Jonathan, b. Oct. 2, 1739; he m. Oct. 16, 1760, Rachel
Moore and d. Mar. 2, 1816, ae. 76-5-. Of his eight children
one was

  3. Nicholas Mason, b. Oct. 4, 1783, m. Apr. 5, 1803, Sally
Eastman, of Gilmanton, dau. of Ebenezer and Mary (Butler)
Eastman, b. June 22, 1784. He was a blacksmith in New
Hampton for 52 years. He d. instantly, Jan. 13, 1861, ae. 77-3-
9. She d. Bristol, Dec. 29, 1864, ae. 80-6-7. They were the
parents of thirteen children, among whom were

  4. Sarah Robinson, b. New Hampton, Jan. 18, 1810; m. Oct. 17,
1833, Dea. Abraham Bodwell Sanborn, of New Hampton and Sanbornton.

b. Nov. 8, 1806. He was for some years acting deacon of the Bristol
Congregational church, and d. Apr. 1, 1878, ae. 71-4-23. She d. in Bristol, Feb. 5, 1899, ae. 89-0-17. No children.
    5. Clarinda Jane, b. Mar. 9, 1815; m. Gustavus Bartlett. (See.)
    6. Anna C., b. Apr. 27, 1817; m. Daniel S. Mason. (See.)
 *7. Cyrus, b. New Hampton, Dec. 18, 1818.
    8. Martha G., b. June 17, 1820; m. Gustavus Bartlett. (See.)
    9. Laura Elizabeth A., b. Aug. 31, 1830; m. George P. Smith. (See.)

(7) Hon. Cyrus Taylor, b. Dec. 18, 1818, m. July 1, 1845,
Martha, dau. of Capt. James Minot (See), b. Sept. 29, 1822.
They res. on Pleasant street. Congregationalists. She was for
many years a member of the choir and an active worker in the
church. She d. Sept. 30, 1894, ae. 72-0-1. He d. May 16,
1898, ae. 79-4-28. When 16 years of age he entered the store
of George W. Smith in New Hampton, and a year later a store
in Meredith. Here he remained till Oct., 1836, when he came
to Bristol and entered the store of I. C. Bartlett & Co., as clerk,
where he remained as clerk and proprietor for 56 years.

In April, 1842, Mr. Taylor bought out Sias S. Sleeper, one of
the partners, and in 1860 purchased the interest of Ichabod
Bartlett and became the sole proprietor. He also purchased the
real estate, and continued in trade here till he sold to Kemp &
Johnson in December, 1892. During all these years, Mr. Taylor
did a very extensive business in this store and was also largely
interested in other enterprises. He was the senior partner of
Taylor & Shaw and of Taylor & Merrill, millers, who did an
extensive business in flour and grain. He was one of the pro-
moters in the organization of the Franklin & Bristol railroad,
and was a passenger on the first passenger train that left Concord for Boston, Sept. 10, 1842. The first freight train that
reached Concord contained freight for him and the first freight
train that reached Bristol contained two car loads of freight for
his store, and from this time for 45 years not a week passed that
did not bring him more or less freight.

During all these years, Mr. Taylor gave his entire personal
attention to his business and confined himself more closely to its
cares than any clerk in his employ. In politics he was a Republican. In 1869, he was elected state senator from this district by
the joint convention of the senate and house, and in 1870 was
re-elected by the people. He was a charter member of Union
Lodge, No. 79, A. F. and A. M., and a prominent member and
liberal supporter of the Congregational church.

Mr. Taylor was universally respected for his many high
qualities. He was a public spirited man and had the best
interests of the community at heart and was a liberal supporter
of all the benevolent institutions of the town. He was honest,
honorable, and upright — a model citizen, and his death was a
great loss to the community.

HENRY A. TAYLOR

CHILDREN

10. Henry Arthur, b. Bristol, June 18, 1848; m. Sept. 28, 1869, Helen Abby, dau. of Warren White (See), b. Jan. 16, 1847. He d. Bristol, of typhoid fever, Sept. 25, 1877, ae. 29-3-7, and was buried with Masonic honors by Mt. Horeb Commandery of Knights Templar, of Concord, of which Commandery he was a member. His widow m. (2) Marcus O. Farrar. (See.) Henry A. Taylor was interested with his father in mercantile pursuits till about three years before his death, when he became connected with the Mechanicks bank, Concord. Child:

  a. Edith Henry, b. Bristol, Apr. 29, 1878; m. Jason D. Emerson. (See.)

11. Abby Maria, b. B., Dec. 11, 1851; m. Ira A. Chase, Esq. (See.)

———

1. James Taylor, son of Mark and Betsey Chase Taylor, was of the third generation from Edward of Stratham, one of the first settlers of Sanbornton (See p. 421) through Jonathan, b. Oct. 2, 1739, and Mark, b. June 19, 1773. James was b. Sept. 1, 1800. He m. Apr. 14, 1825, Eliza Morrison, dau. of John. He was a blacksmith; both were members of the Free Baptist church in Sanbornton. They spent their last years in Bristol, where she d. "after years of terrible suffering," Nov. 20, 1874, ae. 67-2-. He d. Feb. 26, 1884, ae. 83-5-25.

CHILDREN

2. John Perry, b. Sanbornton, May 3, 1826; m. Aug. 23, 1848, Charlotte A., dau. Jacob Smith, b. Sanbornton, Feb. 27, 1826 (1827). He was a trader in Danbury and in Sanbornton. From 1862, was in Bristol; salesman for many years in store of Hon. Cyrus Taylor; was postmaster seven years; fire and life insurance agent; town clerk five years; served on the Republican state central committee; was a Congregationalist and a Mason. He d. suddenly of heart disease occasioned by excitement on account of a small fire in the village, Apr. 8, 1875, ae. 48-11-5. She d. Dec. 2, 1877, ae. 51-9-5. Children:

  a. Eva Eliza, b. Sanbornton, May 3, 1853; m. William Bartlett. (See.)

  b. Annie Lizzie, b. June 6, 1857; d. Bristol, May 15, 1874, ae. 16-11-9.

3. Emily E., b. Apr. 18, 1829; m. Rev. William T. Sleeper.

———

1. John Taylor, son of John and Judith (Cogswell) Taylor, was b. Bethlehem, Nov. 3, 1819. He m. Nov. 28, 1841, Abigail, dau. of Joseph and Mary Thresher, b. Sandwich, July 12, 1817, and d. Bristol, Aug. 16, 1881, ae. 64-1-4. He was a carpenter and wood-worker in Bristol, 1875-'95; since in West Andover and Franklin Falls.

CHILDREN

2. John, } b. Landaff, Sept. 25, 1842; { d. in infancy.
*3. William Thomas, }

4. James Austin, b. Easton, Jan. 9, 1845; served in Co. M, 1st Regt. N. H. Vols., Heavy Artillery, in the Civil war, Feb. 15 to June 9, 1865; d. Haverhill, Feb. 28, 1880, ae. 35-1-19.

5. Royal Herman, b. Concord, May 17, 1847; d. Sept. 20, 1847, ae. 1-4-3.

6. Charles Cogswell, b. Franconia, Apr. 27, 1851; d. ae. about two years.

7. Mary Hackett, b. F., June 7, 1854; removed from Bristol to West Andover, 1895; thence to Franklin Falls, where now resides. Is instituting lodges for N. E. Order of Protection.

8. Sarah Abigail, b. F., June 7, 1858; has been a school teacher; res. Franklin Falls.

9. Clara Emma, b. F., Sept. 22, 1860; d. Bristol, Mar. 1, 1875, of consumption, ae. 14-5-9.

(3) William T. Taylor, b. Sept. 25, 1842, m. (1) Adelaide, dau. Priest and Lydia Young, who d. Franconia, 1864. He came to Bristol, 1865, and here m. Dec. 31, 1865, Sarah Alma, dau. Eldred Roby (See), b. June 12, 1845. He was a skilful pattern maker and wood-worker, and a manufacturer of picker-sticks. A Methodist and Republican. Died suddenly of heart disease, Sept. 17, 1893, ae. 50-11-22. She res. Bristol.

CHILDREN

10. Addie May, b. Bristol, Mar. 31, 1870; d. Bristol, June 22, 1881, ae. 11-2-21.

11. Grace Marion, b. B., Sept. 7, 1873; graduated Simonds High school, Warner; was teacher, now stenographer and typewriter, Manchester.

12. LeRoy Clifton, b. B., Aug. 15, 1878. Professional baseball.

13. Annie May, b. B., July 1, 1884; m. Oct. 24, 1903, Ralph Gray, of Alexandria.

THE TENNEY FAMILY

1. Roscoe Carleton Tenney, son of Charles Herbert and Mary (Phillips) Tenney, was b. Alexandria, Oct. 28, 1879. He m. June 4, 1902, Sarah, dau. of William Rice (See), b. Feb. 3, 1879. He is a laborer in Bristol. No children.

THE THOMAS FAMILY

1. Jacob Thomas, the son of Jonathan, was b. Hampton, Jan. 31, 1763. He went to Sanbornton with his father when three years old. At fifteen enlisted in Continental army as a fifer and served four years. Oct. 13, 1785, he m. Ruth, dau. of Abram Perkins, b. Sanbornton, July 21, 1764. He removed to New Hampton where his children were b. and about 1810 came to Bristol settling in the Locke neighborhood, where he remained ten years or more. In 1829, he was again in Sanbornton, and later went to Avon, N. Y., where he d. in the family of his son, Matthew, Dec. 20, 1835, ae. 72-10-19; she d. Nov. 22, 1852, ae. 88-4-1.

2. Joseph, b. June 17, 1786; d. June 17, 1807, ae. 21-0-0.

3. Abigail, b. May 11, 1789; m. Feb. 23, 1809, Joseph Morse, Bridgewater; res. Salem, Vt., and d. Oct. 8, 1872, ae. 83-1-27. Ten children.

4. Polly, b. Aug. 29, 1791; m. May 22, 1811, Mayhew Sanborn, and removed to Michigan.

5. Elizabeth, b. June 27, 1793; m. 1814, Benjamin Morse, and removed to Avon, N. Y., where she d. Feb. 27, 1885, ae. 91-8-.

6. Jacob, b. May 29, 1795; served in War of 1812; m 1818, went to New York, and in 1836 to Michigan; m. Polly Brown and had three children. He d. Mar. 16, 1892, ae. 96 9-17.

7. Stephen, b. Feb. 5, 1797; d. May 18, 1797.

8. Nancy, b. July 22, 1798; m. 1814, John Dolloff, and d. Apr. 9, 1875, ae. 76-8-17. They had 12 children. Lived in New Hampton, Vermont, Sanbornton.

9. Matthew Perkins, b. July 3, 1800. Went to Avon, N. Y., and in 1821, m. Rachel Harrington, who d. Mar. 23, 1867; he m. (2) Nov. 19, 1868, Mary N. Stone, and d. June 22, 1895, ae. 94-11-19.

10. Esther, b. Oct. 10, 1803; m. Nathaniel Heath. (See.)

11. Jonathan M., b. Aug. 19, 1805; removed to Georgia and had sons in the Confederate army.

THE THURSTON FAMILY

1. John Henry Thurston was b. in Freedom, June 5, 1861. He was a son of Stephen D. and Hannah (Whitton) Thurston. He came to Bristol about 1880, and m. Sept. 20, 1881, Mary Etta, dau. of Samuel and Mary N. (Fleer) Clark, b. Alexandria, June 9, 1853. Was for several years a policeman; d. Bristol, Aug. 15, 1900, ae. 39-2-10.

2. Mabelle Etta, b. May 24, 1882; m. Aug. 15, 1903, Thomas H. Davis, Portsmouth.

THE TIBBETTS FAMILY

1. Alfred Henry Tibbetts, son of Wentworth B., was b. Wolfeboro, Mar. 23, 1860. He m. Nora Bell, dau. of Stephen P. Wiggin, b. Sanbornton, Mar. 20, 1865. Divorced. He m. (2) Jessie Blanche, dau. of Reuben C. Dodge, b. Tunbridge, Vt., Aug. 22, 1879. He is a sawyer and carpenter; came to Bristol from Danbury, Dec., 1899.

2. Lizzie, m. Charles Covey, res. Hill.

3. Hervie, res. Hill.   4. Frank, res. Hill.

5. Alice May, b. Franklin Falls, Apr. 15, 1895.

6. Georgia, b. Danbury, Nov. 4, 1898.

7. Bernard Bishop, b. Bristol, Mar. 5, 1900.

THE TILTON FAMILIES

1. Sherburn Tilton, son of Sherburn, was b. in Kensington, July 31, 1735. Papers left by the late Odlin Sleeper state

that he was with Gen. Wolfe, at the seige of Quebec. In July, 1776, he enlisted in Capt. David Quimby's company, of Col. Josiah Bartlett's regiment, raised for the invasion of Canada ; and in 1777, he marched from Sandown in Capt. Robert Collins's company to join the Northern army at Saratoga. He m. Huldah Prescott, b. Kensington, Nov. 14, 1738, and settled in Sandown. About 1780 they removed to Bristol and he built a log cabin on east side of South Main street, where later stood a hotel and where now is Frank W. Bingham's harness shop. He bought of John Tolford the mill lot, No. 61, First Division, and operated the saw-mill and grist-mill where is now the Train-Smith company pulp-mill. In May, 1794, he sold to Moses Lewis and removed to what has later been known as the Chase farm on north side of Hemp hill, where he had a potash. Later he removed to Wheelock, Vt., where he d. Sept. 20, 1813, ae. 78-1-19. She d. St. Albans, Vt., Apr. 11, 1823, ae. 84-4-27.

CHILDREN, all except last born in Sandown

*2. John, b. Sept. 24, 1761.
  3. Ann, ⎫ b. Aug. 11, 1763; ⎰ m. Daniel Sleeper. (See.)
  4. Dorothy, ⎭   ⎱ worked many years in Lowell, Mass.; d. unm., 1857, ae. 94.
  5. Elizabeth, b. June 26, 1765; m. John Sleeper. (See.)
*6. Sherburn, b. May 12, 1768.
  7. Daniel, ⎫ b. Apr. 20, 1770; ⎰ removed to Vermont.
  8. Sarah, ⎭   ⎱ m. Joseph Ingalls ; res. northern Vermont.
  9. Rebecca, b. July 29, 1772; d. July 11, 1773.
 10. Benjamin, b. Sept. 12, 1774; lived and d. Swanton, Vt.
 11. Theophilus, b. Jan. 15, 1777; m. (pub. Feb. 2, 1801), Comfort Powell; lived and d. Vershire, Vt.
*12. Jonathan, b. Aug. 22, 1779.
 13. Timothy, b. Bristol, Apr. 30, 1783; settled in the northern part of Vermont, where he d.

(2) John Tilton, son of Sherburn, b. Sept. 24, 1761, came to Bristol with his parents, and m. Jane, dau. of Jacob Cass. (See.) He was a farmer in Plymouth 1809-'10, and 1825-'33 ; on the Jeremiah Johnson road near the turnpike in Bridgewater and in South Alexandria, where he d. Sept. 2, 1853, ae. 91-11-8.

CHILDREN

 14. John, was a farmer in Plymouth, 1826-'33.
 15. Henry, b. Nov. 13, 1788; m. Elizabeth Buck. Was a farmer in Alexandria, Hebron, and Plymouth, and d. in family of his dau., Mrs. Charles S. Brown, in Bristol. Children :
        a. Eliza Sage, b. Alexandria, Jan., 1821; m. Joshua Foster, (See.)
        b. Orinda Carpenter, b. Hebron, Sept. 16, 1823; m. Charles S. Brown. (See.)
        c. Ella (Lucy) Buck, b. Plymouth (?), Apr. 28, 1826; m. Nathaniel P. Keezer. (See.)
        d. Charles, went to sea and never heard from afterward.
 16. Sherburn, b. Jan. 30, 1791.   17. Sally, b. Apr. 8, 1794.

18. Benjamin, taxed in Plymouth, 1823-'35. A dau., Sarah Jane, adopted by Abbott Lovejoy. (See.)

19. Putman, d. unm., about 1840.

20. Dorothy, unm. 21. Huldah.

(6) Sherburn Tilton, son of Sherburn, b. May 12, 1768, m. Ruth, dau. of Lieut. Benjamin Emmons (See), b. June 8, 1775. They were the first settlers on the Tilton farm in Dist. No. 7, east of the lake. For years he drove a four-ox team to Boston for supplies for Moses Lewis; removed to what was later the Jonathan H. Johnson farm in Bridgewater. He d. Dec. 27, 1852, ae. 84-7-15; she d. at about 90 years of age.

CHILDREN

22. Huldah, b. Bristol, Feb. 12, 1794; d. unm., Dec. 7, 1821, ae. 27-9-25.

23. Elizabeth, b. B., Jan. 3, 1796; m. Moses Smith, and d. Alexandria, May 6, 1829, ae. 33-4-3.

24. Benjamin Emmons, b. B., Apr. 11 1798; m. Betsey, dau. of Simeon Batchelder (See), b. Mar. 18, 1803. He was a farmer in Bridgewater, where his son Harvey res. He d. Dec. 24, 1871, ae. 73-8-13; she d. July 12, 1889, ae. 86-3-24. Children, all b. in Bridgewater.

 a. Eliza S., b. June 4, 1830; m. Dec. 9, 1858, Lorenzo Flanders (his first wife), and d. in Bridgewater, Oct. 11, 1861, ae. 31-4-7. Child : Anna Eliza, b. Nov. 22, 1860; d. Sept. 10, 1876, ae. 15-9-18.

 b. Harvey W., b. June 11, 1837; m. June 20, 1874, Esther D., dau. of Rodney and Abigail (Spaulding) Hammond, b. Aug. 30, 1838. He was a farmer and a most estimable man. Held nearly all the offices in the gift of the town. He d. Oct. 3, 1898, ae. 61-3-22. No children.

 c. Frank B., b. Mar 6, 1842. Unm. He went to Lowell in 1862, where he res. ten years; thence to Lawrence, where he now res.

25. Sherburn Webster, b. Bridgewater, July 8, 1800; m. Nancy Batchelder, dau. of Simeon. (See.) He was a farmer in Bridgewater, where he d. May 16, 1885, ae. 84-10-8. She d. Jan. 27, 1884. Child :

 a. Lauren C., b. Bridgewater, Aug. 3, 1849; m. Jan. 1, 1872, Mary Comfort, dau. James M. Ames (See), b. Jan. 7, 1852. He was a farmer and a prominent man in the town ; filled nearly all the offices in the gift of the town ; was town treasurer at time of his death, which occurred June 7, 1897, ae. 47-10-4. She res. in Bristol. No children.

26. Ruth, b. B., Nov. 13, 1802 ; d. May 25, 1837, of consumption, ae. 34-6-12. For forty days previous to her death she took no nourishment except hot water.

27. John F., b. B., Apr. 19, 1806 ; m. May 29, 1836, Sarah Jane, dau. John Rollins, b. Oct. 18, 1816. He was a farmer in Alexandria till 1871 ; then settled on the Tilton farm in District No. 9, west of the lake, and there d. July 11, 1888, ae. 82-2-22. She d. Aug. 25, 1894, ae. 77-10-7. Children :

 a. Eliza S., b. Alexandria, Oct. 27, 1839; m. May 29, 1862, John Sanborn.

 b. John Olin, b. A., July 4, 1849; m. Apr. 25, 1882, Emma M., dau. of Nicholas T. Chase. Divorced. No children. Res. on his father's farm till about 1896, when he removed to Concord.

28. David F., twin brother of John F., was a farmer in Bridgewater. He m. (1) Sarah Rowe, of Vermont; (2) Louise Chase, dau. of Dea.

Timothy, of Campton, who d. Nov. 25, 1892, ae. 68 6-0; he d. Aug. 3, 1888, ae. 82-3-14. Children :

    a. Emily A., b. Bristol, Aug. 7, 1845; m. George W. Atwood. (See.)

    b. Marshall W., d. Apr. 17, 1854, ae. 1-8-.

*29. Samuel H., b. Sept. 18, 1816.

(12) Jonathan Tilton, son of Sherburn, b. Aug. 22, 1779, m. Sally Clifford, b. Jan. 21, 1784, and d. Oct. 7, 1833, ae. 49-8-16. Farmer and carpenter (called great barn builder) in Bristol, where Charles A. Gale now res.; Bridgewater, Wheelock, Vt., Bridgewater again, thence to South Alexandria, where he res. about forty years, and where he d. Nov. 27, 1870, ae. 91-3-5.

CHILDREN

30. Dorothy Roby, b. Oct. 7, 1802; m. Capt. Daniel Sleeper. (See.)
31. Huldah, b. May 7, 1804; d. in family of Daniel Sleeper, Jan. 8, 1838, ae. 33-8-1.
32. Timothy, b. Apr. 18, 1806; m. June 30, 1835, Mary, dau. Daniel McMurphy, b. Oct. 15, 1812. He was a farmer in So. Alexandria, where he d. May 12, 1865, ae. 59-0-24. She d. July 29, 1899, ae. 86-9-14. Children :

    a. Jeriah S., b. Mar. 23, 1836; d. Feb. 17, 1841, ae. 4-10-24.

    b. Sarah Elizabeth McMurphy, b. July 22, 1840; m. Isaac Emmons, Hill, and d. June 8, 1878, ae. 37-10-16.

    c. Horace Francis, b. Jan. 19, 1843; m. (1) Jan. 13, 1872, Jennie E., dau. Emmons Lewis, b. Mar. 23, 1852; d. Nov. 30, 1876, ae. 24-8-7. He m. (2) Jan. 1, 1878, Flora S., dau. Moses Noyes, b. Feb. 18, 1854; d. Jan. 1, 1887, ae. 32-10-13. Farmer in So. Alexandria. Several times selectman of his town. Children : (1) Bertha M., b. Nov. 29, 1879. (2) Edith M., b. Sept. 10, 1884.

33. Isaac Clifford, b. Wheelock, Vt., Nov. 18, 1808; m. Oct. 29, 1833, Lydia J. Heath, dau. Samuel (See), b. Dec. 30, 1812. She d. Bridgewater, Feb. 22, 1881, ae. 68-1-22. He was a farmer on the Point in Bridgewater; d. Feb. 12, 1885, ae. 76-2-24. Children, all b. Bridgewater.

    a. Margaret H., b. Oct. 15, 1834; m. Gilbert B. Dolloff. (See.)

    b. Son, d. infancy, Dec. 19, 1835.

    c. Daughter, d. infancy, July 9, 1838.

    d. Hiram S., b. Oct. 22, 1839; m. Lydia P., dau. Samuel and Mary M. (Prescott) Worthen, b. Jan. 30, 1839. Succeeded his father on the farm. Children : (1) Lura Della, b. May 2, 1864. (2) Isaac Samie, b. May 8, 1866; d. June 11, 1877, ae. 11-1-3. (3) Alfred Hiram, b. May 22, 1870. (4) Alice May, b. May 22, 1870; m. George M. Breck. (See.) (5) Frank Hermon, b. Apr. 4, 1877.

    e. Lucy A., b. Oct. 7, 1845; m. Nov. 29, 1866, Curtis Brown. (See.)

    f. Ella M., b. May 11, 1851; m. Oct. 2, 1875, Charles Smith ; d. Tilton, Mar. 22, 1889, ae. 37-10-11.

    g. Lora Jane, b. May 10, 1855; d. Apr. 14, 1864, ae. 8-11-4.

34. Walter, b. Mar. 21, 1811; m. Ruth Webster, Lowell, Mass.; res. many years in Alexandria, where he d. Dec. 24, 1855, ae. 44-9-3.
35. Rebecca, b. Aug. 24, 1813; d. Sept. 25, 1815, ae. 2-1-1.
36. William Sanborn, b. Feb. 1, 1820; m. and settled in Maine where he d. Dec. 31, 1848, ae. 28-10-30.
37. Sherburn Sleeper, b. Bridgewater, Apr. 16, 1822; m. Abbie, dau. Amos Flanders, of Wilmot, and d. about 1884 in South Alexandria. In

1852. He made the trip across the isthmus to California, where he remained nearly twelve years. Res. Danbury. Children:

    a. John Flanders, b. Wilmot, Nov. 25, 1845; m. Grace I. Hazelton. Res. South Alexandria, Wilmot.

    b. Mary, b. W., 1853; d. 1883, ae. 30 years.

    c. Frances Ellen, b. W.; d. about 1857, ae. about six years.

    d. Charles, b. W., 1854; d. about 1859, ae. about five years.

    e. Henry Albert, } b. Andover, Nov. 16, 1864; { res. Danbury.
    f. Alice Sarah, }   { m. George Haines,
res. Bristol. She d. July 25, 1898, ae. 33-8-9.

38. Jonathan Lyman, b. July 3, 1827; m. the widow of William S. Tilton. She d. Concord, ae. about 88; he d. Concord.

(29) Samuel H. Tilton, son of Sherburn, b. Sept. 18, 1816, m. Feb. 16, 1848, Deborah L., dau. Dexter Brown (See), b. Feb. 26, 1831. Farmer, four years stage driver on Groton route; removed from Bridgewater to Bristol, 1868; laborer, res. on Willow street, where he d. Feb. 20, 1885, ae. 68-5-2, and where she still res.

CHILDREN

39. Charles Lee, b. Bridgewater, Aug. 2, 1850. An operative in the woolen-mill; unm.

40. George Scott, b. B., Dec. 27, 1852; m. June 16, 1875. Isabel Eldora Heath, dau. of Stephen N. (See), b. Feb. 23, 1855. Mill operative and trader. Now res. North Carolina. Children:

    a. Edna Isabel, b. Bristol, Jan. 16, 1876; m. Karl F. Bunker. (See.)

    b. Ada Lisette, b. B., Mar. 6, 1878; m. Leon A. Woodman. (See.)

    c. Chester Scott, b. B., Nov. 2, 1880.

    d. Fred Wyman, b. B., Apr. —, 1883; d. Dec., 1883.

    e. Foster Cleveland, b. B., Mar. 11, 1885.

    f. Newell Emmons, b. B., Aug. 10, 1889.

    g. Shirley Floyd, b. B., Apr. 30, 1894.

41. Sarah Emma, b. Hebron, Nov. 15, 1858; m. July 19, 1877, Silas A. McMurphy, a farmer in So. Alexandria. Children:

    a. Lizzie Ina, b. Nov. 28, 1881.

    b. Ella Viola, b. May 3, 1890.

    c. Alvah Edison, b. July 13, 1891.

42. Jennie N., b. Bristol, Aug. 15, 1861; m. May 22, 1879, Alvertus Norman McMurphy, a farmer in South Alexandria. Child:

    a. Helen Aletia, b. Aug. 5, 1882.

---

1. Dr. Timothy Tilton was a tax-payer in that part of New Chester now Bristol as early as 1806, apparently residing on the west side of Newfound river. In 1810, he was residing on the east side of that river on what is now Pleasant street, and consequently, in Bridgewater. That year he served as selectman of Bridgewater. In 1823, he was on Bridgewater hill and was then a member of the District Medical society. The loss of the Inventory books of both New Chester and Bridgewater covering the early years of these towns, prevents a more exact statement in this case as in many others.

CHILDREN

2. William Brackett, b. Feb. 20, 1810.
3. Joseph Chase, b. Dec. 25, 1811.

---

1. David Tilton and Rebecca Green were m. Feb. 8, 1749. They were among the first settlers of New Hampton, and were the parents of 13 children, among whom were :

2. Elizabeth, b. June 10, 1756 ; m. Sept. 7, 1779, Elijah Sanborn. (See.) In the Sanborn family records, she is said to be of Danville.
*3. David, b. Jan. 27, 1755.
*4. Green, b. Kingston, Sept. 9, 1759.

(3) David, b. Jan. 27, 1755, m. ———— Quimby ; was a farmer in New Hampton, had several children, among them

*5. Josiah, b. New Hampton, Feb. 12, 1786.

(4) Green Tilton, son of David, b. Sept. 9, 1759, m. in 1787, Judith, dau. of Cutting Favor (See), b. Sept. 17, 1770. They settled in New Hampton, where he d. Mar. 8, 1810, ae. 50-5-29. She d. June 15, 1850, ae. 79-8-28. Of their 14 children, one was

*6. David, b. New Hampton, Jan. 6, 1810.

(5) Josiah, b. Feb. 12, 1786, m. Sally Keniston, b. Allenstown, May 5, 1781, and d. New Hampton, Apr. 25, 1882, ae. 100-11-20. He d. Mar. 1, 1866. They were farmers in New Hampton. Of their seven children, two were

*7. Salmon Hibbard, b. May 5, 1813.
8. Daniel B., m. Louise E. Cushman. Among their children one was
   a. Harry Warren, b. Lebanon, July 18, 1861. He m. Mar. 28, 1882, Florence D., dau. of Eliphalet G. Kelley (See), b. Sept. 17, 1861. He was a woodworker in Bristol, Apr., 1881-'96, when he removed to Everett, Mass., where she d., Jan. 12, 1903, ae. 41-3-25. Child : Eliphalet Kelley, b. Bristol, May 22, 1886.

(6) David Tilton, b. Jan. 6, 1810, m. Sept. 12, 1843, Polly, dau. of Dea. Levi and Polly (Mason) Carter, b. New Hampton, July 11, 1818, and d. Bristol, Feb. 2, 1895, ae. 76-6-21. He was a farmer in New Hampton : last few years of his life resided on Merrimack street in Bristol, where he d. Feb. 13, 1882, ae. 72-1-7.

CHILDREN

9. Mary Elizabeth, b. New Hampton, Feb. 12, 1845. Res. Bristol.
10. Jane Helen, b. N. H., Aug. 6, 1847 ; d. Bristol, Aug. 11, 1880, ae. 33-0-5.
11. Ruth Anna, b. N. H., Jan. 31, 1850 ; d. Bristol, May 28, 1890, ae. 40-3-27.

(7) Salmon H. Tilton, son of Josiah, b. May 5, 1813, m. Sept. 1, 1835, Joanna J. Hight, b. Feb. 14, 1817. He was a

GREEN L. TILTON

farmer in New Hampton, d. Bristol, Oct. 8, 1893, ae. 80–5–3. She d. in the family of her son, Green L., in Bristol, Jan. 28, 1896, ae. 78–11–14.

12. John Favor, b. New Hampton, Feb. 13, 1838; was 20 years an engineer on Northern road, 8 years in Indiana; since in Bristol; farmer; unm.

13. Green L., b. N. H., Feb. 13, 1840; m. May 21, 1864, Sarah Jane, dau. of Benjamin Q. Fellows (See), b. Feb. 8, 1841. He came to Bristol in 1858, and was a currier and tanner for some years; was for five years making boots and shoes in company with Elijah Sanborn; a job teamster the balance of his life, keeping several teams. He served six years as selectman, many years as highway surveyor, and after the law created the office of road agent, he was twice elected to this office. In 1899 and 1900, he expended the $15,000 raised by the town for macadam road. He was justice of the peace, a trustee of Minot-Sleeper library, a Republican, an Odd Fellow; a prominent member and liberal supporter of the Free Baptist church. He d. Mar. 29, 1901, ae. 61–1–16. Children :

a. Willie, b. Bristol, Apr. 22, 1866; d. Aug. 30, 1866.

b. Ardella Ann, b. B., June 21, 1867; m. Omsby A. Lothrop. (See.)

c. Eva Allana, b. B., Mar. 17, 1870; m. Wesley H. Dicey. (See.)

d. Grace Hannah, b. B., Oct. 11, 1877; m. May 21, 1895, George Frank Trussell, of Orfordville, where they now res. He is a superior mechanic and wood-turner. Child : Marion Emma, b. Orfordville, July 17, 1898.

14. Emily Lucy, b. N. H., Nov. 27, 1844; m. Orrison G. Cass. (See.)

15. George Hibbard, b. Jan. 14, 1852; m. June 2, 1880, Nellie G., dau. James Proctor and Eliza Ann (Gill) Gordon, b. New Hampton, Oct. 24, 1860. She d. Bristol, May 9, 1903, ae. 42–6–15. He was a stone mason in Bristol for 10 years, later in New Hampton and Franklin.

16. Sarah Ann, d. ae. 3–10–26.

---

1. Silas Barnett Tilton, son of Samuel, was b. Andover, Aug. 25, 1795. In Dec., 1819, he m. Abigail Sanborn, dau. of Peter, b. Andover. They were farmers in Bristol, 1836–'44, when they removed to Groton, thence to Franklin. In 1853, with his three sons, he went to California where he remained four years, and then settled in Canaan, where he d. Jan. 13, 1862, ae. 66–4–18. She d. same day.

2. Belinda, b. Andover, Aug. 25, 1820; m. John Nelson. (See.)

3. Elbridge, b. A., Apr. 10, 1822; m. Mar. 25, 1847, Alice, dau. of Daniel and Lois (Kidder) Cummings, b. Groton, Nov. 26, 1827. He was in Bristol with his parents 1836–'44; in California, 1853–'55; res. Canaan and Laconia. In Dec., 1871, returned to Bristol, settling on the farm now owned by his son, Zerah E., where he d. May 6, 1889, ae. 67–0–26. She res. Bristol. Children :

a. Zerah Elbridge, b. Groton, May 23, 1858; m. May 22, 1887, Georgianna, dau. of Charles L. and Francina Weeks, b. Gilmanton, Mar. 5, 1866. He is an extensive dairy farmer west of Newfound river; has absorbed the Aaron Sleeper farm and now owns 600 acres of land; his farm ranks as the best in town and his tax is the largest of any farmer. Is also a manufacturer of lumber. Is a Democrat and prominent in Grange circles. No children.

    b. Della Alice, b. Gilford, Dec. 8, 1867; m. Fred H. Briggs. (See.)

    4. George, b. A., Nov. 21, 1831; m. Aug., 1857, (1) Elizabeth E., dau. Levi Brooks, b. Landaff, Jan. 24, 1832; d. Alton, July 17, 1876, ae. 44-5-23. He m. (2) Mar. 8, 1877, Mary S. Langley, who d. Jan. 19, 1900. He res. California.

    5. Smilie, b. A., Dec. 14, 1833; m. Jan. 12, 1859, Mary Elizabeth, dau. of James M. Bancroft, b. Haverhill, Nov. 24, 1840, and d. St. Helena, Cal., Nov. 13, 1886, ae. 45-11-19. Children:

        a. LaForest Eugene, b. Haverhill, Sept. 13, 1859; d. Oct. 1, 1859.
        b. Villazena Melissa, b. Canaan, Sept. 22, 1860; d. Apr. 4, 1864, 3-6-12.
        c. Katie Abbie, b. C., July 1, 1862; d. Lakewood, N. J., Dec. 4, 1867, ae. 5-5-3.
        d. William Bancroft, b. C., June 12, 1865; d. Lakewood, Nov. 30, 1867, ae. 2-5-18.
        e. George Elbridge, b. Atlantic, Ia., Mar. 20, 1870.
        f. Blanch Arvilla, b. A., Mar. 20, 1872.
        g. Ruby Emma, b. A., Mar. 20, 1875.
        h. Twins, both d. June 9, 1877.
        i. Elizabeth Ambie, b. A., July 9, 1879.

    6. Melissa Ann, b. Bristol, Apr. 21, 1839; m. 1867, Henry Greenough, and d. Lakeport, July 8, 1870, ae. 31-2-17.

---

    1. Lieut. Timothy Tilton, son of Jonathan and Elizabeth (Foster) Tilton, was b. Fremont, May 27, 1836. He served in Co. C, 12th Regt., N. H. Vols. (See Roll of Honor.) He m., Jan. 2, 1869, Martha W., dau. of Alpha C. Jewett (See), b. Apr. 8, 1845. He was a soap manufacturer in Bristol till 1880; a mason and plasterer in Laconia till he d. May 25, 1890, ae. 53-11-28. Republican. No children. She res. Laconia.

THE TIRRELL OR TYRRELL FAMILY

    1. Jonah Tirrell and his brother, Abel, were in Bristol as early as 1787. Jonah had served in the Revolutionary war from Bedford. He settled on the farm now owned and occupied by Samuel K. Worthen, in the Locke neighborhood, and there he d. about 1840, ae. 84. He m. Joanna Lincoln.

CHILDREN

    2. Sally, b. Dec. 11, 1780; res. in Bristol and d. at advanced age, unm.
    3. Whitcomb, b. Jan. 7, 1783; m. Nov. 27, 1806, Susanna Peasley, of Bridgewater, and removed to Stewartstown.
    *4. Samuel, b. May 9, 1784.
    *5. John, b. Bristol, Feb. 27, 1788.
    6. Abigail, b. B., Aug. 27, 1790; m. Ebenezer Darling. (See.)
    7. Daniel, b. B., Oct. 17, 1797. He was in trade some years at Moore's Mills; d. in family of David S. Follansbee, Sept. 3, 1878, ae. 80-10-16, unm.
    8. Emily, b. Oct. 9, 1803; m. Mar. 23, 1826, Jacob B. Sanborn, father of Benjamin F., and d. in Haverhill.

(4)   Samuel Tirrell, son of Jonah, b. May 9, 1784, m. 1806, Polly Pressey, b. June 16, 1788, and d. Hill, Mar. 30, 1841, ae. 52-9-14.   He was a farmer in the Locke neighborhood ; drowned at Parker's eddy in the Pemigewasset, Hill, May 17, 1836, ae. 52-0-8.

CHILDREN

9.   Emily, b. Bristol, Nov. 21, 1806; m. Hollis H. Tirrell, and res. in Plymouth.   Children :

a.   Moses D., b. Bristol, 1827; served in 6th Regt. N. H. Vols. (See Roll of Honor.)   Eight children.
b.   Mercy A.   c.   Samuel.   d.   Mary.
e.   Emily, d. Oct. 27, 1880.

10.   Eliza, b. B., Feb. 7, 1809 ; m. Jan., 1832, Jerry Ward ; d. Hill, Sept. 12, 1859, ae. 50-7-5.   Children, all b. Hill.

a.   Luther A., b. Nov. 10, 1832 ; m. Mary A. Douglass.   Both d.
b.   Anna J., b. July 14, 1834 ; m. Arah W. Prescott ; res. South Hooksett.
c.   Joanna D., b. Apr 12, 1841 ; m. Frank M. Morrill, Manchester, and d. Hooksett, Oct. 26, 1873, ae. 32-6-14.
d.   Amanda Grace, b. Feb. 22, 1851 ; m. William F. Hanaford. (See.)

11.   Parker Plummer, b. B., Feb. 3, 1811 ; m. Rosella Jordan, of Thomaston, Me.   They res. Lexington, Mass., where he d. Dec. 11, 1893, ae. 82-10-8.   Children :

a.   Mary Elizabeth, b. June 20, 1836 ; m. Frank Whitman, and d. Danvers, Mass., June 29, 1899, ae. 63-0-9.   Child : Frank Allen Whitman b. Wenham, Mass., June 2, 1860 ; m. June 20, 1886, Lizzie Rackliffe, Danvers, Mass.
b.   Georgianna, m. E. Frank Keach.
c.   Willie, d. unm.

12.   Nancy, b. B., May 12, 1813 ; m. Elijah Ballou.   (See.)
13.   Rufus, b. B., Apr. 21, 1815 ; m. Susan Avery, Hill ; killed on railroad between Franklin and Andover, July 15, 1862, ae. 47-2-24.   Children :

a.   Mary, b. Hill, Sept. 20, 1835 ; d. East Andover, Aug. 25, 1859, ae. 23-11-5.
b.   Harriet, b. H., Sept. 12, 1841 ; m. (1) Moses Kimball, (2) Daniel Flanders, and res. Concord.
c.   Josephine, b. Bristol, Oct. 16, 1845 ; m. (1) Gilman McAlpine, (2) Edwin Broadley, Tilton.
d.   Lovina, b. Alexandria, Mar. 12, 1848 ; m. William Flanders ; d. Tilton, Dec. 14, 1885, ae. 37-9-2.

14.   Salome, b. B., Aug. 26, 1817 ; m. Joshua Hanscom ; d. Campton, Sept. 9, 1889, ae. 72-0-13.   Children :

a.   Samuel T., b. Plymouth, 1837.   Served in Co. H, 8th Regt., N. H. Vols., and d. of wounds, May 29, 1863, at Port Hudson, La., ae. 26.
b.   Melissa, m. Horace Sanborn ; res. W. Plymouth.
c.   Anna, b. June 7, —— ; d.
d.   Heber, b. May 28, 1853 ; m. Hattie Tirrell ; res. Bristol.
e.   Ami C., b. Dec. 28, 1854 ; m. Ralph Arms, Highgate, Vt. ; res. Franklin Falls.

15.   Jonas, b. B., Apr. 24, 1819 ; m. Dorcas Adams, dau. of Richard, b. Feb. 1, 1821.   He m. (2) Helen Whittemore ; res. Manchester.   Children :

28

a. Henry, b. Hill, Apr. 25, 1843; d. Dec. 29, 1865, ae. 22-8-4.

b. Abby, b. H., Dec. 26, 1844; m. Harvey Huntoon, and res. in Danbury.

c. Victoria, b. H., July 16, 1850; m. Frank E. Mason, Hill, and res. Franklin Falls.

d. George, b. Bristol, July 12, 1856; d. Dec., 1860, ae. 4-5-.

e. Nellie, b. B., Oct. 22, 1859; m. John Allen, of Manchester, and res. Danbury.

16. Daniel, b. B., Apr. 28, 1821; m. Elizabeth Adams, dau. of Richard, b. Hill, Aug. 11, 1824. They res. Hill. Children:

a. Alvin F., b. Hill, May 14, 1845. Enlisted in 8th Regt., N. H. Vols., Civil war; d. of measles, at Manchester, Jan. 26, 1862, ae. 16-8-12.

b. Stephen A., b. H., July 10, 1860; m. Idella A. Couch, and res. Hill. Child: Leona B., b. H., Oct. 21, 1891.

c. Hattie, b. H., Nov. 20, 1861; m. John W. Bartlett; res. Hill.

17. Sarah, b. Hill, May 5, 1823; m. David S. Follansbee. (See.)

18. Martin Luther, b. H., Aug. 23, 1826; m. Emily Tibbetts, of Belgrade, Me. Served in Co. D, 1st Regt., Mass. Infty., Mexican war; d. Belgrade, Feb. 23, 1884, ae. 57-6-0. No children.

19. Levi L., b. H., June 27, 1829; m. Maria ——; served on quota of Bethlehem in Co. C, 15th Regt., N. H. Vols., in Department of the Gulf. Discharged Aug. 13, 1863; d. at Buffalo, N. Y., three days later, while *en route* home, aged 34-1-19.

(5) John Tirrell, son of Jonah, b. Feb. 27, 1788, m. Oct. 10, 1812, Polly Ingalls, dau. of Jonathan (See), b. Oct. 6, 1795. He was a farmer in the Locke neighborhood; removed to Michigan in summer of 1837. She d. Portland, Mich., Nov. 21, 1883. ae. 88-1-15; he d. Sept. 9, 1867, ae. 79-6-12.

CHILDREN

20. Luther, b. Bristol, Feb., 1814; d. 1820, ae. 6.

21. Abigail, b. B., Aug., 1815; d. Michigan, 1845, ae. 30; m., no children.

22. John Fletcher, b. B., July 24, 1817; went to Michigan, 1837; m. Oct. 28, 1841, Sarah Ann Leavitt, of Paris, Mich., who d. Mar. 15, 1845, and he m. (2) Oct. 25, 1845, Mrs. Mary Featherstone, who d. in Aug., 1851. He m. (3) Oct. 30, 1851, Maria Robinson, who d. Mar. 18, 1895. He res. Charlotte, Mich., where he d. Nov. 29, 1902, ae. 85-4-5. "He was a lifelong Methodist, and an ardent Prohibitionist." Children:

a. Olive Mallette, b. Mar. 1, 1843; m.; res. Eugene, Oregon.

b. Sarah Elida, b. Dec. 7, 1844; m. in 1898, Benjamin Davis. No children. Res. Eugene.

c. Judson E., b. Sept. 15, 1852; m. Apr. 3, 1878. Res. Charlotte Chi'dren: (1) Myrtie, b. June 6, 1881. (2) Edith, b. Dec. 3, 1882. (3) Nellie, b. May 20, 1884. (4) Howard W., b. Oct. 18, 1885.

d. Frank L., b. Aug. 28, 1854; m. Oct. 31, 1877, Viola Hall, and res. Charlotte. Children: (1) Elsie, b. July 17, 1881. (2) Clara, b. June 15, 1883. (3) Alice, b. June 29, 1885.

e. Alice S., b. Jan. 4, 1857; d. Aug. 27, 1879, ae. 22-7-23.

f. Mary E., b. May 31, 1859; m. Sept. 21, 1887, Harvey Cole, and res. Chewelah, Wash. Children: (1) Eunice, b. July, 1895. (2) Lois, b. Aug., 1897.

g. Frederick C., b. Nov. 18, 1862; m. Nov. 24, 1885, Lena File She d. He res. Charlotte. Children: (1) Clarence. (2) Kenneth

23. Mary Jane, b. B., May, 1819; m. John C. Smith.
24. Laura, b. B., Feb. 15, 1822; m. Jan., 1839, William Hogle, son of Moses, b. Apr. 17, 1818, who d. Sandstone, Mich., Nov. 18, 1883, ae. 65-7-1. She d. Sandstone, Feb. 27, 1887, ae. 65-0-12. Children:

    a. Gilbert Bruce, b. Sept. 21, 1839; m. Dec. 27, 1866, Malindie Laighton. Res. Parma, Mich. Children: (1) Homer. (2) Alice. (3) Jessie.
    b. Marshall, b. Dec. 23, 1840; d. Feb., 1884, ae. 43-2-.
    c. Josephine, b. Aug. 7, 1842. Res. Parma, Mich.
    d. Emily, d. at two years of age.
    e. Dallas, b. Sept. 22, 1845; d. 1862, ae. 17.
    f. Erwin, b. Apr. 21, 1848. Res. Garden Plain, Kan.
    g. Emma, b. Apr. 17, 1850; m. —— Raymond; res. Jackson, Mich.
    h. Augusta, b. Sept. 9, ——; m. —— Robinson; res. Lamesa, Cal.
    i. Cora, m. —— Howe; d. June 12, 1887.
    j. L. Belle, m. —— Watts; res. Spring Harbor, Mich.
    k. Dora, m. —— Perry; res. Jackson, Mich.
    l. Carrie, m. —— Wellman; res. Parma, Mich.

25. Martha Ann, b. B., May 24, 1824; m. May 24, 1841, David S. Leavitt, son of David, b. Bridgeport, Conn., Oct. 11, 1814, and d. Long Hill, Conn., Mar. 19, 1887, ae. 72-5-8. She went to Michigan with her parents in 1837, spent her life in Grand Rapids, and there d. Feb. 18, 1898, ae. 73-8-24. Children:

    a. Frances Isabella, b. Sebewa, Mich., Nov. 2, 1842; m. Oct. 31, 1861, Levi Shultus. Res. 302 E. Bridge street, Grand Rapids.
    b. Sylvia Elmira, b. Grand Rapids, Aug. 2, 1844; m. June 7, 1867, Lyman Hizer, and res. Lyons, Ionia Co., Mich.
    c. Sheldon, b. G. R., Apr. 9, 1847. Is a physician at 4,564 Lake Ave., Chicago, Ill.
    d. Martha, b. G. R., Oct. 22, 1850; m. Dec. 27, 1870, Rev. W. I. Cogshall. Res. 116 Jefferson street, Benton Harbor, Mich.
    e. David, b. G. R., May 20, 1853; d. Oct. 26, 1862, ae. 9-5-6.
    f. Adelman, b. G. R., Mar. 9, 1856; d. Langston, Mich., May 20, 1872, ae. 16-2-11.
    g. Frederick, b. G. R., Nov. 10, 1861; m. Sept. 3, 1882, Eva Avery. He is a physician, 544 Selby Ave., St. Paul, Minn.

26. Keziah, b. B., Nov., 1833; m. —— Child; res. Grand Rapids, Mich.
27. Martin V., b. Portland, Mich., Nov. 13, 1838; m. Oct. 14, 1863, Rebecca H. Buck, dau. of Hart, b. Avon, Ohio, Aug. 11, 1840. He is a farmer in Portland.

———

1. Abel Tirrell, a brother of Jonah, was first taxed in New Chester in 1787. He was the first settler on the Oliver S. Hall farm where he appears to have res. till about 1812; later, in the northeast part of the town.

CHILDREN   .

    2. Alexander, m. Apr. 12, 1808, Mrs. Sarah Chase, and d. in Haverhill.
    *3. Nathan.

(3) Nathan Tirrell, m. Nov. 12, 1812, Rachel Fuller, dau. of Josiah (See), b. Mar. 10, 1795. He res. southeast shore of Newfound lake, near where is now B. F. Lamb's cottage, as

late as 1822.   He d. Hebron, 1855; she d. Mar. 31, 1871, ae.
76-0-21.

4.   Wooster, b. Andover; m. Judith Veasey.   He was killed in Massachusetts, by falling from his team, a wheel passing over his neck.   Children:

    a.   Charles.   *b*.   Melissa.

5.   Lodema, b. A., Nov. 9, 1813; m. July 4, 1836, Aaron H. Fogg; res. Bristol and Hebron; d. June 22, 1883, ae. 69-7-13.   Children:

    a.   Jefferson, b. Bristol   *b*.   Minot, b. B.
    c.   Milo, b. Hebron.   *d*.   Albert.

6.   Hazen, b. A., 1818; m. Arvilla Varnum. (2) Adeline H. Wise. He d. May, 1901, ae. 83.   She res. Cochituate, Mass.   Nine children.

7.   Russell Plummer, b. Bristol, Mar. 30, 1830; m. Aug. 16, 1855. Emeline Fretts, dau. of Jacob, b Hebron, Oct. 5. 1839.   He has been a farmer in Hebron, Groton, and now in Bristol.   Children:

    a.   Harriet Rhodema, b. Hebron, Aug. 12, 1857; m. Heber L. Hanscom.   Res. Bristol.   Three children: Nettie, Henry, Homer.
    b.   Leona Grace, b. H., Dec. 5, 1859; m. Frank A. Flagg; res. E. Concord.   Six children.
    c.   Frank Ezra, b. H., Jan. 6, 1861; m. Carrie Harriman, Ashland.   Child: Stephen B.
    d.   Dorothy Ann, b. H., May 11, 1863; m. Edwin Hearson.   Res. Concord.   Six children.
    e.   Clara Elizabeth, b. H., Sept. 11, 1864; m. Moses E. Southard. (See.)
    f.   Emma Josephine, b. H., Dec. 11, 1867; m. Charles Leslie; res. Grasmere.   Three children.
    g.   Georgia Augusta, b. H., Feb. 7, 1873; m. George Drew; res. E. Concord.   Four children.
    h.   Emma Rebecca, b. Groton, Dec. 6, 1876; d. May 27, 1880, ae. 3-5-21.

---

1.   Hollis Tyrrell, son of Nathan, was b. in Bridgewater. Nathan was a brother of Abel and Jonah above.   Hollis m. Millie, and d. Hebron.   She d. Haverhill.

2.   Samuel, m. (1) Martha Wescott, (2) Ruth Wescott, by whom he had ten children, one of whom was

    a.   Scott C., b. Plymouth, May 4, 1873; farmer, settled in Bristol, 1889; m. June 25, 1891, Mrs. Augusta A. Emmons, dau. of Oren Nelson. (See.)   She d. Bristol, Dec. 16, 1899, ae. 30-7-26.   He removed to Meredith 1900.   Child: Lynna Mahala, b. Bristol, Feb. 11, 1892; d. B., Dec. 17, 1899, ae. 7-10-6.

3.   Mary, d. Haverhill, unm.

4.   Mercy Ann, m., d. Newbury, Vt.

5.   Moses D., b. Bristol, 1827; m. —— Peaslee, and res. Bridgewater. He served in Co. A, 6th Regt., N. H. Vols., Civil war, and d. on hospital boat "Tycoon" at Cannelton, Ind., Aug. 9, 1863, ae. 36.   (See Roll of Honor.)

THE TOLFORD FAMILIES

1.   Maj. John Tolford was b. in Ireland, July, 1701; came to America and was in Bradford, Mass., in 1724, and settled in

Londonderry. He built the first saw-mill in Hooksett. In 1727, he removed to Chester. He m., Jan. 8, 1734, Jean McMurphy, of Londonderry. In 1736, he was committed to jail for refusing to pay a tax for the support of the settled minister. In March, 1753, he was major of a party sent to survey a route up the valley of the Merrimack from Concord to the Connecticut river at Haverhill. (See p. 24, Vol. I.) At this time he had an opportunity to see the attractions of the territory along the Pemigewasset, and a few months later was a moving spirit in the organization of the syndicate that purchased the town of New Chester. He was one of the proprietors of the town, owning four shares, of four lots each. He was also deeded the mill lot on Newfound river, in consideration of which he erected and set in operation the first grist-mill and saw-mills in what is now Bristol village (See p. 366, Vol. I) ; but he was never a resident of the town. He was a justice of the peace, a land surveyor, and a man of more than ordinary ability. He d. July, 1791, ae. 90 years ; she d. Dec. 29, 1792. Of his nine children, three were

2. Joshua, b. Feb., 1739. He was a surveyor; was one of a party who made a re-survey of the New Chester grant in 1765. (See Appendix E, p. 522, Vol. I.) His map is shown in Vol. I. He settled at Profile Falls in 1769, and had the first saw-mill on that stream in operation in 1773. About 1780 he removed to what is now known as Clark's Corner in South Alexandria, where he was the first settler and where he passed the remainder of his years. He was a prominent man of his day. In the Burns graveyard stands a tablet which reads : "Joshua Tolford died Mar. 4, 1826. Elizabeth Tolford died Mar. 9, 1801."

3. Hugh, b. Dec. 22, 1747 ; m. Elizabeth Patten, of Bedford. Children :

    a. Isaac, b. 1786.   *b.* William, b. 1795 ; res. Bedford.

    c. Jane, } d. Apr. 24, 1823.
    d. Elizabeth, }

4. John, b. Jan. 2, 1750. He made the first clearing within the limits of Bristol. (See "First Settlements," Vol. I.) He settled in Danbury, was a surveyor, and had a family. One son was

    a. John, b. 1783; was in trade where is now White's block as early as 1815, and so continued till his death, Apr. 21, 1823, ae. 40. His remains rest in the Worthen graveyard.

THE TOWN AND TOWNS FAMILIES

1. Henry Town, son of William and Julia Ann (Moore) Town, was b. in Rupert, Vt., Apr. 18, 1871. He m., Oct. 4, 1897, Mrs. Gertie Eva Sherman, dau. of George A. and Abbie (Lathrop) Reed, b. Peru, Vt., May 30, 1873. She m. (1) Oct. 30, 1887, John W. Sherman, who d. Nov. 4, 1892. He has res. in Bristol, employee in paper-mill, since Nov., 1897.

---

1. Joseph Warren Towns, son of John and Eliza (Anderson) Towns, was b. Londonderry, Nov. 4, 1834. He m., Apr.

28a

·

4, 1863, Josephine R. Gaillow, b. May 25, 1837. He came from Hudson and res. in Bristol much of the time for 20 years previous to his death which occurred in hospital at Concord, July 31. 1903, ae. 68-8-27. She d. New Hampton, Sept. 9, 1893, ae. 56-3-14. Carpenter.

CHILDREN

2. Edwin Waldo, b. Lancaster, June 25, 1864. Located in Bristol; m. Mar. 29, 1890, Eva I. Simonds, b. Alexandria, 1873. A fireman in Little Falls, N. Y. Six children.

3. Frank Wilbur, b. Groveton, June 4, 1866; m. (1) Alice E. Waterman. She d. and he m. (2) May 30, 1802, Dora A., dau. of Joseph N. Dickinson (See), b. Dec. 26, 1871. Machinist.

4. Arthur Herbert, b. Windham, Sept. 11, 1868. In Bristol since 1884; job teamster; now operating North End grist-mill; elected road agent, 1902.

THE TOWNSEND FAMILY

1. Ziba Townsend was one of the early settlers in that part of New Chester now Hill, his farm being on Lot 83, First Division, about a mile north of Hill village on the Pemigewasset river. His name appears on a petition to the legislature in 1787, but first on the tax-list in 1800. In 1818, he was taxed as a non-resident. May 5, 1800, he m. Nancy Bartlett.

CHILDREN

2. A dau., who m. a Chamberlain; lived and d. in the West.

3. A dau., who m. a Fellows, res. in Canaan.

4. Luther K., b. in Hill; m. Aug., 1831, Mary True, dau. of Hazen and Catherine (Ash) Call, b. Andover, Mar. 27, 1810 (?). He res. for a time in Franklin, then in Orono, Me., where he was deputy sheriff and where he d. Nov. 16, 1839. Soon after his death, she removed to Bristol and here res. six or eight years. She m. (2) Alvin Fletcher, Aug., 1841, and they res. many years in Tilton. Child :

a. Luther Tracy, b. Orono, Me., Sept. 27, 1838; m. Sept. 27, 1865, Laura C., dau. of Dr. David T. and Sarah F. (White) Huckins, of Watertown, Mass. He res. in Bristol six or eight years in the forties. In a letter to the author he says: "In my childhood, I thought Bristol with its background of hills and its rushing river, was one of the most beautiful places on earth." When a young man, he was a fireman on the B. C. & M. railroad ; studied at Tilton; graduated Dartmouth college, 1859, at Andover Theological Seminary, 1862 ; served as adjutant 16th Regt. N. H. Vols, in the Civil war ; entered the ministry of the Methodist Episcopal church, 1864; was given the degree of A.M., by Wesleyan University in 1866, and of D.D., by Dartmouth college in 1871. He filled chairs at Boston University of Hebrew, Chaldee, and New Testament Greek, 1868-'70 ; of historical theology, 1870-'72 ; practical theology and sacred rhetoric, 1872-'90, when he resigned to devote his whole time to literary work. He was a delegate to the ecumenical council in London in 1881, to the council of all religions at Chicago in 1893, and was dean of The Chautauqua School of Theology, 1882-'85. He has taken a high rank as a preacher and lecturer, has published over 20 volumes and been connected editorially with several magazines and papers. Perhaps his most popular work was *Credo* published in 1869. The merits of *Evolution*

COL. SAMUEL P. TRAIN

or Creation secured for him an election to membership in the Victoria Institute, of London. He is a Mason. Res. Brookline, Mass. Children : (1) Agnes Rich, b. July, 1870; d. Mar., 1880, ae. 9-9-. (2) Helen Webb, b. July, 1873. (3) Fannie Fletcher, b. Watertown, June, 1880.

TRAIN

1. Col. Samuel P. Train, of the firm of Train-Smith company, though not at any time a resident of the town, has been closely identified with its industry for the last 18 years. Col. Train is a son of Samuel F. and Frances G. (Glover) Train. He was b. in Boston, May 23, 1848, and has been connected with the paper business for about 40 years. In 1864, he entered the house of Grant, Warren & Co., Boston, and has been connected with that firm and its successors till the present. This firm was succeeded by H. M. Clark & Co., in 1873, the year after the big fire in Boston. They were succeeded by Thompson, Twombly & Co., and they by Twombly & Co. In 1877, the firm became Train, Horsford & Co., and, in 1880, Train, Smith & Co., which has continued till now. In 1885, this firm succeeded to the property in Bristol of the New Hampshire Pulp and Paper Co., consisting of the pulp-mill on Central street and the paper-mill on Lake street at the North End, and still own and operate them. (See Manufacturing Industries.) In connection with this branch of their business, Col. Train has been a frequent visitor in town, and his enterprise has added materially to the business of the place. It was in his honor that the local company of militia was named Train Rifles.

Col. Train is a direct descendant of Christopher Gore, at one time governor of Massachusetts, and of Gen. Israel Putnam of Revolutionary fame. He served as colonel on the staff of Gov. John D. Long, of Massachusetts, a cousin by marriage.

THE TRUELL FAMILY

1. David Truell was b. in England in July, 1754. He learned the tailor's trade in England and came to America about 1775 and was for a time in Litchfield. He was in New Chester as early as 1796, and at that time lived in a log cabin on the south bank of Smith's river on the old road not far from the first bridge over that stream. A cellar in the woods now marks the site. A few years later he moved to the Bristol side of this stream and lived on the south side of New Chester mountain on the old road over this mountain. Like his first home, a cellar alone marks the spot. He m. Mary Wilson, who d. in Bristol May 27, 1828, ae. 65 ; he d. July 19, 1829, ae. 75.

CHILDREN

2. Polly, b. July 14, 1780; m. Oct. 22, 1799, Jeremiah Hubbard. (See.)

3.   David, b. Jan. 5, 1782; m. Abigail Phillips, of Alexandria, and settled in Grafton, where they spent their lives. He had five children among whom was

    a.   Hiram, m. Nancy Russell about 1830, and d. Jan. 26 1899, ae. 94. He swung the scythe in the hayfield the last season before he d. She d. 1871. Children: (1) Martha, lives in Fitchburg, Mass. (2) Jane, in Fitchburg. (3) Silvia, d. at 10 years. (4) Sumner R., b. Grafton, 1833; d. Grafton, Dec. 29, 1899, ae. 66. Was a farmer and dealer in lumber. He was survived by a widow, two sons, and granddaughter. (5) Abbie, res. Wisconsin.

4.   Susanna, b. Oct. 6, 1783; m. Amos Eastman.
5.   Jonathan W., b. Sept. 11, 1785; m. Esther Watts, of Connecticut.
6.   Jane (Fanny), b. June 26, 1787; m. William Murray, who was drowned in Smith's river. She d. in Lawrence, Mass. Children:

    a.   A. W. Stearns, Lawrence, Mass. He d. May, 1896, aged about 80, leaving $50,000 to the Ladies' Charitable Society of that city to accumulate till it reached $500,000.

    b.   William (Murray).

7.   Samuel, b. Apr. 2, 1789; d. Bristol, unm., about 1863.
8.   Elijah, b. Mar. 20, 1791; d. Bristol, unm., about 1855.
*9.   George Washington, b. Bristol, Oct. 21, 1792.
*10.   Wiseman C., b. B., Aug. 26, 1794.
11.   Lydia, b. B., Apr. 26, 1798; m. Roby Prescott, Grafton. Children: Hiram, Henry, Abbie, Esther, John, and Mary—all deceased.
12.   Sally, b. B., Jan. 17, 1800; m. Benjamin Pevear, of Thornton.
13.   Betsey Smith, b. B., May 12, 1801; m. Alexander Hutchinson. See.)
14.   Hannah, b. B., Feb. 22, 1803; m. Rev. Orrin Whitcomb, of Windsor, Vt., a brother of wife of George W. Truell. He was a Methodist clergyman many years in Maine; about 1850, removed to Ontario, Canada. where he d. about 1884. She d. about 1854. Children:

    a.   Lovitia, m. and res. Ontario.
    b.   Fanny, d.   *c.*   Cynthia, d.

(9)   George W. Truell, son of David, b. Oct. 21, 1792, m. Sept. 6, 1818, in Montreal, Fanny, dau. of Zenas and Eunice (Root) Whitcomb, b. Windsor, Vt., Apr. 17, 1800. He left Bristol when a boy, and at m. returned and was a brick-maker here. About 1828, removed to Vermont, and in 1837 to Barnston, P. Q., where he d. Aug. 29, 1867, ae. 74-10-8; she d. Mar. 5, 1868, ae. 67-10-18.

CHILDREN

15.   Wealthy Jane, b. Bristol, Jan. 18, 1820; m. Stillman Roy, and res. Derby Line, Vt.
16.   Zenas Brooks, b. B., Sept. 6, 1823; m. Carrie P. Hildreth, of Lowell, where he was a spinner. Killed at Battle of the Wilderness, May 8, 1864, ae. 40-8-2. (See Roll of Honor.) No children.
17.   Benjamin Franklin, b. B., Aug. 29, 1827; d. in infancy.
18.   Ira Whitcomb, b. Waterford, Vt., Feb. 14, 1830; d. Lawrence, Mass., Dec., 1875, ae. 45-10-.
19.   George Wilson, b. W., Feb. 5, 1832. Served in 37th Mass. Vols. three years; m. but no children; d. 1878, ae. 46.
20.   Byron, b. St. Johnsbury, Vt., Nov. 23, 1834; m. Sept. 5, 1859, Mary Elizabeth, dau. of William H. and Mary B. (Hannaford) Armstrong, b. St. Stevens, N. B., June 29, 1833. When three years old, he went with his parents to Stanstead, P. Q. In Feb., 1854, he located in

Lawrence, Mass., and commenced life as a clerk in a dry goods store, and four years later became a member of the firm of Bailey & Truell. In 1863, he established the house of Byron Truell & Co., which still continues the leading dry goods house in Eastern Massachusetts, and he is one of the wealthy men of that city. In 1875 and 1876, he served in the state legislature; in 1877 and 1878 in the state senate; 1890 and 1891, member of the executive council of the state and in 1893, he declined the Republican nomination to Congress from his district. He has also filled various city offices and been president of the Lawrence Board of Trade; is now postmaster of that city. Children :

    a. Grace Laura, b. Lawrence, Feb. 13, 1860; m. June 26, 1889, George H. Eaton, a lawyer of Lawrence who d. June 15, 1893. She res. Lawrence.
    b. Gertrude Elizabeth, b. L., Sept. 19, 1861 ; m. Nov. 25, 1886, Albert E. Butler, a banker ; res. Lawrence.

    21. Valorus, b. S. J., Jan. 9, 1837; m. July 26, 1858, Caroline Yemans Hollister, dau. of Harry, b. Feb. 17, 1839, at Derby, Vt., and d. Barnston, P. Q., Feb. 27, 1880, ae. 41-0-10. He m. Mar. 9, 1881, Ada Sutton, b. Kingston, Ontario, Dec. 24, 1855, dau. of Dr. John P. Sutton, L.D.S He spends his winters in Lawrence, Mass., and his summers at his family home in Barnston, where he has been school commissioner, and municipal councillor. In 1872, was appointed one of Her Majesty's justices of the peace for the district of St. Francis, and he was then the youngest magistrate in the Province of Quebec. Children :

    a. Fannie Jane, b. Barnston, Sept. 17, 1859. Is a teacher in Carlisle, Mass.
    b. Mary Ann, b. B., June 10, 1861; m. July 16, 1884, D. Lang Chamberlin, of Carlisle, Mass. Has one son and one dau.
    c. Harry Valorus, b. B., May 18, 1863. Educated at the McGill University and McGill Law School, Montreal, P. Q., and is an advocate, being a member of the bar for the district of Montreal Res. 260 St. James street, Montreal.
    d. Newton Theodore, b. B., May 8, 1866; educated at St. Francis college, Richmond, and St. Hyacinth college, P. Q. Is principal of Lachute academy, Lachute, P. Q., and is a member of the Protestant Board of Public Instruction for Province of Quebec. He m. Dec. 27, 1892, Maud, dau. of I. B. Futvoye.
    e. Mabel Bertha, b. Oct 19, 1883.

    22. Elias, b. Barnston, Dec. 8, 1839; m. Sept. 5, 1866, Lizzie A., dau. Gilman Buzzell, b. Danville, Vt., Sept. 18, 1844. He d. Dudley, Mass., Mar. 20, 1894, ae. 54-3-12. Child :

    a. George Buzzell, b. Barnston, June 1, 1867.

    23. Ellen Amanda, b. B., Oct. 21, 1842 ; m. May 22, 1865, Charles William Vaughan, son of Hiram, b. Barnston, Feb. 19, 1842. Children :

    a. Albert Charles, b. Magog, Stanstead Co., Quebec, Feb. 3, 1866 ; d. June 29, 1882, ae. 16-4-26.
    b. Frederick Walter, b. Coaticook, P. Q., June 24, 1875.
    c. Franklin Truell, b. Stanstead Co., P. Q., Mar. 24, 1877.
    d. Arthur Elias, b. S., Feb. 1, 1879.

(10) Wiseman C. Truell, son of David, b. Aug. 26, 1794, m. Syrene, dau. of Stephen and Abigail (Phillips) Senter, b. Alexandria, Dec. 20, 1803. They removed to Springfield about 1830. He d. Grafton, Feb. 25, 1868, ae. 73-5-29; she d. Grafton, Aug. 20, 1889, ae. 85-8-0.

24. Abigail, b. Bristol, May 8, 1824; m. Dea. Silas Burnham, who d. She res. West Canaan.

25. Mary W., b. B., Nov. 16, 1826. Unm. Res. Lawrence, Mass.

26. Betsey Ann, b. Springfield, Jan. 6, 1834; m. Simon Horton. He d.; she res. Enfield Center.

27. Laura, m. John Honngon.

28. Esther Fannie, m. George C. Chase, and res. Vermont.

29. George Albert, b. Grantham, Jan. 30, 1841; m. Nov. 29, 1863, Marion Alice, dau. of Eben Mitchell, b. Croydon, July 6, 1844. He was a stone mason at Cornish.

30. Henry Washington, b. Grantham, Nov. 7, 1843; m. July 4, 1867, Julia E. J., dau. of Joshua Stevens, b. Springfield, Dec. 30, 1845. They are farmers in Grafton. Children:

    a. Laura, m. George Leavitt, Springfield.
    b. Herbert George, b. about 1882.
    c. Roy Morton, b. about 1889.

31. Hiram Wilson, m. Hannah McCollum, of Sutton, and res. Enfield. He d. Lawrence, June, 1881. Children:

    a. Abbie Lizzie.   *b.* Walter Wilson.   *c.* Elbridge Wiseman.

THE TRUESDELL FAMILY

1. Lucius Elbridge Truesdell, M.D., son of Perley and Mary (Stimson) Truesdell, was b. in Monson, Mass., May 10, 1818. He m., Oct. 10, 1840, Lucy Bliss, dau. of Hezekiah and Keziah (Bliss) Perry, b. Rehoboth, Mass., 1818, and d. Warren, Mass., Nov. 8, 1861, ae. 43. He m., Feb. 22, 1867, Sarah Elizabeth, dau. Andrew and Maria B. (Perry) Mills. By reason of ill health he gave up the profession of medicine and devoted much time to the study of geology and mineralogy. He came from Springfield, Mass., to Bristol in 1876, and, taking a bond for a deed of the Philip S. Drake farm in North Bristol, opened the silver mine there. (See Mines.) He d. Bristol, June 7, 1890, ae. 72-0-27. Mrs. Truesdell returned to her old home in Thompson, Conn., where she now res.

2. Lucius Everett Elbridge, b. Monson, Mass., Oct. 12, 1841. Since 1880, res. Idaho Springs, Colo. Unm.

3. Eugene Ernest Perry, b. M., Sept. 28, 1845; m. 1873, Fannie Page, and res. Belvidere, Ill.

4. Leon Harold, b. Warren, Mass., Apr. 30, 1871. Left Bristol Nov., 1890; m. 1893, Gertrude Boynton, of Boston. He is a sign and carriage painter, 31 Appleton street, W. Somerville, Mass. Children:

    a. Louise Maynora, b. 1894.   *b.* Lucius Boynton, b. 1896.
    c. Richard Eugene, b. 1902.

5. Gertrude Maynora, b. W., Feb. 12, 1874; d. Bristol, July, 1881, ae. 7 5-.

THE TRUMBULL FAMILY

1. Frank Arthur Trumbull is a son of John C. and Mary Ann (Chellis) Trumbull. He was b. Wilmot, Nov. 16, 1866,

and m. Hattie Maud, dau. of Guildford and Betsey Flagg Dotan, b. Canada, June 28, 1874. Came from Canaan, Nov., 1895, and is an employee of Dodge-Davis Manufacturing Company.

THE TUKEY FAMILY

1. Israel Tukey was b. in Canada in 1823. He m., about 1846, Mary —— ; b. Canada, 1826. He was a laborer in Bristol many years, and here d. June 27, 1897, ae. 74. She res. Bristol.

CHILDREN

2. Mary, b. Cornish; m. Joseph Gardner, and res. Franklin Falls.
3. Charles Henry, b. C., Apr. 9, 1850; m. July 3. 1869, Sarah Jane, dau. of John Sanborn, b. Lowell, Mass., Oct. 6, 1853. He learned the saddle and harness business of Judge O. F. Fowler, and since 1873 has conducted this business in Bristol. No children. Democrat, Odd Fellow, K. of P.
4 Julia, m. George Keniston. Child :
    a. Julia Ann, m. (1) William Atwood, (2) Elwood S. Lougee. (See.) (3) W. S. Ferrin.
5. Joseph, b. Lebanon ; m. Hattie Adams, Winooski, Vt. Two children.
6. Clara, b. Boscawen ; m. Edmond Page ; res. Franklin Falls.
7. Eliza, b. B. ; m. —— Gonye ; res. Franklin Falls. Child :
    a. Harry, b. Franklin Falls, July 4, 1888.
8. Almeda, b. Goffstown, Sept. 4, 1863 ; m. (1) William J. Davis ; 2) Nov. 7, 1885, Philip Brooks. Res. Franklin Falls. Children :
    a. Sadie (Davis), b. Franklin Falls, Dec. 14, 1881.
    b. Emma (Brooks), b. Bristol, May 15, 1889.
9. Hattie Belle, b. Bristol, Oct. 28, 1866 ; m. Ira B. Burpee. (See.)
10. Frank, b. Sanbornton ; d. Oct. 25, 1879, ae. 18-7-.
11. Anne Lora, b. 1873 ; d. Bristol, Dec. 14, 1879, ae. 6.

THE VALLA FAMILY

1. Stephen Valla, son of Joseph and Mary (Brovida) Valla, was b. Saliceto, Province of Cuneo, Italy, June 28, 1877. He came to America in 1890 ; was two years in trade in Ashland ; in Bristol engaged in fruit and confectionery trade from Feb., 1900, till summer, 1903 ; now in Alexandria. He m., Sept. 30, 1902, Florence Lydia, dau. of Ira Aland and Clara Adell (Emery) Gale, b. Bristol, Apr. 14, 1884. No children.

THE VARNEY FAMILY

1. Ira F. Varney, son of Chauncey P. and Mary Etta (Page) Varney, was b. Derby, Vt., July 17, 1845. He m., Jan. 15, 1866, Jane Lorenza, dau. George W. and Nancy (Willoughby) Hutchins, b. Rumney, May 11, 1847. He is a carpenter and mason ; has been a dresser in woolen-mill 15 years. Built a residence in No. Bristol in 1895.

2. Albert Ira, b. Rumney, Nov. 12, 1866; m. Jan. 15, 1891, Nellie L., dau. of Hollis B. Hazelton. Is a blacksmith in New Hampton. No children.

3. Henry Chauncey, b. R., Mar. 4, 1870; m. Nov. 2, 1889, Mary Alice, dau. Daniel K. Cummings. (See.) Machinist. Res. in Bristol since 1882; now Franklin. Children:

    a. Nellie Alice, b. Bristol, Feb. 20, 1890.
    b. Herbert P., b. B., Mar. 12, 1892.
    c. Arthur Ira, b. B., Aug. 30, 1893; d. Mar. 31, 1894.
    d. Harry C., b. B., Apr. 13, 1899.

4. Leon Hudson, b. R., July 16, 1874; m. July 27, 1903, Mary Mehitable Sawyer, dau. of Enoch Sumner and Cinderella (Follansbee) Dimond, b. Groton, July 21, 1870. Is a carpenter.

5. Alice May, b. R., July 8, 1876; m. Samuel M. Reid, Nov. 24, 1892. Children:

    a. Pearl Ira, b. Groton, Apr. 24, 1893; d. Aug. 3, 1893.
    b. Eva May, b. Bristol, Dec. 8, 1896.
    c. Maud Dora, b B., Dec. 15, 1897.
    d. Norman Nelson, b. Alexandria, Jan. 22, 1901.

6. Perley Harley, b. R., Mar. 23, 1878; d. Bristol, May (Mar.) 30, 1883, ae. 5-2-7.

THE VEASEY FAMILY

1. Albion Arthur Veasey, son of Lyman F. and Laura (Smith) Veasey, was b. Meredith, Mar. 31, 1861; m. Feb. 3, 1897, Mrs. Alma L. Sleeper, dau. of Roswell Blake. (See.) He came to Bristol from Meredith about 1897. Landlord of Riverside House, and has a meat market. Republican. Odd Fellow. No children.

THE VOSE FAMILY

1. John Francis Vose was a son of Francis and Mary A. (Bracket) Vose. He was b. in Bloomfield, Me., Aug. 19, 1832, m. July 4, 1857, Emily Jane, dau. of Jonas R. Haywood (See), b. Oct. 27, 1835, and d. Alexandria, Oct. 10, 1888, ae. 52-11-13. He settled on the Zerah E. Tilton farm in 1859; later, the Abram Dolloff farm in District No. 6; removing to Alexandria about 1864; now farmer in Manchester.

2. Nellie Marcia, b. Pembroke, Apr. 27, 1858; m. Alba O. Dolloff. See.)

3. Minnie Emma, b. Bristol, June 10, 1860; m. Marcus O. Sleeper. (See.)

4. Hattie Augusta, b. B., May 20, 1862; m. Carl E. Noyes; res. Franklin Falls. Child:

    a. Ervilla Emma, b. Apr. 27, 1886.

5. Frank Reed, b. Alexandria, July 31, 1866; m. Oct. 14, 1890, Lura Augusta, dau. Freeman Hazen, b. North Hero, Vt., Apr. 15, 1864. He is foreman pattern maker Amoskeag Manufacturing company, Manchester. Children:

    a. Alfred Hazen, b. May 12, 1892.
    b. John Raymond, b. May 11, 1896.

6. Christie George, b A., Oct. 20, 1872; m. Annie Wilson, of Bennington. In trade in Tilton. Child:

  a. Donald Thomas, b. Bennington, Apr. 15, 1900.

THE WADLEIGH FAMILY

1. Simeon Hayes Wadleigh was a son of Joseph and Molly (Weeks) Wadleigh, b. Tilton, June 2, 1809. He came to Bristol when a young man, and m., Apr. 13, 1834, Jane B Sleeper, dau. of David (See), b. July 30, 1813. They res. on No. Main street; he was a teamster and laborer, and d. in Bristol. She m. a second time, res. and d. in Canaan.

CHILDREN

2. George Weston, b. Bristol, 1835. A teamster in Boston. Unm.
3. Mary Ellen, b. B., Apr. 9, 1839; m. May 13, 1858, Henry K. W. Currier. Res. 75 Elm street, No. Woburn, Mass. Child:

  a. Nathaniel, b. Canaan, June 9, 1863.

4. Anna T., d. Sept. 3, 1844, ae. 1-4-.
5. John Hayes, b. B., Jan. 24, 1847; m. June 17, 1868, Mary Lela Stiles, dau. of Orrin A., b. Moretown, Vt., Dec. 18, 1850. Res. Randolph, Vt. Children:

  a. Frank Weston, b. Braintree, Vt., Feb. 2, 1869; m. Jan. 23, 1892, Winnie A. Riford. Child: Carroll Riford, b. Apr. 30, 1892.
  b. Jane Bartlett, b. B., Feb. 17, 1874.
  c. Mabel Ellen, b. Randolph, Vt., Mar. 1, 1876.

THE WEBBER FAMILY

1. John Dudley Webber, son of Zachariah H. and Harriet (Abbott) Webber, was b. Groton, Jan. 5, 1843. He m., Jan. 5, 1866, Harriet Adeline, widow of Oscar F. Washburn, and dau. of John and Susan (Ingalls) Fowler, b. Hill, Feb. 19, 1844. He has been a blacksmith in Bristol since May, 1882. Democrat, Odd Fellow, Free Baptists.

CHILDREN

2. Burtis Milroy, b. Canaan, Nov. 7, 1867; m. June 27, 1891, Clara L., dau. of Thomas Parnell. Printer. Res. in Lynn, Mass., Odd Fellow. Children:

  a. Abbott Fowler, b. Lynn, Oct. 9, 1894; d.
  b. Julian Taylor, b. L., Jan. 11, 1898; d.
  c. Dudley Parnell, b. L., June 4, 1900.

3. Myrtle Augusta, b. C., Feb. 19, 1873; d. Bristol, Jan. 30, 1883, ae. 9-11-11.

THE WEBSTER FAMILY

1. George Webster, son of Thomas and Mary (Ordway) Webster, was b. Warner, Dec. 26, 1810. He m., 1841 or '42, Caroline Danforth, b. Warner, 1811. Both were deaf mutes. He was a maker of high grade boots and shoes. They came to

Bristol from Bradford, Vt., in November, 1846. She d. Bristol, Apr. 12, 1869, ae. 58, and he soon after returned to Warner; thence went to Westport, Mass., where he m., Nov., 1870, Lydia S. Macomber, who d. Jan. 6, 1892. He d. Penacook, Apr. 5, 1891, ae. 80-3-9.

CHILDREN

2. Helen Marzette, b. Laconia, June 10, 1843; m. John F. Hastings. (See.)

3. George Arthur, b. Bristol, 1847; d. Jan. 27, 1849, ae. 2 years.

THE WEEKS FAMILY

1. James W. Weeks is a son of George W. and Eliza E. Weeks. He was b. New Hampton, Feb. 23, 1864, and m. May 10, 1897, Addie E., dau. of Madison M., and Addie M. Sanborn, b. Bristol, Apr. 23, 1874. He has been a laborer in Bristol since 1880. No children.

THE WELCH FAMILY

1. William Bradley Welch, son of Thomas and Hannah (Welch) Welch, was b. Plymouth, Jan. 11, 1834. He m., Mar. 16, 1858, Mary Jane, dau. of Daniel S. and Belinda Cass Gordon, b. New Hampton, Aug. 3, 1841. He served in the Civil war on the quota of Holderness, in Co. E, 12th Regt., N. H. Vols. He was conspicuous for cool, determined bravery. At Fredericksburg, Chancellorsville, Gettysburg, Front Royal, Swift Creek, Drury's Bluff, and other engagements he escaped unharmed, but at the terrible slaughter at Cold Harbor, June 3, 1864, when charging the enemy's works, he fell with a severe wound on the side of his head, and while lying insensible and unable to assist himself, he was riddled with balls, no less than six piercing his body. Here he lay for about thirty-six hours, exposed to the hot rays of a June sun, and when he was carried from the field he was considered so near his end that it was useless to dress his wounds. In response, however, to his earnest entreaties, he was placed in an ambulance and carried sixteen miles over a rough road to Surgeon H. B. Fowler's headquarters at White House Landing, where his wounds were dressed. After a few months in hospital he returned to duty where he remained till mustered out with his regiment, May 29, 1865. His terrible wounds undermined his health, and he was a great sufferer the balance of his life. He came to Bristol in 1865, and was a workman for some years in the Mason-Perkins paper-mill, but was finally obliged to relinquish work, and d. Oct. 11, 1883, ae. 49-9-0. She m. (2) Dec. 9, 1886, Miles Hodgdon. She d. while on a visit at Paulina, Iowa, Dec. 9, 1902, ae. 61-4-6.

CHILDREN

2. William Smith, b Ashland, Dec. 9, 1858; m. Fannie Duncan, Maine. No children. Res. Roxbury, Mass.

3. Eddie Gerald, b. A., Sept. 29. 1860; d. Bristol, of pneumonia, Apr. 23, 1881 ae. 20-6-24.

4. Florence Isadore, b. New Hampton, Feb. 28, 1865; m. Aug. 17, 1880, Clarence Irving Gilpatric, in Bristol. He d. Concord, July 3, 1892. Six children. She m. (2) Jan., 1894, William Henry Haskins, b. Pittsfield. They res. Franklin Falls. Child :

   a. Edith Maud, b. May 19, 1895.

5. Cora Belle, b. N. H., Mar. 28, 1874; m. Mar. 28, 1892, Winnifred Walter Gilpatric. She d. Bridgewater, Dec. 23, 1894, ae. 20-8-25. He res. Bridgewater.

---

1. Benjamin Welch, son of John and Elizabeth (Breck) Welch, was b. in Thornton, Jan., 1827. He m Mercy Elizabeth, dau. of Marshall H. H. Breck, b. Wentworth, Feb., 1838. He settled in Bristol, 1867; laborer; removed to the New Hampton side of the Pemigewasset, where he was a farmer; there d. Sept., 1889, ae. 62-8-. She d. New Hampton, July 5, 1888, ae. 50-5-. Free Baptists.

CHILDREN

2. Henry Augustus, b. Candia, Apr. 8, 1855 ; m. Nov., 1878, Carrie I., dau. of Hiram J. and Isabelle Benton Diecy. He was 15 years teamster for the Mason-Perkins Paper company. Job teamster. Three times elected road agent. Removed to Brockton, Mass., in 1903. Child :

   a. Norman A. (adopted), b. Dec., 1895.

3. Fred L., b. Rumney ; res. Franklin Falls. Six children.

4. Marshall Eugene, b. R., Aug. 16, 1864 ; m. Oct. 13, 1885, Cora, dau. of Charles E. and Marguerite (Young) Dixon, b. Streator, Ill., Feb. 15, 1870. For 26 years has been an employee at pulp-mill of Mason-Perkins Paper company. Republican. Children :

   a. Josephine Arabell, b. New Hampton, Sept. 23, 1886.
   b. Ada Elizabeth, b. Bristol, Mar. 31, 1888.
   c. Robert Eugene, b. New Hampton, Jan. 29, 1891.
   d. Nellie Marguerite, b. N. H., Nov. 3, 1893.

5. Leston L., b. Bristol ; res. Franklin. Four children.

6. Claribel, b. B., Nov. 25, 1870; m. Oct. 25, 1891, Nathaniel Kelley, of South Kingston. He d. Alexandria, June 17, 1899. She res. Bristol.

THE WELLS FAMILIES

1. This history of Chester says "Lieut. Thomas Wells, of Amesbury, Mass., m. Elizabeth, oldest dau. of Capt. Samuel Ingalls, b. 1709." Lieut. Wells is named as an heir in the settlement of Capt. Ingalls's estate in 1760. "The name of his [Wells's] wife is Hannah, on record." "He was a man of note." He d. Mar., 1769, and his will, proved May 8, 1769, named as legatees, Sarah Carr, Winthrop, Thomas, Henry, Reuben, Samuel, Ebenezer, Phebe, and Peter. The similarity of these names with the names of "the children of Thomas Wells and

Hannah his wife," found on the records of New Chester, prove beyond a doubt that the two families were identical.[1] Lieut. Thomas Wells was one of the proprietors of New Chester, and six of his sons were among the early settlers of the town, hence the recording of the paper referred to. The following are the children of "Thomas Wells and Hannah his wife" as appears from the paper named.

 2. Sarah, b. Dec. 2, 1739.
 *3. Thomas, b. Jan. 19, 1741.
 *4. Henry, b. Mar. 24, 1743.
 *5. Reuben, b. Aug. 28, 1746.
 6. Samuel, b. Aug. 24, 1749; was a Revolutionary soldier from Chester. Settled in New Chester after the war.
 7. Peter, b. July 26, 1752. "He is dead."
 8. Ebenezer, b. May 3, 1754; m. Sarah, dau. of Cutting Favor (See), b. Dec. 28, 1759; d. May 28, 1843, ae. 83-5-0. He settled in Hill in 1778 or '79, and had at least four children.
 9. Phebe, b. Oct. 14, 1757.
 10. Peter, b. Jan. 20, 1762. Was a Revolutionary soldier from New Chester. (See.)
 11. Timothy, b. May 10, 1765.

 (3) Thomas Wells, son of Thomas, b. Jan. 19, 1741, settled on Lot 64, 4th Division, in that part of New Chester now Hill, in 1774. The name of his wife was Ruth. He d. in Hill, July 29, 1831, ae. 90-6-10.

CHILDREN

 12. William, b. June 30, 1768. When a young man he made his way with Hugh Murray to Canada through the trackless forests and there settled.
 13. Molly, b. Feb. 10, 1770.
 14. Hannah, b. Oct. 23, 1772. "Hannah Wells and Thorndike Proctor, Salisbury, published Dec. 23, 1797."
 15. Philip, b. May 6, 1777; m. Mary Ingalls, pub. Oct. 5, 1799. He was a farmer in Sanbornton; d. Nov. 29, 1850, ae. 73-6-23. She d. Hill. Nov., 1832, ae. 50. Seven children.
 16. Elizabeth, b. July 11, 1780. "Elizabeth Wells and James Murray, m. May 2, 1799."
 17. Ruth, b. Apr. 18, 1784; m. Sethus Forbes.

 (4) Henry Wells, son of Thomas, b. Mar. 24, 1743, m. Nov. 24, 1763, Sarah, dau. of Peter Colby, b. Aug. 26, 1744. They settled on Lot 91, First Division, in Hill village, next south of Carr Huse, in 1771. He perished in a snowstorm, Dec. 26, 1776, ae. 33-9-2. She m. (2) Jan 8, 1778, Ephraim Webster, and d. Jan. 28, 1820, ae. 75-5-2.

CHILDREN

 18. Sarah, b. Aug. 26, 1764.
 19. Hannah, b. May 18, 1768.
 *20. Peter, b. New Chester, Mar. 24, 1771.

[1] For additional facts see affidavit p. 179, Vol. I.

21. Molly, b. N. C., May 3, 1776. The records of New Chester say, "Molly Wells and Aaron Quimby m. June 5, 1794." "Molly Wells and Waite Stevens, pub. Aug. 26, 1794." "Molly Wells and Josiah Evans, of Andover, were pub. Oct. 26, 1801."

(5) Reuben Wells, son of Thomas, b. Aug. 28, 1746, m. Molly ———, b. July 22, 1749. He settled on Lot 64, Fourth Division, in what is now Hill, south part, in 1774. He d. Apr. 3, 1804, ae. 57-7-5.

CHILDREN

*22. Reuben, b. Apr. 3, 1770.

23. Thomas, b. Aug. 14, 1771 ; m. (1) Betty Bean, pub. Sept. 8, 1794 ; (2) Judith Colby, Oct., 1796. Eight children.

24. Moses, b. Mar. 23, 1773 ; m. Sarah Powell, of Hopkinton, pub. Sept. 20, 1796. He d. May 26, 1837, ae. 64-2-3. "Sally, w. of Moses Wells, d. May 19, 1858, ae. 73." Six children.

25. Hannah, b. Jan. 16, 1777 ; m. Ephraim Quimby. (See.)

26. John, b. Dec. 19, 1778. "John Wells and Judith Favor, pub. Sept. 18, 1802."

27. Samuel, b. Sept. 29, 1780 ; m. Rebecca, dau. Ebenezer Carleton (See), published Jan. 13, 1810. She d. Waterford, Penn., Sept. 1855, ae. 66.

28. Henry, b. Apr. 22, 1783 ; d. June 26, 1800, ae. 17-2-4.

29. Molly, b. Nov. 5, 1784.

30. Ebenezer, b. Feb. 17, 1787.

31. Peter, b. May 17, 1789.

32. Joanna, b. Jan. 24, 1792 ; m. Samuel Hoyt.

33. Sarah, b. Oct. 27, 1793 ; d. Aug. 18, 1795, ae. 1-9-21.

(20) Peter Wells, son of Henry, b. Mar. 24, 1771, m. May 13, 1790, Hannah, dau. of Oliver Smith and Deborah (Ingalls) Blake, b. June 30, 1770. After m. they settled in New Hampton and removed to Plymouth in 1805, their farmhouse being on the line between Plymouth and Hebron. About 1830, removed to the farm now owned by H. N. Emmons in Bristol, thence to North Bristol, where he d. Oct. 8, 1841, ae. 70-6-14. She d. Nov. 6, 1850, ae. 80-4-6.

CHILDREN

34. Betsey, b. Jan. 5, 1791 ; m. Robert Glover, May 21, 1807 ; was taxed in Plymouth, 1805-'08 ; d. Rumney, Oct. 29, 1864, ae. 73-9-24.

35. Mary, b. Mar. 13, 1793 ; m. (1) Mar. 12, 1812, Peter Bennett ; (2) Nov. 12, 1829, Ira Webster, of New Hampton ; d. Bristol, Feb. 22, 1867, ae. 73-11-9.

36. Hannah, b. June 30, 1795 ; m. Joseph S. Adams, and d. Bristol, Apr. 14, 1862, ae. 66-9-14. He d. Framingham, Mass., Dec. 12, 1867, ae. 78-8-14.

37. Affa, b. Aug. 21, 1797 ; m. Feb. 29, 1816, Solomon Hodge, Rumney ; m. (2) Jacob Rundlett ; d. Feb. 4, 1843, ae. 45-5-13.

38. Deborah, b. Dec. 4, 1799 ; m. Mar. 31, 1844, Bartlett Gordon, his second wife ; d. Alexandria, Nov. 18, 1893, ae. 93-11-14.

*39. Henry, b. New Hampton, June 28, 1802.

40. Peter, b. Sept. 29, 1804 ; d. Plymouth, Mar. 1, 1825, ae. 20-5-2.

41. Sally, b. Plymouth, Sept. 24, 1807 ; m. Nov. 11, 1834, Asa Drew. (See.)

*42. Kiah, b. P., May 24, 1810.

43. Emily, b. P., Feb. 29, 1816 ; m. Nov. 11, 1834, Michael Hoyt. (See.)

29

(22) Reuben Wells, son of Reuben, b. Apr. 3, 1770, m. June, 1791, Priscilla Sanborn, and d. Aug. 4, 1808, ae. 38-4-1; she d. Mar. 10, 1807.

44. Moses, b. Sept. 19, 1792.
45. Reuben, b. Apr. 22, 1795; m. Mahala, and d. "Mar. 22, 1819, in the 25 year of his age."—Tombstone. One child.
46. Lucy, b. Nov. 8. 1797; m. Moses Sanborn. (See.)
47. Sanborn, b. Oct. 12, 1801. Lived and d. Londonderry. No children.
*48. Sherburn, b. July 31, 1805.

(39) Henry Wells, son of Peter, b. June 28, 1802, m. Sept. 16, 1824, Lavina, dau. of Benjamin Locke (See), b. June 10, 1812. He was taxed in Plymouth, 1826-'29; removed to the Emmons farm, Bristol, with his father in 1830; to No. Bristol, 1836; in 1848, to Merrimack street, where he d. Apr. 26, 1883, ae. 80-9-28; she d. Apr. 1, 1884, ae. 78-9-2. Both were active workers in Methodist church, he a member of the official board. He was a carpenter and builder; served two years as selectman.

49. Peter, b. Bristol, Dec. 21, 1825; d. Oct. 1, 1844, ae. 18-9-10. (Tombstone says d. Sept. 30.)
*50. Benjamin Locke, b. B., Dec. 26, 1831.

(42) Kiah Wells, son of Peter, b. May 24, 1810, m. May 29, 1832, Hannah, dau. of Benjamin Locke (See), b. June 2, 1812. Farmer and carpenter; 1840-'44, manager of town farm, and for thirty-six years in the brick house on east side of Lake street, where he d. May 31, 1888, ae. 78-0-7; she d. same place. Apr. 21, 1894, ae. 81-10-11.

51. John Winter, b. Bristol, May 11, 1833; m. 1853, Rose H., dau. of Stephen and Harriet (Gilman) Boswell, b. Sept. 6, 1833. She d. Laconia, Sept. 6, 1897, ae. 64-0-0. An employee of glove factory; removed to Laconia about 1885; after death of his wife, removed to Alexandria; thence back to Bristol, 1902. Official member of Methodist church; Republican; served several years on police force of Bristol and Laconia. Children :
  a. Henry C., b. Bristol, Feb. 24, 1856; m. 1884, Irene, dau. of Oliver P. Piper, b. Sanbornton, June 1, 1852. She d. of consumption at Laconia, May 1, 1894, ae. 41-11-0. He m. (2) May 30, 1895, Mrs. F. J. George. Has been a practicing physician in Laconia since 1879. No children.
  b. Howard Elgin, b. B., Nov. 24, 1869; m. June 21, 1893, Lillian Winnifred, dau. of Albert and Emily (Gray) Simonds, adopted dau. of William C. Kelley, b. Dec. 15, 1870. He is a farmer in Alexandria Children : (1) dau. b. Jan. 20, 1896; d. two days later. (2) Richard Henry, b. Laconia, May 19, 1897.
52. Charles Wesley, b. B., Sept. 30, 1837; m. July 2, 1856, Sarah Clesby Ferrin, dau. of Philip, b. Concord, July 13, 1835, d. Minonk, Ill., Sept. 29, 1858, ae. 23-2-16. He m. (2) Mar. 2, 1861, Esther Ann, dau. of

William and Betsey (Hoyt) Burleigh, b. Sanbornton, Mar. 16, 1834; d. Apr. 1, 1899, ae. 65-0-15. He res. two years in Illinois, a farmer in Sanbornton, till 1899, when he became member of firm of B. L. & A. Wells, carpenters and builders, Bristol, where now res. He m. (3) Bristol, Nov. 7, 1900, Mrs. Alice B. Jones, dau. of Jeremiah W. Dennett. Child by adoption :

    a. Carrie May, b. Jan. 24, 1867.

  53. Amanda Webster, b. B., May 27, 1849; m. Charles S. Flanders. (See.) She res. Bristol.

(48) Sherburn Wells, son of Reuben, b. July 31, 1805, m. Sept. 28, 1828, Martha Washington Chase, b. Hill, Nov. 15, 1802. He located in Bristol as early as 1838 ; was a custom carder and cloth dresser. Played the bass viol in the Congregational choir. He d. Bristol, Nov. 16, 1874, ae. 69-3-15. She d. July 24, 1889, ae. 86-8-9.

CHILDREN

  54. Martha Ann, b. Hill, Aug. 10, 1829; m. William G. Gould. (See.)
  55. Fletcher Chase, b. Bristol, July 15, 1831; m. Sept. 3, 1857, Sarah S., dau. of Abraham Drake, b. Meredith, June 12, 1832. He d. June 20, 1872, ae. 40-11-5; she d. Dec. 23, 1872, ae. 40-6-11. He was a carriage painter. Children :

    a. Frank Fletcher, b. New Hampton, May 22, 1858. Left Bristol Feb. 22, 1873, and is a manufacturer of patent medicines, Chicago, Ill., res. 811 Washburn Ave.
    b. Martha Ann, b. Bristol, June 20, 1860; m. George P. Everleth. (See.)

(50) Benjamin L. Wells, son of Henry, b. Dec. 26, 1831, m. 1858, Mary B., dau. of David Sleeper, b. New Hampton, d. June 13, 1861, ae. 32. He m. (2) Aug. 12, 1866, Hannah, dau. of Uriah Rollins, b. Andover, Oct. 14, 1841. He is a carpenter and builder, member of firm of B. L. & A. Wells ; Republican and Methodist ; succeeded to his father's homestead on Merrimack street.

CHILDREN

  56. Albro, b. Bristol, July 26, 1860; m. Sept. 15, 1885, Harriet Ann, dau. of George A. Robie (See), b. May 12, 1867. Carpenter and builder, firm of B. L. & A. Wells; Republican; is serving his third year as selectman and his ninth year as member of board of education; member official board Methodist church. Res. Beech street. Children :

    a. Mary Bernice, b. Bristol, July 17, 1886.
    b. Harry Daniel, b. B., Apr. 6, 1888.
    c. Sara Elizabeth, b. B., June 21, 1895.
  57. Ellen Connor, b. B., Apr. 3, 1869; m. Charles A. George. (See.)

---

  1. Daniel Farmer Wells, son of Aaron and Annie (Farmer) Wells, was b. Goffstown, Aug. 5, 1810. He m. Sophronia, a sister of Reuben C. Bean (See), and dau. of Sinclair and Nancy (Quimby) Bean, b. Newport, Aug. 3, 1812. He was a blacksmith and machinist. They res. in Bristol in 1837, and he placed

the machinery in the new woolen-mill at that time. Was for many years in the employ of the Manchester corporation at Manchester. They again came to Bristol in 1857 and made their home with their dau., Harriet Jane, where she d. Jan. 30, 1888, ae. 75-5-27. He d. same place, Oct. 20, 1897, ae. 87-2-15.

CHILDREN, all born in Goffstown

2. Hattie J., b. June 19, 1837 ; m. Alonzo B. Gale. (See.)
3. George W., b. Nov. 22, 1839.
4. Dorothy Ann, b. Mar. 3, 1841.
5. Sophronia A., b. Apr. 29, 1842.
6. Samuel A., b. Aug. 4, 1844.
7. Charlotte E. C., b. May 25, 1846.
8. Frank F., b. July 12, 1850.
9. Thomas F., b. Oct. 18, 1853.

---

1. Jerome Giles Wells, son of John and Susan (Giles) Wells, was b. in Sanbornton, Jan. 27, 1859. He is a grandson of John and a great-grandson of Ebenezer, who m. Sarah, a dau. of Cutting Favor. He has res. in Bristol since 1885 ; engineer, unm. Republican. Mason.

---

1. Frank Bernard Wells, son of George and Olive (Hutchinson) Wells, was b. Franklin, Mar. 17, 1880. He m., Sept. 24, 1900, Arecia, dau. of George M. and Amanda (Patten) White, b. Sandown, Dec. 19, 1883. He is a carpenter and woodworker in Bristol.

CHILDREN

2. Jason Horace, b. Bristol, Mar. 26, 1901.
3. Corinne Arecia, b. B., May 13, 1903.

THE WENTWORTH FAMILY

1. Richard Wentworth, the youngest son of Isaac and Abigail (Nutter) Wentworth, was b. in Rochester, Jan. 14, 1789. He m., Jan. 3, 1814, Betsey Brodhead, b. Northampton Co., Pa., Apr. 15, 1787, a dau. of Capt. Luke, a Revolutionary soldier, and sister of Hon. and Rev. John Brodhead, a distinguished Methodist minister and a member of congress from New Hampshire. He settled on the Homans farm west of Bristol Peak, about 1815, and here he res. till 1828 or later, when he removed to Dover, where he d., Feb. 18, 1854, ae. 65-1-4 ; she d. Oct. 17, 1867, ae. 80-6-2. Methodists.

CHILDREN

2. Elizabeth, b. Rochester, Dec. 5, 1814 ; d. in family of her nephew, Rev. John Wentworth Sanborn, at Perry, N. Y., Mar. 9, 1881, ae. 66-3-4 ; unm.
3. Olive Cross, b. Bristol, Oct. 21, 1816 ; m. Apr. 14, 1841, Jeremiah

Prescott Sanborn, b. Epping, Feb. 19, 1812. He d. Aug. 19, 1893, ae. 81-6-0. Children :

    a   Harriet Elizabeth, b. Epping, Sept. 13, 1843; a teacher for 25 years. Res. Newfields. Unm.

    b.   Sarah Brodhead, b. E., June 22, 1845; d. July, 1877, ae. 32-1-8. Unm.

    c.   John Wentworth, b. E., Nov. 3, 1848; was a clergyman of the Methodist Episcopal church ; made a study of Indian races, and at the World's fair was commissioner on this subject, and has written valuable treatises on same. Is m. and has three children.

  4.   Mehitable, b. B., Apr. 1, 1820 ; d. Bristol, Dec. 16, 1828, ae. 8-8-15.

  5.   John Brodhead, b. B , Aug. 29, 1823; m. Aug. 21, 1851, Clara Mathes, dau. of Stephen Drew, M.D., of Milton. She d. May 2, 1890. He d. in August, 1893, ae. 70. He was a distinguished divine of the Methodist Episcopal church. (See Chapter on Literature, Vol. I.) Children :

    a.   Abby Jane, b. Milton, July 3, 1852; d. Sept. 12, 1853, ae. 1-2-9.

    b.   Lillie Brodhead, b. Perry, N. Y., July 13, 1854.

    c.   Harriet Olivia, b. Buffalo, N. Y., Dec. 15, 1855; d. Apr. 30, 1869, ae. 13-4-15.

    d.   Clara Holloway, b. Williamsville, N. Y., Sept. 12, 1857.

    e.   Stephenia Drew, b. Perry, N. Y., Nov 30, 1859.

    f.   Richard Brodhead, b. P., Dec. 22, 1860.

    g.   David Watson, b. Rockport, N. Y., Nov. 12, 1862 ; d. Nov. 11, 1863.

    h.   John Burleigh, b. Buffalo, N. Y., Aug. 2, 1864.

    i.   Julia DuBois, b. Medina, N. Y., Oct. 4, 1867 ; d. July 20, 1868.

  6.   Harriet Newell, b. B., Apr. 14, 1828 ; m. Nov., 1867, Moses Pettingill, Jr., Newburyport, Mass., where they res. and where she d. Sept. 29, 1888, ae. 60-5-15. No children.

  7.   Hiram Romain, b. Dover, May 16, 1830 ; d. about 1885, unm.

THE WEYMOUTH FAMILY

  1.   Daniel B. Weymouth was b. in Andover, Aug. 25, 1848. He m., Aug. 20, 1882, Ida Adelaide, dau. of William H. and Sarah J. (Tucker) Edmunds, b. Andover, June 19, 1854. His grandfather was Daniel Weymouth, a farmer in Gilmanton, who removed to Andover late in life. His father is Dr. Henry A. Weymouth, b. Gilmanton, Oct. 14, 1820, m. Louise Young, b. Nov. 23, 1819. He has been a physician of large practice in Andover, since 1843, and is extensively and favorably known. With one exception he has been moderator at every town meeting in Andover since 1850. Daniel B. Weymouth commenced life as a bookkeeper for the Sturtevant Manufacturing company, in Lebanon, which position he held for ten years ; he was ten years in trade in Andover, seven years of which time he was town treasurer, and seven years in trade in Penacook, till Jan. 1, 1896, when he came to Bristol, and has since been in trade in the old brick store. (See Mercantile Industries, Vol. I.) Mr. Weymouth is a Democrat, Mason, and a Unitarian. Mrs. Weymouth was a school teacher before her marriage. She has served six years as a member of the board of

education, and three years as superintendent of schools of Union District.

THE WHEET FAMILIES

1.   Dr. John Carlos Wheet, son of Joshua Reed and Huldah (Kidder) Wheet, was b. No. Groton, Feb. 15, 1840, and m. July 26, 1866, Ellen Elizabeth, dau. of Luther and Lucy (Tenney) Hardy, b. No. Groton, July 1, 1845.   He was a practicing physician in Bristol (See Physicians), 1883, till he d. July 11, 1897, as the result of a carriage accident, ae. 57-4-26.   She res. Bristol.

CHILDREN

2.   Edward Eugene, b. Pembroke, May 5, 1868; m. May 21, 1890. Dora Mena, dau. of Frederick W. Prescott (See), b. Mar. 10, 1869.   He was a registered pharmacist; in Fowler's drug store as clerk and partner. She d. Mar. 16, 1901, ae. 32-0 6; he d. Apr. 1, 1901, ae. 32-10-26.   Child:
    a. Geneva Alice, b. Bristol, Oct. 21, 1892.
3.   Nettie Ellen, b. Groton, July 1, 1872; m. Raymond Cavis. (See.)
4.   Von Carl, b. G., July 16, 1879; m. Oct. 8, 1902, at Littleton, Lyle Eaton, dau. of Stephen.
5.   Alice Clara, b. G., Apr. 17, 1883; d. Oct. 26, 1884, ae. 1-6-9.

---

1.   Dr. Fred Eugene Wheet, son of Josiah and Hannah Wood (Southwick) Wheet, was b. North Andover, Mass., Nov. 11, 1867.   He m., Oct. 27, 1892, Hattie Pheobe, dau. of George Kempton and Phoebe (Sisson) James, b. Meredith, April 15, 1871.   He practiced medicine in Bristol from May, 1892, till Aug., 1893, since in Stevens Point, Wis., and Rumford Falls, Me.   (See Physicians.)

CHILDREN

2.   Frances, b. Stevens Point, Wis., Oct. 16, 1893.
3.   Mildred Gertrude, b. S. P., Dec. 28, 1895.
4.   Dorothy Kempton, b. Rumford Falls, Me., Nov. 14, 1900.

THE WHIPPLE FAMILIES

1.   Alexander H. Whipple was a taxpayer in Bristol, 1834-'50.   He res. in a house that stood on the bank opposite the tollgate house on Central street; later where Charles P. George now res., Merrimack street.   He was a house carpenter.

CHILDREN

2.   George W., b. Andover, 1830.   Served as second lieutenant Co. F. 1st Regt., N. H. Vols., and as corporal Co. E, 31st Me. Vol. Infty., on the quota of Sherman, Me.   He was killed at Danville, Va., June 3, 1864.
3.   John P., b. A., 1833.   Enlisted from Nashua in 1st Regt., N. H. Vols., in Civil war.   Sergt. of Co. C, 9th Regt., N. H. Vols.   Was wounded at Poplar Springs Church, Sept. 30, 1864.   Mustered out June

HENRY C. WHIPPLE

10, 1865, and res. after the war at Biddeford, Me.; removed to Sherman, Aroostook Co., Me.

4. Carrie, was a painter and musician ; d. Rockland, Me.

---

1. Henry Chandler Whipple, son of David C. and Clementine (Chandler) Whipple, was b. Hanover, June 25, 1846, and m. June 2, 1875, Lilla Josephine, dau. of Abel P. and Harriet (Jones) Plummer, b. Canaan, Aug. 1, 1852. Mr. Whipple first engaged in manufacturing in Enfield in 1873. In 1884, he came to Bristol as a member of the firm of Dodge, Davis & Co., manufacturers of Shaker flannels, and was assistant superintendent. The company was incorporated in Oct., 1887, as the Dodge-Davis Manufacturing company, Mr. Whipple becoming treasurer and resident manager, and since the death of John W. Dodge in Feb., 1897, Mr. Whipple has been president and treasurer of the company. Since 1890, he has served as trustee of the Bristol Savings bank ; and as president of the First National Bank of Bristol since its organization in 1898, and is a trustee of the Minot-Sleeper library. Has res. on Lake street, but has a residence on Summer street now (January, 1904) nearing completion. A Knight Templar Mason.

CHILDREN

2. Harry Dodge, b. Enfield, May 30, 1876; d. Bristol, Mar. 13, 1893, ae. 16-9-13.

3. Fay, b. E., June 22, 1880; m. Sept. 17, 1903, Grace Mae Louise Barrett. (See Williams family.)

4. Anna Clementine, b. E., Apr. 21, 1884; d. Bristol, Sept. 2, 1887, ae. 3-4-11.

5. Inez Margaret, b. Bristol, July 20, 1886.

6. Ashley Plummer, b. B., Apr. 16, 1891.

THE WHITCOMB FAMILY

1. Joseph Greeley Whitcomb is the son of Daniel and Mehitable (Cowan) Whitcomb. He was b. Francestown, June 26, 1827, and m. Dec. 17, 1854, Ervilla H., dau. Enoch and Polly (Jones) Heath, b. Springfield, Dec. 11, 1829. He res. Grafton ; Bristol, 1876-'84 ; since at Potter Place. Is a Republican, justice of the peace, and pension agent.

CHILDREN

2. Grace Ervilla, b. Canaan, Dec. 6, 1856.

3. Mary Frank, b. Grafton ; m. George H. Emerson ; res. Wilmot.

4. Fred David, b. G., June 7, 1870; killed on railroad, Indianapolis, Ind., Dec. 3, 1889, ae. 19-5-26.

THE WHITE FAMILY

1. Warren White, a son of Stephen and ——— (Hudson) White, was b. Dana, Mass., May 3, 1803. He m. Sept. 14, 1828, Abigail S., dau. Dea. Samuel Danforth (See), b. Nov.

12, 1811. When a young man, he made two fishing trips to the coast of Labrador. At 19 years of age, he commenced to learn the tanner's trade at Cooperstown, N. Y., and later carried on this business at Dana, Mass., at Greenwich, Mass., and at Halifax, Vt. He came to Bristol from Halifax in 1837, having purchased the tannery on Central street of Hon. Nathaniel S. Berry. He continued the business till his death, a period of 38 years, and for 16 years operated a tannery at Woodstock, in company with Richard S. Danforth, and for a time one on Lake street in company with Gustavus Bartlett. (See Manufacturing Industries.) He was also interested in the manufacture of shoes at Bristol, and at Ashland in connection with John H. Thompson. He was also a farmer and dealer in cattle. He was a shrewd business man and a good financier. Probably no other man has done more for the material prosperity of the town than Mr. White. He accumulated a fine property, and was at one time the largest individual taxpayer in town. He built White's block in Central square, and built and occupied the White mansion on Spring street. He was a Calvanist Baptist and a Republican, and twice represented Bristol in the legislature. He d. May 12, 1874, ae. 71 0-9 ; she d. June 8, 1885, ae. 73-6-26.

CHILDREN

＊2.   Marshall Warren, b. Dana, Mass., Aug. 21, 1830.
 3.   Ann Maria, b. June 22, 1833 ; m. David P. Prescott. (See.)
＊4.   George Hudson, b. Bristol, Nov. 14, 1841.
 5.   Helen Abby, b. B., Jan. 16, 1847 ; m. (1) Henry A. Taylor, (2) Marcus O. Farrar. (See.)

(2) Marshall W. White, b. Aug. 21, 1830, m. Sept. 30, 1849, Elizabeth Reynolds, dau. of Rev. Converse L. McCurdy (See), b. Mar. 14, 1830. Mr. White was in the boot and shoe business nearly eight years, then druggist, watch maker and jeweler 25 years in White's block, and operated the tannery some time for the heirs after the death of his father. He is a Methodist, a charter member and past master of Union Lodge, A. F. and A. M., and a Chapter Mason. Republican. He represented Bristol in the constitutional convention of 1876, and the legislature of 1878, and served as town clerk five years. He was one of the committee on the construction of the aqueduct system of water works, and has been for many years treasurer of the Aqueduct Company. He has served since 1876 as a trustee of the Bristol Savings bank, and was one of the committee on building the Bank block, and has been a trustee of Minot-Sleeper library since its organization in 1884. Was several years a justice of the peace. In early life, Mrs. White was a sweet singer and prominent in musical circles.

CHILDREN

 6.   Clara DeElba, b. Bristol, Aug. 21, 1850 ; m. Homer Roby. (See.)

MARSHALL W. WHITE

EDWARD W. WHITE, D.D.S   WARREN WHITE   WILLIAM C. WHITE

CHARLES H. WHITE, D.D.S   KARL M. WHITE

7. Charles Henry, b. B., Nov. 14, 1854; m. Jan. 1, 1878, Etta Belle, dau. Otis K. Bucklin (See), b. Apr. 1, 1859. He studied dentistry at the dental department of Harvard college, 1873-'74; Boston Dental college, 1875-'76, receiving the degree of D.D.S., the latter year. He practiced dentistry in Bristol, 1877-'78, and Jan. 1, 1879, commenced practice in Danvers, Mass., where he built up a large and remunerative business; Jan. 1, 1901, he retired from professional life, to become treasurer of the White Entertainment Bureau, Boston, Mass. Mr. White has filled many positions of trust and responsibility in Danvers. He has been for several years treasurer of the Electric Light Sinking fund commissioners, and for the past thirteen years trustee of the Danvers Savings bank and president of the finance committee. In Jan., 1903, he was elected president of the bank; is trustee of the Peabody Institute. He is a Knight Templar Mason. Children:

    a. Edgar Fowler, b. Danvers, Mass., Oct. 28, 1885.

    b. Cleon Bucklin, b. D., Nov. 8, 1889.

8. Edward Warren, b. B., Jan. 12, 1857; m. Oct. 4, 1881, Kate V., dau. of Henry H. and Luella F. McQuesten, b. Plymouth, Mar. 16, 1861, and d. Tilton, June 28, 1890, ae. 29-3-12. He graduated New Hampton Institution, 1873; Boston Dental college, 1878; practiced dentistry in Plymouth eight years; in Tilton, five; and in Cambridge, Mass., five; now treasurer and director of Reliance Co-operative bank, Cambridge, Mass. Is a Mason — a member of Blue lodge, Chapter and Omega Council. No children.

9. Helen Marion, b. B., Oct. 12, 1863; m. Arthur W. Prescott. (See.) She was later a teacher in the public schools in Lynn, Mass., where she d. Mar. 1, 1897, ae. 33-4-19.

10. William Converse, b. B., May 31, 1865; m. Dec. 5, 1895, Mabel F., dau. of Benjamin F. Johnston, b. Boston, Mass., Dec. 5, 1875. He graduated from Tilton Seminary, 1885; took a post-graduate course of one year in same institution; was clerk in Littleton National bank, 1887-'90; bookkeeper for the Littleton Lumber Company; assistant treasurer of the Bristol Savings bank, 1890-'92, when he became treasurer, which position he still occupies. Was largely instrumental in the organization of the First National Bank of Bristol, and has been a director and its cashier since its organization in 1898. Republican, Knight Templar, and 32° Mason, official member of the Methodist church and for 13 years superintendent of the Sunday-school. Child:

    a. Elizabeth Drew, b. Bristol, May 4, 1902.

11. Karl Marshall, b. B., Feb. 22, 1871; m. Mar. 14, 1898, May Parker, dau. James Henry and Mary (Burnham) Foss, b. Rowley, Mass., July 21, 1875. He learned the printer's art; graduated Tilton Seminary, from Boston School of Oratory, made a tour of the states giving readings; was associate manager of the Central Lyceum Bureau, Rochester, N. Y., 1898-1901; since president and manager of the White Entertainment Bureau, Boston, the largest lyceum bureau in New England. He retains his residence in Bristol. Republican. Mason. No children.

(4) George H. White, b. Nov. 14, 1841, m. Nov. 2, 1862, Roxy D., dau. of Levi Locke (See), b. Apr. 19, 1840. They res. Spring street, where she d. Aug. 29, 1898, ae. 58-4-10. She was for some years a member of the choir and a member of the official board of the Methodist church. He is a Methodist, Mason, and Republican.

CHILDREN

12. Nettie May, b. Bristol, May 26, 1863; m. Oct. 23, 1884, Walter Farr Prince, son of Francis L., b. Amherst, June 10, 1861; was an iron

and brass founder in Bristol in 1889; now superintendent of the International Pump Company, Elizabeth, N. J., at a large salary. Children:

    a. Helen Louise, b. North Andover, Mass., June 10, 1886.
    b. Frank White, b. Lynn, Mass., Apr. 10, 1891.
    c. Marion, b. Elizabeth, N. J., Sept. 3, 1897.

    13. Warren, b. B., Apr. 1, 1867; m. Apr. 8, 1891, in Lowell, Mass., Kate Burns. He was a pattern maker and draughtsman in Lowell; now same in Winchester, Mass.

    14. Harry Grove, b. B., July 2, 1870; d. Apr. 24, 1871.
    15. Fred George, b. B., May 2, 1872. Is a draughtsman. Unm.
    16. Walter Henry, b. B., July 29, 1883.

THE WHITNEY FAMILY

    1. Kimball Whitney was b. in Campton, Oct. 26, 1810. Oct. 13, 1833 he m. Eliza, dau. of Moses Johnson (See), b. Jan. 1, 1808. He resided in Campton till 1842, when he came to Bristol and purchased the blacksmith shop standing on site of the post-office. Here for six years he carried on the blacksmith business. He also owned and occupied the Fisk house at the corner of Central square and Summer street, and a large tract of land connected. He removed from Bristol about 1848 to Plymouth, where he d. Mar. 16, 1894, ae. 83-4-20. She d. in the home of her dau., Mrs. Manson S. Brown, at Plymouth, July 19, 1900, ae. 92-6-18.

CHILDREN

    2. Ann P. E., b. Campton, May 24, 1835; m. Manson S. Brown. (See.)
    3. Sarah, b. C., Apr. 10, 1838; d. Plymouth, Apr. 2, 1893, ae. 54-11-22.
    4. Emma J., b. Bristol, Jan. 8, 1844; d. Plymouth, July 14, 1878, ae. 34-6-6.

THE WHITTEMORE FAMILY

    1. Thomas Whittemore was b. England in 1594. He came to America with his wife and five children in 1642, and settled in Malden, Mass. He d. 1660, ae. 66. Seven children were b. to them in America. One son,

    2. John, b. in England, Feb., 1638, was twice m. His first wife was Mary Upham, by whom he had twelve children, of whom one was

    3. Benjamin, b. Sept. 1, 1669, in Cambridge, Mass. He m., Aug. 17, 1692, Esther Brooks. They res. Concord, Mass. He d. Sept. 8, 1734, ae. 65-0-7. She d. Sept. 16, 1742. They had six children, of whom the youngest was

    4. Rev. Aaron, b. Cambridge, Dec. 13, 1711. He was a graduate of Harvard, pastor of the Congregational church in Pembroke; served in the French and Indian war as a lieutenant, and his house was a garrison. He m., Feb. 2, 1743, Abigail Coffin, of Newburyport, Mass. They had eight children, of whom the youngest was

5. Peter, b. Pembroke, Apr. 2, 1758. He was a Revolutionary soldier. He m., Jan. 25, 1783, Elizabeth, dau. of Deacon Joseph Baker, of Pembroke, b. Feb. 19, 1763. They settled in Salisbury, where he d. Dec. 16, 1836, ae. 78-8-14. She d. Sept. 5, 1826, ae. 63-6-16.

CHILDREN

*6. Caleb, b. Pembroke, Dec. 12, 1783
7. Elizabeth, b. Salisbury, May 7, 1785.
8. Peter, b. S., May 7, 1787; d. May 8, 1870, ae. 83-0-1.
9. Betsey, b. S., Apr. 25, 1789; a tailoress, in Bristol, Feb., 1838, till she d., Oct. 30, 1848 ae. 59-6-5.
10. Susan, b. S., June 3, 1791.
11. Polly, b. S., Aug. 1, 1793; came to Bristol in February, 1838, with her sisters, Relief and Betsey, and res. corner of High and Prospect streets. Polly was a school teacher nearly 30 years. She m. Mar. 3, 1849, Moses Eaton, of Grantham, and d. Salisbury, Jan. 16, 1871, ae. 77-5-15.
12. Hannah, b. S., Sept. 10, 1795; d. Sept. 2, 1872, ae. 76-11-22.
13. Joel, b. S., May 13, 1768; d. Sept. 10, 1800, ae. 2-3-27.
14. Child, b. S., Apr. 7, 1800.
15. Joel, b. S., Aug. 10, 1801; d. Sept. 4, 1855, ae. 54-0-24.
16. Relief, b. S., May 21, 1804; res. in Bristol. She m., Feb. 26, 1844, Daniel N. Haley, and res. Franklin, where he d., November, 1852. Two children, d. young. She m., Oct. 22, 1872, Thomas Haley, and d. East Andover, June 30, 1885, ae. 81-1-9.
17. Child, b. S., Apr. 10, 1806.

(6) Caleb Whittemore, son of Peter, b. Dec. 12, 1783, settled on the Whittemore farm, in Bridgewater, in 1808. He m., May 19, 1809, Dorcas, dau. of John and Susanna Taylor, of Salisbury. They spent their lives on this farm. She d. Jan. 4, 1837, and he m., Oct. 29, 1837, Phebe Chase, who d. Oct. 6, 1859. He d. Sept. 10, 1863, ae. 79-8-28.

CHILDREN, all born in Bridgewater

18. Belinda, b. Mar. 5, 1810; d. Aug. 9, 1831, ae. 21-5-4.
19. Lucinda, b. Aug. 12, 1812; d. Nov. 8, 1841, ae. 29-2-26.
20. Peter, b. May 28, 1815; a farmer in Bridgewater and Plymouth; d. Mar. 10, 1880, ae. 64-9-12.
21. John Taylor, b. Jan. 24, 1818; a farmer in Bridgewater; d. Jan. 26, 1892, ae. 74-0-2.
22. Caleb, b. June 20, 1820; m. Feb. 26, 1856, Elizabeth Patterson, dau. of Moses and Phebe (Gutterson) Burns, b. Alexandria, May 12, 1827. He was a farmer on the Edwin T. Pike farm in Bristol, 1852-1865, when he returned to the old homestead, where he d. Dec. 8, 1892, ae. 72-5-18. She res. Bridgewater. Children:

    a. Laura Ann, b. Bristol, Dec. 1, 1857; m. Dec. 10, 1887, Perry Putnam Elkins, son of Eben. He is a farmer in Thornton. Child: Sadie Winnifred, b. Bridgewater, Feb. 19, 1889.
    b. Elizabeth Patterson, b. B., Feb. 22, 1860; a school teacher. Res. Bridgewater; unm
    c. Daniel Caleb, b. B., June 11, 1862; m. Jan. 15, 1896, Lura Della, dau. Hiram and Lydia Tilton, b. Bridgewater, May 2, 1864. He is a farmer in Bridgewater. No children.
    d. Edwin Baker, b. B., Feb. 15, 1865. Farmer in Bridgewater.
    e. Florence Adaline, b. B., July 23, 1872. Res. Bridgewater. Unm.

23. Luther Baker, b. Feb. 1, 1824; a Congregational clergyman and farmer; d. Dec. 27, 1861, ae. 37-10-26.

24. Dorcas, b. July 30, 1826; m. Hiram Heath. (See.)

THE WHITTIER FAMILY

1. Edwin R. Whittier is a son of Henry M. and Eliza-beth A. (Hughes) Whittier. He was b. Milltown, Me., Sept. 16, 1856, and m. Feb. 18, 1882, Sarah C., dau. of Winthrop and Orpha Fox, b. Compton, P. Q., Sept. 21, 1855. He was a baker in Bristol 1893-'98; removed to Arlington Heights, Mass.; now res. Hopkinton, Mass.

CHILD

2. Mabel Elizabeth, b. Charlestown, Mass., Apr. 10, 1884.

THE WICOM FAMILY

1. Thomas Hardy Wicom, son of Enoch Greenleaf and Sarah (Hill) Wicom, was b. Hooksett, Jan. 19, 1825, and m. Mar. 2, 1852, Marinda N., dau. of Isaac Swett (See), b. July 4, 1836. Has been a farmer on Isaac Swett farm east of New-found lake since m., and there she d. Dec. 11, 1897, ae. 61-5-7.

CHILDREN, all born in Bristol

2. Emma Eldena, b. Aug. 8, 1853; m. May 14, 1870, Charles R. Ham-mond.

3. Evelyn Augusta, b. July 23, 1854; m. Oct. 11, 1873, Frank P. Muz-zey, and d. Hebron, Feb. 23, 1881, ae. 26-7-0.

4. Arzella Elnett, b. Nov. 6, 1856; m. Dec. 5, 1881, Eldorus Smith. Res. Bridgewater.

5. Everett, b. Aug. 28, 1858; m. July 2, 1896, Mabel F., dau. of Charles E. Kemp. (See.) No children.

6. Alice Lovilla, b. Dec. 24, 1865; m. Charles P. George. (See.)

THE WIGGIN FAMILY

1. Rev. George Owen Wiggin is the son of Levi and Bet-sey (Boston) Wiggin. He was b. Pittsfield, Feb. 17, 1859, and m. July 20, 1882, Lizzie May, dau. of Josiah P. and Susan S. Ward, b. Lowell, Mass., May 1, 1858. He is a Free Baptist clergyman. Was pastor of the church in Bristol, Apr., 1882, to Apr., 1886. (See Ecclesiastical History, Vol. I.)

CHILDREN

2. Clarence Ward, b. Lowell, Mass., Oct. 30, 1883.

3. Velma Maud, b. Bristol, Apr. 10, 1886.

4. Ernest Elsworth, b. Sandwich, Mar. 12, 1890.

5. Avelyn Owen, b. Hampton, June 2, 1901.

THE WILBUR FAMILY

1. Rev. Warren Wilbur was b. Westmoreland, May 30, 1795. He m. Betsey Alden, in 1817, and Widow Mary Blake, in

1829, and by them he had seven children. He united with the New England Methodist conference in 1824; was ordained deacon in 1826, by Bishop George, and elder in 1828, by Bishop Hedding. He labored in Massachusetts and Connecticut, but chiefly in New Hampshire. In 1833, he was stationed in Bristol. Of his seven children, one was

2. Warren Wesley, b. Jan. 20, 1827; m. Dec. 29, 1847, Sarah Ann, dau. of John L., and Hannah (Sanborn) Sanborn (See), b. June 26, 1832. He was a farmer, teamster, Methodist, Democrat. Res. Fremont, New Hampton, and Bristol, where he d. Mar. 25, 1893, ae. 66–2–5. She res. Merrimack street.

CHILDREN

3. Hulda Louise, b. Fremont, Sept. 29, 1848; m. Daniel B. Burleigh, b. Dorchester. A farmer in East Andover, where he d. ae. about 68. She res. Bristol. Child:

    a. Fred E., b. Fremont, Sept. 13, 1871; m. Feb. 2, 1890, Alice Cross; res. East Andover. Six children.

4. John William, b. F., Nov. 14, 1851; m. Dec. 13, 1877, Mrs. Octavia W. Moulton, widow of William P. Harlow, and dau. of Nathaniel Moulton, b. Concord, Me., May 21, 1843. He has kept a livery stable in Bristol since 1891. Democrat, Odd Fellow. Child:

    a. Harry John, b. Charlestown, Mass., Sept. 9, 1880.

5. Moses Freeman, b. F., May 15, 1853; m. Jan. 17, 1874, Kate E., dau. James T. Sanborn. (See.) He was landlord Hotel Bristol, 1889–'98, and 1899–1901; since in grain and feed business, Lexington, Mass. Democrat, Mason, Odd Fellow. Child:

    a. Mabelle Lillian, b. Bristol, Sept. 22, 1879; m. Dec. 13, 1898, Levi Bertrand Roby. (See.)

6. Osman, b. F., Jan. 9, 1856; m. Mrs. Vira Norris, Hill. No children. Res. Raymond.

7. Frank Wells, b. F., Dec. 7, 1858; m. (1) Katherine B. Spiller, dau. George H. (See); (2) Mamie Emerson. He d. Abington, Mass., Sept. 7, 1898, ae. 39–9–0.

8. Charles Edgar, b. F., Aug. 2, 1860; m. Jennie L. Nickerson. Res. East Harwich, Mass. Three children.

9. George McClellen, b. F., June 7, 1863; m. Jennie Clement. Res. East Hiram, Me. No children.

10. Harriet Belle, b. New Hampton, July 6, 1871. Res. Bristol; unm.

THE WILLARD FAMILY

1. John Willard lived in a dwelling on east side of South Main street, where later was the Dodge tavern. He m. Rebecca, dau. of Jeremiah Hubbard. (See.) He d. Aug. 30, 1803, and she m. (2) Abel Danforth. (See.)

CHILDREN

2. Betsey, b. Sept. 25, 1796; m. May 24, 1814, Micajah Danforth, and res. in Danbury. No survivors of this family. Children:

    a. John.   b. William.   c. Rufus.

3. Sally, b. Mar. 18, 1799; m. Enoch Coburn; d. in Hebron. No children.

4. John, b. July 18, 1800; d. Aug. 30, 1803, ae 3-1-12.

5. Rebecca, b. June 5, 1802; m. Stephen Bohonon. (See.)

THE WILLEY FAMILY

1. Col. David Cross Willey, son of Ezekiel and Sarah J. (Cross) Willey, was b. Northfield. In 1831, he m. Melina B., dau. Jonathan Dearborn, b. Chester, 1812. Col. Willey came to Bristol and located on the Solon Dolloff farm in 1835. In 1842, he commanded the old 34th Regt., and was a prominent man in his day. About 1847, he removed to the village, and resided on Lake street, till his death. Mrs. Willey d. Concord, May 2, 1878, ae. 66.

CHILDREN

2. Dearborn, b. Chester, Aug. 23, 1833; m. Nov. 28, 1861, Janet, dau. of Peter and Janet (Morrison) Jardine, b. Ayrshire, Scotland, Aug. 12, 1834. They res. 399 South Main street, Manchester. Children :

    a. Frederick Dearborn, b. Manchester, Dec. 4, 1862; m. Sept. 19, 1889, Eliza A. Wheeler. Res. Manchester.

    b. Elsie Jane, b. M., Mar. 4, 1866.

    c. Lilla Belle, b. M., Oct. 25, 1870; m. June 21, 1893, Fred W. McKewin.

3. David Albert, b. Bristol, July 10, 1836; went to Milwaukee, Wis., Nov., 1856; fire men, then engineer on M. & St. P. railroad till 1868; chief engineer Queen city flouring mill till 1888, again engineer on railroad till 1896, then to a farm in Dighton, Lake Co., Ill., where he now res. He m. in Milwaukee, Sept. 18, 1862, Anna, dau. of John and Catherine McFadden, b. Canada, Mar. 15, 1836. Children, all b. in Milwaukee :

    a. Albert, b. Oct. 14, 1863; farmer in Grant, Ill.

    b. Frank George, b. Mar. 21, 1866; killed Nov. 26, 1890, while on duty as fireman on M. & St. P. railroad, ae. 24-8-5.

    c. Truman, b. Nov. 13, 1868. Farmer.

    d. Harry Percy, b. May 1, 1871; d. Aug. 10, 1879, ae. 8-3-9.

    e. Annie Alice, b. Aug. 26, 1874.

    f. Charles Emerson, b. July 18, 1877. Farmer.

4. George Washington, b. B., Oct. 10, 1839. Res. Cincinnati, O. Four children.

5. Sarah Jane, b. B., June 16, 1846; m. May 1, 1864, John E., son of Frank A. and Ona (Hartford) Mitchell, b. Weare, Sept. 16, 1844. Res. Concord 30 years, now Kingston. Children :

    a. Charles Edward, b. Concord, June 27, 1865; m. Sept. 2, 1885, Jessie Keyes, Concord. Res. 8 Grove street, Concord.

    b. Willie Burnham, b. C., July 30, 1868; m. Alice G. Bean, of Newington, Oct. 14, 1887. He is a physician, 7 Temple Place, Boston, Mass.

    c. Bertie Lewis, b. C., Aug. 17, 1873; m. Lillian Mae Stebbins, Apr. 13, 1898. Res. Kingston.

6. Aseneth Ann, b. B., Aug. 1, 1849; m. 1871, John S. Glover. Five children.

7. Charles Henry, b. B., Feb. 22, 1851; served five years, 1873-'78, Light Battery A, 2nd Artillery, Fort McHenry, Baltimore, Md.; five

years, 1879-'84, in Troop B, 6th Cavalry, Fort Apache, Arizona; m. Nov. 27, 1884, Etta, dau. Thomas and Betsey (Brown) Tucker, b. Concord, 1865. He is an employee in carding-room of mill in Belmont. Children :

    a. Grace Beatrice, b. Sept. 22, 1885.
    b. Charles Eaton, b. May 21, 1887.
    c. Alice Mabel, b. Aug. 11, 1891 ; d. Mar. 21, 1892.

    8. Frank Kidder, b. B., Jan. 10, 1854 ; m. Mar. 6, 1872, Fannie E. Whitcomb, b. Orford, Jan. 13, 1852. Child :

    a. Frank Dearborn, b. Bristol, Nov. 18, 1876 ; m. Dec. 23, 1897, Laura Mae Witham, of West Epping. Res. West Epping.

    9. Mary Ellen, b. B., Feb. 10, 1859 ; d. ae. 10 mos.

THE WILLIAMS FAMILY

    1. Amos James Williams is a son of Amos S. and Mary Jane (Lane) Williams. He was b. Sanbornton, May 28, 1860, and m. Nov. 19, 1888, Kate Estella, dau. of Henry and Martha Ann Elizabeth (Smith) Borden, b. York Beach, Me., Sept. 6, 1859. Res. Bristol 1893-1903, now in Concord. Carpenter, Republican, Free Baptist. Served on police force of Bristol.

CHILD of Mrs. Williams by previous marriage

    2. Grace May Louise Barrett, b. York, Me., Apr. 20, 1881 ; m. Fay Whipple. (See.)

THE WILSON FAMILY

    1. Rev. Horatio Ellsworth Wilson, son of Gardner and Maria Elizabeth (Collins) Wilson, was b. Southboro, Mass., Feb. 4, 1862. He m. May 20, 1885, Sadie D., dau. of George and Mary C. (Sanders) Swain, b. Epsom, May 24, 1859, and d. Rochester, May 20, 1901, ae. 41-11-26. He was educated in the public schools of Holliston and Natick, Mass.; under tutors at Lewiston, Me,, and at Cobb's Divinity School, Lewiston, where he graduated 1894. He filled pastorates of the Free Baptist churches at Nottingham, and North Nottingham, two years ; at North Woodstock, 15 months ; at Gonic, four years and nine months, and at Bristol, one year and three months previous to Nov. 1, 1903 ; present business, insurance. In 1902-'03, was Grand Chief Templar of the Independent Order of Good Templars. Member of New Hampshire Prohibition State Committee.

CHILDREN

    2. Myra Elizabeth, b. Epsom, Feb. 7, 1887 ; a student at East Northfield (Mass.) Seminary.
    3. Helen Majel, b. Nottingham, Feb. 1, 1896.

THE WOLCOTT FAMILY

    1. Rev. Robert Thomas Wolcott, son of Loron and Mary A. B. (Wood) Wolcott, was b. Leicester, Mass., Mar. 18, 1858.

He m. Aug. 17, 1887, Alice Manda, dau. of Joseph D. and Betsey B. (Bates) Walton, b. New Portland, Me., Jan. 19, 1858. He graduated from Phillips Academy, Exeter; attended Wesleyan University, Middletown, Conn., and graduated from Boston University School of Theology. He united with the New Hampshire Methodist Conference in 1886, and has been pastor of Methodist churches in Contoocook, Sunapee, Bristol, 1891–'92, Lancaster, Woodsville, Suncook, and now in Plymouth.

CHILD

2.　Robert Henry, b. Sunapee, May 31, 1888.

THE WOODMAN FAMILY

1.　Leon Astor Woodman is a son of Jacob Astor Woodman. He was b. Bridgewater, Mar. 3, 1876, and m. Dec. 24, 1894, Ada Lisette, dau. of George Scott Tilton (See), b. Bristol, Mar. 6, 1878. He was a farmer in Bridgewater till 1894; since a job teamster in Bristol.

CHILDREN, all born in Bristol

2.　Olive Eldora, b. May 27, 1896.
3.　Arthur Astor, b. Oct. 15, 1897.
4.　Gladys Ada, b. Apr. 28, 1899.
5.　Donald Leon, b. June 12, 1902; d. Sept. 25, 1903, ae. 1-3-13.
6.　Son, b. Dec. 23, 1903.

THE WOODWARD FAMILIES

1.　Collins Hill Woodward was b. Waterbury, Me., Sept. 10, 1818. He m. June 20, 1847, Mary Hall Merrill, dau. of Lemuel and Hannah (Thyng) Merrill, b. Groton, May 7, 1821. Farmer in Groton till spring of 1864, when they came to Bristol where he was teamster and farmer. He d. Nov. 29, 1884, ae. 66-2-19. She res. Bristol.

CHILDREN

2.　Frank Willis, b. Groton, May 18, 1853; d. diphtheria, Sept. 10, 1863, ae. 10-3-22.
3.　Mary Anna, b. G., Sept. 10, 1855; d. diphtheria, Sept. 3, 1863, ae. 7-11-23.

————

1.　William Tenney Woodward, son of Lysander M., was b. Oct. 6, 1863, in Hanover. He m. Sept. 30, 1884, Sarah Beede, dau. of Alpheus C. Mitchell. (See.) He res. in Bristol two years, then in Hanover, where he d. Aug. 30, 1894, ae. 30-10-24. She m. (2) Joseph P. Charron.

CHILDREN

2.　Leon Carl, b. Bridgewater, Aug. 30, 1886; d. Bristol, May 27, 1895, ae. 8-8-27.

3. Roy Mitchell, b. Hanover, Mar. 15, 1890.
4. Bessie Jeanette, b. H., Dec. 9, 1892; d. July 8, 1894, ae. 1-6-29.

THE WOOLSON FAMILY

1. John Woolson was b. Dec. 14, 1797, and came to Bristol from Lisbon in 1827; res. next south of present school grounds on North Main street, and was a teamster between Boston and Littleton. He m., July 5, 1825, Hannah P., dau. of James and Ruth Smith, b. Bath, Dec. 19, 1797. He d. Bristol, June 4, 1831, ae. 33-5-20; she d. Bristol, May 4, 1881, ae. 83-4-15.

CHILD

2. Mary Augusta, b. Bristol, May 1 1829. She was a milliner; active in church and society work; d. Oct. 27, 1864, ae. 35-5-26.

THE WOOSTER FAMILY

1. George Merrill Wooster, son of Eleazer and Rosan (Merrill) Wooster, was b. in Campton, Jan. 18, 1834. He settled in Bristol about 1858, and m., Apr. 22, 1858, Mary E., dau. of Isaac K. George, b. Canaan, Jan. 14, 1835. He was a farmer on the Jonathan Merrill farm at Profile Falls, and later a manufacturer of straw board at the North End, residing Union street. He removed to Bow, in March, 1883, where he was a market gardener. Democrat, Mason. He d. Concord, Feb. 21 1901, ae. 67-1-3. She res. Concord.

CHILDREN

2. Rose Josephine, b. Bristol, May 20, 1862; m. Nov. 28, 1888, Charles B. Flanders; res. Concord. Child:

a. Ruth Marion, b. Concord, Sept. 23, 1891; d. June 8, 1900, ae. 8-8-15.

3. Twin daughters, b. B., May 24, 1864; d. June 3, 1864.
4. Mary Diano, b. B., Dec. 9, 1867; d. Sept. 13, 1868.
5. George A., b. B., Sept. 7, 1874; m. Apr. 25, 1894, Eudora Blanche, dau. of Edward P. and Abbie (Stone) Kimball, b. Weare, Dec. 5, 1868. He is a carriage blacksmith at Concord. Children:

a. Mary Ella, b. Cambridge, Mass., May 27, 1895.
b. George Edward, b. Roxbury, Mass., Oct. 2, 1898.
c. Lloyd Kimball, b. Concord, Sept. 1, 1902.

THE WORTHEN OR WORTHING FAMILY

Moses Worthen settled on what is still known as the Worthen farm about three-fourths of a mile east of Bristol village, on the north side of the highway. That he was here as early as 1770 is shown by a return of foreclosure of the township of New Chester, made by Jonas Minot to the Masonian proprietors in August, 1771, in which he states that Moses Worthen had occupied Lot 59, First Division, for one year, that he had a

30

house occupied by his family, and seven acres of land improved. (See chapters on "First Settlements.") From documentary evidence gathered by Prof. George M. Fellows, a descendant, it appears that he was a resident of Sandown in 1763, and that the Moses Worthen who served in Capt. Goffe's company of Indian fighters, in the southern part of New Hampshire, in 1746, and the Moses Worthen who enlisted in Col. Osgood's regiment for the French and Indian war, in March, 1758, at Haverhill, Mass., were probably identical with the Moses Worthen who settled in New Chester, in 1770. At his enlistment in March, 1758, his age is given as 39 years, thus placing his birth in 1719. From the same source we obtain the following probable line of descent to Moses:

1. George, b. England; m. Margaret, and d. in Salisbury, Mass., 1640, leaving a widow and one son,

2. Ezekiel, b. 1635; m. Hannah Martin, and d. in Amesbury, Mass., 1720. He had nine children, of whom the fourth was

3. Samuel, b. 166–, who m. (1) Deliverance or Deborah Heath; (2) Jan. 31, 1720, Elizabeth Johnson. He res. in Haverhill, Mass., and was the father of

4. Moses, b. about 1719; settled in New Chester, as stated above, and there d. as late as 1787.

5. Samuel, son of Moses, was b. Southampton, Mass., 1752. He probably came to New Chester with his father, as he was here in 1771, and Sept 27, of that year, purchased of John Tolford the westerly half of Lot 59, the easterly half being owned by his father. In the deed conveying this land he is spoken o as "Samuel Worthen of New Chester, blacksmith." In 1776, he purchased his father's half of this lot, and subsequently became the owner of 400 acres of land east of Bristol village and 160 acres on the New Hampton side of the Pemigewasset river, which later was known as the Robinson farm. He served in the Continental army. Samuel Worthen m. about 1782, Hannah Ingalls, b. 1759. She was distinguished for her great piety. She was one of the seven who composed the first Methodist class in Bristol, organized in 1801, and it was at her house that it had its weekly meetings for seven years. Years later, after listening to sermons by her two sons in the first Methodist chapel, she arose and testified, as was then the custom, and she then said that she had consecrated her children to the Lord before they were born. Samuel d. in Bristol, Apr. 29, 1824; she d. Aug. 28, 1832, both ae. 72 years.

CHILDREN, all born in Bristol

6. Ruth, b. Feb. 14, 1783; m. Moses West Sleeper. (See.)
7. Sally, b. Mar. 11, 1785; m. Sherburn Sanborn. (See.)
*8. Moses, b. Apr. 12, 1787.   *9. Jonathan, b. Oct. 29, 1789.
*10. Samuel R., b. Sept. 24, 1793.

11. Hannah, b. July 17, 1796; m. Daniel Sanborn. (See.)

12. Polly, b. May 24, 1799; m. Dec. 5, 1819, Cyrus Cass, b. Alexandria, Mar. 6, 1799. They lived a few years in Alexandria, and then emigrated to the West. He d. Feb. 15, 1878, in Oswego, Ill., ae. 78-11-9; she d. Aug. 29, 1883, in Aurora, Ill., ae. 84-3-5. Children:

    a. Mary Ann, b. Alexandria, Aug. 22, 1820; m. Mar. 27, 1842, Gilbert Gaylord. They res. Oswego, Ill., where their children were b., and where he d. Mar. 17, 1879. She d. Monrovia, Cal., Dec. 9, 1891, ae. 71-3-17. Children: (1) Charles C., b. May 24, 1843; m. 1864, Louisa Clark. Res. Greenville, Texas. (2) Cass, b. Mar. 5, 1845; m. Apr. 3, 1867, Angelia Hawkins. Res. Redlands, Cal. (3) Chastina M., b. Aug. 25, 1847; m. Feb. 16, 1870, Orastus Worthing, a grandson of Rev. Jonathan. Res. Redland. (4) Lovina, b. Jan. 5, 1851; d. Aug. 14, 1850. (5) Clinton Gilbert, b. Oct. 9, 1851; m. Jan. 20, 1875, Catharine Loucks. Res. Redland. (6) John L., b. Feb. 19, 1858; m. Sept., 1877, Mary Spangler. Res. Oswego.

    b. Tirzah, b. Dec. 18, 1821; m. Rev. Henry Minard, a Methodist clergyman. No children. Res. Oswego. Their lives and property were given to the church.

    c. Marcia, b. Dec. 17, 1824; m. Aug., 1844, Samuel Collins, and d. Plainfield, Ill., May 30, 1886, ae. 61-5-13. He d. in Plainfield. Children: (1) Frank, res. Plainfield. (2) Henry, d., ae. 20. (3) Nellie, m. Samuel Brainard; res. Aurora, Ill. (4) Cyrus Cass, res. Oak Park, Ill.

*13. Ezekiel Smith, b. Jan. 24, 1803.

*14. Amos Hearnden, b. July 29, 1804.

15. Hannah, d. in infancy.

(8) Moses Worthen, son of Samuel, b. Apr. 12, 1787, m. Dec., 1806, Nancy Sanborn, dau. of Maj. Theophilus (See), b. Nov. 18, 1788. He was a farmer in Bristol till about 1821, when his father gave him a farm on the New Hampton side of the Pemigewasset, and here he res. till about 1838, when he removed West and d. Rock Creek, Ohio, May 17, 1868, ae. 81-1-5; his widow d. same place, Nov. (Feb.) 14, 1871, ae. 82-11-26.

CHILDREN

*16. Sherburn Sanborn, b. Bristol, June 20, 1807.

17. Mary, b. B., May 5, 1809; m. Rev. Caleb S. Beede. (See.)

18. Hannah Ingalls, b. B., July 10, 1811; m. 1834, Daniel S. Batchelder, Manchester. They removed to Ohio in 1854; she d. Rock Creek, O., Oct. 2, 1891, ae. 80-2-22.

19. John Hardy, b. B., Aug. 13, 1813. He went to Ohio, in 1834; became a Methodist clergyman. He m., July 6, 1837, Lucetta Stone, and d. Bloomington, Ill., Mar. 10, 1840, ae. 26-6-27. Child:

    a. Ursula Stone, b. Bloomfield, Ill., Mar. 20, 1839.

20. Orrilla, b. B., Dec. 5, 1815; m. Apr. 20, 1844, Silas Sloat. They res. Rock Creek.

21. Eliza Tilton, b. B., Jan. 4, 1818; m. Apr. 22, 1838, Dr. Amos D. Sargent, b. Feb. 3, 1814. They went to Ohio in 1838; res. Hopkins, Nodoway Co., Mo.

22. Nancy, b. B., July 7, 1820; m. Feb. 11, 1838, William Ruttenbur, b. Ontario, N. Y., Sept. 14, 1818. They res. Hopkins, Mo. Children:

    a. Worthing M., b. Hartsgrove, O., Jan. 25, 1840; m. Feb. 11, 1860, Jane Jones. He went to Cleveland, drew $600 from a bank,

30a

started for home, but never reached there. Supposed to have been murdered. She res. Geneva, O.

   b. Ellen, b. Rome, O., June 15, 1845; m. Apr., 1882, George Nims, who d. Feb. 26, 1893. She res. Pickering, Nodoway Co., Mo.

   c. Eveline, b. R., Apr. 2, 1849; m. Nov. 10, 1869, H. W. Smith. Res. Pickering.

   d. Mary S. P., b. Hartsgrove, O., Mar. 31, 1861; m. Nov. 27, 1883, O. G. Nims. Res. Cosby, Andrew Co., Mo.

23. Samuel T., b. New Hampton, Dec. 11, 1822; m. Belinda, dau. of John Sleeper (See), b. Mar. 3, 1825. Res. Lodi, Wis.

24. Martha, b. N. H., Oct. 26, 1826; went to Ohio in 1834; m. 1844, Edwin Woodruff, and res. Mechanicsville, Ashtabula Co., O.

25. Ruth, b. N. H., Jan. 7, 1828; went to Ohio in 1834; m. 1847, Edwin Bugbee. Res. Steel City, Jefferson Co., Neb.

26. Laura Cass, b. N. H., May 28, 1830; went to Ohio with parents: m. Mar. 10, 1850. Henry C. Hurlburt, b. Litchfield, Conn., Aug. 18, 1830. They res. Bloomington, Kansas. Children :

   a. Clara, b. Ashtabula, Ohio, Mar. 10, 1851; d. Mar. 21, 1851.

   b. John Worthen, b. A., Aug. 10, 1852.

   c. Lizzie, b. A., Sept. 10, 1854.

   d. Henry Roscoe, b. Boone Co., O., Oct. 8, 1862.

(9) Rev. Jonathan Worthing, son of Samuel, b. Oct. 29, 1789, joined the New England (Methodist) conference in 1810, and was sixty-four years in the ministry. He m. (Pub. Apr. 10, 1814), Betsey Hacket, dau. of Walter, of Holderness. She d. in 1821, and he m. (2) in 1821, Sally Robie, widow of John, and dau. of Jacob and Sarah (Eastman) Carter, b. Concord, Aug. 2, 1786; d. at Binghamton, N. Y., Jan. 22, 1870, ae. 83–5–20. He d. same place, Aug. 10, 1874, ae. 84–9–11.

CHILDREN

27. Augustus C., b. Bristol, Feb. 13, 1815; left Bristol in 1833; m. Mar. 16, 1841, Mary Messenger. He res. in Atlantic, Cass Co., Iowa. He was a soldier in the Union army, and this name should have been added to those mentioned in the Roll of Honor. Children :

   a. Martha E., b. Apr. 28, 1843; m. Sept. 29, 1865, Hosea B. Ferryman, of Minooka, Ill. He d. Sept. 26, 1871, and she m. (2) July 4, 1877, Harry Worth. He d. May 26, 1887. He was a soldier in the Union army. She res. Anita, Cass Co., Iowa.

   b. Orastus, b. Fairfield, Iowa, Sept. 5, 1845; m. Chastina Gaylord, Feb. 16, 1870. Res. Bedlandi, Cal.

   c. Libbie, b. Brighton, Iowa, July 3, 1847; m. July 16, 1871, Lieut. Furguson. He d. Sept. 20, 1876. She m. (2) July 28, 1880, at Chicago, Southwell W. Watson. She res. Atlantic, Iowa.

   d. Fannie, b. Seward, Ill., June 5, 1855; m. July 30, 1872, Jerry Leasune, and d. July 20, 1885, ae. 30–1–15.

   e. Ella, b. S., Sept. 28, 1857; m. Dec. 24, 1874, Frank Eldridge, and d. May 18, 1876, ae. 18–7–20.

   f. Sumner A., b. Plattville, Ill., Aug. 7, 1858; m. May 20, 1877, Mary Watson. She d. 1884, and he m., in 1884, (2) Sadie Watson. Res. Redlands, Cal.

   g. Fred P., b. S., Nov. 13, 1869; m. May 19, 1893, Vicia Collins. Res. Atlantic.

28. Solon, b. B., Oct. 26, 1816. He left Bristol in 1834, and m., in 1841, Maria Fannie Messenger, at Mt. Pleasant, Iowa. He was killed at Anita, Iowa, by carriage accident, July 9, 1895, ae. 78–8–13. Children :

   a. William A., b. Mt. Pleasant, Iowa, July 1, 1842 ; res. Atlantic, Cass Co., Iowa.

   b. George S., b. Asmego, Ill., June 26, 1844 ; res. Anita, Iowa.

   c. Rush B., b. A., May 13, 1846 ; res. Anita.

   d. Solon A., b. Plattville, Ill., Aug. 11, 1848 ; res. Anita.

   e. Edward J., b. P., Sept. 5, 1851.

   f. Frank O., b. P., June 8, 1855 ; res. Anita.

   g. Wilbur F., b. Minooka, Ill., June 9, 1860 ; res. Anita.

  29. Betsey Hacket, b. Grand Isle, Vt., May 30, 1821 ; m. in 1839, Derwin Bean. She d. in Denver, Colo., 1871, ae. 50 ; he d. in 1889, in Nebraska. Children :

   a. George, d. at Morris, Ill.

   b. Sarah, b. 1843 ; m. H. Root, and d. in Denver, Colo.

   c. Helen, b. 1847 ; m. Will Perice, judge supreme court, San Diego, Cal., where they res.

  30. John P., b. Burlington, Vt., May 31, 1822 ; m. at Binghamton, N. Y., Dec. 10, 1848, Lydia Hill Tupper, dau. of David, b. Oct. 31, 1830, and d. June 1, 1886, ae. 55-7-0. He served as lieutenant 161st N. Y. Vols., and captain 88th Colo. Infty. in Civil war. Res. Binghamton. Children :

   a. John F., b. Mar. 8, 1850 ; d. Dec. 13, 1856, ae. 6-9-5.

   b. Louis T., b. Mar. 18, 1852 ; d. Dec. 13, 1856, ae. 4-8-25.

   c. Julia Clark, b. Nov. 29, 1853 ; res. Binghamton.

   d. Edward Carter, b. Mar. 30, 1857 ; res. Binghamton.

   e. Harry Preston, b. Nov. 3, 1858 ; res. Binghamton.

   f. Sarah Worthing Rose, b. May 26, 1860 ; res. Sheldon, Pa.

   g. Frances W. Belknap, b. July 27, 1869 ; res. Janesville, Wis.

   h. John P., b. Jan. 24, 1871 ; d. Sept. 20, 1877, ae. 6-7-26.

  31. Frances Sarah, b. B., July 29, 1824 ; m. Rev. George Porter, a Methodist clergyman, b. Berwick, Pa., June 20, 1820, and d. Cowlesville, N. Y., June 11, 1877, ae. 56-11-21. She d. Bayonne, N. J., Dec. 15, 1892, ae. 68-4-16. They were teachers in Wyoming seminary at same time. Children :

   a. Frances O., b. Owego, N. Y., Feb. 13, 1854.

   b. Susan G., b. Waverly, N. Y., June 27, 1856.

   c. George S., b. W., July 10, 1858.

   d. Burtis A., b. Owego, May 3, 1864.

  32. Elizabeth Keth, b. Vienna, N. Y., Nov. 25, 1826. She m. Jan. 26, 1847, Edgar Avery, at Ledyard, N. Y., and res. Fort Collins, Colo. He was b. Ledyard, Apr. 29, 1820, and d. May 27, 1886, ae. 66-0-28. Children :

   a. Edward Robie, b. Oct. 28, 1847.

   b. Franklin C., b. Apr. 8, 1849.

   c. Sarah Louise, b. Mar. 10, 1851.

   d. George Porter, b. Dec. 25, 1852.

   e. William H., b. Oct. 5, 1854 ; d. Jan. 2, 1890, ae. 35-2-27.

  (10) Samuel R. Worthing, son of Samuel, b. Sept. 24, 1793, m. Feb. 23, 1815, Hannah, dau. of Samuel Heath (See), b. May 1, 1796. Was a farmer ; first lived next east of Danforth brook, south side of highway, later in Hall neighborhood, where he d., Jan., 1856, ae. 62-3-. She d. Boston, in the family of George M. Fellows, a grandson, July 3, 1878, ae. 82-2-2.

CHILDREN

  33. Mary Jane, b. Bristol, Apr. 28, 1816 ; m. Calvin Peterson Fellows. (See.)

  34. Martha Adeline, b. B.; d. unm., Feb. 3, 1883, ae. 63-3-.

(13) Ezekiel S. Worthing, son of Samuel, b. Jan. 24, 1803. was a farmer and succeeded his father on the home farm. He removed from Bristol about 1832; was eight years in Amber. N. Y., and two years in Hartsgrove, Ashtabula Co., Ohio, thence removed to Oswego, Ill., where he d. Dec. 28, 1879, ae. 76-11-4. In 1824, he m. Judith Kimball Martin, dau. of Solomon, who was b. Nov. 15, 1801, in Boscawen, and d. Feb. 3, 1882, in Oswego, Ill., ae. 80-2-18.

CHILDREN

35. Sarah M., b. Bristol, Mar. 18, 1825; m. Aug., 1845, Orson Ashley. He was b. in New York state, about 1820, and d. Aug., 1884, in Wamego. Kan., ae. 64. She res. Belvue, Pottawattomie Co., Kansas. Children:
    a. Laura, m. Richard Constable.
    b. Orpha, (deceased) m. Frank Albee.
    c. Martin, m. Ella Judson.   *d.* Leona, m. Clark Taylor.

36. Augustine Samuel, b. B., Oct. 25, 1827; m. Mar. 15, 1855, Esther Ann, dau. of Thomas and Hannah Barron, b. in England, May 25, 1831. They res. in Belvue, Kan. Children:
    a. Edwin Augustine, b. Oct. 19, 1856; m. Letitia Moore. Children: (1) Bertha. (2) Augustine Ray.
    b. Estella Pauline, b. Apr. 15 1861; m. Frank Crabtree. Children: (1) Ethel May (2) Raymond.
    c. Mary Lorinda, b. July 22, 1863; m. Dr. James S. Watt. Child: Ora Lorena.

37. Hannah Maria, b. Apr. 15, 1840; m. H. W. Minard, and d. ae. 27. No children.

38. Joseph Henry, b. May 18, 1845, and d. ae. 14.

(14) Amos H. Worthing, son of Samuel, b July 29, 1804, m. Laura Jacobs. He was a teacher and Methodist clergyman: d. Vairon, Colo., Mar. 31, 1875, ae. 70-8-2.

CHILDREN

39. Helen, b. Bristol: m. Dr. —— Webster, who served in Union army and lost his mind by reason of wound in head. She was principal of Vassar Medical college, N. Y.; is now practicing physician in New Bedford, Mass.

40. Hannah, b. Pembroke, Aug., 1843; m. 1870, Pardon DeVoll. Res. New Bedford.

(16) Sherburn S. Worthing, son of Moses, b. June 20. 1807, m. Nov. 29, 1829, Nancy Sleeper, dau. of Peter (See), b. May 10, 1809 Was in trade in Vershire, Vt.; returned to Bristol, 1835, where he was manufacturer of satinets on Willow street; in trade with N. S. Berry, where Cavis block now is; built on east side of Pemigewasset a saw-mill, which was swept away by a freshet; went to Trumbull, Ohio, with his family in 1848; to Iowa, in 1854; to Redwing, Minn., 1855, where he was blacksmith; to Pine Island, same county, where he was in trade several years. Here his wife d. Jan. 9, 1869, ae. 59-7-29, and he m. (2) Elizabeth A. Pierce. In fall of 1878, emigrated to Grafton, No. Dakota, and in 1881, took up quarter section land

at Medford, N. D., where he was postmaster. He d. Sept. 30 1894, ae. 87-3-10.

41.   Mary, b. Vershire, Vt., Sept., 14, 1830; m. Apr. 13, 1851, Grove Sanders, who d. Trumbull, Ohio, Aug. 28, 1885. She res. Trumbull.

42.   Charles H., b. V., Aug. 22, 1832; d. Mar. 16, 1833.

43.   Ann Orilla, b. Bristol, Jan. 25, 1834; m. Dec. 25, 1853, William H. Andrus, b. Aug. 22, 1821. She d. Meadow Valley, Cal., Nov. 7, 1881, ae. 47-9-12. He res. San Francisco, Cal. Children :

   a.   Frank S., b. Trumbull, Ohio, Oct. 19, 1854, and d. Pine Island, Minn., 1861, ae. 7.

   b.   Nettie M., b. Concord, Minn., July 31, 1860 ; m. Brainard B. Hughes, Nov. 29, 1877, at Meadow Valley, Cal. He d. San Francisco, June 29, 1882.

   c.   William Franklin, b. Drytown, Cal., Apr. 19, 1865; m. Mar. 20, 1889, Phebe A. Webb, and res. Oakland, Cal.

   d.   Charles Bertram, b. Meadow Valley, Nov. 21, 1872, and res. San Francisco; unm.

   e.   Jessie May, b. M. V., Feb. 10, 1875. Unm.

44.   James H., b. B., Nov. 28, 1836; was a soldier in a California regiment during the Civil war. Was shot and killed by Apache Indians at Pinos Altos, New Mexico, May 18, 1866, ae. 29-5-20. Unm. (See Roll of Honor.)

45.   Laura M., b. B., Apr. 5, 1839; m. Mar. 12, 1858, Grant B. Baker. He served in 6th Regt., Minn. Vols., in the Civil war, and d. Redwing, Minn., Oct. 12, 1864. She m. (2) Mar. 29, 1866, Augustus H. Kellogg, b. Aug. 14, 1834. Res. Medford, N. Dakota. Children :

   a.   Annie L., b. Redwing, Dec. 22, 1860; m. Aug. 18, 1882, Geo. W. Millhouse, Luverne, Minn.

   b.   Fred A., b. New Haven, Minn., July 12, 1867.

   c.   Grace G., b. N. H., Oct. 17, 1871.

   d.   Boyd Vernon, b. Pine Island, Minn., June 17, 1875.

   e.   Grey H., b. P. I., May 9, 1881.

46.   Carrie S., b. B., Nov. 9, 1841 ; m. Nov. 15, 1863, Azro Sinkler, b. Mar. 29, 1820, Washington, Vt. Res. Trumbull, Ohio. Children :

   a.   Ida A., b. Trumbull, Sept. 23, 1865 ; m. Apr. 26, 1884, Dr. E. V. Davis.

   b.   Anna Laura, b. T., Mar. 2, 1867; m. Mar. 12, 1892.

   c.   Charles, b. T., Feb. 10, 1872 ; m. June 15, 1889.

   d.   Nina, b. T., Dec. 16, 1876.

47.   Frank D., b. B., Feb. 2, 1845 ; m. Aug. 30, 1865, Sarah Phiiura, dau. Nelson D., and Clarisa (Orpha) Marble, b. Georgetown, N. Y., Nov. 7, 1848. Res. Medford, Walsh Co., N. D. Children :

   a.   Orpha Nancy, b. June 11, 1866.

   b.   Ralph Sherburn, b. Jan. 29, 1871.

   c.   Charles Amsbry, b. Nov. 25, 1872; m. July 18, 1893, Susie Hoyune. Res. Grafton, Walsh Co., No. Dakota.

   d.   Carrie, b. Nov. 16, 1882.

48.   John H., b. B., July 23, 1848; d. Dec. 24, 1848.

49.   Fred H., b. Trumbull, O., Apr. 25, 1852 ; m. Feb. 20, 1877, Clara E., dau. of Thomas E. and Amanda (Locke) Cooper, b. Tomah, Wis., Aug. 16, 1857. No children. They res. Grafton, N. D.

---

1.   Ezekiel Worthen, b. Chester, Oct. 28, 1767, m. June 4, 1792, Elizabeth Batchelder, b. Hawke, Aug. 5, 1770. They

settled on Bridgewater hill, where she d. Sept. 23, 1863, ae. 33-1-18. He m., June 24, 1804, Sally Pillsbury, of Amesbury Mass., b. Oct. 21, 1780. He d. June 14, 1819, ae. 51-7-16.

CHILDREN, all born in Bridgewater

*2.　Elisha, b. Nov. 19, 1793.
3.　Jonathan, b. Feb. 6, 1795.
4.　Theodate Smith, b. Aug. 21, 1797 ; d. Apr. 21, 1829, ae. 31-8-0.
5.　Ezekiel, b. Apr. 7, 1800 ; d. June 16, 1800.
6.　Elizabeth, b. June 9, 1801 ; d. Sept. 23, 1803.
7.　Dolly Batchelder, b. July 17, 1803.
8.　Nancy Auburn, b. Apr. 17, 1805 ; m. —— Adams, Chelmsford, Mass.
9.　Sally, b. Mar. 9, 1806 ; m. —— Boardman, of Lowell, Mass., and d. June 13, 1848, ae. 42-3-4.
10.　Walter, b. May 1, 1807 ; d. May 26, 1833, ae. 26-0-25.
11.　Sophronia, }
12.　Laura,　　 } Mar. 13, 1809 ; { d. Apr. 2, 1838, ae. 29-0-19.
　　　　　　　　　　　　　　　 { d. June 26, 1843, ae. 34-2-13.
13.　Moses Pillsbury, b. Apr. 6, 1811 ; d. Nov. 28, 1859, ae. 48-7-22.
14.　Ezekiel Bartlett, b. Oct. 29, 1816 ; d. Dec., 1883, ae. 67-2-.

(2)　Elisha Worthen, son of Ezekiel, b. Nov. 19, 1793, m. July 29, 1821, Abigail Prescott. He succeeded his father on the home farm, where she d. Oct. 21, 1851. He d. May 22, 1864, ae. 70-6-3.

CHILDREN, born in Bridgewater

*15.　Ezekiel Newell, b. Oct. 20, 1822.
16.　Jonathan F., b. Feb. 21, 1831 ; d. May 2, 1852.

(15)　Ezekiel N. Worthen, b. Oct. 20, 1822, m. Nov. 1, 1848, Abbie P. Gove, b. Wilmot, Jan. 19, 1823. He res. Bristol some years, in employ of Lovejoy & Kelley, and David P. Prescott, and was first sexton of Pleasant Street cemetery ; returned to Bridgewater, thence to New Hampton, where he d. Feb. 13, 1867, ae. 44-3-23. Mrs. Worthen res. Tilton.

CHILDREN

17.　Jerusha S., b. Bridgewater, June 6, 1850 ; d. June 25, 1850.
18.　Jonathan E., b. Bristol, Feb. 25, 1854 ; d. Mar. 21, 1854.
19.　Arthur L., b. B., Oct. 11, 1857 ; had a home after the death of his father with David S. Batchelder, in Bridgewater ; operative in woolen-mill in Bristol ; woodworker in Concord ; 1878-1881, in New Mexico ; m. Dec. 31, 1881, Della M. Phelps, of Danbury. Res. Tilton. Children :
　　　　a.　Carl E., b. Jan. 2, 1883.　　　b.　Chester A., b. Oct. 10, 1885.
　　　　c.　Georgia A., b. Dec. 22, 1887.
20.　George E., b. B., Aug. 19, 1863 ; m. Oct. 5, 1887, Charlotte M. Howland, of Cottage City, Mass. Was a pharmacist in Jacksonville, Fla.; Milwaukee, Wis.; Fall River, Mass., and other cities. A Mason of high degree. He d. Asheville, N. C., Dec. 4, 1902, ae. 39-3-15. Child :
　　　　a.　Florence A., b. Fall River, Mass., June 13, 1893.

————

1.　Samuel Worthen was one of the early settlers on Bridgewater hill, coming here from Chester. He m. —— Libby, and

had three children, two daughters and one son. The son was
2. Samuel, b. Bridgewater, Oct. 10, 1797; m. Nov. 24,
1825, Mary, dau. of Joseph Prescott (See), b. Apr. 20, 1802.
He was a farmer in Bridgewater, where he d. Aug. 11, 1862,
ae. 64-10-1; she d. Bridgewater, Dec. 9, 1883, ae. 81-7-19.

CHILDREN, all born in Bridgewater

3. Harriet Newell, b. Aug. 28, 1827; m. Jan. 2, 1851, Jonathan F.
Morrill, b. Bridgewater, Oct. 4, 1823, and d. New Hampton, Oct. 16, 1892,
ae. 69-0-12. She d. Bridgewater, Mar. 28, 1884, ae. 56-7-0. Children:

    a. Frank P., b. Bridgewater, Dec. 17, 1855; m. Aug. 7, 1886, Car-
rie Rhoda, dau. of J. Ingalls and Elizabeth Ann (Wescott) Wood,
b. Alstead, Dec. 31, 1865. He res. New Hampton. Merchant, justice of the peace, treasurer and trustee of New Hampton Literary
Institution. Has been town clerk, selectman, and represented his
town in the legislature. Child: Frank Maurice, b. Oct. 1, 1887.
    b. Mary A., b. Apr. 4, 1859; was a school teacher, taught five
years in Union District, No. 2; d. New Hampton, 1900, ae. 41; unm.

4. Rufus Lewis, b. Dec. 16, 1828; d. Apr. 7, 1857, ae. 28-3-21.
*5. Samuel Kellum, b. Mar. 8, 1832.
6. Louisa Nelson, b. Aug. 28, 1836; m. July 15, 1857, Alonzo F.
Wheeler.
7. Lydia Prescott, b. Jan. 30, 1838; m. Hiram S. Tilton. (See.)
8. Mary Ann, b. Oct. 7, 1841; d. Sept. 22, 1849, ae. 7-11-15.

(5)   Samuel K. Worthen, son of Samuel, b. Mar. 8, 1832,
m. Dec. 5, 1858, Sarah Frances, dau. of William W. and Mary
A. D. (Adams) Parker, b. Portland, Me., Apr. 14, 1839. He
has been a farmer in the Locke neighborhood since 1868.

CHILDREN

9. Albert Parker, b. Bristol, Sept. 8, 1861; m. Aug. 18, 1892, Harriet
Loud, dau. Quincy L. Reed, b. Weymouth, Mass., Dec. 19, 1860; who d.
Dec. 18, 1893, ae. 32-11-29. He graduated from New Hampton Literary
Institution, 1881; from Boston University Law school, 1885, with the
degree of LL. B. At his graduation he was class orator. He was
admitted to the bar same year; began practice in Boston, and has
built up a large practice, attracting considerable attention through his
connection with notable cases. He has been for some years a member
of the bar of the United States District and Circuit Courts, and Circuit
Court of Appeals, and of the United States Supreme Court. He has been
active in Democratic politics and represented Quincy and Weymouth in
the Massachusetts House of Representatives in 1893, serving on the
judiciary committee. He res. in Weymouth, Mass. Children:

    a. Son,   ⎫   ⎧ d. Dec. 21, 1893.
    b. Albert Parker, ⎬ b. Weymouth, Dec. 17, 1893, ⎨ d. Apr. 8, 1895.
    c. Alfred Reed,   ⎭   ⎩

10. Samuel Everett, b. B., June 1, 1868; graduated from New Hampton Literary Institution, 1889; Boston University Law School, 1894 *cum
laude*, with degree of LL. B.; admitted to the bar of Massachusetts same
year, and commenced practice with his brother, Albert P. After four
years of sickness, d. at Bristol, Feb. 27, 1903, ae. 34-8-26.
11. Hadley Bradley, b. B., Mar. 19, 1871; graduated from New Hampton Literary Institution; is a farmer on the parental home.

THE WORTHLEY FAMILIES

1. Alonzo Henry Worthley, son of Moses and Cynthia (Marshall) Worthley, was b. Weare, Apr. 14, 1839. He m., Dec. 9, 1865, Ruth, dau. of David B. and Mehitable (Chandler) Perkins, b. Hebron, Apr. 2, 1843. He enlisted Aug. 22, 1862, in Co. C, 12th Regt., N. H. Vols., and served till June 21, 1865; was appointed corporal Mar. 11, 1863, and sergeant, Feb. 5, 1864; was wounded at Chancellorsville, May 3, 1863. He was a farmer in Hebron till November, 1890, when he came to Bristol, having purchased the Benjamin Q. Fellows estate on No. Main street. Republican, Odd Fellow, member of G. A. R.

CHILD

2. Alonzo Howard, b. Hebron, Aug. 1, 1867; m. Apr. 15, 1893, Eleanor P., dau. Augustus and Eliza (Prior) Remick, b. Hebron, 1873; d. Bristol, Apr. 1, 1895, ae. 21-6-24. Child:

  a. Harry C., b. Bristol, July 31, 1893; d. Sept. 27, 1893.

---

1. Hiram Moses Worthley, son of Moses and Cynthia (Marshall) Worthley, was b. in Weare, Dec. 17, 1848, and m. Aug. 28, 1871, Sarah G., dau. of Gilman and Wealthy C. Leavitt, b. Gilford, June 11, 1848. She d. Bristol, Mar. 25, 1899, ae. 50-9-14. He m. (2) Apr. 25, 1900, Linnie Maud, dau. of Edward C. and Ella A. (Prescott) Payne, b. Hill, Jan. 1, 1880. He was a farmer in Hebron; an employee in Train-Smith pulp-mill, Bristol. Republican, Odd Fellow, K. of P.

CHILDREN

2. Lena Blanche, b. Hebron, July 4, 1881; m. George W. Cheney. (See.)

3. Louis Edward, b. Bristol, Aug. 1, 1900.

THE WRIGHT FAMILY

1. Andrew Jackson Wright was b. in 1817, in Dunstable, Mass. He m., July 4, 1842, Almira Wright, b. Medford, Mass., 1822. He located in Bristol in 1848; was a conductor on the Bristol branch railroad, 1848-'54. They removed to Chicago, and in 1902 were both living in Passadena, Cal., with their son, Charles A.

CHILDREN

2. Charles Augustus, b. Dunstable, Nov. 29, 1844; m. Dec. 19, 1867, Sarah Jane, dau. of David Brown and Mary Elizabeth McMaster, b. Buel, N. Y., July 11, 1848. Is a bookkeeper in Passadena. Child:

  a. Mabel Almira, b. Chicago, Ill., July 30, 1871; m. Nov. 28, 1894, Horace J. Prince.

3. George E., b. Bristol, 1852; m. Nora Carter, 1895. Res. 2,590 No. Ashland Ave., Chicago, Ill.

4. Harriet A., b. Chicago, Ill., 1858; m. 1885, C. H. Mears. Res. Evanston, Ill.; since 1900, on a seven-acre fruit ranch, Los Angeles, Cal.

THE WYATT FAMILY

1. Rev. Thomas Wyatt, son of Thomas and Martha (Wilson) Wyatt, was b. Campton, Sept. 5, 1818. He m., Mar. 4, 1836, Sarah Ann, widow of Sylvester Sawyer, and dau. of Joshua Clark, b. Candia, Jan. 18, 1814, and d. Rumney, Mar. 29, 1876, ae. 62-2-11. He m. (2) Mrs. Mary Ann, widow of Daniel S. Johnson (See), and dau. of Rodney Hammond. He was a farmer and Freewill Baptist clergyman; res. Campton, Thornton Gore, Rumney, Bridgewater, and, from 1887, in Bristol, where he d. Oct. 24, 1895, ae. 77-1-19. She res.

CHILDREN, all born in Thornton

2. George G., drowned at Campton, May 15, 1867, ae. 26.
3. Ellen A., m. B. F. Smith, Hebron. Res. Amesotta, Iowa.
4. Nathaniel E., freight conductor Boston & Maine railroad. Killed at Woodsville, Aug. 13, 1877.
5. Martha L., b. Aug. 1, 1848; m. Baxter P. Hardy, and res. Rumney.
6. Sarah E., b. Sept. 30, 1853; m. Orlando B. French. (See.)
7. Horace F., is a druggist in Adrian, Mich.

THE YEATON FAMILY

1. Horace Clay Yeaton, son of Eben P. and Mary Tucker Yeaton, was b. Salisbury, July 18, 1858. He m. Hattie M., dau. of Calvin Pattee, b. Enfield, July 21, 1864. He was a paper-mill employee in Bristol, 1885 till 1902, when he removed to Franklin. Republican, K. of P.

THE YEATTER FAMILY

1. George Albert Yeatter, son of George and Lydia (Simmons) Yeatter, was b. Manchester, Nov. 15, 1872, and m. Aug. 3, 1898, Izole G., dau. of Willard B. and Augusta Cawley, b. Hill, Nov. 22, 1877. He is a fellow of the Dental Society; registered in 1896. Is a dentist in Bristol.

CHILD

2. Donald Cawley, b. Hill, Sept. 2, 1899.

APPENDIX A

This appendix contains additional records received too late to appear in alphabetical order in the preceding pages ; a record of births, marriages and deaths that have occurred during the time this book has been in press, and some corrections.

ADDITIONS

THE BLAKE FAMILY

1. Oliver Smith Blake was probably a descendant of Jasper Blake, of Hampton. He was b. Nov. 6, 1742. Nov. 6, 1764, he m. Deborah Ingalls, a sister of Jonathan. (See.) Deborah was b. Apr. 18, 1746. In 1775, Oliver S. served eight months in Col. Enoch Poor's regiment, and was on the rolls as a resident of Sandown. In 1776, he signed the Association Test in Sandown, and the same year served in Col. Joshua Wingate's regiment. He was an early settler on the Caleb L. Clay farm in the Nelson neighborhood, being first taxed in New Chester, in Apr., 1777. One of the early schools of New Chester was taught by Mrs. Blake in their cabin. He subsequently res. several years in New Hampton, and d. in Hebron, Feb. 16, 1823, ae. 80-3-10. She d. Hebron, Mar. 29, 1829, ae. 82-11-11.

CHILDREN

2. Sarah, b. Aug. 26, 1765 ; was unm. in 1808.
3. Ruth, b. Dec. 22, 1767, m. —— James.
4. Hannah, b. June 30, 1770; m. Peter Wells. (See.)
5. Mehitable, b. Sandown, Jan. 17, 1773; m. John Kidder. (See.)
6. Mary, b. Aug. 16, 1775 ; m. James Kidder. (See.)
7. Oliver, b. Nov. 1, 1777. He was for a time landlord of the Dodge tavern on South Main street.
8. Dolly, b. Mar. 16, 1780.
9. Lucy, b. Jan. 9, 1783 ; m. Sept. 29, 1810, Daniel Emerson, son of Judge Samuel Emerson. Res. in Plymouth and there d. Apr. 10, 1856, ae. 73-3-1. He d. June 11, 1866.
10. Deborah, b. New Hampton, Jan. 4, 1785; m. David Fowler. (See.)
11. Abigail, b. May 15, 1787 ; m. a Ferrin.

Add to record of Ada Maria Locke, who m. Rev. Frank D. George, (p. 289, 32 a) the following children :

a. Edith Adeline, b. Worcester, Mass., Oct. 23, 1891.
b. Helen Louise, b. Lowell, Mass., Dec. 28, 1892.
c. Frances Maria, b. Gardiner, Me., Nov. 21, 1895.
d. Carolyn Emma, b. G., Apr. 21, 1899.

Clara Sylvia Osgood (p. 331), who m. Frank H. French, had children :
  a. Carl Herbert, b. Hopedale, Mass., Nov. 6, 1878; m. Oct. 7, 1899, Mary E. Gardner. He served in Co. M, 6th Mass. Vol. Infty. Spanish war, in Porto Rico ; in action at Guanica. Is an expert pattern maker at Milford, Mass.
  b. Paul Thomas, b. H., Aug. 10, 1880. Served in same company with his brother, as above ; d. Oct. 24, 1898, ae. 18-2-14, while en route home and was buried at sea.

Betsey Jane Osgood (p. 331, 3). Add: She m. John R. Bennett Dec. 30, 1871. Res. Medfield, Mass. Children :
  a. Edwin Jonathan Robinson, b. Franklin, Mass., May 14, 1876.
  b. Clarence Raymond, b. Milford, Mass., Jan. 16, 1888.
  c. Beulah Lauretta, b. M., Feb. 14, 1890.
  d. Florence Vivian, b. M., Feb. 23, 1894.
  e. Nelson Appleton, b. M., Sept. 20, 1898.

Fred H. Patten (p. 334, 4). To his record add : He m. Apr. 16, 1898, Annie Belle, dau. of B. Frank and Mahala (Rowe) Robinson, b. Ashland, June 4, 1878. Children :
  a. Fred Seth, b. Apr. 10, 1899.
  b. Frank Louis, b. Dec. 15, 1903

John Page Sanborn, son of Alvah (p. 372, 64), was b. Fremont, Sept. 9, 1844, and m. Apr. 7, 1870, Isa Matilda Higbee (p. 166, 32 a). Children :
  a. Frank Mosher, b. Newport, R. I., Sept. 25, 1871 ; d. Apr. 26, 1875, ae. 3-7-1.
  b Susan Florence, b. N., Oct. 1, 1873; m. June 4, 1901, Albert Sidney Howard ; res. Providence, R. I.
  c. Alvah Howard, b. N., Mar. 28, 1876. Res. Newport.
  d. John Royal, b. N., July 26, 1883. Student at Mass. School of Technology, Boston, Mass.

BIRTHS

William M. Bryson (p. 74). To his children add :
  Ida Katharine, b. Bristol, Aug 16, 1903.

Karl G. Cavis (p. 90, 6). To his children add :
  Morton Hastings, b. Bristol, Dec. 31, 1903.

William E. Cyr (p. 127, 4). Add child :
  Louise Beatrice Joseph, b. Bristol, July 31, 1903.

Herbert E. Hadley (p. 220, 3). To list of his children add :
  Merville Harold, b. Bristol, May 23, 1903.

Frank N. C. Kirk (p. 281). Add a child :
  Aldice Warren, b. Bristol, Nov. 15, 1903.

Daisy M. (Dearborn) Merrill (p. 136, 13) add child :
  Selwyn Dearborn, b. Wentworth, Mar. 9, 1904.

William G. Robie (p. 385, 4). To his children add :
  Ernest Shattuck, b. Bristol, Mar. 15, 1904.

Leon H. Varney (p. 444). Add :
  A son, b. Bristol, Oct. 19, 1903.

31

MARRIAGES

Otis E. Cross (p. 123) m. Apr. 29, 1903, Eva M., dau. of Amos E. Barrett. (See.)

Ionel A. Dickinson (p. 140, 36) m. Oct. 9, 1903, Sadie E., dau. of Charles and Sadie (Reynolds) Colburn, b. Stonington, Conn.

Arthur W. Jewell (p. 256, 2) m. Nov. 14, 1903, Edith Mae, dau. of Leston L. Rollins. (See.)

George W. Gardner (p. 206, 14) m. Apr. 17, 1904, Jessie Loring, dau. of Henry R. and Annie (Tripp) Barker, b. Providence, R. I., Nov. 3, 1873.

Florence Edna Woodward (p. 118, 6 b) m. Nov. 18, 1903 Leo J. Richardson, 45 Chatham street, Worcester, Mass.

DEATHS

George M. Alden (p. 4) d. Bristol, June 9, 1903, ae. 79-8-9.

Jane Alden (p. 4) d. Bristol, Mar. 6, 1904, ae. 69-11-13.

Ichabod C. Bartlett (p. 23) d. Bristol, Jan. 2, 1904, ae. 62-3-22.

Lydia A. Bennett (p. 34) d. Bristol, July 21, 1903, ae 67-0-14.

William L. Bennett (p. 34) d. Bristol, Dec. 5, 1903, ae. 75-11-29.

Silas S. Brown (p. 62) d. Bristol, Dec. 8, 1903, ae. 71-10-4.

Betsey Jane Burleigh (p. 75) d. Bristol, Oct. 8, 1903, ae. 66-9-24.

Laurinda Crockett (p. 118, 4) d. Bristol, Mar. 10, 1904, ae. 88-8-24.

Dorcas D. (Calley) Gordon (p. 80) d. Bristol, Aug. 7, 1903, ae. 54-6-9.

Hannibal Chase (p. 94) d. Lyme, July 24, 1903, ae. 71-2-10.

Oscar B. Davis (p. 133) d. Andover, Mar. 2, 1904, ae. 32-9-2.

Abram Dolloff (p. 143) d. Bristol, Mar. 3, 1904, ae. 85-11-13.

Solon Dolloff (p. 144) d. Bristol, Oct. 28, 1903, ae. 76-0-25.

Nancy A. Durgin (p. 158) d. Bristol, Dec. 29, 1903, ae. 76-2-14.

Judith (Johnson) Eaton (p. 160, 2) d. Jan. 11, 1904.

Rufus Eaton (p. 160) d. Bristol, Aug. 19, 1903, ae. 81-1-19.

Jane (Badger) Everleth (p. 11) d. Bristol, Sept. 11, 1903, ae. 69-1-16.

James D. Follansbee (p. 192) d. in hospital, Concord, Jan. 29, 1904, ae. 57-0-14.

Adeline (Emmons) Higbee (p. 166) d. Newport, R. I., ae 84-4-3.

Helen Louise Ingalls (p. 254) d. Warner, Dec., 1903, ae. 70-9-.

Gustavus W. Ingalls (p 255) d. Worcester, Mass., Nov. 6. 1903, ae 79-5-15.

Joseph W. Johnson (p 260) d. Alexandria Feb. 5, 1904, ae 28-0-28.

William J. Muzzey (p 322) d. Tilton, Mar. 1, 1904, ae 59-8-25.

Sally (Sarah) C. Powell (p 341) d. Bristol Dec. 14, 1903, ae 81-4-1.

CORRECTIONS

William Mudgett (p. 319) first settled on north slope of Hemp hill ; later res. Fowler's river farm as there stated.

For William Leonett Smith (p. 319, 6 *f*) read William Leavitt Smith.
For Sarah Adder Cheney (p. 58, 42) read Sarah Addie Cheney.
For Nathaniel W. Aspenwall (p. 7) read Nathaniel W. Aspinwall.
For Cephus Brown Coolidge (p. 112) read Cephas Brown Coolidge.
For Joanna Melvin (p. 116, 3) read Susanna Melvin.
For Orra Ann Rollins (p. 199,) read Ora Ann Rollins.
For Walter W. Walker (p. 249, 2) read Walter B. Walker.
For Frank W. Towns (p. 438, 3) m. May 30, 1802, read 1902.
For Nancy F. (Lewis) Marsh (p. 9, 20) read Nancy F. (Davis) Marsh.
For William Atwood d. about 1873 (p. 9, 23) read 1874.

INDEX

This index contains the names of all persons numbered consecutively with the Arabic numerals 1, 2, 3, or Roman letter a, b, c, and all whom they married. The only names omitted are the parents of persons marrying into families here enumerated, but having no other connection with these genealogies.

With rare exceptions a name is indexed but once — at birth or its first appearance. If the name is preceded with a star or is accompanied with the word (See), its position elsewhere is thus designated and makes a second reference to it in the index unnecessary.

The first number following a name refers to the page; the second, to a paragraph on that page. The letters a, b, c, if any, refer to a paragraph under the paragraph numbered. Exceptions to the latter will be found where no second number is given, in which case the letters a, b, c, will be found near the top of the page.

32

34

35

511

Musgrove, Susan 320, 4
William A. 322, 12 b
William I. 320, 6
Muzzey, Albert C. 323, 9
Ann A. 322, 2
Arthur P. 323, 8 b
Bertha H. 323 b
Carl 323, 7 d
Frank P. 469, 3
Frankie W. 323 a
Fred C. 323, 7 a
Gertrude E. 364, 28 a
Hannah H. 322, 4
Harry W. 323, 8 a
Herbert T. 323, 9 a
John B. 322, 3
Marion E. 323, 7 c
Merle E. 323, 8 a
Miriam L. 323, 8 a
Orrin J. 323, 7
Orvis T. 364, 28
Ralph K. 323, 7 b
Roy C. 324, 7 c
Samuel 322, 1
Sarah 322, 5
Walter S. 323, 8
William J. 322, 6; 478
Victor G. 364, 28 b

Nash, May E. 386, 3
Nason, Laura E. 238, 2
Neal, Joseph N. 357, 2 a
Nealy, Martha A. 323, 4
Milo A. 323, 3
Walter A. 323, 2
William A. 323, 1
Nelson, Aaron 324, 6
Affa 324, 7
Ai H. 325, 19 c
Albert D. 326, 24
Albert S. 327 c
Alvin S. 326, 21 b
Ann R. 325, 16 a
Arthur V. 326, 21 a
Augusta I. 326, 21 d
Betsey 324, 6 c
Carrie H. 325, 19 c
Charles 324, 6 a
Charles P. 209, 8 a
Clara B. 325, 16 c
Clara P. 325, 17 c
Clora E. 325, 17 d
Cynthia 327, 32
Cyrus 325, 10
Cyrus W. 325, 19
Dan P. 326, 23
Dorcas 325, 12
Electa M. 325, 16 b
Eliza 324, 6 d
Elizabeth 182, 30
Elizabeth A. 284, 3 c
Ellen E. 325, 18 b
Ellen L. 224, 10
Emma 325, 18 a
Finette E. 327, 30
Flora L. 327 b
Hannah 324, 9
Hannah 325, 15
Harriet M. 327, 27
Harrison P. 284, 3
Hattie 327, 33
Henry D. 325, 18
Hiram 325, 16
Ida A. 325 19, b
Ina A. 325, 19 a
Jesse E. 327 d
John S. 325, 17
Joseph 324, 3
Joseph 324, 4
Leo G. 326, 22 b

Nelson, Levi 324, 8
Levi 325, 13
Levi J. 327, 31
Lilla A. 327, 34
Lindsay A. 326, 22 a
Luella L. 284, 3 a
Luella L. 284, 3 b
Lucy N. 284, 3 d
Luther W. 324, 6 b
Lydia 325, 14
Major J. 326, 25
Marcia L. 326 g
Martha S. 327, 29
Martin M. 16, 50
Mary E. 325, 19 d
Miles G. 326 h
Minnie G. 326 f
Nellie B. 325, 17 e
Norman G. 326, 22
Oral S. 327, 31 c
Orea P. 327, 31 b
Oren 326, 21
Philip 324, 2
Ralph W. 327, 31 a
Relief 326, 20
Samantha 369
Sarah E. 327, 28
Stephen 324, 5
Stephen 325, 11
Stephen 327, 35
Thomas 323, 1
William H. 284, 3 e
William S. 313, 13 a
William S. 327 a
Winfield S. 325, 17 b
Winnie A. 326, 21 e
Newcomb, Joanna 262, 6
Thomas C. 420, 3 b
Newell, Mary J. 19
Newhall, Ellen L. 166, 27 d
George S. 166, 27 c
Mary E. 166, 27 a
Richard 166, 27
Richard W. 166, 27 b
Nickerson, Jennie L. 461, 8
Nicholas, Susan A. 22, 12
Nichols, Charles F. B. D. 327, 1
Florence 210, 5 a
Joseph P. 328, 2
Nicholson, Enoch 154, 20
Jonas 96, 7
Nickerson, M. C. 187, 3
Niles, Florence 135 a
Grace 135 b
Mary E. 135 c
William H. 134, 4
Nilms, Thomas H. 134, 2 a
Nims, George 468 b
O. G. 468 b
Nise, Charles E. 170, 70 b
Etta 170, 70 d
Florence J. 170, 70 c
John M. 170, 70
Sarah E. 170, 70 a
Noble, Ellen E. 66, 20
Sarah 265, 1
Norris, Abigail H. 139, 14
Charlotte A. 328, 2 c
George C 328, 2
George W. 328, 1
Harry W. T. 328, 1
Howard C. 328, 2 b
Irving F. 328, 2 a
John 393, 52 c
Minetta M. 224, 8
Nancy 231, 13
Sarah E. 370, 31
Vira 461, 6
Norton, Carrie F. 196, 7 c

Norton, Claude R. 196, 7 a
David A. 196, 7 d
Elsa 196, 7 a
Euphemia I. 344 d
John B. 196, 7
John J. 196, 7 b
Ola 56, 20 b
Phebe J. 32, 4
Ray 196, 7 a
Nowell, Charles A. 130, 5 b
Helen M. 374, 101
Henry P. 130, 5 a
James C. 130, 5
Mary J. 31, 8
Noyes, Carl E. 444, 4
Charles F. 230, 4
Ervilla E. 444, 4 a
Flora S. 428, 32 c
Fred E. 328, 1
Harold A. 328, 3
Helen A. 328, 2
Lulu 186, 3 a
Martin B. 275, 38 a
Mary 34, 9
Nudd, Andrew T. 329, 1
Nutter, Rebecca J. 386
Nutting, Caroline L. 182, 60
Nye, Helen E. 15, 54

Oakley, Charles T. 329, 4
Clara J. 329, 3
Minnie L. 329, 2
Stephen A. 329, 1
William T. 329, 1
O'Brien, Helen M. 256, 3 a
Minnie 145, 32
Thomas E. 256, 3
Obrion, Elizabeth 343, 5 b
Oburg, Mary A. 125, 4
Odell, Jane 49, 9
O'Leary, Arthur 329, 1
Arthur 329, 2
Arthur L. 329, 4
Bert E. 329, 3
Elbon S. 329, 5
Julia 350, 5
O'Neil, Charles H. 300, 10
Charles H. 300, 10 b
Frederick 300, 10 f
George E. 300, 10 a
Henry M. 300, 10 c
John 205, 5
Robert L. 300, 10 d
Stanley S. 300, 10 e
Orange, Henry 283, 3
Ordway, Adeline 216, 1
George R. 330, 3
Giles W. 329, 1
Isaac H. 330, 2
Jennie 330, 4
Polly 226, 4
Relief 57, 7
Orton, Bert 287, 56 e
Osborn, Charles 33, 13
Osgood, Betsey J. 331, 3;
477
Charles H. 254, 18 b
Clara S. 331, 4
Deborah P. 331, 5
Edward F. 331, 3 a
Edward M. 331, 3
Frank 331, 3 c
Harry 331 b
Joseph L. 331, 6
Lydia 331, 3 b
Mahala R. 331, 2
Paul 331 a
Reuben 331, 1
Thomas E. 330, 1
Timothy 330, 2

36

37

CPSIA information can be obtained
at www.ICGtesting.com
Printed in the USA
BVHW031932100321
602009BV00014B/1059